PRAISE FOR *TRIUMPH AND DEMISE*

'A forensic critique of the failings of the Rudd and
Gillard governments.'
Jennifer Hewitt, *Australian Financial Review*

'A masterful overview of Labor's rise and fall, presenting a broad but
intensely detailed examination of the party's ruinous time in office.'
Daily Telegraph

'If you read only one book about these turbulent years in Australian
political history, then this is the one.'
Corrie Perkin, *Weekly Review*

'[An] absorbing fly-on-the-wall documentary narrative ... Few can
write this kind of political history better.'
Saturday Paper

'*Triumph and Demise* is a superbly written book filled with revelations
and sharp judgments that lift off the page with an authority that
is characteristic of Kelly. Its revelations ... are significant and its
conclusions are powerful. It is a compelling book.'
The Australian

'Kelly's books always provide a detailed and accurate reflection of
Australian politics ... [He] dissects the political infighting brilliantly.'
Nicholas Stuart, *Canberra Times*

Paul Kelly is Editor-at-Large of *The Australian*. He has been Editor-in-Chief of the paper and he writes on Australian politics, public policy and international affairs. Paul appears each week on *Australian Agenda* (Sky News) and before that was a regular on *Insiders* (ABC TV) for nearly a decade. He is the author of eight books: *The Unmaking of Gough* (1976), *The Hawke Ascendancy* (1984), *The End of Certainty* (1992), *November 1975* (1995), *Paradise Divided* (2000), *100 Years: The Australian Story* (2001), *The March of Patriots* (2009) and *Triumph and Demise* (2014).

TRIUMPH
AND
DEMISE

THE BROKEN PROMISE OF A LABOR GENERATION

PAUL KELLY

MELBOURNE
UNIVERSITY
PRESS

For my sons,
Daniel and Joseph

MELBOURNE UNIVERSITY PRESS
An imprint of Melbourne University Publishing Limited
11–15 Argyle Place South, Carlton, Victoria 3053, Australia
mup-info@unimelb.edu.au
www.mup.com.au

First published 2014
This edition published 2104
Text © Paul Kelly, 2014
Design and typography © Melbourne University Publishing Limited, 2014

Edited by Sally Moss, Context Editorial
Cover design by Philip Campbell Design
Typeset by Megan Ellis
Printed in Australia by McPherson's Printing Group

National Library of Australia Cataloguing-in-Publication entry
    Kelly, Paul, 1947– author.

    Triumph and demise : the broken promise of a Labor generation/Paul Kelly.

    9780522867817 (paperback)
    9780522867909 (*The Australian* edition)
    9780522867824 (epub)

    Includes bibliographical references.

    Australian Labor Party.
    Political leadership—Australia.
    Political entrepreneurship—Australia.
    Political planning—Australia.
    Australia—Politics and government—2001–

    324.29407

CONTENTS

PREFACE

Triumph and Demise is the story of the six-year Labor Government of Kevin Rudd and Julia Gillard from 2007 to 2013. After eleven long years in opposition the return of Labor was invested with high hopes for policy and political successes. Yet the triumph of 2007 surrendered to the demise of 2013, with many of these hopes dashed or compromised.

This book argues three central propositions: that the destruction of the Rudd–Gillard partnership was the fatal event; that Labor in office was burdened by an institutional malaise that went to identity, policy and strategy; and that the deeper lesson from the Rudd–Gillard years is that Australia's political system is in a crisis that threatens the delivery of national interest outcomes and, without correction, will damage our society and living standards.

The book draws upon my coverage of the Rudd–Gillard years but relies primarily upon more than sixty interviews with the main participants, in particular Kevin Rudd, Julia Gillard, Tony Abbott, Wayne Swan and Malcolm Turnbull. I interviewed more than twenty former Labor cabinet ministers, a number of senior Coalition politicians, other ALP political figures, some ministerial staff, policy experts, corporate leaders and public servants, both retired and current. I made an effort to persuade people to speak on-the-record and I believe this is a valuable feature of the book.

I want to thank those who co-operated, often giving me many hours of their time. I apologise to others to whom I should have spoken. An unfortunate reality of combining journalism with contemporary history writing is the ruthless limit imposed by time and logistics.

This book began as a different project: it was to be the second half of the Howard era from 2001 to 2007 as I explained in my earlier book, *The March of Patriots*. Indeed, I had completed a large amount of research and writing to this objective. In the end, however, I felt the Labor period was so compelling that it had to become the heart of this project.

I owe a special thanks to the Editor-in-Chief of *The Australian*, Chris Mitchell, whose support for this book has been critical and who tolerated my extended absence to complete it. At Melbourne University

Publishing I thank Louise Adler for her belief in the book and enduring support. Cathryn Smith has been a dedicated manager of the project. I thank her and the entire team at MUP.

My son Joe, a journalist who covered some of these events, came up with the title. I liked it from the start. He provided vital help in reading and editing the manuscript and offering advice that led to important changes. There are many other people I should thank for their contributions at various stages: Dennis Shanahan, who covered the Labor Government and whose help and insights were highly valuable, Chris Richardson and Stephen Anthony for helping me to understand better the budgets of the period, Elena Douglas for assistance on editing, Mary Corkhill for interview transcriptions and many colleagues and friends on *The Australian* for their help over the years.

I assume responsibility for the book in its strengths and defects. This was a difficult period to write about because, more than any other era I have covered in book form, it is plagued by contested views over facts, events, conversations and policy assessment. I remain open to further refinements for subsequent editions.

Sydney 2014

INTRODUCTION TO THE NEW EDITION

It is rare in Australian history for a former prime minister to release their memoirs little more than twelve months after losing office. That Julia Gillard was driven to this effort is no surprise. Her prime ministership is remarkable in nearly every sense and is enshrined in her standing as the nation's first female prime minister.

Gillard's memoirs were released a month after the publication of *Triumph and Demise*, my account of the six years of the Rudd–Gillard–Rudd government. In preparing my book I conducted two long interviews with Julia Gillard—in January 2010, five months before she became prime minister, and a four-hour interview in October 2013, the month after Labor lost power. They were supplemented by a further long discussion in February 2014 about her position and attitudes.

The former prime minister was generous with her time and frank in her remarks. She was invariably direct, down to earth, hard-headed, blessed with a good memory and put her case effectively. Many of the arguments, stories and anecdotes she recounted in these interviews reappear in her book. But her memoirs constitute her consolidated view of history and warrant a response—hence this introduction.

Gillard's period in office is unprecedented for another reason: its indelible association with political violence, by her own hand and then against her by her enemies. She became prime minister because of her political assassination of Kevin Rudd and she was deposed when Rudd retaliated in kind. Gillard was prime minister for three years and three days, yet for most of this time she was in minority government and endured an environment more lethal than that of most of her predecessors.

Femininity, brutality and resilience—these are the hallmarks of Gillard's prime ministership. They constitute its drama, tragedy and contradictions. Gillard's period is unique because it involves gender. Her assertion of this is confronting: 'Even if you are the single most powerful person in your country, if you are a woman, the images that are shadowed around you are of sex and rape.' This is Gillard's perspective of Australia from high office.[1]

In the end Gillard's proposition is that she faced more abuse than other prime ministers because she was the first woman. It sounds initially plausible yet it is nonsense. Gillard, undoubtedly, was subjected to sustained and grossly offensive sexist and misogynist attacks for which there is no excuse and no equivalent experience for a man. The reality, however, is that the overwhelming majority of day-to-day criticism of Gillard arose from her policies and political actions, not because of her gender. They included her removal of Rudd, her carbon tax broken promise and the deals she did—some sleazy—to sustain her minority government.

Gillard's experience leads her to the accusation of sexism and misogyny in Australia's culture and its power structures. She is explicit: the problem was not just in society's margins. It came from the mainstream: the Opposition, business and media. By laying this considered accusation, Gillard's gender story becomes inextricably woven into her political story. The two parallel narratives run together and intersect.

This leads to the irresistible question: did Gillard fail the nation as prime minister or did the nation fail Gillard by dishonouring the first woman to hold the highest office? How is Gillard's fate as prime minister to be explained—is it her fault or ours?

This is the explosive conundrum that lies forever at the heart of Gillard's story. She provides no definitive answer but puts the question on the table.

In her manoeuvre Gillard, therefore, raises the question of how she should be judged. Is the test her failure to win government in her own right at the 2010 election and her 2013 political execution by her own party? Or is the test something different that transcends politics—her inspiration to women because she called misogyny when she saw it, thereby empowering women everywhere?

The best preliminary answer is that Gillard became a cultural symbol for many women—yet this was a phenomenon outside politics that neither assisted her standing as a political leader nor substituted for her political and policy failures. Sadly, it entrenched her status as a divisive and polarising figure. The resentment she felt at sexist insults from establishment figures is palpable in the pages of her book, *My Story*, published in September 2014, suggesting that Gillard, despite her toughness, has been personally scarred by these events.

Gillard has the honesty to say that of all her experiences as prime minister, gender 'is the hardest to explain, to catch, to quantify'.[2] Yet as a political professional, Gillard knows she cannot rely upon gender to define her legacy. Her 461-page memoir is, above all, a defence of her

political and policy record in office and virtually every initiative of substance is contained within its pages. In the end, Gillard gives priority to
policy over gender.

With the political body of the Labor government barely cold,
Gillard has rushed into print as the active engineer of her legacy. She
has two opponents in her construction of history—Kevin Rudd, her
arch nemesis, and Tony Abbott, her Coalition opponent every day of her
prime ministership. Having eventually succumbed to the cruel pressures
of Abbott before her and Rudd behind, Gillard is impatient to stake her
claim before history.

The narrative she constructs is that of resilience in the teeth of
adversity that was largely unwarranted. The memoirs of every former
leader are personal. But Gillard's is more deeply personal. She builds a
story around her unique dilemma: the first female prime minister under
a battery of personal and political assault.

Gillard writes: 'Throughout my prime ministership people would
ask me when I met them, "How do you do it?" They would search my
face for clues, wanting to know why I wasn't at home hiding, sobbing,
screaming.' The heart of her answer was her resilience. She called it 'a
modern buzz word, yet a term that came to encapsulate so much about
my life'.[3]

The technique in her memoir is to turn every insult into another
proof of her fortitude. Her writing exposes her emotional inner life: the
tears, anger, frustration and her stoical resistance. Because Gillard is a private person, it would have been difficult to write.

Gillard believes that since the last days of Sir Robert Menzies every
prime minister has had to shoulder 'a crushing constant workload, a
relentless, often negative media, and many road blocks to policy change'.
But she argues, with justification, that her situation was different and
tougher. This was because of three factors—chronic Labor party instability,
the tribulations of minority government and the role of gender playing
into perceptions of leadership.[4]

Gillard invests her memoir with a claim to superior moral virtue.
She presents as a politician of purpose and honour. Her targets are Rudd
and Abbott—but Rudd is the ultimate agent of infamy. It is a variation of
an old theme: the enemy within is the worst enemy.

She sees her prime ministership as subject to an immoral insurgency from a man of irredeemably flawed character. The issues of gender,
virtue and loyalty are fused in June 2013 with Gillard's political execution at Rudd's behest. This is where her book begins. The first sentence

is carefully chosen: 'I felt a sense of stillness and loneliness on the walk from Labor's caucus room to my office, having just been voted out of the prime ministership. Around me was anything but stillness.' Indeed, around her was a media frenzy. Her staff lined the corridor, applauding in sad tribute, some crying.[5]

Gillard depicts her removal as a moral failure on Labor's part. She says that Rudd, as a plotter, left 'nothing to chance', briefing politicians, business leaders, journalists and editors against her. Gillard decided such bad behaviour should not be rewarded. 'I was never going to voluntarily submit to the Labor Party being taken over by Kevin and those who had behaved so disgracefully for so long,' Gillard writes. To allow their victory was to accept 'the ugliest brutality in the pursuit of self-promotion'. By its action Labor invited the conclusion that 'putting the party first means nothing today'.[6]

She cannot leave alone the moral contrast between herself and Rudd. Her disgust is undisguised and undiminished. 'Kevin himself was offering no sense of purpose,' Gillard wrote. 'His whole leadership campaign had been about him and his popularity.' Sitting on the back bench 'he never developed one truly new, original policy idea for our nation's future'. Gillard would bitterly joke to colleagues that if Labor accepted Rudd's logic then Kylie Minogue would be a perfect pick for Labor leader because 'she is popular, has millions of twitter followers and fans gather wherever she goes'.

Gillard knows that leadership contests are dominated by the electoral appeal of the combatants. She argues, however, that in June 2013 Labor took a 'giant step' beyond anything done before. Gillard argues Labor had never previously endorsed as leader 'someone they knew had no talent for governing, someone they knew could not actually do the job, simply because they thought he might do better at an election'. She admitted that she 'could not stomach this rejection of purpose' implicit in the resort to Rudd over herself. She felt sure if Rudd was returned, he would run a 'shocking and purposeless campaign'.[7]

Her self-serving lack of introspection is startling. Does Gillard not grasp that she set the rules by her own behaviour and died by the rules that she made? It is a ritual as old as human nature.

At the moment of her martyrdom, having lost her job, Gillard knew she must project courage without tears. 'I was not going to stand before the nation as prime minister and cry for myself,' she said. 'I was not going to let anyone conclude that a woman could not take it. I was not going to give any bastard the satisfaction.'[8]

The image she cultivates before history is unmistakable: female courage amid betrayal.

What was the final act of 'Julia the honourable'? It was to put the party first and accept its decision, not to create havoc. Again, she invites the moral contrast with Rudd after he had been deposed in June 2010. 'I could have claimed the vote was not truly the judgement of my colleagues, but it was all the work of factional faceless men,' she writes. 'I could have distracted the media, shaped the contest differently and run for Parliament again, demanding a ministry.'

But Gillard 'was never going to do that' because 'it is not the way to show loyalty to the Labor Party'. It would not have shown respect to her colleagues; such destabilisation 'is simply not right'.[9] This closes Gillard's story of honour in her abandonment.

It invites two conclusions. Gillard did stick by her code of Labor loyalty. Her behaviour after losing the leadership was impeccable. She stayed in the shadows and gave Rudd a clear run in sunlight. Yet there is another version, untold in Gillard's memoir. In the end, the party felt obliged to remove her in its self-interest. The caucus did not want to recall Rudd. It neither liked nor loved Kevin. Indeed, many caucus members loathed him. Its preference was to remain with Gillard; its heart was with Julia. But Gillard singularly failed as prime minister to give the party enough reason to follow its preference and its heart. This was an extraordinary political failure on her part.

It is about her failures as prime minister that Gillard either stays silent or offers unsatisfactory accounts. On too many pivotal issues she excuses herself with a blend of sophistry, dissembling and silence. The flaw in Gillard's memoir is her inability to recognise she is the architect of her own problems. There is a delusional theme in this book. She casts the net wide when attributing blame: to Rudd, to Abbott, to the media and to sexists and misogynists. This is part true yet even greater part fantasy. It will appeal to many readers, presumably women readers. Yet at its heart lies the real tragedy of Julia Gillard—she was brought undone by a series of decisions for which Gillard alone is responsible.

These decisions testify to her personal failure and the weakness of Labor as a political institution. And they dominate much of my narrative in this book.

In reality, Gillard is a ruthless, tough and pragmatic political operative. Ultimately, it was Gillard's decisions that shaped the Rudd–Gillard–Rudd era. Her judgements, in particular, determined the three epic leadership events of the period.

It was Gillard who made Rudd the leader of the Labor Party in 2006; it was Gillard who destroyed Rudd as prime minister in 2010; and it was Gillard's political ineptitude in 2013 that made possible Rudd's recall. No previous ALP figure has such a history. These are the events that defined the era. This is what counts, not portentous laments about misogyny.

Gillard is transparent about the foundational event: the rolling of Kim Beazley as ALP leader. This happened only because Rudd and Gillard formed a partnership and attacked Beazley as a team, a story recounted in chapter 7 of *Triumph and Demise*. Gillard was the enabling agent because she decided to run on a ticket as Rudd's deputy.

'I bear the responsibility for creating his leadership,' Gillard said of Rudd. It sounds pretentious yet it is true. Without her support, Rudd had no chance of winning the caucus majority to depose Beazley. Now Gillard, in hindsight, confesses a degree of guilt.

Her view is that her judgement of Rudd's campaigning skill was correct. Yet her judgement of his character 'proved to be dreadfully wrong'. For Kevin, she concludes, 'there was never enough applause, approval, love'. The suggestion of narcissism hangs in the air. Gillard says Rudd's flaws originated in his childhood difficulties. There was 'a hole in him that had to be filled by success and the poor substitute for real love that is political homage'.[10] Her patronising view of Rudd knows few limits.

In truth, Gillard was backing Rudd to deliver her the deputy prime minister's job, a position unavailable to her under Beazley. She felt Beazley lacked the fire to succeed and feared that Howard would defeat him for a third time. The prospect of another Labor defeat consumed Gillard. 'Was I wrong in my judgement of Kim Beazley in 2006?' she writes. 'I fear I may have been.' In politics, as Gillard says, there is no control test, no certainty of what might have been. Gillard comes to the brink, but never says their rolling of Beazley was the wrong option. This is because she cannot. The leadership change was a success. Rudd and Gillard brought Labor to office at the 2007 election.

Gillard says that by anointing Rudd she did not expect to become a future ALP leader. 'In joining forces with Kevin, I accepted the probable consequence that I was unlikely to ever lead the Labor Party,' she writes. 'I had not come into parliament with an ambition to do so.' Many will sneer at this sentiment. But Gillard made the same point in her January 2010 interview with the author. If she was so desperate to be prime minister and was king-making Rudd, then the cynics must explain why she didn't impose a succession pledge on their partnership. Gillard probably realised it was neither prudent nor necessary. In reality, Gillard had ambitions but she knew her succession to the highest position depended upon events that defied calculation. She could live with that.[11]

The second defining event for Gillard—and the pivotal move in her career—was her successful strike against Rudd on the night of 23 June 2010. It is now best seen as high tragedy. This is the misjudgement that defined her character. In an act of abrupt ruthlessness, legitimised by the caucus yet catching the Australian public by surprise, Gillard deposed Rudd and seized the office of prime minister. It was an unprecedented event: the removal of an elected prime minister in his first term by a challenge from his deputy.

Gillard's memoir is strong on her policy activity as prime minister but weak on how she got the job. This omission, ultimately, does not serve Gillard's case. A full disclosure would have been better.

In beginning her account of Rudd's removal, Gillard does not hesitate to sketch his dysfunctional style as prime minister. This sets the scene for her strike. Her charge is that Rudd failed to articulate the government's core mission. She retraces ground well trodden yet nonetheless vital to enable people to grasp what happened.

Rudd's forte was tactics not strategy. Huge policy reforms agendas 'were hostage to a haphazard decision-making style'. Rudd demanded more paperwork and set punishing deadlines, only to then ignore the material provided. Meetings were called but failed to result in decisions because Rudd was too busy to master his brief. Rudd thrived during the global financial crisis but was unable to adapt later. In the end, the four person Strategic Priorities and Budget Committee (SPBC), comprising Rudd, Gillard, Wayne Swan and Lindsay Tanner, virtually replaced the cabinet. Yet Rudd was often absent from its meetings. Gillard reveals she chaired fourteen of the eighty-four SPBC meetings in 2009 and 2010. Gillard said caucus members had no phone number for Rudd and were being diverted instead to a staffer. She tried to facilitate preparations for the 2010 re-election campaign but found Rudd was resistant.

'Time after time I explained to Kevin the need for him to change his way of working and to confront and resolve the major issues before the government,' Gillard said. She would enter Rudd's office, seek to bolster staff morale, fish out papers other ministers were screaming about, get Rudd to sign them or authorise decisions herself. 'The sense that things were out of control was becoming impossible to contain,' Gillard writes.[12]

Gillard correctly identifies the malaise: Rudd was inept as a manager of his government. It is the defect that leads to ruin and the flaw that proves popularity alone cannot suffice. Rudd became 'spooked' by the way the politics of climate change had turned against him. He mismanaged both asylum seeker boat arrivals and the hospital reform package. Gillard said long hours were spent at budget meetings with Rudd refusing to confront the proposal for a super profits tax on mining.

Towards the end she found 'Kevin's demeanour was now unremittingly one of paralysis and misery' such that 'he appeared to hate every minute of his day and to be frustrated by every person and every event'. Gillard felt Rudd was in a catch-22 trap: he bemoaned how little people were helping him but was unable to surrender control to let them help.[13]

This fits into the fuller account of Rudd's malaise documented at length in parts V and VII of this book. In an abject failure Rudd lost the confidence of his caucus. In this period Gillard said she neither canvassed colleagues for a leadership spill nor briefed journalists against his leadership. Finally, however, she moved, upset and then provoked by a newspaper report on the morning of 23 June that left the impression Rudd no longer trusted her. 'If Kevin did not trust me then there was nothing left,' she writes.

Gillard asked to see party elder John Faulkner, and then dissolved into tears over the story. Faulkner held her and consoled her. 'It is the only time I have ever shed tears for myself,' Gillard writes. She seemed ashamed of her indulgence. But tears quickly surrendered to retaliation. Gillard the politician crossed the Rubicon: she decided she must challenge or resign. She confided in senior cabinet minister Tony Burke in a meeting around lunchtime that day.[14] Burke, in his own version to the author, on page 323 of this book, confirms Gillard's account. Another Gillard supporter, David Feeney, who saw her earlier that morning, told the author he left 90 per cent confident she would challenge Rudd.

Gillard barely explains in her memoir how a newspaper story could produce such a complete reversal of her position. Senior cabinet minister Anthony Albanese told the author it was untenable to believe the challenge arose merely because of a newspaper report that morning. It is a persuasive assessment. A fuller explanation, surely, is that Gillard saw an opportunity and seized it—she realised Rudd was weak, she sensed the party was prepared to roll him and she now felt a moral justification for action. It was a perfect trifecta.

In her memoir Gillard is reluctant to confront the magnitude and consequences of her decision. Her strike against Rudd was a mistake. She says she has no regrets. Yet her memoir is unpersuasive on the merits of her decision and, frankly, hardly mounts a case on behalf of her challenge. This absence reinforces the argument in chapter 1 of this book: that Gillard's removal of Rudd was the death warrant of the Labor Government. Within months Labor was reduced to a minority government and never looked like winning the 2013 election.

It is unfortunate that Gillard has declined to tell her full story about these events. Her account of her strike against Rudd borders on caricature. She writes as though she was dispensing an act of kindness to a sick man. She claims she 'truly did believe' that after Rudd emerged from losing his job he would experience 'the feeling of relief'. This is because 'he had been so unhappy' as prime minister and many around him 'were concerned about his psychological state'. Gillard says that even as Rudd wept for himself at his courtyard media conference the day of the removal 'it was my strong belief that after some recovery time, his dominant emotion would be relief—he had become so wretched while leader'.[15]

How convenient. Such sophistry beggars belief. Having conducted a sudden and surprise political assassination of Rudd, having taken his job and offered him nothing, having seen Rudd choking and weeping and his family in grief, Gillard asserts Rudd will feel grateful for the deliverance she provided. The claim is ignorant of human nature and the rich literature of political betrayal. When, pray, does the assassinated leader ever turn to the assassin with gratitude for making their life easier?

The views expressed by Gillard provoke an almost irresistible conclusion—that Gillard has exaggerated Rudd's personal misery and psychological difficulty to legitimise her assault. Lindsay Tanner has made a similar point. He said the removal of Rudd was such an 'extreme' step the perpetrators found it necessary to 'enormously exaggerate the deficiencies in Rudd's leadership'.

When the author interviewed Gillard there was one issue she declined to discuss: the decisive Rudd–Gillard conversation with Faulkner as impartial witness in the prime minister's office on the evening of 23 June. In her book Gillard says she entered the meeting with hesitance. She knew Rudd was 'tragically incapable of changing his behaviour' yet she wished that he could. She wished their 'easy friendship' of earlier days was still alive. Gillard paints herself as the reluctant assassin. Yet Gillard was under no compelling obligation to depose Rudd. Her decision was voluntary. She was a free agent with open options.

Rudd has given his own explosive account of this meeting to the author. He said Gillard initially agreed to his proposal that he remain prime minister for the next several months but would stand down before the election if it was felt, with Faulkner as arbiter, that he was an impediment to Labor's re-election. Rudd says Gillard agreed, left the room, returned, changed her mind and said she wanted a leadership ballot.

In her memoir Gillard fails to provide her account of this exchange. It is a glaring omission. Indeed, she declines to provide her account of many other already documented discussions concerning Rudd and the leadership. She says of this critical conversation, her regret is it lasted too long. But Gillard does concede she gave Rudd 'false hope' because they discussed the notion of 'giving Kevin more time to change'.[16] In fact, the idea that Rudd could have purchased another several months in office was untenable: the media already had the leadership crisis story.

In short, Gillard was hesitant initially in their conversation but this cannot gainsay the reality: Gillard had been gunning Rudd from early that morning. She forced the crisis. She went after Rudd. She had told Burke it was resignation or challenge. And resignation, obviously, was not an option.

Her readiness to strike was discernible. In extraordinary language she likened the conversation with Rudd to that of a 'patient with terminal cancer who is maintaining that it is merely a head cold and they will soon be better.'[17] Yet the idea that Rudd faced certain defeat in the next election was far from established. Indeed, it is too contested to suffice as justification for Gillard's strike. And Gillard's poll ratings as prime minister were consistently far below those of Rudd in June 2010.

My argument in *Triumph and Demise* is that Gillard was unready for the leadership, devoid of any game plan and unable to explain to the people why she felt driven to remove Rudd. Her memoir confirms such judgements. She says her overnight elevation 'allowed no time to brace for the new weight' of high office. Her partner Tim Mathieson, in a rush to get to Canberra for the swearing-in, had dressed with one black boot, one brown boot. Gillard had to borrow a necklace from her staffer, Sally Tindall. Gillard admits she 'did not have the luxury of starting afresh', given the problems of the mining tax, carbon pricing and boat arrivals. She further admits her failure to offer the nation any credible explanation for Rudd's removal in an overnight assault. Gillard concedes the public was taken without warning and left 'shocked'. Finally, she says 'it was the hardest of circumstances in which to become prime minister'.[18]

Yet these were the circumstances she chose. Gillard writes as though this had slipped her mind. If the situation was so hard then that was Gillard's fault. This statement merely brings to a zenith the doubts about Gillard's decision to seize the prime ministership at this point. Gillard had not prepared professionally for the most important decision of her career.

As many of her supporters later conceded, she never recovered from the way she got the prime ministership.

Having rolled Rudd, she felt she had to go to a prompt election and secure her mandate. Yet Labor wasn't ready. No campaign strategy work had been done. Gillard was trapped as a new leader driven to an election with an unprepared party.

From the start, she mismanaged Rudd. She believed he should have done the 'decent thing' and retired at the 2010 election, accepting the judgement of his colleagues. Yet Rudd's premature termination made that highly unlikely. This was not a leader being removed after a long and successful prime ministership. Rudd was consumed by the instinct of unfinished business. He wanted to be Foreign Minister but Gillard reveals her thinking was more in the Indigenous Affairs area.[19] Rudd would have seen this as an insult. In any seizure of power an elementary tactic is management of the deposed leader. Gillard had no such tactic.

Having piled humiliation upon humiliation onto Rudd, she seemed startled when he set upon revenge. Rudd's subsequent undermining of Gillard was unforgivable and caused outrage across the party, but it was not inexplicable. It revealed Gillard's inability satisfactorily to manage the core conditions for a successful change of prime minister.

Gillard survived the August 2010 election by outmanoeuvring Abbott and striking deals that installed her as a minority government leader. It was a brilliant tactical achievement—and Gillard delights in telling this story. Yet her concessions to Tony Windsor, Rob Oakeshott and, less successfully, to Andrew Wilkie weakened her government in the public perception. The pivotal deal was with the Greens under the leadership of Bob Brown. It contained the seeds of her final destruction and the ultimate Gillard tragedy.

Her memoir confirms that the compact with the Greens was to legislate a carbon pricing scheme, provided they could agree on the design. Gillard says she 'bet my future' on two things: getting the Greens to accept a workable scheme and, once legislated, winning public acceptance. The former was achieved but the latter was unrealisable. In fact, she was fatally wounded by Abbott's early 2011 assault on the Gillard–Greens–independents carbon policy/tax framework. Gillard was breaking an election pledge. ALP National Secretary George Wright said 'Julia never recovered' from the broken bond of trust.

Gillard makes a revealing concession: had she won majority government she doubts she would have been able to negotiate and secure an emissions trading scheme during the 2010–13 term. This suggests her carbon scheme was only a function of minority government. And the political price it extracted doomed her government.

The historic carbon scheme passed Parliament on 8 November 2011. It meant Gillard prevailed where Rudd had failed—briefly. She told the Parliament the real test was: are you on the right side of history? Gillard has left a strange hybrid legacy. Having legislated carbon pricing in office, Labor feels it cannot abandon the policy in Opposition. Yet Gillard never persuaded the nation and the Abbott Government repealed the scheme in 2014. The upshot is that Labor is pledged to its resurrection and the seeking of a new mandate at an election.

It is significant that Gillard said the 'greatest' price she paid for minority government was her inability because of the numbers on the floor of Parliament to 'decisively deal with the insurgency and destabilisation' of Rudd and his group of agitators called 'the cardinals'.[20] Gillard had been re-elected leader after the 2010 election. Pointing to the Rudd-inspired media destabilisation against her, Gillard says that over the next three years she faced 150 publicly reported claims that she was about to be deposed very soon or by a specific deadline. No journalist ever apologised when such stories were proved false. Gillard defeated Rudd in a leadership challenge in February 2012. In March 2013 she opened the leadership for a ballot only to find Rudd refused to contest and she was again elected unopposed. Her thrashing of Rudd's perpetual rivalry became resilience personified.

But in June 2013 she succumbed, finally, and was narrowly deposed by Rudd 57–45 in a caucus ballot. Gillard's tragedy was writ large—the absence of clear political air from the day she became prime minister. Her government was consumed by leadership instability, perceived incompetence and Gillard's inability to project authority.

Rudd supporter and former Treasurer Chris Bowen said Labor under Gillard faced an 'existential crisis'—he feared a defeat that 'would cast into doubt the historic mission of the party'.[21] Bowen was not alone. Gillard's bizarre policy and political blunders during 2013 reduced Labor's primary vote to below 30 per cent, an untenable level that gave the caucus little choice but to remove her for Rudd. Given her polls, Bob Carr wondered why Gillard had not resigned. 'Her selfishness struck me,' he said. Incredibly, one of Gillard's final moves was to play the misogyny card, suggesting abortion might become an issue courtesy of 'men who think they know better'. It was an act of desperation; the ALP primary vote among men then slipped below 25 per cent. Upon calling the ballot, Gillard accepted her demise with dignity and discipline.

On election night Gillard sat alone as the results came in. She wanted it that way. George Wright said the switch to Rudd saved Labor at least 25 seats; the Gillard camp rejected this notion.

In her memoir, Gillard enshrines 'sense of purpose' as the life force that sustained her. It is akin to her personal engine-room or her remarkable inner drive. Nobody could doubt Gillard's will or resilience. But 'sense of purpose' is a limited political concept and threadbare as an idea. It is important for many people—footballers, bank bosses and fashion models—as well as politicians. It neither equates to competent governance nor a coherent policy framework. And it was not enough for Gillard, PM.

She sketches her origins within a traditional Labor family in a coal mining district of Wales. Her family values shaped her Labor values. Unionism was an article of faith; the denial of a proper education for her father and mother left in Gillard a passion to locate education 'at the centre of my government'; and her family ethos of hard work became her watchword virtue. From the start she was interested in practical gains. As a left-wing university activist her earliest 'experiences in public action' were in protests against Liberal governments for cutting university education, not global ideological causes. Her guiding stars were: work, education, respect.[22]

In her first speech as prime minister, Gillard said she believed in a government 'that rewards those who work the hardest, not those who complain the loudest'. But 'hard work' is equally a virtue arising within the Liberal Party's middle-class morality championed by Menzies and Howard.

Putting her defining emphasis on personal virtue, respect, work and dignity gave Gillard the opportunity to reach across boundaries in Australian society. Yet this did not happen. The reason is because Gillard, in practice, had a narrow view of Laborism, even arguing she led not a social democratic party—a notion championed by Gough Whitlam—but a Labor Party constituted by its trade union bonds. In this sense Gillard became a prisoner of traditionalism.

Her 'hard work' mantra never converted into a set of policies that backed personal aspiration. Judged by her deeds, she did little to advocate reform of Labor's structure or culture for a more diverse society. In office she failed to strike an acceptable policy balance between unions and business, with a vision of job creation tied heavily to union strategies rather than private entrepreneurship.

In her memoir there is no world view, no sense of Labor's political evolution and little cognisance of the historical challenge the party faced after the Hawke–Keating era. Unlike many previous ALP leaders, Gillard's political formation did not originate in economic policy or national security/foreign policy convictions. Indeed, until she became prime minister, Gillard had displayed little interest in the climate change debate. In the end, she ran a divisive government pushing pro-union laws, anti-business rhetoric, a carbon policy dictated by her alliance with the Greens and a misogynist campaign.

Her memoir rejects the criticism—a theme of this book—that Rudd and Gillard represented a departure from the Hawke–Keating tradition. Yet her argument is feeble and Gillard seems unable to come to grips with intellectual analysis of Labor's past or future. Retreating to cliché, she says while there are 'golden threads' that tie modern Labor governments together, each leader devises their own long-run vision.

Central to Gillard's memoir is unremitting advocacy for Labor's policy agenda. In a personal sense, the National Disability Insurance Scheme and Gonski school reforms take priority. The tears she shed while introducing a bill to increase the Medicare levy to help fund the NDIS revealed a moment of unforeseen emotion tied to a crusading dedication. The NDIS will be realised and become a singular icon in Gillard's legacy. The utility and funding of the Gonski agenda is more problematic. Gillard is methodical in her exposition of My School reforms, the Fair Work Act, the NBN, university reforms, skills and training initiatives, revamped hospitals policy, interventions to protect Aussie jobs and her foreign policy in Asia and America.

Yet the memoir mirrors Gillard's view of politics: get the job done, don't agonise about the past, don't cut the critics any slack, recite the mantra that Labor is for the good and the true, and then show me the next problem to be solved.

In her final press conference as prime minister, Gillard said gender 'doesn't explain everything' about her prime ministership but 'it explains some things'. Yet her book fails to elaborate adequately on those things. In the end, Gillard played the misogyny card not just because she felt ignoring such attacks didn't work, but because her prime ministership was in trouble. We will never know, but the idea of a successful female prime minister resorting to this attack is surely fanciful. Gillard decided to define herself, in part, by accusing Abbott of misogyny. There should have been a better way for the first female prime minister to carry her banner.

Labor in office had avoided a recession and presided over a growth economy. It deserved a stronger electoral position than what it got—the collapse in Labor's vote over two and a half years from early 2011 revealed flaws in Gillard's style and governance. Her memoir concedes tactical mishaps she cannot deny: equating her climate scheme to a carbon tax and the backlash from making Peter Slipper the Speaker (he was later forced to resign and was subject to charges and convicted).

Gillard did make minority government work in that her government passed 566 pieces of legislation, more than in Howard's final term. But minority government had a poisonous perception in the public arena. It was irrevocably tied to the ignominious behaviour of Slipper and Labor MP Craig Thomson, of deals with Windsor and Oakeshott and of an alliance with Greens that contaminated Labor's integrity. Above all, minority government created the impression of Gillard cutting repeated deals to save herself.

Gillard was inexperienced in dealing with the power centres of Australian life, notably business and media. Too often her policy and political judgement was flawed. Gillard's core strategic mistake was that she failed to govern from the centre or middle ground in the established practice of leaders such as Bob Hawke. Indeed, Gillard seemed devoid of any strategic conception of how Labor should govern to succeed. Her memoir is conspicuous because it lacks the self-reflection needed to analyse and confront the bigger mistakes she made that cast a shadow across Labor's future prospects. The Rudd–Gillard generation had its achievements but it looms as a largely negative inheritance for the next ALP generation.

In retirement Julia will not sulk or lament. She gave it her best shot. Her spirits are high. She is proud of her record. She concedes to mixed emotions (how could she not, after such a turbulent ride). She admits to the taste of bittersweet but says the sweet is 'by far the stronger'. This admission, surely, is recognition that it could have happened another and better way.[23]

Sydney
7 October 2014

I

TURNING POINTS

CHAPTER 1

THE DESTRUCTION OF A GOVERNMENT

Julia Gillard's request was lethal—that Kevin Rudd surrender as prime minister, in her favour. 'I have been talking to my colleagues,' she told him. Gillard now knew Rudd had lost the confidence of the Australian Labor Party. She wanted Rudd to resign but if he refused she would seek a leadership ballot. Gillard delivered the final blow only after being assured she had the numbers. Labor was ready to execute Kevin Rudd, hero of its 2007 election victory.

This was the final stage of the Rudd–Gillard meeting on the evening of 23 June 2010 in the prime minister's office. 'In her view,' Rudd later said, 'I could not win the election.'[1] He was angry and shocked. Resentment against Rudd had a long fuse but the detonation came with a brutality and speed unmatched in Labor history. The Rudd–Gillard partnership died that evening.

Gillard, in effect, had signed the death warrant of the Labor Government. It is a contested judgement but the evidence is persuasive. The destruction of Rudd triggered a series of falling political dominoes that would reduce Labor to a minority government within months and would see its convincing defeat three years later. By her action Gillard assumed political responsibility for the consequences.

This became the pivotal moment in the six-year Rudd–Gillard–Rudd Government. Labor would never recover; the destructive forces unleashed assumed a life of their own. There were many dismal consequences: the destruction of Rudd as prime minister; the crippling of Gillard as the new prime minister; the conversion of Rudd into a compulsive insurgent; and a bitter Rudd–Gillard rivalry that would endure unabated until they both left politics. Despite Labor's achievements in office, the public's perpetual image became that of a government consumed by the Rudd–Gillard war.

Gillard's tragedy is that Rudd's flaws provoked her strike. She had an excuse and a rationale. Her justification lay in party sentiment. Gillard acted as agent of a Labor Party that was weak, panicked and faithless. It wanted an end to Rudd. Labor, as a political party, had failed at the task of governing and had misunderstood its responsibility to the nation.

In just a couple of hours Rudd had seen his ambitions and dreams reduced to dust. It was a time of tears, rage and incomprehension. Rudd has given his own account of that night, saying the Rudd–Gillard conversation rambled over a range of Gillard's concerns and for Rudd its essence was the argument that he could not win the election. 'That's the proposition that was put,' he said. 'There was nothing else.'[2]

Towards the end, with Labor veteran John Faulkner in the meeting as an honest witness, Rudd thought he had bargained his way to survival. Interviewed for this book, Rudd said he offered Gillard a compromise and that they reached an arrangement.

He said: 'It was a proposition from me ... he [Faulkner] can be the arbiter of this. I am clearly relaxed about that. I said if he is of the view that I am an impediment to the government winning the election come when the election was due, which is still frankly six months hence, and six months is quite a long time in politics, then of course I would vacate the position.'[3] Rudd proposed to put his leadership into Faulkner's hands on behalf of the party's interest.

It was a bizarre notion. But Rudd was desperate. He was fighting to survive, with the caucus going into meltdown around the building. Rudd wanted a time of grace to re-establish his government's momentum. If that failed, he would surrender to Gillard.

Continuing his account, Rudd said: 'The words I actually used about it were: "So we are agreed upon that?" And she said "Yes".' Rudd said they did the deal.[4] Faulkner was witness to her consent. Gillard left the room.

Rudd felt he had secured his survival. He immediately told his closest caucus supporter, Anthony Albanese, 'It's peace in our time.' Albanese confirms these words. Albanese said: 'Kevin said, it is resolved, yeah, no challenge.' Albanese started to spread the message that all was 'okay'.[5] Rudd felt sure he could recover support among the people of Australia. The threat to Rudd came from the Labor Party, not the populace.

In the preceding months Rudd had governed badly. This flaw, combined with his dismissive treatment of too many caucus colleagues, had produced a unique event: a first-term, election-winning Labor prime minister had lost the confidence of his caucus. This was Rudd's own work, the result of his political incompetence and character defects.

But Rudd was fooling himself. The proposal he put to Gillard was unworkable. The leadership crisis story was in the media, broken on the ABC's 7 p.m. television news bulletin on a tip from one Gillard backer and confirmed by another Gillard backer, cabinet minister Tony Burke.[6] The genie was out of the bottle and the publicity put Rudd under intolerable pressure. Gillard had crossed the threshold to a leadership crisis. After the meeting broke, she went to another room in the prime minister's suite and made some phone calls. The message Gillard received was: things have gone too far, the caucus wants a leadership change, individuals are making commitments. The public façade of Rudd–Gillard unity had been fatally breached.

Gillard then returned to Rudd's office. According to Rudd,

> She came back and said, 'I am now advised that you no longer have the confidence of the caucus and I am therefore requesting a leadership ballot.' To which I just said, 'You are what? We just had an agreement ten minutes ago that we shook on in the presence of Faulkner that these matters would not be dealt with till the end of the year and that Faulkner was to be the arbiter of it.' Then she comes back and reneges on the deal. There's not a word of exaggeration, it's exactly as it transpired.[7]

The history of leadership contests—witness Hawke–Keating—is that the participants have varying accounts of such critical exchanges. In long and frank interviews for this book there was one issue Gillard declined to discuss: this conversation. No doubt she will offer her own version in due course. It is vital, however, not to miss the wood for the trees. Gillard had moved relentlessly throughout the day of Wednesday 23 June towards this decision while keeping her options open. Her supporters confirm this. As a professional she delayed the final blow till assured she had the numbers.

For Rudd, the idea that only Gillard could save Labor was a fantastic concoction. He failed to grasp what had happened: his flawed leadership and contemptuous treatment of some colleagues had turned the once-proud Labor Party into an irrational tribal rampage. The crisis would testify to Labor's collapsing internal culture.

When Gillard eventually returned to her office it was flooded with caucus members. It had become a spontaneous uprising. People were feral to remove Rudd. The treason against him was open and rampant.

One of the right-wing faction leaders involved in his removal, David Feeney (later a frontbencher), gave the author the best summary of the originating impulse:

The events of June 2010 can only be understood with an appre-
ciation of the insufferable atmosphere of fear and intimidation
that prevailed amongst MPs and senators. A supine cabinet and a
caucus routinely subject to punitive abuse meant only a spontaneous uprising could overthrow the tyrant. Incremental reform and
heartfelt advice would only be greeted by a purge.[8]

So comprehensive was Rudd's humiliation that he did not contest the
leadership against Gillard the following morning in the party room. It was
the steepest descent from power of any prime minister in Australian history.

The deal Rudd put to Gillard had assumed, implicitly, caucus tolerance of Rudd's period of grace. But such tolerance was gone. In just two
and half years Rudd had expended the loyalty of the caucus majority.
This invites two insights: Rudd was defective as a leader of people; and
Labor as a party had shrunk to one core purpose—it existed only to
govern and would execute any leader or idea to stay in power.

Gillard is sure the party made the correct decision. Asked why, she
said:

> In my assessment Kevin was not going to be able to come out of
> the spiral that he was in. It was leading to more and more chaos.
> He was miserable. His demeanour in those last few weeks was that
> everything about the job annoyed him, from the woman who put
> a cup of tea in front of him. He was depressed. The show wasn't
> functional. If he had been capable of pulling out of that spiral he
> would have by then. This issue was about more than winning an
> election. The government just wasn't functioning.[9]

Influential right-wing leaders had decided Rudd could not win
the election. Research done in New South Wales in four marginal seats
pointed to defeat: it showed a 7 per cent swing against Labor and a 55–45
Coalition lead on the two-party-preferred vote.[10] But the published polls
were not nearly so bad. The Newspoll conducted before Rudd's execution
showed a 52–48 per cent Labor-winning lead. The three Newspolls
before that averaged at a 50–50 split. The argument of the anti-Rudd
faction chiefs that Rudd was in an irrecoverable position is unpersuasive.
Former prime minister John Howard and his deputy, Peter Costello, said
later they believed Rudd would have won any 2010 election against Tony
Abbott. This was the view of many Labor ministers, including Faulkner.
History is on Rudd's side: the notion that the Australian public would

dump Rudd at his first re-election for an untested Abbott who had been Opposition leader for a mere few months is unconvincing.

The Rudd–Gillard generation went off the rails at this point. The execution of Rudd and elevation of Gillard were premature. Caucus assumed the public had decided against Rudd, yet subsequent events suggest this was dubious. The public was unprepared for the Labor leadership change and reacted with hostility. Rudd was soon the most popular politician in the country—again. The best that Gillard could summon was minority government in 2010 and a landslide polling debacle in 2013 that saw her replaced by Rudd. It is, surely, the most powerful evidence that the June 2010 execution was wrong.

Gillard, far from being Labor's saviour, had a short honeymoon. This leads to the final extraordinary feature of the events of 23 June.

Gillard had no strategic game plan for office. She had no blueprint to revive Labor. Given that she seized the leadership from Rudd close to an election, the expectation is that she was ready with coherent plans. Yet this was not the case. 'I didn't have a plan,' says Gillard, attributing this omission to her innocence of any long-run plot.[11] The Labor Party had failed to conduct its due diligence on Gillard. While an impressive deputy, she assumed the office of prime minister too early and in the wrong way. She was not well known to the Australian public, nor had her credentials for the leadership of the nation been widely or deeply canvassed in public debate. Gillard's ruthless overnight elevation into the job—often called a 'coup'—came as a total surprise to most Australians.

The transition was brainless in its absence of virtually every requirement needed to make Gillard's elevation into a sustained success. Its brilliance was tactical: the swiftness of Rudd's despatch. Yet it was a strategic catastrophe and Gillard was unable to establish herself convincingly in office. There was a recklessness to the act. It was as though the removal of a first-term Labor prime minister after a few months of disappointing polls was a routine move after which Labor's standing was certain to rise again. If only it were so easy! In reality, there were no adults left to manage the party and Labor was consumed by a fatal trifecta: hubris, panic and incompetence.

Many of Labor's experienced warriors were dismayed and when asked for their opinions some years on are still adamant.

Rudd backer and future deputy Anthony Albanese said: 'I told a gathering that evening if you do this you will destroy two Labor prime ministers.' His prediction was fulfilled. Albanese said Rudd's destruction meant Labor could not campaign on his achievements, while Gillard's elevation meant she was permanently tarnished by these events.[12] He was proven correct on both counts.

Finance Minister Lindsay Tanner, one of the 'gang of four', said: 'Panic was a significant factor in the removal of Kevin Rudd.' He believed Rudd would have won the 2010 election. Beyond that, Tanner said, Labor had done long-run damage to itself as a party.

> Removing a first-term elected Labor prime minister by a caucus vote, ostensibly because of his management style, is such an extreme thing to do that those involved have found it necessary to enormously exaggerate the deficiencies in Rudd's leadership. It was impossible to attack the Rudd Government without undermining the Gillard Government.[13]

Former Labor leader and former ACTU president Simon Crean said: 'I said at the time I did not support a challenge. My view is that Kevin would have won the 2010 election.'[14] The Minister for Resources and another former ACTU president, Martin Ferguson, was incredulous and outraged on the night and told Faulkner: 'We've just killed our government.'[15] Faulkner did not dissent; he was appalled at Gillard's actions, the mindlessness of the caucus and saw Rudd's removal as a disaster.[16] Faulkner had previously warned Gillard: 'You cannot assume responsibility for moving against a first-term Labor prime minister just because there is a polling problem.'

Yet it never occurred to the conspirators that they were destroying not only Rudd but Gillard. They were blind to the real meaning of their actions.

Labor's Senate leader at the time, Chris Evans, said:

> I was deeply, deeply worried—I was not in the know—that we could suddenly overturn a prime minister in this way. I think I was the last cabinet minister to go and see Julia the following morning. I told her I was very uneasy about it. I liked her a lot, rated her highly but I didn't think this was a good idea.
>
> There is no doubt as far as I'm concerned these events destroyed both Kevin and Julia. Our inability to recover meant the government was doomed. I am deeply saddened about what happened to what I think could have been a very successful government. I think Julia had the capability to be a good prime minister. The problem was the circumstances of her coming to the job.[17]

Chris Bowen, who was shadow treasurer after the 2013 loss, said:

The big problem with June 2010 is that it was a surprise for the
Australian people. People went to the bed with one prime minister
[in the job] and woke up with another. I believe this fatally
undermined Julia's legitimacy from the beginning. I understand the
rationale of those who did it that way. But I believe, in hindsight, it
was a fundamental error. The case was not made to the people for
a change. I think it was difficult for the legitimacy issue to ever be
overcome, the minority parliament and the carbon issue all rolled
into the legitimacy question.[18]

Passionate Gillard backer and former Australian Workers' Union boss
Paul Howes, who publicly called for the leadership change that night on
television, later recanted and recognised the scale of the folly, unique in
Labor history. Interviewed in mid-2013 Howes said:

The tragedy is that we have destroyed someone who could have
been the greatest leader we have ever had. I think this woman
has an amazing ability to be a great leader but she is consistently
hamstrung by the way she became leader. Of course, it was a stupid
way to do it.[19]

Greg Combet, once seen as a future leader, called the event a 'tragedy'
for the Labor Party. He said:

I think the leadership change defined us in government over
six years. That's how people saw us. What they knew about the
government was Rudd's replacement by Gillard and the divisions
and destabilisation that came with it. If you ask most people, that's
what they remember about Labor in government, despite all the
good things we did. Julia was massively handicapped by it. The
way you become leader in any institution defines you. Coming to
leadership in a way that spoke of secrecy, midnight manoeuvres,
factions, union leaders speaking out, it crystallised a lot about the
way the Labor Party had come to operate. I don't think she ever
really recovered.[20]

One of Gillard's strongest backers as prime minister, Craig Emerson,
said: 'In my view there should not have been a leadership change.' Kevin

was performing poorly and there were huge issues not being addressed. But the change of prime ministers came as a shock and it put Julia on the back foot, particularly in Queensland where we had won many seats in 2007.'[21] Another supporter of Gillard when she was prime minister, Stephen Smith, said: 'I felt that in an election campaign despite all the problems that Kevin would have been able to win. Having been re-elected we could have addressed an orderly transition to Julia.'[22]

Significantly, this was also Treasurer Wayne Swan's preferred position. Swan did not want a leadership change. He felt it would be a mistake and he mobilised against it. The weekend before the change, Swan lobbied senior caucus figures (including Smith) and argued that it was too close to an election to switch leaders. Swan says he spent some time 'letting people know that in my view it was a bad idea'. Swan told the author: 'I felt it would be potentially too disruptive. I conveyed this position to the New South Wales Right. Kevin knew my position.'[23] Swan became Gillard's great supporter as prime minister but he had played no role in instigating the change and joined the push against Rudd only when its momentum was irresistible.

Foreign Minister under Gillard, Bob Carr said:

> It was a crucial error and abnormal behaviour for the caucus to bring down a first-term Labor prime minister. The decision was made by factional bosses. There was no justification for it. The polling showed the normal retrievable position. I believe Rudd's continuing grievance about it was justified and from that time on the government became a Shakespearean tragedy laden with paradox and vengeance.[24]

Interviewed for this book, John Faulkner said: 'It is the seminal moment of the six years in government. My view was that neither of them would survive it—and neither of them did survive it.'[25] ALP National Secretary for the 2013 election George Wright said: 'Without passing judgement on the people, there is no doubt in my mind this is the original sin from which everything else flows for the next three years. What happened in 2010 was an awful mistake for the party and government.'[26]

The Labor leader after the 2013 election, Bill Shorten, a supporter of change at the time, stands by the decision to dump Rudd. Asked in 2014 if he still agreed with Rudd's removal, Shorten said: 'Yes. But it was spontaneous. I certainly formed the view by June 2010 that we were in electoral trouble of a very serious nature.'[27]

Labor's veteran adviser Bruce Hawker, temporarily working in Rudd's office at the time and closely tied to the right-wing faction, was dismayed. His immediate reaction was: 'This would end in tears—and not just Kevin's. Had they thought this through? There will be a massive public backlash and they will blame Julia—one of our best assets. We will be burning two leaders.' For Hawker, the party was ruining the present and the future.[28]

Former New South Wales Party Secretary Senator Sam Dastyari said:

> It was a mistake. In one night Julia Gillard went from being lady-in-waiting to Lady Macbeth. She was never able to get rid of that image. Julia had a legitimacy problem and it sprang from that night. At the time I thought the leadership change would be good for the election and bad for the party. In hindsight, it was bad for both. The damage we did, not just to Kevin but to the legacy of Julia, haunts us to this day.[29]

Albanese described how Labor, at one stroke, had ruined its past and its future:

> It meant Labor couldn't sell what we had done in government. We had protected jobs in the GFC, we had a great story to tell. But the obvious response from voters was: 'Well, if you're so good why did you depose your prime minister?' Looking forward, it meant everything we did from that point was tarnished. Julia Gillard was weighted down by the way she got the job.[30]

For this book the four key factional figures most associated with Rudd's removal—Mark Arbib, Feeney, Kim Carr and Don Farrell—were tested on their retrospective views.

Arbib, national Right factional convenor at the time, was unrepentant: 'The caucus was left with little choice. Unfortunately Kevin's position had become untenable.'[31] South Australian Right leader Farrell says he had always been consistent on Rudd: he opposed Rudd for the leadership in 2006, voted for Rudd's removal in 2010 and voted against his return in 2013. He had no reason to revise any of these decisions.[32] Left-wing faction leader and cabinet minister Kim Carr, who backed the change, conceded his blunder: 'This event was the key in the destruction of the Labor Government,' he says. Carr later re-joined the Rudd camp and became a fierce Gillard opponent. He lamented his role, saying he wished he had gone to see Rudd on the day.[33]

The most nuanced response comes from Feeney:

> The decision to switch from Kevin Rudd to Julia Gillard saved
> the Labor Government from impending political defeat. It was the
> right decision. The execution of the leadership change, however,
> was flawed in that we had learnt the wrong lessons from the
> Hawke–Keating transition. The swiftness of the decision and broad
> base of caucus that supported it was no compensation for the fact
> that the wider community and even the political elite were left
> bewildered and even shocked.[34]

The ALP National Secretary at the time, Karl Bitar, argued that his
research pointed to Labor's defeat under Rudd. This remains his view:
'While I was convinced we would lose the election under Rudd, I was
not convinced that if Gillard was leader it would enable us to win. We
would need to demonstrate a clear change in direction through our policies and action.'[35]

How should blame be allocated? It should be shared. Rudd is culpable because he lost the confidence of the caucus and Gillard is culpable
because she decided, ultimately, to step into the breach and overthrow
Rudd.

Evans insisted on a wider responsibility: 'I take the blame, my fair
share of the blame, for what happened in the Rudd Government. In the
final analysis cabinet should have been braver, we should have used the
cabinet to pull Rudd into line. And we didn't.'[36] As an agitator for change,
Howes insisted on collective blame on the part of the conspirators: 'We
are all in on it. You can't just blame Julia Gillard. It is our naivety. The
naivety of the party to think we could execute a leader in such a way
that there wouldn't be credibility problems for her. That is the tragedy of
Julia Gillard.'[37]

The sheer extent to which ALP figures see the event as terminating Rudd but dooming Gillard justifies the death warrant description.
The Labor Government would linger for another three years but Labor
did not recover from this night. It is rare in history that the timing of a
government's death warrant can be so exactly identified, but that is the
meaning of 23 June 2010.

Throughout his leadership, Kevin Rudd had assumed that Gillard
would succeed him; this was also the universal view in the Labor Party.
The transition should have been managed in Rudd's second term. Labor
was blind to the lessons of history: Bob Hawke had won three elections

before Paul Keating confronted him on the leadership and had four election victories under his belt before Keating deposed him. By contrast the caucus of 2010 was consumed by haste and was devoid of judgement.

There was no compulsion in Gillard's move. It was a voluntary act. Her supporters applauded her courage in stepping forward to 'save' the government. Yet she created a new and deeper series of problems. The truth is, Rudd and Gillard needed each other. They had succeeded as a partnership. They could not succeed when that partnership was ruined. This was not Rudd's era; it was not Gillard's era. It was the Rudd–Gillard era. They came to the Labor leadership in a joint enterprise. They would succeed or fall as a joint enterprise. When their enterprise was detonated in 2010 it was the end of their alliance and their government.

To this day Faulkner is one of the few prepared to confront the truth: 'They were both at their best and the Labor Government was at its best when they worked as a team. Kevin was a better PM when Julia was with him. Julia would have been a better PM with Kevin's support.'[38] Together they succeeded; separated they were diminished.

Labor had never executed a prime minister in the first term. The issue will remain in dispute but the evidence is that the leadership change would not have happened in a properly functioning political institution. It testifies to deep flaws in the culture, values and power structures of Labor in government. If the mistaken execution of a Labor prime minister does not prove this point to the party then it is hard to imagine what else would do the job. Some corrective measures have since been taken but they are not enough.

Rudd and Gillard were the brightest stars of their generation. Yet the true nature of this Labor generation was deceptive. It was unusual because it was a shared leadership. It was different from the recent ALP norm, which was one of a dominant leader with authority in his own right (witness Gough Whitlam, Hawke and Keating). In December 2006, Kevin Rudd had become ALP leader in a 49 to 39 defeat of Kim Beazley. But he won only because of Gillard's numerical support as his deputy; neither Rudd nor Gillard could have defeated Beazley in their own right, yet they prevailed as a team. 'The point is that we needed Julia Gillard,' said the pivotal New South Wales Right organiser and Rudd champion Mark Arbib. 'We couldn't win without her.'[39] Beazley said his survival depended upon Rudd and Gillard remaining rivals: 'Once they united, then I was finished.'[40]

As leader, Rudd lacked the internal authority of Whitlam, Hawke or Keating. As prime minister he had the opportunity to establish such a power base in his own right but failed to do so. The source of Rudd's power lay outside the party—it was with the Australian people. In 2007 Rudd became the third Labor leader since the Great Depression to bring the party into office at a general election. But Kevin's internal position was vulnerable: it still rested on his unity ticket with Julia.

The same limitation applied to Gillard. At the November 2007 election victory Gillard began her dramatic rise to high office when she became Australia's first female deputy prime minister. Around the nation women applauded. Yet Gillard won this honour only because of her deal with Rudd. Most of her enthusiastic backers denied reality: Julia's success depended upon her unity ticket with Kevin. As a realist Gillard had known this. In 2006 she put the party's interests first and deferred to Rudd. 'I made a clear decision,' Gillard said. 'I put it to Kevin, and I believed it, that he was ready to go, that he was the right person to lead us into the contest against Howard.'[41]

It was a far-sighted decision by Gillard. It created the Rudd–Gillard team, the essential step in Howard's defeat. The power reality that was obscured at the time was that Gillard was the key actor. 'I was the change piece for Rudd in running against Beazley,' she said. 'Without my support, which was probably greater numerically than his at that time, he couldn't have become prime minister.'[42]

Rudd proved a more successful campaigner than his backers had dared to hope. Howard was convinced that Rudd made the difference, saying Labor 'would not have won the election' under Beazley.[43] Faulkner says: 'I would rate as Opposition leaders Whitlam as number one pre-1972 and then little to pick between Rudd and Abbott.'[44] Gillard, as his female deputy, played a complementary role in Rudd's victory but he did not need Gillard to win the election. Rudd needed her in order to become ALP leader, and he needed her in order to stay ALP leader; it was their compact.

Interviewed towards the end of his first year as prime minister, Rudd told the author he talked with Gillard 'all the time' and that 'it is a very good relationship'. He said: 'There is complete transparency, trust, common analysis of politics. I think that's based on a high degree of mutual respect.' Asked what quality he most admired in Gillard, Rudd nominated her loyalty. This was 'her most remarkable quality'. 'I have taken that as a given because I have seen it so often,' Kevin said of Julia's loyalty.[45] For Rudd in late 2008, the idea of betrayal by Gillard was inconceivable.

Interviewed six months before she removed Rudd and having no premonition of such an event, Gillard praised their partnership. Her description of its significance is remarkable. 'This has been a stable government and that stability will be there for the long term,' Gillard said. 'I think there is a natural equilibrium within the government.' Julia, in effect, was saying that she and Kevin had created the right internal balance for long-run success. She said she trusted and respected Rudd.

Gillard was explicit: when their agreement was sealed in 2006 she brokered no deal with Rudd on her own leadership succession. As a realist, she knew it was likely. But Gillard was content to remain deputy while Rudd remained a successful leader. 'If I do this current job [deputy prime minister] for the long term, that will be enough for me,' she said.[46] People will scoff but it is true: Gillard could have lived happily without being prime minister. This is not to deny her ambition. The truth is that in early 2010 Gillard was not plotting to roll Rudd.

There is indeed a Shakespearean quality to this story: Rudd and Gillard were a brilliant team before their destruction born of human frailty. From the start they seemed possessed of a maturity. Labor's two stars had united in mutual interest; yet Howard and Costello were locked in unresolved rivalry. Labor had moved to the next generation; the Coalition was trapped with Howard and unable to secure generational change to Costello. Many argued the Rudd–Gillard team was doomed from its inception but such claims are nonsense. It was a real partnership and, for three years, it was highly successful. In this period it was the most successful Labor team since the early days of Hawke and Keating.

However, in politics the lure of power can blur the reality. It became too easy to forget the foundational axiom: if the Rudd–Gillard partnership fell apart the Labor generation and its government was in jeopardy. A brainless caucus did not grasp the first rule about its government: as long as Kevin and Julia worked together, Labor faced a potential golden age. Gillard was positioned to ascend at the desired time.

Rudd and Gillard needed each other not just because of caucus numbers; they needed each other because of their complementary strengths and characters. Each substituted for the other's weakness. It was a strange but profound truth.

Kevin and Julia were polar opposites. For many caucus members their partnership had been improbable. Beazley said Gillard had 'no particular regard' for Rudd.[47] The main facilitator of their compact was Victorian Socialist Left powerbroker Kim Carr, who spent months during 2006 working on them both. 'Kevin and Julia were very different people who distrusted each other,' Carr said, looking back. 'Bringing them together on a joint ticket was not easy to achieve.'[48] The extent of their contrasting lives and outlook was remarkable.

Kevin came from outside the Labor Party while Gillard was born into a Labor family. Kevin hailed from a southeast Queensland farm and was raised in a conservative family, his father, Bert, being a Country Party supporter and his mother, Margaret, being DLP. There was no Labor birthright, no trade union ties, no class consciousness.[49] Kevin came from one of the nation's deepest conservative heartlands with a long National Party suit. He was born into an understanding of conservative Australia.

Julia, by contrast, came from a working-class family steeped in Labor faiths located initially at Barry, a coal-exporting and industrial port for the Welsh mines. Her father, John, admired the Welsh political hero Aneurin Bevan and, after migrating to Australia in 1966 and doing it tough in Adelaide, he became a hospital nurse and active trade unionist. The family thrived on the glory days of Whitlam in Canberra and Don Dunstan in Adelaide. 'Dad was pro-Labor, Mum was pro-Labor, that's just who we were,' Julia said. Labor politics were in her blood and in her home.[50]

Kevin was a Christian while Julia embraced atheism. At university Kevin's membership of the Christian evangelical group was as conspicuous as Julia's plunge into student politics, the Labor Club and a campus job with the Australian Union of Students. Kevin met his future wife, Therese, in his first week of university, aged eighteen. 'I think you're the first Kevin I've ever met,' she told him. Meanwhile Julia at sixteen told her mother she had no wish to have children; she didn't see herself as a wife and mother.[51]

Julia thrived in Melbourne working at the AUS office on the corner of Grattan and Lygon streets, the social and intellectual heart of the inner city, a focus of progressive and left-wing politics. She absorbed its values and had a relationship with another AUS organiser, Michael O'Connor, later National Secretary of the Construction, Forestry, Mining and Energy Union (CFMEU), to whom she paid tribute in her maiden speech. Julia learnt the factional and networking skills for Labor politics in her early twenties. She was a radical activist, whereas Kevin was conventional and traditionalist, a natural right-winger.

Kevin and Therese married at beautiful St John's Anglican Church at Reid, just off Anzac Parade, in 1981 and had three children. At the Australian National University, Kevin had lived at Burgmann College among future politicians and public servants. He shunned the fun-loving bar crowd and had no interest in student politics. The scholar Pierre Ryckmans, who supervised the Asian Studies student's thesis, said Kevin was 'neat, courteous, sound, reliable and articulate'.[52] He was too perfect to be true. Kevin studied Mandarin, lived in Taiwan for a year and then became a diplomat with postings in Stockholm and Beijing. Former DFAT chief Dick Woolcott said he was a future secretary. From university their divergent paths were set—Julia was being socialised into Labor politics while Kevin headed towards a lofty career in public policy.

Julia chose law, kept her focus narrow and joined Slater & Gordon, a firm specialising in trade union briefs where, after only three years, she became a salaried partner at age twenty-nine. The firm was a Labor stronghold, wired into the party's factional and union players and represented, among other unions, the powerful right-wing Australian Workers' Union. Julia's professional and social life became intertwined. Acting for an AWU Victorian official, Bruce Wilson, with whom she had a relationship, Gillard gave advice leading to the establishment of a legal entity on Wilson's behalf that, unknown either to her or the AWU national leaders, was used by Wilson to defraud companies. The upshot was Gillard's resignation; it would be the only shadow on her relentless path to the Lodge.

In personal terms, Julia was unpretentious, smart, devoid of vanity, a tough woman succeeding in a man's world. She would not be intimidated but knew when to defer to power. In the office she dressed conservatively, embraced a punishing work schedule and was known for calmness under pressure. She was a feminist but never ran on feminist issues. She had charm and an appealing frankness. Her style was captured when, handing out political material in Melbourne, an older bloke looked at her photo, looked at Gillard and said, 'Taken on a good day, wasn't it, love?' She shot back: 'And you'd be bloody Robert Redford, would you, mate?'[53] This was pure Julia; what you saw is what you got.

Rudd came at Labor from the outside. At each step he was an irresistible force: a smooth-talking atom of intelligence and ambition. As a fifteen year old he wrote to Gough Whitlam saying he wanted to become a diplomat. He joined the Labor Party not by virtue of tribalism but because of intellectual commitment to Whitlam's China policy. He landed the top position with a surprised Queensland Premier Wayne Goss by answering a newspaper advertisement. When he decided to enter politics everybody was shocked except Therese.

Gillard's progress, by contrast, came from within the ALP beast, the legacy of years wrestling with factional and union powers. At university she worked part-time with the Socialist Forum, a rallying point for left-wing ideas. Yet Julia was more pragmatist than ideologue. She had a tense time with Victoria's Socialist Left faction, headed by Kim Carr, who was hostile to the Socialist Forum and suspicious of her. Her ascension to Parliament was highlighted by bitter factional feuds, her relentless determination and a pre-selection where she was opposed by Tanner and Carr but put together a coalition of both Left and Right support. The O'Connor brothers, Michael and Brendan, were important, along with the Right powerbrokers.[54] Julia had proved her stamina, pragmatism and intra-party skills.

Kevin was an outsider and Julia an insider. As politicians, Rudd's success was his appeal to the public while Gillard's strength lay within the party. Their complementary qualities made them a powerful team but, if left alone as individuals, exposed their deficiencies. In the end they tortured each other as enemies because their rivalry defied resolution.

Rudd was grounded in the Australian community and Gillard was grounded in the culture of the Victorian Labor Party. Rudd was a conservative God-fearing family man, though a modernist with the ability to appeal to both conservative and progressive voters. Gillard was an unmarried Leftist with a radical past, possessed of emotional fortitude, superior at party management, a heroine for some party loyalists but viewed with suspicion by many from the Labor Right and Left. Gillard was hardly representative of wider Australian society.

Once they were united, they were formidable. Rudd and Gillard took control of the Labor Party, steamrolled Howard and, in office, looked set to ignite a brilliant chapter in Labor's saga. Their tragedy lay in the wilful, unnecessary and premature destruction of their partnership. This event doomed the Rudd–Gillard generation. It would destroy the Labor Government they had won and provoke recognition that the party faced a deeper crisis.

CHAPTER 2

THE MAKING OF AN OPPOSITION

On 26 November 2009, Liberal frontbencher Tony Abbott, reluctant yet determined, confronted his party leader Malcolm Turnbull in his office and instigated an upheaval that would shape Australian politics for years. Abbott asked Turnbull to abandon his support for carbon pricing. He was accompanied by Senate leader Nick Minchin, the ideological spearhead of the campaign against Turnbull and the engineer of this encounter. This meeting would unleash unpredictable winds that would ruin Turnbull's leadership, catapult Abbott into the office of Opposition leader and eventually destroy both Kevin Rudd and Julia Gillard.

It triggered the remaking of conservative politics in Australia under Abbott's leadership. The upshot is that the conservative side strengthened its electoral base yet excited huge hostility from the progressive political class. There were furiously contested views about what the rise of Abbott actually meant. However, by 2013 the consequences were manifest: the remaking of conservative politics under Abbott had been pivotal to the eclipse of the Labor Government. It is a story of resurrection from the ashes.

By late 2009 the Liberal Party that Turnbull led and the Coalition he headed were in crisis. After the Turnbull–Abbott–Minchin meeting, events would spiral out of control. For the next week the Liberals became a cauldron of chaotic manoeuvres driven by wilful politicians and clashing beliefs. When the dust settled the participants struggled to grasp the full meaning of the leadership transition from Turnbull to Abbott. This event became the great fulcrum of Australian politics, the point at which the system shifted, leaving a confused political class and media shaking their heads in disbelief.

Abbott's election as leader mocked the idea of master tacticians controlling results. His elevation saved the Liberal Party, but it was an accidental event. On 1 December, Abbott was elected leader with a party-room vote of 42 to 41 against Turnbull, a result nobody in the party would have believed possible when Abbott had entered the leader's office with Minchin five days earlier. Looking back from the perspective of 2014, Abbott said: 'It may seem odd to say so now, but I became leader by accident.'[1]

A humble man with a turbulent personality but inner strength, Abbott has always excited conflicting emotions. Much of the Labor Party and political media believed he was unelectable as prime minister, yet his four-year record as Opposition leader would offer an alternative view: that only Abbott could have maximised the Coalition vote at the general elections of 2010 and 2013. It was a conclusion that Labor preferred not to comprehend. There is no precedent in the past half century for so many experts and participants to so comprehensively misinterpret the nature and impact of a political leader. His record suggests Abbott was the most successful Opposition leader since Gough Whitlam forty years earlier.

The Abbott–Turnbull struggle was never about popularity, a fact that distinguished it from the long Rudd–Gillard saga. Rather, it was about ideas and political identity and, as a result, it was a far more important contest: it arose from a profound internal crisis within the Liberal Party.

Minchin believed that Turnbull had to be stopped. He was convinced that Turnbull threatened the stability and unity of conservative politics. This dispute about climate change policy had a deeper meaning—it went to the identity of the Liberal Party. Minchin's immediate purpose was to prevent Turnbull from realising his declared objective of voting in the Parliament to pass the emissions trading scheme (ETS) proposed by Rudd as Australia's prime response to the worldwide problem of global warming. Minchin judged that if Turnbull proceeded then 'all National Party senators and at least a dozen Liberal senators if not more would have crossed the floor'. The impact would vary from serious to catastrophic. Minchin said:

> This would have resulted in the biggest crossing of the floor by Coalition senators in the history of the Coalition. It could well have meant the end of the coalition with the National Party. It could cause an irrevocable split, a literal split, in the Liberal Party. I foresaw thousands upon thousands of resignations from the Liberal Party if we had supported Rudd. I believed the consequences for the party would have been devastating.[2]

Minchin was not alone in this assessment. The Federal Director of the Liberal Party, Brian Loughnane, was alarmed at the consequences of Turnbull's push for the Liberal Party to support Rudd's Carbon Pollution Reduction Scheme (CPRS). Interviewed for this book, Loughnane said:

> With an unresolved situation on how to handle the ETS and potential for a significant number of senators to move to the crossbenches, our concern was this could spiral out of control into one of the worst crises in the history of the Liberal Party. If you have a group of senators move to the crossbenches then you essentially have a split in your party.[3]

Loughnane's nightmare was the prospect of being caught at an election in the worst possible circumstances. At the time he told senior party figures that they faced one of the most dangerous internal situations since the founding of the Liberal Party by Sir Robert Menzies.

The most comprehensive survey of party sentiment had been made by deputy leader Julie Bishop over the previous two months. She had spoken to nearly all Liberal MPs and senators and probably had the best grasp of the mood. Bishop told the author:

> I believe had we attempted to support Rudd's scheme before the Copenhagen conference it would have led to the dissolution of the Liberal and National coalition. There would have been a very substantial number of Liberal parliamentarians, and in particular Liberal senators, who would have crossed the floor or abstained. I think Minchin as leader would have taken a lot of people with him.[4]

In short, the conservative side would have sunk into disunity, indiscipline and bitterness. Bishop's survey revealed other powerful sentiments: a burning resentment of Rudd's tactics and an emerging belief that if the Coalition surrendered to him it would sacrifice its integrity, reveal its weakness and become easy prey for Labor.

The depth of the 2009 crisis in conservative politics is rarely appreciated. But senior Labor minister Anthony Albanese, a student of the Parliament's mood, told a caucus social event on the evening of 26 November that: 'We've now got the Libs on the canvas and they are more internally split than any major political party since the great Labor split of the 1950s.'[5] It was an extraordinary claim, but Albanese was right. He had picked the trend. There was much evidence to buttress his comment.

Abbott was steeped in the cultural dynamics of Australian conservatism. He realised, eventually, that the division over climate change had ignited every fuse within conservative politics—economic, cultural and political. Interviewed for this book, Abbott said:

> It threatened to split our party and it threatened to break the Coalition. If Malcolm had remained leader and had asked us to vote for Rudd's proposal there would have been a lot of former frontbenchers voting against his position and there would have been, I think, a united vote by the National Party against his position. It may well have broken the Coalition on this issue. Thank God it didn't happen. The aftershocks would have been serious. The perception in the public's mind would have been that on this critical issue we were utterly divided and, to use the immortal phase of Bob Hawke, if you can't govern yourselves then you can't govern the country. This was by far the most divisive crisis in my time in the Liberal Party.[6]

The late 2009 Liberal Party showdown is the most misunderstood event in recent political history. Yet it is the key to the politics of the period. It is, above all, a struggle for internal unity. In early October, Bishop made a note of what Abbott had told her: 'The first duty of the leader is to keep the party together.' In the end, this is where Abbott took his stand. He says: 'My view in late 2009 was that we needed to find a position on the ETS that, as far as humanly possibly, kept the party together. This was the priority. This wasn't a division about leadership. It was a division about policy and ultimately about belief.'[7] That made it more dangerous. Abbott feared that if a satisfactory solution could not be found the result might be a Labor government, by default, for a number of years. The defining Abbott–Turnbull difference in the crisis was that Abbott was able to unite the Liberals when, under Turnbull, they were only becoming more divided.

Much of the media analysis over 2009–14 centred on the fact that polls showed Abbott was relatively unpopular while Turnbull was relatively popular. Such polls, however, were actually irrelevant as long as the over-arching reality remained: that Abbott could unite the conservative side and Turnbull couldn't. The evidence lay in the record of Turnbull and Abbott as leaders. Ultimately, Turnbull's intelligence and appeal were insufficient because he was unable to command his own army, a guarantor of defeat.

'Tony made the point to me about unity,' Turnbull said. 'When we were cycling around the lake one day he said, "Sometimes preserving unity is more important than getting the policy right." That is true, unity is important. But at the time I felt a majority of the party room wanted the ETS.'[8] The irony is that Turnbull's support for an ETS had been John Howard's 2007 election policy. This is the reason he began with majority support from his own side. Turnbull's problem was the tide running against him.

With Rudd's bills before the Parliament, a new mood was apparent in parts of rural, regional and suburban Australia. Prominent National Barnaby Joyce saw this and began waging an effective anti-ETS grassroots campaign. For the first time people began to realise climate change action meant higher taxes and higher power prices. There was a sceptical cultural backlash from conservative voters suspicious about alarmist edicts from the scientific and political establishment and hostile to moralistic lectures demanding sacrifice now to save future generations from catastrophe. And there was mounting fear that Australia might be locked into action, short of any global deal, that would damage the economy. Yet this growing resistance had no political home. The Coalition was nominally lining up to back Rudd's ETS scheme while the National Party was turning against the policy. The conservative wing of the Liberals saw the problem: there was a grass-roots revolt against carbon pricing within its constituency but Turnbull was on Rudd's side.

Abbott had wrestled all year over his position. His internal struggle was later described by Turnbull on his blog:

> Tony himself has, in just four or five months, publicly advocated the blocking of the [ETS], the passing of the ETS, the amending of the ETS and, if the amendments were satisfactory, passing it, and now the blocking of it ... every time he announced a new position to me he would preface it with, 'Mate, mate, I know I am a bit of a weathervane on this but ...'

Abbott's confusion had become a point of discussion among colleagues. Yet there was no shame in searching for the best path from a complex forest. When Abbott did decide, with much persuasion from Minchin, he found his political anchor. Abbott said of the ETS: 'It was one of those things where the more you thought about it, the less you liked it.'[9] And there was a redeeming feature: Abbott would call the politics right for the Liberal Party.

For much of the year Turnbull's strategy had been persuasive. His real aim was to neutralise the climate change issue, which he saw as Rudd's political strength. Turnbull said: 'I felt the best way to deal with climate change was to get the legislation amended, get the scheme passed and get it off the table. That meant we could return to our core narrative, the economy, debt and deficits. This was our strength.'[10] Turnbull's constant fear was that Rudd, if denied, would call a double dissolution election on his climate change scheme and smash the Coalition.

The problem—as Abbott, Minchin and Loughnane saw—was that the conservative grass roots were staging a revolt against the price hikes and cultural symbolism of Rudd's scheme. The more Rudd lectured people about their moral obligations, the more Barnaby Joyce was able to raise a populist backlash. The conservative wing of the Liberal Party concluded that implementation of Turnbull's approach would crack the party's foundations. This crystallised into a simple question: why are we supporting Labor? One of Abbott's fiercest supporters, Bronwyn Bishop, later nailed this sentiment when she said Turnbull was trying to steal their party and they wanted it back.

Abbott's message to Turnbull was simple: our task is to fight Rudd, not support him. Minchin explained the essence of their 26 November meeting: 'I said Tony and I could not support Rudd's bill and, as a consequence, we would resign from the frontbench.' Minchin said the Senate deputy, Eric Abetz, would also resign. Turnbull asked Abbott: 'Are you clearing the way for a leadership change?' Abbott said the issue was not the leadership. 'My aim is to change the policy,' he said. 'That's why we're here.' Ensuring Turnbull was left in no doubt, Abbott said: 'If you change the policy then I will support you as leader.'[11]

It was a face-to-face dispute over policy. It is hard to imagine a greater contrast with the popularity-based sleaze of the Rudd–Gillard feuds. The cynics will scoff but the facts are irrefutable. There was no personal vanity in Abbott's decision. Abbott's behaviour over the next few days revealed that his prime motive was, in his view, to save the Liberal Party by reversing its climate change policy. He was ready to back Turnbull, and then Joe Hockey, as leader if they delivered the policy change. Abbott only contested the leadership when first Turnbull and then Hockey refused to turn against the ETS.

Turnbull was never for turning. Carbon pricing was one of his deepest beliefs from his time as Environment minister under Howard. He was well versed in this policy and the international experience. Convinced of the reality of human-induced global warming and a market response as the superior solution, Turnbull could not retreat. He told Minchin and Abbott: 'How can I change the principles I have championed? What reputation would I have left?' Turnbull was going to fight. It was the honest and honourable decision. Those cynics who say politics is only about power know nothing of real political motivation. As leader, Turnbull took a courageous stand and almost saved his position.

Turnbull knew that this request of Minchin and Abbott, with resignations in their pockets, constituted political blackmail. 'Their aim was to kill the ETS,' Turnbull said. 'When I asked them what our alternative policy was going to be they had no idea.'[12] At one point Turnbull left the room to ring his wife, Lucy. Abbott looked across at Turnbull's office chief, Chris Kenny, and said 'Sorry mate.' But Turnbull's house was built on a cracked foundation. He based his position on a bitter party meeting two days before where there had been a narrow majority for supporting Rudd's scheme. The conservative wing of the party refused to accept the decision. Minchin had called for the issue to be reconsidered by the shadow cabinet.

In a shock move, Kevin Andrews, convinced Turnbull was unfit to be leader, had challenged for the leadership in the party room on Wednesday 25 November where his leadership spill motion was rejected 48 to 35 votes. It was a strong vote for Andrews, who was not considered a serious contender. This event told the conservative forces that Turnbull was at risk. The numbers had a deep effect on Abbott. The next day Minchin pulled the trigger. He decided that he, as Senate leader, would not vote in the Parliament in favour of Rudd's scheme. That meant he had to resign from the shadow cabinet. As soon as Minchin told Abbott of his decision Abbott said he would adopt the same position. Minchin had been the decisive agent.

The Minchin–Abbott position was a declaration of political war against Turnbull. When Turnbull refused to buckle, the upshot became a three-way struggle for the leadership between Turnbull, Abbott and Hockey. In this contest Turnbull supported an ETS, Hockey supported a conscience vote on an ETS and only Abbott rejected carbon pricing.

The Liberal Party, just two years after Howard's 2007 election defeat, had reached a crossroads. This issue transcended climate change and went to identity and values. Howard's genius as leader had been to openly proclaim his party as a 'broad church' representing two great political traditions, the liberal and conservative traditions. This was the single greatest lesson Howard had learnt from his failed leadership during the 1980s. Upon his return and for eleven years as prime minister, he ran his government and selected his cabinet to harmonise these two traditions, liberal and conservative. Howard promoted a large number of liberals or moderates—namely, Robert Hill, Philip Ruddock, Brendan Nelson, Julie Bishop, Turnbull, Amanda Vanstone, Michael Wooldridge, Kay Patterson and Hockey—and in doing so secured a new internal peace. For Howard, this strategy went beyond mere unity. 'We are the custodians of both traditions in the Australian polity,' Howard said of liberalism and conservatism.[13] His broad church aimed to occupy enough of the voting spectrum to put Labor under permanent pressure and create a Liberal Party with far wider support than that enjoyed by its counterpart, the British Conservative Party.

The Abbott–Turnbull showdown now threatened this broad church. Climate change had become the ideological wedge between liberals and conservatives. Turnbull and Abbott represented these warring outlooks. For Turnbull, the policy debate was a no-brainer. He 'knew' the ETS was the 'right side of history'. Accepting the economic argument that the market was the most efficient means of containing emissions, Turnbull saw any retreat as a policy and political blunder. He asked his colleagues: Are we really saying Howard, who backed an ETS, was too green?

Turnbull represented the Sydney seat of Wentworth, one of the richest, most socially progressive, most climate change–sensitive areas in the nation. By contrast Abbott was sceptic enough to call climate change 'absolute crap', realist enough to distrust prospects for a global deal on emissions trading, smart enough to see the coming populist revolt over higher power prices and, because he was a conservative suspicious of grand plans, increasingly of the view that Rudd's new carbon apparatus would increase domestic power prices without any tangible impact on the global problem. Abbott concluded that Rudd's ETS was flawed as both a policy and a political instrument.

The politics of climate change had been transformed since the 2007 poll. For Rudd, climate change was a weapon to be mobilised by Labor to smash the electoral standing of the Coalition. Abbott grasped that Labor owned the issue of carbon pricing. He saw the consequences: if the Coalition under Turnbull voted for Rudd's scheme then Rudd would be vindicated. The Liberals would get no thanks from Labor or the voters. They would be left vanquished and broken, nursing a deepening internal row and facing an even greater election defeat. How crazy was that?

Before the leadership ballot, Hockey sought Howard's counsel. He stayed neutral but offered critical advice: the task was to keep the Liberal

Party united. Howard got to the essence. This test became the key to Abbott's success.

Abbott's judgement was that only one policy—rejection of Rudd's ETS—could hold the Liberal Party and its constituency together. Abbott's insight was to discern that the anti-ETS side, then a minority in the country, could become a majority over time and furnish a viable platform for the Coalition parties. This was a prescient judgement, as proven by events. On 1 October, during a long car trip, Abbott formed the view that opposing Rudd's policy would invest the Coalition with a new hope: a campaign against Labor's 'giant new tax on everything'.[14]

In September 2009, after Turnbull returned from talks with Britain's Tory leader, David Cameron, he nailed his faith to the wall. 'I will not lead a party that is not as committed to effective action on climate change as I am,' Turnbull said.[15] Abbott saw immediately that it was a most unwise formula. He said: 'I found myself thinking: "Mate, you've just given an ultimatum to the party and you may not like the way it responds."'[16] This was Whitlamesque in its fatalistic grandeur: Turnbull purported to define the party's values and tied his leadership to this view. But as the divisions deepened, Turnbull was stranded.

'We thought Joe Hockey was the person who should lead the party,' Abbott said. 'We all knew Joe was popular. I only decided to contest the leadership ballot after it became clear that Joe was not ready to change the policy should he become leader.'[17] With Turnbull pledged to the ETS and Hockey seeking a middle way, only Abbott was committed to sinking the ETS and reversing course. He stood to represent that position.

In the end Abbott emerged as leader not by calculation but by accident because Turnbull and Hockey split the pro-ETS vote. 'I'm a bit overwhelmed,' Abbott said on leaving the party room as leader. It was a surprise result. Many Liberals were stunned. A Newspoll published the day before the party meeting showed Abbott by far the least popular of the three candidates. It had Hockey 33 per cent, Turnbull 30 per cent and Abbott 19 per cent.

As soon as the leadership was settled, Abbott moved to a vote on the ETS, the trigger for the crisis. A secret ballot on a policy issue was a highly unusual process and the vote was extraordinary—a resounding 54 to 29 vote against the ETS. Many Liberals were surprised by the size of the vote against Rudd's scheme. The party, recognising Abbott's victory, had accepted its policy logic. The truth is that Abbott's position was far stronger than his personal one-vote margin implied—the party was behind his crusade to destroy Rudd's scheme. They had completed a leadership and policy revolution.

Turnbull, a progressive liberal, had been eclipsed by Abbott as a conservative populist. It was one of the wildest events in politics for decades, triggering a range of emotional and confusing reactions. The core judgement, however, was manifest: that in the interests of unity and self-preservation the Liberal Party had to recast itself against Rudd's scheme.

There was a deeper reality at work. With his origins in the conservative wing of the party, Abbott was in the tradition of Howard and Fraser, both tied to the party's conservative ethos and philosophy at the time when they became prime ministers. Indeed, it was Turnbull, a classic progressive, who constituted the radical departure from the tradition of successful Liberal prime ministers. The ETS demonstrated that the Liberal Party and the Coalition were more comfortable with a leader whose roots lay in the conservative rather than the progressive wing of the party. It is the core insight.

Much of the political class had a different view. Laura Tingle, writing for the *Australian Financial Review*, called the transition 'a disaster of epic proportions' for the Liberals because they had taken 'a major step to the Right' and 'away from mainstream voters'. Peter Hartcher, in the *Sydney Morning Herald*, said the Liberals had decided it was more important to be 'combative than to be electable'. He followed up by branding Abbott as 'aggressive, unpredictable, unsettling, perhaps even a little creepy with his well-publicised talk about female sexuality' and compared Abbott to Mark Latham. David Marr quoted a National Party senator saying of Abbott that 'even my mother won't vote for him'. The *Sydney Morning Herald*'s political correspondent, Phillip Coorey, wrote on the weekend after Abbott's election that: 'Abbott is on notice. If polling does not improve by early next year, he might become the third Liberal leader to succumb to climate change policy.'[18]

Such assessments capture the bedlam surrounding what is best called the great conservative revolt. Abbott's elevation was a high-risk move, and to pretend otherwise is nonsense. These media commentaries were neither aberrations nor without justification. They revealed the challenge that Abbott's elevation posed to entrenched orthodoxies of Australian politics as seen by much of the media and virtually all of the Labor Party.

The above commentary may have been vindicated had Kevin Rudd done what was expected of him: stand up to Abbott. But Rudd backed off—and *made* Abbott.

The orthodoxies would linger for years; namely, that a populist conservative leader was outside the mainstream and would never be accepted by the Australian people; that a leader as personally unpopular as Abbott with such socially conservative views and overtly religious commitment must fail; that the only viable course for the Liberals was to support carbon pricing, not oppose it; that Abbott, because of his alleged extremist views, could not unite his own side; and that Rudd and Gillard were closer to the norms of contemporary Australia and enjoyed a decisive advantage over Abbott.

Each of these doctrines would be disproved. But their tenacity revealed a culture war around Abbott that would only intensify with his election as prime minister. Progressives in the media and politics had a deep investment in Abbott failing because his success contradicted their view of the nature of Australia as a nation. Abbott succeeded brilliantly as an Opposition leader—but his ability to succeed as prime minister is a separate issue.

Within days of Abbott's election, Rudd said the Liberals had embraced an 'almost Joh-for-Canberra agenda'. Gillard said the Liberals were 'spitting in the face of the Australian people'. Bob Hawke said Abbott would be a 'temporary' leader. Greg Combet said 'extremists, climate change deniers and conspiracy theorists' had taken over the Liberal Party. The near-universal social media response was to condemn Abbott as a Catholic extremist. In response a joking Abbott said his daughter mocked him as a 'gay, lame, churchie loser'.[19] One of Rudd's press secretaries, Sean Kelly, said: 'We were thrilled when the news came through that Abbott was leader. We had stunned grins on our faces.'[20]

Interviewed for this book, Turnbull was magnanimous. As he reflected on events over 2009–13, he said:

> I did not want a climate change election and I didn't envisage the next four years of our narrative being about the abolition of the carbon tax. Now I recognise this has been politically successful. In that sense, you can say the challengers to me were proven to be correct in political terms. I would have to say their judgement on the potency of an anti-carbon tax campaign turned out to be correct and my reservations were ill-founded.[21]

Personal relations between Abbott and Turnbull survived the leadership transition. Turnbull told the author: 'I never found Tony to be slippery or treacherous or disingenuous. In so far as he was a stabber, he was a front stabber with ample warning. My differences with him have always been straightforward.'[22] There is no greater contrast than with the

Rudd–Gillard battle. Labor destroyed itself at this point; the Liberals made themselves at this point. The Labor contest was purely about power; the Liberal contest was about substantial issues of policy, unity and identity. Personal relations between Rudd and Gillard were poisoned while Abbott and Turnbull retained a mutual respect and working relationship. This contrast became fundamental to the Coalition's defeat of Labor.

By mid-2010, just seven months after the Abbott revolution, the course of politics was defying the orthodoxies. Abbott had prevailed where Turnbull failed by uniting his own side. He had made the rejection of carbon pricing an electoral plus, exposed Rudd's lack of nerve, proved that attacking Labor from a conservative stance was the superior strategy and cast doubt on views that his social conservatism was an insuperable obstacle to electoral success.

What if Turnbull had stayed leader, as many experts had preferred? The answer is speculative, by definition, yet the likely result is not hard to discern. The psychology of politics would have been transformed; Rudd would have carried his carbon scheme and become a Labor hero for the ages worshipped as another Whitlam or Keating; Rudd would have remained undisputed leader through 2010; the risky carbon pricing issue would have been taken off the table with Turnbull co-sponsor of Rudd's policy; the conservative side would have sunk into crisis with bitter relations between the Liberals and Nationals and a poisonous mood inside the Liberal Party with Turnbull's leadership in permanent jeopardy; the media narrative would have focused on the internal Liberal crisis, making the Coalition unelectable; and in this situation Rudd would have won the 2010 election. Labor would have avoided minority government, the alliance with the Greens and Gillard's destructive carbon tax broken promise. For Turnbull, the tragedy is that he could not hold his party together behind a pro–carbon price policy in 2009 or at any other time before the 2013 election.

Asked which leader—Abbott or Turnbull—would have constituted Labor's most formidable opponent, the ALP's National Secretary, George Wright, said in 2014: 'I think Abbott, though Turnbull is very capable, popular and may have broader appeal. But Abbott delivers; he gets the job done. He has been a very formidable opponent for us. Abbott is disciplined and highly effective in situations of combat.'[23] Rudd's chief media adviser, Lachlan Harris said: 'There's no doubt Abbott was much more formidable against Rudd—Turnbull may have been better suited against Gillard.'[24] These are revealing, but not typical, opinions.

Much of the progressive political class was sure Turnbull would have been a superior leader to Abbott. That Rudd's main political adviser, Bruce Hawker, was actually worried in the 2013 campaign that the Liberals might switch leaders and return to Turnbull is an illuminating commentary on the misjudgement of the political class. It bordered on delusion.

It misunderstood the nature of Liberal Party politics and the conditions for unity within conservative politics. The Abbott–Turnbull dispute did not originate in popularity but in the best climate change stand for the Liberals. Indeed, it could not be separated from that judgement.

Abbott may succeed or fail as prime minister. But there is no denying his remarkable success as Opposition leader. He proved the orthodoxies to be wrong. The elevation of Abbott became the making of the Opposition. It was the decisive step within the Liberal Party leading to the 2013 victory.

II

THE LABOR MALAISE

CHAPTER 3

FIGHTING ON TWO FRONTS

T
he Rudd–Gillard governments were under assault from both sides—from the Greens on the Left and populist conservatives on the Right. This was unprecedented in Labor's history. Facing a structural change for which its culture provided no answer, Labor fiddled with tactics and spin as its core vote eroded. The feature of contemporary politics is Labor's strategic failure. The Labor centre was stretched too thin and could not hold.

Rudd's victory in 2007 was based on a Labor primary vote of 43.4 per cent. At its 2013 defeat that vote had fallen to 33.4 per cent. It is not easy to lose 10 percentage points of your vote over two elections in office, but Labor achieved it. The Green vote in 2013, by contrast, was still above its 2007 level while the Coalition vote was substantially above its 2007 level. George Wright, the ALP National Secretary since mid-2011, sketched the dimensions of the problem:

> The Greens are completely focused on taking votes and seats from Labor. They do not compete with the conservative vote. Fighting the conservatives is left solely to Labor. So Labor now must fight for the conservative vote on the Right with fewer resources than it used to have and also defend against the Green vote on the Left. It's hard going.[1]

Former New South Wales premier and former Foreign Minister, Bob Carr says social democratic parties around the world are under assault from the populist Right and pro-green Left. 'The stresses for social democratic parties are intense,' Carr said. 'They need exceptional leaders, like Bob Hawke and Neville Wran, to straddle these contradictions, to hold left-leaning middle-class voters yet keep the blue-collar voters thinking you are protecting their jobs and upholding law and order in their streets.'[2]

On the Left, the Greens constitute a global ideological movement fanned by a grass-roots populist idealism that appeals to inner-city students, teachers, academics, progressives and environmentalists, many once ALP voters. On the Right, Tony Abbott duplicated the proven Howard technique and stole both working-class Labor supporters and 'aspirational' voters from Labor. Many of the Howard 'battlers' became the Abbott 'battlers'.

Labor failed to meet either challenge. It was complacent about these threats and resistant to change. Yet these challenges went to Labor's historical mission. The question raised by the Rudd–Gillard failures is whether Labor survives as a party that governs in its own right. Have the structural changes in Australian politics terminated Labor's historic mission as a stand-alone force?

As long ago as November 1995, Tony Abbott told the Parliament during a censure motion against then Prime Minister Paul Keating: 'Next year, 1996, is going to be a watershed in Australian politics. It is going to be a watershed like 1949 because Howard's battlers are going to be to the 1990s what Menzies' forgotten people were to the 1940s and 1950s. It is on their shoulders that a new generation of Liberal dominance is going to be created.'[3]

This was not merely prescient in predicting the basis of Howard's success. Abbott predicted eighteen years before the event, the strategy he would deploy to win the 2013 election. It is proof that what counts in politics is long-run strategy, not spin. It is where Labor has unravelled.

There was no secret about the technique Howard and Abbott would apply to achieve success. They believed a mix of aspirational economics and social conservatism would ruin Labor at its base. What does the record show? It shows that Howard and Abbott, in succession, were the Liberal leaders at the seven elections held between 1996 and 2013. The Coalition won five of these seven elections and in 2010 it won more seats than Labor. In only one of these elections did Labor win majority government—in 2007 under Rudd. This is a dismal record that points to profound problems. Yet Labor has repeatedly fallen for its own propaganda. It has been intellectually weak and psychologically paralysed.

The centre-Left spectrum is shared by Labor and the Greens. The two parties are locked into a mutual support system via preference deals with Greens Senate victories depending on ALP preferences and Labor MPs relying on Greens preferences. Labor is divided about how to manage the Greens because it is confused about its own values. The cultural factor is pivotal to this failure.

Australia is split along rigid cultural lines. Its progressive opinion makers in the ABC, Fairfax, SBS and the education, arts and cultural sectors, along with social media, project an ideological view hostile to Howard–Abbott values. This accentuates Labor's dilemma: it needs the backing of the progressive establishment yet it also needs to appeal to what Howard once called 'the mainstream mob' with its more traditional values.

Fighting on two fronts was a challenge the Rudd–Gillard generation never mastered. The initial damage was done at the 2010 election when Labor's majority position was destroyed. It never recovered from this event. The main carnage at that election came on the Left, where Labor's weakness against the Greens proved fatal. At this election the Coalition primary vote increased by 1.5 percentage points. But the Greens primary vote increased by an extraordinary 4 percentage points. It rose from 7.8 per cent in 2007 to 11.8 per cent in 2010, a remarkable surge over Rudd's first term. Much was a protest vote from disillusioned ALP voters (with only 80 per cent of lost votes returned via preferences). Rudd had raised expectations on climate change sky-high and then smashed them.

In 2010 Labor's primary vote fell to 38 per cent, an alarming drop from 43.4 per cent in 2007. If the Greens primary vote surge had been denied and its 2010 vote been the same as its 2007 vote then Julia Gillard would have won office in her own right, minority government would have been avoided and Labor would have continued in power with a reduced majority.[4]

In political history the 2010 election has a unique status. For the first time a national Labor government lost its majority position primarily because of attack from the Left. It became, literally, too embarrassing to suggest in polite company that the Greens had shot the ALP government. Election analyst Malcolm Mackerras affirmed the historic moment: 'This election was the only occasion where a federal Labor government lost a majority because of voting attrition on the Left and loss of votes to a party to Labor's left.'[5]

Greens leader Bob Brown says the party took votes from both Coalition and Labor. Asked if he felt the high Greens vote was a factor in reducing Labor to minority government he said: 'I think that's right.'[6] With his intimate grasp of inner-city politics, Finance Minister Lindsay Tanner said:

> As the focus has shifted from material concerns to more abstract issues of environmental degradation, international cooperation and human rights, the Greens have prospered at Labor's expense. The groups of people who helped reinvigorate Labor in the 1970s

and 1980s have defected en masse to the Greens. They won't be coming back in a hurry.[7]

In 2011, John Faulkner tried to inject a dose of reality into Labor: 'We are a small party getting smaller, we are an old party getting older … we have lost some of our base and could lose more. We are facing our first electoral challenge in history from the Left, in the Greens. And we are a declining political force.'[8]

He was wasting his breath. Labor was paralysed, intellectually and politically. It is astonishing that Labor refused to respond as the Greens stole the ALP vote. Bob Brown, like Abbott, advertised his intentions. 'We're here to change the dynamics of politics and that means to become Opposition or government in the future,' Brown said.[9] Interviewed for this book, he said:

> This is about power. I say to people we are not here to green up the other parties. We are not here to do a Don Chipp and keep the bastards honest. Our job is to replace them. The Greens are the third party now and I think there's an inevitability about the Greens becoming one of the major parties. I read history. We once had a very different party structure to what we have now. That changed with the rise of the Labor Party. So the change I am talking about is not unprecedented and I think history will repeat itself. A time will come when Greens are in the cabinet at the national level, it's inevitable. It is a gradual process—you gain parliamentary representation, you participate in power sharing and, down the line maybe, you form government.[10]

Such dreams are unlikely to be realised. The Greens vote fell at the 2013 election after Brown's departure. But this misses the point—Labor was guileless and gutless in its response to the assault from the Greens. It is sad that Gillard's reaction, after being put to the sword by the Greens at the 2010 election, was to enter an alliance with them to consolidate her minority government position. Many commentators, incredibly, applauded this as astute. That alliance, involving carbon pricing with an upfront fixed price, killed the Gillard Government. Gillard had her obvious tactical reasons for this decision. Yet it betrayed a deeper problem: Labor was confused over whether to treat the Greens as a friend or an enemy.

Labor's 2010 election humiliation by the Greens had multiple dimensions. The Greens gained more than 20 per cent of the primary vote in 8 seats and they won the prized inner-city seat of Melbourne, held by retiring ALP minister Lindsay Tanner, giving them a crossbench role in the minority government. Tanner said that if he had contested the seat the Greens would have won anyway. They are now entrenched in that seat, with Adam Bandt re-elected in 2013. In the Senate the Greens primary vote reached 13.1 per cent, enough to give the party a Senate seat in each state at the 2010 poll and long-term influence in the Upper House.

While Labor gets back 75 to 80 per cent of the vote that it loses to the Greens, the net loss is material. George Wright says because public funding of campaigns is based on the primary vote share, such funding on the progressive side is split between Labor and the Greens. In addition, the Greens' tactics are to concentrate their resources on a few ALP-held seats where they are able to mount formidable campaigns.

The ineptitude of the Labor Party in the new structure of Australian politics was exposed in the horror story of carbon pricing. There is no parallel in Labor history for the climate change saga over the 2007–13 period. When Rudd came to power, climate change was his issue. He owned it, he controlled it, he manipulated it against Howard. Yet Labor blew it—climate change became its lethal virus at the 2010 and 2013 polls.

In 2010, with Labor having abandoned its climate change scheme, the ALP saw a voting haemorrhage to the Greens that ruined its majority. In 2013, having legislated Gillard's scheme in alliance with the Greens, the ALP suffered a more virulent loss of votes to the Abbott Coalition.

Labor mastered the art of losing both ways: it lost votes to the Greens when it failed to legislate and it lost votes to Abbott when it did legislate. Fighting on two fronts, it was punched from one side of the ring to the other. The problem was that Labor faced aggressive parties on both sides—the Greens exploited its retreat and then Abbott exploited its flawed commitment. Bob Carr pointed to the international dimension of Labor's dilemma: 'This is happening everywhere you look. The once-great Scandinavian, German and Austrian parties, they are losing votes to populist conservative parties on the Right and green or left-wing parties on the other side.'[11]

Because the Greens are not worried about governing in their own right they have two assets over Labor: they are purer, and they can promise more. On climate change they pledge to shut down the coal industry and demand higher emission-reduction targets. Tanner said: 'The Greens can always outbid us because they are not weighed down by the need to deal with the material concerns and to win majority support in order to form a government.'[12] Bob Brown and his successor Christine Milne had a standard taunt: Labor always sells out. It is the Greens gospel.

Unsurprisingly, Bob Brown said: 'The real question these days is not for the Greens; it is for Labor.' What is the Labor strategy? Is it to move to the left and work with the Greens in future progressive alliances against the Coalition? Or is it to move to the right and offer a decisive alternative to the Greens?

The 'fighting on two fronts' trap is not a new event. It was basic in the demise of Mark Latham as ALP leader. In the final tight week of the 2004 campaign Latham turned John Howard into a blue-collar workers' hero. That was when Latham lurched into an alignment with Bob Brown by moving to end logging in Tasmania's old-growth forests. This triggered a fierce backlash, provoking what Howard called 'one of the more remarkable events in my political life'. Some 2000 burly timber workers gave him thunderous applause at Launceston's Albert Hall when he announced a Liberal Government forest policy that satisfied both the forestry industry and one of the nation's most powerful trade unions, the Forestry Division of the CFMEU. It was the most electric moment of the 2004 campaign.

It is significant that Latham's miscalculation was not his alone. He acted on the near unanimous advice of Labor's campaign brains trust to make a final-week pro-green pitch to win the election. They hoped to pull off a masterstroke. The result: Labor lost 2 seats in Tasmania, and across the nation the Howard battlers decided Howard was the genuine workers' friend and kept voting against Labor.

'History will record it as an act of folly,' Latham said later.[13] But it was much more: it proved that Labor was divided between its traditional workers and its inner-city pro-green believers. Latham rose as an economic policy realist and died in the embrace of Bob Brown. It was a modern Labor tragedy.

The Hawke–Keating model saw Labor occupy the centre Right, confident that voters on the Left were captive. Holding the centre Right, the Hawke–Keating model delivered office by pushing the Coalition too far right. But the battle on two fronts has transformed this situation. Labor has not figured how to battle both the Greens and Abbott/Howard populist conservatism at the same time.

A clear exposition of Labor's blunders came from Chris Bowen in his 2013 book *Hearts and Minds*, where he said Labor stood for economic growth, nationbuilding and job creation—yet the Greens rejected material-based economic growth as incompatible with the planet's finite resources.[14] They were an anti-growth party. 'We are different parties that believe in different things,' Bowen said. While he avoided direct criticism of Gillard's 2010 'alliance', he made clear his disagreement with it. It was one thing for Labor to form government with support from independents, as Curtin did in 1941 during wartime, but it was a mistake to offer concessions to a political party with a different philosophy in order to form government. Bowen said his conclusions sprang from Gillard's lived alliance with the Greens from 2010 and the Greens dumping the deal in 2013.

'We must govern alone or not at all,' Bowen said. For Labor's future, it is the essential principle. It is the foundation required to save Labor as a stand-alone party. Bowen saw the weakness in Labor's heart: its drift to accommodation of the Greens. The consequence would be the end of Labor's mission as a majority governing party. When Labor struck an alliance with the Greens, the Labor brand got tainted. The public asked: What does the ALP stand for?

'People need to be very clear in their understanding,' said Bowen. 'If you vote Labor you will not get Greens polices by default. If you vote Labor, you get Labor's pro-growth policies, not the Greens' anti-growth policies.'

Tasmania is proof of this warning. After years of close collaboration with the Greens, the ALP has seen its vote reduced to the low 20s and Tasmanian Labor has jeopardised or even terminated its stand-alone future. Labor has engaged in two disastrous alliances with the Greens—one following the 1989 election and the other following the 2010 election. Before the 2014 state election, Labor Premier Lara Giddings terminated the Labor–Green coalition she had championed, saying Labor supporters had told her 'we don't like the Greens'. For Labor the lesson from its Greens alliances is that they are guaranteed to diminish the ALP vote.

Labor's betrayal of the Tasmanian people has resulted in a fearful economic plight. Giddings' belated and cynical move came amid an anti-Green backlash from the young Turks of the New South Wales Right led by its former secretary, Sam Dastyari, and former AWU boss Paul Howes. Their aim is to kill any Labor deals with the Greens at state and national level. Howes said Gillard's 2010 deal with the Greens was 'a nonsense deal, a ridiculous deal', though he was more critical of the Tasmanian situation. For Howes, Labor has only one option: to build a strong centre. 'The Greens do not share our values,' he says.

They are fundamentally opposed to the essence of what it means to be Labor. Tying ourselves so closely with them is bunkum. It might sound a bit controversial but there was actually more in common between Labor and the Communist Party than there was between us and the Greens. They are actually opposed to our base having a decent standard of living. For Labor to be successful in the future we have to be a multi-tendency party, we need to hold the centre across economic and social issues.[15]

Reviewing Gillard's decision, Dastyari says:

The mistake we made is that, effectively, we went into coalition with them. It was an unmitigated mistake. It was a positioning mistake for the Labor Party. We didn't sufficiently recognise these people aren't our friends; they have their own agenda. The idea that they are our natural bedfellows is wrong. They are not a centrist party. To get a winning majority in politics you need to keep your base and appeal to the centre ground and being associated with the Greens didn't allow us to do that. Hindsight will show this decision was a huge mistake. I don't think it will ever happen again.[16]

The cabinet minister most experienced in dealing with the Greens was Greg Combet, who conducted a long negotiation with them over carbon. What had Combet learnt about the Greens? 'They have a disregard for the economy,' he said.[17] 'This was the single outstanding takeout for me. Large regions, industries, businesses and workers can be profoundly affected by carbon pricing. I was determined to look after them. But this just wasn't a factor for the Greens. They are driven by ideology.' But Combet lays another charge against them—sheer irresponsibility: 'The Greens have wrecked carbon pricing and climate change policy twice in this country. Once is when they voted with Abbott to finish Rudd's scheme and the other is by their insisting on these targets that are economic lunacy. This is why, in the scheme I negotiated, we had to have a fixed price at the start.'

Labor's 2013 defeat opened the way to a far tougher and more realistic view of the Greens and how to cope with the threat they posed to the ALP.

Bob Brown believes the Labor counterattack is too late. He thinks the Labor 'stand-alone' cause is doomed. When Giddings severed the Labor–Green alliance, Brown said the Dastyari–Howes tactic was a Labor 'death wish'. Brown issues a sharp warning: if Labor cuts off the Greens and moves to the right it will find the Liberals do pulp mills, mining and extractive industry policies better than Labor and Labor will only lose more support. Brown believes Labor is trapped. He warns of the consequences if Labor, after the Gillard experience, moves to the right: 'This will bring Labor to grief. They are not the Labor Party they used to be, they are not the Light on the Hill. They have no way back.'[18]

The Greens will continue to be tactically flexible. They will continue to offer Labor deals, trade-offs and alliances—and Labor, keen to govern, will be tempted. It is the path to decline via seduction. Meanwhile, the arrival of the Abbott Government may empower the Greens as a party spearheading anti-Abbott sentiment.

The Rudd–Gillard story shows that the 'two fronts' dilemma confounds Labor. On climate change, boat arrivals and the mining tax, Labor was wedged between the Greens and the Coalition—whether it went left or right, it ignited a battle.

Seen in historical context, Labor has reached a turning point. Gough Whitlam created modern Labor by grafting middle-class constituencies onto the party's working-class base, thereby enhancing Labor's appeal. Under Whitlam, Labor became tied to academics, teachers, environmentalists, the NGO sector, migrants, Aborigines, the arts and media industries, feminists, civil libertarians, the human rights lobby and gays. It was a sprawling coalition for a trade union–based party. This coalition delivered much success before it began to unravel. It would fracture along a new fault line: old politics defined by interests versus new politics defined by identity.

The Greens offered identity-based politics. The post-1960s era saw rising prosperity coupled with a more consumer-based and individualistic political culture. It was about 'new generation' values, personal identity divorced from class consciousness and the endless mantra of human rights. The cult of individual identity meant Labor's idea of civilising capitalism was in retreat. Integral to this process has been the rise of single-issue campaigns via social media for same-sex marriage, refugees and the environment. The explosive pluralism of progressive politics has made this phenomenon more difficult to contain within the Labor tent.

John Faulkner warned about this revolution. 'When I joined the ALP it was the political face of a broad social movement,' he said in a 2011 lecture. Labor politics in the 1960s was about ending the Vietnam War, fighting apartheid, free education, health care and defending unions. Yet the social movement that Faulkner had hailed split into many pieces.

In 2011 he lamented that too many activists now found their home out-side the ALP. 'We have lost a generation of activists from Labor,' he said. Unless the party reformed itself 'we will risk losing a generation of voters as well'.[19] By this stage senior ministers would confess in private their fears that their staff were voting Green.

The argument for a Labor strategic reappraisal is irresistible. The Greens are a deeply flawed political force, far weaker than many realise. Their ideological essence is too extreme and their internal divisions are potentially fatal. With Brown's departure they will struggle to find a long-run effective national leader. If Labor targets and attacks the Greens primary vote such a strategy will accentuate Labor values and assist its contest against them.

This battle will break one way or the other: either Labor will reverse the electoral momentum of the Greens or the idea of majority Labor government will die. At that point Labor will begin to fold its 100-year-old tent.

Meanwhile, on the Right, John Howard had re-made the Liberal Party to express his deepest faith: that Labor was divided between its better-educated progressive vote and its traditional working-class heritage. It became the strategic foundation of the Howard/Abbott Liberal Party. Since Howard's 1995 return as Liberal leader the aim has been to wedge Labor on this fault line—in other words, to fracture its vote by highlighting the party's internal contradictions.

It was Paul Keating who gave the kiss of life to the Howard battlers. ALP National Secretary Gary Gray said: 'Howard didn't steal the Labor base vote. Paul Keating drove people away because of his style, outlook and language.'[20] Keating's flaws bequeathed a Liberal success proven at the 1996 election with the defection of blue-collar voters. According to Andrew Robb, who was Liberal Party director at the time, 'There was a deep sense of Keating's alienation from Labor voters who felt their concerns and interests were being ignored.'[21]

The research told Robb that Labor faced a cultural crisis: Keating's passion for the republic, Mabo and minority social interests violated the living tradition of Labor as a party of social conservatism. Howard made this a pillar of his ascendancy.

Tony Abbott arrived in Parliament at a by-election in 1994. The timing is pivotal. He saw the return of Howard to the leadership, Keating's blunder in courting the progressive vote and Howard's wedge over four election victories. Abbott would follow Howard and become convinced that Labor was in an identity crisis between its progressive and traditional voters. 'I think this split has become a fundamental conflict,' Abbott said in 2011. 'It is virtually impossible for the current Labor leadership to reconcile these two constituencies.'[22] For Abbott, it has been a twenty-year-old axiom.

Fundamental to Howard's success was turning the Liberals into the party of social and cultural attack, an event that took Labor by surprise and remains the subject of denial within sections of the ALP to this day. Before his 1996 victory Howard declared: 'I give you this pledge: I want to do everything in my power to preserve the social fabric of this nation.' This idea became a political weapon, reflected in Howard's use of the term *mainstream*, a code that linked Howard to the people. Latham grasped what was happening: Howard was taking control of the 'outsider' culture and turning it against Labor.[23]

Howard's social and cultural offensives were based on family tradition, Australian patriotism, law and order, Christian values, a 'fair go', mateship and individual responsibility.

The policies and symbols tied to these ideas included family tax benefits, Work for the Dole, mutual obligation, welfare reform, upholding traditional marriage, gun controls, the Northern Territory intervention, national security laws, backing the constitutional monarchy, flying the flag, honouring the Anzacs and Don Bradman, championing the Western canon in school curriculum, a crackdown on drugs and—above all, with asylum seeker boat arrivals—the principle that government, on behalf of the people, 'will decide who comes to this country and the circumstances in which they come'.

Howard's conservatism transcended a defence of the status quo; it became a populist attack on Labor progressivism. Convinced that progressives had exaggerated their public support, his tactic to wedge Labor on the fault line was implemented for eleven years with many successes and some failures.

The two politicians Abbott studied closely were Menzies and Howard, the most successful conservative leaders in Australia's history. 'They both appealed to a section of Labor's base that Labor had apparently abandoned,' Abbott said. 'Menzies appealed to the anti-communist working class. Howard appealed to the aspirational battlers.' This technique was built into Abbott's political DNA given his past as a Democratic Labor Party sympathiser whose initial hero had been anti-communist trade union organiser B A Santamaria. This cultural history located Abbott closer to Labor's roots than any previous Liberal leader. He felt comfortable campaigning with blue-collar workers. For Abbott, this was his natural terrain.

The Santamaria story tutored Abbott to see Labor's weakness. This was Santamaria's pivotal and enduring legacy to Abbott as Opposition leader. The story was about how to steal the Labor base vote. Menzies achieved this with Santamaria's help through the formal defection of the DLP, an anti-communist breakaway party from Labor that collaborated to keep Menzies in power for a decade. Howard replicated the technique using aspirational economics and social conservatism. Abbott, again, sought to repeat the same Menzies/Howard tactic.

Abbott recognised the risks implicit in Howard's method. The main risk was that the Liberals would lose small-'l' liberal voters—and this materialised at the 2007 election. But Abbott decided, overall, that the strategy worked, saying in his 2009 book: 'With Howard, it was keeping the support of the "blue collar conservatives", not the "doctors' wives" that had always made the difference between winning and losing.'[24] This was Abbot's bottom line: the votes won exceeded the votes lost.

In Abbott's hands two main instruments were deployed in this strategy: the carbon tax and boat arrivals. He used them to throttle the political lifeblood from the Gillard Government.

Abbott didn't just campaign against the carbon tax; he recruited the tax to buttress his theme, that Labor was betraying working families. Abbott said Labor was penalising households to further its carbon pricing ideology sealed in its post-election deal with the Greens. Only a populist conservative leader with working-class credibility could mount this campaign. It would have been possible for Howard but not for Malcolm Turnbull. Turnbull was too much a progressive in his own right. Abbott was outrageous in his taunts to Labor. 'I've often said that if Ben Chifley were alive today he'd be more likely to vote for the Coalition than the ALP,' Abbott said. It became his propaganda flourish. Would Chifley have imposed the carbon tax? Would Chifley have welcomed asylum seeker boats? Abbott told Labor's base he was a better representative of its interests than Gillard.

For Abbott, Gillard's alliance with the Greens was a dream. It was the perfect illustration of his accusation against Labor. He exploited the alliance for three years. 'I am effectively saying if you are interested in a strong economy as opposed to green gestures you should be voting for the Coalition,' Abbott said. 'I expect Bill Shorten understands that deals with the Greens are fatal for Labor but he cannot bring about the divorce. Labor tries to say that green policies will create jobs. It's rubbish. They will never provide the long-term employment [that] Labor's working-class base knows is necessary.'[25]

For Labor, the boats issue became a long-run trauma. Its progressive wing aligned with the human rights lobby to assert that Australia had legal and moral obligations to accept boat people, regardless of numbers, under the 1951 United Nations Convention Relating to the Status of Refugees (the Refugee Convention). It said this constituted the ultimate test of the party's integrity. Labor's pragmatic wing felt the boats had to be stopped in the national interest but vacillated over the severity of the response according to the flow of boats and depth of public anger.

Labor's tragedy in office is that it lost control of the nation's borders with more than 45 000 boat people arriving during its watch. This broke a non-negotiable border security expectation the public held of its national government. The anti-Labor backlash was most pronounced in Western Sydney. The extent of voter alienation was a factor in the removal of Rudd and Gillard as leaders. Asylum seeker policy constituted one of Labor's worst political failures in the past half century. Once again, the 'betrayal' concept was integral to Abbott's campaign. He said because Labor was deluded by progressive values it had abandoned its border security obligations to the Australian public.

For Abbott, the catholicisation of the Liberal Party was influential in detaching the ALP vote. It is easy to dismiss this trend as nothing more than Catholics voting Liberal as they became more prosperous. Abbott had a different view. 'I think the catholicisation of the Liberal Party and the Coalition is critical,' he said. At the time of the 2009 leadership struggle the three candidates—Turnbull, Hockey and Abbott—were Catholics. This was an unprecedented situation in Liberal history and it matched the sharp decline of Catholic influence in the Labor Party, once a rock of its working-class consciousness. The demise of the DLP became the bridge that saw many Catholic families move their support to the Liberal Party. 'When this happened it gave the Liberal Party a much deeper political culture,' Abbott said.[26] As a Catholic and social conservative Abbott's mind was forever geared to dividing the Labor vote along the fracture of social values.

Abbott's 2013 victory was based upon his application of the Menzies/Howard technique. Liberal Director Brian Loughnane said:

> The electoral coalition that Tony Abbott has built was informed by and reflects the electoral coalition that was the basis for success of the Menzies, Fraser and Howard governments. Tony Abbott reflects the mainstream of the party's traditional success. History shows the successful Liberal leaders—Menzies, Fraser, Howard and

Abbott—have come from the conservative side of the party. They secured the base and then built upon it.[27]

The progressive critique of Abbott—that he was an aberration as leader—missed the point entirely. Far from being an aberration, Abbott was implementing his own version of the traditional Liberal leadership model. This is the reason he won the 2013 election. He ruined Labor on the fault line between progressive and traditional ALP voters.

The Coalition primary vote increased from 41.8 per cent in 2007 to 43.3 per cent in 2010 and to 45.4 per cent in 2013. It was steady progress. Abbott was not a popular leader but he had a consistent strategy to penetrate the ALP base. Abbott's approach may or may not work in government. That is a separate story. He will find, as Howard did, that the implementation of tough economic policies in office will make it difficult to retain the Abbott battlers.

This is the political significance of the first Abbott Government budget. The budget inflamed public hostility for breaching the fairness ethic with voters. It means that Abbott, at the start, has risked losing the battler vote—a vote that Howard retained into his fourth term despite a tough first budget. For Abbott, being able to penetrate the Labor base was pivotal to his election success. Losing this ability early in his time in office would constitute a far-reaching setback.

Meanwhile Labor in Opposition faces a choice. It can decide that the more volatile short-term electoral cycle will restore, almost naturally, the ALP vote and make a return to office possible at the 2016 election. That would constitute a denial of the problem. Unless Labor confronts the structural dilemma besetting progressive politics it will fail again in office. The lesson from the Rudd–Gillard generation is that the battle on two fronts against Greens and populist conservatives needs to be confronted. It ruined one ALP generation; it should not ruin another.

CHAPTER 4

SHUNNING THE POLICY CHALLENGE

The Hawke–Keating years constituted Labor's most fabulous run of victories but left the party in the smoking ruins of an identity crisis. The question posed by the policies of Bob Hawke and Paul Keating is whether they presaged the permanent decline of the Labor Party. These leaders deregulated the economy, floated the currency, cut tariffs and promoted structural change: this put the old Australian model of protection and state controls on the escalator to extinction.

It also put the old Labor Party on the road to extinction. Old Labor had no future in the emerging contemporary Australia. It was a shocking thought—that traditional Labor, the oldest, most romanticised party, was finished. Yet the evidence seemed irresistible. Formed in the nineteenth-century class struggle and marooned in the globalisation of the twenty-first century, Labor as a majority governing, trade union–based party faced inexorable decline. Its primary vote, state and federal, proved the problem.

It was the old Australia that had called the Labor Party into existence, along with the trade union movement it represented in Parliament. It was the old Australia that invested Labor with its tribal meaning. It was the old Australia that defined Labor's identity and became the platform for its class appeal. When the old Australia died Labor faced an existential question: Would it die or would it re-invent its mission in contemporary Australia?

The Labor Party had to make an historical choice. It was a nasty, unpalatable choice, the sort of choice faced by many institutions and companies: reform or wither. Reform meant accepting the Hawke–Keating values and logic: that Labor must change its structure, policies and culture to become a different party for a different nation. The alternative was to cling to the fading icons of the past: its identity as a 50 per cent trade union party, preferring public enterprise over private enterprise, sceptical of markets, faithful to state power, and pledged to a more regulatory polity to advance its ideology. The first option was difficult; the second was the comfort zone.

There was one certainty: Labor could not do both. It could not be the party of modern Australia and remain the creation of old Australia.

In his heart and in his bones, Kevin Rudd knew this. Interviewed for this book, he said of the ALP he was elected to lead: 'I think the party by the end of 2006, after a decade in Opposition, had become politically moribund. Therefore, the leadership of the party had to occupy that vacuum.'[1] This captures perfectly the Labor crisis. But having Rudd's persona conceal the party's weakness was no basis for long-run success. Rudd ran on his leadership persona when he won in 2007 and when he lost in 2013. But the Kevin 07 cult merely swept the historical baggage under the carpet.

Gillard's senior political adviser, John McTernan, said of Labor's pre-2007 election position: 'The focus groups told us that people were voting for Kevin Rudd despite him being Labor. We had not restored the Labor brand. There was no love for Labor as a party, brand, movement or anything else. It was all Rudd.'[2] If McTernan's analysis was correct, it meant Labor would fail in office. And that is what happened.

The Hawke–Keating era, in effect, had posed the historical question. It fell to the Rudd–Gillard government to provide an answer. Its response was understandable but inadequate. It evaded the question, pretended there was no strategic crisis and governed without any perceptible game plan.

Labor's young Turks, not participants in the government, were aggressive in their self-criticisms. Newly elected New South Wales Senator Sam Dastyari said: 'The tragedy is we took over in 2007 at a unique moment in Australian history. We had this opportunity to re-shape the nation and have a golden age of Labor, and we botched it. The question for Labor is: what are the lessons? How do we ensure it doesn't happen again?'[3]

The exhaustion of Labor's governing model became irrefutable during the 2013 horror year. In a defining moment Gillard told the annual conference of the Australian Workers' Union that the party she led was not called progressive or social democratic. It was called Labor because 'that is who we are'. This assertion of the party's trade union identity sent a message of exclusion to corporate, entrepreneurial, small business and self-employed Australians (far outnumbering unionists). At the time the ALP primary vote was 30 per cent. Labor's 2013 demise came against a lethal backdrop: sustained policy appeasement of the union base and the worst collapse in business and industry confidence in a national government since Whitlam.

The ride to this debacle had been wild and unpredictable yet wilful. It began in 2007 with 'The Rudd Experiment', a remarkable yet flawed project in prime ministerial power. Despite Rudd's achievements and the aura he generated, his poor judgements and missed opportunities resulted in his premature termination by the caucus. From 2010 the party under Gillard, in the straight-jacket of minority government, reverted to an introspective mindset, appeasing the unions, pandering to the Greens, alienating business, indulging in end-of-empire spending and creating too many enemies in a retreat to tribalism. Finally, with no time left, a recalled Rudd, halfway down the Damascus road, tried to readjust policy in a government long lost. Rudd talked about the future and made some progress on economic policy, boat arrivals and climate change policy. In the 2013 campaign, with his old magic almost gone, Rudd saved some furniture but was unable to conceal the hollowness at Labor's heart.

The Rudd–Gillard era misread the policy and political needs of contemporary Australia. As its electoral situation progressively unravelled during the four years from late 2009, Labor seemed puzzled about what had gone wrong.

The problem had been concealed initially by the intelligence, flair and freshness radiated by Kevin and Julia in their first golden eighteen months after Labor's 2007 victory. Goodwill towards them was near universal. Yet the speed with which the Rudd and Gillard governments disintegrated was a shock. It caught most people by surprise. Political professionals were agog at its rapidity. The media naturally focused on the drama of leadership and personality clashes. Yet this concealed as much as it explained. There was a deeper cultural and policy malaise. At first people were shocked at the extraordinary collapse of Rudd. The shock was repeated with the extraordinary collapse of Gillard. How could this have happened, not once but twice?

The truth is that Labor as an institution was no longer equipped to govern successfully. Rudd's press secretary, Lachlan Harris, a young staffer often prepared to challenge Rudd, puts it starkly:

> To govern a country, an institution needs to be very strong. Labor has been eroding its processes for a long time. If you have to sum up what happened to Labor in six years it's fairly simple: the party cracked under the pressure of government. In fact, the party as an institution cracked twice. Interpreting why that happened goes beyond the personalities of Rudd and Gillard.[4]

The institutional Labor crisis preceded Rudd and Gillard. During its eleven years in Opposition from 1996 to 2007, Labor had chosen the 'comfort zone' default option. It let the Hawke–Keating agenda slip but failed to embrace a new position. It looked at Tony Blair's Third Way—and then looked away. Aware of its vulnerability, it shunned policy revitalisation as too risky. It specialised in the tactical imperative of attacking John Howard's agenda—that was easier. It kept the party united—that was good for Labor's diminished soul and substituted for the bigger task of self-analysis and renovation. So Labor began to destroy, by default, its political and intellectual capital.

After Keating's defeat, Labor chose to be the party of the old Australia, preferring its old policies, structures and traditional habits. It was a wilful decision founded on a false assumption: that Labor could succeed without having to change itself. The rationalisation was that Howard wasn't too formidable. Assuming the ALP leadership after the 1996 loss, Kim Beazley had to hold the party together, nurse its grievances and keep Howard under pressure. Beazley was an effective Opposition leader whose technique was to shun policy rethinks and affirm the existing power structure. Unpopular and isolated in his Sydney retirement exile, Keating became a fierce private critic of Beazley and of Labor's 'do-nothing' malaise. Keating and Beazley were polar opposites on Labor's future.

For Keating, the issue was a no-brainer. He said Labor must modernise from the ground up. He proselytised for Labor to champion the new aspirational class that its pro-market policies had helped to create. He believed that the power of capital and entrepreneurship was the means to realise Labor's enduring values. But this ran slap bang into Labor's nature as one of the most conservative institutions in the country. 'Labor must recognise what it has created,' Keating said of the Hawke–Keating de-regulatory agenda.

> It has created a new society and it has to be the party of the new society. It can't be the party of the old society. Labor must be the party of those people who gained from the pro-market growth economy that we created. Labor must be open to the influences of this middle class, to people on higher incomes.

Interviewed in 2011 when Gillard was in the Lodge, he lamented: 'I don't think it is [open in this way].'[5]

Becoming the party of a new society was an idea beyond the imagination of most ALP politicians. The most fervent apostle of Keating's legacy was Mark Latham, a ferocious critic of Beazley. Latham saw the Hawke–Keating economic reforms of 1983–96 as one of Labor's finest achievements since Federation. They created the settings 'for 20 years of low inflationary growth and unprecedented wealth creation'.[6] The workers moved into better jobs, improved their living standards or obtained capital to start their own enterprises. Moreover, all boats had been lifted. For Latham, walking away from the Keating settlement had been one of Labor's epic blunders.

It went to bedrock belief. In 2002 Keating slammed his successors, saying to Latham: 'They don't get it, they don't actually support the model I put in place.'[7] During a private lunch in November 1998, Keating's former adviser, John Edwards, told an anecdote that Latham, a lunch guest, recorded in his diary. Latham wrote:

> The boss [Keating] was just back from a cabinet meeting where he had pushed through a new deregulatory policy and he said, 'Yeah, I got them to agree to it, but they don't really believe in it.' That sums up the dilemma perfectly. As soon as Keating left, caucus lurched to the Left on economic policy. They never really believed in it.[8]

Labor's lack of belief is revealed in its absurd official pledge that members be committed to 'the democratic socialisation of industry, production, distribution and exchange to the extent necessary to eliminate exploitation'—an effort to echo socialism yet reject Marxism. Few Labor MPs believe in this credo, yet the party is unwilling to construct a replacement.

The abandonment of the Hawke–Keating legacy endured from Beazley to Rudd to Gillard. An astute leader, Beazley was steeped in ALP tradition. For Beazley, the retreat to orthodoxy was in his blood. 'I'm an ideological Social Democrat,' he said.

> I'm about the world view of the Labor Party in a way that they [Hawke and Keating] were not. I think in a way both Bob and Paul were ... not necessarily within the Labor Party tradition. They have a radical perspective on the world—a view that wants to change things ... Bob's a bit less than Paul that way. I am more

conventional in the sense of having a view in the first instance
which is an ideological, Social Democrat view.[9]

Such sentiment offered no answer to Labor's problems. One of Labor's
elder statesmen, John Faulkner, hardly a crusading deregulator, said:
'I think we made a massive strategic error in turning our backs on the
record of the Hawke and Keating governments. To a large extent we
squandered the Hawke–Keating legacy.'[10] Faulkner's charge, in effect, is
that a Labor generation took the wrong path.

Beazley's leadership won more internal approval than Keating's
leadership. Beazley respected the unions, recognised the factions and
honoured Labor orthodoxy. He was seen as stable, reliable and trustworthy.
His tactic was to ensure that Howard, not Labor, was the issue. He grasped
the imperative to distance the party from Keating, who had become
electoral poison. Beazley was not a pro-market reformer by belief, nor
did he see any logic in adopting a credo guaranteed to provoke political
woes inside and outside the party. The trouble is that this consigned the
bigger issues to the freezer.

Labor conducted no formal inquiry after its 1996 defeat. It is no
surprise the party avoided any rethink; the core problem went to its
existence. It was too hard to answer intellectually and almost impossible
politically. Former Finance Minister Lindsay Tanner saw the premonition of demise: 'Social-democratic parties like ours are slowly unravelling.
While circumstances inevitably vary around the world, there is an underlying factor that is common: loss of purpose.'[11]

The economic base that formed Labor culture was being demolished by globalisation, a process illustrated by the 2014 decisions that signalled the end of car production in Australia. The party's response under
Bill Shorten—defending the industry status quo—suggested that it had
learnt nothing and was lagging behind public opinion. It was as early as
1990 that Tanner said: 'The 25-year-old secretary, a very typical Australian
worker in the 1990s, tends not to see herself as a "worker" or see her
employment relationship as the overwhelming dominant factor in her
life.'[12] In short, social change was ruining Laborism.

The two factions whose perpetual wars had defined Labor's existence became empty volcanoes. The Left was rendered bankrupt since
the Hawke–Keating era had demolished its fading ideas of socialisation, nationalisation and public monopoly. The Right was also bankrupt
since it lacked the will to sustain the Hawke–Keating market credo
but had no alternative framework. With their ideological purpose gone,

these factions declared a truce, their rivalry reduced to personal power contests.

The tragedy of the New South Wales Right was writ large. It was the party's greatest faction, the power house that saved Whitlam as leader, sustained Hawke and launched Keating. Since the 1950s it had been nourished at a cultural level by two pervasive ideas: the anti-communism of the Cold War and the values arising from the religious and Catholic establishment. The demise of the Cold War and decline of religious faith sucked the life forces from its machinery.

As Labor degenerated, the factions reverted to vehicles of pure self-aggrandisement. The single most unforgiveable atrocity perpetrated by the machine came in 2008 when the New South Wales ALP turned against the Labor Government of Premier Morris Iemma over his electricity privatisation reform agenda. The party conference, led by New South Wales Party President Bernie Riordan and the head of the New South Wales union movement, John Robertson, repudiated its government, openly mocked its ministers and, when Iemma subsequently stood his ground, the party machine cut off his political head, thereby signing the government's death warrant. In an immortal letter to Robertson in 2008, Keating said: 'You have behaved with reckless indifference to the longevity of the current government … let me say that the conscientious business of governance can never be found in a soul so blackened by opportunism … I am ashamed to share membership of the same party with you.'[13]

Meanwhile trade hostility towards the former ALP–ACTU Accord was rife. The unions decided it had been a blunder and they wanted to strike out on their own. They felt they had become too dependent on government and lost too many members. This created a magnificent opportunity for Labor: it could distance itself from the unions. It was handed the invitation but was too timid to accept.

Former ACTU president Martin Ferguson described the mood: 'When I first went into Parliament we would have union officials and secretaries sitting across the table damning the Accord as a sell-out. Both the Left and Right, for their short-term interests, demonised the Accord. Yet it had been the most rewarding period of achievement in the history of the Australian trade union movement.'[14] The logic of the new situation was not for Labor to recreate the Accord but to recognise that it needed to reform its trade union link. Ferguson saw this and he wanted a 'complete overhaul' of the 50–50 rule, saying 'there is too much union representation in the governing of the party'.[15]

Beazley correctly discerned Labor's mood: there was no appetite for transformation. Indeed, there rarely is such an appetite.

The retreat to the old mindset became entrenched in Beazley's first term, with the message highlighted in a March 1997 *Business Review Weekly* article 'Labor buries Keating'. The theme was the necessity for greater government intervention, planning and subsidies. Beazley hammered market failure and praised government action to create jobs; shadow treasurer Gareth Evans said he would not be dictated to by financial markets; and Simon Crean, later Beazley's successor, outlined an across-the-board agenda of government intervention.[16]

It was in 1997 that the central economic idea of the Rudd–Gillard era was enunciated: the notion of 'market failure'. It was a rationalisation to conceal Labor's retreat from a pro-market position. Under Beazley, 'market failure' became a mantra. At one time or another nearly every senior figure embraced this wonderful truism. More than a decade later it was endlessly recycled by the Rudd–Gillard government to justify its labour market, financial system, climate change, NBN, media and industry policies.

Beazley visited his old friend from Oxford days, Tony Blair, not long after the 1997 election put Blair into Downing Street behind a massive majority. Tony entertained Kim at Chequers. What did Kim learn from his friend Tony, who was keeping much of the Thatcher settlement and ditching old Labour faiths for middle-class voting support? 'Look, he's only just catching up with what Hawke and Keating did,' Beazley said on his return. 'Blair's experience doesn't have lessons for us now.'[17] Labor shut its mind to the most successful British Labour leader in history. Within Labor, strategic policy debate was ditched in favour of the 'small target' tactic to win on Howard's mistakes. This almost delivered Beazley victory at the 1998 election. But 'almost' is not good enough.

Beazley defined himself against Howard: he opposed most of Howard's 'return-to-surplus' spending cuts and his privatisations, denounced his GST-based tax reform, rejected his industrial relations changes, rallied the party's class consciousness during the waterfront dispute, played to class envy with higher taxes on caviar and more tariffs on four-wheel-drive vehicles. On tax, Labor was to the left of the Australian Democrats, who accepted the GST and made it fairer by insisting food be excluded. On IR, Labor was again to the left of the Australian Democrats in rejecting statutory individual contracts, which were supported by the Cheryl Kernot–led Democrats. Beazley sought to make fairness the issue of the 1998 election, a tactic intrinsic to Labor identity yet mostly unsuccessful in its own right.

The narrow 1998 election defeat, with Labor winning 51 per cent of the two-party-preferred vote, seeded the next term of denial. 'It's within reach,' Beazley said late on election night about his prospects at the 2001 election.[18] Howard was more prophetic: 'Beazley totally misread this result. The 1998 election did not represent the rebirth of Labor.'[19] The result mirrored Labor's strategy: it accumulated useless majorities in safe ALP seats but failed to win enough marginal seats where the middle ground was located. In the autumn of 2001, however, Beazley was supremely confident of victory later that year based on ALP research. 'We're going to win this,' he told Labor intimates in May 2001. It was before the *Tampa* crisis and the 9/11 attack.

In November 2001, John Howard won his third election with a 1.9 per cent swing. Beazley had campaigned well to ensure the swing was not bigger. The Labor denialists used *Tampa* and 9/11 as excuses. But the hard heads knew Labor had fooled itself for too long. 'We were just far too confident after the 1998 result,' Gillard said. 'My view going into 2001 was that our vote was soft. The conventional analysis was that all we needed to do was keep our house in order and we'd get over the line next time. The whole party succumbed to far too simplistic an analysis.'[20]

Labor had become a phoney tough party—strong in its attacks on Howard but weak in deciding its policy beliefs and putting muscle into its structures. Latham was disgusted. In June 2000 he wrote: 'We have spent four of the last eight years concentrating on a GST scare campaign and people wonder why we have no policies.'[21] Tanner saw that in fighting Howard the ALP had, by default, become 'defenders of the status quo'. Labor was the anti-Howard party. Nothing else.[22]

But Beazley made a contribution that shaped Labor's thinking for more than a decade—his 2001 Knowledge Nation policy, a manifesto for office. Its central idea was that the next wave of economic reform would arise from public investment in education, skills and technology. Beazley was seeding agent for the Rudd–Gillard 'education revolution'. His starting position, critically, was that the Hawke–Keating pro-market reforms were completed. In their place the next Labor generation would commit to a different strategy to generate productivity and nation-building: a government-driven agenda that backed schools, universities, scientists, researchers, enhanced R&D, universal broadband access and an industry policy to boost new information and environmental industries.

For Labor, it was the perfect synthesis—reinventing education as the heart of its new economic policy. This was extremely convenient but it proved to be too convenient. The party put no real money behind the idea and it never gained traction. But the notion rationalised the party's rejection of markets and invested Labor with a reform agenda that was an alternative to the Productivity Commission's message of market pricing, structural reform, competition policy, tax reform and IR de-regulation. It implanted a false choice in Labor's head: investment in education was essential but not as the substitute for the next round of market-based economic reform.[23]

Faulkner offered Beazley a generous tribute: 'Lack of a hard edge and sheer bad luck are the two things that really cost Kim the prime ministership.'[24]

Simon Crean replaced Kim Beazley as Labor leader but he was subjected to searing internal attack as the caucus descended into rancour and turned against itself. Crean promoted a modest reform: the proportion of union delegates at state and national conferences was cut from 60 per cent to 50 per cent. 'The impact on the character and control of the ALP was zero,' said ALP historian and former Wran minister Rodney Cavalier.[25] The reform implied a bigger shift but nothing more happened.

Unrest and division within the caucus drove two generational leadership experiments during the 2003–07 period: the Latham experiment that failed and the Rudd–Gillard experiment that succeeded in bringing Labor to power.

Abrasive, gutsy, intellectual and erratic, Latham lacked the temperament to manage the euphoric highs and crushing lows of political leadership. He launched his leadership with a brilliant metaphor—'the ladder of opportunity'—but finished sick and consumed by despair, raging against what he called the business, media and foreign policy establishments, the power elites that he hated. After giving Howard a fright, Latham succumbed in 2004 to an eclectic and confused agenda.

Latham accentuated the contradictions that plagued Labor—he tried to uphold the Hawke–Keating legacy, fiscal responsibility and welfare-to-work reform but ran a left-wing 'scuttle and run' line on Iraq, resurrected old-fashioned Whitlamism by reliance on Gillard's Medicare Gold policy and indulged in class-based rivalry with his private school 'hit list'. Suffering from ill-health, Latham resigned the leadership in January 2004 in a bizarre television event in a suburban park.

In a brutally honest admission nine years later, Latham said of his leadership: 'I made no lasting progress in the development of new Labor thinking.' He felt he got the job too early, aged 42, with much of his thinking still a work in progress.[26] Latham left a demoralised party reeling from its fourth loss to Howard. Labor's policy malaise only deepened.

A shocked party chose stability and returned Beazley to the leadership. It was a natural response. But within two years lack of faith in Beazley triggered the second experiment with the rise of Rudd and Gillard. Neither had been in the Parliament with Hawke or Keating. They had no direct involvement in the Hawke–Keating era, its achievements, struggles and political strategy.

Rudd and Gillard constituted a new generation keen to leave its mark. The party they inherited was intellectually lazy, organisationally ossified and entrenched in its ways. Labor was hungry for power but ill-equipped for power. In 2003, before he became leader, Latham had nailed the disease: Labor was wedded to an obsolete class-based politics and a lust for big centralised bureaucracies imposing 'top-down' solutions in the name of equality, a prophetic insight into the coming flaws of the Rudd–Gillard era. Yet in real life 'the boundaries between capital and labour [had] blurred, with the number of share owners (54 per cent of adults) exceeding the number of fulltime workers (43 per cent).'[27]

In 2006, the year before he became Rudd's Finance Minister, Lindsay Tanner warned that Labor's 'real point of vulnerability' was economic management. Tanner said the party was trapped, 'trying to be Old Labor and New Labor at the same time'. He felt it had neither repudiated Hawke–Keating economics nor embraced them: 'the end result has been confusion and outcomes that satisfy no one'.[28] He warned that Old Labor was being 'drastically weakened' or 'destroyed' by globalisation. Yet the ALP seemed frozen, 'saddled with a political culture dominated by arrogance, exclusivity and intellectual rigidity'.[29]

Machine politics were corrupting the heart of the caucus. Martin Ferguson described the party's strangulation at the hands of factional power: 'In the old days at New South Wales conferences we put trade unionists into the New South Wales Upper House. Then it extended to the Senate and to federal seats. The Senate is now the prime example of our failure as a party. It has become a retirement pasture for union officials.'[30] This was the chamber that once shone with Lionel Murphy, Gareth Evans, Peter Walsh, John Button and Jim McClelland. An analysis of the Labor Senate that terminated in mid-2014 revealed the debacle. About two-thirds of ALP senators had worked as union officials and only six out of thirty-one senators had not previously had a job working for an ALP politician, the party or the unions.

In 2002 John Button, the Senate leader under Hawke, said: 'The union–ALP relationship has degenerated into a bad habit. It damages the ALP. It damages the unions even more. It may be time for the formal

relationship to end, to have a friendly divorce.'[31] Rodney Cavalier subsequently offered this uncompromising conclusion: 'Belonging to the ALP
is not part of the life of a modern Australian worker.' Cavalier reckoned
that the proportion of members of affiliated unions who belonged to the
Labor Party was fewer than 0.5 per cent.[32] A majority of Australian workers saw no need to join a trade union, with union membership falling
from about 50 per cent of the workforce after World War II to less than
20 per cent by 2007 when Rudd took office.

Yet Rudd and Gillard united the party and disguised its flaws at
the 2007 election. This perfect summer of concord began with Rudd's
brilliant conception of how to beat Howard. He offered Howard-lite
reassurance to the public plus a heavy dose of New Labor Blairism. Rudd
put a fresh gloss on Labor's fading canvas. He made Labor respectable
and even fashionable—no mean feat. To enable Rudd to overcome voter
suspicions about Labor, the party decided on a presidential campaign
exceeding that of Hawke in 1983.

Labor gave Rudd its soul. It didn't know much about him but that
didn't matter. Rudd would deliver office to Labor—this was the pact, a
pact with a shelf life of less than three years.

The key to the concord was the WorkChoices legacy: it brought
Labor and the trade unions together. More significantly, it broke the
trend: instead of the unions being a negative for Labor, they became a
plus. The unions and Labor ran on a unity ticket against heartless Howard
and, for a briefly bright two years, the strategic tribulations of Labor
seemed an over-written hysteria. The return of realism, however, could
not be denied indefinitely.

Former AWU boss Paul Howes said:

> I think in 2007 John Howard united the Labor Party—it was
> united around defeating Howard and WorkChoices. He was so
> universally abhorred. Fighting Howard helped us to mend our
> divisions. The party and the movement locked in together. We
> were clear on what we opposed, but God knows what we actually
> stood for. We had to have a summit on that. We had been in the
> wilderness for eleven years and we didn't have a clear agenda back
> in office.[33]

Chris Bowen said: 'Time in Opposition is best spent not just developing discreet policy ideas but also doing serious thinking about an
over-arching purpose, a theme to sustain you through the first term in

office and beyond. In hindsight, not enough was done during our time in Opposition to developing that over-arching theme.'[34] This is a balanced and persuasive critique.

The Young Turks were less forgiving. Sam Dastyari said:

We went to the 2007 election with four ideas—repealing WorkChoices, ratification of Kyoto, the apology [to the Stolen Generation] and an education revolution. That's all. But as a movement we were obsessed about Howard. The brilliance of Howard is that he dominated us as well as his own side. We failed to use the 1996 to 2007 period to articulate what was our purpose. It wasn't sorted.[35]

In a sense Labor's paradox was its weakening as a party yet its success at winning elections—at state level. It got weaker and smarter at the same time. For too long Labor relied upon its campaign professionalism to cover its policy flaws. The day of reckoning, however, cannot be indefinitely deferred. When it came, above all in shattering election defeats in New South Wales and Queensland, the public recognised that Labor's policy framework had collapsed.

Lack of policy development and lack of belief were tied together. Latham understood this from the inside. He saw the fatal nexus: 'Machine politics has not only produced a crisis of methodology within the ALP; it has also led to a crisis of belief.'[36] The party that lacks belief in itself lacks the ability to persuade the public about its policies. It is a perfect description of the Rudd and Gillard governments: they were unable to persuade the public.

Indeed, after Rudd's 'fair weather' phase ended in 2009, Labor failed to persuade the public on virtually anything (Gonski school reforms and the National Disability Insurance Scheme being qualified exceptions late in Labor's life). But the failures were lethal: the climate change scheme that Rudd abandoned, the mining tax that Labor had to weaken, the fiscal stimulus that bequeathed debt and deficits and the carbon tax that the public loathed. Keating's skill had been able to persuade the public about economic policies. But Labor during the Rudd–Gillard era lost this art. Even when Labor had a strong case—its response to the GFC—it was unable to win the policy debate. The party had lost its resolution. Gillard knew this; as prime minister she tried, but failed, to rekindle the fire of belief.

Under Rudd and Gillard the Labor crisis became a governing crisis in that they failed in their different ways at the task of effective government. Inexperience was one element, a weak party another and character yet another. Rudd was too much the talking head without conviction while Gillard was too transactional, obsessed with deals inside the beltway that she could never explain outside the beltway. But the deeper problem was policy. Rudd and Gillard became prime exhibits of Labor's unreformed post-1996 policy culture. Both products of their party, they were improvisers within the Labor tradition but neither was a genuine policy innovator.

In his content Rudd was elusive and contradictory. Who was the real Kevin? It was a question his colleagues asked. Rudd paraded as a policy wonk but had an incorrigible populist streak. He purchased policy options across the spectrum—he was pro-business but also pro-union, pro-government intervention but also pro-market, a friend of China but also tough on China; he preached humanity towards asylum seekers but declared he would stop the boats, presented as a fiscal conservative who also mounted the greatest spending spree in the nation's history, paraded as a nation-builder but went to war against the resources sector, enshrined climate change as the moral test of the age but walked away when the public's enthusiasm faltered. The public wanted to support Rudd but, in the end, felt it didn't know Kevin. He was a follower of opinion rather than a leader who shifted the nation's thinking. The problem with Rudd was not his strength but his weakness.

When the disguise was removed and Rudd acted from instinct he was an old-fashioned champion of state power. This is the philosophical hallmark and enduring legacy of the Rudd Government 2007–10. He presided over Gillard's partial re-regulation of the industrial system, expanded manufacturing industry assistance, delivered an exaggerated Keynesian stimulus in response to the 2008 global crisis that left the nation with a protracted deficit and debt burden, authorised construction of a hi-tech, government-driven National Broadband Network without adequate cost accountability and widened regulation across economic, social and environmental domains. This was not a Hawke–Keating reform agenda.

The defining achievement of his government—Australia's passage through the 2008–09 global crisis—was Rudd's triumph. It consumed his brain, energy and time in a remarkable phase of chief executive activity. Economists will dispute the extent to which Rudd's policies saved the day—but Rudd will always be accorded credit because the challenge came on his watch. The issue, however, is the price paid in terms of the long-run painful budget reckoning imposed across the nation to discharge Rudd's debt.

Gillard had the ruthlessness to put Rudd to the sword, the skill to form a minority government and a survival instinct that enabled her to stay leader nearly an entire term with the lowest ALP primary vote in history. Operating one-on-one or in a small group, Gillard was often persuasive and charming. On the larger stage she lost traction and was too wooden. She disappointed the party and dismayed the public. As an orator Gillard lacked the didactic inspiration of Whitlam, the charismatic intelligence of Keating or Hawke's projection of strength in consensus. She was down to earth, better organised than Rudd and had little trouble taking decisions. Unfortunately, she took too many bad decisions, the result of what Crean called her 'tin ear'.

Unlike that of most ALP leaders, Gillard's formation did not arise from economic policy or foreign/security policy. Her major reforms— carbon pricing, the Gonski school agenda and the National Disability Insurance Scheme (NDIS)—were substantial but flawed, plagued respectively by the absence of public support, poor implementation and funding uncertainties. She failed to establish credible economic policy credentials and lacked a convincing governing strategy.

During Gillard's final two years Labor's primary vote fell to the 30–33 per cent range, probably the worst in a century. Labor had shrunk its appeal. Its policies were too narrowly based. It had done lethal damage to its brand. The public distrusted Labor as an institution.

Gillard's policies gave rise to a serious critique: that her organising principle was actually about doing deals and shaping policies for her own political survival, a charge she would reject. Gillard was a victim of circumstance yet she tended to create those circumstances: she chose to remove Rudd on the eve of an election; she negotiated an alliance with the Greens; she chose to break her election promise on a carbon tax; she chose a close alignment with unions; and she framed relations with business based on a class-war mentality that left a toxic aftermath. Her improvisations in the cause of survival weakened her position in the country. Gillard became an unpopular PM running an untenable policy framework. She became a case study in how Labor should not govern.

Gillard's failures had a profound effect on Rudd. When he was recalled in June 2013, Rudd, with little time and few tools, tried to project a new direction. 'When I became prime minister in 2013,' Rudd said when interviewed for this book, 'I was elected on a platform of new leadership which was our way of saying New Labor.' Rudd dismissed Gillard's government as Old Labor—because 'the primary source of power was unions and union-based factions'. He attacked Gillard for treating business as a 'class enemy', saying this was 'Old Labor thinking' and that 'it had never been my view'. Rudd said class warfare was not the basis on which he had won the 2007 election. He accused Gillard of betraying the principles that had guided the first Rudd Government. Upon his return, Rudd said, he moved at once to contact the Business Council of Australia to devise a fresh approach and terminate 'this ridiculous outdated language'. At a meeting with business and unions, Rudd said that, if successful at the 2013 election, he would govern by seeking common approaches across business and unions. It was a repudiation of the Gillard method.[37]

It is impossible to know how different a second fully formed Rudd Government might have been and difficult to gauge how much Rudd had learnt from his earlier mistakes as prime minister. But one thing is certain: he had learnt there was a need for the most sweeping recasting of Labor since its creation in the 1890s. He said that his 2013 decision to give the rank and file a 50 per cent say in electing the leader was just step one.

Interviewed for this book, Rudd set out the next three steps. He envisaged a rank-and-file vote on Senate pre-selection; the innovation of primaries for pre-selection involving ALP supporters, not just members; and, critically, complete embrace of the principle that 'the party has to reflect the society at large'—which meant union representation in party forums could not exceed 25 per cent if union workforce representation stayed below 20 per cent. As Rudd left politics he was pledged to bust Labor's foundational identity as a 50–50 trade union–based party.

This agenda, if implemented, would change Labor decisively. It would liberate the party from having former trade union officials dominating its caucus and having the unions dominating its conferences. The irony is supreme: on his departure from politics, Rudd belatedly pledged a transformation of the ALP.

Rudd's simple conclusion that Labor must 'reflect the society at large' was actually radical because Labor did not operate by this principle in practice. It was too infatuated with 'true believer' ideology in both its Left-progressive and its union dimensions, along with the vast array of public-sector interest groups it cultivated. This meant the party's base was too narrow and, in office, it was not equipped to govern effectively. The ministers were usually smart and diligent. But the whole never exceeded the sum of the parts. There was a strategic flaw at the centre.

The Rudd–Gillard–Rudd era was witness to two related defects: Labor as an institution was ill-equipped to govern, and its leadership proved inadequate during 2007–13.

It is impossible to ignore the comparison with Hawke. He had a philosophy of consensus that he applied in office, an accord with the unions, the view that business was essential to his purpose, an approach of market-based growth with equity, and a strategy of governing from the middle ground. Yet Labor when it returned to office in 2007 showed not the slightest interest in how Hawke and Keating had fashioned the most successful ALP government in history.

From his intimate position during the Rudd era, Lachlan Harris said:

> The conclusion is that Labor doesn't have the strength any more to sustain the pressure of government. Those pressures have been growing. The temptation for Labor is to look back on those six years and say it was just a personality challenge. I'm not arguing that leaders didn't make mistakes; of course they did. But you can't explain what happened just in terms of personalities. I'm arguing that Labor must honestly accept that it cracked under the pressures of government and it needs to rebuild to ensure that doesn't happen again.[38]

However, Rudd and Gillard as leaders must carry responsibility for their government. They were the best of their generation. They failed in their different ways, in the joint job of managing the party and governing the nation. This is not to dismiss their achievements or their legacy. It is no disgrace to fall short of the Hawke–Keating summit. This is a high benchmark but it is the benchmark.

Their policies were too narrowly based, too reliant upon state power, too reluctant to focus on individual economic empowerment and, ultimately, lacking a convincing over-arching strategy. Rudd and Gillard were burdened by the inadequate ALP policy culture that had prevailed from 1996; yet, for all their abundant intelligence, they failed to think sufficiently about how they would govern. Towards the end Labor ran a crude pro-union, anti-business model. Denialists in the party—and there were many—said Labor's problem was just leadership division, nothing else. The truth is that Australian governments do not sustain landslide defeats having got the policy settings right.

After its 2013 defeat Labor was still faced with its post-1996 problem: it was trapped, refusing to decide between Old and New Labor. In an ideal world the Rudd–Gillard–Rudd era should have answered this test. But it evaded the issue, bequeathing the question about Labor's future to yet another generation.

THE CRISIS OF
THE SYSTEM

CHAPTER 5

THE DEATH OF REFORM

T he first decade of the twenty-first century saw the death of the economic reform age that was inaugurated in 1983 with the election of the Hawke Government. It was symbolised in the struggle over John Howard's two most significant reforms—the GST and WorkChoices. These reforms sparked polarised battles that lasted for years. They bequeathed a new political culture shaped by reform timidity, the power of negative politics and recognition that long-run reform faced Herculean obstacles from a new regime of short-run, sectional-interest, media-driven tyrannies.

The death of economic reform was part of a larger story: the decline in the quality of government. If this decline went unchecked the consequence was certain: weaker economic growth and the undermining of Australian living standards.

During its 1996–2007 wilderness years Labor had been destructive of the reform cause. In office after 2007 Rudd and Gillard were not helped by Labor's obsession with opinion polls and focus groups. Their policy failures as prime ministers are tied to their reforms debacles— pricing carbon, the mining tax, the lost surplus and counter-productive government interventions. They succumbed on the 'big picture' issues that had once *made* Hawke, Keating and Howard.

At the 1998 election the incumbent prime minister, John Howard, and his deputy, Peter Costello, became heroes by carrying their historic GST-led reform. They had sacrificed a stack of seats and the fallout was rarely mentioned: having come to the brink of defeat in 1998 they were reluctant to risk another mega-reform on tax. Howard almost became a 'oncer'. Howard's chief adviser, Arthur Sinodinos, said of another mega tax reform: 'We had just survived the last round.'[1] Enough said.

But there was one exception. In 2005 Howard aspired to realise his lifetime dream of putting the old industrial system on the escalator to extinction via WorkChoices. His final reform impulse ended in catastrophe for the Coalition. It revived the trade unions, vested Rudd and Gillard with a winning campaign and gave them a mandate to partially re-regulate the industrial system. WorkChoices was a defective policy; it put industrial reform into the freezer for a decade. Howard never conceded he was wrong.

The paradigm of the reform age—change in the national interest— was being smashed. Howard had calculated that national interest factors— the key to Hawke–Keating success—would prevail. The GST meant a more efficient tax system and the public accepted this. It was a close-run thing but Howard won that debate. In the case of WorkChoices, Howard asked the public to tolerate greater employer power in favour of a stronger economy and more jobs. The public was hostile to the trade-off that Howard proposed and he lost that debate. For the first time since 1983 a legislated reform was rolled back and it would become a symbol, though not the cause, of the eclipse of the reform model.

The Rudd–Gillard era affirmed this conclusion with deadly conse-quences. The iconic Labor reform was pricing carbon to combat climate change, a highly fashionable idea. Yet it was resisted with ferocity by the Tony Abbott–led Coalition. In a saga of tragic comedy Rudd was ruined off the back of his carbon policy retreat and Gillard was destroyed by legislating her program in a breach of trust.

There is no disputing the dismal record. Three successive prime ministers—Howard, Rudd and Gillard—lost office because they either failed or mismanaged the reform challenge. This testified to a transfor-mation of politics against reform agendas. The balance of risk had shifted dramatically. The broad consensus surrounding the post-1983 reform agenda had collapsed. Economic reform had moved from being a unify-ing idea to being a divisive idea. The new political culture was defined by hatreds: Labor in Opposition detested the GST and de-regulation of industrial relations while the Coalition in Opposition saw Labor's carbon pricing schemes as frauds that would damage competitiveness for little environmental gain.

The unique factors that gave birth to the post-1983 reform age had disappeared. They can be summarised under three headings: first, a wide-spread recognition that the status quo had failed, a sentiment driven by the deep recessions of the 1970s and early 1980s; second, a consensus in the political system in favour of new ideas such as the utility of markets and the need to de-regulate, wind back protection, increase savings and impose more discipline on the public sector; and third, a political cul-ture that was able to prioritise the public interest. This gave governments an electoral incentive to look beyond narrow policies catering to their traditional voters and seek fresh supporters in the middle of or from the opposing side of politics.

The post-1983 reform age was built on sentiments that took decades to mature, but from the late 1990s two defining trends emerged to erode its foundations. The first was the power of the negative, a global phenomenon that attacked the heart of Western democracy. Its essence lay in a truism: it was easier, given modern communications, to win votes by being negative than by being positive. This was tied to the weakening of political parties. With fewer voters loyal to Liberal and Labor, leaders had to earn voter support, a task more easily accomplished by discrediting your opponent than by projecting your positives. The ingredients that empowered interest groups to run negative campaigns were obvious: a grievance to be exploited, a smart advertising executive and the luxury of deep pockets.

The second trend was the evolution of two separate and competing reform agendas: a Liberal reform agenda and a Labor reform agenda. These agendas were spearheads for party rivalry and they meant the idea of a single bipartisan national reform agenda was destroyed.

The Liberal reform agenda involved industrial de-regulation, lower tax rates with a broader base, smaller government, privatisation, cost reductions, fiscal prudence and market-based policies. The Labor agenda involved more human capital spending, investment in education and skills, carbon pricing, re-distributive taxes, government-based industry and innovation policy, more tolerance for public spending and large-scale public enterprise investment—witness the NBN. These competing agendas were tied to ideological competition, interest group support and electoral tactics. Reform politics became defined by dispute, not agreement. The competing Liberal and Labor agendas dissolved the legacy of the 1980s.

By the time of the Gillard Government it was game over. The framework to sustain reform had literally ceased to exist. This was obvious to Howard, a proposition he argued in his memoirs. For Howard, the post-1983 story was that reform only came via two pathways—either by bipartisanship (witness financial de-regulation and tariff cuts) or by the prime minister being strong enough to expend reserves of political capital (the GST) to carry the debate. 'Gillard has neither of these,' Howard said.[2]

Nothing was the same after WorkChoices. This ill-conceived venture destroyed more than Howard's IR policy. It ingrained in Labor culture the idea of election victory by attacking Liberal support for industrial de-regulation. It intimidated the Liberals. It left both sides with a deep awareness of the electoral rewards to be had from brutal negativity, provided there was an opening. It became a template to be applied across the political system. The extent to which Labor attributed its 2007 victory to the anti-WorkChoices campaign was remarkable. Julia Gillard told the author: 'I do not believe that without WorkChoices Howard's standing would have deteriorated quickly enough for Labor to win the 2007 campaign.'[3] Gillard had said it—for many Labor figures the anti-WorkChoices push was the difference between success and defeat. It was that vital.

In a sense Labor tolerated but never accepted the GST. It campaigned against the GST at the 1998 election; it voted against the GST in Parliament when Howard implemented his mandate; it pledged GST rollback at the 2001 election (yet was actually keeping 97 per cent of the revenue); and in office it excluded the GST from the Henry tax review, signalling that it rejected both its extension and its increase. Labor kept the revenue but still loathed the tax. In office, it was waiting to run another GST scare against the Coalition. Labor saw tax reform in more specific and re-distributive terms. The GST became a symbol of the breakdown between the parties on any hope for tax reform consensus.

The Rudd Government's review, headed by Treasury chief Ken Henry, raised expectations about major tax reform. The report provided the intellectual framework: it was comprehensive and ambitious and it constituted a huge effort. Yet Labor never gave any serious consideration to using the report for a significant across-the-board reform because its recommendations were too ambitious for a government that preferred a cherry-picking approach.

Terry Moran, who was secretary of the Department of the Prime Minister and Cabinet under Rudd, said:

> When Howard was PM the Labor Party under Kim Beazley decided for political reasons to go all out opposing the GST. Labor didn't destroy the reform and retained it on coming to office. But Labor weakened bipartisan support for reform in the national interest and it has never really recovered since.[4]

Heather Ridout, chief of one of the major business lobbies, the Australian Industry (or Ai) Group, had been a member of the Henry tax review. The Ai Group invested resources, time and hopes in a major tax reform and was bitterly disappointed. Ridout's successor, Innes Willox, said: 'We felt the Rudd Government missed a major opportunity to re-make the tax system. We were deeply disappointed. Frankly, we felt they lacked the courage for the task.'[5]

The next great blow to the reform cause arose from the turbulent and unpredictable saga of pricing carbon. At the 2007 election the prospects looked good—both Howard and Rudd campaigned on carbon pricing platforms. It seemed the urgency of a warming planet had driven a Labor–Liberal concord. It was impossible to imagine the idea would be denied in the next Parliament. Yet this is what happened.

Labor's initial pledge came in 2006 when Beazley and shadow minister Anthony Albanese combined to commit to a carbon price with a national carbon trading regime, a position Rudd seized with brilliance. Howard's resistance to this policy was broken only under extreme pressure, forcing the single greatest policy reversal in his eleven years as prime minister. Howard was driven by a perfect storm: the drought gripping Australia; the popular Al Gore movie *An Inconvenient Truth*, one of the greatest polemics in history; and, at the higher reaches, the *Stern Review* in the United Kingdom arguing the economics for carbon pricing. Howard moved because the politics of resistance were killing him.

Inside the government, senior public servants staged one of the most assertive reform campaigns for a generation. The key actors were the head of the Department of Prime Minister and Cabinet Peter Shergold and Treasury chief Ken Henry. In Australia the commitment to carbon pricing policy came not from the environmental lobby but from the Treasury, and it was conceived as an economic policy reform.

In November 2006, at a meeting of departmental heads that Shergold convened to examine the issue, Henry declared: 'the Prime Minister is right to think he's behind the curve'. The upshot after more policy work was a Shergold-instigated meeting in the cabinet room between Howard and senior public servants. When Shergold reached the bullet point advocating an ETS, Howard asked: 'What's that doing here?' It was the decisive moment; the next exchange was a classic in the advisory art.

Henry said: 'Prime Minister, I'm taking as my starting point that during your prime ministership you will want to commit us to a cap on national emissions. If my view on that is wrong, there is really nothing more I can say.' It was a threshold moment. 'Yes, that's right,' Howard said cautiously. Henry continued: 'If you want a cap on emissions then it stands to reason that you want the most cost-effective way of doing that. That brings us to emissions trading, unless you want a tax on carbon.'[6] Howard did not want a tax on carbon.

Each public servant then spoke in favour of the ETS as preferred policy. The pieces were being assembled. Shergold was the organiser, Henry the spearhead. But the ultimate sanction came from Michael Chaney, president of the Business Council of Australia. 'I decided the BCA would lose credibility if it didn't take a position,' he said. Invoking the insurance principle, he led the business lobby to shift position to favour pricing carbon.[7] That closed the circle. Howard confidant Arthur Sinodinos later said: 'The switch by the business community was the key. This was the driver. When the BCA brokered their new position it was a tipping point for us. I think the country had reached tipping point.'[8]

So a formidable stakeholder alliance for reform was assembled: the Coalition, Labor, the BCA, Treasury, the pro-market lobby and, of course, the environmental movement. Rarely has such a remarkable coalition been forged for such a difficult reform. This great opportunity was given to Rudd to implement. It was his 2007 winning mandate. Rudd's personal dedication to the cause was extraordinary. Yet he mismanaged the politics. Rudd delayed too long, failed during 2009 to sell the cause with sustained passion and lost his nerve when the Coalition reversed direction and threw up Abbott as a demolition agent. Put crudely, Abbott did a WorkChoices on Rudd.

Labor's retreat from its carbon pricing package during 2010 constituted a new low tide in the fading waters of economic reform. It was all the more crushing because the ducks had been lined up. Rudd had misunderstood the nature of reform: the window is only ever briefly open. Abbott's arrival meant that bipartisanship on carbon pricing quickly turned into bitter partisanship. For Labor, the lesson was that carbon pricing had devoured its political capital yet had become an electoral dead weight.

The final setback to the reform cause was the 2008 global financial crisis (GFC) and its meaning as presented to the Australian public by Rudd. He exploited the crisis to attack Howard as the local version of the neo-liberalism that had brought the world to the brink of ruin. Writing in the national magazine *The Monthly*, Rudd put his proposition about the crisis in sweeping terms: 'It has called into question the prevailing neo-liberal economic orthodoxy of the last 30 years—the orthodoxy that has underpinned the national and global regulatory frameworks that have so spectacularly failed to prevent the economic mayhem which had now been visited upon us.' Depicting the Liberal Party as the 'home of neo-liberalism in Australia', he put the Howard Government in the dock—despite the fact that our banks and financial system had avoided the US and European disease. Rudd recruited the crisis against the Liberals and on behalf of Labor, saying that the coming epoch might be called 'social capitalism' or 'social democratic capitalism' with the state taking on a greater role.[9]

This was playing with fire. The 2008 crisis was an external event imposed upon Australia; there was no domestic policy fault; there was no market failure in Australia, just the reverse. The historical truth, as economist Ross Garnaut wrote, was that Rudd's 'past 30 years' in Australia encompassed the reform era that had contributed to a distinct improvement in economic performance. This had seen roughly equal periods of Liberal and Labor rule, with both sides contributing to market-based reforms and liberal economics. The risk Garnaut identified, typified by Rudd's essay, was that the need to better regulate the North Atlantic financial systems might translate into 'a generalised justification for increased government intervention in the economy' of individual nations undermining open and competitive markets.[10]

There was no worldwide lurch into protectionism but Rudd's effort to distort the history of the reform age in Australia was highly counterproductive. He denied the real history: that Australia's strong position was because of the combined post-1983 effort of Labor and Liberal governments in a shared project of pro-market reform. By inserting a false and partisan wedge into this history, Rudd recruited the GFC to polarise the economic policy debate in Australia.

Leading up to 2013, in the final four years of Labor government, intense conflict erupted over economic policy and reform along this fault line. Labor's message was that government intervention and spending had created economic activity, income and jobs. The Coalition's message was that Australia's future was compromised by excessive spending, rising debt, and pervasive government intervention and regulation. Given this philosophical split, agreement on reform measures became a forlorn hope.

A former chair of the Productivity Commission, Gary Banks, lamented the policy corrosion tied to the GFC and its role in a rent-seeking resurgence: 'It radically heightened the inclination of governments to spend rather than save. Suddenly politics and economics were in harmony—spending was generally seen to be good, almost regardless of its productive potential (and much of it was not very productive).' The handout was extolled as good policy.[11]

Australia seemed headed towards rival models of governance. Labor governed in alliance with the unions while the Coalition in Opposition aligned closely with business. Labor was seen as anti-business; the

Coalition was seen as anti-union. The ability to reach across the divide to negotiate inclusive deals disappeared and the common political and intellectual ground for reform was torn apart.

The turmoil of the Rudd–Gillard–Rudd era had a meaning beyond a Labor power squabble. Its tribulations arose from multiple problems: executive instability, the real-time media cycle, the entrenchment of short-term politics, the tyranny of the polls, the disintegration of party loyalty and a more pluralistic society defying 'top-down' pyramidal style initiatives. The effect was to make political leadership more difficult. It is a crisis of the system.

The economic difficulty facing Europe and the United States after the 2008 GFC betrays fissures in the established democracies. Australia has enjoyed a superior economic performance and better decision-making than most northern hemisphere democracies but this is not guaranteed. Australia's recent history offers no grounds for complacency. Just the reverse—it suggests cracks in quality decision-making that, unless corrected, will lead to growing social divisions, diminished economic performance and either a fall in living standards or a decline in their rate of increase.

The death of reform in Australia is a symptom of a far larger story: the decline of good government. The decision-making system has become more susceptible to special interests, professional lobbyists, single-interest campaigns and media mobilisation based on deep pockets. The litany of unjustified 'gesture' policies spans both sides: ethanol subsidies, Cash for Clunkers, the baby bonus, the Renewable Energy Target, the fuel and grocery watches and huge solar subsidies.

The two most senior public servants of the Rudd–Gillard years, Terry Moran and Ken Henry, felt obliged, after leaving their jobs, to speak out about the crisis. They were convinced Australia's political culture was degenerating and both saw communications at the heart of the problem.

'I can't remember a time in the past thirty years when the quality of public policy debate has been so poor,' Henry said. 'A leader who is pre-occupied with following public opinion is, of course, not really going to offer any leadership at all. The best political leaders I've observed like to be just in front of where they think public opinion could possibly move to.'[12] Henry argued that politicians were willing victims of the media and media quality was in decline. He told the story of a minister confronting a political bushfire, who told him: 'You know, if I haven't dealt with this issue by ten in the morning it will consume my whole day. There won't be any policy work.'

Henry said debate 'has become increasingly short-term', a flaw induced by media. The example he gave was close to his heart: Treasury's 2002 Intergenerational Report drawing attention to the long-run impact of population ageing and the need for a new policy narrative based on better workforce participation and productivity. 'Here we are, more than ten years on and we are no closer to having put in place the policy requirements,' he said. 'We've in fact lost our way. There's something missing in the way in which public policy debate is conducted in this country.' Henry was specific: the truly big issues were put on the backburner. Having been at the centre of decision-making for thirty years, Henry put out the message that the decline in public policy quality, unless addressed, would diminish the nation and the living standards of its people.

Moran told the author:

> I believe that reform has got much harder in Australia's political system. During the Rudd–Gillard period there were a large number of successful public policy initiatives but also more than the usual number of failures. It's the failures that stigmatised the Labor Government because the failures often had a very significant impact on public sentiment. Other than in major crises, explicit or implicit acceptance of major, high-impact reform is necessary. The loss of bipartisanship hurt both Rudd and Gillard and the signs are that it may hurt Abbott as well.

Moran saw a nexus between poorer government and poorer policy results. He identified the flaws: erosion of the cabinet system, excessive centralisation in the prime minister's office, the rise of abuse of power by ministerial advisers, and short-term media pressures. The trend 'to obsess and fret' over media and media management was undermining good government.[13]

The warnings by Henry and Moran were given extra impetus by the outgoing chair of the Productivity Commission, Gary Banks, who by 2013 was alarmed at the regression in the political system. Banks feared a return to the 'bad old days', with an excessive focus on redistribution rather than wealth creation and a priority on political preferment rather than productivity. The essence of the 'bad old days' was the insider political fix that gave a firm or industry a special deal at a net cost to the public—the supreme example in Australia being the massive subsidies to an uncompetitive car industry. At the end of the Rudd–Gillard era, Banks said: 'In my view the re-emergence of a "rent-seeking society" poses a bigger threat to the future living standards of Australians than the ageing of our population or the vicissitudes of world markets.'[14]

It was a frightening commentary on the decline of politics. It is a reminder, as Banks said, that 'often there is nothing easier for governments to do than to introduce bad policies'. Once a political system rewards bad policies, then the rot is seeded. The Abbott Government, in its early months at least, seemed to recognise the urgency of terminating government handouts fed by a political culture that tied vote winning to endless pledges of expanded state power.

Labor ministers knew that the heart of the crisis was the communications revolution. It had changed the pace and nature of politics and the problem was systemic. Their individual accounts are part self-serving, part depressingly accurate.

Former Treasurer Wayne Swan was the most damning. He told the author after Labor lost office:

> I think our political journalism in this building [Parliament House] is largely broken. It's a number of things—the business model breaking down, a generation of journalists who haven't been mentored properly, the viciousness of News Ltd and its culture. But in some ways the ABC was just as bad. It became a media frenzy—it was pretty frightening. Economic reform is far more difficult today. The pace of political life is driven by technological change in the media. Vested interests have a lot of weapons available to them, notably via the media. Much of what happens in business is short-term. Major companies just focus on short-term share prices movements.[15]

After retiring from politics Lindsay Tanner, one of Rudd's 'gang of four' ministers, offered a scathing assessment: 'The two key rules that now govern the practice of Australian politics are: (1) Look like you're doing something; and (2) Don't offend anyone who matters.' Tanner exaggerated, but he had a valid point. Describing the corrupting legacy of the technological revolution, he said: 'Winning today's micro-argument is all important and tomorrow can look after itself. This breeds a collective mentality of cynicism and manipulation. Policy initiatives are measured by their media impact, not by their effect.'[16]

Drawing upon his experience selling the carbon price package, Greg Combet said:

It was hard for Hawke and Keating to get reforms up and make them stick but, you know, they were tremendous politicians. I think reform has got harder. It's partly because of the daily media cycle. Things are battled out at a more puerile level. It's much harder now to prosecute and win a long-term argument.[17]

Former faction boss Graham Richardson, now a Sky News commentator, described events outside Parliament House on the morning of the Gillard–Rudd February 2012 challenge:

My time was divided between the outside booths of Channel 7 and Sky News set up for the purpose of covering the leadership ballot. Channels 9 and 10 were there as well. Even SBS joined in before the close of play. A parade of ministers (Bowen, Burke, Smith, Emerson, McClelland, Conroy, Roxon are the names I can remember) turned up to pass judgement on the combatants. They were joined by Tony Windsor, Rob Oakeshott and Uncle Tom Cobley.

The media frenzy was amazing. Reporters were stationed all over the nation to give us vox pops from the punters. Kevin Rudd himself returned to the *Sunrise* set where, with sparring partner, Joe Hockey, he had built a media reputation. Between my media contributions I watched this passing parade with ever increasing astonishment. There had never been a more public brawl in the more than four decades I have closely observed Australian politics.[18]

The media invaded everything. Gillard blamed the media for undermining her government. Rudd used the media relentlessly to undermine Gillard's leadership. He had recruited the media brilliantly in his earlier campaign against Beazley. In office, however, Rudd got confused between projecting spin and delivering substance.

The most dramatic evidence of transformation in political pace and corruption of the culture is the leadership story. The pressure is greatest on the Opposition leader: this is the death seat. In the twelve years between the 2001 and 2013 elections, there were seven changes of Opposition leader. The list reads: Beazley, Crean, Latham, Beazley again, Rudd, Brendan Nelson, Turnbull, Abbott. If anyone wants proof of the short-term nature of politics, this is it. There was an iron rule: an Opposition leader either gets on top of the prime minister or is removed. It made sensible policy development a distant option.

The hypocrisy of the media that demands substance from an Opposition leader yet knives that leader to the point of execution when the polls head south is nauseating.

Under Labor the disease extended into the office of prime minister. Once the virus takes hold it will kill governments. This is the story of the Rudd–Gillard–Rudd years. Neither side of politics is immune, but the virus has been more prevalent within Labor. Over the 2001–13 period Labor engaged in six leadership changes in Opposition and in office. The leadership became a contested issue in each of the four parliaments over this period.

During these years, Crean became the first ALP leader since World War II to be denied the opportunity to lead the party to an election. The 2001–04 Parliament saw two leadership contests as part of the three-way Crean–Beazley–Latham struggle. The 2004–07 Parliament saw three Labor leaders: Latham, Beazley and then Rudd. The 2007–10 Parliament saw Rudd become the first elected prime minister in history to be removed by his own party during his first term. The 2010–13 Parliament saw a permanent Gillard–Rudd leadership struggle, with Rudd returning to power at the third showdown. In 2013 the nation had three prime ministers: Gillard, Rudd, Abbott.

This depth of instability is unique in Labor history. Labor has had a leadership change at every election for the past five elections: in 2001 Beazley, 2004 Latham, 2007 Rudd, 2010 Gillard and 2013 Rudd again.

It is true that many leadership changes were justified. Yet Labor has been too cavalier in deposing prime ministers and premiers. The 2010 Rudd removal and the 2008 decision by the New South Wales ALP organisation to destroy the Labor premiership of Morris Iemma are the most grievous examples.

The problem transcends personality and lies in the political system. No genius is required to identify the impulse at work—it is the opinion polls, published and private. The main polls—Newspoll, published in the *Australian*, and Nielsen, published in the Fairfax papers—set the rhythm of politics to an extent that is astonishing. Governments regularly organise announcements to coincide with pollsters being in the field to boost their poll rating. The national Parliament is hooked on polls akin to an addictive gas circulating throughout the building. No leader and no policy has immunity. When leaders are threatened the next step is guaranteed: the leaking of private party polling against them. In this environment the quest for serious policy is under pressure.

An important improvement has been the change in ALP rules to consolidate the position of the ALP leader in Opposition, instigated by Rudd in 2013. It establishes a 'change' threshold of 60 per cent of caucus, a rule that should serve to shift the culture and create much-needed stability. However, the Rudd-imposed 75 per cent caucus threshold for removal of an ALP prime minister is a gross over-reaction and risks the reverse problem: too little accountability.

The fading of party ideology means Labor now exists to govern. In a post-ideological climate Labor is driven by its stakeholder interests, not abiding faiths. Labor has little interest in any policy that jeopardises its voting coalition. For Labor, the worst fate is not loss of belief but loss of office. In this sense Labor and the Liberal Party have become more similar: their legitimacy is found in office because they lack an ideological cause that makes Opposition a tolerable fate.

For Liberal and Labor alike, nothing substitutes for the lure of success—not personal loyalty, policy belief, cherished icons or being the first female prime minister. The transformation in Labor has been marked. The old Labor Party is dead and its rituals seem unfathomable. This was the Labor Party that retained both Dr HV Evatt and Arthur Calwell as leader for three election defeats each. Recent ALP leadership contests are conspicuous for the absence of any policy factor. The only test that counts is the prospect of election victory. In 2006 Rudd prevailed against Beazley because the party, after four defeats, was desperate; in 2010 Gillard was able to remove Rudd only because the caucus lost faith in his winning ability; and in 2013 Rudd was recalled because Labor faced 'calamitous defeat', a view shared by a caucus majority. On each occasion the motive was self-preservation as informed by opinion polls.

Abbott had the best grasp of the new rules of politics. He saw that an Opposition leader had only two possible fates: you establish a polling lead or you lose your job. Integral to this process was the operation of the political media. Like the currency market, it overshoots by exaggerating the trend. The political media guarantees an Opposition leader is untenable once consigned to an opinion poll deficit position. Leadership speculation stories flourish. The media fans internal division and finally breaks the incumbent.

This leads to a more brutal political competition. Leaders now actively pursue the destruction of their opponents. Rudd's destruction of Turnbull's standing over the Godwin Grech affair is a classic in the genre. Labor proved this technique at state level, where the generation of

ALP premiers from Bob Carr onwards made destruction of their Liberal opponents into a Roman amphitheatre art form.

In a contest of first-strike destruction Abbott replied with an assault that contributed to the removal of Rudd in 2010 and Gillard in 2013. From the time he became leader of the Liberal Party in 2009, Abbott knew that if he failed to establish an ascendancy over Rudd then he would be eliminated. It was the same story with Gillard. The media hypocrisy surrounding Abbott has been unparalleled. If Abbott had taken the advice of his media critics and 'gone positive' much earlier he would possibly have lost both his bite and his polling lead and triggered a crisis over his job.

The political culture now enshrines 'safety first' tactics because the trick is to avoid blunders. Any blunder will be magnified, courtesy of the media's 'overshoot' modus operandi. The iconic event in this genre was John Hewson's calculated Fightback! blueprint at the 1993 election, the riskiest agenda ever put to the public by an Opposition leader. With Keating leading the anti-GST onslaught and winning re-election on this basis, the lesson was absorbed by Labor. It was also absorbed by the Liberal Party: Howard, Costello, and Abbott as Hewson's press secretary. It proved that negative pyrotechnics could defeat a party that had unnecessarily exposed itself. Opposition leaders followed the rule for the next generation—don't make yourself the issue—and Abbott gave a practical demonstration of this lesson at the 2013 election.

Tied to the exploitation of grievance has been the rise of third-party politics in Australia. The two great examples are the ACTU campaign against WorkChoices and the 2010 mining industry campaign against Rudd's proposed mining tax. Both were lethal: they proved the clout of sectional interests with deep pockets, astute research and smart advertising agencies. Neither the Howard nor Rudd governments could withstand the assault. Indeed, their effort on behalf of the alleged public interest was simply overwhelmed. The ACTU campaign was integral to Howard's defeat and the killing of WorkChoices, and the mining campaign defeated Rudd's tax and had the unintended consequence of contributing to Rudd's removal.

Greg Combet was architect of the former campaign and victim of the latter. Asked if he had started the rot, Combet said:

> I think it's true. Some of the mining executives said to me 'You showed us how to do it.' Well, it's a democracy and that won't change. Third-party interests are only going to campaign more

effectively in future. Governments will have to respond better but I am not certain what the answer is.

In a chilling insight into the limitations of government in this type of battle, Combet said:

> The resources available to me in government were less than I had at the ACTU looking at the people, the advertising and the politics. The guidelines in government about the use of public funds are very tight. And that's appropriate. But what is the recourse then? It gets down to me getting up at 6 a.m. as Climate Change Minister, my staff having been up at 4.30 a.m., reading the papers, getting me on the radio between juggling meetings and maybe getting the PM to put a line in an interview she does later. We do this in a hectic schedule with Parliament, stakeholder meetings and legislation. It is a clear weakness in governance of the country over how to get up reforms in the national interest. We are competing against well-financed third-party interests free to pitch their appeal in any manner they want. Hundreds of millions of dollars of advertising may be spent in a sectional interest. This issue has got to be flushed out and debated. In this generation it will take a leader or leaders of immense maturity and capacity to achieve anything like what Hawke and Keating did.[19]

The transformation of Western political culture traps governments on the killing ground between the needs of short-term politics and the demands of long-run policy. The time span over which policy must succeed just gets longer—consider the challenges arising from demography, infrastructure, climate change, tax and industrial reform, education and health, productivity and competitiveness. Yet such policies must be devised, sold and implemented in a ferocious media-driven and short-term political environment where the 24–hour news cycle requires immediate evidence of success.

Rudd was the great victim of this trap. He tried to succeed on both fronts—as master of short-term politics and champion of long-run policy. His failures will be seen in better context after the record of his successors is known.

The related conundrum is the conflict between expectations and delivery. Again, this is where Rudd came undone. He was psychologically incapable of limiting expectations to the zone of realistic delivery. Abbott's attack on Rudd's 'over-promise and under-delivery' became devastating. The deeper parable is the ambivalence of power, with President Obama being a prime exhibit.

The American scholar Moises Naim, in his book *The End of Power*, argues that 'power is harder to use—and easier to lose'. Naim argues that leaders today still wield immense power but 'less so than their predecessors' because they face more challenges and more competitors 'in the form of citizen activism, global markets and media scrutiny'. Leaders, he says, find that 'their tenure is getting shorter and their power to shape policy is decaying'.[20] Once again, Rudd's tragedy only gives credence to such analysis.

Tony Blair said that the political contest has become more ferocious while the ideological chasm has narrowed. Australia must be the prime example: the Labor–Liberal divisions over 2007–13 were real yet exaggerated by the demands of the political system and erosion of the culture.

Politics, however, moves in cycles. The death-of-reform cycle will surrender, at some point, to the revival-of-reform cycle. As one age dies a new age is born. Because Australia is a stand-alone nation running an open and competitive economy, it will be driven back to the reform path by the public-interest imperative. This was the impulse for the post-1983 reform era. It is as relevant today as it was then. There is no future in retreating to the abandoned, introspective fortress of the past. The Abbott Government, sensing this, is attempting to embark upon its own reform agenda. The real art of political leadership is to change the established order in necessary and enduring ways.

The issue is the price Australia will pay and the damage that will be done before it restarts the reform engine. This penetrates to what sort of catalyst, crisis, recession or mere change of government is needed. That means confronting the pluses and negatives from the recent age of prosperity.

CHAPTER 6

THE CURSE OF PROSPERITY

From 2003 the world economy turned in Australia's favour and offered the greatest surge in national income in the nation's history. Arising in John Howard's third term, this seismic event transformed Australian politics. The task became management of prosperity, distribution of its benefits and appeasement of the non-resources economy. Prosperity made Australians fat but often unhappy. The resources boom lifted household incomes and wealth and killed any hunger for economic reform or sacrifice for the common good.

The erosion of Australia's political culture was deep and dramatic, best captured by community anger towards the Abbott government's 2014 budget. After years of expanded entitlements across all income levels, Australian society was in denial when confronted by fiscal reality—that it had been living beyond its means. It seemed to lack either the intellectual or moral ability to grasp what had happened over the previous decade.

The China-driven terms of trade extinguished the national challenge that had propelled the post-1983 reforms. The rhetoric of self-improvement remained, but the bold deeds were gone. From the suburban street to the inner-city financial district, new mantras arose—grabbing the spoils, demanding redistribution and imposing new demands upon the public revenue to feed ludicrous expectations.

In economic terms there was a fatal legacy. The China-led commodity boom from 2003 largely replaced domestic productivity improvements as the driver of higher national income. This unlocks our understanding of the next decade of Australian history. Most Australians were much richer than before, courtesy of a mining boom rather than the harsher road of economic reform and productivity enhancement. Yet such booms, by their nature, are temporary.

The moral is writ large: prosperity is a gift and a curse. This has been the story of Australian history. For decades economic students read in their textbooks that our terms of trade (export prices compared with import prices) would boom and the boom would disappear nearly as quickly as it appeared. The post-2003 boom would be distinguished by its sheer force and longevity but, ultimately, it would also retreat. The Gillard Government suffered from the boom's slowing; the Abbott Government may suffer even more from its protracted retreat.

In 2011 Reserve Bank Governor Glenn Stevens said the boom was 'a once-in-a-century event' and 'potentially the biggest gift the global economy has handed Australia since the gold rushes of the 1850s'.[1] The previous year Treasury Secretary Ken Henry had suggested it may become 'the largest external shock to the Australian economy in its history'. Such words by the senior economic officials captured the boom's ambivalence: it was a 'gift' yet a 'shock'. It could deliver riches but bring ruin.

Never has Australia's dual position been more striking: it belongs to the West as a civilisation but is tied to the East as an economy. Australia is a major resources power linked to the industrialisation and middle classing of Asia, an exciting yet daunting fate.

Australia's post-2003 boom came like a surging locomotive whose rolling thunder kept exceeding the expectations of waiting passengers on the platform. It arrived not on a weak but a strong economy, already enjoying a ten-year-plus growth cycle. It was akin to a turbo charge that would drive Australia's momentum for another decade at least.

The national income boost was dramatic: estimated by the Reserve Bank at 12 to 15 per cent of GDP in extra income running on an annual basis compared with the 100-year price trend line. The gains went to mining producers, local shareholders, employees, consumers via a higher exchange rate, and the taxman as fantastic tax payments rolled into Canberra's vault. In 2011 Governor Stevens famously said one shipload of iron ore exports could now buy 22 000 energy-intensive flat screen television sets compared with only 2200 sets five years earlier.[2] That is resource power leverage, a literal depiction of what higher terms of trade meant: Australian income and dollars had far more global buying power. It was this strength that helped Australia to combat the 2008 global financial crisis without recession.

The prominent economist Ross Garnaut said the main effect of the terms-of-trade boom was to raise potential government revenues by about 10 per cent. He calculated the total impact was to raise potential average incomes of Australians by more than one-eighth, measuring the 2011 peak of the boom against the 1983–2002 price average.[3] This meant that Australia's average income levels moved ahead of both the EU and the United States.

The boom brought about a transformation in Australia's political culture. How could it not? It shaped the tenor and content of our politics throughout the post-2003 decade, it dominated Howard's last four years in office and it set the conditions for the entire Rudd–Gillard–Rudd era. It began before the global financial crisis and it peaked in 2011 after the worst of the crisis. It guaranteed that during this decade Australia's economic experience would be divorced from the rest of the West. For Australia, the management task was daunting because booms unleash a process of creative destruction as other industries are rendered uncompetitive off the back of higher costs and a high dollar.

The cultural change from greater wealth became a fantastic story. People lived in bigger houses and increasing numbers owned investment properties. Confident of their rising incomes and rising asset prices, they took more debt to boost their wealth and were rewarded with even higher asset, share and property prices. Peter Costello asserted that in his time as treasurer net household wealth (taking account of debt) tripled from $1.7 trillion to more than $5 trillion.[4]

What was the political consequence of such wealth? Was the community more ready to accept sacrifice to lift productivity and the economy overall? No, there is no such evidence. Indeed, the evidence points to the opposite. As the political arteries began to harden, prosperity bred a change in national psychology. Yet a vicious trap lay at the heart of the prosperity surge.

The clearest exposition came in 2010 from Reserve Bank Assistant Governor Phillip Lowe:

> If we look back over recent years we see that productivity growth has slowed ... Normally, slower rates of productivity growth would lead to slower increases in average living standards. But this has not occurred ... The reason for this is that the prices of Australia's exports have risen relative to the prices of our imports, lifting the purchasing power of Australia's national income ... This has allowed our living standards to increase at a faster pace than if we had to rely upon productivity growth alone. Looking forward, this situation cannot continue indefinitely.[5]

In 2012 Treasury Secretary Martin Parkinson offered the same analysis with biting clarity:

> After the significant improvements in productivity flowing from
> the post-1983 reforms, the beginning of the 2000s saw a marked
> slowing in labour productivity growth. More disturbing still has
> been the sharp deterioration in multi-factor productivity—how
> clever we are at combining labour, capital, resources and ideas ...
> After almost all of our growth in national income coming from
> productivity in the 1990s and early 2000s, over the last decade
> the contribution from productivity has more than halved—we
> have maintained the same rate of growth in living standards only
> because of the huge rise in the terms of trade.[6]

The new wealth was based not on productivity but higher terms of trade.
The latter had substituted for the former. Over a period of years the
Reserve Bank, the Productivity Commission, the Treasury and prominent
economists all described the remarkable transition at work.

One of the nation's academic experts in the field, Dean Parham,
constructed the story. During the 1990s productivity growth was basic to
the rise in average real wages. Prosperity grew in parallel with productivity. But this nexus was broken early in the new century. Productivity
growth slumped in 2003–04 but the commodity price boom took off
at that time. The continuing rise in real incomes came from the China-
driven terms of trade.[7] It was a gift, though a hard-earned gift.

Australia had avoided, perhaps postponed, a retreat in living standards. Addressing a business economics conference in 2010, Productivity
Commission chair Gary Banks had said:

> The productivity slump of the 2000s could have been expected to
> bring with it a decline in incomes. In fact, thanks largely to our
> rampant terms of trade, income growth for most of that period
> was at historical highs. Both history and economic logic tell us
> that this cannot go on indefinitely.[8]

In fact, as productivity faded, Australia experienced first a housing boom
fuelled by debt and when that was contained, a far bigger China-driven
resources boom. The political class was given a holiday from having to
initiate more productivity-enhancing reforms to boost national income.
East Asia was doing the job for them.[9] The 'lucky country' was lucky
again. But the luck came with a curse.

Parkinson issued the warning: the terms of trade had to fall. Sooner
or later, that would impact on living standards. It meant that the nation

needed to rekindle a productivity-enhancing strategy. The longer the delay, the harder it would get. He was discreet enough to avoid the obvious: the political class was facing a showdown with economic destiny.

Governor Stevens closed the argument: 'There is only one source of ongoing higher rates of growth of real per capita incomes and that is higher rates of growth of productivity … It is now just about impossible to avoid the conclusion that productivity growth performance has been quite poor since at least the mid-2000s. So everything comes back to productivity. It always does.'[10]

In 2012 Parkinson told then-treasurer Wayne Swan: 'You didn't cause the productivity problem but you own the consequences.' No doubt he gave the same advice to Tony Abbott and Joe Hockey when they came into office. As the terms of trade ease under Hockey, the government needs a new growth strategy to maintain jobs, activity and government revenues. That task will make or break the Abbott Government.

It was true that declining productivity was in part attributable to the resources boom itself because it generated huge investments without near-term output growth. This meant that as the boom receded productivity would improve, a truism that did not negate the case for the re-kindling of economic reform.

The sharpest early warning of a decline in the political culture came from Ross Garnaut, Hawke's former adviser and a guardian of the reformist creed. An expert in trade and resources policy, Garnaut went for the jugular at a conference in March 2005, in Howard's last term. After asking what was going wrong, Garnaut said:

> The deterioration had its origin in a Great Complacency that descended upon the country after a decade of exceptional economic growth. As a community, we accepted the excellent economic performance as evidence that we had changed enough … The links were forgotten between earlier economic reform and the contemporary prosperity.

He cast the blame net wide. For Garnaut, populism had become 'bipartisan' and was evident in state government as well as federal. The rot had been seeded; the terms-of-trade boom was eroding the mettle for hard decisions. Garnaut's label for the post-2003 years—the 'age of complacency'—took hold.[11]

These years fanned inflated and unsustainable community expectations, a psychology that was often called 'reform fatigue'. By 2010 more than half the workforce had never seen a recession. For several years Australians had read about the recession tribulations of a range of EU nations and the United States without having much understanding of why they had escaped. In Australia public demand continued for almost endless government programs in health, education, disability, child-care, pensions, family support and green industry subsidies, guaranteeing a bitter collision with fiscal reality. There was an entrenched sense of entitlement.

The high dollar and high costs from the boom made much of Australian industry uncompetitive. The resulting two- or three-speed economy saw intensified demands for more public subsidies to compensate some industries under pressure due to the resources boom. Yet using this pretext to pour taxpayers' funds into uncompetitive or declining industry was financially irresponsible and constituted long-run political fraud. The car industry was being backed by more than $1 billion annually yet was able to hold less than 10 per cent market share.[12] The resources boom hastened the showdown: it heightened the unsustainable nature of such subsidies yet accentuated the demands for them. Politicians had to decide whether to let the structural changes caused by the boom flow through the economy or try to deny them by protecting ailing firms and industries. Such tensions ran across the entire economy as the boom generated new winners and losers.

The problems that booms create for politicians are long established. Many people become unhappy because they are missing out or feel they are missing out. This sentiment worked against Howard at the 2007 election. Beyond that, boom conditions make it extremely difficult for politicians to take decisions that generate losers since this is seen as outrageous during such times of prosperity.

The decade to 2013 revealed a critical nexus in Australia's recent history: the link between the terms of trade and economic reform. The equation is lethal: sustained low terms of trade drove the will to reform and high terms of trade eroded such political will.

History tells the story. The early 1950s to the mid-1980s saw mounting resource price pessimism when Australia seemed caught on the wrong side of history as manufacturing prices rose (for imports we had to buy) and primary produce prices sagged (for exports we sold). Pressure tightened around the nation's financial arteries. Australia was branded 'the poor white trash' of Asia. The nation was living beyond its means in a deluded Fortress Australia of protectionism, an uncompetitive industrial system and weak export prices.

Such pessimism became a national convulsion in May 1986 when Treasurer Paul Keating gave the interview of the decade to radio king John Laws. Keating's warning that Australia risked becoming a 'banana republic' was prompted by the previous month's balance of payments figures based on low commodity prices. 'We are importing about $12 billion more than we are exporting on an annual basis,' Keating said. 'We are living beyond our capacity to meet our obligations ... it's the prices of our commodities—they are as bad in real terms [as] since the Depression.' Unless Australia confronted its core economic problems, he said, then 'you are gone, you are a banana republic'.[13]

Low terms of trade provoked the banana republic crisis. It was fear that Australia was no longer able to finance its living standards that compelled its leaders into radical new policy. This crisis helped to initiate the reforms implemented over time by Labor and the Coalition. Glenn Stevens said: 'The will to reform was probably most powerful when the terms of trade reached a long-term low in the mid-1980s.'[14]

But the post-2003 boom inaugurated a different era. Pessimism was banished from Australia's psychology to be replaced by a borrowing orgy involving households and business. It was cheap money that stimulated the consumer boom and then higher terms of trade that lifted national income. Keating's 'banana republic' siren had become an irrelevant footnote. Nothing so corrodes tough policy choices as the combination of easy money, a consumption boom and record terms of trade. The year 2003 was a dividing line in the nation's political culture.

Howard's prime ministership offered a variation on the same Keating theme because Howard had his own 'mini banana republic' episode. In the frenzy of the late 1990s dot.com share market boom, Australia was dismissed as an unfashionable commodity-based economy. Nations with capacity in information technology became the rage and prophets of the future. In October 2000 the dollar fell below US$0.52 (it would later sink to US$0.48) and a concerned Howard called then Reserve Bank Governor Ian Macfarlane to a meeting.

'The Prime Minister and Treasurer were worried,' Macfarlane later said. 'A constantly falling exchange rate makes people think: What is wrong with us?' The governor told Howard the dot.com craze was a global play that hurt Australia; it sent money into nations with strong ICT manufacturing and away from commodity-based economies; there was little that could be done.[15]

Howard attacked the World Economic Forum meeting in Melbourne in late 2000 for pushing 'much of this rather fatuous nonsense' about new and old economies. He was angry and frustrated. Australia, again, seemed caught on the wrong side of history. 'The conclusion was drawn that the Australian economy had little future because of its heavy reliance on both agriculture and mining,' Howard lamented. He was held prisoner by financial markets that kicked the currency to death.[16]

The correction came in 2001 when the dot.com asset bubble deflated. Once the 'tech wreck' ran through global share markets and the dollar rallied, Howard and Costello clamed vindication: they had focused on the economic fundamentals, not fashion. 'We had been on the right course in Australia,' Howard said. The moral, Macfarlane argued, was that a country did not have to manufacture IT products to be a success because what counted was its ability to utilise such equipment for productivity gains.

Howard recalled this as 'the last period' when Australia's economy would face difficulties 'in the time that my government remained in office'. Yet Howard remained in office for another six years.[17] This is an incredible statement. It testifies to a remarkable transition. Within 18 months the resources boom appeared and terminated any talk of Australia as an outdated economy. Howard and Costello had the last laugh on the markets. One of the epic events in world history had transformed Australia's position.

This was known as the Great Convergence—the twenty-first-century industrial revolution in China, India and many other emerging economies that was reducing the vast income gap between rich and once-poor nations. It was likely to become the pivotal economic event of the century. Australia's role was as a commodities powerhouse for the Great Convergence, notably in iron ore, coal and liquefied natural gas.

In short, the terms-of-trade boom divided the reform age from the age of complacency.

The post-1983 reform model involved a number of policies which, although discreet, were underpinned by a coherent set of ideas: the value of free trade, the utility of markets, an independent central bank, a surplus budget, low inflation, a competitive tax system, privatisation of public enterprise, a flexible industrial system, means-based welfare, national competition policy and engagement with Asia. By 2003 the reform age had run for twenty years and had delivered the longest unbroken economic expansion in Australia's history, then in world history among developed nations. It took Australia from the bottom third to the top third among OECD nations in per capita income. Under Howard and Costello, Australia had survived the 1997–98 East Asian financial crisis and the

US 2000–01 dot.com recession, while under Rudd it would survive the 2008 global financial crisis. This was an unmatched record of economic resilience and it arose not from luck but from quality policy settings.

The reform-based economic model was the reason Australia survived so long without a recession—that model hinged on a floating exchange rate, a more flexible economy, low inflation and sound macro settings. As history told, the old Australian economy could not have survived the turbulence of the resources boom without falling into recession.[18]

Yet the ability to keep the wheel turning only grew harder as the lure of prosperity persisted. Access Economics director Chris Richardson, like Ross Garnaut, had the core insight at an early stage, seeing beyond the prosperity to the corrosion that lay beneath. 'Our prosperity is under threat and we've run out of reform juice,' Richardson told *The Australian* and the Melbourne Institute conference in April 2005. 'Something's got to happen. This is not just about the federal government; it's about the Opposition and it's about the states. The good times are rolling but the reforms are not. The risk is that the current boom is being squandered.'[19]

Gary Banks said that 'real reforms' involved 'some losers at least in the short term'. This required effective mobilisation for the cause. He feared that the legacy from the resources boom was 'one of complacency about pursuing reforms'. Without political leadership, the cause was lost. Yet if productivity-enhancing reform was a no-goer, he said, 'Australia is in for a tough time.'[20]

Ken Henry was worried about the policy implications of full employment. In March 2007, in an address to his staff, Henry said that with the unemployment level the lowest since the June quarter of 1976 'the community appetite for reform is considerably smaller'. He told his officers to beware the economic consequences of complacency. In this climate, with pressures against good policy, they should strive to make their advice to ministers compelling and convincing.[21]

At one point Glenn Stevens floated a radical idea: that Australia should lift its productivity performance while its terms of trade were high. As Stevens saw it, this would offer 'the most secure base for strong increases in living standards'.[22] It was doubtful, however, whether the political system was capable of such a feat.

The terms-of-trade boom proved more enduring for Australia than the 2008 global financial crisis. It is no surprise that the political system succumbed to the boom. It merely reflected the social and community values of the time. Having the terms of trade substitute for productivity gains was good fun and a lucky ride. As the music slowed, though, the collective national hangover began. The age of complacency extracted a toll that will eventually demand repayment. The task is to re-create the courage and honesty of the reform age.

IV
THE RUDD TRIUMPH

CHAPTER 7

THE RUDD–GILLARD PACT

The Rudd ascendancy is a story in the will to power. Kevin Rudd had no party base. He was loyal to neither the Right nor the Left in the Australian Labor Party. He arrived in caucus with no champions. He was a loner unsympathetic to Labor's tribal rituals. He looked a geeky bureaucrat with no popular appeal, and he quickly had powerful rivals swearing he would never be leader. Rudd began his run starting behind Swan, Smith, Gillard and Tanner but he blitzed his rivals. He became leader in 2006 just eight years after his election to Parliament in a quest remarkable for its intensity.

'I have no intention of being here for the sake of just being here,' Rudd said in his prophetic maiden speech. Kevin and his wife Therese had worked on the speech till about 3 a.m. the night before, Kevin as wordsmith, Therese at the word processor. At the start nobody saw him as a future leader. Yet Rudd was a freak, a solitary man with a consuming purpose. Kevin lobbied, networked, gave speeches, wrote articles, lived on his mobile phone, and cultivated editors, journalists, caucus members and union leaders. He went to bed late and got up early in the endless cause of self-advancement. Nobody, not Keating, not Howard, as young MPs had such a relentless drive.

Yet in the Labor Party will-to-power is not enough. Rudd was a Queenslander and an outsider, remote from the big blocs of factional votes. He became leader only because of a series of bonds that he forged— the three most important being with Julia Gillard, with New South Wales right-wing ALP secretary Mark Arbib and with left-wing broker Kim Carr. The deal with Gillard was the critical event. The Rudd–Gillard pact had the potential to set up Labor for a decade in office.

Kevin craved media publicity and popularity. From his early months in Parliament Rudd cast his net wide. He attracted attention courtesy of his intelligence and compulsion to network. Over the years he won an eclectic range of friends and supporters: New South Wales Premier

Bob Carr; the Left's Anthony Albanese; the *Australian's* editor-in-chief, Chris Mitchell; World Bank president Bob Zoellick; New South Wales union boss John Robertson; big-name journalists Laurie Oakes and Peter Hartcher; young New South Wales MP Chris Bowen; ABC journalist Maxine McKew; and South Australian Premier Mike Rann, as well as Arbib and Kim Carr. Such names verified the singular truth about Rudd's appeal: it was personal, not based on faction. It was about Kevin.

The Rudd–Gillard pact was a remarkable deal, heavy with insights about Julia. Gillard believed in Kevin: she genuinely felt he could win the election. By sealing this deal she put a Labor victory ahead of her personal ambition. Julia knew she was Rudd's successor but she also knew she may never win the prime ministership since deputies had been known to wait forever. Julia could live with that. There was no Kirribilli pact, no timeline after which Rudd would stand aside for Gillard. She could have asked for, and extracted, such a guarantee. Many other politicians would have done so. Julia didn't.

By the time of Rudd's second parliament, 2001–04, it was obvious to the journalists who dined with him that Kevin was chasing the leadership. He was a media junkie. There was tabloid Kevin and broadsheet Kevin; he thrived on elitist *Lateline* and became a hit on Channel Seven's *Sunrise* tabloid television. He penetrated the policy forums—impressing at the Australian–American Leadership Dialogue, attending the free-market Centre for Independent Studies Consilium, cultivating business and, aware of his outsider status, seeking advice on Labor—who counted and who to cultivate. He presented as an expert in federalism, beat the education drum, promoted a religion-based moralism in politics and began to run on climate change. Rudd was a man for all seasons and he was everywhere. In summer Kevin and Therese, along with their kids, would sometimes take a holiday in Sydney and visit a collection of friends in the media, politics and business. They were always entertaining company. The mix of brain power, success and family seemed almost too perfect. The Tony Blair comparison was inevitable.

Latham and Rudd loathed each other. Latham distrusted Rudd's 'posh accent' and believed Rudd was a chronic leaker with a media mania 'worse than heroin'.[1] Rudd saw Latham as erratic, over-rated and a leadership skyrocket destined to crash and burn.

Yet as Rudd's profile rose so did the suspicion he generated. Some colleagues were shocked when they saw his hunger for the leadership. He was cooler and more hardworking than his rivals—rivals that he ultimately wore down and trampled over while praying to God. He refused to take 'no' as an answer when he pitched for the leadership. Latham called him 'a force of nature' as he laid siege to the Labor Party. Cartoonist Bill Leak drew him as the comic-strip adventurer Tintin, 'a little nerd who prevails in the end'.[2]

Rudd started to land punishing blows against the Howard Government. Alexander Downer watched Rudd and decided he was a conceited phoney. Downer told the story of how, in 2004, after an anti-Australian terrorist attack in Indonesia, he decided to visit Jakarta as Foreign Minister and offered Rudd, as shadow minister, a seat on the VIP plane. Downer said: 'There was a message to call Rudd. He was furious. The fucking VIP plane wasn't going via Brisbane to pick him up. It fuck-ing had to. He ordered me to change its fucking flight schedule.' Downer told Rudd he wasn't his travel agent. The Foreign Minister concluded that people had died 'but for the Member for Griffith it was about one thing: himself'.[3]

Labor's internal crisis was fundamental to Rudd's rise. He became leader only because of the trail of failures and hostilities. After Beazley's 2001 election defeat the caucus descended into a whirlpool of personal animosity, angry at its inability to throttle Howard. The internal culture was being torn apart. ALP National Secretary Tim Gartrell said: 'From 2002 a number of senior organisational figures were alarmed about the growth of personal hatreds in the caucus. Our fear was that caucus animosities might reach beyond the point of no return.'[4]

It nearly happened. Simon Crean, as successor to the leadership, was unable to settle and was challenged, in turn, by Beazley. Paul Keating told Latham that the current ALP generation—represented by Beazley and Crean—was finished. For Keating, the hope lay in generational change. He meant Latham; but generational change would put Rudd and Gillard into the frame.[5] After the Latham experiment failed, the party returned to Beazley in early 2005—and this became a critical moment for Rudd and Gillard. They put their names forward.

Interviewed in 2010, Gillard said:

I had not envisaged myself being a potential leader until the time of the Latham implosion. I knew intellectually that Beazley was coming back to the leadership. I understood what people might say about me having exercised poor judgement about Latham. But I felt we had to make a break from the past. It wasn't personally fair to Kim but I thought he embodied the past. I had that sentiment when I put my name forward. I think Kevin felt the same. We knew we weren't going to succeed. But we wanted the Beazley section of the party to think about this.[6]

Latham had previously signalled his preference for a Gillard ascension. At 8 p.m. on 30 November 2004, Latham had told Gillard that if he could not survive as leader then they should organise a strategy around her as successor in order to halt Beazley.[7] They did the numbers together and concluded that Beazley would still beat Gillard. She did not take this discussion too seriously.

Rudd was incensed about the events of January 2005. Indeed, they had a profound impact on his views about the Labor Party. He saw the Labor Establishment—faction chiefs, union leaders and ALP premiers—unite for Big Kim and slap him down. In truth, it was a sensible decision. After its fourth successive loss to Howard, a traumatised party acted to stabilise the ship.

'The factions fucked me over completely and they fucked Julia as well,' Rudd said in 2008. He was angry for years, almost ranting about these events even when in the Lodge. Rudd saw Beazley's recall as Labor at its worst. He condemned it as factional thuggery, outside intimidation and proof of Labor's loss of nerve.[8] Rudd had pushed harder at this time than people realised. Things had got brutal, with the party chiefs combining to deny him. Kim Carr estimated that Rudd had no more than 7 votes. Gillard, by contrast, had backing based on factional support.[9] Rudd had trailed his coat with the media and looked a fool.

'Beazley was the only choice,' said Arbib in 2010. 'I thought, "We've just taken a big risk with Latham, why the hell would we take another risk?"' The right-wing—notably Swan, Conroy and Smith—slammed the door on Rudd. Gartrell said: 'I was relieved when Beazley returned as leader and we got stability back into the party. We were reeling.'[10] Yet Arbib had been given an insight into the depth of Rudd's passion. He found that Rudd had made more progress than people realised. 'Kevin wouldn't give up,' said Arbib.

> He'd be on the phone to me till two or three in the morning. He was so persistent and such a good lobbyist that he'd have you doubting your own position. This is when I first got to know Kevin. I told him, 'Sorry, Kevin, it's not going to happen' but he didn't give up.[11]

Beazley knew he was on notice. Rudd wanted his job and Gillard wanted his job. The event had inaugurated the Rudd–Gillard dialogue. And Labor was a mess: a divided caucus, an interfering machine, assertive unions and a party organisation doubting its parliamentary arm.

Party elder John Faulkner doubted that Beazley could endure. Faulkner said: 'I had made my decision about Kim some time before, driven by nothing but genuine fondness and admiration for him. I thought his time was past. I didn't believe he could win the prime ministership against Howard, Costello or anybody else.' Faulkner wanted a leadership change before the 2007 election—'otherwise we were heading to a categorical defeat'.[12]

It took only months for Arbib to reach a similar conclusion. He could pinpoint the moment when his faith in Beazley began to erode: it was when Labor responded to the 2005 budget. Costello had surprised all with a post-election tax cut budget. What followed what a classic Labor blunder: Beazley and Swan decided to block the tax cuts on the grounds that they were unfair. Labor put redistribution before higher post-tax incomes. In the end, Costello stared Labor down.

Arbib said: 'After that, it was over. People said: "What? There're blocking tax cuts? This is the old Beazley." Things went off the cliff. For me, it was the turning point. I thought, "How could we make this mistake?" The public decided Kim hadn't changed, that he wasn't a prime minister.'[13]

Guess who was waiting in the wings? Arbib had stayed in touch with Rudd: 'Kevin was smart. He was cheesed off when we backed Beazley but we kept talking. Our relationship was building.'[14] One of the key New South Wales Right figures, Tony Burke, said of the leadership change: 'The key was Mark Arbib. He broke away early and formed the view that Kim couldn't win.'[15] At one point Arbib met Beazley at a Chinese restaurant, the Golden Century, near ALP headquarters. 'The trend isn't good,' he said. Arbib's message was that 'he couldn't guarantee the future'. Beazley understood. Arbib commissioned some of the most extensive research in the party's New South Wales history. It covered every demographic. The upshot is that Arbib became certain that: 'It wouldn't happen for Labor under Kim.' Howard would win a fifth time.

Arbib confided in Gartell and found a fellow traveller. In 2006, Gartrell commissioned his own research and found that leadership was Labor's biggest negative. 'The result was lethal for Kim,' he said. 'The risk we faced was a repeat of the previous pattern: another Howard victory because Labor failed to get its act together.' Gartrell met Beazley to brief him. 'It was painful, not something any sane person would enjoy,' he said. 'Kim's chance to win had passed. There was no way Labor could project a credible story about the future with Kim as leader.'[16]

Gartell asked Faulkner what he should do. 'Leave it to the caucus,' Faulkner said.[17] Meanwhile Arbib decided to promote Rudd's cause.[18] He went to Swan and Albanese. But hell would freeze over before Swan would ditch Beazley for Rudd. Albanese told Arbib: 'Kim is a close personal friend. I think we can still salvage it.' Arbib understood: Rudd had no way through. Kevin must sort it out with Julia.

The Rudd push was devoid of any policy or ideological position. It was only about winning. Labor was desperate to deny Howard a fifth term. It was the polling that doomed Beazley.

Rudd was already dealing with Gillard. 'We were more alike on policy issues than some outsiders may have realised,' Gillard said. Eight years in the caucus, Gillard was now a pragmatic realist. If she had learnt one core lesson it was Labor's unfailing ability to deceive itself about its election prospects. She felt the anti-WorkChoices protest vote wasn't strong enough: 'We had to get people to actively turn to us. It wasn't happening with Kim.'[19]

Gillard's path to realism had begun when she was shadow Immigration Minister post-*Tampa*. At that point she grasped what most of the Left still denied: that border protection was integral to Labor's tradition and values. 'In immigration, Labor had never been a soft touch,' she said in 2010. The party's other high-profile woman, former Western Australian premier Carmen Lawrence, quit the frontbench in protest at the Crean–Gillard asylum seeker policy. It was this policy that triggered the demise of Lawrence and the rise of Gillard.

Gillard came to her talks with Rudd with two convictions: Labor must have another generational change and it had yet to persuade the public it was a safe option. 'I felt people had parked their votes with us but they weren't grafted onto us,' Gillard said. 'In my view governments don't just lose elections. Progressive political parties need to give people permission to vote for them.'[20]

The agent who facilitated the Rudd–Gillard dialogue was Left factional chief Kim Carr. He decided Beazley lacked the will to discipline the Right and had no affinity with the Left. Beyond this, he was sure Howard had Beazley's measure.[21] Carr sensed Rudd was a fellow traveller. In their long talks, Rudd, despite his moderate image, convinced Carr he was a state power interventionist who held industry policy beliefs virtually identical with those of Carr and was hostile to free markets. 'Rudd believed in the social transformation of Australia,' says Carr. 'He saw the importance of manufacturing and the blue-collar base. He was committed to investment in education, greater equity and an agenda for climate change action. He had an acute interest in the power of ideas.'[22]

Carr invited Rudd to Lygon Street, Melbourne, to dine with the Socialist Left. The event went like a dream. 'He was charming and they liked him,' says Carr. Rudd's support for manufacturing was pivotal given the influence of the Australian Manufacturing Workers' Union as a bastion of the Left's power. Now Carr had to seal the deal.[23]

'I think Gillard was suspicious at first,' Carr says. She was being asked to make the sacrifice. Carr felt that Gillard's profile as a single, childless, left-wing atheist put strict limits on her marketability. He felt the public would not accept a Gillard–Rudd ticket and he knew this ticket would not defeat Beazley in the caucus. Therefore, Gillard had to accept the deputy's slot.[24]

'Kim Carr played a strong role in discussions with myself and Kevin,' said Gillard. 'He was centrally involved in putting to me that I needed to think about my position, about Kevin, about a partnership. He pushed us both to think it through.'[25] Would they have got together without Carr? Probably but it was not certain.

As 2006 advanced, the deadline approached. 'Kevin and I had a number of discussions,' said Gillard, 'and it became apparent we had the same analysis. The choices stared us in the face. The issue was: should we challenge and what should the arrangements be? I made a clear decision about this.' Gillard became the crucial actor.[26]

'Kevin is right, he's ready, it's his time,' Gillard said. She told Rudd she would back him for leader. 'I have no kids and a radical past,' she told one colleague. Rudd would be able to deny these lines of Liberal attack. Kim Carr said: 'She knew she needed time to allow the public to get used to her personal background.'[27] Gillard told the author that, as a result of their talks, she saw no policy problem in giving the leadership to Rudd— another insight into Rudd's views.[28]

Gillard took two decisions. The easiest, she said, was stepping aside for Rudd. 'That was not an agonising decision for me,' she said. 'I'm not much given to agonising personal journeys.' The second decision was tougher: to destroy Beazley's leadership.[29]

The point is that in 2010 Rudd was not the first ALP leader Gillard had pulled down. The first was Beazley in 2006, the consequence of her partnership with Rudd.

Rudd said in 2008: 'Neither of us could contemplate just bouncing around politics waiting for some mystical law of succession politics to prevail. For all his virtues neither of us, in our honest minds, could see Kim winning.'[30] While Beazley fought, he was fatalistic. He believed Gillard had nearly 40 per cent of the caucus and Rudd had no more than 20 per cent. This exaggerated Julia's strength and under-estimated Kevin's. Beazley said: 'Kevin could not get the numbers while Julia was in the race.'[31] Once they had joined forces, though, Beazley could not save himself.

In the prelude to the forming of the Rudd–Gillard pact, Rudd's performances scaled a new peak. His appearances with Joe Hockey on the *Sunrise* program showed Rudd could, in Keating's words, 'throw the switch to Vaudeville.' Arbib said: '*Sunrise* was probably the thing that most convinced me about Kevin.'[32] The other issue was Rudd's assault on Howard and Downer over the bribery scandal involving the Australian Wheat Board and Saddam Hussein's regime, with the government forced to establish a public inquiry. Kevin proved he could prosecute a government.

The New South Wales Right, Beazley's base, began to crack. Chris Bowen, from the New South Wales Right, became a confidant and adviser to Rudd. He did the numbers and kept the lists. Bowen felt Beazley was too close to union power. Tony Burke came on board: he argued the leadership switch must be made before the 2007 election year. Arbib and other pro-Rudd defectors from the Right came under strong internal assault. Union secretaries told Arbib he had lost the plot.

In the first of her interviews for this book, conducted in January 2010, Gillard explained the reason she refused to seek a Kirribilli-style leadership succession agreement from Rudd:

> I had watched the tortured Costello assertions about what he believed had been agreed by Howard or what he felt he was owed by Howard. I thought this was dreadful for Costello personally in terms of what he felt about himself and how happy he was in life. It was bad for the Liberal Party and bad for Costello's standing. The public increasingly didn't see him as a successful treasurer but as a failed leadership aspirant. I saw this as a salutary lesson.
>
> I made a decision that Kevin should be the leader. If he succeeded I would become deputy prime minister. In that capacity I would be serving in portfolios I cared passionately about—and education and workplace relations were the two things that had

motivated me to enter politics in the first place. I felt that would be enough for me to view my career as a success and as bringing to me everything that I could have dreamed it would do. That was my mindset in 2006. It is my mindset today [January 2010].[33]

It is easy to sneer at such comments. At the time, however, they were verified by Gillard's deeds. If Gillard was a singular, ruthless agent for the prime ministership as alleged, then her detractors must explain why she did not lodge her claim at this point when Rudd had no option but to grant it. Gillard's judgement was that such agreements caused more trouble than they were worth. Her deal with Rudd was to challenge Beazley and his deputy, Jenny Macklin, as a team and campaign against Howard as a team.

Gillard's judgement was right. A leadership deal would have carried risks for no gain. Her statement is not a rejection of leadership ambition. It is, rather, recognition that her elevation to the top job would depend upon events that defied calculation and should not be assumed. Kim Carr said the partnership had an obvious logic: Gillard would succeed Rudd in office. It was the political glue that sealed the deal and was universally assumed within the party.

In her January 2010 interview, Gillard told the author there were bigger issues at stake than her own future. She said: 'I never saw this as being about me.'

This is the truth, even though it might sound twee to say it. It was about more important things—the future of the country, the fate of WorkChoices, the future of the Labor Party. When I am asked about the leadership, the answer I give is genuine and heartfelt— that if I do this current job [as deputy prime minister] for the long term that will be enough for me.[34]

Gillard requested that Crean be treated 'with respect' and Rudd slotted him into the Trade portfolio. A number of Gillard backers were looked after. Carr would be Industry Minister, the job he had long sought. Gillard would hold the Industrial Relations portfolio, thereby spearheading the campaign against WorkChoices.

Events coalesced in the final week of November 2006 when Rudd and Gillard decided they would probably challenge in the first week of December. Operating as Rudd's numbers man, Bowen said to bring it forward. 'I remember telling Kevin that it's time,' he recalls.

I said we have to bring this to a head. I recall he rang Julia, I think he spoke to Arbib as well. Alister Jordan was involved. On the Thursday night he agreed to press the button for the next morning. He rang me and I went to his office and it was 10 p.m. before I left. We wrote his announcement speech in the office that night.[35]

The next day, Friday 1 December, Rudd went to Beazley's office to inform him.

The lions of the Right—Swan, Conroy and Smith—stuck with Beazley but the faction was deeply divided, with younger right-wingers joining the Arbib–Bowen–Burke breakaway for Rudd. Nearly all the unions stayed with Beazley. Albanese co-ordinated the Beazley vote and worked tirelessly against Rudd. Gillard and Carr delivered a core of Left support. The ballot on Monday 4 December was still relatively tight. Rudd defeated Beazley 49 to 39 and Gillard took Macklin's deputy's post unopposed. It was three years, almost to the day, since Latham's election as leader.

The strong Beazley vote was a pointer: much of the caucus rejected the Arbib–Gartrell analysis that Beazley could not win the election. This led to a subsequent hypothetical: if Beazley could have beaten Howard then he would have delivered more stable government than Rudd. Stephen Smith lamented: 'Kim would have been a solid and cautious PM. It would have been a very different government to that of Kevin's.'[36]

Beazley's vote testified to residual alarm at the Rudd persona. 'I had known Kevin a long time,' Swan said after Labor lost government at the 2013 federal election. 'He was difficult to work with. He didn't value friendships and was prone to bitter hatreds. I didn't think he was right for the leadership. We made a mistake.'[37] Chris Evans said: 'I voted for Kim. I felt Rudd didn't have the stability or personality for the job.'[38] These were the views of the future treasurer and government Senate leader. Much of the ALP Right was unpersuaded. Rudd had prevailed by dint of his appeal, intelligence and drive. But his power base in the caucus was weak. Most senior players said Gillard delivered more votes than Rudd, a view Bowen rejected.

In terms of numbers it was a dual Rudd–Gillard leadership, a strange hybrid, unparalleled in recent ALP history. There was one critical conclusion: Rudd could not prevail in his own right, unlike Whitlam, Hawke or Keating. He became leader only because of Gillard's good grace. This power reality should have informed Rudd's leadership tactics and strategy.

The caucus got it right. The Rudd–Gillard pact was founded in mutual self-interest. Rudd and Gillard, in that order, were the two superior figures from the next generation. They had confidence in each other. They complemented each other, almost perfectly: male–female, Queensland–Victoria, Christian–agnostic, family man–single professional woman. In addition, they offered stability to a caucus ravaged by five years of rancour.

Having a ballot had been important. Gillard later said Beazley did the right thing: it helped to unite the party because it established the legitimacy of the Rudd–Gillard majority. Beazley decided to leave politics at the election, giving his successors a clear run, and Rudd and Gillard offered all the Beazley backers senior jobs. 'Everyone had a place at the table—it was brilliant,' Arbib said.[39] Rudd's vital decision was to appoint Swan as shadow treasurer to lock in the Right and Beazley camp. He broke his promise to Lindsay Tanner several months earlier that he would be shadow treasurer. The case for Swan was too great. While Swan was a Rudd critic, he accepted the outcome.

The party closed ranks. The second project in generational change had begun. In its opening pyrotechnics the Rudd experiment would succeed beyond Labor's dreams.

CHAPTER 8

RUDD AND THE UNIONS: AN ALLIANCE OF CONVENIENCE

R udd and Gillard came to power off the back of the most formidable alliance seen at an Australian election—simultaneous campaigns by the trade union movement and the Labor Party against the Howard Government. Howard was not just beaten by Rudd. He was beaten in a unique display of power by the wider Labor movement when its survival instincts were aroused.

While Rudd led Labor to victory, his most vital ally was former ACTU secretary Greg Combet, who organised the union campaign that had crippled Howard even before Rudd was elected ALP leader. Rudd was an unlikely Labor leader to inherit this trade union campaign. He accepted the gift gratefully. But Rudd, politically and psychologically, was worried about the role of the unions. During and after the campaign he was anxious, almost desperate, to repudiate impressions that he was beholden to them.

Gillard, by contrast, was the chief mechanic on the Labor side of the ALP–ACTU policy collaboration. She saw Howard's WorkChoices as the pivotal event of the 2007 election. It was Gillard, not Rudd, who dealt with the unions, earned their respect, negotiated the Fair Work Act in office, oversaw its passage, kept the business backlash to tolerable dimensions and won kudos from both party and movement for her fidelity to their interests.

In the prelude to the 2007 election the union movement became the most influential third force at any poll in Australian history. The joke was on Howard. He believed the movement was in decline, yet he found himself fighting both its wings, political and industrial. Whether Rudd could have won in 2007 without WorkChoices and the ACTU campaign is a speculative question. Gillard had a neat view: 'I believe we couldn't have won if John Howard hadn't enacted WorkChoices and we wouldn't have won if the Labor Party hadn't elected Kevin Rudd as leader.'[1]

The $28 million ACTU campaign transformed Australian politics. The biggest third-party campaign in election history, it cast a shadow likely to last a generation and testified to the vulnerability of governments to astute third-party assaults.

The key was the asymmetrical nature of the 2007 election. Howard was merely promoting a critical reform while Combet felt unionism faced a moment that went to its viability, even survival. 'It was a point of no return had Howard won,' Combet said of the election.[2] The unions and Labor had far more at stake than Howard. For Howard, it would be another victory: his fifth. For Labor, in Gillard's words, 'the election had a make-or-break element to it'.

> If we lost it would give the Libs time to re-invent themselves to the next generation with a Costello government. It would have cemented the WorkChoices legacy. It would have been seen as a collapse of confidence in Labor about what we stood for. This was our core issue. It had been our political bread and butter for the past one hundred years.[3]

Every aspect of Labor's effort betrayed this urgency.

Rudd had a quite different range of perceptions. He loved to channel Britain's Tony Blair as a Labor moderniser. But where Blair distanced himself from the unions Rudd presided over a policy that brought Labor into a tighter trade union embrace. Blair promised to keep the Thatcherite anti-union laws and 'the most lightly regulated labour market' of any leading economy while Rudd gave the unions most of what they wanted. In an ideal world Rudd would not have chosen this course since it violated his instincts. But Rudd was a conscript of history.

Rudd's genius was to present himself as a modernist while presiding over an industrial policy that constituted a victory for trade union authority. In effect, he struck a bargain with the party and unions: if they applauded him, he would win a mandate to remove WorkChoices. So Rudd rode the anti-WorkChoices caravan to the Lodge. Yet he paid a high price: this alliance would help to determine the character of his government, a reality Rudd was loath to concede. It meant he institutionalised suspicion from business and became the first Australian prime minister to roll back any of the post-1983 reforms. Rudd was no Blair.

Combet's aim was to make the election a referendum on WorkChoices and he had two campaigns to conduct. The first was to turn the public against WorkChoices and the second was to persuade the Labor Party to legislate a new pro-union industrial settlement. He had to win on both counts. His tactic was to discredit WorkChoices such that Labor had no option. At this point the full magnitude of Howard's gamble began to materialise.

By carrying WorkChoices, Howard was putting at risk the reforms of both the Keating and Howard governments. The former chief of the Australian Industry Group, Heather Ridout, said:

> Howard opened up his flank. If he hadn't done WorkChoices the unions would have been profoundly weakened. But he opened the door for them. WorkChoices unravelled a consensus that had been building over a long period in favour of the de-regulation of industrial relations. It was a slowly built consensus, very delicately built, but Howard and Costello unravelled it.[4]

For Labor, the key lay in the negotiations between Combet and Gillard as shadow minister for Industrial Relations (IR). Rudd, unfamiliar with the arcane world of industrial policy, delegated this task to Gillard. It was Gillard who had to devise the new ALP policy. Would Gillard have become prime minister without WorkChoices? Probably. Yet Gillard's successful management of the industrial issue in office was fundamental to her soaring reputation as deputy prime minister leading to her 2010 elevation as prime minister.

Explaining the stakes at the 2007 election, Combet said:

> I believe we would have ended up with a labour market much more akin to the United States with very low and ineffective levels of safety-net protection and where employers would have an enormous amount of bargaining power, effectively a sort of monopoly right to determine terms of employment. I think Howard massively underestimated the capacity of the labour movement to respond.[5]

An analysis of WorkChoices suggests this is an exaggeration. Yet there is no denying the scale of Howard's miscalculation. In retrospect, what he could have done is obvious: follow the position preferred by Tony Abbott. 'We should have legislated the measures that had already been knocked back,' Abbott said.[6] Indeed, before Christmas 2004, when Howard knew he had won control of the Senate, he ruminated to his new Workplace Relations Minister, Kevin Andrews: 'if we could just legislate all the industrial measures blocked in the Senate it would be a significant reform'.[7] This included Howard's cherished effort to exempt small businesses with fewer than twenty employees from the unfair dismissal laws.

Senate resistance had turned workplace relations reform into a desert of lost hopes. Stretching back to the 1996 election, there were almost a hundred changes for which Howard had election mandates but which the Senate had denied. The 2001–04 Parliament alone had three significant IR reforms on its double dissolution list. Election analyst Malcolm Mackerras noted that Howard inherited in 2004 a powerful moral case to legislate his previous bills, a position he abandoned by embracing WorkChoices.[8]

Interviewed in 2008 after losing office, Howard was emphatic: the two elements he regarded as the 'great changes' were the unfair dismissal laws and the national industrial relations system—both vital elements of WorkChoices.[9] Yet these were not the primary focus of the coming political battle. If Howard had settled on a package that legislated his previous bills plus implemented a national IR system, an idea backed by Combet, there would have been resistance but not the great ideological showdown that occurred.

The key to Howard's position was the labour market. It was the fullest employment for three decades, with unemployment falling below 5 per cent. Howard judged that 'it was the ideal time to bring about these changes and that any adverse impacts would be cushioned by the powerful bargaining position of employees'. He was seduced into WorkChoices by his success in delivering low unemployment.[10]

For Howard, the industrial system was the final bastion of the old Australian Settlement, the ultimate symbol of the protectionist past denying the nation full entry into the globalised age. His ambition, literally, was to become architect of Australia's new enterprise culture, a step also decisive in weakening the institutional power of the unions and the Labor Party. His vision owed more to Margaret Thatcher than to Sir Robert Menzies.

The core aspects of WorkChoices were the national IR system, long championed by figures such as Gough Whitlam and Neville Wran, based on the corporations power of the Constitution affirming Howard's status as a centralist; the unfair dismissal provision where Howard shocked and dismayed Andrews by insisting that the exemption apply to firms with up to one hundred employees, thereby extending the reach to medium-sized companies—an idea that Howard pushed on the eve of the cabinet meeting, forcing the rewriting of the documents; a reduction and

simplification in awards; and the contentious heart of the package—
the promotion of agreements by weakening the 'no disadvantage' test,
thereby allowing employers to trade off conditions such as penalty rates,
overtime, annual leave loading, rest breaks and public holidays. It meant
employers could make workers worse off as well as better off. The safety
net still existed but was being weakened.

There were two forms of agreement: collective and individual
(Australian Workplace Agreements, or AWAs), the latter introduced in
1996. The aim was to promote agreements at the expense of awards and
to promote, in particular, AWAs then representing only 4 per cent of the
workforce. The then Finance Minister, Nick Minchin, said:

> The critical point in the cabinet debate was at the start, when
> Kevin Andrews said the main problem in advancing AWAs was
> that the 'no disadvantage' test had become a brick wall. It was
> halting their spread. We felt we had to confront this. I believe this
> is where the Howard Government committed political suicide.[11]

The most susceptible workers would be the weak and vulnerable in
small firms. Howard knew exactly what he was doing: his purpose was
to create more jobs and higher productivity. When WorkChoices was
being marketed, Howard insisted upon the inclusion of the Billy cameo.
Billy had been on unemployment benefits since leaving school but got
a job by sacrificing penalty rates and overtime. It was the heart of the
WorkChoices philosophy and moral position. Howard's adviser, Jamie
Briggs, said: 'Some people had to take a safety net sacrifice to enable
others to get jobs.'[12] Howard gambled the public would accept this trade-
off, agree that Billy was better off and conclude the policy was justified.
He proved to be wrong.

Having studied the Liberal Party research, Howard concluded: 'The
depressing reality from this and all other research was that the contribution made by industrial relations changes to lower unemployment
meant nothing to the voting public. The individual citizen was interested in unemployment only to the extent that it affected him or her or
their family.'[13] Amid prosperity the public rejected viscerally any idea of
employers being allowed to cut working conditions. Howard's notion of
sacrifice lacked public legitimacy in the boom time.

When Howard became PM in 1996, unemployment was 8.2 per
cent; in February 2008, just after his defeat, it stood at 3.9 per cent. The
public would have been more ready to accept Howard's medicine to create

jobs if the unemployment rate had been much higher, thereby generating a sense of urgency.

However, ideology was also pivotal to Howard's thinking. 'The main reason the Labor Party didn't like AWAs,' he said, 'was that they took away the compulsory insertion of unions into the workplace. This was, in a sense, my single biggest philosophical argument—it has been for 25 years. They [unions] should not have a monopoly in the bargaining process.'[14]

Stripped bare, Howard's aspiration was to substitute the idea of employer–employee bargaining for union involvement and control. He wanted to make AWAs more attractive, not to punish workers but to smash union bargaining monopolies. It was a dispute over power, philosophy and society.

In this sense Combet and Gillard were right—at stake were not just wages and conditions but the institutionalised power of the Labor movement. Howard was offended by the legal privilege attached to trade unions. 'I thought it was a wholly legitimate civic goal because I don't think any section of the community should have a privileged position,' Howard said.[15]

Combet's mentor, Bill Kelty, who had been ACTU secretary in the 1980s, saw the flaw in Howard's scheme:

> Howard decided to fuck over the unions. I said to people at the time: this might kill him, he's doing what he wants to do, indulging himself. Why would people complain about the unions? They weren't doing anything. They had accepted 4 per cent for ten years. There was no problem to solve. Nobody was complaining about unions. People said, 'What's Howard doing this for?'[16]

Incredibly, Howard never saw the real enemy. Having taken lethal aim at the unions, he misread their survival instincts. What did he expect? Combet merely acted on the logic of the situation. As Minchin said: 'We grossly under-estimated the capacity of the trade union movement to mobilise on this issue. We didn't think that through. We misjudged the opportunity we gave our opponents to destroy the government.'[17]

Jamie Briggs said:

> People should not re-write history. When WorkChoices was finalised there was no sense we had gone too far. The Treasury and Finance departments had wanted to go further. The party room was overwhelmingly positive about the package. The only person I know who expressed concern to Howard was Tony Abbott.[18]

Abbott was the cabinet dove. Howard told the author that 'some people in cabinet were whinging that we weren't going far enough'.[19] In retrospect, Howard's mistake can be precisely identified: he weakened the 'no disadvantage' test such that he lost control of the politics. Most people, including the author, failed to appreciate this at the time.

At no stage did the cabinet grasp the political risk it was running. There was no analysis of winners and losers. Howard believed that, because he had created a vast number of new jobs over four terms and run a growth economy, he would not be sacrificed on the altar of individual negative stories. This is exactly what happened.

Combet was hardened in the 1998 waterfront dispute when he led for the unions. WorkChoices would be a reversal of the waterfront showdown: this time the unions would surprise Howard. Combet believed excessive reliance on strike action was obsolete. Unions had to master the modern methods—media skills, deep pockets, grass roots mobilisation and a vision to carry public opinion. Above all, Combet learned from Reith that 'you get out of the blocks early'.[20] In the WorkChoices race, he left Howard for dead. The policy was discredited even before it was legislated, a remarkable outcome.

'I knew this might kill Howard if Combet was smart,' Kelty said. 'And he moved quickly, he did the job.'[21]

Combet knew the unions had to reach out to the community. Relying on the ALP was futile. By early 2005 Combet and his ACTU colleague (and future ALP National Secretary) George Wright had devised a strategy, prepared a funding plan and commissioned a firm, Essential Media Communications, headed by Tony Douglas, to run the advertising campaign. They would regain the battlers Howard had stolen from Labor. It was the research conducted by Douglas that enabled the unions and then Rudd to re-brand the Howard battlers as Labor's 'working people' or 'working families'. These were people earning under $60 000 a year. WorkChoices would become the lever that turned the political culture. Douglas found that any risk to job security alarmed workers. 'This is where 30 years of anti-union rhetoric came home to roost,' he said. 'I told George Wright at the ACTU, "You've got a live campaign on your hands."'[22]

That campaign—with research, television and marginal seat strategies—cost the trade unions nearly $30 million. Combet said $25 million 'would be the ballpark number'.[23] Other reports suggested $28.5 million.[24] Either way, it was more than the Liberals spent at the 2004 election.[25] The ACTU campaign was framed not in defence of unions but *for* worker rights and family values. Douglas said: 'When we framed it as your rights at work, it suddenly tapped into a nerve.' The ads defined WorkChoices as being about the right of the boss to sack you and to cut your conditions. The creative expression of this position on television would grip the nation and appeal to working women.[26] 'This was the union movement going to the people,' George Wright said. 'Our aim was to move ahead of the politicians and bring the politicians with us through our public campaign.'[27]

The ACTU was helped immeasurably by the government's appalling timetable. There was a six-month gap between Howard's parliamentary announcement of the reforms on 26 May 2005 and introduction of the legislation on 2 November that year. Howard conceded that this allowed 'a fear campaign to gather momentum'.[28] The battle was lost before the bill hit the Parliament. The unions neither waited for Labor nor relied upon Labor. As Howard conceded later, it was the ACTU, not the Labor Party, that did the damage.[29] When Howard's office began work on the government's own advertising campaign, the initial idea was to run ads saying nobody would be worse off. After Jamie Briggs pointed out that this was inconsistent with the policy, Howard's office chief, Tony Nutt, replied: 'So we're selling cancer.'

The symbol of Labor's intentions boiled down to whether AWAs, legislated in Howard's first term, would also be abolished. For Combet, this was a non-negotiable red line. Heather Ridout put the alternative: 'I kept saying to Greg Combet, "Just put the 'no disadvantage' test back in the AWAs."'[30] But the unions wanted to kill AWAs, not reform them. Combet had never forgotten that the mining industry had used AWAs 'to de-unionise the economy and destroy collective bargaining'.[31] It was an issue of power.

The Labor Party decided that in the twenty-first–century economy—with union coverage falling to below 15 per cent in the private sector, growing job mobility and small business demands for union-free flexibility—it was time to declare illegal the right of an employer and an employee to enter a statutory individual contract. This had electoral logic amid the anti-WorkChoices rampage. But in the long run it would leave Labor a problem. In 2007 there were 3 million small business owners, franchisees, consultants, farmers and self-employed—the people Howard called enterprise workers—and only 1.79 million union members.[32] Labor would purchase victory but it was locked into the past.

Meanwhile Andrew Robb, chair of the backbench taskforce to help sell WorkChoices and a believer in IR reform, had his worst doubts confirmed. By early 2006, Robb had decided that this package was unsaleable. He was dismayed by Kevin Andrews. 'I doubt he has a political bone in his body,' Robb told colleagues. Robb believed the two defects were abolition of the 'no disadvantage' test and setting the unfair dismissal threshold at 100 employees. 'Howard loaded the gun and gave it to the unions,' he said.[33]

In late 2006 Howard removed Andrews as minister in favour of the avuncular New South Wales moderate Joe Hockey. For months Hockey had made clear his views: 'We were melting on WorkChoices; it was a disaster.' But Howard told him, on his appointment, 'there's no way we are changing'. He wanted Hockey to sell WorkChoices more effectively but Hockey knew the policy was the problem.[34]

In March 2007, Hockey floated in cabinet the idea of a policy retreat. He didn't tell Howard before raising it. Some ministers thought it essential; others said very few people were raising personal complaints. Hockey wanted the 'no disadvantage' test restored. He was astonished that a number of ministers were unaware that people could be worse off. The upshot was that Howard and Hockey worked on the revision.

'I had in my drawer a piece of paper setting out what was needed,' Heather Ridout said. 'Hockey's office had rung. I had been waiting. I saw Howard not long afterwards and he thanked me and I said, "Well, this is what we wanted in the first place." I suppose it is the closest I have ever come to saying to a prime minister "I told you so".'[35]

On the night of 3 May, Howard rang half a dozen senior journalists to brief them. He was introducing a 'fairness test' for workers on less than $75 000 a year to guarantee that they faced no disadvantage when moving onto an agreement. He sold it as an effort to retain faith with the Howard battlers. But the real reason Howard briefed was to avoid stories that he was in headlong retreat. He was desperate to kill the perception of a backflip. In truth, the battlers were gone.

As a political animal, Gillard decided that Howard lost government because he upset the balance between reform and security: 'I think the battlers felt he was broadly in touch with where they were. Then he did WorkChoices and people said, "What on earth is this? We thought he got us, knew what gave us security and now he's doing this."'[36] Gillard absorbed the political message: reform could not threaten job security. It became an axiom for the Rudd–Gillard era.

Labor's policy 'Forward with Fairness' was unveiled in 2007 in two stages—initially in April at the ALP National Conference and then with modifications in August. Gillard went too hard at first. Her package was too pro-union, provoking an intense business backlash. An angry

Heather Ridout, heading the most moderate business group, was 'deeply disturbed'. The media were highly critical. It was a dangerous moment for Labor. Having attacked Howard for an ideological frolic, Gillard had succumbed in the reverse direction. 'I don't sweat much,' Gillard said of the business attacks.[37] It was a learning curve for her.

Rudd had to intervene, assuring business leaders and political journalists in private that 'I will take responsibility for this'.[38] Combet said Rudd's pro-business rhetoric has 'concerned my colleagues'.[39] The author had a long lunch with Rudd on 15 May 2007 when he made two points: he would 'fine tune' the IR policy, working with Gillard; and, significantly, he saw no evidence that Howard's policy delivered better productivity and he rejected outright the idea that labour market de-regulation delivered better productivity.[40] This would become the intel-lectual platform of the Rudd–Gillard governments.

Labor took to the 2007 election an alternative IR system drawing upon the Keating and Howard models but constructing a new edifice. Gillard remained the principal architect. While dressed up as economic reform, the unifying idea was fairness.

Labor accepted the High Court's upholding of the constitutional basis of WorkChoices and backed a national industrial relations system. A new safety net covering all industries would be created on a dual basis— it would have ten legislated employment standards with ten minimum employment standards provided by awards. Employees would get both a stronger safety net and award strengthening. It reflected Labor's ideology: only heavily mandated employment provision could deliver fairness in Australia, an obsolete view in the twenty-first century.

AWAs were abolished—the philosophy was denial of choice. Collective bargaining to deliver gains above the safety net was enshrined as the heart of the negotiating system. The Keating–Kelty model of enter-prise bargaining was retained, with the policy providing a two-year tran-sition to Labor's model. A new, independent, powerful, central body, Fair Work Australia, would be resurrected to oversee the system and repudi-ate Howard's effort to downgrade the operation of a strong umpire. The power to set minimum wages would be returned to Fair Work Australia, which would have a role in settling disputes and ensuring compliance with the new laws.

Howard's unfair dismissal laws were swept away. Labor accepted neither his 100-employee threshold, below which business would be exempted, nor his principle that small business deserved an exemption to assist them to hire staff. Union views on employee rights came before the interest of the small business sector. Yet Labor offered a tangible concession—for many small businesses, employees would need to have twelve months' service in order to make an unfair dismissal claim. Labor retained strong rights of entry to workplaces for union officials.

Combet called his dialogue with Gillard 'very constructive' and praised her as 'a very smart person' able to master the industrial relations culture and language. In turn Gillard praised the ACTU campaign, saying it 'rightly encapsulated everything that made people concerned about WorkChoices'.[41] Asked what he thought of the final ALP policy, Combet said: 'I didn't have any concerns. I appreciated that Labor adopted a policy they were prepared to implement in office.'[42] He had succeeded in his original aim: the 2007 election became a referendum on WorkChoices, with Rudd the ultimate beneficiary.

The Howard era finished in a way that neither Howard nor the Labor Party could have imagined in 2004. The ACTU had staged a revival—it subjugated WorkChoices, was pivotal in Howard's defeat and won an ALP policy to restore trade union rights and a degree of IR re-regulation. The lesson Briggs drew as Howard's adviser was that the government had failed to make its case: 'I believe this failure was the biggest setback for our economic project since 1983. The lesson was you can't get too far ahead of people. Old truths need to be re-argued.'[43]

WorkChoices gave the union movement a new energy. Yet its alliance with Labor to suffocate WorkChoices was based upon mutual convenience, not long-run sustainability. Rudd pocketed the electoral gains delivered by the ACTU but was ambivalent: he was suspicious about the consequences of union power and misjudged the extent to which industrial relations would damage his ties with business. Rudd, however, repudiated the argument made by Howard, his advisers and the business sector: that de-regulation would deliver a stronger, more productive economy.

Labor and the unions did more than win an election: they won the battle of ideas. Howard chose to stage this epic battle and he lost. Rudd won two great mandates at the 2007 election: on climate change and industrial relations. In office, he mismanaged the former but Gillard delivered the latter. Australia's industrial relations model for the twenty-first century has become a Labor model—a legacy that mocks, haunts and challenges the Abbott Government.

CHAPTER 9

RUDD'S TRIPLE TRIUMPH

In November 2007 Kevin Rudd set up Labor for a 'new generation' government with a brilliant campaign that smashed the tottering Liberal edifice. It was the most presidential campaign in Labor history. Rudd now took control of Labor. This was the true meaning of the election.

The campaign determined the government. 'Let me clear about this,' Rudd lectured on 27 September. 'I'll be determining the composition of the Labor ministry.' He was seizing this 100-year-old power from the caucus. Desperate to win, Labor gave Rudd his head. It would become a Rudd Government as much as a Labor Government. The authority the party surrendered it would reclaim only with Rudd's 2010 execution.

Interviewed years later Rudd, high on hubris, said: 'They embraced a leader who believed in New Labor, in a pro-business New Labor. I think, in embracing that, the party bit off more than it could chew. It got someone as leader who wouldn't just tap the mat, tug the forelock and do what the unions wanted.'[1] He was exaggerating but the point had validity.

Yet the campaign would become pivotal to Rudd's undoing because the Rudd who campaigned was not the Rudd who governed. Rudd presented as a highly saleable package: a social moderate, a fiscal conservative and a dedicated economic reformer. In office, Rudd proved to be very different, leaving a chasm between promise and reality.

John Howard's 2007 defeat constituted the greatest loss amid prosperity in Australia's history. After the election Peter Costello said of Howard: 'The fact that his government's economic achievement was so strong makes the defeat worse, not better.'[2] Rudd turned the boom against Howard, casting him as an unconvincing manager of prosperity after a decade of economic success.

Rudd was the perfect Labor leader to fight Howard—he defied the Liberal stereotypes and deflected every attack—while the nation's conservative hero, the slayer of Keating, Beazley and Latham, was unable to land a serious punch. In mid-June 2006, Howard hosted one of his periodic off-record dinners with senior journalists at the Lodge. At one point he asked the journalists if they believed Labor would change leaders. Everyone said 'no', except for the *Australian's* Dennis Shanahan. 'Who would they change to?' Howard asked. When Shanahan said Kevin Rudd, Howard laughed. His media aide, David Luff, said later: 'We should have listened.' Rudd took command of the Labor Party, seized the political agenda from Howard and won the public's trust in a performance that confounded Howard and left his government marooned.

'Rudd's election surprised me,' Howard said. 'I had thought his style would grate too much with ALP members who didn't appreciate being lectured to on a regular basis.'[3] In fact, Howard never recovered; he completely misjudged Rudd's appeal. During 2007 he waited for Rudd to unravel, as Latham had unravelled three years earlier. But Rudd and Latham were two extremes. Howard was sunk in a *Waiting for Godot* futility.

'Kevin wasn't an orthodox Labor man,' said ALP National Secretary Tim Gartrell. 'He was more eclectic and that helped us and made it difficult for the other side to get a bead on him.'[4] Rudd did not fit the ALP mould that Howard was used to beating and this was the source of his strength. He was not a leader from ALP Central Casting. It is the reason the ALP was suspicious of Kevin and why the public was intrigued by him. 'Kevin's view as Opposition leader in tactics meetings was usually the opposite of the Labor orthodoxy in the room,' his press secretary in office Lachlan Harris said. 'We only won because of Kevin's unique qualities.'[5]

Those qualities seemed a disconnected jumble—no union ties, an outsider from Queensland, a former diplomat, married to a rich business-woman, intellectually arrogant with a capacity to bore people, remote from Labor's 'mates' culture and with the gift of fluent reassurance. Like Tony Blair, Rudd fell outside the emotional heartland of his own party.

In private Rudd was critical of his own party and the foibles of the leaders who preceded him. He grasped that being an orthodox ALP leader was the kiss of doom. His instinct, from the start, was to market himself under a new leadership banner. Rudd had no truck with Old Labor. 'I am not a socialist, I have never been a socialist,' he declared within days of becoming leader. His tactic was to push Howard off the centre ground. Blinded by a series of Houdini-like escapes, Howard took too long to grasp that this time there was no escape.

It was difficult to categorise Rudd. Therese said she found the young Kevin to have a sense of humour, to read *Hansard* and to dance the Pride of Erin. Rudd was too complex to stereotype. This is where his critics came undone. As Opposition leader Rudd emerged as astute on policy, alert to community, clever with words, always the elusive target. Nobody had Kevin sorted out.[6]

The party had little option but to tolerate his insufferable 'know all' mentality. The outsider, advertising director Neil Lawrence, who devised the superb paid media campaign, recalled their first shoot together. Rudd asked: 'Who wrote this rubbish?' Lawrence replied: 'That would be me, Kevin.' The leader was unhappy. 'It doesn't read well,' Rudd said. Lawrence told him: 'It's written to be read out loud, Kevin. If you read it, I think it will work.'[7]

The eighteen-year generational difference between Rudd and Howard was significant. Howard had seen Bradman bat and attended Churchill's funeral. Rudd was the first prime minister to have finished school in the 1970s and was at ease with digital-age symbols. Mark Arbib would never forget Rudd's act of campaign genius: he held aloft a computer in a classroom, a simple act with a symbolism that captured perfectly the education revolution that Rudd wanted the public to imagine. That Howard would think of such symbolism was inconceivable.

Howard never got a line of sight on the target. Rudd presented himself on issue after issue as Howard-lite in a fashion impossible for any other ALP figure. His tone and look were reassuring. Rudd was calmness personified. He projected as a moralist and a leader who believed in principles when Howard's government had begun to look tawdry. Yet Rudd was adept at channelling the changing currents in Australian life. In his espousal of climate change action, an education revolution and a more caring society, he captured the modernist wave.

Gartrell said: 'Many of Kevin's ideas were socially conservative, yet he was obviously a modern person in his outlook, committed to education, equality for women and an inclusive society.'[8] Rudd persuaded the public that under his leadership Labor was an acceptable option—that change was desirable and, above all, safe. The Liberals were agog when Labor began to project Rudd as a cult figure. 'The party did a fantastic job,' Gillard said. 'Arbib and others bolted Kevin 07 onto Kevin Rudd the person. It became a masterful safe-change proposition—if you want the new John Howard then you want Kevin Rudd. It was a bit of jazziness without jeopardising safety, very clever.'[9]

Rudd destroyed the values wedge that Howard had used against each of his Labor opponents. He abandoned Latham's private school 'hit list', accepted Howard's SES funding model for private schools and backed a national curriculum for schools based on core disciplines. On national security, while pledging to exit Iraq, Rudd would make Afghanistan Labor's war. He projected as a national security hard-liner and US alliance champion, backed practical reconciliation and endorsed in principle Howard's Northern Territory intervention to confront family violence. He got briefings from the BCA and then gave speeches to business that recycled their own ideas back to them. The most vivid example in weight of money was his first–campaign week decision to match Howard's $34 million tax cut with a $31 billion tax cut. If the ALP thought by the campaign's end that Rudd's 'me too'-ism was exhausted, it was wrong. In the final week Rudd pledged to turn back asylum seeker boats and declared he was 'more than prepared' as prime minister to fight trade unions in the national interest. 'There will be times when we radically disagree with the trade unions,' Rudd said, lest anybody was silly enough to think his abolition of WorkChoices constituted a pro-union stance.[10]

This was far from the ALP rule book; it was Ruddism as a political tactic. Rudd was remaking the party in his own image. It was clever in the campaign but a risk in office.

In Rudd's critique of Howard there was a subtlety based on party research. Rudd wasn't a Whitlam pledging to sweep away the old order— the public wanted most of Howard's order to be kept. Neil Lawrence said:

> I felt Labor had got obsessed about hating Howard. I told Kevin—I think it was my first conversation with him—that saying people were wrong about Howard wasn't a smart marketing strategy. He asked me how I would describe Howard and I said I'd call him a very clever politician.

Lawrence and Gartrell told Rudd: 'Don't say Howard's out of touch; say he's *lost* touch.' It conveyed the idea that Howard had walked away from the battlers he once loved.[11]

Arbib felt Labor's post-2004 position was better than it seemed. 'I think Howard misunderstood the 2004 election result,' Arbib said. 'He felt it was about people endorsing him. The truth is he won because we weren't good enough.'[12] But Arbib confronted Rudd with Labor's defects: Howard stood for hard work, small business, enterprise and initiative and Labor was for none of that. It was this perception that Rudd needed to change.

The notable feature of Rudd's campaign from early December 2006 up to the November 2007 election was his consistency. There were four central themes: new leadership, the restoration of the 'fair go' by abolition of WorkChoices, climate change action and the embrace of fiscal conservatism. But Rudd's effort transcended the sum of these parts. He created a new atmospheric: that he had the reliability to improve the lot of working people.

The economy remained Howard's issue yet his core frustration. Costello's May 2007 budget, his last, was one of the best received in history. The economy was humming. 'We were all imbued with the belief that the public would not throw us out against the background of such a powerful economy,' Howard said.[13] Yet Liberal research showed the economy had been so strong for so long that the public began to take it for granted. Newspoll showed the Coalition slaying Labor on the 'best economic manager' question with its October 2007 lead at 53 per cent to 29 per cent. But Rudd's tactics had decoupled this test from the party vote.

Rudd's most brilliant achievement was to turn economic success against Howard. The feature of the resources boom was that the Howard Government spent all its proceeds in a 2:1 ratio between government spending and tax cuts. The boom seduced Howard. He financed foreign wars, gave huge assistance to families, backed seniors and retirees and poured funds into health, education and water. At the 2007 election, with the boom running strong, Howard offered big tax cuts and a vast spending agenda. A damaging article by the *Financial Review*'s Laura Tingle the day after Howard's launch said he spent at the rate of $667 million a minute.[14] It dramatised rising cynicism about Howard.

Costello, who spoke before Howard at the launch, had warned 'there is no clear sailing in economic management', an effort to put Rudd under pressure. He had no hope. Howard pretended it was all blue sky. He warned that Rudd could not be trusted on the economy, and then delivered himself into Labor's hands. Rudd now played his master stroke.

He offered spending of $2.3 billion, less than a third of what Howard offered. It was the symbolism, not the figure, that counted. Having presented as a fiscal conservative for a year, Rudd now closed the circle: 'Mr Howard is putting his own interests ahead of working families by risking further increases in their mortgage rates ... Today I am saying loud and clear that this sort of reckless spending must stop.' At this point the Labor faithful cheered, not because it distrusted spending but because it knew Rudd had checkmated Howard. It was Rudd, not Howard, who was listening to the Reserve Bank. It was Rudd, not Howard, who embraced fiscal prudence. The prime minister who had eliminated Labor's $96 billion debt was being ruined, depicted as an agent of fiscal irresponsibility. How could Howard and his advisers have let this ignominy occur?

At this point the mantle of prime ministerial authority passed to Rudd. Howard became a victim of the politics of prosperity. The further ignominy came in the middle of the campaign when the Reserve Bank under Glenn Stevens lifted interest rates, the latest step in the long tightening of monetary policy provoked by the resources boom. This cycle ran from May 2002 to March 2008 and saw rates lifted twelve times, with the cash rate increased from 4.25 per cent to a high 7.25 per cent. Having exploited low interest rates against Latham in 2004, Howard was now humiliated by the high interest rates of 2007. 'It did hurt us,' Howard said. 'It just hung over the whole campaign.'[15]

In the end, the boom smashed Howard's claims on fiscal prudence and·interest rate superiority. Rudd's judgement and timing were superb. The young and better fiscal conservative was replacing the older and tired fiscal conservative. How could the public not accept the trade-in?

Nobody could foresee that Rudd's claims would prove to be fickle. As he became the biggest-spending prime minister in the nation's history, Rudd never fathomed a satisfactory explanation for his turnaround. His prudence in 2007 would become hypocrisy by 2009.

However, Rudd was masterful is his campaign guise as Mr Compassion while strong economic growth was forcing up prices and cost-of-living pressures. He sympathised with 'working families' (a focus group concept) sitting at the kitchen table and he pledged gimmicks (Fuel Watch and Grocery Choice) to help consumers. Labor was immeasurably helped by Howard's March 2007 blunder when he declared 'working families in Australia have never been better off'. It was true—by any measure. But Rudd proved in 2007 that the public preferred kitchen–table spin over macroeconomic reality. Prosperity brings its own strains from higher expectations and rising social envy. The economy was no longer able to win Howard an election.

In advancing his claims, Rudd's campaign contained the seeds of inflated expectations. His rhetoric was sky high and his pledges were many. Rudd would 'fix our nation's hospitals', 'fix the Federation', make Australia part of the 'global climate change solution'. His 'education revolution' would 'build the best education system in the world' to produce 'the most innovative, the most skilled and the best trained workforce in the world'. There would be revolutions ad infinitum. He made it sound easy. Rudd's admiration for Whitlam was known; the pity was his naïve lurch to replicate Whitlam's folly.

What did Rudd do on election night after victory was clear? He said: 'I did, with the family, pause for a moment of prayer and reflection—these are large responsibilities for which considerable grace is required.' He joked later that 'Labor Party members may be horrified at the thought'.[16] The next morning Kevin and Therese attended church, giving thanks once more.

Re-reading Rudd's election-night acceptance speech is enough to make ALP voters weep. It is a litany of failed hopes and dashed promises. Rudd invoked the concept of new leadership: 'I want to put aside the old battles of the past, the old battles between business and unions, the old battles between growth and environment, the old and tired battles between federal and state, the old battles between public and private.' In retrospect the speech is heavy with irony. In office Rudd floundered at each of these specifics. His speech hailed Gillard and Swan, the duo that deposed him; he hailed 'my great friend' Mark Arbib, leader of the factional thrust that would destroy him.

There was no rallying of true believers. Rudd finished by saying 'We're ready for hard work', suggesting that people have a 'strong cup of tea' or 'even an Iced Vo Vo'. End of story. ALP supporters were left flat. Kevin gave them no red meat and no red flags. Although unfair, it is irresistible to suggest this was an omen: the coming prime ministership would be about Kevin and not them.

It was on the leadership test that Rudd staged his great strategic victory. He drove Howard into a crisis of confidence necessitating a retirement pledge for the coming term. The reality is that Howard had to be beaten; Labor could not creep back into office by walking around Howard.

Consider Rudd's achievement: he defeated the Howard Government, saw Howard lose his own seat and had the successor, Peter Costello, foreshadow his own exit. Rudd became a giant killer; at the one poll he eliminated both Howard and Costello. He had the chance to ruin the Liberal Party for a decade at least. Newspoll for Rudd's early phase was devastating for the deposed Liberals. In the first four months of Rudd's leadership his average two-party-preferred lead was 56.5 per cent to 43.5 per cent. It proved that Howard had misjudged the leadership transition.

In July 2006 Howard announced to the world that he would stay in politics for the next election, his fifth in succession. His decision arose from the mid-year Howard–Costello leadership crisis that saw Howard test party sentiment and deny Costello any transition. Howard took this decision sure that Beazley would be his opponent. But as Loughnane noted: 'Towards the end of Beazley's time as leader there was a fundamental change in our research—previously the public had liked him but now he had lost their respect. I think if Beazley had stayed leader that Howard would have beaten him.'[17]

Howard had every chance to depart in a trifecta of glory—the ten-year anniversary of his prime ministership in March 2006, the January 2007 onset of the election year and the launch of his $10 billion Murray–Darling water rescue on Australia Day. He could have orchestrated a hero's exit in the Liberal Party's most emotional moment since Menzies, with Costello arriving as the bright version of generational change. But there was a shortage of will to leave. 'I don't think he ever really wanted to go,' Costello said later.[18]

Yet Howard's prime ministership was in decline and by autumn 2007 the evidence was convincing. Secretary of the Department of the Prime Minister and Cabinet, Peter Shergold, told confidants he believed Howard's performance deteriorated from the time of his decision to stay. 'I've got a whole department here for you,' he told Howard. 'We should be doing more.'

The art of politics is anticipating the next trend before it arrives. In December 2006, Labor punted on generational change; the Liberals should have done the same. That it never happened revealed the decaying condition of the Liberal Party in Howard's final term.

Costello had a choice. After the 2004 election he could strike or retreat to the backbench—but he did neither. Abbott confided: 'Peter was unable to resolve what to do. In public he tried to play the loyal deputy but in private he was an aggrieved and agitated rival.'[19]

The leadership crisis of July 2006 terminated Costello's hope of becoming prime minister.

It was triggered when News Ltd correspondent Glenn Milne revealed a secret statement Howard had made to Costello in 1994 that he would want only one and a half terms as prime minister. Costello authorised the story that was provided by former cabinet minister, Ian McLachlan, who had been privy to the discussion and had made a note. It triggered a Howard–Costello showdown, with party sentiment strongly behind Howard. 'Not one minister expressed to me the view that I should go,' Howard said when he tested opinion.[20]

At 6.30 pm on 30 July 2006, Howard rang Costello to say he believed the party wanted Howard as prime minister and Costello as treasurer for the election. Costello told him it was the wrong decision. He said the best interest of the Liberal Party was an orderly transition.

He warned Howard that Beazley might not be his opponent. But Costello had no leverage: he buckled to accept Howard's decision. Most Liberals were relieved.

Yet the crisis had forced Howard's hand too early. He had intended to make a final decision at the end of 2006. Howard conceded: 'It was the wrong time and the wrong set of circumstances' to make this decision. He blamed Costello for imposing this timetable upon him. Facing the need for a decision, Howard calculated he could prevail with a fifth election victory. He was confident that he would beat Beazley and convinced that he was a better leader than Costello.

Howard took his decision in July 2006. Labor switched horses five months later, in December, and Howard now faced not Beazley but Rudd. He was trapped. Or was he?

The fact is that no leader is trapped into staying in office. Howard, if he had had the will, could have orchestrated his resignation in January 2007 in favour of Costello. The problem was being seen as a coward. 'Once Rudd became leader it was very hard for Howard to resign,' Nick Minchin said. 'There was nothing in Howard's character that would enable him to go.'[21] Howard felt that if he resigned in January 2007 Rudd would be hailed as the 'world-beater' who had 'scared' the second-longest-serving prime minister into retirement.[22]

In fact, Howard had under-estimated Costello's ability to be a generational-change circuit breaker for the government. If Howard had gone, his career would have looked better, not worse, and Costello would have had his opportunity against Rudd—whom he regarded as a poseur.

Interviewed by the author in January 2008, Howard made a remarkable claim: it had been his intention to resign as PM in favour of Costello over the 06/07 summer. He said: 'We [Janette and himself] were moving in that direction. But this McLachlan thing just came from nowhere. It was a disaster. I would have gone at the end of 2006 if it hadn't been for the McLachlan thing. We were talking about going.' It was a joint John–Janette position.[23] In his subsequent memoirs Howard repeated this statement: he would have gone at Christmas 2006 had not the McLachlan crisis forced his hand earlier.[24] It meant Costello would have fought the 2007 election. Costello did not believe it.

Yet in September 2007, close to election eve, Howard momentarily lost his nerve. The Newspoll published on Tuesday 4 September showed a 59 to 41 per cent two-party-preferred annihilation. Against the backdrop of the historic APEC Leaders' Meeting, Howard called his closest cabinet confidant, Alexander Downer, to his office. 'My best judgement is that we will lose the election and I'll lose my seat of Bennelong as well,' Howard told Downer.[25]

Downer agreed: 'I don't think we can win. Perhaps we have to give Costello the opportunity. It will give us the chance to re-brand the government.'[26] Having been Howard's strongest backer, Downer now favoured change. Deeply pessimistic, Howard was of the view that if the cabinet wanted Costello they should have him. Howard asked Downer to consult the cabinet: he opened the door on resignation. For Howard, it was a crisis of nerve.

On Thursday 6 September at 11 p.m. Downer gathered nine ministers in his suite at the Quay Grand Hotel in Sydney, lit a cigar and opened with a thunderclap: Howard didn't believe he could win and was thinking of resignation. It was the night Howard's authority in the Liberal Party died.

Only two of the nine ministers wanted Howard to stay. The overwhelming sentiment of cabinet was for Howard's departure by choice without duress. Yet there was little enthusiasm for Costello. The two ministers most insistent on change were Joe Hockey and Malcolm Turnbull. Hockey said Howard's pessimism 'made the decision easy'. Turnbull said: 'The impression I had was that Howard was seeking our permission to leave.'[27]

But that was the problem. Howard's actual position, as conveyed by Downer, was that cabinet must take the political responsibility. That is, Howard would resign because the cabinet wanted his resignation. The onus would be on the cabinet. Ministers rejected this position. Their reaction exposed its absurdity. The idea of Howard being tapped on the shoulder and forced out by his cabinet would have been electoral suicide, the worst form of leadership change. 'We would have bled to death,' said Minchin, a Costello supporter. The majority view was clear: a leadership change was the best option. But this had to be Howard's choice and responsibility. It could not be 'owned' by anybody else.[28] The meeting had failed to meet Howard's 'responsibility' condition. Abbott had missed the meeting. He rang Downer the next morning to say, 'We stay with Howard.'

On Friday evening Downer visited Kirribilli House to report. The meeting involved three people: John, Janette and Downer. Downer was on Howard's home territory. He reported a sentiment for change in cabinet but 'there is no way they will own a request'. Downer didn't press Howard to leave. He sensed the mood had changed. The glint of Howard defiance was back. Given that his condition was not met Howard said he would not walk. 'That would be an act of cowardice,' he said. 'You're not a quitter, John,' Janette said. The waters were choppy but the issue was settled. Costello believed the family had been important in the decision.

Downer knew what to tell George W Bush as the US President was leaving Sydney: 'When we meet next I doubt John Howard and I will be holding our current jobs.' The impossible problem was what to tell the public. On Saturday a number of ministers told Costello that Howard had to go. On Monday Howard made the mistake of revealing that his family had advised him to stay. With these dramatic events beginning to leak, Howard now had to devise a new public formula on the leadership. He delivered it to ABC TV's Kerry O'Brien on *The 7.30 Report* on Wednesday 12 September. Howard's performance was agonising: he announced that, if re-elected, he would retire in the coming term. He had just killed his fading election prospects.

Finally, six months short of twelve years in office, John Howard waved the retirement flag. In the interim the 68-year-old Prime Minister would lead the campaign against Rudd. It was the worst of all worlds: the cabinet preferred his resignation, Howard decided to remain, but he was a lame duck forced into a post-election retirement statement. Costello asked Howard of the cabinet fiasco: 'If your position was that you wouldn't go voluntarily, why did you ask their opinion?'

With the Howard leadership devalued, Rudd's 'new leadership' pitch soared higher and Costello would lament in his memoir: 'We mismanaged generational change. The electorate did it for us.'[29] Howard later conceded that re-opening the leadership issue was a 'serious mistake'.[30]

Gartrell said of Howard's retirement declaration: 'Why would anybody vote for him?' Labor research showed, Gartrell said, 'Swinging voters just felt that Howard's time was up. They weren't too angry; they just felt it was over.'[31] Labor's ad director, Neil Lawrence, confirmed Joe Hockey's view: 'The Liberals should have changed leaders. I think the election was very winnable for Costello.'[32] Brian Loughnane summed up: 'A simple way to tell the story of the 2007 election is that John Howard had two great assets—he stood for certainty and for fairness. The leadership issue made it difficult for us to run on certainty and Labor had painted WorkChoices as unfair.'[33]

At the start of Rudd's 14 November policy speech he said: 'Mr Howard has no plans for the future because he's not going to be there to deal with the challenges of the future. It's official—Mr Howard's retiring.' The rest was easy: 'After eleven years Mr Howard has become stuck in the past. He simply doesn't understand the new challenges that we face in the future.'[34]

Howard's liability as an 'old generation' politician was exposed on two symbolic issues: his refusal to ratify the Kyoto Protocol and his opposition to the apology to indigenous Australians over the Stolen Generations. Costello would have done both. The full consequences of these Howard refusals was only apparent after Rudd won the election.

Howard gifted Rudd as prime minister, turning him into a hero. Rudd's Kyoto ratification and the apology gave him an aura of brilliance that defined his early months, enhanced his standing and highlighted at home and abroad that Australia was under new management. Howard had played to Rudd's strength: his genius at symbolism.

Howard's 2007 climate change policy was founded on a contradiction that frustrated much of his cabinet, notably Turnbull, his Environment minister. Under political pressure Howard had made immense concessions on climate change: he had embraced an emissions trading scheme to begin by 2011–12 and cover a whopping 75 per cent of emissions— far beyond the EU scheme. He branded climate change 'the biggest economic challenge of our time' and he backed a renewable energy target of 15 per cent by 2020. This positioned Howard's Australia as a leading nation in climate change action.

Neither the public nor the media believed it for a moment. Howard had staged the biggest policy reversal of his career but won virtually no electoral kudos for it. He had changed his policy but felt unable to embrace the moralism and symbolism of the issue. That was understandable, given that it was riddled with hypocrisy. But in the media-induced hysteria of 2007, climate change was a moral issue: it was about saving the planet and politicians were required to perform semi-religious acts of faith to affirm their virtue. No matter that the public didn't know what emissions trading or Kyoto really meant. Rudd loved this cathedral while Howard was outside his comfort zone.

Rudd launched the 2007 election year with a parliamentary attack on Howard for running a government 'full of climate change sceptics'. It played beautifully. Having been provoked, Howard followed his instinct in defending the coal miners! While Howard's loathing of climate change fanaticism was palpable, Rudd kept rolling out climate change initiatives: he appointed the former activist Peter Garrett as shadow minister for Climate Change, commissioned Ross Garnaut to conduct the local version of the *Stern Review* and held a mid-year climate change summit. Rudd controlled this agenda.

The drought across four states reached its zenith in 2007. It was widely seen as proof of changing climate and public officials began to talk of a 'one in a thousand year drought'. Howard had no hope in this rhetorical contest. Resorting to a famous Australian cliché, he merely labelled it 'the worst in living memory' and was promptly ridiculed.

Howard's problem was that he had changed his policy but not his political strategy. He refused to genuflect before the icons: Al Gore's scare, the drought as proof of a climate transformation, and Kyoto sanctification. For the ABC, Howard was now a figure of undisguised ridicule. His *Lateline* interview of 5 February 2007 began with this mocking question from Tony Jones: 'Can you recall exactly when it was that you ceased being a climate change sceptic and became, in effect, a true believer?'

In January 2007, Howard had appointed Turnbull as Minister for Environment and Water and announced a $10 billion water initiative. Yet Howard could not project the moral conviction that came so effortlessly to Rudd. The symbol of virtue had become acceptance of Kyoto; Rudd had merely to utter the word *Kyoto* to be acclaimed.

Because Kyoto represented a deeply flawed treaty there was a good reason not to ratify. Its binding targets applied only to developed nations, while emissions increasingly came from developing nations such as China and India. The existing Kyoto Protocol was obsolete and Australia's public service advisers knew the framework was untenable. It would need to be re-designed post-2012, a proposition Rudd had accepted.

Yet the politics were a no-brainer. Howard had pledged to meet Australia's Kyoto target of 108 per cent of emissions from 1990s levels. Consider Howard's position: he refused to ratify the protocol of a treaty whose domestic provisions he was pledged to uphold. How crazy was that? Where was the principle in that? Ratifying Kyoto imposed no further obligations. Rudd had turned 'me too'-ism into an art form, but Howard couldn't 'me too' even when it mattered.

In late 2007 Turnbull raised in cabinet the option of a death-bed conversion on Kyoto. He agreed that the protocol was ineffective but said 'Australia should be magnanimous' and alter its position. 'Whenever Rudd was asked what he would do as PM, the first thing he said was ratify Kyoto,' Turnbull said.[35] Yet most ministers felt it was too late. 'We made a mistake not ratifying Kyoto earlier,' Downer said. 'But it's too late to change now.' Costello felt it should have been ratified before but agreed—Howard would look too desperate if he changed now. Costello had told Turnbull, 'If I become prime minister I'll ratify Kyoto.'

What was Rudd's first step after being sworn in as prime minister? It was Kyoto ratification, an event he orchestrated to the world as a symbol of a changed Australia. Rudd owned the issue. That meant, in political terms, that Rudd owned the future—the key to election success. The National Broadband Network was mere icing on the cake. In Rudd's policy speech he patronised Howard, saying Howard had 'spent a decade' in climate change denial. 'Even now, Mr Howard still opposes Kyoto,' Rudd said. Gartrell called climate change 'the perfect fit for us'.[36]

For a politician reluctant to admit mistakes, Howard, interviewed post-election, did concede a mistake. Asked if he should have ratified Kyoto, for instance, at the end of 2006, he said: 'Yeah, I do.'[37]

The apology for the Stolen Generations rarely touched the surface of the election. Yet the same Rudd–Howard syndrome was repeated, almost exactly. The second great reversal of Howard's prime ministership had been his commitment to Aboriginal reconciliation, both practical and symbolic, culminating in his 2007 election pledge to hold a constitutional referendum to recognise the indigenous peoples.

It was under Noel Pearson's influence that Howard, in his October 2007 Sydney Institute speech, said he fully accepted 'my share of the blame' for his government's flawed dialogue with many indigenous leaders and promised a bill within the first 100 days of his fifth term. But he never recanted his opposition to an apology, a stand that left the nation divided and unresolved.

There was nothing in Liberal Party policy that prevented a Liberal prime minister making the apology on behalf of the nation. Costello would have done so. By his refusal Howard handed Rudd a unique opportunity and gave Labor the discharge of this historic moment. The Liberals in Opposition supported Rudd's February 2008 apology.

Written in Rudd's own words, the apology was cast as an act of contrition and a new beginning. It was the finest speech of Rudd's prime ministership and revealed the heights to which he could rise. The vision agreed upon by Rudd and his Indigenous Affairs Minister, Jenny Macklin, was that the apology must not remain a statement about the past: it had to project a new future. The speech had claims to greatness not just for its eloquence but because Rudd tried to shift indigenous policy onto a more realistic platform.

The apology entrenched the Closing the Gap national objectives over a range of measures: literacy, numeracy, infant mortality, life expectancy. Rudd followed the spirit of the *Bringing Them Home* report on the Stolen Generations but accepted neither its demand for financial compensation nor its accusation of genocide.

He wrote the speech longhand in the study at the Lodge. Suffering from writer's block, on the Saturday he felt he needed to speak to a person from the Stolen Generations and visited Nanna Nungala Fejo at her Canberra home. She told Rudd the story of how she was removed as a four year old in central Australia to be located at the Bungalow at Alice and then removed again to the missions. 'Mothers are important,' was her message to Rudd and he relayed that to the Parliament.

His speech began with these words: 'There comes a time in the history of nations when their peoples must become fully reconciled to their past if they are to go forward with confidence to embrace their future. Our nation, Australia, has reached such a time.' Rudd said it was 'unfinished business' to remove 'a great stain from the nation's soul' and open a new chapter. He delivered an apology without qualification 'for the hurt, the pain and the suffering'. Looking across the chamber, he said: 'I say to honourable members here present: imagine if this had happened to us.' The 'business as usual' approach to indigenous Australians was not working; there had to be firmer measures of success or failure. Rudd said the apology must not degenerate into a 'moment of mere sentimental reflection' but should become the occasion for reconciliation writ large 'across the entire history of the often bloody encounters between those who emerged from the Dreamtime a thousand generations ago and those who, like me, came across the seas only yesterday.'[38]

Facing a difficult task, Liberal leader Brendan Nelson delivered his own side, thereby reversing a decade of Howardism. His failure to achieve this would have been catastrophic for the Liberals. 'I thought his speech was poor,' Rudd told the author.[39]

Rudd excited the nation with his triple triumphs—the election victory, Kyoto ratification and the apology. He gave people confidence that their decision to change the government was correct. The 2007 election became an 'It's time' event.

Rudd's victory was greater than Whitlam's but less than Hawke's. In 1983 Hawke won 53.5 per cent of the two-party-preferred vote, compared with Rudd's 52.7 per cent. Hawke had a 25-seat majority, compared with Rudd's 18 seats. The Coalition still had 65 out of 150 seats in the House, a competitive position. Howard had lost his seat. But his defeat fitted the description of a 'respectable loss', particularly since he was attempting a fifth victory.

In Rudd's first year the focus fell on the polls. In twenty-one successive Newspolls during 2008, Rudd's worst result was a 54 to 46 lead, a superior outcome to the 2007 election. The average revealed a further significant pro-Labor swing, suggesting an entrenched period of ALP government. This could only unravel if Rudd's 2007 campaign was based too much on illusion and too little on reality.

V

THE RUDD PROJECT

CHAPTER 10

THE RUDD EXPERIMENT:
A CRISIS IN GOVERNING

Once in office, Kevin Rudd defied the orthodoxy and engaged in the most centralised, novel and risky experiment in prime ministerial power since Gough Whitlam. Rudd had two critical weaknesses—managing people and running a government. In Opposition he was a master but those skills did not translate easily into office, a story that perplexed the Labor Party and sent it on a voyage ending in panic.

The inexperience of Rudd's government was masked by its veneer of competence. Yet none of the four most important ministers—Rudd, Gillard, Swan or Tanner—had been ministers before. From the moment of ascent Rudd radiated confidence that quickly translated into hubris. He spent most of his waking hours giving orders, requesting papers, calling meetings, mastering detail and travelling at home and abroad. He seemed to know what he wanted but that impression was deceptive.

Rudd was the most popular Labor leader since Bob Hawke yet he had little of Hawke's cunning, judgement or smell for power. The difference was critical. Hawke knew popularity was not enough and set out to institutionalise his power in the government and in the party. Rudd did neither. His grasp of human nature was defective.

Rudd inherited an elaborate system of prime ministerial government. This model had been evolving since Whitlam until under Howard it became, in the new Parliament House, a formidable machine for executive dominance. Indeed, it seemed ideal for Rudd's ambition. But in less than three years Rudd seized it, pushed it and broke it. He pushed people too far and too hard. Yet he imposed even more strain upon himself—it was too much, physically and psychologically.

The Rudd experiment ended in busted dreams and broken governance. His removal as prime minister in 2010 was a revolt against the way he had run the country and managed the party. In truth Rudd was better than this and had many policy achievements but they were overshadowed by his political defects. The Rudd prime ministership, therefore, is a truly tragic tale of a leader with the potential to become a great prime minister brought undone by his flaws. The explanation lies in Rudd's complex personality. Kevin was a brilliant solo player but not an effective team leader. This was the heart of the problem. It is the best explanation for the extraordinary saga that saw Kevin in just two and a half years transition from Labor hero to repudiated prime minister. It is a unique fall.

In office Kevin rated high on the PM's score card: impressive IQ, rational mind, phenomenal work ethic, ability to absorb data, grip of detail, comfort with high policy and, when motivated, a capacity to strike an immediate rapport with people. The record, however, suggests he was weak on emotional intelligence, deficient in the 'human factor', too impatient, unable to prioritise, inept at inspiring his peers in a common mission and so obsessed about being prime minister that he treated too many people badly.

The Rudd story is proof yet again of the axiom advanced by Professor David Kemp in his famous 1973 essay 'A Leader and A Philosophy'—that the fundamental test of leadership is not popularity but the relationship between the leader and his party. A leader cannot succeed in the nation unless he or she succeeds with their party. At the end of Rudd's career, former ALP operative Graham Richardson would say: 'I have been a member of the ALP for 47 years and I have not known a more hated figure.'[1]

From her position of proximity Gillard identified the problem:

> In his organisational style Kevin was unable to adapt to government. Opposition suited him to a T. Kevin's absolute forte is management of the media agenda, quick tactical decisions. Nobody will ever work harder than Kevin so he might be in Sydney for a meeting and then see a tactical advantage in being in Darwin tomorrow and jump up and go there. In Opposition, you can operate like that. But that is not what government is about and Kevin never shed that organisational style. It is not just about your own time management. It is the sense of using the full power of government and he never got that.[2]

Gillard's point is that Rudd was a brilliant individual performer but defective in running a government. The prime ministership that he conducted was both furious and imperial—furious in its pace and chaotic processes, and imperial in that Rudd was dominant: he selected his ministers, shaped the agenda and fashioned the government's character. The defect was manifest: because Rudd was the sole source of authority, the only way to change the government was to execute him.

Rudd failed to deploy cabinet power to solidify his own position. This management flaw was multiplied by his erratic personality. Over time Rudd saw his relations either decline or degenerate with nearly every major institutional figure in the system: Gillard as deputy, Swan as treasurer, Moran as his departmental head, Bitar as National Secretary, Arbib as his sole Praetorian guard and even Quentin Bryce as Governor-General.

Interviewed for this book, his cabinet ministers disagreed on the extent to which Rudd ran a dysfunctional government. There is no dispute, however, that his process and decision-making were defective. Bad process means bad results: that is an iron law. It is as though the Labor Party in its eleven years of Opposition lost the art of effective government. Under Rudd, then Gillard, it failed to deliver quality decision-making. The then secretary of the prime minister's department, Terry Moran, says:

> There were serious defects in the Rudd cabinet system. On the public service side cabinet submissions were too long, complex, often impenetrable and written very often by junior people. But over time Rudd's office corrupted good process. They went around the system, disregarded the rules designed to support good quality decision-making, put items on the agenda very late and allowed a large number of informal papers which came forward outside the usual process.[3]

The head of Swan's office, Chris Barrett, later Australia's ambassador to the OECD, wrote a private twelve-page analysis of Rudd's operational approach as prime minister that identified the core problem: his failure on proper process led to poor policy.

Barrett wrote:

> The Rudd Government was never and could never have been a functional government because of the man who ran it. So there's no way of avoiding the fact that this account lays the central responsibility for these wasted policy ambitious on Kevin Rudd … I am hardly on my own in this judgement … In public policy terms the big story of the Rudd prime ministership will not be what he achieved but the gap between what he ventured and did not achieve. The list is long. It is headed by action on climate

change but there is a long tail of efforts begun and not finished: Commonwealth–State relations, health reform, industry policy, innovation policy, drought policy just to name a few.

Barrett identified Rudd's six governing flaws:

(1) The PM radically centralised the decision-making of government drawing decisions towards himself and then often failing to make them; (2) he ran a terrible cabinet process that ignored or wasted the skills of his ministers or officials; (3) he tried to do too many things and (4) tried to do them too quickly; (5) he neglected policy and focused overwhelmingly on political and media considerations; and (6) he propagated a culture of blame and retribution that stifled honest advice and undermined decision-making … Kevin Rudd came to the job of PM with something of a reputation as a policy wonk. This was something we never, ever saw behind closed doors. His instinct was invariably for the politics of a policy problem.[4]

This critique goes to personality, character and judgement. The critique is contested but Rudd's problem is that too many people make the same case. This is the critique mounted by Gillard and Swan, the two ministers closest to Rudd's decision-making.

A convenient but unhealthy Rudd–Gillard process developed: Gillard did the cleaning up after Rudd, a fact that became notorious across the government. When Rudd was overseas and Gillard was acting prime minister—and that happened a lot—ministers and officials got a host of delayed decisions and paper work done. The word spread: Gillard, unlike Rudd, could take a decision.

Gillard said:

Kevin's operating style was dysfunctional. It was a great pity. Kevin is a highly intelligent man. If you wanted to talk to someone over dinner about the geopolitics of the region for the next twenty years, then you couldn't have a better companion than Kevin Rudd. But Kevin's fatal flaw was that he couldn't delegate, he couldn't manage his time, he couldn't plan strategically as opposed to plan tactically. Under pressure he was a great prevaricator. His reaction to not being able to decide was to ask for more and more briefs and more and more paperwork that would never get read.

Then he felt the pressure more and more; there was more paper and more chaos. It would get worse, not better.[5]

The same story often occurred at cabinet meetings or the 'gang of four' SPBC (Strategic Budget and Priorities Committee) meetings. Gillard recalls: 'I saw him treat the whole National Security Committee badly. He'd keep them waiting endless hours. He'd come in late, grumpy, carrying around his bloody cushion, looking miserable, treating them like school children.' On one occasion there was a raised-voice encounter with the Chief of the Defence Force (CDF), Angus Houston. It looked like Rudd hectoring Houston. Some ministers were appalled. A prime minister doesn't hector the CDF in front of others, especially not Angus Houston. On many occasions Rudd would be late for cabinet or the SBPC. 'I would be the one who had to go in and deliver the message,' says Gillard. 'Oh, he is going to be another half hour, the meeting has been delayed to six o'clock or whatever.'[6] On one occasion Ken Henry, a cool individual, snapped; it wasn't satisfactory. There was only one conclusion: Rudd as prime minister didn't show respect to the people on whom he had to rely.

Gillard would joke about Rudd's operational dysfunction. She would take home 200 briefs on the weekend. The system began to look to her. 'I was clearing briefs and correspondence in a routine way,' she says. 'People would say: Have you done all those briefs? It's only 11 a.m. It was as though I'd turned water into wine.'[7] Senate leader Chris Evans said: 'Julia spent the first two years of government running around cleaning up the mess, day after day. She was not given enough credit for that.'[8] This was a highly unsatisfactory modus operandi, guaranteed to strain personal relations and lead to trouble.

It meant Gillard lost respect for Rudd. In 2010 when Bruce Hawker was recruited to Rudd's office, he engaged with Gillard and found her deeply frustrated, now struggling to cope with 'what she saw as dysfunctionality' in Rudd's office.[9]

Greg Combet was promoted under both Rudd and Gillard. He had good working relations with both of them as prime ministers. He offers a practical yet alarming view of Rudd's style:

You'd have to say the government had become dysfunctional. It was still functioning as a government. But Rudd's approach to governing was the real reason he was replaced. That's not often appreciated. Rudd failed in his management of his colleagues on any assessment. He tried to take it all on himself. He was terrified of leaks and wanted to keep everything tight; colleagues were not engaged, cabinet processes were not followed. The SPBC system led to very poor process. Ministers were travelling around from city to city trying to get an audience with the SPBC; as a minister that's where you had to go. So Rudd would have a full day in one city, then all the SPBC members, all the public servants, the deputy secretaries, the advisers would be rushing out to buy underpants and toothbrushes because they were now staying the night, then we'd decamp the next day to yet another city in the hope of getting in, waiting all the time for huge decisions to be taken.[10]

When their relations died, Swan revealed some of his concealed views about Rudd, once one of his closest family friends. He became Rudd's sharpest critic:

The central problem with Rudd is that he didn't listen to people, he treated people badly. His tendency was to be unfocused, jumping from issue to issue, handing down dictates to people, not consulting, over-reacting, trying to run a 24–hour news cycle. This really started to emerge after we came out of the global financial crisis from June–July–August in 2009. He got smashed by the *Oceanic Viking* at that stage.[11]

Swan had known Rudd longer than any of the ministers. He said he was unsurprised. Interviewed for this book, he said:

The problem, to be extremely frank, is Kevin is not suited to lead a team, if you want to sum it up. He had neither the temperament nor the interpersonal relations. And it is a pattern of behaviour that has been repeated in his career. It is one I chose to ignore for a number of years. But, you know, anyone who has worked closely with him is acutely aware of it. And it doesn't matter who you are talking about, whether you are talking about the former premier of Queensland [Peter Beattie] or political colleagues or public servants. It is the same pattern.[12]

The Finance minister, Lindsay Tanner, was far closer to Rudd than Gillard. Yet Tanner's restrained assessment of Rudd's style by one of his strongest supporters conceded Rudd's 'slightly manic habits' and suggested a cabinet system bordering on chaotic:

By the beginning of 2010 the SPBC process was deteriorating. Meetings were called, rescheduled and cancelled with great regularity, so that I lost the ability to schedule diary appointments any more than two or three days in advance with any confidence. Individual matters of middling importance were left unresolved for extended periods, and ministers and public servants were sometimes kept waiting for hours before getting a chance to enter an SPBC meeting to discuss their particular issues. In some cases the issues weren't even discussed because of the logjam in the agenda.[13]

Despite these concerns, Tanner rejected the idea that Rudd's flaws justified his removal.

This summarises the views from 'inside the gang of four'—Gillard, Swan and Tanner—the ministers closest to Rudd's decision-making. They range from moderate critique to excoriation. To an extent their lens is distorting. These are retrospective judgements made after Rudd's removal. The truth is that for most of their time in office Rudd, Gillard, Swan and Tanner worked well together. Yet this period was too short. The problem is that Rudd fell out with his two most senior ministers, his deputy and his treasurer.

Because the Gillard–Swan critique originated in Rudd's personality they decided it was incurable. Swan didn't buy the argument that the cabinet could have reformed Rudd: 'Having known him long enough I knew he wasn't going to change the way he operated.'[14] Gillard made the same point as Combet: the real reason for Rudd's removal was his failure of governance. Since she launched the challenge, she must know. Asked if Rudd's problem was the character issue, Gillard replied:

I think that is absolutely right. If you genuinely like someone you will forgive them more than someone you don't like. Kevin had treated so many people so badly for so long that there was no bond. When things get bad there is no shield to protect you. He never got that. And because he never got it, that ultimately broke people, it broke some individuals, particularly political staff and some bureaucrats. It broke his relationships with people and with ministers.

The heart of the Gillard–Swan critique is Rudd's fusion of poor process with his difficult personality. In the end Gillard, like Swan, decided that Rudd wouldn't change.[15]

Terry Moran had a different assessment: 'By June 2010, Kevin's private office was disliked. But Kevin should have been given the chance to mend his ways. There were problems in the way he governed and the sensible course would have been to raise them with Kevin. I am sure he could have changed things.'[16]

The Gillard–Swan view is rejected by other Rudd supporters in the ministry. John Faulkner was contemptuous of the argument that Rudd had to be removed because of his personality. He would ask people: Have you forgotten what Whitlam and Keating were like? He insisted the attacks on Rudd distorted the reality. 'I didn't think it was grossly dysfunctional,' Faulkner said of the government. 'The committee that grew up, the SPBC, I think worked pretty well. There is no question Kevin was dismissive with some people. I think he did become more and more isolated. But it is unfair to say that ministers didn't have an opportunity to express their views.'[17]

Chris Bowen, a junior minister under Rudd, said:

My experience was a positive one. When I needed to see the Prime Minister I got to see the Prime Minister. He didn't keep me waiting. If I had an item in cabinet, it was a proper group discussion. I found Kevin's management style to be open and inclusive. If you texted him he would text back. If you rang him he'd ring back.

Bowen said he was unaware of any talks among ministers about Rudd's dysfunctional style.[18]

Anthony Albanese, who had a special relationship with Rudd and easy access as leader of the House, was impatient with the cabinet hand-wringing. He said Rudd had 'massaged' people to get the leadership and then stopped the massaging. The upshot was that people were upset because they weren't being listened to enough. 'You just knock the door down if it's a big enough issue,' Albanese said.[19] It was easier for him.

Rudd took to dizzy and unsustainable heights what is best called the cult of prime ministerial governance. He gave priority to his personal office over cabinet, a cardinal mistake for a prime minister. One of his press secretaries, Sean Kelly, said: 'Kevin liked the idea of being courted and he enjoyed having young people around him.'[20] The symbols of this youthful office were chief of staff Alister Jordan, economic adviser Andrew Charlton and press secretary Lachlan Harris. Each was impressive and dedicated, but they operated in a political environment where inexperience was accentuated.

Rudd's office lacked some older and wiser heads that Fraser, Hawke, Keating and Howard as prime ministers felt it essential to employ. Martin Ferguson said: 'Kevin's bright and he's a policy person but he should have had a few more hard heads around him.'[21] The office took its cues from Rudd's policy centralisation and compulsion for activity but it could not manage the obligations imposed upon it by Rudd. It had to carry too much to the exclusion of other power centres: the cabinet, the ministers, the department and, fatally, Julia Gillard. By June 2010, Gillard felt that 'the degree of chaos and dysfunction was above and beyond anything to do with Labor as a political outfit'.[22] Her criticism was targeted at Rudd's office.

The chief of Rudd's office until late 2008, David Epstein, offers a chilling account of the Prime Minister's habits:

> Kevin Rudd's work pattern was eratic. He would push himself to the limit. Convinced he needed little sleep, almost seeing this as a badge of honour. But he would get over-tired, his temper would fray, then he would need a day's break to recover. His office was chaotic. Briefs would just pile up and be arranged across the floor. He would commission multiple briefs and then not read them because other issues became more pressing.[23]

The cabinet had talent but it was pathetically weak as a unit. It bowed before the exceptional authority that Rudd had established as Opposition leader, a level of authority unparalleled in ALP history. Senate leader Chris Evans said: 'We gave Rudd complete licence as Opposition leader and that set the pattern.'[24] As Combet put it: 'Rudd had beaten Howard, a huge achievement. He was accorded tremendous authority.'[25] Gillard said the election-year victory meant that people accepted the 'command and control' model as run by Rudd.

According to parliamentary secretary Gary Gray, the key to Rudd's demise was his misreading of the source of his authority: 'Rudd's view was that his power was derived not from his caucus or from his government but from his ascendancy in the opinion polls. Kevin's translation of political power was very American, very presidential.'[26] Yet Australia is a Westminster system. The prime minister was elected by the caucus and it is the caucus that makes or breaks Labor leaders. In Rudd's case caucus disenchantment came in advance of public disillusionment.

The only minister prepared to stand up to Rudd was Gillard, hardly a surprise given her power base. 'Kevin was never as rude to me as he was to everyone else,' says Gillard. 'He couldn't afford to be rude to me. And because he couldn't afford to be rude to me he didn't meddle in my areas.' Gillard had a clear go in industrial relations and education.[27] Faulkner would challenge Rudd in certain areas. After Gillard and Faulkner there was daylight. Tony Burke said only two people could help a cabinet minister with a problem—Gillard or Alister Jordan.

The weakness of cabinet mirrored the new power system. Rudd, not caucus or factions, selected the ministers. Having a power base in caucus mattered less than it did before. Rudd's staff would routinely issue humiliating orders to senior ministers in a fashion once unthinkable in an ALP government. It was an iron rule: more power for Rudd meant less respect for ministers.

After Rudd's demise there was an undercurrent of resentment at the hypocrisy of some wailing ministers. One senior figure, given Swan's fierce criticism of Rudd, said: 'Here is a person [Swan] who is in cabinet for over two years while Rudd was prime minister, not once taking Rudd on over anything and then declaring later that Rudd had no Labor values. Now that perplexed me.' Many ministers later blamed Rudd for their own weakness. Gillard backers had an interest in exaggerating Rudd's dysfunction to justify their decision. Nonetheless, the system was defective and Rudd's personality was a serious problem.

The flaw in the system was the absence of internal 'checks and balances' on Rudd. This testified to Labor's failure as an institution. Two prominent Gillard backers, parliamentary secretary Gary Gray and Right faction leader David Feeney, said the leadership change was essential to restore effective cabinet government. Rudd's dominance of a mostly compliant Labor Party ultimately brought him undone.

A former minister in the Hawke–Keating Government and right-wing factional boss, Robert Ray, likened Rudd's government to 'Nelson's Column with Rudd at the top'. He said that within Westminster terms it was 'an extreme centralist outfit bordering on a command regime where decisions are made at the top and percolate downwards'.[28] This was an insight into Rudd's personality: he was a loner. Rudd often felt things wouldn't happen unless he did them. This personality trait guarantees erratic government.

It was fused with his intellectual arrogance. 'Kevin did believe he's the smartest guy in the room and did react badly when challenged,' says Sean Kelly.[29] James Button, briefly his speechwriter, said Rudd's advisers saw him at close quarters and identified 'his need to be the smartest guy in the room'—a trait that 'made him treat people poorly'.[30] It meant Rudd resented unpalatable advice; he didn't like being told things couldn't be done. He would put people 'in the freezer'. Gillard would joke about it with colleagues such as Mark Arbib after he was consigned to the freezer.

Lachlan Harris, Rudd's senior press secretary, identified the essence of the crisis:

> Having lived and worked inside the government, I saw the structural problems at first hand. You really only have two sources of power in the party—the leader or the party itself. Labor's trouble is that it had only one accountability mechanism left— termination of the leader. If the only accountability mechanism in an organisation is regicide then you've got a big problem. It's proof of a weak institution.[31]

This is a perfect description of the Rudd Government. Rudd had created a model that put his own survival at risk. The risk would only materialise if sound decision-making fell apart and Rudd alienated much of the party. Both conditions were met.

All recent prime ministers, Howard aside, have had temper tantrums. But Rudd's temper tantrums were different: they left the impression he did not respect people. In a group with intense feelings about Rudd, none had more intense feelings than frontbencher and former ALP National Secretary Gary Gray. Interviewed for this book, Gray revealed that he was contemplating leaving politics because he could no longer tolerate Rudd as prime minister.

Gray said: 'I recall it like yesterday. When I came home from the session before Easter in 2010, I sat down with my wife and I said, "I actually don't want to continue in this government." I could see it had designed a model in which it was comfortable and I was not.' Gray, who had other job options in the resources sector, said he was 'absolutely serious' in re-thinking his position, though he would not walk away in any fit of pique. He believed Rudd's approach as prime minister was domineering and unacceptable, the cabinet was weak and the system would not endure.[32]

But Gray had deeper complaints: he felt Rudd, because of his character, had forfeited the goodwill of the caucus. Gray felt personally insulted by Rudd's behaviour during an exceptionally difficult period for the Gray family in 2009, the details of which he did not want published in this book. He concluded that Rudd was a damaged person and said that 'nothing can really explain the offhand way in which he would treat people'.[33] This trait reached a revealing extremity in Rudd's decision not to attend the funeral of ALP icon John Button but to visit Cate Blanchett's new baby instead, a faux pas repeatedly mentioned by many ALP figures. Gray has affirmed the view of Gillard, Swan and Combet: the real reason for Rudd's removal was to save the country from the way he governed. 'I made that decision,' he says, 'not because of popularity but because it was the right decision for the government, for the country and for the Labor Party.'[34]

Chris Evans worked professionally with Rudd but he had long-established views about his character. Evans, who replaced Faulkner as Senate leader, recalls a discussion with Rudd after the 2004 election:

> We actually had a discussion: he asked me why don't we get along? I told him. I said he is brilliant. He works hard. He is seriously capable. But he is not a team player. I was honest with him. Robert Ray had told me he would be the next Labor prime minister, so I didn't do it without knowing. But after that we never had a relationship.

Evans is one of many to conclude that Rudd nursed grudges within his heart.[35]

In many ways Simon Crean was the most experienced minister in Rudd's government. A former Labor leader, he had served in the Hawke–Keating years. Crean started off 'hugely optimistic' about the government but he grew disillusioned with Rudd on grounds of character and process. 'Rudd was carried away with the euphoria and personal accolades, the popularity, call it what you like, it was all about him,' says Crean. 'He fell for the classic deception, that you can do it all without the party. The point is you work with the party and you add value.'[36]

'I had a dispute with Kevin over FuelWatch and I almost got sacked,' Martin Ferguson said. 'I argued it was all show, no substance.' Rudd was furious over the leak of a letter from Ferguson urging cabinet to ditch the election promise. Ferguson, a Rudd supporter, came under intense pressure. 'There was a full investigation of myself and my staff,' he said. 'People were interviewed, phone records analysed. I was disappointed but we got on with life.'[37]

Some ministers grew angry and frustrated because they were marginalised by Rudd. That meant exclusion from genuine participation. Chris Evans, then Senate leader, said: 'He had no interest in the Senate. I just did my job. We didn't have any close engagement.'[38] When Rudd was deposed, the attorney-general, Robert McClelland, once close to him, felt Rudd had abandoned their past friendship.

For Rudd, the most dangerous instance of exclusion was with the Minister for Agriculture, Tony Burke. Burke stuck his neck out in 2006 to back Rudd against Beazley. He found himself quickly marginalised. 'I probably only had three or four calls from him in three years,' Burke said. Rudd stopped taking his phone calls 'very quickly' after becoming leader. Burke had been appointed Agriculture minister only after Rudd had asked whether he wanted to be in cabinet. Burke heard he had been consigned to the outer ministry in the initial planning. 'I kept hearing stories of him furiously bagging me,' Burke said of the period in government. 'I approached him on three separate occasions. It was hard to ever get him one-on-one. He'd say, "No, there's no problem." This idea of trying to make people feel they weren't secure—that's certainly how he operated with me.' Burke sensed it was high risk to discuss such sensitive issues. 'If you stepped out of line, you'd be gone in an instant,' he said.[39] Eventually Burke gave up on Rudd: he cultivated Gillard, whom he hardly knew, and influenced her to challenge.

Rudd had wanted to get the cabinet right. He appointed Special Minister of State John Faulkner as cabinet secretary with responsibility for signing and checking cabinet minutes and providing informal advice. In the cabinet room Gillard sat to Rudd's right and Faulkner to his immediate left. Faulkner strove to bring out the best in Rudd and repress the worst. That needed mature management. 'Kevin is a very, very good instinctive politician, disciplined and very bright,' says Faulkner.[40] When Joel Fitzgibbon resigned as Defence minister both Rudd and Angus Houston were keen to see Faulkner take the portfolio. But Faulkner warned Rudd: 'It might be the right thing for the government but it is the wrong thing for you.' It was an assessment Gillard shared. Yet Faulkner went off to Defence.

Stephen Smith, the Foreign Minister put into the portfolio at short notice by Rudd post-election, was in a hot seat, with Rudd expressing opinions on every aspect of foreign policy. Smith took the smart approach from the outset: 'My operating principle was to ensure there was not a crack of light between the Foreign Minister and the Prime Minister.'[41] It was the only viable option.

Gray felt Rudd's elevation of his staff over frontbenchers had become untenable. For Gray, the trigger event came when, as parliamentary secretary, he requested meetings with ministers to sort out issues concerning electoral law and process. In the end he was told by Alister

Jordan that he was, in effect, exceeding his authority. Gray says the attitude of Rudd's office was: 'We will tell you who you will talk to and in what circumstances you will talk to them.' According to Gray, Rudd's office 'was incapable of managing the power put into their hands by the Prime Minister'.[42]

Senior public servants were alarmed not just at ministerial staff numbers but at their political (as distinct from policy) orientation, which was eroding good government from within. Few people were as concerned as Terry Moran. Interviewed in 2014, he said:

> We have a particular Australian problem at present. We have come to accept a ministerial office system with hardly any experienced public servants or people with deep policy expertise engaged alongside political and media advisers. This puts ministers at a significant disadvantage. It contributes to governments having a shorter life span because, frankly, it puts more pressure on ministers.[43]

It is hard to imagine a more serious warning about Labor methods coming from the top public servant.

At the start Rudd had told Moran he wanted the prime minister's department to be a pre-eminent policy institution not just in Australian terms but in international terms. This was typical Rudd: he used such hyperbole when appealing to individuals. Yet Rudd failed to properly utilise his own department as serious tensions grew between his office and Moran. Moran was worried at the ministerial staff appointment process, fearing it was a Labor spoils system based on family and party networks.

Moran recommended to Rudd that he establish a new cabinet committee sitting alongside the National Security Committee and Expenditure Review Committee to determine priorities. The idea was modified and came to fruition as the SPBC, cutting its teeth during the global financial crisis. It became Rudd's pet instrument and the source of resentment from non-members.

There is universal agreement about the erosion of the cabinet process. Anthony Albanese said: 'This was a busy government. It had a lot on. You had the SPBC and it continued after the global crisis to make decisions effectively as an inner cabinet. It had too much power for too long. And that annoyed ministers.'[44] Gillard has given her own version: upon arriving in government everybody was 'bubbling with enthusiasm' but Kevin's style was irritating. 'People could have cheerfully strangled him when he called the 2020 Summit,' she said in 2013.

Then we got the global financial crisis and this was both a great boon and a great burden for Kevin. The boon is that in that sort of crisis Kevin's organisational style is actually okay. People accept a fair bit of command and control in times of crisis. They don't mind working long hours for a real purpose. But it was a burden because he never reverted from the crisis organisational style to a version of normality. The situation just reinforced his belief in this dysfunctional style. He never moved into a normal, organised pattern of decision-making. We never got there under Kevin. The other difficulty is that the politics were getting harder. Kevin's style became more chaotic and people got more infuriated with him. The harder the challenge got, the more chaotic he got.[45]

Moran identified the flaw: Rudd thrived amid the global financial crisis, with its urgency, adrenaline, and late-night and early-morning briefings. Rudd, Swan and the 'gang of four' were in overdrive. Moran said of the SPBC process:

It took decisions in real time in a rapidly moving situation. Kevin seemed enthusiastic about the process and became keen about it as an approach to governing. He understood the issues and made his late-night phone calls to other leaders. It was what he loved doing. After that, he couldn't easily return to normality.[46]

It is the core insight: Rudd couldn't return to normality. He thrived on urgency and emergency and would engender such atmospherics when they were unnecessary. The Rudd Government never settled: it had no normality. It had, instead, three phases: adjusting to office, the global financial crisis and then the drift to dissension and paralysis.

Stephen Smith confirms the point: 'Kevin thrived on the sense of crisis, the 24-hour media cycle, requests for immediate advice, urgent phone calls and briefings. The GFC decision-making format came to define the government permanently. We never reverted to orthodox decision-making.'[47] In short, there was no normal. Rudd had become an addict; his drug was crisis. He could never let go.

Centralisation of power in the prime minister's office had been a forty-year-old story, from the Whitlam days onwards. Rudd's defect wasn't just excessive centralisation—the real problem is that he centralised decision-making but often failed to make the decisions. That led to paralysis. The great exception was Rudd's management of the GFC, yet that exception tends to prove the rule. Ministers testify that Rudd had two speeds: full forward or disengaged.

Stephen Smith again nailed the point:

Many people blamed Kevin for micro-management but I don't think that was the real problem—it was indecision. One of the risks for ministers was having Kevin or his office say to you, 'No, you can't do that' because that raised the question 'What *could* you do?' If you got trapped in that deadlock it could take months to resolve.[48]

In his analysis, Chris Barrett lamented:

Too often in the Rudd Government advice would go to the PM for a decision (all too often when it didn't need to) requiring action by a certain date. Despite the very best efforts to follow up, a decision would not be forthcoming and options would simply disappear because the time for exercising them had passed.[49]

The 2012 dissection of Rudd's decision-making by Health Minister Nicola Roxon assumed legendary status. Roxon's critique was about Rudd's governing, not his treatment of her. She experienced Rudd in 'fully engaged mode'. She said he contemplated vast changes in health policy without proper assessment or advice, imposed unrealistic dead-lines, elevated politics above policy substance, wanted a referendum for a Commonwealth takeover of the hospital system in circumstances that made such a move irresponsible, delayed proper cabinet consideration and drove her to seek support from Gillard and Swan to curb the Prime Minister's excesses. A strong supporter of the leadership change, Roxon said: 'I did have to stand up to Kevin on many, many occasions when he was keen to take a path which I thought was going to be destructive for the government.'[50]

Moran had earlier come to grief with the prime minister's office over his complaints about their corruption of the cabinet process. 'The system isn't working,' he told Rudd's office. He issued a firm warning: poor cabinet process would get Rudd into trouble. Their reply was: 'The SPBC is Kevin's forum—he will run it as he wishes.' Ironically, it did kill Rudd politically, in April 2010 over climate change, in an SPBC decision-making fiasco. David Epstein said that 'over time he froze Moran out'.

Over time the full cabinet process deteriorated. Tony Burke said: 'There was an inability to take decisions and an unwillingness to tolerate dissent. [Rudd's] style was to comment on each participant's contribution, not to encourage debate.' Burke believes Rudd's obsession about leaks helped to terminate cabinet government: 'In the end we stopped making decisions at cabinet. The official business of cabinet took no time and then we'd have a political discussion, but with no agenda, no direction, no decision.'[51] Burke was dismayed by Rudd, as a prime minister and as a person.

Barrett offered an account of Rudd in action:

Cabinet and the committees chaired by the PM were extraordinarily inefficient. Meetings did not start on time, frequently ran too long and accomplished too little … The PM generally wouldn't submit to a pre-briefing session. Officials and private staff would give him briefing notes for cabinet, but unfortunately these very frequently were not read … The Rudd practice was to arrive at the cabinet table and either ask what was on the cabinet agenda or who could explain the item to the room. He would often be the first to ask questions (i.e. he used the cabinet meeting as a personal briefing session) and far too often would discover some problem with the proposal and defer it for consideration … Even very short agendas could take three or more hours of cabinet debate and not be completed. Unresolved issues were put on the agenda for the next meeting and frequently not resolved then either. Unsurprisingly, urgency then became the principle of cabinet agenda setting. Things would only be decided when they were right up against deadline … It became standard practice for most ministers to arrive with minutes to sign or papers to read for the long unproductive hours in cabinet.[52]

Meanwhile relations between Rudd's office and department went into a freeze. Moran felt the problem was not Rudd but his staff. After being told on one occasion that Rudd could not see him, Moran stopped asking for meetings with the Prime Minister. At one point the journalist Brian Toohey wrote an article saying Rudd hadn't spoken to Moran for several months. It was right in substance but not technically, since they would still see each other at cabinet. Rudd asked Moran to deny the article. 'But it's true,' Moran protested. Rudd seemed genuinely surprised.

At the end of 2009, Moran initiated a review of the cabinet system by an outsider, Colin Carter, formerly from the Boston Consulting Group. It recommended a series of reforms. In April 2010, Moran had a long talk with Rudd about the need to improve the cabinet process. Rudd agreed. They decided it would happen post-election. But Rudd was removed pre-election.

While Rudd's supporters defended his decision-making, nearly everyone agreed there was a fracture between Rudd and his cabinet. Kim Carr said: 'It wasn't a dysfunctional government and Rudd was a competent chair of cabinet. But ministers became cut off from one another and from Rudd.'[53] It is a classic problem: cabinet members did not confide in one another; ministers functioned in silos; there was no internal rapport, no collegiate spirit. Faulkner said: 'There was a failure on the part of ministers to talk frankly to the Prime Minister.'[54] Faulkner and Carr blame the ministers, not Rudd. 'Too often on major issues, ministers would not press their views on the Prime Minister,' Carr said.[55]

Crean has affirmed the dysfunctional nature of the government. Although he personally never had trouble working with Rudd, he said the Prime Minister operated a 'hub and spokes' system; he dealt separately with ministers. 'He never used the collective of cabinet properly,' Crean said. 'Kevin didn't have faith in the ability of his ministers to initiate policy.'[56] Gray was lethal on the cabinet: after the struggle to win office, nobody wanted to rock the boat. He said the culture was 'everything in the world will be set right if only I am called minister'. Labor existed to hold office. That had become its rationale.[57]

Chris Evans was scathing of the cabinet. 'I take my fair share of the blame,' he said when interviewed. 'I and my cabinet colleagues have got to take responsibility. It is easy to blame Rudd for everything. The grown-ups should have taken more action.' Alluding to the intimidation, Evans said:

> Ministers weren't quick to share their views about their frustrations because one had to be a bit careful about that. I wasn't aware how badly some of the other ministers had been treated. We should have done more as a cabinet, much more, to pull Rudd into line. But our failure to take on Kevin and save him from himself was a failure of all of us.[58]

Nicola Roxon agreed: 'It's right that cabinet never found a way to address the Rudd problem. Ministers would talk about the problem but nobody found a way to bring it to the table.'[59] The cabinet was rendered spineless by Rudd. Yet it gained him nothing. Rudd's defective cabinet system neither sustained him in office nor saved him from the revolt of the dispossessed. It was a double negative.

The great contrast between Rudd and Gillard as prime ministers was their relationship with the Labor Party. Rudd played down his Labor identity—he shunned the unions and factional chiefs and patronised the caucus. On each score, Gillard was the opposite. Neither got it right, erring in opposite directions. Rudd's mistake was to think he could be the prime minister he wanted to be regardless of the Labor Party.

Former AWU boss Paul Howes, representing the most influential union inside the ALP, described Rudd's style: 'I remember having my meetings with Kevin at a round table. If he glanced up at me it might be to say hello or goodbye. It was the Emperor sends his message and off you go. And if you dare to disagree, you are on the outer forever.'[60] Swan said: 'The unions never got any love out of Kevin. He didn't tend the base. He turned his back on whole slabs of the caucus.'[61]

This is where Rudd's hubris led to recklessness. A Labor prime minister doesn't need a factional base, provided he remains strong across the party. Yet Rudd had no factional base and no pacification strategy with his caucus. The exception was that Mark Arbib initially operated as his Praetorian guard in a solo capacity. After the pair fell out, Rudd's defensive trenches were empty. He was, literally, without fortifications. It was as though he believed his ascension had abolished the normal laws of politics. Rudd paraded his distaste for factions and was keen to reduce their influence. Kim Carr said: 'Rudd assumed that governing the country well was enough. He didn't look to factional support to sustain his leadership. When his standing with the public declined, his weak internal management was exposed.'[62] As the tide ran out he was naked and friendless.

The contrast with Hawke could not be greater. Hawke enjoyed the support of two of the greatest right-wing factional figures in ALP history, Graham Richardson and Robert Ray. The slightest sign of any tremor was quickly detected and addressed. By comparison Rudd seemed an innocent. Chris Evans explained the difference: 'If you are a right-wing PM, like Kim Beazley would have been, you must deal with the New South Wales and Victorian Right. Ray and Richo did this job for Hawke and he listened to them. Under Rudd, nobody had that power. He didn't have those bulwarks.'[63]

For Rudd, the dramatic encounter came in 2009 when a six-strong delegation of faction convenors saw him to make representations against the reduction of printing allowances for members of Parliament. Rudd listened politely but exploded when Victorian right-wing organiser David Feeney argued that if the decision went ahead the government would need to find another communications strategy for MPs. Feeney had been lobbied by Rudd in his campaign for the leadership; he and his wife knew Rudd socially. They had been impressed by Rudd, and Feeney felt close to him. Confronting Feeney, Rudd said: 'I don't give a fuck about you and I don't give a fuck about what you think.'[64] It was pure anger and what stuck in Feeney's head was that Rudd kept saying it.

The delegation left shaken. Feeney was particularly shaken. He thought he had a relationship with Rudd. Now he realised he didn't matter. Indeed, he was held in contempt. 'Rudd only cared about himself,' Feeney said later. He never forgave Rudd. Combet said later that Rudd 'went off his block when things didn't go right'.[65] The staff would try to say something better about Kevin. 'He did have temper tantrums and he did freeze people out,' Sean Kelly said. 'But Kevin is not the monster in personal relationships that is often depicted.'[66]

Yet this cross-factional group from Left and Right did matter. It included Senator Don Farrell, a former secretary of the Shop Distributive and Allied Employees Association. Farrell said:

> Rudd just flew at David [Feeney]. It was an incredible attack and very personal. David was humiliated and we virtually had to carry him out of the room. I don't think any union official would tolerate a manager speaking to a staff member the way Rudd spoke to David. And David was one his backers from 2006. I think Rudd lost control at this meeting. I believe he spoke like this because he felt he could, because he was the boss.[67]

A member of the group, Senator Carol Brown, said to Feeney, 'That's what he thinks of all of us.' The story spread across the caucus. Gillard later went out of her way to see Feeney, trying to cover Rudd's arse. There was another aspect: Kevin was a wealthy man ready to make life financially more difficult for his MPs. From this day Feeney saw Rudd as a tyrant; Farrell would move against Rudd whenever the chance came. Feeney and Farrell would become two of the four key factional figures in Rudd's removal.

The Rudd experiment in governance failed, ultimately, because Rudd lacked the skills for prime ministerial leadership. The cabinet was ineffective, the factions were alienated and the caucus felt disrespected. Rudd failed to grasp that a leader's authority derived from the consent of his colleagues.

CHAPTER 11

RUDD FINDS HIS MISSION

The 2008 global financial crisis gave Kevin Rudd the grand purpose for which he had been searching. Rudd seized the crisis like a leader possessed. He rushed forward with meetings, briefings and war games, and was endlessly on the phone to world leaders. Rudd said later that this was 'the year when I didn't sleep'—an exaggeration with meaning. It was his finest performance yet only helped to expose the flaws in his make-up.

Rudd authorised one of the strongest fiscal responses of any government, initiated a range of new programs and intervened to protect the financial system. There were two fiscal packages—in October 2008 and February 2009—and it was Rudd, not the Treasury, who led the way. The Treasury, if given its discretion, would have been more modest.

As the world confronted the deepest financial risk since the Great Depression, Rudd was fixated by one idea: the need for rapid audacity. His instinct and his intellect were in perfect harmony. Rudd's impulse was to act, to fight and to intervene. He was shameless in telling world leaders what to do—and then, in case they missed it, telling them again and again. Rudd was brazen but methodical. Indeed, the methodical nature of Rudd's response invites another conclusion: that he had been awaiting such an event. He was psychologically ready.

The keys to Australia's response lay in the fact that it had a new government and that government was Labor. Being new meant Rudd was cloaked in the arrogance of inexperience; he was not afraid to be bold. The fiscal conservative became a raging Keynesian. At this point Rudd acted from the deepest well of Labor traditionalism—desperate to avoid the failure of the Scullin Labor Government in the Great Depression when it became a prisoner of financial caution.

Rudd said of his government's response:

I took charge of it and drove it. I did not see it as a technical exercise. I saw it as a profoundly political exercise in leadership of the country. This was a phenomenally difficult challenge and I found it the most intellectually and physically demanding part of the prime ministership.[1]

He knew a deep recession soon after Labor's coming to power would lead to electoral annihilation. The timing seemed a terrible historical joke, given the challenge facing Scullin soon after his 1929 election victory. Rudd's fighting instincts were aroused:

I said to the cabinet, as this loomed closer, that we had every prospect of becoming the second Scullin government. I used the terms directly and advisedly. I was acutely conscious this could be a very, very short-term Labor government. Therefore, I said to the cabinet I am not about to stand idly by and not have a go at this, because everything we have fought for over the last decade now hangs in the balance just months into office.[2]

The nation was in the hands of two Queensland boys, Rudd and Swan, who had the same response. For Swan, the 2008 challenge was monumental, coming only months into his job as treasurer. Given his roots, there was never any doubt about Swan's response: 'The experience of the early 1990s recession drove me personally. The unemployment rate in my electorate at that time reached 11 per cent and in the working-class areas it was far higher.'[3] The crisis would reveal Swan as a Labor traditionalist.

The sanctioning agent for Australia's response was the Treasury, headed by Ken Henry. By 2008 Henry was a veteran, having been appointed by Costello in 2001 and reappointed in 2006. Educated at Taree High School, the son of a timber worker, Henry typified a remarkable Treasury tradition: departmental heads from humble origins ascending by merit. Rudd, from the start, wanted to prove his government's credentials by listening to Henry and recruiting Treasury's imprimatur for his policies.

It is critical to grasp, however, that Rudd merely drew sustenance from Henry; in the end he made his own call and Rudd went beyond Henry's position. It is equally true that Treasury accepted and backed Rudd's judgement. In effect, it legitimised the stimulus. Years later its officials were reluctant to criticise Rudd's response.

Interviewed for this book, Henry said of the big February 2009 $42 billion package:

I was a little surprised at the overall quantum of the stimulus. Around $30 billion would not have surprised me. However, at the time I didn't think the government's decision was inappropriate. This is a fine judgement. It was always better to err on the side of doing too much than too little. I think Rudd's judgement on the stimulus required was as good as anybody could have made and better than just about anybody else would have made.[4]

Accounts from the 'gang of four' ministers are explicit: Treasury was with them. If Henry had taken a stand against the extent of spending, it would have had an impact on their decision-making. But he didn't. Asked later if he believed Australia was heading into recession, Henry replied emphatically: 'Yes.'[5] Asked the same question, Swan said, 'Yes, we thought we'd go into recession. I mean eight of our top ten trading partners were in recession.' Pressed again about whether he believed a recession was certain, Swan said: 'Absolutely.'[6] But Rudd said later he thought they might pull through. 'In my heart of hearts I thought we had a chance. I am just telling you. That is not a retrospective call—and more than just a chance, up there with 50:50.'[7]

Australia survived the financial crisis without a recession because of two factors—the pre-crisis strength of its financial position and soundness of its banks; and the speed with which monetary and fiscal action was taken when the crisis hit. The former was due to Howard–Costello and the latter to Rudd–Swan. The element usually underestimated is that this crisis was external to Australia. The nation did not suffer the banking rupture that tore apart the financial systems of the United States and the United Kingdom, and as a result Australia was likely to be less affected.

The other pillar on which Labor relied was the Reserve Bank under Glenn Stevens. The bank had to combat two problems: panic leading to a possible run on deposits, and a collapse in confidence that demanded interest rate cuts. The government offered a guarantee for retail bank deposits and for wholesale funding by the banks. The Reserve Bank, led by Stevens, cut the cash rate overall by 4.75 percentage points, a decisive response. Rudd and Swan proposed a scheme to lend to commercial property ventures (the 'Ruddbank'), which was eventually abandoned. Rudd did, however, implement a fund managed from Treasury to finance car dealers caught in the credit shortage. Throughout the crisis Rudd was on the prowl, ceaselessly looking for more potential trouble spots he could fix with more public funds or guarantees.

In the end, Australia spent too much. The deep downturn Treasury anticipated, even with the stimulus and interest rate cuts, did not eventuate. Such a judgement on Rudd may seem unfair; it is somewhat akin to saying because the problem didn't occur you were wrong to try to avoid it. On balance, however, the judgement is warranted. Labor's response assumed a far deeper domestic downturn: the size of the stimulus was too big, its composition was flawed and it ran for too long.

The crisis had an epic political consequence. It set up the Liberal campaigns for the 2010 and 2013 elections. Indeed, Tony Abbott rode into office on the back of Labor's prolonged deficits. The most important decision Malcolm Turnbull made as Liberal leader was to oppose the February 2009 stimulus as excessive and accuse Labor of plunging the nation into unjustified debts and deficits. This defined the economic policy split between Labor and the Coalition for nearly the entire Labor era.

In the nine months before the crisis, Rudd and Swan ran an economic policy caught between two risks: halting domestic inflation and taking insurance against the growing rumble of global financial instability. Henry's assessment when Rudd took office was that 'while we recognised the sub-prime problems in the US, we didn't think this would lead to a failure of global financial markets.'[8]

On 29 February, flying to Gladstone with Swan, Henry and other advisers, Rudd initiated the sort of conversation that he loved: probing Henry to range over the potential overseas financial risks. Henry said: 'He wanted to know the worst that could possibly happen. I realised he was crisis planning.' The potentially catastrophic scenario that Henry described was Australian banks losing access to world financial markets and being unable to fund the current account deficit then running above 6 per cent of gross domestic product (GDP). Henry did not believe it feasible. Yet within the year such fears had materialised.[9]

Less than three weeks later the fifth-largest US investment bank, Bear Stearns, was rescued from bankruptcy by the US Federal Reserve, which had facilitated its sale. Its stock market value had fallen from $20 billion to $3.5 billion over a year. On separate overseas trips, Rudd and Swan now sensed a financial crisis was looming.

Swan's most vivid memory was of a lunch at the Australian embassy in Washington when a former Treasury officer, Tim Stewart, now a senior manager with Fortress Investment Group and an important source for the Australians, told the Treasurer that the Bear Stearns event 'was not the end of the crisis, it wasn't even the beginning of the end, it was just the beginning'. Swan said of Stewart's warning: 'It stuck with me.'[10] In fact, it changed Labor's first budget.

The upshot was a 'steady as she goes' May 2008 budget with the economics editors complaining it wasn't tough enough. Labor forecast a surplus in 2008–09 of 1.8 percentage points of GDP, a mild tightening. Asked why he hadn't acted more boldly against inflation, Swan said: 'I wasn't prepared to slam the economy into the wall.'[11]

Meanwhile, under Rudd's direction, the war-gaming continued. At one meeting Henry warned that if US financial instability triggered a downturn then Australia might need a fiscal stimulus as well as interest rate cuts by the Reserve Bank. Pushed by Rudd, he nominated a possible stimulus of 1 per cent of GDP, or about $10 billion. Implicit in Henry's stance was a profound rethink in Treasury driven by himself and his former deputy and subsequent successor, Martin Parkinson. Treasury had been haunted by the early 1990s recession, one of the most debilitating events for the department in the past half century. It was recognised that Keating's One Nation fiscal stimulus was delivered too late and was too geared to time-consuming infrastructure. Henry and Parkinson decided that when the next downturn came the correct response was not to abandon the technique of fiscal stimulus but to get it right. They embraced two ideas. Firstly, a fiscal stimulus was vital in the period before lower interest rates had any impact; and secondly, one-off payments and government spending were superior to tax cuts in delivering 'bang for the buck'. 'The view was that the Treasury should be the first to say to government "do something"; we shouldn't be the last,' Henry said of the next recession.[12] Swan said:

> What drove me, and I think both Ken and Kevin, was that we didn't want a repeat of the early 1990s, the capital and skills destruction, the difficulty when unemployment goes above 10 per cent with some people never getting a job again. We wanted to avoid the destruction that had characterised the last recession in Australia. I was deeply alive to this.[13]

The machinery of government was geared to the crisis. From an early stage there would be a daily meeting at 8.30 a.m., mainly of Rudd, Swan, Moran, Henry, Finance Department chief Ian Watt, and deputies. Above all, it meant Labor was ready when the crisis hit.

On 15 September, Lehman Brothers, once the fourth-largest US investment bank, announced it would file for bankruptcy after the

US Treasury declined to bail it out. Lehmans fell over without government support, leading British Chancellor Alistair Darling to believe that the US administration was 'in a state of panic'. The alarm went through the global banking community: the United States had signalled it would let banks fail. There was only one question: how many more banks would fail?[14]

On the afternoon of that same day Swan spoke to the Treasury, the Reserve Bank and the Australian Prudential Regulation Authority and was assured that Australia's financial system was sound. As the US political system struggled to respond, Australia's own plans were about to roll out.

On 7 October the Reserve Bank Board, facing a recommendation to cut the cash rate by 0.5 percentage points, went instead for a huge one percentage point reduction. Swan said he was 'surprised, happy'. Henry said: 'I was initially a little surprised but then I was deeply impressed.'[15] Swan was now pushing for a stimulus package of several billion.[16] It was a new world. The Reserve Bank was the first central bank to take action, thereby setting the global trend.

The next day Swan left for Washington to attend the spring meetings of the International Monetary Fund (IMF) and the World Bank. On Friday 10 October the share market fell more than 7 per cent and there were signs of a run on the banks. Rudd decided to act. He convened an SPBC meeting in Canberra over the weekend of 11–12 October. Moran, Henry, Watt and their senior advisers attended with Rudd and Gillard. Rudd felt ready to press the button and was keen to make history. Cameras were invited in at the start.

Henry gave a rundown and said a fiscal stimulus was a conventional response in this situation.[17]

Henry said if ministers wanted an impact, they had to spend immediately. He had to fight to convince Rudd that funding infrastructure would not work. 'I know you want infrastructure,' he said. 'You think you get a double bonus, you get the stimulus and then you have the infrastructure project as well. But it doesn't work. The infrastructure projects ready to go don't exist and the lags from infrastructure are too long. This is what we learnt in 1991.' Rudd was resistant but in the end he accepted the case. 'Go early, go hard, go households' was Henry's famous message. So Rudd did, eventually. He would endlessly recycle Henry's mantra.

Henry's opening proposal was for a stimulus of about $5 billion. But Rudd pushed beyond this. He kept driving the issue. He didn't want half-measures and he didn't want a recession. 'The worst thing you can do in public policy terms is to half-act,' Rudd said.[18]

Swan's intervention from Washington buttressed Rudd's case. Having the Treasurer at the IMF/World Bank meetings and the emergency G-20 finance ministers meeting meant Australia was at the epicentre of the crisis. Swan's notes from these meetings refer to a 'psychology of confusion, frustration and fear' with nations' fates 'bound together in a way unimaginable a decade ago'.[19] IMF managing director Dominique Strauss-Kahn told the G-20 ministers that the world faced an 'unprecedented liquidity problem' that would become an 'insolvency problem'.[20] For Swan, the decisive event was the briefing by the IMF chief economist, Olivier Blanchard: 'It sent a fair bit of terror around the room. He said unambiguously there will be a need for significant stimulus across a range of economies because global demand is tanking. It solidified my thinking that not only do we need this package but that we would need more.'[21]

Swan rang in to the Canberra meeting. 'My message was: be absolutely under no doubt, this is bigger than any of you think,' he said. 'It is going to have a devastating impact on the global economy. It's going to hit our trading partners. Australia will cop it. We will need a significant fiscal stimulus and we will need to stabilise our financial system.'[22]

The SPBC decided upon both bank guarantees and a fiscal stimulus worth $10.4 billion. Henry proposed to the meeting that the government guarantee all wholesale funding by the banks plus all retail bank deposits. He feared that other nations might give such guarantees and this would disadvantage Australia or risk capital flight.

Early on Sunday morning Henry took an urgent call. It was from his mother, a full-rate pensioner. 'I'm really worried,' she told him. 'What's this stuff about how our bank deposits aren't safe. I want to know if I should go down to the bank and take my money out.' Henry was aghast. 'Mum, don't be silly,' he said. 'The NAB is the eighth-safest bank in the world, it's okay.' But Henry's mother was hard to convince. As he went into the meeting Henry thought: If I'm having trouble convincing my mother, how close are the conditions for a bank run? Henry told Rudd about the phone call. 'You have to announce the bank guarantee today,' he said. 'It needs to be this afternoon.' He told the author: 'I formed the view there was a significant risk of a bank or every bank facing … an inability to raise wholesale funding and/or a run on deposits. I communicated this to the Prime Minister.'[23] The guarantee had to be capped a few weeks later, but Rudd believed this decision earned 'near universal applause'.

The driving force on the stimulus was Rudd backed by Swan. Tanner was sceptical and took persuading. Announcing the decision,

Rudd set the tone: the situation, he said, 'is the economic equivalent of a rolling national security crisis'. It was affecting not just banks but 'the real economy, jobs, growth, overseas and here in Australia'. In one hit Labor was spending nearly half the previously estimated budget surplus of $22 billion.[24] And Australia had loads of ready ammunition—courtesy of a budget in surplus.

The bulk of the stimulus was direct cash payments to pensioners, seniors, carers, family support and assistance for first home buyers. Swan told the media: 'we are in the midst of the worst financial crisis ever to confront the modern market economy'. Rudd and Swan got over one critical message: the crisis was external to Australia. Rudd was fixated on Henry's advice about sequencing—the interest rate cut would boost activity from the second half of 2009 but that left eight long months before. 'The first stimulus was what we could get out the door to put a floor under confidence before Christmas,' Swan said. It worked. Consumers went Christmas shopping.

'We certainly did more than Treasury recommended,' Swan said. 'But the package wasn't opposed by the Treasury. The point is there isn't a precise figure where anybody can say "that's it". The Treasury was on board 110 per cent for a classic Keynesian response. And if you look at the impact, we got it about right.'[25]

Interviewed for this book, Henry paid tribute to Rudd, saying: 'I think Rudd's judgement on the first stimulus package was better than mine and I told him this. I might have gone for something smaller, probably would have. But I walked out of that meeting confident the decision to go for $10 billion was the right decision.'[26] Henry also said 'the instincts that made Rudd a problem in normal times worked brilliantly in the crisis'.

The October decision was difficult at the time. In retrospect, it looks easy. It was pre-emptive—before the impact on the real economy was apparent. Henry put the October decision into context: 'At this point [the government] got their stimulus and they kept their surplus. In that sense it wasn't hard.'[27] The package was passed by Parliament on 24 November and the first payments were made on 8 December.[28] Malcolm Turnbull supported the package while saying he would have structured it differently. He said Australia's strong budget position meant Labor should 'stay in surplus' but this was never going to happen.

Meanwhile Rudd and Swan were intent on doing more. During 2008 Swan read Ross Fitzgerald's biography of Scullin's ill-fated treasurer, 'Red Ted' Theodore, the moral of the story being that 'the Keynesians were cut off at the knees'. Rudd would not be Scullin; Swan was not going to suffer Theodore's fate. Modern Labor would get to implement Keynesian policies and purge Scullin's ghost.[29]

But they recognised the political negative—the shift of the budget towards deficits and debt. 'I felt what we did had a high political risk,' Swan said. 'But we had no choice. We knew we would be criticised for wasting money and spending too much.'[30] Meanwhile Rudd wanted the best of all worlds—he said the global economy had been transformed but all Labor's policies were still deliverable. Both propositions could not be right.

In early November the IMF issued new pessimistic forecasts predicting a recession in the United States, the Eurozone, Japan and Britain. It was the first time since World War II that growth across the advanced nations was expected to contract. In the same month Swan attended the G-20 finance ministers' meeting in Brazil and found the alarm had engulfed the developing world. 'It became apparent to me that we were stuffed, we were looking at a global recession or depression,' Swan said.[31] Rudd and Swan then attended the Washington G-20 leaders' emergency summit called by US President George W Bush. The Australians pressed for a global fiscal stimulus and this was the consensus of the meeting. China had already moved, announcing on 9 November a huge US$586 billion fiscal stimulus. Beijing had gone Keynesian, to cheers from Rudd's office and the Australian Treasury.

The Washington summit was one of the most important meetings in the past half century. The IMF called for a global fiscal stimulus of 2 per cent of world GDP, proof that it believed the world was on the brink. An action plan was agreed upon for what Strauss-Kahn called the 'worst economic situation' for sixty years. In reality, it was seat-of-the-pants improvisation, with IMF chief economist Blanchard saying: 'If we say 3 per cent we'll scare people to death; and if we say 1 per cent, it will be taken as the IMF is doing nothing.'[32] The IMF had given Rudd full sanction to follow his instinct. When later criticised for the size of his next package, Rudd immediately referenced the IMF. He left the meeting firmly disposed to another stimulus package, and a bigger one.

This time there was no escape: it would be Rudd's deficit. He agonised, but the outcome was predestined. In truth, Rudd was thriving amid the rolling crisis. He had become obsessed, drilling down to the details, talking endlessly and at length about its dimensions. The polls showed Labor with a substantial lead. This was the mood in which the February 2009 package was devised. Its construction was chaotic. Swan said of this next package: 'It was driven by fear of recession. It got bigger as we became more alarmed about where things were going.'[33] In late January the IMF released new forecasts that output in advanced nations would shrink by 2 per cent in 2009, the first such contraction for sixty years.

Much of the February package was shaped in Rudd's and Swan's offices with backing from the departments. At this point Rudd took an iron control of his government. With the focus on jobs, the 'gang of four' approved the decisions, the main voice for restraint being Tanner. Much of the work was done on the run as Rudd travelled around the country, visiting Papua New Guinea with ministers and officials following him. One official said: 'We found that, under the media-management culture, it was impossible to have four senior ministers sitting in a room without having at least one of them leave to conduct media interviews. It didn't matter that serious issues were being decided. The non-negotiable priority remained—to feed the media beast.'

The 3 February package, called the Nation Building and Jobs Plan and costing a huge $42 billion across the forward estimates, dwarfed the October 2008 decisions. It was equivalent to about 2 per cent of GDP, a stimulus unmatched for many decades. Henry's model was largely gone; Rudd's infrastructure vision had prevailed. Rudd said the package was filled with 'practical nation-building measures'. There was $13 billion in cash payments but the centrepiece was a $29 billion infrastructure agenda spearheaded by a $15 billion investment, under the absurd heading Building the Education Revolution (BER), for assembly halls, libraries and other improvements for primary schools plus building for science and language laboratories for secondary schools. In addition, there was $7 billion for the construction of 20 000 new public and community homes and $2.7 billion for a program to provide free ceiling insulation and installation for home owner–occupiers.

Rudd said Labor 'will never haul up the white flag on the inevitability of a recession' and declared: 'We will throw everything at this.' Treasury announced that the global downturn was expected to be 'the sharpest collective decline in GDP in the post-war period'.[34] It believed Australia's downturn, originating in the global financial system, would be a more severe event than witnessed for many decades, a serious error as it turned out. Incredibly, the $42 billion figure was more the sum of the decisions rather than the pre-determined best number. In private, Rudd claimed ownership of the numbers. That he went so far testified to political courage and his faith in spending.

David Epstein said: 'Rudd was a spender and it rationalised his desire to spend. During the crisis Ken Henry became tutor-in-residence but he cut Rudd too much slack.'[35]

What if Treasury had resisted the stimulus number? Swan says that would have been 'diabolical' but the government would have proceeded. 'What guided this package was the spectre of a global depression and the spectre of a severe domestic recession. I don't think the $42 billion was out of whack with where we were.'[36]

Rudd was sensitive to cash handouts being seen as wasteful. The philosophy now was nation-building via 'shovel-ready' infrastructure. Rudd drove this hard. Yet the strategy brought him undone and became a critical step in the ruin of his leadership.

Henry said of the roof insulation idea: 'The Prime Minister insisted the package must contain an energy efficiency element. He was quite fixed on this.'[37] Rudd told the author the proposal was recommended by his department. The plan was to insulate 2.2 million homes over three years, a high ambition. Rudd personally drove the roof insulation scheme—it incurred four fatalities; it was beyond the administrative competence of the national government in the speed required; and it should never have been embarked upon in this fashion, as documented in subsequent reports.

This was an insight into Rudd: he had pushed too far and too hard. The tragic incompetence of the roof insulation scheme crippled the electoral gains from stimulus overall. It was a question of judgement.

In relation to the BER, Rudd, in an interview with the author, claimed personal responsibility for the scheme and dismissed Gillard's role:

> The school building program was entirely my idea. You need to know that … I knew the demands in my electorate. I knew all my fifty or sixty schools … I have done so many speeches out in the blazing sun, speech days out in the blazing sun … for me it made sense as a demonstrable need … So I drove this one hard. And the truth is she [Gillard] had no view. I don't exaggerate it. She was supportive of it when, you know, we did it. I don't criticise her for that at all. But she didn't have a view on it going forward.[38]

In fact, while Rudd took the lead, Gillard was actively involved in the final design and when the political attacks were being mounted it was Gillard rather than Rudd who defended the scheme. Henry said he accepted the purpose behind the BER—to hold up construction industry jobs. Swan was unapologetic:

You've got to be realistic. When you invest in thousands of projects around the country you pay a price. I always felt we would pay a price for having the courage to take this on. But the place was collapsing. We needed to find shovel-ready projects and the point is: if you did this you had to do all schools.[39]

Gillard backed Swan's argument: she was amazed to find that the government did not have a list of the poorest schools. She felt the scheme had to be universal. In terms of holding up construction industry jobs, the scheme delivered.

Yet the BER was inefficient, failed to deliver value for money, and its waste became a political issue exploited by Abbott. Evidence was that quotes were inflated and work was often sub-standard. The educational value in the classroom was limited given total funds. Terry Moran felt that the BER should have been done in tranches to create flexibility to halt the process.

The February 2009 package was not just an economic stimulus—it was a spending mechanism to deliver Labor's political aspirations, notably its commitment to clean energy, education investment and fighting homelessness. This is how Rudd presented his package. But it was too smart by half—he was chasing a double dividend and therein lay the trap.[40]

In electoral terms the package became a macroeconomic success and a microeconomic negative. 'We understood with the second package the political risks were even higher,' Swan said.[41] Consider the consequences: the wastage in the BER discredited the Education Revolution slogan; the home-insulation fiasco branded Rudd as an incompetent; the problem was that the specifics discredited the package overall. It was one thing to offer cash handouts; it was another to embark upon large-scale public works spread across the nation in small-scale investments. Blunders occurred on a scale nobody in government anticipated. The 'micro' mistakes branded Rudd as reckless with taxpayers' funds, an impression reinforced by a budget deep in the red.

Treasury believed the stimulus prevented a serious recession. The department's David Gruen estimated that the stimulus delivered economic growth over the March, June and September quarters of 2009. Without the stimulus 'real GDP would have contracted not only in the December quarter 2008 (which it did) but also in the March and June quarters of 2009'. He argued that the policy response was large and quick enough to convince consumers and businesses that the slowdown would be 'relatively mild (indeed much milder than most forecasters, including the Australian Treasury, had earlier expected)'. Gruen said the stimulus reduced the peak unemployment level by 1.5 percentage points and he believed this was an underestimate.[42]

In a fifty-page analysis Chris Barrett concluded that without the stimulus there would have been 'two large negative quarters'. He repudiated the view that Australia could have survived merely with lower interest rates, a lower exchange rate and China's stimulus. Barrett said that, given that the economy grew at only 1.7 per cent over five quarters and unemployment rose 1.1 percentage points, it is hardly a surprise that recession would have eventuated without a $40 billion stimulus.[43] He deemed that Rudd and Swan had made the right call in giving priority to growth rather than fearing a deficit.

There are three connected arguments against Labor's policy: they spent too much, the stimulus ran for too long and its composition was flawed. Central to the critique is that Labor devised a stimulus for a downturn the severity of which did not materialise. The May 2009 budget forecast, with the stimulus included, was for unemployment to reach 8.5 per cent, a significant Treasury misreading of the impact of the global downturn on Australia.

Saul Eslake, the chief economist for Bank of America Merrill Lynch, said:

> Hindsight is always 20/20. Once the government decided to implement a fiscal stimulus in order to manage a deep recession it had to make one of two mistakes. The stimulus could be too little, forcing the government to try again, or the stimulus could be too big. The chance they would get it exactly right was zero. In the end, Labor made the right mistake. In retrospect, it is obvious they did spend too much. I think the stronger criticism is that the design of their schemes was faulty and once it became clear the economic damage was not as great as feared, Labor should have wound back the spending, particularly on schools halls, the biggest single item.[44]

The principal of Deloitte Access Economics, Chris Richardson, refers to both the scale and the timing: 'I think the February package was too big. About $20 billion would have been more appropriate. The reason we spent too much was because too much of the spending came too late.'[45] In this sense it fell outside the idea of emergency stimulus. Chief of the Macroeconomics consultancy, Stephen Anthony, said:

Wayne Swan deserves credit but it was too much. A fiscal stimulus is about the 'here and now'. It should be reviewed according to the progress of the economy. No hindsight is required to say that when the danger had passed by late 2009 they should have scrapped whatever stimulus was still built into the forward estimates. That would have reduced the stimulus by half and cut the debt level by up to $40 billion, a significant figure.[46]

Former Reserve Bank board member Warwick McKibbin, an internationally recognised economist, said Australia did not face the financial problems of the United States and United Kingdom, that it was in a strong position to meet the challenge, that its stimulus should be 'less than the world average' and certainly less than the 2 per cent of GDP recommended by the IMF. To be precise McKibbin said the stimulus was 'twice as large as required'.

Asked whether the stimulus ran on for too long, Henry was cautious. 'It's a hard call, possibly,' he said. 'But are we talking six months or twelve months? I don't know. In the situation of late 2008 and early 2009, with the IMF urging such a strong stimulus, it would have been an extraordinary exercise of judgement to have designed the package so it ended six or twelve months earlier and to have come through without a recession.'[47]

The February stimulus was a bridge too far for the Coalition. Under Turnbull's leadership it offered a competing story. 'We in the Coalition do not reject the need for a stimulus at this time,' Turnbull said. 'But our judgement is that $42 billion is too much right now. A more appropriate stimulus would be in the order of between $15 billion and $20 billion dollars.' Turnbull wanted to bring forward the announced tax cuts. He called Rudd the most reckless spender since Whitlam.

The shadow cabinet was initially divided. 'I don't think anyone felt it was a great idea,' Turnbull said. 'But people like Minchin and Abetz took the pragmatic view we shouldn't stand between a bucket of money and the Australian public.'[48] Hockey was opposed. Julie Bishop begged Turnbull not to support it. Within the day, the issue was settled. In the party-room debate Costello strongly opposed the package, a critical pointer for Turnbull.

There were risks for the Coalition. Rudd was offering the biggest gravy train in history, with benefits for business, consumers, unions, premiers, and the education and green lobbies. Turnbull said:

> When this ended in tears, as we believed it would, we would
> be the party left with economic credibility. We opposed not just
> the size of the stimulus but programs like school halls and pink
> batts. The biggest political mistake Labor made was not having a
> co-contribution with the pink batts scheme.

'I think it was a benchmark moment,' Turnbull said. The Liberals signed
up to campaign on Labor's deficit, debt and waste at the 2010 election.
It became their position for the rest of the Rudd–Gillard era and was
pivotal to Labor's eventual destruction. 'In the end,' said Turnbull, 'they
looked ridiculous, even pretending the NBN was part of the stimulus.'

But Rudd and Swan were far from finished. Swan enshrined the
May 2009 budget as a project in nation-building with a $22 billion
infrastructure package for new investments in roads, rail, ports and
education. The biggest cash item was a huge pension payoff—an increase
in pensions and related reforms worth a hefty $14 billion across the forward
estimates. The budget was the proof: Labor now had a spending disease.

The budget papers announced in a thunderous declaration: 'A recession in Australia has become inevitable with unavoidable consequences
for Australian jobs.' The day after the budget, Swan said: 'Before we come
through, more Australians will have lost their jobs. More small businesses
will have gone under. Many older employees will have to postpone
retirement. It will be years before Australians are as well off as they were
two years ago.'[49]

The 2009–10 budget deficit was revised upwards yet again, with a
forecast of $57.6 billion or 4.9 per cent of the GDP. A year earlier this
forecast had been for a $20 billion surplus. The nation was deep in the
red. It would not emerge from the red during the six years of ALP government and Labor would never deliver a budget surplus.

The Opposition was handed a gift—large budget deficits across
the forward estimates. The Howard–Costello hefty surplus was gone.
Australia had entered a new deficit world though its debt position was
low compared with the OECD nations and incurring debt to avert
recession is a rational and responsible move. Turnbull asked: 'How many
years, how many decades will it take us to pay off hundreds of billions of
dollars of Rudd Labor debt?'

Post-budget, Rudd and Swan looked scared. Swan left the deficit
number out of his budget speech. Rudd and Swan declined to attach
the words 'dollars' and 'billions' to either the deficit or new debt figures
in their public comments. They looked like frightened children; it was a

shocking example of Labor defensive spin. Meanwhile Rudd's old enemy, Mark Latham, remarked that with cash, tax cuts, pension rises, incentives for business, school infrastructure, investments in clean energy, roads and rail, 'most Australians are having a happy recession'.

The economy had shrunk in the December quarter of 2008. But on 3 June 2009, three weeks after the budget, Rudd and Swan unveiled the March quarter figure of 0.4 per cent growth. Australia had avoided the classic measure of recession. It was the euphoria moment.

Rudd and Swan worked to repress their grins. Swan said his reaction was 'enormous relief'. He said later: 'I regarded the publication of those accounts as the most significant period in my treasuryship.'[50] Rudd said it was the best day of his prime ministership. The Queensland boys had got home. 'We are not out of the woods yet,' Rudd repeatedly cautioned. Yet the positive March quarter was pivotal. From this moment 'confidence rebounded sharply and kept rising'.[51] By late 2009 it was apparent the economy had taken only a mild hit, with unemployment peaking at 5.8 per cent.

'I believe we did get the political credit,' Swan said of the GFC. 'I think people felt we got the response right and that's why we got re-elected. People understood that Australia had done better than virtually any other country in the world. We had avoided mass unemployment.'[52] Yet Swan knew political damage had been done. He admitted that debt and deficits were 'political poison', saying: 'The counter factual—what would have happened if we hadn't done this—wasn't obvious to people.'[53]

Rudd said he felt there was 'grudging acceptance' from the public that this was a 'reasonable achievement' but that over time people 'just said well thanks very much, what's next?' Rudd drew a nexus between Australia's survival in the GFC and being ditched as prime minister. How could he not? Rudd must have asked himself a thousand times: How dumb was Labor to execute the leader who delivered its re-election platform? Rudd told the author his removal undermined Labor's ability to run on its record. There is much validity in his claim that 'Labor trashed the opportunity to campaign on having saved the national economy' and that this was 'a grave strategic error' for the 2010 election.[54]

Interviewed in 2014 former Finance Minister Lindsay Tanner offered two messages: Labor's response to the GFC was overwhelmingly correct but the party must grasp that fiscal responsibility determines political survival. On the fiscal stimulus, Tanner said: 'As Finance Minister I was nervous initially about spending anything. But I accepted the case for a very big stimulus and what influenced me was Ken Henry's support. On the quantum, that debate will last forever and there will be no resolution to it. The bank guarantee was critical. If we had not done this, one bank would have been in trouble by the Monday.' But Tanner has a deeper message. 'The lesson for Labor is that fiscal rigour is everything,' he said. 'Our modern history shows, time after time, when Labor is hard headed on fiscal management it will be given a licence to govern. The election defeat of 2013 had multiple causes. Yet of all the issues, including leadership dissension, it was the Opposition's debt and deficit message that was the foundation for its success.'

Why did Australia avert recession when many other advanced nations succumbed? First, the local stimulus was large by world standards, only behind China and South Korea. Australia was able to respond strongly because its fiscal position was sound and the Reserve Bank had plenty of scope to cut interest rates. Second, the stimulus was implemented very fast by world standards. Third, Australia's financial and banking system was not impaired. Fourth, the economy had momentum from the terms-of-trade boom. These factors together represented a situation different from virtually every other advanced economy.

On Henry's advice, Rudd and Swan locked in an exit strategy. Aware that financial confidence in Australia depended upon them offering a credible 'return-to-surplus' path, Swan projected a surplus in 2015–16. The stimulus was temporary: it phased out across the forward estimates. Labor pledged that, as the economy recovered, it would limit spending to 2 per cent a year in real terms.

Swan was proud: 'We put our exit plan in the announcement. We are the one country that did that.'[55] The cynics joked: maybe Rudd planned to return as a fiscal conservative. Then Swan delivered one of his most famous lines: 'We took a decision: to be Keynesians on the way down and then Keynesians on the way up.' Having spent big in the down-turn, Labor's pledge was to impose discipline in the recovery. It sounded brilliant.

There was only one problem. Swan didn't do it. Neither Swan nor Gillard were Keynesians 'on the way up'. It was easy to say but hard to do. Labor never kicked its spending habits from fighting the GFC. Its most grievous economic policy mistake came in its second term, under Gillard, when Labor lacked the mettle to regain the budget surplus it had sacrificed in order to deny the recession.

CHAPTER 12

BLUNDER AT THE BORDERS

In October 2009, Labor's Immigration Minister, Chris Evans, was at Bunbury in Western Australia for a weekend soccer tournament for his eleven year old when he received a call on his mobile phone from Rudd's office chief, Alister Jordan. He was told Rudd had done a deal with Indonesian President Susilo Bambang Yudhoyono to stop seventy-eight Sri Lankan asylum seekers from coming to Australia. They would be put on an Australian vessel instead and sent to Indonesia. It was the start of the *Oceanic Viking* fiasco that sent alarm waves through the cabinet about Rudd's chaotic style and poor judgement.

'I wasn't being asked for my view,' Chris Evans said. 'I was being told. The decision had been taken. Rudd had done the deal with SBY.' Neither the minister nor his department was consulted. Evans immediately rang his departmental head, Andrew Medcalfe, and briefed him. 'Minister, they won't get off the boat,' Medcalfe told him.[1] This was the start and end of the *Oceanic Viking* story.

Rudd thought he was being clever and tough. In fact, his decision was foolish. Medcalfe, experienced in these issues since the *Tampa*, could have told him the move would fail. Evans said his conversation with Medcalfe offered 'the best insight' into the *Oceanic Viking* saga. With the government near its two-year mark, this crisis would send Labor's polling numbers into a spiral.

Medcalfe was appalled by the scale of the blunder. 'This was rule 101 when it came to boat people,' he told colleagues. 'You didn't put people on a ship unless you had a cast-iron agreement to get them off. And it wasn't followed. Rudd calling SBY wasn't enough. Thinking this would suffice was just naïve.'

The humiliation of the Rudd Government would last nearly four weeks. Indonesia played Australia for a bunch of fools. It was cruel to watch. While the asylum seekers had refused to leave the Australian Customs vessel the *Oceanic Viking* when it reached Indonesia, the

Indonesian authorities were obstructionist, even hostile, and had no intention of removing them. Rudd declined to force the issue. The Sri Lankans threatened self-harm and suicide unless sent to Australia.

The project exposed Rudd as a phoney tough. He wanted to prove he was a robust border protectionist to combat the upsurge in boats. But the *Oceanic Viking* became the symbol of an asylum seeker policy now unravelling. Senior ministers saw the crisis as an emerging nightmare: Labor was trapped between its once proud softer asylum seeker policy and an increase in boats shattering its border-protection credibility.

The other three members of the 'gang of four'—Gillard, Swan and Tanner—saw this event as decisive evidence of Rudd's flaws as prime minister. 'It moved the asylum seeker issue from a drumbeat in the background to being flashpoint centre stage,' Gillard said. 'It became emblematic of the lost-control-of-the-borders test, the Howard test. As Medcalfe said, they wouldn't get off the ship, they had our boat. We had lost control of our own boat. It happened because Kevin decided it and ordered it without proper consultation.'[2]

Gillard called the four-week deadlock in the Indonesian port an 'ongoing catastrophe'. Years later she would recount the Evans–Medcalfe story as Labor folklore. Tanner believed the *Oceanic Viking* was a significant moment in Rudd's decline. He felt it exposed Rudd as weak and uncertain: he believed Rudd had to intervene to get people off the boat. For Swan, the issue confirmed his doubts about Rudd: 'The *Oceanic Viking* was a thundering disaster. He went off doing mad stuff on his own, always wanting to direct operations, summoning the military and police and giving direct instructions.'[3]

The *Oceanic Viking* was the start of a four-year rolling public policy failure for Labor on boat arrivals that ended only in its 2013 election loss. It saw policy twists and turns, growing public disenchantment, agitation inside the government, the collapse of border protection, polarisation in the Parliament, the intervention of the High Court, the savaging of the reputation of Rudd and Gillard and, after four years of self-laceration, the abandonment by Labor of its previous principles and its subjugation to offshore processing and denial of residency to boat arrivals, a harsher stance than adopted by Howard in 2001.

Like no other issue in half a century, border-protection policy captured the conflict between Labor's morally superior self-image and its desperation to appease public opinion for votes. From the *Tampa* in 2001 to its election victory in 2007, Labor engaged in a cycle of compromises trying to satisfy both its conscience and its political needs. When the crunch came in office, it was psychologically unprepared. In the end, in 2013, facing 3000 boat arrivals a month, it threw overboard most of its principles to embrace border protection as an essential commitment for an Australian government.

This process saw many politicians revise their views. Nobody displayed more fickleness and hypocrisy than Rudd. He began by invoking Christian principles to attack Howard's policy, exalted in superior compassion as he dismantled Howard's framework, obfuscated as the boats returned, denied on the floor of Parliament the special deal Labor authorised for the *Oceanic Viking* asylum seekers, invoked humanitarian principles against the Gillard forces on the eve of his removal and then, upon returning as prime minister, completely reversed his previous stance.

In truth, Rudd was two-faced from the start. Only forty-eight hours before the 2007 election, with Labor pledged to soften Howard's policy, Rudd, in an interview with the *Australian*, declared 'you'd turn them back' when asked how he would combat any resurgence of boats. Rudd said he believed in 'orderly migration' enforced by deterrence.[4] The author and Dennis Shanahan, who conducted the joint interview on Rudd's plane, had no doubt he was sending a message on election eve. Evans branded Rudd's comments 'a bolt from the blue'.[5] Rudd was Mr Tough.

He had earlier sent a different message. In late 2006, when campaigning for the ALP leadership, Rudd wrote an article for *The Monthly* titled 'Faith in Politics', declaring his hero was the German theologian and pastor Dietrich Bonhoeffer, hanged by the Nazis at the end of the war, whose life exemplified the need to speak 'truth to the state'. According to Rudd, Bonhoeffer's message was that Christianity must side with the oppressed. Rudd said: 'The parable of the Good Samaritan is but one of many which deal with the matter of how we should respond to a vulnerable stranger.' This is why, he argued, Howard's so-called 'Pacific Solution' and excision of the mainland from the Migration Zone 'should be the cause of great ethical concern to all Christian churches'. At this stage Rudd was Mr Compassion.[6]

To be fair, it was a Labor problem, not just a Rudd problem. Rudd won office in 2007 on a compromise Labor platform—Labor would end the Pacific Solution, abolish Temporary Protection Visas (TPVs) and limit the length of detention, yet it would keep detention, retain excisions from the migration zone that restricted judicial review and, overall, protect the borders. It was a 'fair weather' policy.

The aim was to solve Labor's internal problem, not address Australia's dilemma. It appeased the party's conscience and pretended to champion border protection. It was a house of straw and, in office when the boats returned, it fell apart.

For Evans, making Howard's policy less repressive was a personal mission. A left-wing realist, he moved with purpose and relish. The cabinet was unanimous in backing him. 'When we came into government people were tired of Howard's policies, tired of seeing refuges self-harm and worried about the punitive nature of the system,' Evans said.[7]

The reality was different. The rift in Australian politics over asylum seeker boats was disguised but unresolved. As ever, it was driven by the rate of boat arrivals. The boats had virtually stopped and this had two contradictory consequences. It left the Coalition convinced that offshore processing, TPVs and detention were a proven formula for halting the boats—yet it encouraged the Rudd Government into the convenient delusion that the situation had changed and Labor's softer policy was viable.

The subsequent political crisis under Labor had its origins in Australia's identity as a nation. The Australian mind was shaped by geography—by water, ocean, bush and desert. Being an island gave Australia a special ability to protect its borders. This was instrumental in shaping the nature of Australian nationalism and the first major law of the national Parliament—the White Australia policy based on the idea of racial sanctuary. When Australia underwent a transformation to become a society of mass immigration and then multiculturalism, the idea of border protection remained. The distinctive Australian approach to immigration was based on a legal intake and defined labour-market entry criteria (a program serving the national interest), resistance to illegal entry and a generous offshore refugee program that rarely raised any controversy. (The government makes a distinction between 'offshore resettlement' refugees and 'onshore protection' refugees, the former being people not already in Australia, who have been identified as refugees by the United Nations and who typically come from refugee camps around the globe, and the latter being people who are found to be refugees after arriving in Australia seeking asylum.)

The resurgence in the late 1990s of asylum seeker boats became a humanitarian, political and legal dispute. It was also an ideological contest—between the rights of asylum seekers under international law and the right of Australia as a constitutional democracy with a large-scale migrant program to decide who was allowed entry and given residence. In this contest the Coalition stood for border protection while Labor, literally, could not make up its mind and stood for compromise. But compromise was not a tenable position once the boats were running.

The Howard Government had commissioned a new $400 million detention facility on Christmas Island. When Medcalfe showed the facility to Evans he was distinctly unimpressed. 'We'll never use it,' Evans said dismissively. 'Well, it's ready and fit for purpose,' a defensive Medcalfe said. Labor's distaste for Howard's policy and his 'white elephant' was palpable.

The Immigration Department was in retreat, its standing battered and its integrity in tatters. The department's wrongful decisions and mistreatment of individuals in two infamous cases—Cornelia Rau and Vivian Alverez Solon—produced an inquiry by former Australian Federal Police chief, Mick Palmer, apologies to the women from Howard and removal of the department's senior officers. The Palmer Report attacked the department's culture and the operations of the detention system. Medcalfe was appointed to clean up the mess.

A career public servant, Medcalfe had been an immigration official and then worked in senior positions in the Department of the Prime Minister and Cabinet. He knew the Immigration Department had faced the gravest crisis in its history and had come to the brink of a Royal Commission into its performance. Medcalfe understood that Evans, unsurprisingly, was suspicious of a discredited department. This background is critical to the pivotal question arising from Rudd's policy: Did the Immigration Department warn Labor of the consequences, namely, that a softer policy might promote the flow of boats by weakening the disincentives among pull factors? Was Labor warned?

'We never said, "Don't do this",' Medcalfe told colleagues. 'If we had, we would have been shown the door.' The department had lost its authority to offer such advice to an incoming government. How would such advice have been seen? It was a bridge too far to think a discredited department could have offered a credible critique against a new Labor government pledged to moderate Howard's policy on the basis of its election mandate.

Labor now belatedly took its revenge against Howard. It made three decisions: it closed offshore processing at Nauru and Manus Island, it abolished TPVs and it sought to improve detention conditions and lessen their duration. Evans denounced TPVs as the symbol of Howard's 'punishment of those found to be owed our protection'. Detention was to be limited to security, health and identity checks on arrival. This wound back not just Howard's policy but that of the Keating Government.

The Rudd Government wore its humanity on its sleeve. Conditions in detention henceforth would uphold 'the inherent dignity of the human person'. Cabinet endorsed these exact words and Labor warmed its soul.

There was fervour in the denunciations Evans laid against Howard. With virtually no boats on the water in 2008 there was little limit to Labor's self-righteousness. Evans said the Rudd Government believed that 'strong border security and humane and risk-based detention are not incompatible'.[8] The wheel had turned: the absence of boats made punitive detention into a political negative. Yet Evans was measured in his moderation. Although the Pacific Solution was abandoned, Labor had Christmas Island, and mandatory detention was retained as a system. 'I was under enormous pressure from the Left to end mandatory detention and I didn't,' Evans said in 2013. Excision of offshore islands remained to limit rights of asylum seekers who arrived there. 'Our approach was to remove the punitive aspects of Howard's policy,' Evans said. 'But Labor still believed in a strong border security regime.'[9]

The refugee lobby gave Labor two cheers and the Coalition hardly tried to defend Howard's system. Evans was more a realist than later depicted. In a speech given in 2008, he said, 'We will still see people coming to this country unauthorised, either by boat or by plane.'[10] He felt people movement was a permanent twenty-first–century condition.

Evans knew the risk: if the boats returned, the blame would be sheeted home to Labor. 'It's true that higher numbers will put our system under pressure but I think our policy changes are sustainable,' he said in August 2008.[11] It was a declaration of hope but it proved to be wrong.

As minister, Evans was proud of the changes he made and he never revised that view. 'I make no apology,' he said after Labor lost office. 'I don't retreat from what we did.' He refused to endorse the harsher Rudd policies after Rudd's return as prime minister in mid-2013.[12]

In the endless debate about whether push or pull factors drove the boats, Labor prioritised push factors. In November 2009, Rudd said that Australia, Europe, America and South-East Asia were 'dealing with the same global push factors'.[13] However, given the sophistication of the smugglers and their knowledge of Australian events, it was false to pretend pull factors had no role. In truth, Labor's new policies encouraged more boats like a magnet.

The turning point came in 2009 when sixty-one boats arrived with 2850 people, though this was a mere prelude to almost 7000 arrivals in 2010 when destabilisation in Afghanistan, Sri Lanka and Iraq were the originating forces. In the 2009–10 budget Labor announced a $654 million 'whole of government' strategy to combat people smuggling. Christmas Island had capacity for 800 people and surge capacity for 1200. Labor was upgrading Villawood in Sydney, the largest centre on the mainland.

The higher boat arrivals alarmed yet paralysed the government. Rudd was anxious on two fronts—to keep asylum seekers detained on Christmas Island, not the mainland, and to achieve better regional cooperation to stem the arrivals. The upshot was policy chaos and political drama.

Labor, having mocked the Christmas Island centre, was now reluctant to use anything else. Security on Christmas Island was being degraded. Looking back, Chris Evans said: 'It was difficult for the government politically to say that numbers had reached a point where Christmas Island wasn't coping.' He said Rudd was 'reluctant' to face this reality.[14] With the department responsible for detention, Medcalfe was confronting a crisis. It flowed from the 'iron rule' laid down by Rudd's office: nobody was to be brought to the mainland.

The department told Evans the situation was untenable. Medcalfe pushed for Baxter to be re-opened but got nowhere because its history was too toxic and it was being utilised by the Department of Defence. Convinced Rudd and his office were in complete denial, Medcalfe ordered his department to ensure that everything on this issue be written down, notably advice to ministers. Fearing deaths, injury or security breakdowns, Medcalfe wanted the department to have proof of its repeated warnings so it would have political and legal protection. As the deadlock continued, Evans became frustrated and angry. The pushback from Rudd's office was relentless. Meetings were scheduled and then cancelled.

Finally, in autumn 2010 the issue was scheduled for an SPBC meeting in Sydney. Evans was bringing forward a cabinet submission. Rudd was absent because of his schedule of hospital visits and Gillard was in the chair.

About thirty minutes before the meeting, Evans, Medcalfe and Rudd's adviser Phil Green had a terse exchange in a side room. An angry Evans unloaded his frustrations. He said the government had a responsibility to address the issue and resolve it. Further delay would be irresponsible and intolerable. Medcalfe rammed the message home. 'This is completely unacceptable,' he said. 'The situation is dangerous. People are at serious risk, some might die. I am not interested in the politics. You will have to take responsibility for what happens because I won't.' Medcalfe felt the issue had reached breaking point.

Gillard said:

> Kevin had given a commitment that if you came unauthorised and ended up at Christmas Island you would not get to the mainland. I had instructions through Alister Jordan from Kevin that Chris

Evans would arrive and seek permission for people to be transferred
to a mainland detention centre. I was told this should be resisted at
all costs because it would breach what Kevin had said.[15]

Evans said: 'The prime minister's office had been asking me to try to
contain arrivals on Christmas Island. My submission argued that logisti-
cally this was no longer possible. We could no longer accommodate the
numbers. My submission went to the risks in just allowing numbers to
grow.'[16] It would become a classic case of Gillard having to resolve the
deadlock—the type of situation that highlighted her skills.

Evans came into the room and presented his submission. 'He made
this impassioned plea,' said Gillard, 'that people had to be moved, that he
couldn't predict what would happen if they weren't moved … riots, fires,
people could die, all the rest of it. I looked at his face [and thought] Evans
is going to cry. He was at absolute breaking point.'[17] Wayne Swan was
there—he knew the instructions. Gillard looked at Swan, then passed him
a note saying, 'He is going to cry.' And Swan wrote under it, 'He is going to
resign, give him what he wants.'

Gillard had the same view. She gave instructions in front of all the
officials and asked them to minute it: the Minister for Immigration had full
authority to implement what he believed was the best approach to manage
pressures at Christmas Island. Gillard had overruled Rudd.

'Did you see him, Al?' was her comment to Jordan. 'He is broken. This
is breaking him.' Gillard said Jordan accepted the decision.[18] He wasn't
happy, though, because he was the one who had to tell Rudd.

Interviewed for this book, Evans said: 'I'm not a dramatic type. But
the situation was no longer tenable. Would I have resigned? No.' Yet he
said the stakes were 'high' and he felt 'very strongly' about the issue.[19]
Eventually all the mainland detention centres would be filled to excess as
well. The saga revealed the extent to which Rudd would push situations
to protect his own standing.

Rudd's main boats strategy in 2009 focused on the region, notably Indonesia. By mid-2009 Evans had visited Jakarta four times. Rudd
scaled upwards Australia's effort and resorted to personal diplomacy
with President Yudhoyono. In October 2009, Rudd said he was working towards a 'new framework' with Yudhoyono and that the President
'is facing a large new inflow himself, therefore he's looking to us to help
with his problems as well'. Disrupting the smugglers before they put to
sea became a priority for Australian intelligence operations and Australian
Federal Police in cooperation with Indonesian authorities. Despite media

talk of a so-called Indonesian Solution there was a tension in political relations that came to a head over the *Oceanic Viking*.

On 18 October, Indonesia asked for Australian assistance following distress calls from a vessel just 20 nautical miles from an island off South Sumatra. Headed for Christmas Island but in Indonesian waters, the boat was sabotaged to force HMAS *Armidale* to take on board the seventy-eight Sri Lankan asylum seekers and refugees. In Jakarta for the inauguration of the President, Rudd pursued the issue with Yudhoyono, who gave in-principle agreement for Indonesia to accept the people, who had been transferred to the *Oceanic Viking*.

A farcical journey ensued, with Indonesia diverting the vessel from the nearby port of Merak in west Java to another port where the asylum seekers were to be disembarked and transported to an Australian-funded detention centre, Tanjung Pinang, on the island of Bintan near Singapore. This centre suffered from inadequate infrastructure, water and electricity and the Sri Lankans began a hunger strike in protest at not being allowed to enter Australia.

The Rudd–Yudhoyono deal was met with antagonism across most of Indonesia's system. Local Indonesian officials were hostile to acting at Australia's behest; the provincial governor and other Indonesian authorities refused to cooperate and the Indonesian police refused to forcibly remove the Sri Lankans, saying this was Australia's task. The upshot was a prolonged stalemate off Bintan Island. A Foreign Ministry spokesman said: 'These people don't want to be helped, so the ball's now back in Australia's court. They don't want to come to Indonesia.'[20] Foreign Minister Natalegawa said if the people refused to budge then Australia must take that reality into account.

Urgent talks were undertaken at a formal and informal level to resolve the deadlock while the Sri Lankans refused to contemplate going into detention in Indonesia. Senior immigration officials felt that Australia was 'used and then abused by Indonesia'. The humiliating alternative for Rudd was to order the *Oceanic Viking* to take the Sri Lankans to Christmas Island. That would become an iconic declaration of his weakness. 'In effect, the Indonesians told us we'd have to remove the *Oceanic Viking* if we couldn't talk the people into coming ashore,' Evans said.[21] Australian intelligence had voice surveillance on the boat. 'They were talking about a mass suicide,' Gillard said. 'It was awful.'[22]

The tragedy highlighted the ugly reality of the asylum seeker issue. People coming by boat to Australia originated outside the South-East Asian region, travelled half way around the world, paid substantial monies to an illegal people-smuggling industry, passed through several nations during their transit and destroyed their documents before arrival as part of a chaotic system designed to realise Australia as the destination. Some boat people were genuine refugees; others were economic migrants. The phenomenon was based on the idea of country self-selection, a right not available under the Refugee Convention.

In early November, during the *Oceanic Viking* crisis, there was a one-off or rogue Newspoll showing Labor's massive two-party-preferred lead cut from eighteen points to just four points. It was an omen. While that lead was re-established in mid-November, by early 2010 the one-off Newspoll began to look the norm. The boats crisis was a prominent factor in Labor's polling shakeout.

Evans chaired a sub-committee of the National Security Committee of cabinet to oversee the crisis. Process began to deteriorate. Sometimes Jordan was sitting in the Prime Minister's chair giving instructions that began with the words: 'The Prime Minister wants …' Evans said: 'Rudd never came to any of the meetings. He sent Alister Jordan. The leadership group didn't meet. I either dealt with Alister or I went through Julia if I needed to get something.'[23] Prominent Australian refugee advocate Paris Aristotle was flown to Indonesia to act as an intermediary and played a decisive role in persuading the Sri Lankans while Australian diplomats offered them generous terms in writing. Finally, they agreed to disembark.

The deal was authorised by the cabinet sub-committee. The Sri Lankans had won a preferential deal. Any person already found to be a refugee would be resettled in four to six weeks; any person already registered with the UNHCR would be resettled within twelve weeks; any person not yet registered and found to be a refugee would be resettled in twelve weeks. These timetables were far in advance of normal delays in Indonesia, typically running beyond twelve months. Evans said Australia would get 'the larger proportion' of refugees as third-country settlement was worked out. Canada would also become a settlement point.

Under fierce attack from Turnbull, Rudd denied point-blank that the Sri Lankans got preferential treatment. 'Absolutely not,' he told 3AW's Neil Mitchell in response to this proposition.[24] He made the same denial in Parliament. Rudd's claim was false. The *Oceanic Viking* people had to be separated from others after disembarkation because of resentment at their favourable treatment. Everyone involved from Australia, Indonesia and Canada knew it was a special deal. A spokesman for the Indonesian Foreign Ministry said: 'If it was normal it would take years for the Sri Lankans to be resettled in third countries.'

Rudd told Parliament he was unaware of the terms of the offer and was not involved in its approval. At its kindest, this was disingenuous. The offer was authorised by a cabinet sub-committee of his government chaired by Evans, with Foreign Minister Stephen Smith a participant.[25] Rudd wanted a solution but he also wanted clean hands.

Rudd's office asked Medcalfe to write a letter covering the terms of the deal. Under attack in Parliament Rudd tabled the letter, claiming it showed that 'these are not preferential arrangements'. The letter did not verify Rudd's claims. Medcalfe was prudent enough to alter the draft he was given. Gillard said: 'I wasn't involved in this personally but it is obvious to anybody who looks at it, as a government we did a deal to get them off the boat. They got a favourable deal.'[26]

The month-long saga damaged the Rudd Government publicly and internally. Rudd's initial intervention was flawed, the refusal of the Sri Lankans to disembark was highly predictable and Rudd exposed his government to Indonesian resentment and Sri Lankan brinkmanship. With his government forced into a preferential deal, he tried to deny the obvious to protect his personal image. Senior ministers were dismayed by his poor judgement and dissembling. Rudd only succeeded in elevating to new heights public worry about his boat people policy.

The story is a classic case of Labor being mugged by reality. The politics are vicious. When there are no boat arrivals the politics are driven by human rights concerns; when the boats are running they are dominated by border protection.

Should Evans have softened Howard's policy in the first place? He had no choice. Labor was always going to implement its alternative to Howard; it was a political imperative.

By 2010 the debacle had deepened, with 134 boats containing 6879 people arriving in Australian waters. Gillard would inherit this problem from Rudd when she became prime minister, with the tempo driven by global and regional events. But Labor was finally forced to another concession: recognition that Australian policy mattered and, if imposed with willpower, could halt boat flows. Interviewed for this book, Evans said:

> I think our responses were proving to be ineffective. We vastly increased AFP resources in Indonesia. We used the security agencies. But despite these efforts we were fighting a losing battle against increased numbers. There are huge barriers to success in Indonesia that include corruption but also include the fact that the police and army are paid so little. There's evidence elements

of the Indonesian army and police have on occasions facilitated or
organised boat departures.[27]

Ironically it was during the *Oceanic Viking* saga that Rudd delivered
one of his defining speeches as prime minister—his declaration of faith
in a 'big Australia' at the October 2009 Business Council of Australia
annual dinner. It was a courageous speech and a statement of vision.
Rudd nominated three reasons for a big Australia: national security, long-
term prosperity and 'enhancing our role in the region and the world'.

The backdrop, however, had been his attendance a few weeks earlier
at the Pittsburgh heads of government meeting that enshrined the G-20 as
the world's main economic decision-making body. As Rudd savoured this
diplomatic triumph over celebratory drinks with Australian journalists that
night, he reflected on how he had looked about the room that afternoon
and decided that fundamental to the future of Australia, now sitting for
the first time in the big league, was the need to expand its population base.

Projecting current trends, Rudd nominated 35 million people by
mid-century as a tenable concept. 'The century ahead stands to be the
greatest century of economic growth and nation building in Australia's
history,' Rudd said in his BCA speech. He spoke with passion, yet the
vision was challenging: 'Most of these 35 million people will live in our
cities. By 2049, Sydney and Melbourne will each hold almost 7 million
people, adding around 3 million to their current populations. Brisbane
will more than double in size to reach 4 million. Perth will reach almost
3.5 million.' He wanted a greater role for the national government in
urban planning.

With the borders under assault, the speech was a bolt from the blue.
It was brave and valid, yet it revealed Rudd's complete inability to devise
effective strategies for long-run policy change. This speech invited a backlash, and the backlash came. Making declarations to business about a 'big
Australia' was the last way to bolster public support for immigration.

The fact is that Rudd, despite the dramas since 2001, was arrogant
and ignorant about the politics of people movement to Australia. He had
a model to follow: it was staring him in the face. It was the system created,
by trial and error, under John Howard. Yet Rudd's intellectual hubris
meant that he was never interested.

By the time of Howard's 2007 defeat there was a new unwritten law
of politics—a successful prime minister must master people-movement
policy. Howard's legacy was enshrined: safe borders and strong immigration
went together. It was obvious—yet most of the media and the ALP shut

their minds to the story. Under Howard, border protection came from the *Tampa* crisis and ambitious immigration came from the economic growth cycle, with its tightening of the labour market. In Howard's final year the figures were remarkable: boat arrivals were close to zero and net overseas migration was 277 300, probably the highest such annual figure in Australia's history to that point. It was a threefold increase since Howard's first year in office. By 2007, 25 per cent of Australia's population was born overseas, compared with 9 per cent for the United States, the Australian figure being nearly double that of most European nations testifying to its migrant profile.[28]

Howard's border-protection stance, dramatised by the *Tampa*, was depicted as ruthless and xenophobic. The Labor Party and the media were fixated by his destruction of the boat trade. They paid virtually no attention to the increase, year by year, in the immigration intake to the point where more Asians, Muslims and people of different cultures settled in Australia under Howard than under any previous Australian prime minister. Long after Howard's departure this statement of fact provokes widespread and emotional disbelief. Such is the power of the exclusionist image that Howard cultivated. He began by cutting the immigration intake, fretted about the divisive potential of multiculturalism and never let the phrase 'a Big Australia' pass his lips. Howard would have found the label unwise and pretentious.

'Howard's profile as a strong border protectionist purchased him political immunity on immigration,' said Peter Shergold, who headed the prime minister's department under Howard. 'The consequence of *Tampa* was important—it put Howard in a much safer political position for a significant expansion of immigration. Howard delivered far higher immigration with little political blowback. It is a major and unrecognised achievement.'[29]

It is also an enduring point of confusion in the politics of immigration. The foundation of Australia's immigration program, from the 1940s onwards, was government control of an authorised intake in the national interest. Settlement was a gift extended to migrants on behalf of the Australian people. Protection of the borders was not an act of hostility towards immigrants. On the contrary, safe borders went hand in hand with a robust immigration intake while weak borders that promoted illegal arrivals only doomed public confidence in immigration.

In the end, Rudd grasped the obvious.

He had felt he had nothing to learn from Howard. In truth, Rudd was far too slow in realising the transformation of people-movement policy post-2001. Howard had managed the politics skilfully and achieved practical results. When Rudd came to office in 2007 he had a different approach. He denied Howard's tough line on border protection and his stealth on a large immigration intake.

Under Rudd, Labor succumbed to moral vanity and then a panicked retreat on asylum seekers. It displayed courage on immigration yet Rudd's naïve declarations fuelled a backlash. Within just two and a half years as prime minister, Rudd mismanaged the politics of people movement to Australia. This failure, which was largely self-inflicted, was basic to the ruin of the ALP government.

CHAPTER 13

LABOR'S NEW CAUSE

Kevin Rudd was Whitlamesque in his speed. Within hours of being sworn in on 3 December 2007, he attended his first Executive Council meeting with Governor-General Michael Jeffery to give effect to Kyoto ratification. That afternoon, when Australian official Howard Bamsey announced the change to the United Nations Climate Change Conference in Bali, he was interrupted for nearly a full minute by applause. Rudd travelled to Bali the next week as prophet of a new Australia—the 'pariah nation' of the Howard era had recanted its sins.

Bamsey described the mood:

> At Bali, Rudd is a global figure instantly. He surprises people with the extent to which he understands climate change issues. The Secretary-General [Ban Ki-Moon] and his office immediately identified Rudd as somebody, almost more than any other leader, who understood the politics, economics and social dimensions of climate change. At Bali and from then on, people would come to me and say, 'What's Kevin Rudd's view about this or that?' The Secretary-General saw Rudd as a critical global figure right through to Copenhagen. He was seen as a star.[1]

The idea that climate change, more than any other issue, might destroy Rudd's leadership fell outside the wildest imagination. A team of Labor ministers descended on Bali. In this arena Rudd rose to the moment. He came not just to transform Australia's position but to help broker the global solution. Rudd was playing his way into global diplomacy.

'Australia now stands ready to assume its responsibility,' he told representatives from 190 nations. 'Our inland rivers are dying, bushfires are becoming more ferocious and more frequent, and our unique natural wonders—the Great Barrier Reef, Kakadu, our rainforests—are now

at risk. Climate change is the defining challenge of our generation.'
Unilateral action was not enough. Only a global solution would work:
'The community of nations must reach agreement. There is no Plan B.
There is no other planet that we can escape to. We only have this one.'[2]

With such language Rudd kicked Howard into the dustbin of
history. His ambition for a major global role looked realistic.

Yet there was another Australian who excited attention at Bali—
Penny Wong. Here was a young, competent, gay, Malaysian-born woman
suddenly materialising as the Australian Minister for Climate Change
and Water. What was going on? The NGOs loved it; so did the official
delegates. At Bamsey's suggestion, Wong was asked to lead the dialogue.
She later called it 'a baptism of fire'.

Bamsey captured her impact:

> I knew she was clever. But it became a tour de force. In the closed-
> room negotiation she was a brilliant chair, extraordinary; she had
> the skill of summing up in a way that did bring people closer.
> She would move around the room picking off the troublemakers
> [and] she established at once a great relationship with the US
> negotiators. It was a universal view that she'd done a brilliant job.
> She didn't get the meeting to the outcome we wanted but she did
> better than anybody else would have.[3]

For Australia, Kyoto ratification was painless. The new Liberal
leader, Brendan Nelson, backed Kyoto ratification. The audience Rudd
addressed at Bali overwhelmingly comprised developing nations. They
had no binding targets and opposed binding targets for all countries. This
was the flawed Kyoto model whose flaws the Australian media had been
scrupulous to play down for years. It fitted with the narrative of Howard
as demon and Rudd as hero.

At Bali, Rudd repudiated pressure from the Europeans to commit
Australia to 25 to 40 per cent emissions reductions by 2020. He retaliated,
telling the Europeans he would not be 'fucking' pressured by their
tactics.[4] Australia's decisions on 2020 targets, Rudd said, would be made
after a full assessment by his government and not before. The European
demand, backed by an NGO chorus, was invited by Rudd's rhetoric.
Rudd's response was telling: when decisions went to Australia's economy,
he would be cautious. There was another lesson: Rudd would always
be outbid, at home and abroad. He could never satisfy the escalating
demands of the 'climate change push'. It was the nature of the auction.

The 25 to 40 per cent target originated with the UN's Intergovernmental Panel on Climate Change (IPCC) and reflected the scientific analysis. On the eve of Bali, IPCC chair Rajendra Pachauri, said: 'If there's no action before 2012 that's too late. What we do in the next two to three years will determine our future.'[5] This type of intimidation only guaranteed a backlash. Rudd made clear that many states 'do not necessarily accept those targets'. Amid the madcap mood of activists, Rudd went from being hero to a figure of suspicion within forty-eight hours. The lesson was that the conflict between the scientific/green lobby on one hand and the Rudd Government on the other would only escalate.

The Bali conference ended with a mandate for a post-2012 negotiation. But the chasm remained between developed and developing nations. 'We got something that was half workable,' Bamsey said of Bali. Any early resolution to meet the targets wanted by Pachauri was fantasy. The worlds of politics and science ran according to different laws.

During 2008 the Rudd Government became climate change central. Former Treasury officer Martin Parkinson, head of Wong's department, presided over much of the process while Ross Garnaut, with his support team, aspired to produce the most important document since the *Stern Review*. The 'best and the brightest' climate change talent was being mobilised in Canberra. This flurry of analysis and policy-making during 2008 saw a green paper in July, the Garnaut Report in September and a white paper in December. No other nation generated such Rudd-style activism.

Garnaut produced a report of range and insight that would be cherry-picked as convenient.[6] He said while the science was characterised by 'large uncertainties', there was no rational choice but to accept it. Unlike any other policy challenge, Garnaut said the solution had to be global. With Australia's contribution to greenhouse gas emissions being less than 1.5 per cent of the total, any idea that Australia could solve the problem was fanciful. This led directly to a 'prisoner's dilemma': each nation benefited by doing less of the mitigation and allowing others to do more. It was in each nation's interest to have the climate change problem solved, yet in no nation's interest to penalise its economy ahead of others. Australia's response, therefore, should be proportionate to the action the world takes or fails to take. Garnaut stressed the need for a new global bargain post-Kyoto.

Since 2000, emissions from developing countries had been growing eight times faster than those from developed countries and were now responsible for 85 per cent of emissions growth. Yet the Kyoto model did not require binding commitments from the nations who would become the main emitters. The origins of this absurdity, justified by fairness, lay in the underestimation of future economic growth in developing nations when the UN Framework Convention was adopted in 1992 leading to the Kyoto Protocol in 1997. By 2008 the political crisis was obvious: the Kyoto-based solution put the onus on developed nations, yet the emissions problem was caused by developing nations. Garnaut was blunt—'no global agreement would be effective unless China took on binding targets' and no international progress would be made until the United States adopted a credible long-term target.

Garnaut argued for Australian ambition. The economy had to be restructured away from carbon. He recommended that Australia's unconditional pledge without any new global agreement be a 5 per cent emissions reduction from 2000 levels by 2020. If there was an effective global agreement then Australia must aim higher. It should support the idea of an ambitious international deal to hold concentrations at 450 ppm, the estimate calculated to limit the global mean temperature rise to 2 degrees Celsius above pre-industrial levels. Australia should signal its willingness to reduce emissions by 25 per cent in the context of such an agreement, though Garnaut admitted such a compact was next to impossible.[7] He said the benefits of mitigation outweighed the costs; yet the costs came early and the benefits came later.

In summary, Garnaut was brutal. His long experience drove his warning that climate change was a 'diabolical policy problem'—'harder than any other issue of high importance that has come before our polity in living memory'. In a prophetic passage Garnaut said: 'Observation of daily debate and media discussion in Australia and elsewhere suggests that this issue might be too hard for rational policy making. It is too complex. The special interests are too numerous, powerful and intense.' The time cycles seemed too punishing—the science said radical decisions were needed now, yet the effects of such decisions fell on generations far into the future. Pricing carbon was different from other economic reforms—their aim had been to raise incomes, while this reform sought to minimise income losses from limiting emissions.

Any intelligent politician reading Garnaut's report would have been put on notice. This was a uniquely difficult political challenge—yet the message was not absorbed by Labor.

Rudd was relentlessly optimistic. In a July 2008 interview with the ABC's Kerry O'Brien, who asked whether he had the 'bottle' for the tough decisions on climate change, Rudd said: 'The resolve of the government which I lead is clear. We will be introducing an emissions trading scheme.' When O'Brien said, 'We're going to judge you on it', Rudd retorted: 'Good on you, and so you should and I know you will.'[8]

The event that could have derailed the scheme was the 2008 global financial crisis. The irony is that Garnaut handed his report to Rudd on 30 September as they were absorbing news of the biggest ever one-day loss on Wall Street. Rudd's judgement was that delaying climate change action would be a mistake. He was firm on this point. Rudd decided that if Labor retreated, it would not be rewarded for prudence but condemned as weak.

The white paper, the formal statement of government policy and another huge document of nineteen chapters, was released on 15 December 2008, with Rudd delivering a rallying speech to the National Press Club. Two conflicting ideas dominated—Labor's boldness in tackling this historic challenge and relentless caution in the scheme's design to curb the electoral backlash.

The key was the Rudd–Wong political strategy to legislate the scheme. 'I had come to the view pretty early on the Greens were going to oppose whatever we did,' Wong said in 2010. 'They locked in so hard on differentiating from us.'[9] The Greens were riding the high tide of climate change activism knowing Labor must fall short of such virtue. Labor looked to the Turnbull-led Coalition, not the Greens, as its parliamentary partner. This sensible decision would have epic consequences.

In a landmark speech, Rudd now re-defined Laborism to enshrine climate change action. Rudd presented as a figure of destiny. He said:

> Climate change is nothing less than a threat to our people, our nation and our planet. The incontestable truth of climate change is that a decision not to act is in fact an active decision—an active decision to place the next generation at grave risk. Today, this generation—our generation, stands at the crossroads of history. Do we act on the knowledge that we have in our possession? Or do we wait—knowing our grandchildren may never see the grandeur of the Great Barrier Reef or experience the wonder of the wetlands at Kakadu? I say we can wait no more. The time has come for action.

The risk to Australia, Rudd said, was rising sea levels that threatened people living along the coasts. The longer Australia delayed, the more mitigation would cost. Rudd then announced that the Carbon Pollution

Reduction Scheme (CPRS) would begin in July 2010, a fast and crazy timetable. Labor locked into Garnaut's 5 per cent below 2000 levels as a minimum unconditional target. It would go to 15 per cent in the context of a meaningful global agreement. It said an ambitious agreement based on 450 ppm was in Australia's interest but felt any such deal was 'unlikely'. Rudd called Labor's 5 to 15 per cent targets 'serious and credible'.

Within days they were trashed: the majority media orthodoxy was that Rudd's targets were a sell-out. The Greens killed Labor on this propaganda push, claiming Rudd was denying the implications of the science. The fact that, in per capita terms, Australia's targets more than matched those of Europe and President-elect Obama was barely raised in public debate. The 5 per cent target was a significant reduction from business-as-usual levels for Australia yet was largely dismissed as inadequate.[10]

Under the CPRS, permits would be needed for every tonne of gas emitted. The number of permits would be limited and tied to the cap, thereby delivering the environmental outcome. Firms would have a choice—cut emissions or buy permits for emissions, whichever was cheaper. The scheme would be limited to about a thousand companies and the initial price would be about $25 per tonne.[11]

The most dramatic break from Garnaut was the significant expansion in assistance to industry and the power generators. It became an issue of furious dispute. The assistance to trade-exposed industry facing a disadvantage with other nations that had not priced carbon would now be broader and longer. Aluminium, iron and steel production, liquefied natural gas and petrol refining were being accommodated. Coal excepted, Labor was keen to cut deals with the major companies. In addition, coal-fired generators won support as a 'strongly affected industry' worth $3.9 billion over five years via permit allocation. Generators had warned that without such help security of electricity would be threatened.

The most substantial early assistance went to households, costing $9.9 billion over the first two years. Given that the initial carbon price was estimated to increase the cost of living only 1.1 per cent—less than Howard's GST—the compensation was highly generous. About 89 per cent of low-income households would receive assistance equal to 120 per cent or more of their cost-of-living increase. About 97 per cent of middle-income households would receive some direct cash payments.

In addition, Rudd exempted fuel from the scheme for three years by promising to cut fuel taxes. This gave motorists five years to plan for higher petrol prices, a concession driven totally by politics. The white paper showed the government raising a huge $23.5 billion from selling permits over the scheme's first two years. Rudd boasted that 'every cent' would help households and businesses adjust. The overall fiscal impact was revenue neutral.

Rudd predicted Labor would be attacked by the 'far right' for acting and the 'far left' for not going far enough. He was correct on both counts. The problem was soon apparent: Rudd wanted to help save the planet but not at any political risk to himself. He was a risk-averse hero addicted to complex policy, a dangerous mix. In trying to satisfy environmentalists, industry and pro-market reformers, Rudd risked satisfying nobody.

Within days Rudd was outflanked on the Left—and he never recovered. The Greens were infuriated, angry that Rudd had ignored them and hostile to his scheme. They were agog that there was no mention of the 25 per cent reduction target that Garnaut had flagged. They saw the CPRS as ineffectual in tackling climate change, insufficient to generate investment into new technology and indefensible in compensating polluters to keep polluting.

Not even the more moderate green groups—the Climate Institute and the Australian Conservation Foundation—were satisfied. The ACF decided to campaign against the scheme, proof that the entire NGO movement was alienated. The absence of a 25 per cent qualified target was a crippling blunder for Labor since the scientific/green push had enshrined this as the minimum needed. Wong said:

> In hindsight I think we didn't pre-position on the 5 to 15 per cent targets enough. Bob Brown was saying if we didn't have 25 to 40 per cent on the table it wasn't worth having. We should have explained to people the targets the Greens were talking about were simply unachievable.

As Rudd knew from his success against Howard, climate change politics was driven by emotions, simplicity and symbolism. Yet Rudd faltered when facing an attack from the Left based on these very techniques.

The unfolding GFC made business highly risk averse. Yet Rudd was better placed with business than he was with the green movement. Both the Business Council of Australia and the Australian Industry Group offered qualified support, a significant platform.

Special Envoy on Climate Change Howard Bamsey felt Rudd was losing the plot.

He was losing touch with the public on the issue. I felt this quite strongly. We abandoned the storyline about why we were doing this. The new storyline became 'we have the world's best ETS'. At the public service level this became the paradigm for a lot of the people coming into the new Department of Climate Change. There was a deep and enthusiastic commitment to devising the world's best ETS. Kevin Rudd was very taken with this, very interested in this magical instrument we were now devising. The idea of the 'world's best' was powerful. I got alarmed because it was clear that we were alienating the natural support base.[12]

Yet there was a deeper problem. After Rudd delivered the white paper he flew overseas, so there was no concerted selling strategy at home. Rudd was, literally, too busy. He was too busy to sell his policy to save the planet. The GFC would consume him for the next six months. What of Garnaut's warning that climate change was the most diabolical policy and political problem? Labor seemed to assume that the political war had been won at the 2007 election and that the task now was just about the politics and policy of implementation. Yet this was a false reading.

In Bamsey's words:

We started to lose political momentum from an early stage. After the white paper I think we lost those on the Right, worried, if you like, about damage to our prosperity, and we lost those on the Left because we forgot our story about climate change action, why we were doing this. For example, Rudd announced the CPRS one day and instead of spending two weeks on the road with it, he got in a plane and went overseas.[13]

The critique, again, goes to Rudd's style. It was brave to say 'let's do climate change despite the GFC' but it was futile if Rudd was unable to find sustained commitment to his CPRS. And that is what happened. 'He didn't give enough attention to the issue,' Bamsey said. 'Because of the way he tried to run every detail in other areas of government, he failed to give it the priority needed.'[14]

Meanwhile Garnaut attacked the CPRS as a corruption of good policy. He was outraged by the financial support extended to the electricity generators. For Garnaut, this was a wealth transfer from taxpayers to generators. He was alarmed about the extent of support for trade-exposed industry and the cult of political lobbying. Garnaut drew attention to a reported comment from the chief of Woodside, the American

Don Volte, who talked about buying a ticket to Canberra and getting a better deal for his company. Garnaut hated what he saw as publicised rent-seeking. 'This sort of talk disgusted me,' he said.[15]

Wong said: 'The difficulty I found with Ross was [that] while his advice was very good, his disagreement with the decisions of the government when we didn't take his advice was so public and so strident.' It was Terry Moran who was worried about the situation of the generators and commissioned a Morgan Stanley report to address their difficulty, a result Garnaut called a travesty.

Garnaut thought the 5 to 15 per cent targets dependent upon global action were 'dumb'. 'Why not offer 25 per cent and show we support stronger global action?' he asked Rudd during a phone call.[16] They met at Kirribilli House at 5 p.m. on 7 January 2009 and Garnaut presented an aide-mémoire. It was a good discussion but settled nothing. Rudd told Garnaut his strategy—get a scheme in place, get through the economic downturn, seek a mandate for more ambitious targets at the 2010 election. It made sense. They agreed that the outlook for the Copenhagen conference was not favourable.

By early 2009 Wong sensed Labor was sinking in the centre under criticism from business and greens. She feared a slow death. A GFC-sensitive business community was going lukewarm. The fight over the targets was lost. In March she met Rudd in Brisbane. 'We have to re-prioritise,' she told him. A born negotiator, Wong said Labor must re-negotiate both with business and greens; stakeholder backing for the CPRS must be revived. She envisaged a new negotiating process with business and NGOs. In April, Wong flew to Noosa to see BCA chief Greg Gailey and discover what terms business wanted in order to offer its backing. She went from group to group to fix the new bargain. The package was finalised at a Sydney meeting involving Rudd, Swan, Wong, Arbib and Combet.[17]

On 4 May Rudd announced what he called 'significant changes' to the CPRS. The CPRS would be delayed a year and have a one-year fixed price of only $10 per tonne. The real scheme would begin only in mid-2012. Rudd said a 'recession buffer' would provide extra support for trade-exposed industry. The government now pledged to the 25 per cent reduction target if the world agreed to the 450 ppm deal, though Wong conceded such a deal would be 'hard' to achieve.

The package was endorsed by the BCA, Ai Group, the ACTU, the Australian Council of Social Service (ACOSS), and both the Australian Conservation Foundation and Climate Institute. 'We had to do this,'

Wong said. 'We had lost the political argument on targets and the GFC made business a lot more stressed. It wasn't the easiest situation in which to bring down a whole-of-economy reform.' The key to legislating the CPRS now hinged on holding this coalition together.

Wong was a pragmatist who wanted the legislation. 'The easiest way to kill a Labor reform is to have a united business voice against it,' she said. 'This was demonstrated by the Resources Super Profits Tax. I knew the most we could expect was muted acceptance. We wouldn't get people cheering for it.'

Labor had given up on the Greens. Wong said: 'I had come to the view at the beginning of 2009 after my discussions with Bob Brown that they weren't just positioning to look a bit different. They wanted a funda-mental differentiation.' Wong felt Brown suffered from too much praise for too long. She was astounded that most of the media took the Greens at face value and suspended criticism when dealing with them. Wong's plan was to negotiate with the Coalition. That had an extra advantage: 'With these whole-of-economy reforms it is best to have them bipartisan because you don't want business thinking there is any uncertainty.'

Wong understood the tactics of the Greens. 'They thought Turnbull would vote for the scheme, so it would pass,' she said. The Greens would then be positioned as heroes—the purists who stood aside from the Labor–Coalition grubby deals and still backed a 25 to 40 per cent target.

Rudd called his scheme 'the biggest structural reform since the opening up of the Australian economy in the 1980s and 1990s'. Yet the price in compensation and 'buying off' political resistance was absurdly high. Rudd and Wong felt it justified for the goal. Wong said:

> It was my political choice to focus on the industry side of the argument. I felt we needed to think how this will look ten or fifteen years down the track, not how it looks in one, two or three years. If you have this perspective then you are prepared to accept more transitional assistance at the start.

In short, get the scheme 'up and running'.

Finalisation of the CPRS mocked any idea of climate change idealism as a force when it counted. If the cause had actually been about saving 'our people, our nation and our planet' then Rudd might have offered less bribery and the Australian public might have accepted a greater sacrifice. But nobody acted on this basis. The rhetoric was just rhetoric: in the end it made no difference. There was no transformative spirit at work beyond the song sheets of the converted. The policy formation was merely time-honoured Australian expediency hitched to a new cause. Labor invoked idealism but traded in cash, compensation, special deals, compromises and spin. There was no new politics and such claims were fraudulent. Rudd wasn't mug enough to actually ask the people to make a genuine sacrifice to save the planet—that was far too risky. He got that call right.

But it exposed the essential problem. Public support for climate change action was fashionable. But public commitment was weak and acceptance of higher power prices and lower living standards in the cause was weaker still. Rudd operated on this assumption. He seemed to think that saving the Barrier Reef and the planet was best accomplished on a safety-first basis. Meanwhile legions of Green activists stood with Bob Brown in denouncing Rudd's revised scheme.

Consider Rudd's first-term agenda: he was saving Australia from the global recession and delivering a blueprint for climate change action to influence global mitigation. This went beyond stoking the reformist fires; Rudd was stoking the furnace. A wiser judgement might suggest it was too much, too difficult and risked something going badly wrong.

The longer the climate change issue ran, the more elemental it became. Beyond the fine words, policy action meant imposing higher costs on people. It was that brutal. It seemed such an uninspired solution to such a thrilling problem. Yet as the 2009 winter crept over the capital, Rudd and Wong were in fine spirits. 'We had a lot of groups now backing the scheme,' Wong said. 'I think at that point the momentum was with us.'

CHAPTER 14

THE QUEST FOR CONTROL:
FROM THE MEDIA TO YARRALUMLA

Kevin Rudd's operations as a control freak knew no limits. His quest for control ranged across cabinet, ministers and public servants and even extended to the Governor-General at Yarralumla. Channelling and controlling media coverage of his government was a daily preoccupation. In office, the job of Rudd's staff was to control the daily media message in a whole-of-government project on a scale no prime minister had attempted before. Most ministers fell into line, fearing retaliation.

Yet the strategy failed the ultimate test: it became an end in its own right. The irony is that Rudd won public relations battles but lost the bigger political wars—a prime example being the climate change issue, where he conquered Malcolm Turnbull on the public relations front but failed to secure his prized policy in a humiliating defeat.

Rudd's two press secretaries, Lachlan Harris and Sean Kelly, admitted the problem. 'As we became uncertain about the policy agenda then activity began to fill the void,' Harris said. 'At the end there was just the media strategy. It was all that was left.'[1] Kelly said: 'I think we did fall into the trap of having the media process become the issue. There's always the risk the media strategy is what counts, not the outcome.'[2]

These are brave and shattering comments. They point to a classic blunder. Instead of being the servant to publicise good policy, Rudd's media strategy too often came to define the government's hollowness and manipulation. Rudd rarely seemed to grasp this point.

Lindsay Tanner, reflecting on his time in office, said: 'I sometimes joked with my colleagues that we should experiment with governing well: maybe that would go down well in the focus groups and the polls. The creation of appearances is now far more important for leading politicians than is the generation of outcomes.'[3] Tanner, who quit politics for family reasons, said he was content to leave, one reason being the 'sideshow syndrome' in which the politicians and media debased each other.

Rudd's office chief for most of his first year as prime minister, David Epstein, said:

> While Kevin Rudd presented as a policy wonk, his real focus was politics and the tabloid media. He governed on a tabloid basis and was obsessed about his personal popularity. It often felt like government by what were called 'announceables'—endless stunts intended to draw media attention [away] from stories likely to embarrass the government. Sometimes they reverted to the worst aspects of the New South Wales Labor Party in attempted media manipulation.[4]

The Foreign Minister in Rudd's government, Stephen Smith, affirms this obsession, well known in the cabinet. Smith felt that Rudd pushed too hard to shape media coverage. 'The Prime Minister in my view exerts much impact from just turning up,' Smith said. 'But Kevin's office was obsessed about "announceables". The wheels of government were repeatedly set in motion in the cause of finding "announceables".'[5]

It is an ugly word and an even more ugly idea. Rudd's media fixation repeatedly undermined good government. His problem was that daily media manipulation did not equate to persuading the Australian public on the big issues: carbon pricing, the fiscal stimulus, hospitals reform, the mining tax and boats policy. Rudd was an astute manipulator but, as prime minister, a poor persuader.

In his analysis of Rudd's obsessions with the media, Swan's office chief, Chris Barrett, argued that this was a systemic problem:

> He geared the entire government's decision-making process to the media cycle ... It meant every substantial policy deliberation became not a matter of solving a public policy question but a cluster of potential attack points or announceables. Nothing had a coherent whole beyond a succession of nights or mornings won or lost in the evening news bulletins or newspaper front pages ... The PM had a reflex fear of even momentary unpopularity, so that he became an easy target for every lobbyist in town on the Carbon Pollution Reduction Scheme. They could all see that anyone who could get a nasty story up for even a day was getting concessions and they wanted in on the action.[6]

A telling example of this flaw was the early 2010 push by Rudd and his political advisers to stage a referendum on a Commonwealth takeover of responsibility for hospitals. This struggle went on for months. Rudd's advisers were explicit: the Prime Minister didn't expect the referendum to pass. Indeed, he didn't seem to care whether it passed. The motive was public relations and media manipulation—to whip up concern about hospitals to assist Labor to win the 2010 election by coupling the poll with a referendum.

It sent the Health Minister, Nicola Roxon, into dismayed fury. What most alarmed Roxon was that such an epic change in the Australian Constitution and public policy was treated like a 'play thing'. She was appalled, saying 'this is actually a really serious issue'.[7] Yet the referendum was a public relations stunt.

The first lesson of the Rudd media project is obvious: a prime minister who governs according to the dictates of the 24-hour media cycle actually runs a high risk. The assumption underpinning modern media tactics is that the side winning most of the daily media cycles during a three-year term will be re-elected. It usually works, but Rudd disproved the theory. By any test Rudd won the vast majority of daily media cycles—yet, in the end, he lost his job. His tactics had a negative dimension. Rudd and his staff deluded themselves that they were winning the public when they were seeding doubts about the prime minister and his government.

Harris described the daily schedule:

> There would be a national hook-up at 5.15 a.m. That was the senior press secretaries and Alister Jordan. That was, pretty much, every morning seven days a week, 365 days a year. For a while it went to 6.15 a.m. The junior press secretaries would have prepared a brief for us from the morning's news, having picked up the papers after 4 a.m. We would break up the issues we wanted to elevate and defend. I would do that from home and get into work about 6 a.m. The first conversation with Rudd would be about 7 a.m., after we had more clarity on how things were looking. We created a system to stop ourselves being pulled apart. A lot of the early morning focus was about discipline, clarifying what the government's view was on issues. It was a defensive system. It was about shaping the media coverage. We would have another hook-up at 6.30 every night, getting ready for the next cycle, a recap on the TV news that night and what's coming up in the papers next

day. We would wrap by 8.30 p.m. on most days. The aim was to do better than the opponent each day.[8]

Harris spoke with Rudd's authority. He would regularly instruct the cabinet ministers selected to carry the message on any particular day. It was often demeaning. They were told what to say by Rudd's office. Ministers were simply subordinated to Rudd's grand design. On an infamous occasion Tony Burke, bedridden in Darwin, was abused when he said he had laryngitis and could not do a media interview.

Only Rudd operated as the spokesman for the entire government. His communications skills were highly rated yet his performance became erratic as the pressure grew. 'If Rudd had a clear sense of what he wanted to communicate he was as effective as anyone I have ever seen,' Harris said.[9] 'More often than not we succeeded in the daily media battle, and that was largely because of Kevin's media skills,' Kelly said.[10]

The key to Rudd's approach was discipline and keeping his government on-message. Media tactics are built around the elimination of negatives and repetition of the chosen message each day. Nobody is exempt. The frustrations of one of Rudd's favourites, Maxine McKew, an experienced broadcaster who won Howard's seat, revealed the nature of Rudd's control system.

A high-profile ALP candidate, McKew, who became a parliamentary secretary, ended up virtually invisible. She found no solution to the conundrum she faced: conforming to the daily Rudd office media dictates was compulsory but McKew, because she could not stomach them, often preferred to stay below the radar. She declined to become an 'operational robot'.

In early 2008, when McKew proposed a policy message to Gillard's office, she was told: 'That's not the story we want out there today.' McKew's responsibilities came under Gillard and she soon concluded that Gillard's office was 'far more effective' even than Rudd's office in 'courting support or freezing out alternative voices'. McKew found that the daily talking points from Rudd's office were a moronic way for Labor to communicate. She felt the repetition of the nonsensical phrase 'working families' had become counter-productive and she junked it from her material. McKew was disgusted at the dumbing down of politics, saying 'it meant that we introduced a whole new era of Labor Brutalism'.[11]

When an interview McKew had done appeared on page one of the *Sydney Morning Herald*, she got a message from Lachlan Harris at 6 a.m.: 'This is not what we wanted on the front page.' McKew noted the assumption: that Rudd's office expected to determine the front page. She concluded 'that parliamentary secretaries are not supposed to occupy prime real estate in national newspapers'—unless sanctioned by the prime minister's office.[12] McKew nailed the problem: Rudd's and Gillard's offices operated with little finesse. She said: 'I've lost count of the number of people—normally Labor allies—who still talk about the high-handed and arrogant way they were treated by senior staff in the leaders' offices.'[13]

Before Epstein left Rudd's office in late 2008 he was convinced the obsession with short-term politics was corrupting the system:

> Properly functioning cabinet government ceased to exist. More and more the discussion was about politics and the real business was not conducted. The decision-making process just fell away. Rudd would speak to Alister Jordan before 7 each morning, commissioning all sorts of things—the PM's office just cut across all lines of authority within executive government.[14]

Under Rudd, decisions would be fast-tracked, packaged before they were ready or merely given a new coat of paint. Once a technique used during election campaigns, the 'announceables' practice became the daily business of the prime minister's office. This was at Rudd's personal insistence. It occupied immense time for staffers and public servants, distorted priorities and distracted from policy work. The government lost track of what mattered and what didn't matter. It is no surprise the public became confused about what Rudd believed. The obsession with media controls and polls will limit a prime minister's options and induce timidity.

Howard had conducted a constant dialogue with the people, spending more time on the media than in the Parliament or cabinet. Like Rudd, he was a media addict, morning, noon and night. But Rudd took the process to another extreme: he worked old media but thrived on social media. Under Rudd the 24–hour media cycle became continuous.

Rudd's obsession about leaks crippled the government's decision-making. Simon Crean said: 'He always used the argument about leaks to close things off.'[15] Tony Burke reported: 'At one point, Kevin said: "I could just make all the decisions myself if this room is going to leak." Kevin felt people could not be trusted. There were two results: decisions were made without being properly assessed, and decision-making was grinding to a halt.'[16] Chris Barrett described a process of exclusion as Rudd narrowed the circle of influence: he began to exclude firstly public servants, then ministers. 'He was obsessively concerned about leaks,' Barrett said. 'Some of the most important issues were taken out of cabinet for this reason.'[17] Ministers later shook their heads in disbelief at Rudd's hypocrisy—as prime minister he was fixated on killing leaks, but as Gillard's rival once she became prime minister, he was river master of leaks.

Rudd's performance demands a re-think by political leaders of the conventional wisdom about media 'spin'. The Rudd record suggests: (1) that winning the 24-hour media cycle is not enough and comes at a price; (2) that real leadership means persuading the public on issues, not just re-cycling what the focus groups report; and (3) that retreating from core policies because of polls, focus groups and media pressure can be counterproductive and even destroy a prime minister in his or her first term.

Rudd's speechwriter, James Button, quit disillusioned after twelve months. The account he later gave of his dealings with Rudd is moving in its capture of his intense but flawed leader, locked in a quest for endless control:

> I think that personal connection, that intimacy, was not possible for
> Rudd. How he spoke, wrote and presented himself was somehow
> existential for him. He had to control it. And that was why he
> would always be awake in the Lodge at 3 a.m. fighting for the
> words that said who he was and cursing everyone else for failing
> to find them for him.[18]

Button described a meeting with Rudd and his key advisers, Alister Jordan and Andrew Charlton, at Kirribilli in January 2009. Rudd's plan was to deliver six Australia Day speeches, one in each state capital, over six days on four different aspects of the GFC seen through the same six themes. Each speech was to have what Rudd called a 'detachable module of announceables' and each speech needed a cover page containing four or five dot points that captured its essence. As he listened, Button said, 'My head swarmed with thoughts. Six cities, six speeches, six themes, four elements in each, five dot points … how could the story of the GFC be cut up this way? … Maybe this was the day I realised that writing for Rudd probably wasn't going to work.'[19] For anyone who knows Rudd, the story is unsurprising. A dismayed Button felt his job as speechwriter was merely to lock in the parts to the model Rudd designed and controlled.

Harris defended his former boss:

He had the capacity for intense warmth but there were definitely some prickly edges on him. Does that slip into a medical condition that made him a manic? No. Was he a nightmare the whole time? No. He could be very warm and we saw that a lot. Was his personality a reason to sack him? No.[20]

But David Epstein offers a more alarming view of Rudd: 'He treated many people badly. As prime minister he would shout at people and sometimes humiliate them. I heard him say to people, "You'll have no future while I'm here." He would make promises to individuals and then break them.'[21]

Rudd gave a high priority to personal ties with newspaper editors, with his primary focus being News Corporation, its capital city tabloids and its national broadsheet, the *Australian*. His focus in Melbourne was editor-in-chief of the *Herald Sun*, Peter Blunden, who became managing director of the Melbourne operation about the time Rudd became prime minister.

Blunden said:

We saw a lot of each other when Kevin came to Melbourne. He didn't know the city and he wanted to learn and that was smart. His determination to get his message over with newspaper editors was unlike anything I've ever seen and I've been in the business for thirty-five years. I'd dealt with John Howard and Paul Keating but Kevin was something else. His ambition was so obvious. Kevin spent years coming and going into this organisation.[22]

The usual modus operandi was a phone call or text message when he was coming to Melbourne.

It was similar in Sydney when he was meeting the editor-in-chief of the *Australian*, Chris Mitchell, a fellow Queenslander. Mitchell had previously had a long stint as editor-in-chief of the *Courier-Mail* and knew Rudd well. When Rudd was campaigning for the ALP leadership he would periodically meet Mitchell and the author over a meal in Sydney to canvass his plans and the caucus numbers. The *Australian* gave substantial support to Rudd. At the 2007 election under Mitchell's direction the paper abandoned its long-standing endorsement of Howard and switched to Rudd after many discussions where he argued he was an economic reformer and fiscal conservative.

Once Rudd was prime minister, relations became problematic. On one occasion there was a dinner for six at Nobu, a Japanese restaurant in Melbourne's Crown complex, the party including Rudd, Blunden and his successor as *Herald Sun* editor-in-chief, Phil Gardiner. It was a constructive evening until Gardiner showed Rudd on his mobile phone the paper's page one for the next day with the headline, 'Abbott: "I'll stop the boats"'. Rudd snapped. Blunden said: 'Rudd just went off with plenty of expletives.'

> He had made a health policy announcement that day and asked in the most voracious fashion why he wasn't on the front page. The longer he talked, the angrier he got. I tried to slow him down, saying it was a legitimate story. But he just kept going. He was looking daggers and said, 'I won't be fucking intimidated by Murdoch editors.' At one point he thumped his fists on the table. I would judge the tirade lasted for a full ten minutes and bordered on a public display. The next day or a few days later he rang me to apologise. He was embarrassed, there's no doubt.[23]

Rudd's staff later conceded that he had lost control, but Rudd and Blunden maintained their cordial ties.

Mitchell believes his relations with Rudd frayed from the June 2008 publication of an article by John Lyons headed 'Captain Chaos and the workings of inner circle', the first exposition of Rudd as a dysfunctional prime minister. In a prescient article just seven months into Rudd's term, Lyons described his insulting behaviour towards senior officials and ministers and his obsession about media control. Lyons quoted Laurie Oakes saying: 'I have been told that Rudd's people insist there must be something positive for him to announce or do every day and that this creates strains. It is hard to determine how much truth there is in this.' Lyons quoted a senior journalist who nailed Rudd's defect: 'Everything's either for the next 24 hour news cycle or 2020.'[24]

The Lyons article began a culture war within the media between those who championed Rudd and those who felt his government was deeply, perhaps fatally, flawed. Mitchell said: 'I felt Kevin was making the same mistakes he had made in Queensland with Wayne Goss. I had got a lot of feedback from inside his office and asked John Lyons to find out what was happening. I think relations between the paper and Kevin broke down after the Lyons piece.'[25]

Rudd was running into trouble over authenticity. He had pushed FuelWatch and Grocery Choice as schemes to help consumers get the best prices. Yet he planned to combat global warming by a carbon pricing policy that would deliberately lift power prices across the board in Australian households. How did the electoral cosmetics relate to the policy substance? It was never explained. In early 2009 the story broke that Rudd, unhappy about the service he got on a VIP flight, had shouted at an airforce attendant—an extraordinary act by a prime minister. Laurie Oakes said the story was 'dangerous' because 'it is the first public confirmation of claims there are two Rudds'—happy Kevin from the *Sunrise* show and 'darker' Kevin who lurked backstage.

Despite tensions over the *Australian*'s coverage, Rudd and Mitchell continued to talk, and on 10 October 2008, Mitchell and a senior editor, Nick Cater, were at Kirribilli House with Rudd. They had a beer and cup of tea together. Rudd said he was talking that night to US President Bush and Brazilian President Lula. Cater left but Rudd insisted that Mitchell stay. Mitchell said:

> Kevin went into the study and left the door open. The conversation with Bush was on the speaker phone. I heard the entire conversation. He had a note taker in the room who hadn't been with us and who didn't join us later. I was taken with how forceful Kevin was with Bush. I had expected the dynamic to be a bit deferential. But Kevin was quite hectoring, I thought. It was about the G-20 and the need for a broader approach to the GFC than just the G-8. Kevin argued there was a lot to be gained for Bush and for America in being seen to lead the way with the economies of Asia.[26]

After the call Mitchell said he had been 'surprised' at how forceful Rudd had been in pursuing Australia's case with Bush. Rudd, in fact, was passionate about the G-20 and anxious to ensure that it became a heads-of-government group. Indeed, this became his most important foreign policy success as prime minister. Rudd made some derogatory remarks to Mitchell about Bush. Mitchell said Rudd's phone call would make an excellent 'inside' story for the paper and asked whether it could be written. Rudd agreed but said a delay was best. Mitchell said:

> I subsequently had a long discussion with [political correspondent] Matthew Franklin who produced a story [about it]. He sent it to Lachlan Harris and Alister Jordan. He emailed all the quotes

to them. Some changes were made. Two people in Rudd's office cleared the story. On the Friday night, just before 7 p.m., Kevin rang me and said, 'Just read me the intro and tell me the headline' and I did. He said, 'That's great', and that's where we left it. Of course, the story became a big issue later.[27]

Franklin's well-sourced story of the phone call ran on 25 October 2008. Rudd appeared in a highly favourable light, forcefully advising Bush. By this stage, Bush had called an historic G-20 leaders summit in Washington, exactly what Rudd had wanted. It became a breakthrough moment for Australia. But in the middle of the story was the line: 'Rudd was then stunned to hear Bush say: "What's the G-20?"' Bush was depicted as an idiot. It was a political fuse that detonated.

The White House was surprised and angry. It used a *Washington Post* story to deny that Bush had made such an ignorant remark—obviously, as US President, Bush would have discussed the G-20 on many occasions in public and private. When questioned by the media, Rudd's office denied Bush had uttered these words. Unsurprisingly, Rudd got a frosty welcome from Bush at the G-20 White House arrivals ceremony for the summit. Mitchell's recollection was that Bush had asked a question about the G-20. 'I'm not sure exactly what it was,' he said. Mitchell's point, however, was that Rudd's office gave the story the green light.[28]

There are several take-outs. The core point is that Rudd's behaviour on the night of the phone call was reckless. He wanted to solidify relations with Mitchell after a rocky phase. Perhaps at a more shallow level, he wanted to show off. His behaviour in allowing Mitchell to listen to the phone call was probably unprecedented for an Australian prime minister. It reflected Rudd's obsession with the media, with News Corporation and with the *Australian*. Mitchell said of the Kirribilli evening: 'Kevin had wanted me to stay for Lula as well. By this stage it was getting late but he wanted me to listen to the Brazilian. I said, "Mate, I've got to go home. I've got to take the kids to the zoo tomorrow."'

Soon afterwards, in late October, Rudd hosted a lunch at Kirribilli House for Rupert Murdoch, News chief executive John Hartigan and the Sydney editors. The editors (but not Murdoch) were kept waiting outside the gates to Kirribilli, distinctly unimpressed, for twenty minutes. Rudd, of course, was busy. At lunch they canvassed the Beijing Olympics and the best response to the emerging GFC. Towards the end Murdoch began to rise from the table and started to thank Rudd. But the Prime Minister had been telling a story. Pushing out his forearms with pointed fingers and looking straight at Murdoch, Rudd said: 'Sit down and let me finish the story.' It was an unforgettable moment. Murdoch and his editors departed a few minutes later with Rudd's story well and truly completed.

At critical times Rudd would contact Mitchell: it was a pattern over six years. A few weeks before he was deposed, Rudd asked Mitchell and the paper's political editor, Dennis Shanahan, to Kirribilli House. The mining tax issue was raging. Mitchell and Shanahan gave Rudd a message: the mining tax was doing him huge damage and, as prime minister, he must take control from Swan. At one point Mitchell went to the bathroom: 'Does he think I can win?' Rudd asked Shanahan. And Shanahan felt he knew why they were there: Rudd wanted to harness Mitchell's support for the 2010 election campaign.

Sean Kelly said: 'Politicians are often disproportionately focused on their media enemies who were once their friend. Kevin was no different. After the *Australian* and the *Daily Telegraph* withdrew the support they had previously shown, it was a source of anguish for him.'[29]

Although Rudd hardly knew Quentin Bryce and had only met her on two social occasions, he offered her the office of Governor-General, an inspired choice. She would be the first woman in the post, the sort of gesture Rudd loved. Bryce had a near-perfect résumé for the job: academic, lawyer, public servant, administrator, she had been Governor of Queensland for the previous five years. She had high expectations about the proper relationship between a prime minister and a Governor-General. She found Rudd to be elusive and unsupportive.

Bryce began at Yarralumla on 5 September 2008 and exactly a fortnight later she received a letter from Rudd dated 19 September that dismayed her. He said her overseas travel as Governor-General would be 'closely aligned with our national foreign policy objectives'. He bluntly said that countries he was not able to include in his own travel schedule should be included on her schedule. He wanted her to travel to Germany and the Czech Republic because they were important in Australia's quest for election to a non-permanent seat on the United Nations Security Council (UNSC). Her job was to assist in this campaign. Rudd would be a highly controlling prime minister.

The letter contained an attachment A that listed the nations Rudd wanted her to visit. Under Africa it listed: Nigeria, Senegal and Cameroon. The Latin American nations were Argentina, Ecuador and Costa Rica. With the Nordics and the Baltics, it listed Sweden, Norway and Lithuania. Jordan and Lebanon were the two countries nominated from the Middle East. From Central Asia the named countries were Kazakhstan, Uzbekistan and Kyrgyzstan.

On 8 December 2008, without consultation with Government House, a cabinet minute was authorised specifying a 'whole-of-government' approach to the UN bid. It specified a 'strong and active involvement by the Governor-General' and ministers. Bryce's attention was drawn to the decision when cabinet papers were sent to Yarralumla as part of administrative routine. She was being recruited by Rudd as a diplomatic emissary for the bid and was required to travel to a number of African nations. Bryce was worried: she had reservations about being used as a diplomatic lobbyist and, because the Opposition criticised the bid, she feared being locked into a partisan role. Rudd seemed to assume her job was to follow his orders.

Bryce now found the vice-regal office assuming a complexion different from what Rudd had foreshadowed. When she had been offered the post her conversation with Rudd had been encouraging. He told her that she 'would probably be the last Governor-General and the first president of the Republic'. Obviously, Bryce didn't accept the role on that basis but such statements from prime ministers usually carry some intent. It was a Rudd technique: talking up jobs when he offered them and doing little or nothing to realise the talk. As prime minister, he made no effort whatsoever to advance Australia's transition to a republic.

Bryce got alarmed when the Opposition and the media began saying the Governor-General should not make the proposed African visit, by now an odyssey to many nations. On 9 March 2009, the *Australian's* Greg Sheridan said Rudd was in danger of 'politicising and misusing' the office.[30] The Coalition was attacking the way Rudd pursued the UN campaign and the costs of the Africa trip. Bryce had become a target in the political brawl. There is no doubt she was highly sensitive to the situation; she feared the office was being compromised. Bryce felt the trip was wrong and decided she must talk to Rudd directly. Her office tried but failed to set up a meeting. Rudd was elusive. No doubt the Governor-General felt frustrated and even demeaned; Bryce was unable to talk to the prime minister who had floated the idea that she might be president one day.

The secretary of the Department of the Prime Minister and Cabinet, Terry Moran, was despatched to Yarralumla. He arrived 5.05 p.m. on 13 March 2009. It was a tense and difficult meeting. Moran, nicknamed 'the Cardinal', could be charming or aggressive, depending on the need. Bryce's staff concluded that Rudd 'wanted to put the woman back in her slot'.

The record of conversation shows that Moran suggested Bryce was 'hyper-sensitive to media criticism' and told her that 'media criticism is part and parcel of her life'. His advice was 'she needed to resist taking it personally'. Bryce replied that she was not taking it personally. She told Moran the issue was the role of the Governor-General and 'the integrity of the office'. Moran disagreed. He said there were 'many occasions on which the Governor-General would be speaking on behalf of the government', such as outlining its legislative program. But Bryce was not persuaded.

She told Moran 'she had come to the view that she should not proceed on the visit to Africa'. This visit had been organised at Rudd's will; he had selected the countries. She argued that 'in the absence of robust public support from the Prime Minister over a week she could not see how the trip could continue'. This penetrated to one of Bryce's main concerns.

Her office had spoken to Rudd's office during the past week. They expected Rudd to defend Bryce and explain she was travelling at his behest. When Rudd said nothing Bryce felt she was being hung out to dry. She had spent much of that day trying to contact Rudd. Moran explained he was at the funeral of Geoff Gallop's wife. Bryce told Moran that 'several calls had been promised' but they had 'not eventuated'. Bryce repeated her request: 'She wanted to speak directly to the Prime Minister'. Moran said he had the draft of a minute providing advice to the Prime Minister on the G-G's trip and, as Secretary, he was prepared to go on the record supporting the trip. Bryce said she looked forward to Rudd providing 'that clear advice'. At 5.40 p.m. Rudd rang in.

Bryce raised the media attacks on her and the politicisation of her visit, and said she was 'willing to postpone or cancel the trip'. The journalists mentioned were Andrew Bolt, Piers Akerman, Glenn Milne and Greg Sheridan. Rudd called them 'right-wing rat pack misogynists'. That hardly helped Bryce. He suggested a response by him would only make it worse, saying it was 'a judgement call' whether he should speak out. Bryce said she was worried Rudd would not publicly support her. Rudd then said that 'all governments make intelligent use of their heads of state'. Bryce asked Rudd whether he would defend her personally over this trip and Rudd said his defence would be 'watertight, absolute, definitive'. The Governor-General subsequently felt Rudd did not honour this statement to the full.

Bryce told Rudd the Opposition was now briefing the media critically on the costs of her trip. Bryce sought confirmation that Rudd was advising her that the trip should proceed. He affirmed this was his advice, saying that 'under no circumstances' would the government leave her undefended.

The next day, 14 March, Bryce wrote to Rudd saying she was 'grateful' for his commitment. Bryce confirmed she would raise the Security Council seat in her talks in Africa but the purpose of this letter was to shift the focus of the visit away from the UN bid.

Bryce was unhappy about the institutional and personal relationship between the Prime Minister and the Governor-General. She was acting on Rudd's advice despite her misgivings; that meant the government took political responsibility for her trip; yet when the media heat was turned up Bryce saw little sign of Rudd's public support for her. Instead she had been given lectures about the need to toughen up. The 2009 trip involved ten nations in eighteen days with over eighty official engagements. While the shadow minister for Foreign Affairs, Julie Bishop, said it 'compromised the position' of Governor-General, Foreign Minister Smith defended Bryce.

Six months after the trip on 8 November 2009, Bryce saw Rudd at one of his very rare meetings with her. She raised comments by columnist Piers Akerman made on ABC TV's *Insiders* program to the effect she had been advised by Rudd to confine her role to rural and regional Australia. 'The report was insulting and damaging,' Bryce said. Perhaps she was too sensitive. Bryce recalled Moran's visit to Yarralumla. She said she sought to uphold the Constitution and the conventions surrounding the office. 'I have had too much flak about Africa,' she said. Bryce made detailed notes of this discussion with Rudd. She wrote that Africa was 'a visit I made on his advice'. She had to request his support 'several times' over the African visit and now she was communicating to Rudd her concerns about the comments made by Akerman on *Insiders*, comments that could only be damaging to her office.

Bryce told Rudd of the 'serious responsibility' with which she undertook her role, of 'its gravity and the need for his support', stressing that she 'always acted on advice'. She referred to Rudd's expansive phone conversations before she accepted the office. The sub-text was apparent: Bryce felt that Rudd had not lived up to those lofty statements. Looking for encouragement, Bryce took heart from Rudd's comments that she spoke for the nation and he spoke for the government. 'I had the impression he had been reflecting on the Governor-General's role,' she ruminated.

In the time during which he was prime minister, Rudd made eight calls on the Governor-General. His contact was infrequent and irregular.

Their discussions were uncomfortable and Bryce remembered that, on one occasion when he was leaving, Rudd made a passing reference to her rural and regional commitments. In June 2010 when Rudd was removed by the caucus he did not visit Government House to resign; he sent his resignation with a driver.

There was logic in Rudd's view that the Governor-General's travel should be used to advance foreign policy. But this was implemented in a casual and contemptuous manner. The prime minister's office was also concerned about the increase in spending at Yarralumla. This account, however, suggests that Rudd gave little attention to the office; that he was prepared to manipulate Bryce for his own ends; and that Bryce felt repeatedly dissatisfied with her prime minister. From Bryce's perspective, it was a relationship defined by Rudd's penchant for distance but control.

In summary, the irony of Rudd's quest for control is that politics had passed a threshold: a leader's ability to control communications was eroding given the digital age and the decline of old media. Rudd was fighting against the tide. Gary Gray said: 'Government is far more challenging today than it was thirty years ago. When Cyclone Tracey hit Darwin in the 1970s we didn't see it until film could get to a broadcast point. When Cyclone Yasi hit Cairns people were filming it on their iPhones.'[31] Gray said the Parliament House media environment had been transformed: old mastheads were fighting for their lives, journalists were under greater pressures, facing tighter budgets yet having to meet web, video and traditional demands. The days when Paul Keating as treasurer could brief five senior journalists confident his message would be transmitted around the nation were gone. That world no longer existed.

'There used to be a playbook to run these media operations, but the playbook is in doubt,' Harris said.

> I sat in Canberra for ten years and watched and listened. The media cycle changed. The hard, nasty opinionated part of the media came to dominate. And it changed the way people thought and talked about politics. The days of people thinking about a competent government don't exist any more. The story from the media now is dissatisfaction with government. What is achievable in policy terms is far more limited.[32]

Rudd's quest for control coincided with the decay of the established media apparatus. He was caught between two worlds—desperate as prime miniter to control media coverage and events around him, yet perpetually frustrated because complete control was unachievable and its pursuit often backfired. His unhappy record suggests future prime ministers need to find a different and better approach.

CHAPTER 15

AUSTRALIAN SETTLEMENT NOSTALGIA

T he Rudd and Gillard era brought to a fresh peak Labor's faith in state power, centralised government interventions and interest group politics. The global financial crisis had an enduring legacy—it affirmed Labor's instinct to enshrine government at the heart of economic life. Rudd and Gillard escalated public expectations and tried to satisfy them by regulation, spending and grand schemes.

It is rare that a government misinterprets the historical nature of the period in which it governs. Yet this happened to Rudd and Gillard. It is their tragedy and the intellectual failure of their era. The result was a legacy of squandered opportunity, uncompetitive industry and a serious budget imbalance. Labor's post-2013 future hinges on its ability to reassess much of the Rudd–Gillard record and change direction.

By their actions Rudd and Gillard did not see themselves as inheritors of the Hawke–Keating mantle. They lived by the notion of 'market failure' as the rationalisation for virtually every major policy. Rudd often tried to 'buy off' business but by the twilight of Gillard's government Labor ran a naked pro-union line hostile to the business community. Rudd invoked a series of Labor traditions—Andrew Fisher, Whitlam and Hawke–Keating—to cherry-pick as he went. Yet his default option was invariably the lure of state power. With the arrival of the GFC he seized this notion with passion.

By Christmas 2008, Rudd was convinced he was governing in a world that had reached a new epoch—he felt the Reagan/Thatcher de-regulatory excesses had been exposed by market failures and elitist greed. He saw the policy paradigm of the previous generation collapsing, liberal and neo-liberal economics in eclipse and a new age of social democratic wisdom emerging in Australia and the West. This was the ideological conclusion Rudd imposed on the GFC. Yet the vision he embraced was a mirage.

The Keynesian stimulus and low interest rates were essential to counter the financial emergency. Yet it left the public sectors in many nations staggering under huge debts and unprecedented deficits and trapped in an entitlement vortex where spending exceeded revenue. The key to recovery was private-sector revival, the return to sound credit provision, greater economic efficiency, enhanced productivity and, over time, disciplined moves to restore public-sector balance sheets. This was not a social democratic nirvana.

The actual world Rudd lived in meant that the revolution in emerging economies—China, India, Brazil and other nations—created a far more competitive global marketplace. For Australia's domestic economy there were two defining events: the GFC and the resources boom. The latter would prove to be more important, starting before the GFC, with its impact enduring far longer. The boom delivered a high dollar, drove punishing structural change and rendered sections of the economy uncompetitive. This was Labor's real challenge.

In his 2013 book *Dog Days*, Ross Garnaut warned that 'business as usual' meant a serious hit in living standards and jobs. Garnaut identified the challenge: because the boom had left much of the nation uncompetitive and with the Howard Government having spent its pre-2008 proceeds, Australia needed a new wave of economic reform and a lower dollar to combat the 'dog days' it confronted.[1] This was a variation of the warnings that Treasury chiefs Ken Henry and Martin Parkinson had also sounded for some years.

Yet much of Labor's policy had taken the nation in the opposite direction. The government seemed mesmerised by the magic of new rules, regulations and programs that burdened the private economy. There was no secret about the required task: reform on the supply side of the economy to lift competitiveness, improve transport and infrastructure, boost workforce productivity and participation, and limit regulatory costs. Yet many of Labor's decisions had the reverse impact. The party lacked a consistent reform philosophy to achieve a more competitive economy. The sheer range of Labor's government-inspired interventions was astonishing.

Consider the record. Labor engineered the partial re-regulation of the industrial relations system under Gillard's supervision in a gain for the trade unions; it offered new financial support for the car industry under Industry Minister Kim Carr, with Rudd's authorisation; it created a multi-billion-dollar government-owned National Broadband Network monopoly under the supervision of Communications Minister Stephen Conroy; its fiscal stimulus, overseen by Swan, was excessive in quantum and flawed in its interventionist detail—witness the $2.7 billion home-insulation scheme and the far too protracted $16 billion school halls program; infused with green politics, it expanded green energy schemes and subsidies in the name of clean energy, forcing up energy prices and costs across the board; it imposed tax rises on a range of industries; it abolished the Australian Building and Construction Commission despite its restoration of order in the industry; in relation to road transport and shipping, it took a series of decisions that meant more regulation and protection; in the teeth of documented damage in cost and time, Gillard upheld the dual system of Commonwealth–State environmental authorisation for resource projects; under union pressure it legislated new restrictions on 457 Visa entrants; and it engaged in spurious oversights on behalf of alleged consumer interests called FuelWatch and Grocery Choice. This list is far from exhaustive.

The issue here is not activist government. Activist government is essential in modern democracies and in meeting emergencies such as the 2008 GFC. The issue is effective government in the cause of a productive economy and successful society.

A range of independent analysts, some sympathetic to Labor, voiced their concerns about Labor's philosophy. Productivity Commission chair Gary Banks signalled his alarm in 2010 that 'productivity-enhancing reform' as the mainstay of economic progress had become a non-option. Banks reminded his audience that Hawke–Keating reforms hinged on leadership—'identifying, prioritising and building political support for structural reform'. The implied contrast was obvious: Rudd lacked such commitments. Given Labor's passage of the Fair Work Act, Banks nominated industrial relations as 'arguably the most crucial to get right'.[2]

Ross Gittins, the *Sydney Morning Herald*'s economics editor, said in 2009: 'Mr Rudd is no economic rationalist because he simply hasn't absorbed "the economist's way of thinking". From his chronic inability to set priorities or to delegate, you see he has no inherent conception of opportunity cost. He has no inbuilt suspicion of interventionist solutions.'[3] Gittins offered a sharp insight into Rudd's cynicism: Rudd saw economic rationalists not as arguing over 'propositions that are either right or wrong' but as merely 'another interest group needing to be squared away'.

Garnaut, angered at the interest group appeasement in Rudd's scheme, branded his ETS 'one of the worst examples of policy making we have seen on major issues in Australia'. The underlying issue was Rudd's defective grasp of public interest reform. Two months after Rudd's removal, Garnaut called for 'the restoration of the role of transparent, independent authoritative analysis of policy issues'. He believed Rudd had 'abdicated the leadership of Australia' because he gave preference to short-term politics and sectional interest groups on climate change. Yet this was not an aberration—it was Rudd's core method of governing.[4]

A classic mini example was the Rudd cabinet's 2009 decision to keep restrictions on imported books in an appeasement of local publishers, authors and unions. As former ACCC chief Allan Fels said, if Rudd refused to show courage here, how could he possibly defy far more powerful interests? He said Labor voted to uphold 'a government-mandated import monopoly market which is grossly overcharging Australians'. Such decisions did not occur by oversight. They happened by dint of belief and calculated political tactics.

The minister with the deepest ties to the Hawke era was Craig Emerson, who served on Hawke's staff and held a series of economic portfolios under Rudd and Gillard. An abiding supporter of Gillard, Emerson said he believed 'both the Rudd and Gillard governments were in the Hawke–Keating reforming traditions' yet he imposed a series of qualifications on this view. Emerson said reform under Rudd was sometimes 'faltering or reversing'. While Rudd had managed the GFC well and the G-20 negotiations, 'he left the impression we needed to re-think market-based economics [and] that was a pity'.[5]

Emerson said Rudd's car industry initiatives were 'bad', that his green car policy 'was more about politics', that the Henry taxation review was a 'missed opportunity', that his hospitals reform 'hadn't quite worked', that his mining tax was a 'misstep', that his GFC response 'probably spent a bit too much' and was undermined by the roof-insulation scheme, and in general terms that 'we could have done more on the de-regulation side but the political environment and the GFC made that hard'. And this is the view of a loyalist.

The veteran from the Hawke–Keating generation, Simon Crean, began 'hugely optimistic' about the Rudd Government's prospects. 'We had the resources boom and an economy in transition,' Crean said. 'We had to be competitive and productive.' But Crean, like many others, found his assumptions were wrong. Rudd's head was elsewhere: he was neither a consensus reformer like Hawke nor a pro-market innovator like Keating.[6]

The former chair of the Industries Assistance Commission, Bill Carmichael, accused both sides of politics of moving away from policy transparency. With Labor, he identified the paradox: 'While the government is turning to the Productivity Commission for advice on social policy challenges (such as aged care and disability) it is turning away from it on major issues affecting national productivity (such as the National Broadband Network, industrial relations and assistance to individual manufacturing companies).[7]

Rudd was a modernist in style but a throwback in content. Gillard was a Labor traditionalist. They shared Wayne Swan as treasurer—he was focused on the disadvantaged, orthodox in his economic management, weak in reform. For most of the first government, Rudd and Swan worked closely together. For the second government, Gillard and Swan operated from the same page. There was an ideological and policy unity at the top for most of the Labor era.

Yet Labor had missed the challenge—or perhaps, it just failed to respond adequately. From the Treasury, Ken Henry and Martin Parkinson had nailed the task. There was no excuse. It was the coming crunch from weak productivity, slowing revenue growth and the fiscal blowout from an ageing population and huge new spending agendas. In 2012 Parkinson warned that public expectations about government services were in conflict with fiscal reality.[8]

Within months of Labor's departure from office the full scale of the economic task was tabled. Parkinson identified the two related problems. First, the nation faced falling growth in living standards because productivity was unlikely to compensate for the declining terms of trade. Treasury calculated a gap of $13 000 per person between what Australians now expected and what was likely to happen, a serious political problem. Second, a decade-long budget deficit outlook and a fiscal sustainability crisis would require spending restraint and tax reform. If Australia 'kept drifting along' it would be vulnerable to the next global crisis. Parkinson said unless the task was confronted then 'our children may really end up "doing it tough"!'[9]

Labor, in office, had failed to act upon the challenge of the times. Claims that it could not be expected to know were nonsense. The productivity/terms of trade challenge was on the table before the 2007 election and the structural budget problems were canvassed from Gillard's first budget in 2011. Rudd and Gillard failed to get the priorities right.

In late 2013 and early 2014, after the transition to Abbott, Labor was exposed as the party of Old Australia. It championed corporate welfare, taxpayer subsidies for an uncompetitive car industry and protectionist policies in the name of 'Aussie jobs', stood with the trade unions in opposing Abbott's inquiries into union rorts, opposed spending cuts, ran scare campaigns on the GST and, to a large extent, defended the 'green scheme' status quo. It is true that much of the competitiveness problem flowed from the high dollar off the resources boom. It is equally true that Labor's policies were not geared to ameliorate the currency impact by promoting a more efficient economy.

In office, Rudd became a victim of his success; his mind never escaped the GFC. Karl Bitar's research told him the public had moved on, yet Labor seemed frozen in time. The public wanted the next story but Rudd's bookshelf only listed Keynes. He had no new story to offer. Rudd's priority was what he did each day—but that meant the absence of real priority. His effort to mobilise the GFC for ideological purposes left a damaging legacy. The chief executive of BCA, Jennifer Westacott, said:

> The GFC allowed politicians to argue for government intervention in markets virtually all the time by saying markets either did not work properly or could not be trusted. The idea was that government was at the centre of wealth creation. The great success of this country during the GFC was attributed to government, not our well-run and regulated banks and sound businesses making prudent decisions. Then after the GFC, when we could have done more to make ourselves competitive, we did the opposite. We went out of our way to impose inflexibility in the workplace and obstacles to resource projects. We sent a message to global investors [that] this was a hard place to do business. American companies told us they were holding back from investing in Australia.[10]

By 2013 and 2014 the evidence was embarrassing. The car industry had fallen over; projected budget spending could not be remotely financed by the tax base; Gillard loyalist and onetime AWU chief Paul Howes declared that the IR system was 'dragging us down', while former cabinet minister Martin Ferguson called for revision of Gillard's Fair Work Act. The bell was tolling: mere defence of the Rudd–Gillard legacy had become untenable in political and economic terms.

Labor, in office, had done many worthwhile things. It had many competent and reforming ministers: Jenny Macklin, Lindsay Tanner, Penny Wong, Craig Emerson, Nicola Roxon, Greg Combet, Martin Ferguson, Chris Bowen and Tony Burke—a list that could be extended. But what counts are the central economic outcomes and reform structure to deliver the future. The culture of a government comes from the centre—this was the central organising defect.

Labor's record is the subject of much confusion. There are two conclusions to be drawn on the 2007–13 era: Labor delivered economic stability and growth during an exceptionally difficult period marked by the GFC yet it was weak on economic reform, leaving a truckload of unfinished business. When Labor lost office in 2013, economic growth was running at 2.5 per cent, a below-trend result, having motored above 3 per cent for much of their time; unemployment was above 5.5 per cent and forecast to reach 6.25 per cent; inflation was contained at 2.5 per cent; Australia's performance had been superior to most other OECD nations but it was rapidly coming back to the field. Labor's reputation derived from surviving the GFC. 'What we have achieved is, by any measure, significant and will stand the test of time,' Swan told the author.[11]

While Garnaut rated Swan highly on the test of macro-economic management, he ranked him below both Keating and Costello as a reformer. It is a commentary not just on Swan but on the leaders he served. Rudd faced two great reform agendas—climate change and tax reform off the back of the Henry review—and left them in burning ruin.

Having raised expectations by commissioning the 'root and branch' Ken Henry review, Rudd failed to devise an ambitious reform. Swan constructed a package with a mining tax as its financing centrepiece, yet that mining tax unravelled. Labor never remotely tapped the potential of the Henry Report for a comprehensive tax reform package, an omission that became more glaring each year. It should have been a priority for Rudd's second term if events had gone to plan. When Labor lost office in 2013 the gap between spending and revenue made such a tax reform imperative, yet Labor had consigned this to Abbott.

Stephen Anthony, the principal of the Macroeconomics consultancy, of the Henry review: 'It was Swan's chance to make history. If Swan had an ounce of Keating in him he would have relished this. Labor should have done a major reform involving income tax, company tax and micro-economic reform.'[12] In March 2014, referring to Gillard's disability insurance and school funding initiatives, Henry said: 'We cannot afford new social policies with the current revenue base. We can't.'[13] The previous year, venting his frustration, Henry had said of the post-resources boom challenge: 'You would feel more confident about the Australian economy's ability to be resilient to these negative external shocks if you thought we had done everything we could in respect to domestic economic reform. Clearly, we haven't. There is a massive productivity agenda that needs to be prosecuted.'[14]

In early 2014, Parkinson defied Labor's blind orthodoxy that the GST must not increase. The Treasury chief said the budget situation meant genuine tax reform was required; he argued for a shift towards more indirect taxation, including the GST.[15] Labor's attempt to quarantine the GST for electoral gain constituted one of its most indefensible reform denials. A few weeks earlier Henry, tired by the political dishonesty, had flatly said the GST rate 'will be raised' at some point.[16] Labor refused to tell the public the truth—that not adjusting the GST would force people into paying more income tax or having spending programs wound back.

Rudd lacked a frame of reference to determine whether policy was good or bad. He was not a good conceptualiser; his mind defaulted to detail. He would drill down to specifics and focus on them. His office had good people but no policy heavyweights. From the start his ideological bias was documented.

Rudd was proud of his 1998 maiden speech. It launched the theme he repeatedly invoked: the power of the state as applied to individuals. In the second paragraph he was quoting Keynes. By the fourth paragraph he repudiated 'the death of ideology' and argued a 'fundamental divide' between Labor and Liberal over state power. He accused Howard of being 'Thatcherism writ large'. He rejected labour market deregulation, backed an 'activist role' for the state and said the public interest dictated that in some areas there should be 'no market at all'.

Rudd the moderniser was actually an orthodox social democrat. He felt Labor's mission was to reassert state power against the rise of economic liberalism since the 1980s. In coming years he would seethe with passion about this deeply conservative notion. He gave token recognition to the pro-market Hawke–Keating agenda; it had not penetrated him in any meaningful way. He was obsessed about depicting Howard as an agent of Milton Friedman and Friedrich von Hayek. It was a touch crazy. Ross Gittins said the idea of Howard as a neo-liberal was 'laughable'.[17]

Advancing his claims for the ALP leadership in late 2006, Rudd penned two essays for *The Monthly* casting himself as a social democratic moralist arguing that the battle of ideas was between 'market fundamentalism and fairness'. Under the title 'Howard's Brutopia', Rudd hammered the themes of market failure and declared Labor had 'a rich policy terrain in which to define a role for the state' and restore balance to Australian politics.[18]

The first signal of Rudd's interventionist intent had been his appointment of Kim Carr as shadow Industry Minister. Carr and Rudd found a meeting of minds. Upon becoming leader, Rudd asked: 'Will Australia in the future be a manufacturing country? Will we still make things?' Rudd's answer was that manufacturing had a bright future.

He declared himself a heretic among economic rationalists on these issues—the solution was activist government. On one occasion Rudd explained his philosophy to the author saying 'we cannot wait for the invisible hand of Adam Smith'.

Together Rudd and Carr launched a more intensive chapter of car industry assistance that would end in a shattering crash shortly after Labor's 2013 defeat. The Productivity Commission estimated that about $30 billion in taxpayers' subsidy was provided to the car industry in the fifteen-year period 1997 to 2012.[19] It is one of the epic failures in public subsidy in Australia's history.

In a 2013 interview with the author, Carr branded his strategy an innovation 'for what I call a richer, greener, fairer Australia'. Car subsidies were part of a much bigger idea. Who could disagree with innovation, clean energy and workplace fairness? These values were invoked to advance sectional interests. Carr insisted on including 'Innovation' in the name of his department. He was clever and not interested in reversing the tariff cut schedule. He sought instead hefty budget subsidies tied into matching investments from the car companies. 'During the GFC the industry was on the brink of collapse,' Carr said. 'Without the new car plan it would have collapsed.' Carr had no doubt: in 2008 he and Rudd had saved Australia's car industry.[20]

Labor appointed former Victorian Premier Steve Bracks to chair its car industry review, not the Productivity Commission. Sidelining the commission was essential. The Carr–Rudd tactic was to dress up protectionism as a 'feel good' green car project. It was a proven marketing technique: protectionism for environmental progress. In June 2008, Rudd went public: 'We do not just want a green car; we want a green car industry.' It was the worst brand of gesture politics.

In November the government unveiled a $6.2 billion package titled 'A New Car Plan for a Greener Future', with $3.2 billion extra funding, the plan running to 2020. It included an expansion of the Green Car Innovation Fund to total $1.3 billion. It was classic Labor industry policy: the bargain saw the government, the unions and the companies walk away with gains. Only the public lost out. The objective was to have, by 2020, a self-sufficient industry producing greener cars.

Carr revealed that the package was negotiated at the Lodge over a dinner hosted by Rudd in October 2008 with chief executives of the big three: Holden, Toyota and Ford. It was the corporate state on steroids. The government required investment commitments from the companies in writing. 'We sent the first letters back,' Carr said. 'They weren't good enough.' It is hardly a surprise: the multinational car companies were struggling and some faced bankruptcy. 'I took the view the government had to be deeply interested in the welfare of individual companies,' Carr said.[21]

His claim that Labor saved Holden's operation in Australia is true. Its commitment extended to provision of a $200 million line of credit to Holden when the Commonwealth Bank withdrew as the company's banker. It came on the condition that Holden retain its local operation. For Rudd and Carr, the test of success was 'whether the industry exists'. It was protectionism in its purist sense. The public was supposed to underwrite the proposition that Australia's economy was so weak that the exit of an uncompetitive industry in decline was intolerable. Rudd was ebullient because Australia would 'still make things'. There was never a test of whether the public investment was justified.

Productivity Commission chair Gary Banks warned in August 2008 that, on current assistance levels, each job 'saved' in the car industry came at a cost to the community of $300 000 annually. Banks said: 'The goal should not be to promote any particular industry or sector as an end in itself.' This was Rudd's precise policy and it failed.[22] In 2013 and 2014 Holden and Toyota announced their closures because they were unable to make their operations profitable. At the end of Labor's period in office Banks said car industry assistance was worth more than $1 billion annually; he called the industry 'the most successful rent seeker in Australia's history'. As for Rudd's alarm about not 'making things', the evidence was clear: 'the richer the country, the greater the share of services in its total output'. The public preference for an expanded services sector—whether restaurants, tourism or health services—was not a crisis demanding state intervention on behalf of car workers.[23]

In its January 2014 position paper the Productivity Commission, with Holden and Ford having announced their closures, recommended that all car industry funding should cease from 2020. It enunciated a story now obvious: global forces were driving changes in car making; subsidies to 'ride out' tough times would not work; scale in local plants was far short of numbers to be cost competitive; and capacity was shifting to lower-cost nations.[24]

Labor, in Opposition, blamed the Abbott Government for the closure of the industry and demanded that subsidies continue. Its leader, Bill Shorten, accused Abbott of having 'a dislike of manufacturing jobs' and claimed that his negligence would be 'felt for generations to come'. The public seemed more intelligent than Labor. The pertinent questions now had obvious answers. What was fair about subsidies to support car workers as distinct from other workers? Why should capital and labour be locked up in such an inefficient industry? Labor's culture was tied to union interests, corporate welfare, failed industry policies and an electoral politics whose time had gone.

The range of special protectionist deals for unions and sectional interests was vast. One example was creation of the Road Safety Remuneration Tribunal. It had the power to fix haulage rates in a way that favoured large incumbent freight companies with unionised workforces over the contractors and owner drivers who competed against them.[25]

Protectionism was conspicuous in what Gary Banks branded the Carbon Abatement Industry. Vast bureaucracies had been created in the name of clean energy to appease green politics. In 2013 Banks said: 'On the last count, there were over two hundred different programs to support this "industry" Australia wide. At the Commonwealth level alone, budgetary expenditure on such programs amounted to around $1.7 billion in 2011–12. All told, the transfers now dominate most other categories of industry assistance.'[26] Taxpayer subsidies in the cause of clean energy and higher prices usually guaranteed favourable and sometimes euphoric media support.

The 'Big Wind' turbines and solar panel industries were viable only because of taxpayer subsidies and the Renewable Energy Target (RET), which aimed to deliver 20 per cent of power from renewables. The RET was a high-cost method of emissions abatement. Gillard's 2011 legislated scheme had two arms: carbon pricing and government-sanctioned special deals. Big Wind, for instance, was a beneficiary of the $10 billion budget from the Clean Energy Finance Corporation. The Productivity Commission had urged the abolition of 'direct' measures once carbon pricing was introduced. Yet the clean energy renewable companies typically claimed a 'right' to taxpayer support.

The fusion that did the most political damage to Rudd was linking economic stimulus to energy-efficient homes. If you want a tragic example of Rudd being too smart, it is the perfect instance. Anxious to make his $42 billion fiscal stimulus as acceptable as possible, Rudd included a $2.4 billion program for rebates for insulation installation, the aim being to create jobs and secure an environmental dividend. The installation industry was weak and largely self-regulated and came under the authority of the states. Its rapid expansion through consumer-subsidised demand was fraught with risk, and when four people died at work in roofs a political outcry ensued, together with the scheme's termination in early 2010.

Rudd had personally insisted on an energy efficiency component to the stimulus. His department gave two officials in the Environment Department the 2009 Australia Day holiday weekend to cost and assess the scheme, keep it secret, avoid contact with the industry and have the finished product ready by the Monday public holiday. Their recommendation that the rollout extend over five years, not two, was rejected. It didn't fit the speed needed for the stimulus.[27] The report into the scheme by former senior public servant Allan Hawke made clear that the department lacked the resources and expertise to manage the scheme. Hawke found that the inherent risk 'could never be fully mitigated'.[28] Public servants were put in an untenable position, having to implement at speed a scheme that needed more time, regulation and safety. The Auditor-General's report found that, after Rudd came to office, the Environment department had responsibility for 107 new policy initiatives, including ten new renewable and energy efficiency programs.[29] It captures the madness of Rudd activism.

Attempting to use roof insulation as part of a speedy stimulus response was naïve and dangerous. The policy should not have been launched in this way, a judgement available at the time in the form of public service concerns. Environment Minister Peter Garrett, who had to oversee the scheme, was later demoted by Rudd. Asked what explanation Rudd gave him, Garrett said that, 'the issue was politically damaging for the government'. Garrett believed he was offered up as a sacrifice.[30] The most lethal comment comes from Greg Combet, brought in by Rudd to 'fix' the situation:

> The federal government, to my knowledge, had never run a program like that and the federal public service was ill-equipped to be running a program like that. Service delivery to a home is state and local government, not federal government. As a consequence, given the lack of systems—administrative, IT and financial—running that from Canberra was easily penetrated by fraudsters. I felt very sorry for Peter Garrett. He hadn't designed it but it got parked in his department. He was a political victim of it.[31]

The decision betrayed Rudd's inability to comprehend the limits of public administration and his uncritical faith in stimulus and spending agendas to deliver their aims devoid of unintended consequences. He paid a high price. The success of his fiscal stimulus overall was badly undermined by two programs: the $2.7 billion home-insulation scheme and the far too protracted $16 billion school halls program.

A classic in interest group appeasement was the bizarre late-2009 cabinet decision against allowing cheaper book imports as recommended by the Productivity Commission and advocated by Allan Fels. The commission recommended repeal of parallel import restrictions that protect Australian books and limit the sourcing of overseas editions. The opponents constituted a dream coalition of Old and New Labor sectional interests: the printing unions, the local book publishers, writers and the culture lobby.

The lions of Australian literature began their roar. Tim Winton said: 'Australian rights are fundamental to the maintenance of our literary culture, our publishing, our printing, our writing and teaching.' Richard Flanagan said the proposal was 'like handing the Obama children to be baby-sat by the Taliban' and, in case the public was too stupid to grasp his point, he likened the risk to Australia having 'its tongue torn out'. Evidently the enhancement of Australian culture depended upon the public being ripped off at the bookstore.

Gillard, who chaired the meeting, told cabinet that Rudd, who was overseas at the time, preferred to absent himself because a family member (Jessica) was writing a book for an Australian publisher. The numbers were extremely close; ultimately, the decision went against cheaper books. Craig Emerson who had put up the cabinet submission made a valiant effort to win some change. Fels said the overcharging was 'hundreds of millions of dollars' in a $2.5 billion industry. Gillard told a colleague that 'Kevin got the result he wanted'—and kept his hands clean. Rudd as prime minister could have turned this issue if he had had the inclination. That meant defying the jungle drum of the culture tribe and much of the Left in caucus; Rudd was not such a leader.[32]

Labor's great edifice to innovation was the National Broadband Network (NBN), the largest infrastructure project in the nation's history. It involved bringing optic fibre to homes or premises for 93 per cent coverage with a broadband speed capability of up to 100 Mbps and remaining premises accessing wireless or satellite networks. The project was run by NBN Co, its job being to design, build and operate the network with a timetable to reach all Australians by 2021. The NBN is a government-owned entity categorised in budget terms as a government business enterprise. Because it was expected to return a future profit, its funding fell outside the budget. The government would retain full ownership until the network rollout was complete, and its expected funding commitment in 2013–14 was $30.4 billion. The idea was to sell the NBN in future, enabling government to regain some or all of its costs.[33]

There was no independent cost–benefit analysis of the NBN. In 2010 Reserve Bank Governor Glenn Stevens said some projects ought to be done even if the private sector would not finance them—Labor's justification for the NBN. However, Stevens said, 'there ought to be, of course, a proper cost–benefit analysis of that case in those circumstances'.

Rudd promised a $4.7 billion government commitment at the 2007 election for the network but the Communications Minister, Stephen Conroy, didn't find any of the proposals submitted for the network to be adequate. Telstra had bombed out, though it was widely assumed that only Telstra could do the job. In a famous story, journalist Peter Hartcher revealed that Conroy had to fly around the country with Rudd in order to brief the prime minister and seek an answer from him. Hartcher reported that when Conroy explained, Rudd 'barely hesitated' and decided at once 'that if the private sector was unable to build the system the government would'.[34] For Rudd, it was a familiar situation: another market failure.

The NBN had a deceptive beauty. It offered faster broadband and more electoral kudos and the idea was carried through the SPBC and the cabinet. There was a catch, though: the cost. The initial estimate for the new scheme was $43 billion. Tensions between the NBN as a commercial venture and Labor's exploitation of it for political needs ran throughout the project at many levels. The rollout was inefficient, the costs escalated hugely and its commercial basis was compromised.

In his over-arching criticism made in 2013, Malcolm Turnbull said:

> Literally, nobody else in the world has done this. Nobody else has said we'll do fibre to 93 per cent of the population. When they decided this they had no basis for knowing what it would cost or how long it would take. I mean, to actually start a whole new project like this was fraught with huge risk. The smartest company in the world would find it risky. For Labor to embark upon this from scratch is staggering folly.
>
> I think this reveals an extraordinary arrogance, a megaloma-nia. Across the world, countries are upgrading their broadband networks. In almost every country the model is essentially the same: the private sector is doing it and the government is provid-ing subsidies to ensure regional and remote areas get better broad-band. The virtue of this is government knows what it's up for and all the risk is with the private sector. This is what New Zealand had done. I think it just shows how nuts they were. In its own way it's the maddest single thing they did.[35]

Meanwhile fibre to the home had become a Labor hi-tech ideology, a notion sold as a productivity enhancement. The NBN brought to a zenith an idea Rudd had long championed: the articulation of a unique Labor productivity agenda reflecting Labor values. It was first unveiled in his January 2007 blueprint for an Education Revolution. This remains the deepest insight into Rudd's approach to productivity.

He argued that future gains from pro-competition, pro-market policy would be limited because 'market settings in Australia are competitive'. That is, the job was largely done—a ludicrous claim. As a result, Rudd said, future productivity gains lay elsewhere—in technological innovation, in improving public infrastructure and in investment in education and skills. He called this the 'third wave of economic reform' after the dismantling of tariffs and national competition policy. This was Rudd aspiring to prove Labor's economic credentials by devising an alternative to the Hawke–Keating model—witness his Education Revolution and the NBN. It was a clever yet flawed construct. The nation, in truth, needed both options; it needed more market reform plus Rudd's third wave.

One of Rudd's pivotal claims came when in April 2007 he unveiled Labor's historic Fair Work Act pledge, saying the new IR system would be more productive, not just fairer. The ultimate justification of Labor's IR re-regulation is productivity; the Fair Work Act will stand or fall on its economic impact.

The FWA was the most important policy legislated by the Rudd Government off its 2007 mandate. Passed in 2009, it came into effect in January 2010, though many workplace agreements would not feel its impact till their expiry. Looking back, Greg Combet said: 'We had a number of key objectives and the Fair Work Act delivered on all of them. Julia's motivation was to get stuff done.'[36] The lesson was Labor's irrevocable attachment to interventionist IR machinery as the essence of its political identity. Nearly thirty years after the opening up of the Australian economy, Labor's rejection of a deregulated workplace remained its abiding faith. For Labor's political class, climate change policy could be sacrificed but workplace protection laws were non-negotiable. It was core business.

Gillard aimed high: she wanted to achieve a new status quo. The key to her law is the historical context. In the past generation there have been three IR phases: the great Keating–Kelty 1993 shift to enterprise bargaining; the 1996 Reith–Kernot model that entrenched enterprise bargaining, limited awards and created individual contracts (AWAs) with a 'no disadvantage' test; and Howard's WorkChoices, putting more emphasis on agreements and facilitating the growth of AWAs by removing the 'no disadvantage' test.

Gillard's model, while incorporating elements from the three previous models, most resembled the pre-1996 system. It significantly turned back the clock. The Fair Work Act championed collective enterprise bargaining, revived a range of trade union powers, abolished AWAs, removed employer discretions (notably on unfair dismissal provisions), strengthened awards and the safety net and vested the new umpire, Fair Work Australia, with more influence.

The 2007 policy was conceived in a period of economic prosperity, yet the Fair Work Act's operation coincides with high domestic costs and a competitive crisis off the high dollar. By 2013 much of the business community, big and small, had decided the model was untenable in the damage it would exact on jobs, profits and productivity. This resistance solidified in 2013 when Gillard legislated more pro-union measures covering penalty rates, workplace bullying, stronger union entry rights and greenfield agreements. Hostility in small business, services and resources is most pronounced.

The head of the Australian Chamber of Commerce and Industry (ACCI), Peter Anderson, pointed out:

> The reality is that the Fair Work Act did not just repeal Work Choices. It repealed central elements of the 1996 Howard laws and even some of the 1993 laws. This was done opportunistically because the political moment allowed it. The Rudd Government misrepresented the fact that AWAs had existed since 1996 and were not a creation of WorkChoices. We now have an industrial relations system that is incompatible with Australia's economic structure and an open economy. The Fair Work Laws are a flaw running through our entire economic framework. They don't work for a trade-exposed economy that is geared to the services sector. The irony is we are losing an industrial base yet we have an IR system designed for that base, a collectivist system built for the old economy when our needs are in the new economy, in services, small business and innovation.[37]

Innes Willox, the chief of the Australian Industry Group, says the FWA was 'fundamentally flawed', got worse the longer it operated and was contributing to 'business closures, redundancies and more jobs moving offshore'.[38] The BCA's Westacott says business did not accept government claims that the FWA was not undermining productivity and that 'the mood has become one of huge frustration'.[39]

The law has become a permanent new battleground hardly restrained by Tony Abbott's cautious 2013 mandate. Labor says there is no evidence that the FWA hurts productivity, a position buttressed by the 2012 review completed by Ron McCallum, Michael Moore and John Edwards that found the FWA was 'operating broadly as intended'. While expressing concern about poor productivity growth, the review concluded this was not due to the Fair Work Act.[40]

This makes Abbott's pledge to have the Productivity Commission review the Act a pivotal event. Winning political support for major revision of the FWA will be extremely difficult with only two likely pathways: a convincing Productivity Commission argument for reform or a recession that transforms the IR debate—a high price to pay.

The rift over the IR system, which is now unbridgeable, was basic to the collapse in Labor–business relations during 2012 and 2013. This is not simply posturing over ambit claims. Just as unions were able to destroy Howard's 2005 system, so business insists Labor's current model cannot work for the economy. This view is now seeded in much of the corporate culture, big and small. The conflict between Gillard's law and the demands of a competitive economy has just begun. It will be played out with serious, perhaps brutal, consequences. It is doubtful whether Labor grasps its full import: while Labor remains tied to the Fair Work Act it has mortgaged both its economic credibility and its hopes of constructive ties to business.

For Labor, the immediate showdown will come in the construction industry. Its abolition of the Australian Building and Construction Commission (ABCC) gave fresh sanction to 'fear, intimidation and coercion' on sites and revealed its craven and fatal appeasement of the CFMEU's rogue behaviour, an issue before the courts in 2014. It is rare in ALP history to identify a more blatant case of the party's commitment to union power ahead of the public interest.

In the late twentieth century, Australia decided to dismantle the Australian Settlement ideas of racial exclusivity, protection, arbitration, excessive reliance on state power and subservience to great and powerful friends. The recent lesson is that this separation is harder to make than many people appreciated. The Labor Party was fundamental in initiating this break and it will be equally fundamental in completing that break.

While the Rudd–Gillard era accepted the opening up of the Australian economy, it failed to recast Labor policy to sustain this trajectory. On too many fronts Labor retreated to a default position based on tradition and its instinct for state power rather than policies to sustain a competitive economy. Labor's job in Opposition must be to re-discover its reformist mission. If this does not occur then Australia's prospects will be jeopardised.

VI

THE CONSERVATIVE CRISIS

CHAPTER 16

TURNBULL: THE FATAL ASSAULT

As dawn broke with the temperature near freezing, the two cyclists were visible near the lake, pedalling fast, riding tight then pulling apart, occasionally talking while they rode. They were close yet distant—friends now, but such friendship had been transitory. As long as they had known each other they had been rivals and occasional enemies. As they cycled towards Parliament House the stars had left the morning sky but the personal stars of Malcolm and Tony were about to burn in fierce competition.

Turnbull and Abbott would become the principal figures in a chaotic, almost crazed phase of Coalition politics that threatened to rupture relations between the Liberal and National parties, split the Liberal Party and render the conservative forces unelectable for years.

As Liberals, they had so much in common and so much that divided them. If the Liberals were a broad church then Malcolm and Tony were the proof. These were both Sydney boys, aggressive, passionate and intellectual. They were GPS boys—Tony was St Ignatius, Riverview, and Malcolm was Sydney Grammar—and, from school days, they shone as natural leaders. Just three years apart, Tony was heading towards fifty-two and Malcolm would soon turn fifty-five. They were both law graduates from Sydney University, Rhodes scholars from New South Wales, Oxford University graduates, initially drawn to the excitement of journalism (Malcolm at the *Bulletin* and Tony at the *Bulletin*, then the *Australian*), both married independent and highly capable women on whom they depended, adored their kids and became dedicated 'family men' in the genuine sense. Malcolm and Tony were addicted to politics, possessed of frightening energy, wild emotions and, in their younger days, a raging ambition for advancement that left their colleagues reeling. They were self-made opportunists, men of action, authors dripping with passion and intensity, firm in their views about society and the world, preoccupied by

Australia's fate, from its Constitution to its spiritual dimension, with Tony a Catholic by birth and Malcolm a Catholic by conversion.

Yet they were complete opposites. They would provoke strangers to express amazement 'that they could belong to the same party'. Malcolm lived in a dazzling multi-level Point Piper waterfront castle while Tony lived in dullsville at down-to-earth suburban Forrestville. Malcolm was a rule-breaking entrepreneur who operated as Sydney's Renaissance Prince, carrying a flashing smile and a cold blade (used interchangeably), terrifying in the prosecution of his interest, the 'boy' adviser to the feared Kerry Packer, business partner of Labor's illustrious Neville Wran, wheeler and dealer with the city's media, financial and legal barons, attracting everywhere he went big names, big money, big friends and big trouble. Malcolm was your best friend at breakfast until he threatened to bankrupt you by dinner, always too mercurial to typecast, too restless to be complacent, with an intellectual outlook that astonished by its fantastic range. The richest man in Parliament (Kevin Rudd apart), he became Liberal leader just five years after entering the chamber.

Tony, steeped in Catholic culture and Jesuitical method, genuflected before tradition yet was an addicted rule-breaker. He glorified and romanticised the heroism and physical courage from the eighteenth and nineteenth centuries, a stupendous age when the British Empire ruled the world and heroes were writ large on the earth, their followers now having to settle instead for the tame offerings of the early twenty-first century—the volunteer fire brigade, the surf club and triathlon. Tony carried a humility that recalled the biblical giants, a charm that won patrons from B A Santamaria to John Howard, possessed little instinct for business and money-making but conducted a restless search for personal fulfilment from the seminary through the media to Parliament, worrying about his mortgage, dreaming about the leadership, working in Cape York among the indigenous peoples but becoming a hate figure within progressive politics for his views on God, the monarchy, women and cultural values. Tony presented himself as a conservative by belief yet he was a populist by deed, above all in his mobilisation of people power as a battering ram against the Labor orthodoxy. A myriad of contradictions, Tony, widely seen as both a values-laden dogmatist and a ruthless pragmatist, was elected Liberal leader in December 2009 on his pledge to crusade against Rudd's climate change ideology.

Malcolm and Tony had led opposing sides in a previous battle: the great constitutional referendum of 1999, with Malcolm as head of the Australian Republican Movement and Tony as head of Australians for a

Constitutional Monarchy. As with climate change, Malcolm sought radical change while Tony preferred a variation on the status quo. The author once sat between them chairing a debate on the republic. Beneath the surface they puzzled over each other—Malcolm struggling to accept Tony's intellectual credentials ('How did he ever become a Rhodes scholar?') and Tony forever struck by Malcolm's impatience ('his problem is that Australians will never trust him'). Each had acute insight into the other's weaknesses.

Still they became friends. Even when divided by the leadership, they were able to reconcile.

In November 2007, Brendan Nelson was elected Liberal leader over Turnbull with 45 votes to 42. The decisive event had been Peter Costello's refusal to accept his obligations and nominate for leader. Costello's firepower meant he would have taken the Coalition to the 2010 election. Having been denied by the party at its convenience, Costello would now deny the party at his convenience.

'I pleaded with Peter to stay and take the leadership,' said Senate leader Nick Minchin. 'I think it very regrettable that he declined.'[1] Turnbull said: 'I thought Costello's abandonment of responsibility after the election was terrible. Everybody expected he would step up.'[2]

Abbott had been anxious to stand but pulled out with less than a handful of votes. It was a humiliation that left him more determined. For many Liberals it confirmed that Abbott's ambitions would never be realised. The odds in early 2008 that Abbott would become leader that term would have been upwards of 50 to 1.

Turnbull expected to win but misjudged the party's conservatism. Minchin, who had worked against Turnbull, was pleased; he ensured that the party's conservative wing backed Nelson. 'I told Turnbull why I thought he wasn't qualified to lead the party at that time,' Minchin said. 'The point was, "You've been here five minutes, mate."'[3]

Turnbull was appalled by Nelson's emotional acceptance speech in the party room. As the party room broke, Turnbull was on the phone to a journalist saying Nelson's only honourable option was to resign because he was out of his depth. Immediately Turnbull went to Nelson's office, where the new leader was surrounded by packing boxes. 'You can't talk like that,' Turnbull said. 'That speech was funereal. You've got to toughen up.'[4] The subtext was that Nelson wasn't fit for the job.

Minchin said: 'When I went to Brendan's office to have a celebratory drink with him and his wife, he told me that Turnbull had already been around, confronted him and told him what a dickhead he was. Malcolm couldn't believe he had been beaten by Brendan. He couldn't accept the decision.'[5] Interviewed for this book, Turnbull said: 'It is right to say I didn't think he was cut out for leadership.' Turnbull defended his tough approach: 'I think you've got to tell people the truth.'[6]

Nelson was widely seen as a stopgap. With Howard gone and Costello about to go, the Liberals were sinking into crisis. Nelson lacked the strength to repel Turnbull, yet the Minchin-led conservative wing would never accept Turnbull. Minchin captured the resulting bedlam: 'Brendan told me how Malcolm would just tell him any time what an idiot he was and how he had to resign. In the end it really got to him.'[7] Meanwhile Nelson struggled over climate change.

In opposition, the Liberal Party's right wing began to treat climate change as an ideological issue—they saw Labor's agenda as a new economy-wide intervention that fused lost socialist dreams with a quasi-religious faith based upon a green scare about global warming. It embodied the two conservative demons: the reds and the greens together. Nelson's office chief Peter Hendy and senior adviser Tom Switzer told him to resist Rudd. Under Nelson's name they co-wrote an op-ed published in July 2008 warning that a unilateral Australian ETS would damage the economy. The policy ground was shifting; some Liberals were delighted, others terrified.

As Rudd's popularity soared and Nelson's position weakened, Costello faced renewed pressure to reverse his decision. The party longed for Costello. Nelson said: 'I'd be very happy if he changes his mind.' Julie Bishop said: 'Costello could have had the leadership on a platter.' Minchin told Costello that 'by allowing speculation to run you are undermining Brendan'.[8]

Just a few weeks before Costello resigned from Parliament, Joe Hockey and Costello dined together at a Kingston restaurant. 'I felt very confident he was going to stay,' Hockey said. 'He asked me if he ran for leader would I run as his deputy.' Hockey said yes. He assumed Costello was serious. 'In my view, with Costello as leader we would have won the 2010 election,' Hockey said.[9] But in mid-September 2008 Costello again announced that he would not be a candidate. The door was open for Turnbull and the Turnbull camp promptly briefed that Nelson was finished. Nelson decided to bring the issue to a showdown.

Minchin advised Nelson he would lose. 'Brendan just told me he'd had enough,' Minchin said. The Minchin nightmare—a Turnbull leadership—had arrived.[10] By calling for the contest, Nelson took Turnbull by surprise, but it wasn't enough. Turnbull prevailed 45 to 41, a slight turnaround on the earlier vote. He told the party room that the Coalition had to stay disciplined and competent.

Many people assumed Turnbull's wealth was his major problem; in truth, it was his electorate. Harbour affluence and inner city fashion defined much of Wentworth, putting its values at distance from many of the rural and suburban areas that voted Coalition. The label 'Wentworth Man' was deployed against Turnbull, a reference to the gulf between his seat and the wider Coalition constituency. 'I doubted he would be a successful leader,' Minchin said. 'My assessment was that for all Malcolm's brilliance, team play was not his forte.'[11]

As leader, Turnbull's strategy was sensible: to fight Rudd on the economy as the Coalition's strength and neutralise climate change as Labor's strength. That meant allowing Rudd to legislate his scheme, thereby removing the ETS as an issue of party division. It fitted perfectly with Turnbull's belief in pricing carbon. Turnbull's strategy enjoyed the support of Bishop, Hockey and most of his frontbench. Beneath the radar, however, internal turmoil over climate change was deepening.

The key to the politics of 2009 lay in Rudd's misjudgements. Rudd was untroubled by Nelson but saw Turnbull as dangerous. Yet his attitude to Turnbull was contradictory. He wanted to discredit Turnbull as an opponent by exploiting climate change scepticism within the Coalition yet also have Turnbull legislate his Carbon Pollution Reduction Scheme (CPRS). Rudd's refusal to resolve this contradiction proved fatal for him.

The government's CPRS bills were introduced into Parliament in May 2009 by the parliamentary secretary for Climate Change, Greg Combet, who said they were 'one of the most significant environmental and economic reforms in the history of the nation'. Turnbull's aim was to negotiate passage of the bills by winning from Rudd pro-industry concessions that made the policy more acceptable to the Coalition. It was a classic 'insiders' tactic.

But Turnbull would be caught short by a grass-roots rebellion among the 'outsiders', the foot soldiers of conservative Australia, the rank and file, their local regional networks and the emerging voice of 'outsider' sentiment, the powerful shock jocks led by the Sydney-based Macquarie group that broadcast throughout New South Wales and Queensland, its spearheads being Alan Jones and Ray Hadley.

The Coalition party room on 26 May decided to oppose the CPRS bills the first time and then consider its final position upon the second introduction of the bills. It was a stalling tactic to disguise internal divisions.[12] If the bills were defeated a second time, Rudd would have the trigger for a double dissolution election on his scheme. Rudd immediately taunted Turnbull for 'an absolute failure of leadership.' It became the standard Labor attack. Penny Wong said:

> I thought we could get Turnbull to the point where he would pass the bills. The question was always whether he could carry his own party. The setting up of the double dissolution trigger was a strategy. It was to put pressure on the Opposition to pass the scheme. My judgement was—and I think Turnbull's if you ask him—that his people wouldn't vote for it until they were placed under this pressure.[13]

Turnbull, in fact, didn't want to wait until later in the year. He didn't like the party room decision. 'We are going to be attacked as deniers between now and November,' Turnbull told his office chief, Chris Kenny.[14] Turnbull pushed in the shadow cabinet to start negotiating amendments with Labor as soon as possible. In the end, he had to back off, but Turnbull's sentiment was revealing. The Coalition negated the measures in the Senate in August. The pivotal debate would come in October 2009 with the measures introduced a second time. The Coalition, however, endorsed Rudd's reductions targets: the 5 per cent emissions reduction by 2020 from 2000 levels.

'I took the view we should be constructive and improve the legislation,' Turnbull said. 'Business was in favour of it. There wasn't a business lobby telling us to reject it.' But business worried about the scheme's design. Turnbull's tactic was to urge business leaders to speak out backing his improved scheme, not Labor's original model.

In June, however, Turnbull made a near-fatal blunder when, after evidence to a Senate inquiry from a Treasury officer, Godwin Grech, he accused both Rudd and Swan of seeking an advantage for a mate in relation to a car-financing GFC scheme and misleading the Parliament. Turnbull, convinced that the Prime Minister and Treasurer were finished, called for their resignations. He never recovered from this mistake.

Grech had been the source of Turnbull's confidence. Grech was a pro-Liberal leak in the Treasury with a history of providing highly reliable material. In an improbable saga, Grech had a memory of sighting a damaging email from Rudd's office but, unable to locate it, he later 're-created' the message and despatched it from home. Grech subsequently briefed Turnbull in person on Labor's car dealership fund but did not reveal that the email in question was a false document. Turnbull relied upon this incriminating document, over-reached, made his accusation and triggered a brief panic inside the government. But when Rudd and Swan confirmed that a search had shown no email, Labor had Turnbull trapped. They launched one of the most ferocious onslaughts in years.

Rudd set out to destroy Turnbull in the Parliament and in the media: Turnbull had relied upon a forgery to call for the resignation of the Prime Minister. Rudd's attack was methodical, merciless and awesome to watch. Sean Kelly said: 'The next morning it was crazy. We were calling gardening shows in Tasmania, ringing radio stations that had never heard from us. Everyone wanted to hear about Turnbull's incredible blunder.'[15] This event should have had a great consequence: it should have allowed Rudd to dictate terms to carry his ETS.

In a remarkable action, Turnbull, after he lost the leadership, went to Rudd and apologised over this event. Interviewed for this book, Turnbull said:

> While I had been the victim of an extraordinary deceit in the case of this forged email and while Grech was the last person likely to do something like that, I felt very, very bad about making those claims based on that email, however innocently or honesty. I was strongly of the view, deeply committed, that I should make an apology to Rudd. My colleagues and my staff urged me not to—they said, 'No that would be absolutely fatal.' They made the point that Rudd had made terrible allegations against Alexander Downer and John Howard that were clearly wrong. But after I lost the leadership I did apologise to Kevin. I spoke to him. I am strongly of the view that if you get something wrong like that and you cause offence you should apologise. It was a bad period.[16]

It is a remarkable testimony to Turnbull's character. What was said about Turnbull in Labor's counter-attack was worse in many ways than what Turnbull had said about Rudd. Very few senior Australian politicians would have had the integrity to apologise in this way.

Meanwhile the first internal domino to fall against Turnbull was the National Party. His most vehement opponent was Queensland National Party Senator Barnaby Joyce. Nationals leader Warren Truss had branded the ETS 'a job-destroying rabid dog that should be put down'.[17] An accountant and a maverick with a nose for populism and common sense, Joyce was the precursor to Abbott. Interviewed by Laurie Oakes in August 2009 Joyce was lethal: 'Everywhere there is a power point in your house, there is access to a new tax for the Labor Government, a new tax on ironing, a new tax on watching television, a new tax on vacuuming.'[18] At this time Joyce told the author:

> The mood is changing. I am now getting hundreds of emails a day from people. They hate this policy. They just hate it. And they actually get the gist of it. They know it's a new tax and they are asking: 'How does putting another new tax on me change the temperature of the globe?' Our constituency is demanding a position from us.[19]

The Nationals were tapping rural populism, working-class resentments, price pressures and climate change scepticism. Rudd's scheme was demonised as an exercise in cultural elitism and political correctness. But Joyce was prescient; he predicted that the revolt would extend into Labor's industrial heartland. 'It is cutting through in the blue-collar regions,' he said. 'It's in the Illawarra, in Newcastle and the Hunter and Central Queensland.' He was writing the script that Abbot would seize.

National Party Queensland Senate veteran Ron Boswell was a fierce opponent. He told the joint parties meeting in September: 'the Nats won't vote for it'. Truss privately told the Liberals that the Nationals could not be held—they must go their own way. It is time, Joyce said, for the Nationals to 'burn the boats'—à la Cortés—and take an irrevocable stand.[20] The Nationals had defected and a bigger revolt was coming.

The agony within the Liberal Party was a slower burn with a bigger explosion. In July 2009 Abbott emerged, to the surprise of many conservatives, as a Turnbull supporter. Abbott and Turnbull had been talking a lot during their riding exploits. For months Abbott had been musing about the issue, changing his mind from one month to the next. On 24 July 2009 Abbott, in an op-ed for the *Australian*, warned against provoking an election on the issue. 'Turnbull's assessment that the government's ETS should ultimately be allowed to pass is his attempt to save the Coalition from a fight it can't win,' Abbott said. His motive was pure politics: he feared Rudd would win any election contest.[21] When the author expressed the same view in a column, Abbott rang to say: 'Mate, you're right, we have to give Rudd his policy because we have no hope in a double dissolution election on climate change.'

But Abbott remained unconvinced by the science: 'We can't conclusively say whether man-made carbon dioxide emissions are contributing to climate change.' At heart, he was still sceptical.[22] The Newspoll coinciding with Abbott's op-ed had Labor's lead at 57 to 43 per cent on the two-party–preferred vote. The Coalition confronted a landslide defeat that might consign the Liberals to the wilderness for years. This was the assessment in mid-2009 of Turnbull, Hockey, Abbott and a number of senior journalists.

But Minchin disagreed. He became the rock upon which the conservatives rallied:

> I never accepted Tony's political view on a double dissolution and I tried to persuade him it was wrong. As a former campaign director I felt public opinion on this issue was relatively fickle. The sentiment of middle Australia was that it was crazy to act if nobody else was acting. People would never buy that argument. I argued in shadow cabinet I was more than happy to fight an election on this issue and I believed it was winnable.[23]

Minchin's assumption was that the late 2009 Copenhagen climate change conference would fail. He saw this first and he was vindicated.

The second domino to fall against Turnbull was the revolt of the Liberal senators legitimised by Minchin as their leader. This was more serious than the National Party revolt. During his career Minchin, at various times, had been close to both Howard and Costello. While on the conservative wing, Minchin did not have the temperament of an extremist. On the policy front, he had several objections to Rudd's scheme: he was unconvinced that anthropogenic carbon dioxide was the main cause of global warning, he saw pricing carbon before the other nations as an assault on Australia's economic competitiveness and he believed such action would have almost no environmental benefit since Australia contributed only about 1.5 per cent of global emissions. Minchin felt the broader Left was deploying climate change as an ideological weapon to revive its stalled fortunes and achieve an anti-business interventionist framework that had long been its goal.

'We were psychologically damaged in 2007 by the combination of drought, Al Gore and the *Stern Review*,' Minchin said. 'But I felt the situation was changing fast. The Liberal base had a different view and we had to be careful about our core 35 per cent base vote. I was convinced Liberal Party members would accept Australian action only as part of global action.'[24]

Minchin, unlike Abbott, was not for turning. Minchin said Coalition support for an ETS had to be conditional on progress at Copenhagen (which he believed would not materialise). The progressive media mocked Minchin as a climate change sceptic out of touch with public opinion when, in fact, Minchin's nexus with Copenhagen was a winning position. Sitting behind Minchin was a loose group fired by hostility to Rudd's scheme. Those who were named as likely rebels included Senate deputy Eric Abetz, Cory Bernandi, Alan Ferguson, Mathias Cormann, Mitch Fifield, Brett Mason, Julian McGuaran, Judith Adams, Alan Eggelston, Michaelia Cash, David Bushby and Chris Back.[25]

Alerted by an article written by Peter Van Onselen in the *Australian* that party-room sentiment was moving against Turnbull's position, Bishop told Turnbull: 'If this is half true, we have a problem.' They agreed she would take soundings. Bishop later reported to a shadow cabinet meeting: there was mounting opposition to supporting Rudd; the sentiment to wait until after Copenhagen was strong; people were not opposed to climate change action but there was resistance to 'caving in' to Rudd; and many Liberals felt the Opposition would gain nothing by supporting Rudd and that he would still denounce them as sceptics. These were dangerous omens for Turnbull.

In early October, Wilson Tuckey, a ferocious Turnbull critic, told Bishop: 'We're in the grip of a madman. I am on the precipice of calling a leadership spill to bring things to a head.'

In September 2009 Turnbull visited Britain, where he met Tory leader David Cameron, a symbol of climate change activism as a natural stance for conservative parties. Upon returning, Turnbull, more impatient than ever, put his leadership on the line. 'I will not lead a party that is not as committed to effective action on climate change as I am,' he said. It was a most unwise formula.[26]

Turnbull would 'do a Whitlam'—crash through or crash. He calculated that, in a showdown, he would prevail. Few were more stung by Turnbull's comment than ETS spokesman Andrew Robb. He felt Turnbull would railroad the party. But Robb had a more serious issue: suffering from depression, he had stood down from the frontbench.

The conservative wing had two complaints about Turnbull: he lacked the personal skills for leadership and he failed to grasp the nature of conservative politics and belief. Across the party, Liberals began to discuss Hockey as an alternative. In early October 2009, after weeks of pressure, Hockey adopted a new position: he would not oppose Turnbull for the leadership but was prepared to stand if Turnbull's leadership failed—that is, if he was removed. The complication, of course, was that Hockey backed the ETS.[27]

The pivotal moment, however, had come a few days earlier. Abbott visited the 1200-strong Victorian country town of Beaufort to speak to local Liberals over the night of 30 September. The local newsagent, Jim Cox, recalled that Abbott 'was rooted' when he arrived at the meeting.[28] It was hardly a surprise since Abbott had flown early that morning from Canberra to Adelaide for a shadow cabinet meeting. The CPRS was canvassed and it became obvious to Abbott 'that the Nationals would oppose the legislation'. For a coalitionist like Abbott, the earth was moving. That afternoon he flew from Adelaide to Mount Gambier, where he was met by the veteran Liberal MP for Wannon, David Hawker. They flew by charter to Ballarat, where they were met by Hawker's wife Penny, who drove them to Beaufort. Hawker told Abbott that regional Liberal MPs were facing a bush revolt on the ETS. As Abbott walked through the door of the community complex at Beaufort, he looked exhausted.

Abbott spoke for about twenty minutes, plugged his book *Battlelines* and asked for questions. The main topic was the ETS and Craig Wilson, editor of the *Pyrenees Advocate*, was sitting at the back of the room. Branch secretary Margaret Barling said it was a 'very happy night' and Abbott felt comfortable. He asked for a show of hands on whether the Coalition should support the ETS and 'only a handful voted yes', journalist Stuart Rintoul later reported. As he canvassed climate change Abbott, finally, said the science was 'crap' and Wilson had his story. Abbott relaxed later over a brandy.[29]

Next day a refreshed Abbott left for Melbourne about midday in a government car. He had plenty to think about during the 160-kilometre trip. He was soon on the phone to Minchin for a long conversation that Abbott said 'crystallised my new thinking'. He was returning to his conservative base. Abbott decided on the car trip: voting for the ETS would 'fracture the Coalition and split the Liberal Party'. It was too high a price. Opposing the legislation would invest the Coalition with a new opportunity: to campaign against Labor's 'giant new tax on everything'.[30]

Abbott's two-day trip would transform Australian politics for the next five years. He told Bishop: 'Our heartland is incandescent with rage.' Abbott believed the central task of leadership in this crisis of conservative unity was to hold the party together. Interviewed for this book, Abbott said:

In the latter part of 2009 there was growing unhappiness about an ETS in conservative sections of the community. There was unhappiness in the party rank and file. It was obvious that support for the government would only come at a very heavy price in terms of Liberal Party division. I tell you, it is a very big call by a leader to deliberately do something that will seriously divide his party.[31]

For Abbott, the issue was resolved: it was a question of unity.

For years Abbott had been one of Australia's most poorly understood politicians, perhaps because his formation lay outside the beltway. Abbott was a community-based politician, less impressed by Canberra-orientated policy doctrines and more impressed by the outlook of people beyond the beltway. More than most politicians, he was prepared to carry the views of 'outsiders' and impose them on political 'insiders'. Abbott's task now was to persuade Turnbull.

'Over the next two months I had many opportunities to put this to Turnbull,' Abbott said. 'In phone conversations, in shadow cabinet discussions, during a meal at his home and even on morning bike rides around the lake in Canberra. Malcolm was easy to talk to but impossible to persuade.'[32] It is doubtful Turnbull took Abbott very seriously.

In early October, Peter Costello, a Turnbull critic, told Bishop of the ETS: 'Seventy per cent want to vote it down but the leadership wants to vote it up. If the bill passes this is a big win for Rudd. Nobody trusts Turnbull any more. This issue is undermining him badly.' He asked Bishop if she would become a candidate for leader. 'Malcolm is in a death spiral,' Costello said. 'He's a wounded beast running on three legs.' With talk of Hockey as an alternative leader, Turnbull told Bishop: 'Joe's so sloppy, he's a lightweight. Of course I like him a lot and he's a friend but he's so insubstantial.' At the same time Turnbull, significantly, said: 'Rudd is unbeatable.'[33]

At a special party meeting on Sunday 18 October the Opposition agreed to a series of amendments to Rudd's scheme. It was a conditional victory for Turnbull. Its terms, however, were vital: the party room authorised negotiations with Labor to improve the ETS bills but this did not pre-judge its final decision. For Minchin and Abbott, this provision was critical. Combet introduced the bills into Parliament on 22 October. He said there was 'no need' to delay pending the Copenhagen meeting. Rudd's plan was to attend Copenhagen in triumph, having just won parliamentary approval for one of the world's most comprehensive ETS schemes.

Labor's negotiator was Penny Wong. With Robb on sick leave, Turnbull gave her Ian Macfarlane. It was hard to imagine two more different people than the tough Queenslander and the Adelaide feminist. Yet they came to trust each other.[34] Wong's worry was that she might cut a deal with Macfarlane that would be rejected in the Coalition party room. This was exactly what happened. Macfarlane knew her fears. At their first meeting he said: 'I want to tell you we can deliver—there are enough senators on side to pass the bill.'[35] As negotiators they established a trust—yet there was a problem.

Not far into the process Wong suddenly fronted Gillard. 'I'd like to know if I'm supposed to be negotiating this deal or crashing this deal,' she said. It was a remarkable question. 'Well Penny, I don't bloody know,' Gillard said. This was serious: Wong was tearful, emotional and worried, confused by talks either with Rudd or with his office. It went to the essence: was Wong's job to get the CPRS passed or discredit the Coalition by proving its refusal to accept climate change legislation? The fact that Wong was unsure was an astonishing omen. What was going on? The issue got sorted—Rudd wanted the CPRS passed. The point, however, is he had other aims as well: he wanted to use the issue to discredit Turnbull. Rudd wasn't operating as a conviction politician. Where was his campaign to sell his scheme to the Australian public? It didn't exist.

Having made little public effort for the previous three months, Rudd now engaged in overkill. In an address to the think tank, the Lowy Institute, he escalated the ideological war over climate change, affirmed it was the 'greatest long-term threat' to mankind and signalled that he would fight the sceptics, deniers and delayers in the Coalition. Turning the screws on Turnbull, he warned it was only twenty days until the Senate vote and only thirty-one days from the Copenhagen conference.

'This is a profoundly important time for our nation, for our world and for our planet,' Rudd said. His tactic was to intimidate Turnbull— if the Coalition destroyed the scheme then it was playing with 'our children's fate and our grandchildren's fate'. Indeed, the sceptics were 'quite literally holding the world to ransom', he said. If the Coalition found another excuse for delay it would constitute 'absolute political cowardice'. It would, Rudd said, targeting Turnbull, be 'an absolute failure of leadership' and such failure would 'echo through future generations'. This gamble with 'our jobs, our houses, our farms, our reefs, our economy and our future' was 'too big a risk, too radical a departure from the basic conservative principles of public policy'. Rudd demanded that the Turnbull-led Coalition back down and pass his scheme.[36]

What on earth was Rudd trying to achieve with such rhetoric? He needed Turnbull's support for the CPRS. But this speech had the opposite effect: branding Turnbull as a weak leader if he didn't fall into line behind Rudd? For becoming his legislative partner, Rudd offered Turnbull nothing but a truckload of humiliation. If Turnbull agreed to Rudd's public intimidation he would be seen by the conservative side as submitting before Rudd. In truth, Rudd was greedy; he wanted a win–win. He wanted Turnbull to pass his bills but he also wanted to discredit and smash the Turnbull Coalition as sceptics and deniers. Perhaps Rudd couldn't decide what he really wanted.

What should Rudd have done to secure the CPRS? He should have engaged in a leaders' dialogue with Turnbull and cut the deal one on one. Yet it was never done. They had a shared interest—they both wanted the bills passed. Rudd should have helped Turnbull to carry the coalition parties. It was obvious to Gillard. 'We should have thrown our arms around Turnbull,' she said. 'And not sought to keep taking a chip out of him.'[37] Rudd did the opposite.

Turnbull told Chris Kenny that 'if Rudd and I could only get together, I'm sure we could sort this out in an hour'. They decided to approach Rudd. Kenny said:

> I rang Alister Jordan and told him the issue was dragging on need-lessly and that if the two leaders could get together they could resolve it inside an hour. We offered a meeting, on the quiet, just to finalise the outstanding points. Alister said he would speak to Rudd. The next day he rang back. The message was: 'No go.' The negotiations would remain in Penny Wong's hands. There was no Rudd–Turnbull meeting.[38]

On reflection, Kenny said: 'I think Rudd was enjoying Malcolm's pain. It seemed Rudd was more intent on splitting the Coalition than "saving the planet". It made no sense because unless he wanted a double dissolution he needed Malcolm to pass his climate change legislation.'[39]

Mark Arbib alluded to the same point: 'Kevin had a lot of success using the ETS to wedge the Coalition. He expertly used it to end Nelson's and Turnbull's leadership, because their party was so deeply divided.'[40] In the end Rudd did destroy Turnbull but he failed to secure his policy, a pyrrhic victory. Rudd's press secretary, Sean Kelly, said: 'We missed the main game—what mattered was the passage of our scheme, not further discrediting Turnbull. I think Kevin Rudd misjudged the priority.'[41]

By mid-November, as the showdown approached, the odds still narrowly favoured the scheme becoming law. Turnbull said:

I thought if Rudd didn't get his scheme he would go to a double dissolution election in early 2010 and win. I felt allowing this to happen would be madness. We had lost a climate change election in 2007. Going back in 2010 to another climate change election was just nuts. If the Parliament ran full term then I felt we were in a strong position to campaign on debt and deficits and economic management. But Rudd's approach, frankly, was baffling. Maybe he was still dripping with anger over the Godwin Grech stuff, I just don't know.[42]

Turnbull's plan was to lock in his shadow cabinet, carry the party room, absorb the shattering spectre of Coalition defections in the Parliament, declare that Coalition amendments had made Rudd's scheme tolerable, get the issue off the agenda and announce mission accomplished. If the party room voted down his position then Turnbull was finished as leader.

In the last week of November an ebullient Macfarlane took the negotiated deal to shadow cabinet. Turnbull won a majority 14 to 6 vote to back Rudd's scheme as amended. But such division was ominous. The six dissenters included the three Nationals, the two Senate leaders Minchin and Abetz, plus Abbott. Minchin complained about Macfarlane's briefing to shadow cabinet: 'It was all wonderful, Labor had made lots of concessions. But I believed public sentiment was hardening and that Copenhagen was shaping as a failure.'[43]

In a powerful speech the previous week, Minchin told the Senate:

The government has no justification whatsoever for forcing this bill through before the Copenhagen conference. The government itself has delayed the actual commencement of this scheme until July 2011—eighteen months away. Frankly, Mr Rudd is prepared to sacrifice Australia's national interest on the altar of his vanity. It is also, frankly, idiotic of this country to legislate an emissions trading scheme before the US Congress does so.

The argument for legislating before Copenhagen was to satisfy Rudd's political needs.

The Wong–Macfarlane deal offered lots of 'bait' for Turnbull to exploit—an extra $1.28 billion over the forward estimates and $7 billion to 2019–20. Assistance to electricity generators was boosted. Emission-intensive trade-exposed industry won more help. The coal industry saw its support doubled to $1.5 billion. Extra assistance went to the LNG sector. Rudd's scheme was top-heavy with handouts. Treasury estimates showed that household and industry compensation would cost a fantastic $116 billion in the twelve years to 2019–20, testimony to the extent of churn from pricing carbon and ploughing the proceeds back. The viability of this design had to be questioned.

Rudd and Wong calculated they had probably done enough. But there were two problems: the process had taken too long and it was too public. The Coalition was near boiling point.

The pivotal event was the Coalition party meeting of 24 November to consider the shadow cabinet recommendation to support Rudd's amended scheme. This meeting determined the future of conservative politics for many years, and its consequences for Australia were far-reaching. The debate began at 10 a.m. with a briefing from Macfarlane who called the deal 'exceptional'. Most backbenchers struggled with its complexity. The meeting ran for more than seven hours, with two breaks. Its disputed outcome was an insight into the arcane nature of political rituals.

Turnbull's problem arose from the undisputed fact that a Coalition backbench majority opposed the shadow cabinet position. Several counts inside the room had 40 speakers against Turnbull's position and 35 in favour. Brandis, as official note-taker and briefer, had the numbers 40 to 33 against Turnbull. This is the sentiment that mattered, because the purpose of the meeting was to test backbench views of the shadow cabinet recommendation. However, a majority of backbench Liberals did back Turnbull, with Brandis scoring this 33 to 29 in favour of the package.

There is wide agreement about the turning point—it came when Andrew Robb attacked the deal, drawing upon his insiders' knowledge of the negotiations, given that his staff had been involved. Robb made no effort to talk to Turnbull beforehand and believed Turnbull had forfeited such courtesy. 'I could have claimed ill-health and just sat here,' Robb told the party room. 'But this is the biggest structural change in our history.'[44]

Robb said he supported pricing carbon from an 'insurance' rationale. He said: 'It was a mistake for Australia to get far ahead of the rest of the world. There are a lot of people, average people, who started off concerned about the issue who now felt like becoming deniers because they'd been lied to, defamed and kept in the dark.' Robb repudiated Turnbull's claim that the Coalition had got 75 per cent of its position. Then he tore the package apart: the coal industry had not got enough, many industries would be severely disadvantaged, small and medium-sized business would be damaged, the electricity generators still said it was a 'dog' and their loss of asset value was not addressed. 'I find this package unacceptable,' Robb said. 'It is bad policy. It goes nowhere near meeting what the party room wanted. And it raises sovereign risk issues.'

His message was that the Coalition was being conned. Loud applause greeted Robb's remarks. Turnbull was rocked. He later called Robb's speech 'an act of treachery'.[45]

The debate finished in the evening when senators were attending a division. Turnbull declared the result in their absence—he said there was a narrow majority for his package. He counted frontbench as well as backbench numbers to get the narrowest of majorities for his position. This provoked uproar. Brandis said that when the senators returned from their division 'there was pandemonium'. After a break the meeting was reconvened at 8 p.m., with Turnbull saying in a defiant speech: 'the decision I am making as leader is that there is a majority' for the legislation. With this call he put his leadership into jeopardy.

Minchin said later:

A number of us had gone to Malcolm's office during the break. I said to him, 'You're crazy to call this as support for your position. You cannot do that.' I urged him to tell the party room he'd take it back to the shadow cabinet. But he didn't want to do that.[46]

Later Turnbull said of Minchin: 'In effect, he was saying, "We've created an insurrection, now you must appease the insurrectionists."'[47]

Minchin described the situation after the meeting reconvened: 'I said we must find a way through that keeps this show together. I urged we say the Wong–Macfarlane proposition be sent to a Senate committee. That would allow Copenhagen to take place and full public consideration of the deal. But Malcolm rejected that out of hand.'[48] Turnbull's declaration generated white-hot emotions in the party's right wing. Its case against Turnbull was elemental: he was trying to 'steal' the Liberal Party. Kevin Andrews said a leadership spill was a 'possibility'.[49]

For Turnbull, counting the total numbers was rational. It was also in his own interests. Turnbull later pointed out that total Liberal Party numbers, including both the frontbench and backbench, were a strong majority for the ETS. There was no dispute on that point.[50] When the Nationals were added, this was reduced to a slender majority.

Minchin repudiated this view:

The tradition in the party room is that with contentious issues it is the leader's call but that prerogative assumes the leader acts in the interest of party unity. In this case a majority spoke against. For the leader then to say, 'We will support the legislation' meant there was uproar. The view that you just roll in the shadow cabinet numbers is outrageous. It had never been put before in my experience. The process is the party room comes to a view of the shadow cabinet recommendation. The issue should have been reconsidered by the shadow cabinet.[51]

The next day, 25 November, three Liberal senators—Brett Mason, Mathias Cormann and Mitch Fifield—resigned as shadow parliamentary secretaries. They intended to defy Turnbull and vote against the legislation.[52] It was proof that Turnbull could not stabilise the party. The conservative resignations from Turnbull's frontbench had begun.

The crisis over climate change policy now became a leadership issue. The next several days would be some of the most important in Liberal Party history.

CHAPTER 17

ABBOTT: THE ACCIDENTAL VICTORY

C onvinced the crisis must be lanced and unafraid of personal embarrassment, former Howard minister and social conservative Kevin Andrews decided to challenge Malcolm Turnbull. Andrews had no chance and his doorstop announcement was met by a mocking media. But Andrews made two calculations: the party wanted to vent its frustration; and he might destabilise Turnbull. He was right on both counts.

'I didn't think Kevin would beat Malcolm,' Minchin said. 'It was Kevin's own decision. I knew he felt Malcolm was unfit to lead the party.'[1] Turnbull brought the issue to an immediate contest on Wednesday 25 November. The party room rejected the leadership spill motion by 48 votes to 35. It was a strong vote for Andrews, the anti-Turnbull forces proving their strength with a candidate nobody saw as a viable leader. A switch of only 7 votes would have finished Turnbull. The Liberal Party was a smouldering mass of rumour, rancour and rebellion.

Hockey had offered strong support for Turnbull. He said after the ballot, 'Malcolm was very humble.' Continuing the tragic farce, Turnbull told the media he would work on his 'interpersonal skills' and confessed that 'even somebody as quiet and unassuming as myself can improve'.[2] 'Kevin did a lot better than I thought he would,' Minchin said. 'It showed the extent of anger towards Malcolm.'[3] The vote had a big impact on Abbott. Andrews had run in his own right; he was a stalking horse for nobody. But Abbott knew a bigger showdown was coming.

The pivotal play now came from Minchin. He refused to accept Turnbull's decision that the Coalition would vote for Rudd's ETS. Emboldened by Turnbull's vulnerability, Minchin now crossed the Rubicon. His decision not to vote for Rudd's ETS meant Minchin could not remain as Senate leader or in the shadow cabinet; he would resign. Minchin knew this would guarantee a full-blown showdown. 'There was a minority not prepared to accept the view of the majority,' Turnbull said in a summary of the assault upon him.

Minchin asked Abbott to come to his office. 'I made it clear to Tony that I could not vote for the legislation,' he said. 'Therefore, I had to resign from the shadow cabinet. Tony immediately said that was his position as well. We decided the proper thing was to see Malcolm and hand him our resignations.' Abbott confirmed that it was a joint decision. The purpose of his action, Minchin said, 'was not to knock off Malcolm as leader'.[4] Abbott said the same: his aim was to change Turnbull's policy. Yet Minchin and Abbott, as realists, knew the consequences. It was a declaration of war against Turnbull.

For Abbott, it was the biggest step of his career. The gulf in the party was now unbridgeable. Nobody was sure of how it could be resolved or repaired. Abbott said:

> A key moment for me came in late 2009 when Malcolm said during a radio interview that he would not lead a party that did not have the same views on climate change as he did. I found myself thinking: 'Mate, you've just given an ultimatum to the party and you may not like the way it responds.'[5]

Anxious to justify his actions, Minchin said: 'I knew this could have very serious consequences for Malcolm. My concern was that Malcolm was going to take the whole Liberal Party over the cliff. I had already offered him a way out and he declined to take it.'[6]

There was no personal rancour between Turnbull and Abbott. 'Tony had been a strong supporter of mine during that terrible Godwin Grech week,' Turnbull said. 'He helped then, he gave me a lot of good advice. My only complaint about Tony was inconsistency: he did change his mind a lot.'[7]

At 4 p.m. on Thursday 26 November, Minchin and Abbott saw Turnbull in his office. The situation was not complicated. 'I said Tony and I could not support the bill and, as a consequence, we would resign from the frontbench,' Minchin said. His deputy, Eric Abetz, would resign along with Senate whip Stephen Parry. They wanted to fight Rudd, not submit to him.

'It was a tense meeting,' Abbott said. 'Malcolm was calmer than I expected. I thought he would become quite angry.'[8] Turnbull made furious notes in his black notebook on the conditions of their resignations. In his rebuttal, Turnbull said: 'If I change the policy now, it will be the end of me.' Interviewed for this book, he said: 'I told them I could not maintain any reputation by buckling to this. I would just be a laughing stock. They were inviting me to a course of action that would have annihilated my credibility. I knew by this stage the die was cast.'[9]

Turnbull asked Abbott: 'Are you clearing the way for a leadership challenge?' Abbott told Turnbull the issue was not about the leadership. 'My aim is to change the policy,' Abbott said. 'If you change the policy then I will support you as leader.' Abbott said at the end he 'implored' Turnbull to refer the issue to a Senate committee until February. If Turnbull deferred the vote until February—the position Turnbull had already rejected—then the leadership would be unaffected. This was also Minchin's final plea: defer Rudd's legislation until the Copenhagen conference had taken place.[10]

Turnbull was going to fight; it was an honourable decision. He would stand by his principles and integrity. For Turnbull, it was an easy decision. Turnbull was fatalistic: he would 'crash through or crash'. 'Their aim was to kill the ETS,' he said. 'They were happy for me to remain as leader. When I asked them what our alternative policy was going to be they had no idea.'[11]

It would have been easy for Turnbull to purchase a three-month reprieve from the crisis, and many other leaders would have grabbed this delay. Not Turnbull. He knew that if he could not prevail now, then he could not prevail in February. Turnbull was prepared to die on his feet rather than live on his knees.

'Turnbull kept a poker face for most of the meeting,' Minchin said. But Turnbull was thinking clearly—his priority was the bills. He asked Minchin to remain as Senate leader to meet his responsibility to manage the climate change bills and Minchin agreed. Turnbull then summoned a group of senators. Brandis had arrived before several others. Turnbull's initial hope was to pass the bills as soon as possible. Once they were law, Rudd and Turnbull would have achieved their goals. Kenny spoke briefly to the Leader of the House, Anthony Albanese, about trying to keep the House sitting that night. It was too late. MPs were leaving the building to fly home. Yet the notion of Coalition cooperation to pass the bills in that environment was fanciful.

Minchin called a Senate party meeting to explain what had happened but more senators and members now insisted on backing the conservative position by resigning from the frontbench. Shadow ministers Tony Smith and Sophie Mirabella were resigning. Liberal MPs and senators were besieged by phone calls and emails from members and financial backers demanding they turn against Rudd's scheme. 'This isn't a leadership issue,' Abbott told the media on Thursday evening before writing an op-ed for the next day's *Australian* saying he wanted a new policy, not a new leader. But with Turnbull defiant the leadership was in play.

Turnbull had earlier called a media conference in the Opposition party room where he gave an electrifying performance. The entire building was glued to Sky News as Turnbull was simultaneously persuasive and defiant. Under pressure on a great policy issue in which he believed, Turnbull rose to the occasion in a show of desperate magnificence.

He defended his policy and signalled he would fight to the end. 'We must be a party committed to action on climate change,' he declared. 'Anything else is irresponsible.' As a matter of political integrity he was pledged to pass Rudd's scheme. 'This is about the future of our planet and the future of our children and their children,' he said. 'It is the responsible thing to do and it is the honourable thing to do.' He warned that if the party turned its back on climate change action that 'will be a catastrophe for us'. Denying reality, Turnbull said the mass resignations had not weakened his leadership.

In private Turnbull said he would fight a spill motion and contest the leadership if it was carried. 'If they want to remove me they must take ownership of the decision,' he said.[12] The next day Abbott said he was prepared to contest the leadership but would withdraw if Hockey ran. Meanwhile Julia Gillard said if the Coalition failed to pass Labor's legislation it would have been conquered by 'sceptics and deniers'.[13] Labor had its script on the great conservative revolt. It was an act of betrayal—of Turnbull, of the nation, of responsibility, of the planet.

The Liberal Party had reached a crossroad. The broad church Howard had championed of liberals and conservatives was shattering over climate change. Howard may have found a path forward but Howard had retired. Turnbull was seen as too liberal by the conservatives and Abbott was seen as too conservative by the liberals. The struggle was about the values and ideology of the Liberal Party in the age of climate change.

'Have we learnt nothing from 2007?' Turnbull asked. 'The people that have sought to tear me down do not even believe in the policies that we took into the last election. They basically believe or regard John Howard as being too green.'[14] Yet the party's base was being mobilised in a fierce campaign, with Sydney's most popular breakfast announcer, Alan Jones, launching broadsides against Turnbull. A Nielson poll showed public support for the principle of an ETS running at 66 per cent in favour and only 25 per cent against. Yet on timing the public wanted to delay legislation until post-Copenhagen.[15] Abbott recalled an exchange on radio between Jones and Turnbull: 'Malcolm was getting quite angry towards someone who is greatly admired by many members of the Liberal Party. Disagree with him if you must but don't get angry with him.'[16]

At the weekend Turnbull launched a premeditated strike during his Sunday morning interview with Laurie Oakes. Referring to his enemies as Minchin-ites, he said: 'There is a recklessness and a wilfulness in these men which is going to destroy the Liberal Party.' He said their views 'are completely wrong and are contrary to the best interests of our nation, our planet and indeed the Liberal Party.' Branding Minchin as a climate change denier, Turnbull said 'if he wins this battle, he condemns our party to irrelevance'. His target was Minchin, not Abbott.

This confirmed that a Turnbull victory would deepen the internal divisions. Indeed, he seemed fatalistic about the future, saying of the Minchin forces: 'They will not give up. They will not give up until they are crushed in an election and the bizarre thing is they mightn't give up then … these men are leading us into an electoral catastrophe.'[17] Kenny was alarmed, sure that Turnbull had gone too far. But Turnbull had merely polarised the divisions, hoping to frighten the waverers back to him.

Turnbull's problem, though, was that the party base was moving against him. The crisis was generating an atmospheric that led to Joe Hockey. Hockey was Turnbull-lite on policy, while substituting camaraderie for abrasion. Many Liberals felt his style was more appealing than that of Abbott, who excited polarisation. Hockey tweeted: 'Hey team re the ETS. Give me your views please … I really want your feedback.' Hockey was in play. Over the weekend of 28–29 November he finalised his position: he would support Turnbull and not directly challenge him but if the leadership became vacant then Hockey would nominate. Hockey told Turnbull of his decision.

Hockey was appalled by the party's downward spiral. He wanted the ETS to pass and he preferred Turnbull to stay leader. For Hockey, with three young children, this was not the right timing to ascend as Liberal leader but he recognised that politics is not designed to suit the convenience of the players. Hockey had criticised Costello for walking away from the leadership and knew he could not make the same mistake himself. After discussing the issue with his wife, Melissa, Hockey was ready to nominate.[18] The judgement of many Liberals was that Hockey was a better choice than Abbott to re-unite the party; this was certainly Minchin's view.

'My assessment was that in any contest Joe would beat Tony,' Minchin said. 'I also felt Joe had the best prospects of being a healing leader.'[19] Abbott was ready to cooperate. He told Minchin and Hockey he would not contest the leadership on the assumption that Hockey would take over.

Minchin praised Abbott's decision. 'Tony, to his credit, accepted the best thing was for Joe to have our support [the Liberal right-wing support] to take over the leadership,' Minchin said. Tony would defer to Joe.[20]

There was, however, a catch. The unresolved question remained: how would any new leader deal with the ETS legislation? After all, the legislation had triggered the crisis. This penetrated to Howard's test: what was the best solution to unite the party? Hockey and Abbott had different answers to this question and, in the end, that determined the result.

The leadership was coming towards Hockey. The prize was within his grasp. The moderates preferred him to Abbott and the right wing was ready to accept him over Abbott. Hockey would be elevated to the leadership as a consensus candidate by a party desperate to find stability. On Monday 30 November the Liberals were engulfed in a series of meetings mainly around Hockey's office. But Minchin and Abbott had a demand: the conservative wing wanted Hockey as leader to defer any vote on the ETS legislation until February and then vote it down. For Minchin and Abbott, the supreme objective remained the defeat of Rudd's ETS. It was the non-negotiable price they demanded from Hockey to make him leader.

But Hockey refused to meet their demand. He was prepared to delay the vote; he was not prepared to defeat the legislation. This was for two reasons. Hockey's support for the legislation was on the public record and he had backed Turnbull's position in private and in public. He saw his leadership would be compromised from the start, perhaps fatally, if he was seen to have bargained away his climate change principles to win party-room votes to become leader. If he did this deal, Rudd would destroy him as 'puppet of the climate change deniers'. Hockey's second reason was that he felt the best electoral position for the Liberals remained support for the legislation, operating from the middle ground and getting the main political debate onto the economy.

Faced with this dilemma, Hockey proposed a free vote (or a conscience vote) on the scheme. Minchin and Abbott were dumbfounded. 'When Joe floated his notion of a free vote, Tony and I reacted very strongly against that,' Minchin said. 'I thought we had convinced him it was a bad idea.'[21] Despite the pressure, Hockey refused to buckle. He knew doing this deal meant his leadership would be doomed from its inception and he would be mocked by Labor as a Minchin–Abbott stooge. Hockey stood by his free vote idea. An incredulous John Howard rang Hockey to say a free vote wouldn't work.

By any calculation it meant the legislation would be passed since there would be enough Liberal moderates in a free vote to give Rudd the numbers in the Senate. Minchin and Abbott saw this at once. For Hockey, it was a neat idea but conceived in weakness.

Minchin said: 'Joe was effectively saying that his first act as leader would be not to lead. It would have been untenable for the party to have no view on such an important issue. Tony then told me very strongly that if this was Joe's position he would not accept it. In this situation Tony said he had no option but to nominate for leader.'[22]

Before the meeting broke, Abbott said he would contest the leadership as the anti-ETS candidate. Just after 7 p.m. the evening before the ballot he emerged to announce this decision. Abbott said it was 'not possible' for the Liberals to offer a free vote on this policy and stay credible.

This was Abbott's answer to Howard's unity test. It was to re-group and re-unite the Coalition around a new position that repudiated Rudd's scheme. It was to terminate Turnbull's belief in the ETS. Abbott's instincts left him convinced this was the only viable solution for the conservative side of politics. He was sure that supporting Rudd's ETS would destroy the Coalition at its base.

Abbott had read the mood of the party members. He disagreed with Turnbull that to reject the scheme would be a catastrophe for the Liberal Party. On the contrary, Abbott saw the tide running fast: support for Rudd's ETS would betray the Coalition base, weaken the conservative side for years, hand Labor an immense propaganda victory and make Rudd into a political hero. Having finally settled on his position, Abbott was immovable. He saw that the party wanted to fight Rudd, not embrace him. Of the three contenders, only Abbott was ready to burn the boats. Endorsement of Rudd's scheme meant the Liberals would have joint responsibility for its defects.

The Newspoll published on Monday 30 November was sobering. On the question of best candidate to lead the Liberals the results were: Hockey 33 per cent, Turnbull 30 per cent and Abbott 19 per cent. On the ETS, the public backed Turnbull with a 53 per cent to 32 per cent split in favour of the Coalition supporting the ETS. In two-party-preferred terms Labor led the Coalition by a massive 57 to 43 per cent. If the party room followed the polls it would vote for Turnbull or Hockey and forget Abbott.

'There was disappointment we could not reach agreement with Joe,' Minchin said. 'I know Joe was concerned about his own integrity.'[23] Minchin was backing Abbott but without much confidence. Abbott did not expect to win but did not rule it out. During the meetings in Hockey's office Hockey said he wanted Peter Dutton as his deputy. Bishop was rocked; it was the first she had heard that the deputy's position would be spilled as well. After the meeting broke Abbott came to her office. He asked her to stay deputy if he won the ballot. Bishop agreed.

When Hockey entered the party meeting on the morning of Tuesday 1 December he still expected to emerge as leader. He knew the combined Turnbull–Hockey vote was greater than the Abbott vote. Moreover, Hockey believed he had an understanding with Turnbull that, if the spill motion was carried, then Turnbull would not nominate and the leadership contest would become a Hockey–Abbott two-horse race. Hockey would win such a contest. But Hockey's understanding proved false. Indeed, it was this misunderstanding that brought the moderate wing of the Liberal Party undone.

'I have a very clear recollection that Malcolm told me on more than one occasion that if the spill was carried then he would not be a candidate,' Hockey said the day after the ballot. Interviewed for this book, Hockey was emphatic: Turnbull had given him and others this assurance.[24] A number of Hockey's backers confirmed it. Minchin said: 'Joe had categorically told our meeting that he had been told by Malcolm that he would not run against Joe if the leadership spill was carried.'[25] For Hockey, it was a form of quid pro quo. He would support Turnbull on the spill motion but, if it was carried, then Turnbull would not nominate, allowing Hockey to compete against Abbott with the support of the combined Turnbull–Hockey forces.

Turnbull rejected Hockey's version of this so-called understanding. The day after the vote, Turnbull confirmed Hockey had asked him to stand aside if the spill was successful. 'I didn't give Joe an undertaking that I wouldn't run if the spill was carried,' Turnbull said. 'I came to the view that if there was only one other vote for me, I didn't want to deny that person the opportunity to vote for me.' Turnbull was as emphatic as Hockey about his own interpretation.[26] Turnbull's supporters believe Hockey had convinced himself about what he had wanted to hear. The previous Friday when the author and editor-in-chief of the *Australian*, Chris Mitchell, had lunched with Turnbull at Tabou restaurant in Surry Hills, Turnbull's firm disposition was to fight to the end and keep fighting if the spill was carried. Interviewed for this book, Turnbull said: 'I had made it clear that I intended to stand.'

The absence of any agreed Turnbull–Hockey tactic fatally weakened the moderates. The spill motion against Turnbull was carried 48 to 34, suggesting he was finished as leader. But when nominations were called for leader, Turnbull nominated with Hockey and Abbott. In the first ballot Abbott polled 35 and Turnbull 26. Hockey, with 23 votes, was eliminated. This sent shockwaves through the party room. The combined Turnbull–Hockey vote was 49, signalling a majority against Abbott. It was obvious that in the final ballot Hockey would have been in a better position than Turnbull to retain more of these 49 votes. In any Hockey–Abbott ballot, it is almost certain Hockey would have won.

Many Liberals were shocked to find the choice they now faced was Turnbull or Abbott. In the end Turnbull came to the brink of a remarkable victory, losing to Abbott only 42 to 41 in the second ballot. Abbott said later he had won by accident. 'When I went into the party room I didn't expect to walk out leader,' Abbott said. 'Nick had done a lot of counting and I knew he didn't think I'd win. I expected the final ballot would be Abbott v Hockey, with Hockey winning.'[27] It was only with Hockey's elimination that Abbott realised he would probably win. 'My God,' he thought. Abbott began scribbling notes for an acceptance speech. 'I'm a bit overwhelmed,' Abbott said leaving the meeting. Hockey said he was surprised by the result.

Turnbull was surprised at his vote. 'I thought I would run last,' he said. 'I felt I had zero chance. I was fully resigned to my fate. There turned out to be more support for me than I thought.'[28]

Minchin said he worked hard for Abbott on the assumption that Hockey would win.[29] His nightmare was a possible Turnbull victory. Some Liberals reported Minchin turning grey in the meeting when Hockey was eliminated. Minchin said if Turnbull had not nominated then Hockey would have won. 'Yes, I was surprised when Turnbull nominated,' Minchin said. 'With this bloke anything's possible, but I was surprised he did that to Joe.'[30]

There was a pivotal second stage to the meeting. As soon as Abbott had won, Kevin Andrews had written out a motion on the ETS. In a remarkable event, a secret ballot on the ETS was held, the result being 54 to 29 against. Most people were surprised at its magnitude. It was as though the party, recognising Abbott's elevation, got behind his rejection of Rudd's scheme. In later years people remembered Abbott's one-vote margin over Turnbull but forgot the convincing majority for his rejection of the ETS. The Coalition had completed a policy and leadership revolution.

In his address to the party room Abbott said:

> The most important task is to heal the wounds. I will do my best to be as collegial and consultative as possible. This has been the most tumultuous week in the history of the Parliamentary Liberal Party in the past thirty-five years. We can win if we play as a team.

Abbott said the party had to avoid a repeat of the Peacock–Howard experience of the 1980s.

As they left the party room, two Turnbull backers, Brandis and Pyne, were shocked. 'I felt we had to see Tony as quickly as possible,' Brandis said. 'As Turnbull supporters we offered him our support. I think he appreciated that.' Pyne and Brandis became part of Abbott's inner sanctum.

At his first media conference Abbott played to the psychology of transformation. 'I cannot promise a victory but I can promise a contest,' he said. The Churchillian tones were unmistakable. Abbott was a fighter and he would command attention. The equivocation of Nelson and the progressiveness of Turnbull were gone. Abbott laid down his benchmarks: the Coalition would meet Labor's 5 per cent emission reduction by 2020; it would campaign against the ETS; and Abbott would devise his own alternative policy. It was a new political world.

Turnbull retired to the backbench. Quitting politics at that point became a likely choice. He had different attitudes towards Minchin and Abbott. 'Minchin was in the shadow cabinet,' Turnbull said, 'and he set out deliberately to undermine the policy the shadow cabinet had adopted. Tony did not do that. At the end Tony became the candidate against the policy.'[31]

How important was Rudd's role in these events? By any test, it was critical. If Rudd had brought the vote on several weeks earlier by engaging directly with Turnbull then the bills may have passed. It would have been Rudd legislating a carbon price in 2009 rather than Gillard in 2011. Rudd's hard line drove a fusion between the ETS and the Liberal leadership that saw Turnbull fall. The longer the debate lasted, the weaker became Turnbull's internal position.

Gillard, in retrospect, was critical of the tactics: 'If we had thrown our arms around Turnbull early enough and hard enough we could probably have got something that was at least a viable start.'[32]

'We didn't take Turnbull down,' Penny Wong said. 'His party took him down. They chose to execute a leader rather than take action on climate change. That was their decision.'[33] There is, however, no denying that Rudd misjudged the high politics of this issue. When he lost Turnbull, he lost his policy. How clever was that?

How serious was the 2009 situation for the Coalition and Liberal Party? Speaking for the conservative wing Minchin said it was a moment of historical crisis: 'In my view Turnbull's determination to do a deal with Rudd would have done potentially irrevocable damage both to the Coalition and to the Liberal Party. I argued in shadow cabinet that nobody should underestimate the potential for a split in the Liberal Party. I argued strongly to Tony that this had to be averted.'[34]

This was not Turnbull's assessment: 'I didn't think our base was as agitated as they claim. There was a ferocious email campaign conducted. Most people wanted to see us with a credible climate change policy and an ETS had been John Howard's policy.'[35]

On 2 December the Senate voted down Rudd's scheme 41 to 33. The Greens, the independents and the Coalition voted against. There were only two Coalition defectors in Senator Judith Troeth and Senator Sue Boyce. 'There'll be no recriminations,' Abbott said of the defectors.

Rudd's dream of passing his scheme in Parliament with Liberal Party votes was dead. Even more significant, the Liberals had staged a revolution—they had changed their leader, their policy and their strategy.

THE DEMISE OF RUDD

CHAPTER 18

HOW RUDD GIFTED ABBOTT

Kevin Rudd's leadership came under stress for the first time when a pugilistic Tony Abbott taunted him to call a climate change election. Like the boxer he once was, Abbott came to intimidate. It was obvious what Rudd must do: mobilise his capital, exploit Abbott's vulnerability and prepare for an election. Yet Rudd did none of this. He lost his nerve and gave Abbott a sniff of victory.

The opening story in the politics of 2010 was a shock: it was how Rudd created Abbott. And Abbott never lost this early momentum.

It took months before many of Rudd's colleagues realised that something had malfunctioned with their leader. Yet the insiders saw it quickly. In December 2009 Rudd faltered, battered by the destruction of his CPRS scheme and the dismal outcome from the Copenhagen conference. Gillard, Swan and Wong realised Rudd was damaged. There was an element of psychological paralysis.

Abbott concealed his weakness by projecting strength. 'The early election that he [Rudd] has threatened us with: bring it on and we will be ready for you,' Abbott said.[1] His aggression would be either brilliance or folly. 'I think he lives in his own world,' Abbott said of Rudd. As a boxer and rugby union front-row forward, Abbott had been raised in the techniques of intimidation. He felt Rudd might succumb under pressure. Few agreed with him, yet Abbott would be vindicated.

'When I became leader I knew I was facing a tough opponent,' Abbott said. 'But I was never over-awed by him. I felt his support in the community was very brittle. I remember somebody writing that Rudd's only friend in the caucus was Mr Newspoll.'[2] Abbott drew inspiration from a deeper conviction: 'I was absolutely convinced by the end of 2009 that the ETS was a political dog. My gut feeling was that if we managed to keep people focused on it, we had quite a good chance of winning the 2010 election.'[3] Abbott had become Liberal leader on this gamble.

In truth, support for the ETS was far from finished. The conventional wisdom was still against Abbott.

Abbott's eruption from stage right was sudden, almost shocking, as he swung hard at Labor and discussed in interviews his faith, his family and his hopes. For many Labor loyalists Abbott seemed like a mad bull wrecking their understanding of how the world was supposed to work. Rudd staffer Sean Kelly said: 'It is absolutely true that Abbott was under-estimated. I recall being with a senior ALP figure and staff when the news came through that Abbott had won the leadership. We were thrilled. We sat there with stunned grins on our faces.'[4]

Rudd felt Abbott was a poor choice as leader, too elemental and too extreme. Labor fell for its own propaganda: that the Liberals had been conquered by sceptics and deniers. Much of the ALP believed Abbott would not last as leader and assumed he fell outside the norms for successful leadership. The Labor prejudice towards Abbott ran deep: it was assumed he was too religious and too sexist to be accepted by the public. Labor was so emotionally hostile towards Abbott it had trouble thinking rationally about him. Abbott, by contrast, had an insight into Rudd's flaws.

Having destroyed Rudd's climate change policy in the Parliament, Abbott's mission was to destroy the policy in the nation. There was only one method of fighting Abbott: to stand up to him. It was the option Rudd rejected. This blunder would turn Abbott into a giant killer.

Moving quickly, Abbott recast the ETS debate. With audacity, he said the issue was not climate change but tax. Not climate change? What had the past five years been about? As Abbott re-defined the test to the hip-pocket nerve, Labor seemed clueless. The most startled observer, however, was Malcolm Turnbull. Turnbull's entire 2009 assumption was that Rudd, if denied, would call a climate change election. But Rudd was immobilised; he didn't want to fight.

Turnbull said:

> If Rudd had gone to a double dissolution election in early 2010 I am sure he would have won it. What none of us ever imagined was that Rudd would lose his nerve the way he did. Why he did that is beyond me. You know, Tony Abbott has made the most of his luck. But Kevin Rudd made a pretty sizable contribution to Tony's good fortune.[5]

In Parliament, Labor had been torn apart by the Coalition and Greens coming from different sides. The destruction of its CPRS had been a brutal affair. Emboldened by Abbott's election, Barnaby Joyce mocked Labor:

> Will the ETS fix the drought, minister? No, it will not. Will the ETS cure the Great Barrier Reef? No, it will not. Will the ETS stop Greenland from thawing? No, it will not. … I say to the Australian Labor Party: bring it on. We welcome the opportunity to go to the Australian people to clearly spell out to every man, woman and child that what the Australian Labor Party proposes for the future of our nation is a massive new tax.[6]

The Greens lanced Labor for appeasement of polluters. Christine Milne said:

> This is a craven cave-in to coal-fired generators. It is a disgraceful public policy … The earth will not wait. In 2015 global emissions must peak. The government's own modelling says that we are not going to see a reduction in emissions from the energy sector until 2034, well beyond the tipping point. We will have lost the Arctic ice by then. We will have had ocean acidification. Once we go across those tipping points there is no coming back.[7]

Milne kicked Rudd's scheme to death. Bob Brown danced on its grave. Venting his hostility to Rudd, Brown said: 'We [the Greens] were not taken into account at any time. Rudd didn't see me despite my requests.'[8] The Greens were never part of Rudd's plan. He relied on the Coalition and he lost. Despite this, the Greens had the chance to make carbon pricing the law of the land. They refused. Many ALP figures never forgave them. 'They were an irresponsible bunch, a teenage fantasy bunch of irrational fundamentalists,' Lachlan Harris said.[9]

But Labor lacked the stomach to fight. When asked about a double dissolution, Gillard, as acting prime minister, merely said 'all options are on the table'. She said Labor would introduce the bills for a third time when Parliament resumed in February to give the Liberals a 'chance' to rethink. The *Sydney Morning Herald*'s Phillip Coorey reported that Labor sources said 'it was hoped that a combination of a long dry summer and growing public concern about climate change would pressure the Liberals to reconsider'. It was a joke. There was no end to Labor self-delusion. Abbott saw the weakness in Labor's soul and each day he gained confidence.[10]

Since 2007, Labor had enjoyed too much success for too little conviction. The fire of Whitlam, the mettle of Hawke, the fight of Keating—all were gone from the ALP.

The Liberals were nervous, still shaking from their internal crisis. Abbott was a new and risky commodity for the public to absorb. Yet Abbott knew that causes are the lifeblood for parties. He had given the Coalition a cause. 'We had a fight on our hands and political parties are at their best when they have a fight,' he said.

From 2 December the choice facing Rudd was obvious: given that the Coalition and Greens had killed his CPRS he had to either accept such defeat or take the issue to a 2010 election. If he decided on an election the tactical question became whether to strike with an early double dissolution against Abbott or to hold a normal election later in the year. Given the momentum Abbott was likely to build, the argument for an early double dissolution was persuasive. Of course, a dash to the polls was always a risk. A strong leader would have pencilled in the possibility of an early March 2010 double dissolution and moved onto the offensive to maximise his options. Rudd should, at least, have tried to generate serious alarm within the Coalition. He made no such effort.

Labor's reading of Coalition politics had been defective for years— witness its litany of misjudgements about Howard. Rudd assumed that Abbott's difficulties would intensify over time. He missed the psychological recasting of conservative politics. Where Turnbull had been desperate to prevent an election Abbott dared Rudd to call an election. Morale was being transformed and unity was growing.

Penny Wong had wanted Labor to devise a Plan B if the bills were defeated. She had advocated a meeting of senior ministers to prepare a fallback. Such a meeting was unobtainable.[11] Rudd had been pre-occupied for weeks by Copenhagen conference planning.

Wayne Swan said:

> He [Rudd] had spent months in the leadup, doing all these midnight video things, he couldn't stop talking about it, he was obsessed with it. I think he really thought he was going to play a critical role in bringing together the grand bargain. I honestly think he felt it was going to be his moment on the world stage.[12]

Gillard said: 'I think he had written up Copenhagen as being a grand success and him playing a starring role.'[13]

In October it had been announced that Rudd, along with the UN Secretary-General and Mexican President, would become 'a friend of the chair' to assist Danish Prime Minister Lars Rasmussen achieve an outcome. Pessimism about Copenhagen was rife yet Rudd needed a credible result to keep his momentum against Abbott. He should have lowered expectations before the meeting but that would have contradicted his own role.

The Special Envoy on Climate Change, Howard Bamsey, said: 'I was summoned back from Copenhagen to brief him. Penny and I saw him. I told him things were very grim. He seemed to be realistic.'[14] Wong said: 'When I arrived in Copenhagen I thought it would be pretty bad. I knew we would politically fail because Copenhagen couldn't get the outcome that was publicly being called for.'[15]

The Copenhagen task was to work towards a new global legally binding agreement to replace the broken Kyoto model. But the conference was a shambles. Rasmussen, as chair, was out of his depth. The realpolitik of climate change based on competing national interests was rampant. Upon arriving Rudd said Australia wanted 'a grand bargain'— a compact for the first time between rich and poor countries. While nobody was satisfied with the result, President Obama sorted out the basis for an accord. It was a weak patch-up job but Obama was the key. The hope of a legally binding treaty involving rich and poor nations was postponed—for years, perhaps for decades. Rudd and Wong were prominent players.

Wong said: 'Within the room Kevin was brilliant. But this stuff never gets written. I don't think we would have got the outcome we did without Australia.'[16] Bamsey said of his boss: 'I think it fair to say there wouldn't have been a Copenhagen accord without Rudd.'[17] In technical terms it was the first agreement for climate change action involving both rich and poor nations. But there was no agreement on emission reduction targets or timetables.

Bamsey said:

When Penny and Rudd came out with the accord, my first thought was 'It would have been better to bring down the house.' I said to Penny 'Why didn't you just say no?' But I was wrong. It wasn't the time to collapse the system. Rudd's immediate instinct was to be positive and he was right. His message was: not perfect, but better than nothing.[18]

Abbott branded the outcome an 'unmitigated disaster'. Referring to the CPRS, he said Rudd had been 'very unwise to try to rush Australia into prematurely adopting a commitment in the absence of similar commitments from the rest of the world'. Wong said:

> Copenhagen gave Abbott enormous momentum. It was critical. It bought into one of his main arguments—that Australia was moving ahead of the rest of the world. The argument that China has the largest renewable capacity in the world and that others are moving didn't matter. Copenhagen allowed Abbott to argue this version of anti-reform economic nationalism.[19]

When the Australian delegation returned Bamsey felt sure, knowing Rudd, that after his holiday break, the Prime Minister would want a new plan looking to the next meeting in Mexico. Australian officials were busy over the break, travelling to New York and Mexico, confident Rudd would want to stay on the front foot. But something had gone wrong. Bamsey said:

> We gave him a strategy. But nothing happened. There was no appetite for action. In my view after Copenhagen, the right approach for the government, domestically and internationally, was to stay on the front foot. Frankly, I couldn't get much interest in that. Something had changed in the Rudd Government due to Copenhagen.[20]

Wong felt Copenhagen had left its mark on Rudd: 'I saw him in the room and I think it had a significant personal impact. He was very committed to getting an outcome. It wasn't achieved because of events beyond his control. "Disheartening" is not a strong enough word.'[21]

For Gillard, the Copenhagen debacle was decisive. She said: 'He came back from Copenhagen really hurting. I actually think it was emotionally scarring for him. It wasn't just a vanity or a folly. Kevin is a man who, for all his foibles, has invested a lot of his life's work in diplomacy and he wanted the world to be better than it had been. The result hit him psychologically very hard.'[22] Swan felt Copenhagen was a turning point for Rudd. 'He came back as best can be described as completely devastated,' he said. Swan felt the government now entered a phase of Rudd-induced paralysis on two crucial issues: climate change and the Henry Report on tax.[23]

Such comments suggest Rudd was not able to function effectively. Labor's problem, however, transcended the impact on Rudd.

Copenhagen shattered one of the grand delusions of Australia's recent political life. This was the idea that, because urgent climate change action was a moral imperative, Australian action was part of a common utopian cause to save the planet. Rudd had cultivated and exploited this sentiment. Now he would become its victim. Copenhagen was the dawn of another reality: that climate change was riven by the rules of old politics. It was about competing national interests because nations did have competing interests and about global negotiations that were driven by the quest for economic advantage. The viability of Australia's ETS depended upon the extent to which other nations also priced carbon and traded permits. The global talks were about deals, trade-offs and compromise. Developing nations refused binding targets, making clear that any serious action they took required a financial bribe from rich nations. Despite Obama's efforts, the US Congress would not legislate 'cap and trade' without, at the least, binding commitments from China.

The greatest shock, however, was the public's realisation that climate change idealism led to old-fashioned, unpopular solutions in the form of higher taxes, higher priced electricity and huge subsidies for renewables. The public was justified in probing the ethics and practicality behind such actions. The chair of the Productivity Commission, Gary Banks, said: 'In retrospect, it is clear that initial public support for an emissions trading regime was essentially predicated on ignorance about how it worked. That was hardly a sustainable basis for policy success.'[24] The morality of climate change finished on the slag heap of old politics. This reality hit Australia with a thud and it hurt Rudd.

Upon his return Rudd faced a decisive political decision: the election question, the ultimate judgement test.

In the week before Christmas, on 23 December 2009, a leadership strategy group comprising Rudd, Gillard, Swan, Faulkner, Arbib, Bitar and Alister Jordan gathered at Phillip Street, Sydney. Accounts of this meeting differ widely and significantly. Yet the central thrust seems clear. Arbib and Bitar say they wanted an early 2010 double dissolution election to be announced around Australia Day 2010.

Indeed, Bitar had been looking for such an opportunity. Now Labor had a climate change trigger. With an early 2010 election an option, Bitar had done his research. Advertising concepts had been prepared and tested; preparations had been made for the campaign headquarters, computers, desks and databases; the National Secretary would be ready to press the button.

Bitar's research showed public distrust of the Liberals, with their 'revolving door' leadership occupied by four people over the past two years: Howard, Nelson, Turnbull and now Abbott. It revealed that 64 per cent of people felt the Liberals were not ready for power and two-thirds believed they were disunited. Bitar's plan was to slaughter the Liberals over their instability. His conclusion was clear: if there is an early 2010 poll 'then Labor will win'.

Interviewed for this book, Bitar said: 'Going to a double dissolution in early 2010 was Labor's best chance at re-election. I have no doubt we would have won. That was my view and a view shared by everyone in the leadership team I spoke to.'[25]

At the meeting Bitar said he expected either a relatively slim victory or about the size of the current majority. Arbib argued for a 2010 poll. Swan said: 'My view and Faulkner's view was that we should go to a double dissolution.'[26] Faulkner was the pro-election hawk in the cabinet. Arbib and Bitar felt the consensus of the meeting was for an election—but this is disputed by others who claim the mood was not this firm.

The issue was left as Rudd's call. Arbib said later he did not believe the Parliament would reconvene in February. The bottom line is that Rudd did not say 'no' to an early election but neither did he say 'yes'. 'There was no decision taken,' Swan said.[27] But Arbib left more confident: 'Kevin seemed to agree with the arguments put for a double dissolution election called at the end of January.'[28] Bitar felt an early election remained an option but that Rudd, on balance, would not take it. What stuck in his head was Rudd's line: 'I don't just want to win. I want a convincing victory.'

Interviewed for this book, Rudd declined to discuss the meeting in detail and played down its importance. 'I had a genuinely open mind,' he said of the election. Rudd confirms he made no pre-Christmas election decision.[29] Others said the push for the early election was not as great as claimed.

Swan was scathing: 'It was one of the more bizarre meetings I have ever been in with Kevin. He left the meeting in the middle of it in a traumatised state, went away for a while. He obviously didn't want to bite the bullet on the election.' For Swan, it was a failure of nerve and Rudd 'just basically retreated'.[30] Others claimed Swan was not a forceful advocate for an early election.

Wong was not involved in these talks, but just before Christmas, Jordan rang her. 'We need to prepare for a February election,' he said. It was an alert; not a final decision. Wong wanted to fight the cause. But she was worried about Rudd. Abbott would only be beaten by a ruthless campaign based on conviction. But was this Rudd? Wong was starting to have her doubts.

Rudd, however, reveals he had previously raised the early election option in cabinet. It was in late 2009. Rudd said:

> It was unusual for me to canvass election timing in cabinet but I did. And on this question, there were only two ministers who were directly arguing in favour of such a double dissolution: John Faulkner and Kim Carr. I just reserved my position. I wanted to hear what they were all saying.[31]

Rudd saw no sign of an early election groundswell. His claim that early election enthusiasm became inflated in hindsight is surely true. There was only one senior minister pushing hard. Faulkner told the author:

> We needed to go at the earliest possible opportunity. The history shows this—from the Whitlam, Fraser and Hawke experience, but not Kevin, oh no. I said at the time I fear I am part of the greatest strategic fuck-up ever made by a Labor Government, words to that effect. I could see the writing on the wall for us not taking the opportunity to have an early election that we could win. I made an impassioned plea as much as I could.[32]

Yet there was no urgency from Rudd. Interviewed for this book, he said:

> When I say I had a genuinely open mind I meant that. In politics there are those questions upon which you have an absolute clear view, a deep instinct and a deep level of rational logic underpinning it. On this one, I confessed to all colleagues I had a very open mind ... on the conservative side of me was the view that, a bit like Howard, you are elected to serve full terms ... On the other side, I was acutely conscious of the fact that Abbott would never change his position and that, if the government was returned then we would face a similar adversarial environment on it although we would have the legitimacy of a further election [victory].[33]

Rudd's 'open mind' was a euphemism for 'no'. He was wary of a February–March double dissolution as opposed to an orthodox general election around October. He feared the public would not accept its validity. Interviewed for this book, Rudd asked: 'Would the country at large, as opposed to those passionate about climate change, get the gravitas of needing to act, needing to basically pull the entire Parliament down in order to get the thing through which would get through anyway under a deferred CPRS with a new Senate?'

The question provided the answer. Rudd felt the risk was too great. He rationalised he would get the CPRS through a Labor–Green-dominated Senate post-election.[34]

In retrospect, it was the turning point of his prime ministership, although Rudd could not have foreseen this at the time. He did not know how fateful his refusal would become. It was inconceivable to him in late 2009 that this was his only chance for re-election because he would be deposed in June.

Bitar's research showed rising public concern about the ETS. He felt Labor could still win an election with an ETS but that became highly improbable if Rudd waited full term. Bitar's message was: if you want to win on the ETS then go now; you can't wait and still win on an ETS. Over Christmas the election option sat on the table. 'I knew we had to be ready in case Rudd rang in mid-January,' Bitar said. Sam Dastrayi got married on 30 January 2010 and was told 'to be ready' for a possible election.

What would have happened had Rudd triggered an election? It is improbable to think that Abbott, Liberal leader for only weeks, would have won. Rudd had a proven record from 2007 and, given the public's reluctance to discard a first-term prime minister, would surely have prevailed. Re-election meant he would have dictated passage of the CPRS in the new Parliament or at a joint sitting following the double dissolution. Rudd would have been a prime minister who had defeated his opponents and secured his climate change laws.

Interviewed for this book, many ALP figures felt Rudd should have called the election but most conceded this was a judgement in retrospect. Chris Evans said: 'In hindsight, we should have gone to an election.'[35] Swan said Rudd would have won an early 2010 climate change poll.[36] Kim Carr said: 'The greatest political failure was not to call a double dissolution. My regret is that I didn't prosecute that case more firmly.'[37] Anthony Albanese said that 'we should have gone but that's a judgement in hindsight'.[38] Press Secretary Lachlan Harris said: 'We should have gone to a double dissolution. I think it was a genuine miscalculation. But you see the clarity more in hindsight.'[39] Faulkner didn't muck about: he said in private that Rudd 'lacked the ticker' to take this essential step.

Over summer Rudd went on holidays and then visited New Zealand. Upon his return to work he opened the new political year on 18 January 2010 by launching a children's book. Arbib was aghast. 'What was Rudd doing?' Arbib asked himself. Bitar was prepared for war without a general to lead the battle. Rudd had no taste for combat—and he was not alone.

In early January 2010 Rudd was unnerved by a meeting at Kirribilli House with his deputy, Julia Gillard. This is one of their decisive encounters—complex, psychological and prone to contested interpretations. They talked on the verandah overlooking the harbour. They were still friends and confidants. Yet a dark shadow was falling across their relations. Interviewed for this book, they agreed on the basics but provided a different emphasis. Rudd described the meeting this way:

> She explicitly said to me that under no circumstances could she support the double dissolution on the CPRS. I remember the conversation clearly on the verandah, the first meeting we had in 2010 ... she said under no circumstances does she support an early election. Her argument was that the government had comprehensively lost the debate because Copenhagen had been perceived as a failure and secondly because Barnaby Joyce had begun to mount a campaign on the pricing impact of an ETS. That was her presentation. By the way, at that stage I had not ruled out a double dissolution. I just listened intently. But her position was dogmatic. And knowing the Deputy Prime Minister as I did, as being a person of firm and fixed views when she chose to adopt them, I was taken with the vehemence of her position.[40]

Asked whether he had seen Gillard so vehement ever before, Rudd said: 'Maybe once or twice, but not a common occurrence. It stood out. And also, it was the specific purpose of the meeting. That is what she came to discuss, that and nothing else.'[41]

It seemed Gillard had lost faith in the electoral viability of the CPRS. The real problem, however, was far deeper. Gillard had lost faith in Rudd.

Gillard offered her own version of this meeting:

> Kevin retreated to Kirribilli to plan the election year. We had troubles everywhere. I went up to Kirribilli and we sat on the

verandah. He had a grid and modules, health reform, Henry, carbon, and we were talking about the sequencing. He put to me Faulkner's argument for an early election on carbon. I would have said I don't agree with Faulkner. I had already come to a conclusion but I wasn't going to blurt it out in front of Kevin— that he was not in the zone to fight an election campaign.[42]

This penetrated to Gillard's view of Rudd's condition post-Copenhagen: 'He was not in the frame of mind where you could have put him out for an election.'[43]

It is an astonishing situation. The Deputy Prime Minister had decided the Prime Minister post-Copenhagen was not mentally or psychological equipped to fight Abbott and call an election. This is Gillard's real position. She may have been right or wrong, but this was her conclusion.

Gillard was unimpressed by the meeting; her recollection of Rudd fiddling with A3 sheets of paper was scathing. Interviewed for this book, she explained her assessment and defended her decision not to tell Rudd what she really thought. 'Call me perhaps lily-livered,' she said. 'But do you sit there and say to the Prime Minister: "You're not in the right state to run this election campaign"? Or do you just concentrate on seeing if we can start to plan the election year?'[44]

Gillard felt that while the Copenhagen failure was the gravest cause of Rudd's malaise it only accentuated an existing condition: 'I think he had been in pretty bad shape for a long time because of the wear and tear of his organisational style. He had been in the wars for a bit. Copenhagen really knocked him around.'[45]

Yet the strength of Gillard's view did penetrate Rudd. He told the author this meeting was 'decisive'. Did he sense Gillard's real position— namely, her loss of faith in him? The vehemence of his recollection suggests, maybe, that he did.

Asked about the impact of this conversation, Rudd said:

It was huge. Because as the period wore on between mid-January and the decision to defer [the climate change policy] in April— through February, March, April—the position of the Deputy Prime Minister became much more entrenched even though it was unequivocal on day one. It was reaffirmed in direct messages to me that under no circumstances could she or would she support not just a double dissolution on the question but could or would she support a continuation of our current policy.[46]

It is false to think Gillard vetoed an election, because there is no evidence Rudd wanted an early election.

Interviewed for this book, however, Gillard added another layer to her election assessment. She drew a distinction between the ideal world and the actual world. 'In a perfect world what we ought to have done is called an early election,' Gillard said. Pressed on this, Gillard said: 'Should we have gone early and hard, to salvage what we could? Yes.' But this was an 'ideal world' view. In practice, because Rudd was politically disabled it was a 'non-option'.[47] She was knifing Rudd: his personal failing meant Labor could not do what was best.

Gillard felt sure the post-Copenhagen politics had turned against Labor: 'For Mr and Mrs Average it looked like a circus. Copenhagen was a disaster. It was starting to look bad: the drought had broken, the emotional impetus in Australia had changed. The politics were going sour for us very quickly.'[48]

On 11 January, Bitar emailed Alister Jordan: 'Is there still a chance of going in February?' He had indirectly heard about the Rudd–Gillard meeting. Jordan replied: 'February is becoming softer by the day—as are the early March options.' He added: 'the thinking a bit later—ie April.' Rudd was ruling nothing out and nothing in. It was a 'no-election' decision by default.[49]

Rudd was tactically adrift, unsure and undecided about when he would hold the election and what political strategy he would run. The uncertainty was corrosive and from early 2010 Rudd's government went into a trajectory of rapid decline.

By declining an early election Rudd faced a new dilemma: what happened to his climate change policy? The ETS was left hanging like a ghost in the cupboard. It was facile for Rudd to pretend, as he did, that he could run full-term, have the ETS as an election policy and, post-election, just team up with the Greens to legislate his scheme. Given their hostility towards him, the Greens would demand a huge price.

The early election was dead. That was not necessarily fatal for Rudd. The art of being prime minister lies in finding the best options. What was disastrous for Rudd was that he rejected the early election but failed to find an alternative political strategy for his ETS. This second failure, in retrospect, made his spurning of the early election a fatal mistake.

CHAPTER 19

CLIMATE CHANGE RETREAT

On Monday 8 February, ALP National Secretary Karl Bitar was summoned to Rudd's office and told to prepare a new political strategy on climate change. 'This is very confidential,' Alister Jordan told him. 'Kevin has decided to delay the CPRS. We want urgent research on how to go about it and how we present it.'[1]

Bitar commissioned focus groups in Brisbane for the evening of Thursday 11 February. The next day he reported to Jordan by email. At the top of the email he wrote: 'Given how hard KR has supported and defended the CPRS it is important to get the timing, justification and language right or delaying it might neutralise the CPRS as an issue but do KR a lot of damage in terms of what he stands for.'

Under the heading 'justification', Bitar wrote:

a. KR needs a clear trigger and reason to change his position. We should only announce the CPRS delay after it has been rejected by the Senate a 3rd time. That way he can argue that while he still believes a CPRS is still the best way to reduce emissions significantly in the long-term, he is a realist and he accepts that parliament has now rejected it 3 times ... KR is a realist who is more interested in results.

b. He must argue that he still strongly believes a CPRS is the best way to reduce emissions significantly in the long-term. (Important to counter arguments of flip flop or not standing for anything. He does stand for something but as PM he must be a realist.)

c. He must make clear that he isn't ditching a CPRS forever but is delaying it until there is bipartisan support and the major international countries sign up to a binding agreement.

d. It's absolutely critical that we put a massive emphasis on what we will be doing in the short to medium term to reduce emissions. So we have to say something strong like: we will act immediately to cut emissions and protect our environment with a new Renewable Energy Strategy. I can't emphasise how important this is. As soon as we tell them that KR would introduce a renewable energy strategy asap we get nearly everyone on side. I'll send you more notes on language but Renewable Energy Strategy worked much better than Clean Energy Strategy.

Bitar's warning was stark: unless Rudd got the timing and explanation right the delay would be disastrous. He wanted Rudd's announcement 'on the day the Senate rejects it a third time'.[2] Bitar was alert to the potentially huge damage for Rudd if delay was mishandled.

Yet it was, and Rudd lost the leadership.

Bitar saw Rudd on 12 February to brief him on the findings. 'You can't just roll out of bed one morning and do this,' Bitar said, before going on to tell Rudd about the risks.[3] Rudd listened. Ultimately, he did not heed the message. More than two months later, in April, the full catastrophe unfolded, with Rudd completely unprepared. As they talked, Bitar was aware that Rudd's focus had shifted. His restless mind was turning to health policy. After leaving the office Bitar heard nothing on climate change for two months.

Rudd continued to dither. He failed to finalise a decision with senior ministers, and a series of ad hoc meetings was held that went nowhere. Penny Wong felt he wanted a 'fix'. Rudd would call for more work to be done, more papers, more analysis, as though the answer would somehow materialise. He had three options—defend it, ditch it or delay it.[4] Wong told Rudd: 'A carbon price means we cannot avoid a cost-of-living political contest. We need to face this.' Ultimately, Rudd refused.

During February journalists would probe cabinet ministers: what's happening on climate change? And the ministers would bluff or admit being clueless. Rudd's indecision was holding his government hostage. Meanwhile he had a new cause.

Rudd now elevated hospitals policy to centre stage in his bid for re-election. In the 2007 campaign Rudd pledged that if the public hospital system was not fixed by mid-2009 he would hold a referendum for the Commonwealth Government to take over full funding responsibility. It was a classic over-promise, political folly and financial nonsense. By

June 2009 the report on health and hospitals reform headed by Professor Christine Bennett was presented to the government. Enunciating his new mission, Rudd said:

> In the first three months of the 2010 year I made it very plain to people that having received the health and hospitals commission report the previous year we had to bring it to a conclusion. This was a major priority for the government because I had been so explicit about the [election] commitment and, frankly, the need was so great.[5]

Health Minister Nicola Roxon was a competent minister who liked clarity. She wanted to use the report to collaborate with the states and ditch the 'takeover' option. There was a tension between her and Rudd over process and direction, a tension that would ultimately shatter their relations. Roxon knew that any referendum was pure folly. She believed that if Rudd wanted to proceed he had to obtain cabinet approval for such a decision. But for Roxon dealing with Rudd was exhausting and inconclusive. Rudd alienated Roxon and lost her support. Called a 'fiasco' by Gillard, the protracted hospitals saga would bring Roxon and Gillard together.

Before Christmas 2009 Rudd, Roxon, staff and officials met in Sydney with working documents. Roxon found Rudd had not read the material, yet he demanded some of it be rewritten before Christmas. 'Kevin, you haven't read this; it's crazy having things rewritten,' Roxon said. But Rudd was immovable. Roxon's staff worked till 3 a.m. on the eve of Christmas to meet Rudd's demands. 'I doubt he ever read it,' Roxon said. 'People were exhausted all the time.'[6] Gillard knew all about the incident; it became infamous.

Roxon's complaint was that hospital policy differences were not resolved because 'things did not go to cabinet'.[7] It became her main charge against Rudd. 'Kevin as PM simply refused to list contentious and often strategic items for cabinet,' she said. 'Health and climate change were the two longest running "non-discussions" for the first term of government.'[8]

Beyond this, Roxon found Rudd's work habits near impossible. In early 2010 she and her advisers flew with Rudd across the continent and then to Darwin working on hospitals policy. Finally Roxon got off the plane; she had had enough. 'It was a crazy way to make policy.'[9] As his leadership entered its most decisive months Rudd exhibited a series of bizarre contradictions: he was paralysed by some issues (climate change) yet obsessed by others (hospitals). As prime minister, he was unable to order his priorities or balance his responsibilities.

Rudd convened a series of meetings to discuss hospitals policy and his push for a referendum with the 2010 election. Roxon was dismayed, then appalled. On St Valentine's Day, 14 February, Rudd convened a small group at the Lodge, including Gillard, Swan, Roxon and Bitar. Bitar said a takeover announcement would show strength, responsibility and honouring of promises. Rudd was pushing for a decision within days. According to Roxon:

> Knowing full well and agreeing that that referendum would be lost, he [Kevin] thought it would be a good tool to be able to win the election. So he was prepared to have such a cynical approach to this. I think that would have been a disaster … He sat there with Karl Bitar and others and said, 'Look, this [referendum] is a really popular thing to do; we'd win the election.'

Roxon rejected it outright.[10]

Gillard testified to 'numerous meetings' on hospitals policy. 'Nicola played me in to try and help her,' she said. 'The referendum thing was crazy. My approach was to back Nicola because I thought she was at least thinking about things rationally.'[11] Roxon said:

> He wanted, with four days notice on one occasion that I can recollect, to take over the entire health system, didn't have any materials for cabinet, didn't have legal advice, I think it was on the Wednesday or Thursday that we could prepare something to take to cabinet on Monday to announce on Tuesday. Now this is just a ludicrous way to run a government.[12]

At one point there had been a Kirribilli House meeting to canvass the issue. The push from Arbib and Bitar, backed by Rudd's office, was extraordinary: announce the referendum, conduct a short four- to five-week campaign with health as the spearhead, and enshrine the theme 'It's us against the states.' This reflected a shallow 'state government' tactical culture that plagued the Rudd camp. The idea was cosmetic; the ploy was to make Rudd look strong in a caring cause. His concession that the referendum would fail meant the plan was a fraud. Even as a re-election tactic it was dangerous and assumed voters were mugs. The referendum would have split the Labor Party along federal–state lines. ALP premiers, led by Victoria's John Brumby, would have opposed it. Many state-based media outlets would have fought the idea. It would have triggered huge financial issues for Rudd. It was an idea best buried.

After one late-night meeting at the Lodge, Roxon retreated to Parliament House and summoned a meeting with her closest advisers. 'In good conscience I can't be minister and prosecute this referendum,' she said.[13]

Roxon saw Rudd's proposal as 'one of the biggest reshapings of the Federation' ever, with 'huge political consequences [and] immense financial consequences', yet he was not prepared to address the issue properly. Ministers would periodically ask her: 'Surely we're not taking over the hospital system?' Roxon correctly saw it as flawed strategy. She said Rudd was consumed by the notion that 'Canberra could do it better', yet the policy experts 'didn't support him'. He 'wouldn't let officials properly prepare the pros and cons', she said.[14] Reviewing the entire saga, Roxon said: 'I asked for it to go to cabinet on a number of occasions. That wasn't agreed mostly because he [Rudd] wanted there to be an agreed position between him and I.'[15]

Finally, Rudd was persuaded against the idea. Roxon said that Gillard, Swan and she managed to talk him out of it.[16] In early March the policy was unveiled. It was typically Rudd—risky, complex and raising expectations. The politics were laid on with a trowel. Rudd pledged to 'end the buck passing and blame game' on hospitals; reform must 'begin now'. The policy, naturally, was 'the largest single reform since Medicare' with 'the Commonwealth assuming a fixed and dominant share of public hospital funding of the country'.[17]

Hospitals were to be funded nationally and administered locally. The new shares of hospital funding were 60:40 on a Commonwealth–states split, a significant lift in the Canberra contribution. One-third of GST revenue (all of which went to the states) would now be earmarked by Canberra for health.

The package was relatively modest despite Rudd's huge spin. Medibank co-author John Deeble said: 'Will this reduce the blame game? Of course not. This policy document is full of it.'[18] Rudd's claim was nonsense, driven totally by politics. Rudd said the buck stopped with him but this was also nonsense since hospitals under this model remained a shared responsibility. No new federal funds would flow until 2014, four years away. Rudd, once the champion of cooperative federalism, dumped this package on the states with a deadline and a threat. Putting a political gun to their heads, Rudd said he expected the states to approve the package at the 11 April COAG meeting and, if they refused, 'we will take this reform plan to the people at the next election', along with a referendum to empower the Australian Government. The referendum had been downgraded from a commitment to a threat.[19] The message was: farewell emissions trading, welcome hospitals policy.

Brumby staged a breakout repudiating Rudd's design. Western Australian Premier Colin Barnett said losing a third of GST revenues was a deal-wrecker. From the start, the GST proposal, included at the last minute, made universal agreement impossible.

Terry Moran was appalled by the GST provision: 'It was a straight political fix from ministerial offices. The idea was to create the impression the Commonwealth was calling the shots on hospitals because it contributed most of the revenue. It became the factor that undermined the entire package.'[20]

The conflict revealed Rudd's weakness on policy. He was prone to getting the big calls wrong, lacked the patience to work through issues and had a naïve faith in the ability of the national government to both solve and fund major policy challenges. David Epstein said: 'His knowledge of a number of areas of public policy was weak and superficial.'[21]

Rudd launched an extraordinary campaign of hospital visits with full media exposure to sell his policy. The public was confronted on the television news with Rudd and Roxon, in surgical outfits, talking with doctors and nurses. It can be asserted that no prime minister has ever visited so many hospitals, testifying to Rudd's boundless energy. There comes a point of diminishing marginal returns when any gains cannot be justified as a call on the prime minister's time. Roxon estimated she personally visited thirty-seven or thirty-eight hospitals in this process but there were more than a hundred visits to hospitals and health services, taking into account Rudd, herself and three junior ministers.

'Often on the day before,' Roxon recalled, 'we could not get confirmation from the Prime Minister which hospital or which city he was going to be in [the next day].' This made it difficult to plan her movements, not knowing which state was the next day's destination. Roxon said doctors and nurses welcomed the PM but the uncertainty would often 'wreak havoc' on their agendas.[22]

The hospital visitations, a measure of Rudd's sincerity, became a monument to his dysfunction. On his visits Rudd would sometimes conduct seminars, including PowerPoint presentations. In April 2010 in Brisbane, still refusing to make a final decision about climate change policy and only ten weeks before being deposed, he waxed lyrical:

Together with Nicola [Roxon] and Justine [Elliott] we have visited more than 100 hospitals across Australia in the last six months or so, big ones, little ones, every state of the Commonwealth and in both territories. Myself, I've conducted seminars of three hours at a stretch in about 20 to 25 hospitals across the country ... I feel as if I am now so part and parcel of how hospitals work on the ground and the great work which is done in them that when I turn each corner I am now greeting something which is no longer foreign to me but entirely familiar.[23]

Rudd was losing his grip on reality. He confused activity with strategy. He confused the role of a policy bureaucrat with the job of a prime minister. Would his policy have been diminished if Rudd had cut his hospital visits by three-quarters? No, it would not. Rudd used false measurements to judge policy success. His obsessions crowded out the space and time for sound decision-making. He projected a personal element, saying of Brisbane hospital: 'I remember coming here as a child. My father was admitted here suffering road trauma and he died here.'

Swan felt Rudd's hospitals saga was political escapism. 'It was almost deliberate, to avoid pressing decisions on carbon and the Henry tax review,' Swan said. 'We couldn't get him to focus. It was painful, it was mad, it was unhinged in various respects.'[24]

Rudd denies the assertion that his embrace of health policy was a substitute for the climate change deadlock. The evidence, however, makes this irresistible as a conclusion. Those senior ministers closest to Rudd felt his psychological need for a new crusade. Invoking a new crisis saw Rudd enter his 'fully engaged' mode. In March, Rudd defeated Abbott in a televised debate on health policy. This was a glimpse of the old Rudd who had eclipsed Howard: confident, persuasive and constructive. He proved his superiority on Labor's terrain. It seemed, briefly, the health strategy might succeed for him.

At the April COAG meeting a number of ALP premiers extracted concessions from Rudd as the price for agreement. But Western Australia's Barnett held out—he refused to accept the departure from the original Howard–Costello GST allocation. Barnett pointed out that the GST was state revenue: 'We're not willing to hand over an important part of our fiscal autonomy ... Frankly, the West Australian public, the West Australian Parliament would never agree to the state handing back its GST.'[25] Rudd had misread the politics of the West.

This Rudd–Barnett GST breach was unresolved when Rudd was removed as prime minister. As for Roxon, her alienation from Rudd was irrecoverable. Subsequently Gillard, as prime minister, revised the hospitals package and secured a unified agreement accepting Barnett's stance. But the hospitals issue could not keep the climate change wolf from the door.

Explaining the fateful tolling of the bell, Rudd said: 'Having concluded our [hospitals] work at the COAG special meeting in April 2010, I was then told a Strategic Priorities Budget meeting [the "gang of four"] had been convened specially to discuss the future of the Carbon Pollution Reduction Scheme.' In a rare concession Rudd admitted: 'I was physically exhausted after two days of solid negotiations led by me with the six premiers and two chief ministers.'[26] The showdown had arrived, yet Rudd by his own admission was not ready.

The budget was pressing. By April 2010 a decision was needed on how any CPRS would affect the May budget forecasts. Swan recalled: 'I said, "Look, I've got a budget. So are we going ahead or not? I have got to have a decision."'[27]

This April meeting of the 'gang of four' was a turning point for Rudd. It produced the worst single policy mistake of Rudd's prime ministership, a decision that ruined his authority. The event will be debated as long as Rudd is remembered. On balance, it is probably the most ignominious policy retreat by a prime minister in half a century. It is hard to believe Rudd would have been deposed in June without the polling damage from this decision.

The SPBC decision was that Labor remained committed to its ETS but would delay the scheme to coincide with the end of the Kyoto period at the end of 2012, when nations would be assessing their new pledges. This would save the budget about $2.5 billion across the forward estimates. Labor would only proceed with the scheme at that point provided there was sufficient international progress from the big emitters such as China and the United States. This took the scheme off the agenda for one election, but more realistically two elections, and possibly beyond that point. That Rudd succumbed to this decision revealed his impaired judgement. The great moral challenge was slated for postponement.

Moran felt that Rudd's defective decision-making trapped him: 'My recollection is that Kevin was very tired and probably came late into the meeting. He would have been better equipped with a briefing beforehand. I think this decision is closely tied to abandonment of good process, which can bring too many surprises to the table.'[28]

Interviewed for this book, Rudd said he was debilitated because he 'had to run a national campaign about public hospital reform up and down the length and breadth of the country to get it right'.[29] Yet if Rudd got exhausted, that was his own fault. If he was unready to take other decisions, that was also his own fault. This is the job of being prime minister.

The ETS deferral was pivotal in the collapse of relations between Rudd on one hand and Gillard and Swan on the other. The proof is Rudd's statement to the caucus the day he was deposed. 'I changed our position on the emissions trading scheme and I'm responsible for that change,' Rudd said. He told the party room that Tanner and Wong argued against the change and 'equally strong was the advice from Wayne and Julia that the emissions trading scheme policy had to be abandoned'.[30]

Beneath this statement lay a chaotic struggle. Since her early January meeting with Rudd at Kirribilli, Gillard had wanted to beat a climate change retreat. Rudd later became obsessed by Gillard's demand and tied it to his loss of office. Interviewed for this book, he claimed Gillard 'indicated to me in writing that she could not and would not support the continuation of the CPRS as a matter of government policy', an interpretation Gillard disputes.[31]

Gillard had put before the committee a two-page paper titled 'The Bipartisan Solution'. She argued Labor should not try to price carbon until the Coalition changed its mind. It was a retreat and recognition that Abbot had won the immediate contest. 'I felt at this point we couldn't proceed without a change in the politics,' Gillard recalls. 'I believe we needed a broad political consensus and that we needed to put some pressure onto Abbott. But it is wrong to say I simply refused to support the policy any more.'[32]

Gillard was alarmed at the damage being done to the government. Her 'bipartisan' position became the policy she took to the 2010 election as prime minister. She felt Labor could not fight carbon pricing against both the Coalition and Greens. She wanted a tactical retreat to neutralise Abbott's 'great big new tax' campaign.[33] Tanner claimed it was tantamount to making Abbott the climate change minister.

Interviewed for this book, Rudd said: 'I faced a split, a deep split in the government.' He said Gillard was dogmatic and Swan backed her for policy and budgetary reasons.[34] Swan rejects this account: 'My position in April was you either have it in or out, give me an answer because I have a budget to put to bed.'[35]

Over time Rudd, exposing his angry heart, escalated his attack on Gillard and Swan. In February 2012 he said Gillard and Swan advocated retreat 'very bluntly and very directly'.[36] He later told the author he had been 'stunned and surprised' by their vehemence.[37] On another occasion he alleged that Gillard 'had virtually vetoed the idea'.[38] Interviewed for this book, Rudd went further: 'Had I taken that position [sticking by the policy] I ran a real risk of the Deputy Prime Minister resigning, which would have fractured the government completely.'[39] In short, Gillard and Swan gave him no option; and Gillard made his position impossible.

Gillard dismissed with contempt the idea that she might resign and threaten Labor's stability. But her frustration ran deep.

> You couldn't get Kevin on the phone. Was I frustrated? Absolutely. Could I have sent Kevin a few sharp text messages? You bet. You should see some of the emails. I argued for my bipartisanship option but I distinctly remember at that meeting and on other occasions saying to Kevin this is the central judgement call of the campaign and you have to make it. There are only two options: either we get our stack hats on—and I used that term—and we fight this issue knowing we may well lose, or we mitigate our losses and move on. What we can't afford to do is drift.[40]

Interviewed for this book, Gillard kept returning to her frustration over Rudd's paralysis in the early months of 2010. Referring to climate change, she said: 'I had a view about what the political plan should be but, at the end of the day, I would have taken any plan over no plan. I just wanted a decision.' Rudd couldn't decide on an election and he couldn't decide on climate change.[41]

The row had been underway for many weeks and Rudd had faced competing streams of advice. The political advisers Arbib and Bitar said the time zone for the CPRS had expired; having decided against an election, Rudd had to 'get it off the table' because the cost-of-living negative was too great. They stood by Bitar's February advice to bring down a renewables package.[42] Gillard said: 'Bitar wanted to kill the carbon pricing idea. He was just doing his job by reporting how he saw the electoral impact. Bitar and Arbib were saying manoeuvre out.'[43]

For Wong, this sort of advice was hopeless. She became impatient with the New South Wales Right. Wong asked the counter-factual: had anybody done polling asking what happens if we walk away from the CPRS? Wong felt research had become an instrument to kill good policy.

Rudd's problem, however, was not just the decision but the manner of its release. The story was broken by Lenore Taylor in the *Sydney Morning Herald* on 27 April when she reported that the ETS had been shelved 'for at least three years'.[44] The leak to Taylor was devastating. Rudd was taken by surprise and left without an explanation. 'It was a very damaging leak and hard to retrieve,' Wong said.[45] 'It derailed our government,' Martin Ferguson said.[46]

One reason the damage was so great was Rudd's claim that the decision-making was not finished. He told the author he planned to take the SPBC decision to full cabinet. The leak, however, meant that was 'blown out of the water'. Rudd argued further that the leak cost him the chance to sell the policy as a two-year deferral. The leak meant it was depicted as a 'sell-out'.[47]

Yet if Rudd was so unhappy at the time, he could have gone to the cabinet; it would have been messy but he may have prevailed. Ministers such as Tanner, Wong, Ferguson, Kim Carr and Burke would have supported him. After Taylor's story, Carr said to Rudd: 'Your opponents are stripping you naked.'[48] The truth, surely, lies elsewhere: Rudd at the time was prepared to see the CPRS off the table.

The Taylor 'backdown' story was running across all media. Rudd felt there was no way back. His press secretary, Sean Kelly, described his frustration: 'Rudd was furious before he announced the retreat after the Taylor story. He felt he had to do this for political reasons but never really wanted to do it.'[49] Yet, as the prime minister, Rudd did it. And he is responsible for it.

Rudd cannot use Gillard and Swan as an excuse. Implying he was bullied by them won't work. On defining issues a prime minister carries the day. While the circumstances of his retreat have plagued Rudd ever since, trying to shift the blame to others is a false construct. Rudd's subsequent rage is understandable: Gillard told him to back off but that blunder weakened him sufficiently to allow Gillard to seize his job. It is a saga worthy of Shakespeare, but Rudd cannot shift the blame elsewhere.

Lachlan Harris felt guilty: 'The advice to dump the CPRS was incredibly bad. At the time I held out for a long time but, in the end, I felt it was necessary and that was a terrible mistake. The CPRS was all we had left.'[50] In fact, Rudd did not grasp the full dimensions of the horror.

Watching Rudd struggle through his public explanations was agony. He justified the retreat on two grounds: Abbott had torpedoed domestic bipartisanship and Copenhagen had revealed slower global progress than people had anticipated. He stood by the CPRS principles.

Rudd seemed oblivious to the absurdity—he wouldn't abandon his ETS but he wouldn't fight for it; now on the eve of the 2010 election he was saying he would consider it on the eve of the 2013 election but he couldn't make any promise. The politics in 2013 would probably be harder than in 2010. Rudd had turned Abbott into an even bigger giant killer. Labor was intimidated. It shrank in naked political fear. No wonder it hated Abbott.

Wong left no doubt about the qualifications on the 2013 timetable: 'We will only introduce it if there is sufficient progress internationally, particularly from China, India and the USA.'[51] This probably meant a more substantial delay; the aim was to deny Abbott the chance to argue that the scheme would happen anyway.

Wong grasped the full Rudd tragedy. It was wrong to think Rudd didn't care. Nobody watching Rudd work his guts out at Copenhagen could think that. But the change in politics left him uncertain. He didn't know how to fight the cost-of-living issue or his scheme's descent into unpopularity. 'Kevin cared but he couldn't fight,' was Wong's summation.

After he lost the leadership Rudd conceded his mistake. 'I made the wrong call,' he said. 'I accept full responsibility for having made the wrong call.'[52]

What should Rudd have done? Interviewed for this book, he said: 'What I should have done was stick to my guns on sustaining the policy, taking it to the next general election and then saying: once the Senate changes we will legislate this thing.'[53] It was a long second-best answer after his previous failure to call an early 2010 poll.

Swan said the event exposed Rudd's reluctance to confront difficult issues. 'The decision was taken almost de facto by Kevin's refusal to actually take a decision,' he said.[54] Tony Burke said: 'The policy that was our most emotional commitment was abandoned without cabinet discussion.'[55] 'I think cabinet would have said "no" to dumping the package,' Ferguson said.[56] Tanner warned Rudd there was no escaping his dilemma: 'The public ... will either decide you're running a great big new tax or that you've retreated and undermined your credibility.' Tanner called it 'our most serious policy misstep'.[57]

Wong believed Rudd's retreat would probably destroy him as prime minister. She felt Labor had not framed the debate properly: the focus was on the risks of acting, not the risks in retreating. In public, she conceded the decision made it 'difficult for Kevin to retain his credibility'.[58] Wong felt sorry for Rudd yet she saw Labor was in a weak position to fight the cost-of-living argument. Forced to defend a position she found deeply unpalatable, Wong, unsurprisingly, considered the resignation option. She never discussed this with Rudd. She raised it with two trusted staffers and with her partner, Sophie. But Wong was a professional. She saw that resignation would only precipitate more trouble for the government, achieve nothing and perhaps ruin her career.

Wong recalled a line from Paul Keating: 'Once you put it up in lights you can't take it down again.' Rudd had missed the simplicity of the test. 'When we tried to take it down this struck at the heart of public belief in us,' Wong said of the CPRS.[59]

'Labor as a party wasn't as committed to the CPRS as many people believed,' Lachlan Harris said. 'Support from the unions and factions was tenuous. I doubt it was in Labor's DNA. The problem was [that] after the global financial crisis this was all we had left. It was a "bet the farm" issue but there wasn't the belief you need to push it through.'[60]

Having told the Lowy Institute in November 2009 that 'there are two stark choices: action or inaction', Rudd now chose inaction; having attacked the Coalition for political cowardice in failing to legislate the ETS, Rudd's retreat suggested he was such a coward; having exploited climate change when it was popular, Rudd went missing now that it was unpopular; having attacked delay as 'the least responsible path', Rudd was now the architect of delay; having insisted that industry and business needed certainty, Rudd left them with the deepest uncertainty; having invoked 'our children's fate and our grandchildren's fate' Rudd could hardly complain when people, having taken him seriously, decided to make a moral judgement against him. Rudd invited the standard by which he should be judged.

How could Rudd and his advisers miss all this?

How serious was Rudd's retreat? Think of Whitlam backing down on Medibank or Keating on the tariff cuts. Yet the issue had transcended policy to become a matter of character. It had been obvious for months; that Rudd missed this was astonishing.

Wong stated the case for Labor to have fought in 2010: 'Climate change is an issue that we must deal with. This debate won't go away. It is as much a part of the Labor reform agenda as our other reforms: opening the economy, floating the dollar, reducing tariffs. It is as much an economic reform as an environmental reform.'[61]

The retreat was authorised by Rudd and advised by Gillard and Swan. In the end, the price became Rudd's leadership. The decision would define Rudd's character and that of his government. It became a parable for the lack of conviction at the heart of modern Labor.

CHAPTER 20

THE MINING TAX: THE FATAL BLOW

As a policy mistake perpetrated by the Rudd Government, nothing matches the mining tax for its scale of failure. The combination of Treasury expertise and Labor clout, so successful during the global financial crisis, unravelled at this point. Labor got the timing, design and politics wrong. For Kevin Rudd, it was one fiasco too many.

A profits-based mining tax was feasible and saleable. Despite the damage done to Rudd by his climate change retreat, he would probably have led Labor to the 2010 election if not for the mining tax. The problem this time was Rudd's disengagement; he failed to give the issue the attention it deserved. This project revealed Labor as inept at reform and incapable of dealing with business. The decision-making was a shambles and the tax saw relations between Rudd and Swan irretrievably damaged. The head of the prime minister's department, Terry Moran, said: 'It's one of the biggest own goals I've seen.'[1]

Every rule of established tax reform practice—consultation with stakeholders, ministerial assessment of bureaucratic advice, cultivation of the terrain for reform—was breached. Yet this was the central tax reform of Rudd's first term.

The Rudd Government chose to ambush the mining industry with a tax it believed was a political winner based on redistribution and fairness. Rudd and Swan had taken the justified idea of a resources tax on profits and botched it. They provoked the mining sector into a political war and left much of the business community convinced they were untrustworthy. Labor was haunted by this failure right up to the 2013 election. Once again, the Rudd–Swan approach was the antithesis of Hawke–Keating reformism.

The states were treated with the same contempt as the industry. Given the constitutional view that the states owned the mining resources and the Henry taxation review recommendation of negotiating with the states, the government assumed such strictures could be surmounted.

Its ineptitude triggered doubts about Labor's ability to manage the biggest resources boom for a century. Finally, when the industry engaged in massive retaliation, the Labor government was resentful at the blowback it had provoked.

The Henry taxation review arose from Rudd's 2020 summit recommendations. Anxious to produce a tangible result, Rudd announced the tax inquiry during a post-summit television interview. 'Kevin essentially had a brain snap,' Swan said. 'I went along with it.'[2] The terms of reference were sweeping.

This review was notable for three features. First, unlike the Hawke and Howard governments, whose tax inquiries were designed to deliver specific reforms, the Rudd Government had no tax reform strategy in its mind. Rudd, notably, seemed clueless about what he wanted. Second, the review was headed by the government's principal economic adviser, a situation bound to create problems in the reporting phase. Who would evaluate the report? The Treasury, yet the Treasury head had done the report. The further difficulty was that because the report was chaired by Henry, the government would be saddled with a degree of ownership of the recommendations. Finally, in the terms of reference Labor ruled out any extension of the GST or reduction of superannuation tax concessions, both critical issues. It was an omen: Rudd and Swan had no stomach for tough decisions.

Interviewed for this book, Rudd insisted that the Henry review was Swan's responsibility. 'The Treasurer ran the review from the time of its announcement in the middle of 2008 through to the report at the end of 2009,' he said.[3] Swan said it was an 'independent inquiry'. He admitted to 'grave fears' that some of the proposals would be very challenging.[4]

During Henry's inquiry the budget went from surplus into heavy deficit courtesy of the GFC. Henry's experience told him that any package had to be revenue negative—that is, it had to reduce the overall tax burden to be saleable. That needed a surplus, and the surplus was gone. It is obvious what Swan and Rudd needed to do: they had to defer implementation of the Henry Report until after the 2010 election. This was an easy step. It should have been one of many policy changes required by the financial crisis. Given the fiscal upheaval, a major tax reform package was always high risk done on the run in 2010. In the end, Labor was trapped and overwhelmed.

The report, delivered on the eve of Christmas 2009, had 138 recommendations. It was presented to a government in a state of confusion, with Rudd's climate change scheme having just been defeated. The report involved a rethinking of the tax system. 'I spent the whole of Christmas reading it,' Swan recalls. 'It spoilt my Christmas. Some of it was achievable and some was not.'[5]

Swan rightly said, once the report was delivered: 'It was never an option not to release it. But once released, there had to be an agenda coming out of it.'[6] Swan concluded that sweeping reform of direct or indirect taxation was unrealistic. Aware that his credibility as treasurer was at stake, Swan decided to run on the resources tax—hardly a surprise. It validated his deepest instincts about fairness. The Hawke Government had introduced the Petroleum Resources Rent Tax, a similar concept. State royalties, largely imposed on volume, were an inefficient tax. A new profits-based tax was justified by equity and efficiency. This was not a case of Labor running on a bad idea but, rather, of mishandling a good idea.

The Henry Report proposed a uniform resources rent tax of 40 per cent, administered by the national government that, taking into account corporate tax changes, would mean a combined statutory tax rate of 55 per cent. The tax would apply to oil, gas and mineral projects. Existing projects would be transferred into the new system. Under the complex and contentious design of the tax, the government, in effect, became a silent partner, sharing 40 per cent of the costs and profits. Henry offered two options for dealing with existing state government mining royalty regimes—either the new tax would replace state royalties (with an appro-priate revenue deal done with the states) or a parallel system would apply, state royalties would stay and companies would be credited for their roy-alty payment.

Swan had what seemed to be a plausible strategy: 'It was obvious we were going to have a mining boom Mark Two. The May budget wouldn't have addressed this challenge unless, from the very start, we had decided to have a resources rent tax. The tax was going to fund infrastructure and national superannuation.'[7] The benefits of the boom would be shared. Swan, in effect, had devised Labor's 2010 election framework but he had trouble getting the package approved. 'He [Rudd] kept avoiding the issue,' Swan said.[8] Rudd was very busy.

In January 2010, Swan had a meeting with the Resources Minister, Martin Ferguson. He gave Ferguson the brief extract from the Henry Report that recommended the tax. Ferguson agreed with the concept although he was given no details of the design. Swan asked Ferguson to reassure the mining industry that it would be fully consulted on the tax. 'He asked me to talk to the mining companies and get their agreement,' Ferguson said.

The message was that we want to develop a profits-based tax but give the industry an undertaking on behalf of the government there will be full and proper consultation. Swan had said to me, 'I will do nothing without full and proper consultation.' When the Treasurer asked me to talk with the industry he said, 'You are the only one who can pull off this arrangement.'

Ferguson agreed.[9]

I had discussions at the most senior levels with BHP, Rio and Xstrata and also the Minerals Council. I said this will be the agreement: you give the government time to think this through and nothing will occur without full and proper consultation. I reported back to the Treasurer within a couple of weeks that I had secured the total agreement of the industry on that basis.[10]

In assuring the industry, Ferguson used the example of the Hawke Government's extensive consultation in the early 1980s leading to a Petroleum Resources Rent Tax. The upshot was that between February and May the industry kept quiet. Swan purchased an excellent deal off Ferguson's goodwill.[11]

After the event Swan had a different view when Ferguson and Rudd became his critics. 'It is possibly true that Martin told the mining companies stuff he shouldn't have,' Swan said. 'That's because he wasn't in our discussions. Kevin had banned him.'[12] Ferguson was not involved in the decision-making, a mistake made by Rudd. According to Swan, 'Kevin wouldn't have him in the room.'[13] Pressed later, Ferguson said: 'Kevin denies this. I've challenged him on it.'[14]

Critically, the Minerals Council accepted the principle of the profits-based tax in its submission to Henry. 'We put that on the table,' Minerals Council boss Mitch Hooke said. 'I said the concept of a profit-based system and the principles of that are almost incontestable. But getting to that point is huge.' Hooke said it was folly for the industry to just say 'No, no, no, you can't do that.' He said: 'You can't allow yourself to be pitched into the troglodyte category. But I said you must deal with the states.'[15]

Having the industry accept the principle of the tax was an important foundation for a negotiation, even a deal. But Labor did not want a deal. Hooke was suspicious of the Henry review process. 'When it came to meeting the Henry review we were last cab off the rank,' he said.[16]

In January, Ferguson spoke to Hooke when the minerals chief was in the United States. 'Ferguson was giving assurances on behalf of the Prime Minister and the Treasurer,' Hooke said. 'Consultation will be on the table. There will be a process. We will work it through. Ferguson has always been absolutely straight with me.'[17] But Hooke, in turn, was putting Ferguson on notice. 'Some of my companies were getting very nervous. There was stuff in the press. I said, publicly, it is really a Neville Chamberlain. You have to give peace a chance.' Hooke wanted to keep the industry disciplined. But he warned Ferguson: 'I said, Martin, you asked me to put my finger in the dyke and hold back the flow. I have got five fingers in the dyke.'[18]

On 10 February, Hooke outlined the core principles that the Minerals Council wanted upheld. It had three fears: that new taxes would be imposed on the grounds that the industry was 'not paying its way'; that Treasury might assume resources capital was 'immobile' in response to higher taxes when, in fact, the world was awash with capital redeployment in the sector; and that new taxes might aim to slow the pace of resources-driven structural change in the economy.

On 12 February, Hooke and his deputy, Brendan Pearson, met with Swan. Hooke outlined the industry's views. He warned Swan against including the rate in any announcement since this pre-empted the key decision. But he found Swan non-committal. Hooke said the message was: 'It hadn't been settled; we would be consulted.' When Swan said it would not be possible to signal minerals-specific consultation ahead of other processes for other sectors, Hooke became concerned.[19]

Explaining the origins of the tax for this book, Rudd said:

He [Swan] briefed Julia [Gillard] and I about it. We had reservations but Wayne's view was that without it his credentials as a reforming treasurer would have been shot to pieces … I was not running it or any other tax. There is no doubt in anyone's mind: the carriage lay with the Treasurer.[20]

Swan, however, had a tight timetable. He was planning a package to be unveiled before the budget, not a twelve-month or two-year industry consultation. The thinking was embodied in an email sent on 30 March by Swan's office chief, Chris Barrett, to Treasury officers Ken Henry and David Parker. Barrett said he had held 'further chats with the boss' in the run-up to the next SPBC meeting on tax. He wrote:

> What we're trying to work towards is the set of core principles
> we would announce and not resile from, given we will need fairly
> extensive discussions with companies around implementation and
> legislative design, but don't want the key elements to be seen as in
> some way negotiable through that subsequent process.[21]

This is the decisive insight. The core design would be unveiled upfront
and would be non-negotiable. In his email Barrett also named the four
core elements 'we need to nail down and stick to': the tax rate, the uplift
factor, treatment of existing investments and the tax point in the chain.
They constituted the absolute heart of the tax. They would be decided by
Labor without consultation.

Barrett's email made clear that the post-announcement consultations, while vital, had a strictly limited scope. They were about 'creating
a process to discover the genuine anomalies we know will be thrown up
by the new policy' and partly about giving miners 'a process for raising
their concerns other than doing so publicly'.

This revealed a chasm between Swan's plan and the industry's hopes.
Labor was devising a new resources tax whose core elements were non-
negotiable yet it was telling industry there would be full consultation.
Both could not be right. This went to the contradictory versions from
Swan and Ferguson. The contradiction was compounded by appalling
process. Rudd was disengaged and Ferguson was excluded from the policy
decision. Yet Labor was grossly underestimating industry reaction. It was
playing with fire. It was imposing a significant new tax on Australia's most
globally important industry without the courtesy of meaningful dialogue.
For a government obsessed by politics, it was a brainless miscalculation.

Labor's assurances were not confined to the top-tier miners but
extended to the 'second tier', notably Rudd's friend and Fortescue Metals
founder Andrew Forrest, who was assisting the government with an
indigenous employment program. Forrest said he was tipped off about
the tax by the unions. 'I rang the Treasurer three times,' he said. 'Each time
he assured me the tax would be benign, that it would be no problem for
Fortescue. Frankly, I was not reassured.'[22]

Meanwhile Ken Henry was struck by Labor's political judgement.
'They thought the resources tax was a dead-set political winner for
them,' he said. He was amazed at the time invested to sort out its name.[23]
Interviewed for this book, Rudd said the 'gang of four' laid down two
conditions: Swan had 'to secure the support of the major miners or a
significant proportion of them' and also secure the support of the states.

He claimed Swan 'told us that they [the miners] would be supportive of the proposal' that was eventually put forward.[24]

This leads to the second dispute: the Rudd–Swan conflict. Of course, neither the industry nor the states were 'on side' (notably West Australian Premier Colin Barnett) and this opposition destroyed the mining tax. Swan has denied Rudd's claims. He says Rudd's office was kept informed throughout and that they knew the state of play, adding that many documents testify to this. Swan has said that 'there was discussion between Kevin's officials and Barnett's officials, discussions between him, me and Kevin at various times about what we wanted to do and how'. The conflict between Rudd and Swan over who said what remains unresolved.[25]

On 7 April Swan's office sent Rudd's office an email summarising the Treasurer's recent meeting with the West Australian premier. It says Barnett 'put on the record his full opposition to a new federal resources tax, said he wants to keep his royalties structure and his current plans for it'. Unsurprisingly, Barnett said if the new federal tax was imposed he wanted 'a share of it'. This document confirms that Rudd's office knew what was happening and knew Barnett would fight the tax.

Rudd cannot shirk responsibility. 'I am led to believe Kevin had very little hands on,' says Ferguson.[26] What on earth was Rudd doing making countless hospital visits while spending so little time supervising the mining tax?

Hooke had another meeting with Swan on 1 April, after which he concluded he was getting nothing substantial on the tax design and knew the industry was being strung out. Again he issued a warning to Ferguson. 'I made it clear to Martin we were not getting anywhere despite assurances about full-blown consultation,' Hooke recalled.

> I said to Martin, 'Mate, if this stuff comes out the way it is moving there is no way I will be able to hold back the industry even if I wanted to.' I said we will mount the most ferocious and vigorous advertising campaign. I mentioned $20 million. I gave him that figure.[27]

Having tried appeasement, Hooke went for a touch of intimidation. Neither worked.

Minerals giant BHP Billiton had long seen this tax coming and Labor's most formidable foe would be its chief executive, the South African Marius Kloppers. BHP was universally known in Australia and had an iconic status somewhat similar to that of Qantas. It was the world's largest mining company and it was the largest taxpayer in Australia. Yet it was treated with barely disguised contempt by Labor in this process.

The miner had engaged many consultants in preparatory work: KPMG, Deloitte Access Economics and McKinseys. By January 2010, Kloppers had identified the four principles he felt should guide the new tax: it must be prospective only; the companies must remain internationally competitive; the tax must differentiate between different minerals; and the tax must apply at the mine gate and not to infrastructure. Kloppers pumped out this message, later saying: 'I told it to my children, my wife, everybody that wanted to listen to me, ad nauseam.'[28] But Labor was not listening.

On 16 February, BHP Billiton briefed Treasury on its four principles. On 10 March at 4.30 p.m. Rudd met Kloppers and his key advisers in his Parliament House office. He was curt and demanding. 'Okay, what have you got to tell me?' he began. The body language was unmistakable. Kloppers outlined the company's four principles. The miners felt Rudd was uninterested. He launched an attack on Steve Knott, one of the industry lobby leaders. It was a short meeting, no more than twenty minutes. Rudd's disenchantment with the miners was unmistakable. Senior BHP Billiton executive Gerard Bond later said that the company was unable to get details of the proposed tax 'despite our repeated effort to engage with government and Treasury'.[29]

In mid-April Rio Tinto Managing Director David Peever saw Swan in Sydney and had an exchange that would become legendary in the mining tax saga. Peever wanted to discover Labor's tax thinking and, in particular, to establish whether the mining tax would be built into the May 2010 budget. For Peever, the critical part of this meeting was Swan's assurance—later denied by the Treasurer—that no tax revenue numbers would be included in the budget. Peever told the author:

> We were assured both by Wayne Swan and his chief of staff that whatever tax policy was settled upon, it would not be in the budget's forward estimates. I left the meeting re-assured on that vital point. It meant there would still be time after the tax announcement and the budget to work through the proposed policy because the numbers were not settled upon.[30]

Pressed on this point, Peever was sure. There was no doubt about Swan's assurance.

The tax policy release date was set for Sunday 2 May. It would be a media lockup at Parliament House, a budget-type event. The policy was being put up in lights. Critical meetings were held late the week before the release.

On Thursday 29 April, Ferguson and his senior adviser were briefed on the tax by Swan and his officials. Ferguson was dismayed. 'When we suggested changes we were told the document was at the printer,' Ferguson said. 'We went back to our office and our view was "It won't work." I felt like resigning, especially when I got the companies in and saw their reaction. It was one of disbelief.'[31] Ferguson was angry because he had been exploited. 'I was misled by Swan,' Ferguson said.[32] Acting on that basis, Ferguson felt he had misled the mining sector.

Hooke has a graphic recall of the industry being briefed: 'We were at the Treasury and it was like Fort Knox. I remember saying to Martin, "Well, this flies in the face of all the assurances we have been given. You have put a 40 per cent tax rate on the table." He was very diplomatic.'[33]

Swan briefed the corporate executives, including Kloppers and Peever.

Swan has put great store in these briefings of the corporate executives. In 2012 he told the author: 'The dominant theme is that they [the miners] were left out, that there was no consultation. What I want to dispel very clearly is this notion that significant sectors of the industry were unaware of it [the tax] until it was announced.'[34] But this comment mistakes form for substance. Swan did tell the industry. It was a briefing about a decision taken, not a consultation that might shape the decision. Ferguson dismissed Swan's argument: 'This is rubbish. He met them once. That's not consultations. It's not what I was I led to believe would occur.'[35]

When Peever and his Rio team were briefed he was appalled. At one point they caucused among themselves and then returned. 'We implored them to re-think,' Peever said. The Rio team felt the tax design wouldn't work. They felt Swan didn't comprehend and that Treasury officials were too theoretical. Peever's final message was to appeal to the government to leave itself some flexibility. This request was ignored. The miners could scarcely believe what was happening.

These events triggered an even greater Rudd–Swan conflict. It was apparent the full tax numbers were in the budget. Peever believed the industry had been misled and ambushed. This was also Ferguson's view. Referring to the issue of the forward estimates, Ferguson said: 'Peever had asked the question and the Treasurer said "no". The company executives believed he misled them.'[36] The entire point of the tax, of course, was to finance initiatives across the forward estimates so the numbers had to be in the upcoming budget.

Interviewed for this book, Swan said: 'On 29 April we had a briefing with the main companies on a confidential basis. The numbers were in the budget. It is absolute nonsense I said to anyone the revenue numbers wouldn't be in the budget. That's beyond comprehension.'[37] Swan said the industry had spread the story and there was no basis to it. Yet Rudd took it up.

Rudd told the author:

> The subsequent unfolding of the debate was a huge surprise both to myself and I think to the Deputy Prime Minister. When we choose to find out why and got Martin Ferguson to go and find out, the answer was this: the miners had been told in briefings by the Treasurer that the policy would be announced but it would not contain numbers in it for the forward estimates. Martin Ferguson will confirm this version of events.[38]

Ferguson did. Obviously, if the numbers were not in the budget, that would open the way for serious consultation and negotiation about the tax design.

Rudd even claimed he was 'stunned' when the tax package was released as a detailed proposal with numbers.[39] This is surely an untenable remark. Rudd had attended 'gang of four' meetings on the tax. How could the Prime Minister not know the tax had numbers attached to it? Swan said Rudd knew because he had been involved in 'endless meetings' about the package.[40] Beyond this, Swan denies ever giving the industry grounds for thinking the mining tax would be unveiled as a general policy, not a costed budget measure. He says the mining tax was basic to the budget. 'What else would have been in the budget?' he asked rhetorically.[41]

Asked to explain the contradiction between his version and Swan's, Rudd said: 'Either there was a profound miscommunication between the Treasurer and the miners—profound—on whether numbers would be attached or not, or we were misled. I am not in a position to judge which of these is the case.'[42] From this comment, it is obvious who Rudd blames. The whole saga is an irrefutable instance of a decision-making shambles.

On the morning of 2 May, before the lockup, Swan and Rudd were in the prime minister's office going through the press releases. 'Kevin wanted to change the press releases,' Swan later recalled. 'We were due in the lockup. I said, "No, Kevin, it has all been done and approved." He wanted to recast some of it. It was unbelievable.' Swan had not expected Rudd to attend the media conference. He envisaged it would be 'one of the biggest press conferences I will do as treasurer'. Now Rudd said he was coming. For Swan, it was a blatant discourtesy.[43]

In the media lockup, Labor released its tax package and the full Henry review. The optics were bad. Labor had accepted less than half a dozen of Henry's 138 recommendations. This was a narrow conception of tax reform—no taxes were eliminated, most areas of tax were untouched, and the tax burden was not reduced. The centrepiece was the mining tax, wearing its populist title the Resource Super Profits Tax (RSPT). It was to start in mid-2012, raising a total of $12 billion in its first two years, with the revenue used to finance a cut in the corporate tax rate from 30 to 28 per cent, assistance for small business, a new infrastructure fund for the states and superannuation concessions for low-income earners. Swan said it would stand or fall as a package.

Compared with those in the Henry Report, the tax changes were modest. Labor did not accept, even as a goal, Henry's recommendation that the corporate rate be cut to 25 per cent to make Australia competitive. Labor's statement offered no road map for future tax reform. Even worse, Rudd and Swan signalled that this package would constitute their second-term agenda.[44]

The increase in the superannuation guarantee rate from 9 to 12 per cent was included in the package but would be funded by employers, not the RSPT. This was a significant move. It was also deliberately misleading. A false impression was left that the mining tax was financing the lift to 12 per cent super. ACCI's Peter Anderson said: 'It was one of the most brazen misrepresentations by a government in the past twenty years.'[45]

In their media conference Rudd and Swan argued the reforms would improve efficiency and equity. From the start a presentational conflict arose that plagued Labor: would it sell the tax as economic reform or as a populist 'soak the rich' bandwagon? To be on the safe side, it tried both.

In his guise as aggressive populist, Rudd said mining companies were not paying their way and predicted a 'fear campaign' against Labor. He said mining profits had risen by $80 billion in the past decade but royalty revenue had increased by only $9 billion. Rudd asked rhetorically: 'Why should we put up with a tax system for the next decade that has cost us $35 billion in lost revenue?'—money that could have been spent on rails, roads and ports. Labor's proposition was that mining was under-taxed and needed to pay more.[46] Every message from Rudd and Swan was that Australians must get a 'fairer share of the boom'—they had their election pitch.

Industry consultation would be tightly limited. The panel involved was not to consult 'on the overall merits of the RSPT or the key parameters'. Labor was playing it very tough.

There was hubris in the air. The documents said 'the RSPT is world class' and was setting a 'new benchmark for resources taxation'.[47] That no other nation had the RSPT model, however, would become a double-edged proposition. Swan told the media: 'If you think about reforms of our economy and the economic system in our lifetime, this is more significant than any I can think of.'[48] It was an invitation to ridicule.

For the industry and BHP Billiton the tax exceeded their worst-case scenario. The company had never conceived of the idea of government being a 40 per cent project partner. The sense of betrayal was enduring. There were nine days between the release of the RSPT and its incorporation into the forward estimates via the budget—so much for consultation. Labor was moving much too fast, betting its reputation on the tax. Yet a perfect storm was coming. There were three connected problems: industry anger, the absence of agreement with the states, and design flaws in the tax.

Hooke accused the government of a tax grab that would undermine the nation's investment reputation. He said mining was a global industry where projects were rated and 'capital deployed where it is strategically opportune to do so'. Getting ready for war, he replaced his Chamberlain persona with a Churchillian one. Hooke was consumed by Labor's breach of faith. 'It was an act of betrayal in terms of the assurances we were given,' he said. 'This was an ambush.' Hooke felt the industry had been treated like fools. He had told Labor not to come with a rate. But Labor decided it would get a better tax rate by pre-emption rather than dialogue.[49] It had to live with the consequences.

Hooke's sentiments about Rudd became the industry orthodoxy: 'All the pennies had finally dropped. Rudd got mugged by the GFC, seduced by redistribution, found the politics of envy and believed that governments knew best. I said, "They wanted a fight and it looks like they are going to get it."'[50]

Some people claimed the industry exaggerated the extent of the government's deception. The problem with this theory is Ferguson: Ferguson said the mining chiefs were ambushed and the blame lay with Swan. 'The industry was promised full and proper consultations. But Swan had no intention of that. Wayne does not like meetings and argument. He likes to ambush you with the numbers. He is a political apparatchik, not a policy person.'[51]

Within days of the policy's release Ferguson knew major changes were essential. The 'big three'—BHP Billiton, Rio Tinto and Xstrata—were alarmed. Kloppers said the tax would 'threaten Australia's competitiveness, jeopardise future investments and adversely affect the future wealth and standard of living of all Australians'. Kloppers did not oppose a resources rent tax in principle but he disputed the design, saying BHP's effective tax rate had been 43 per cent in 2009 and that it would rise to 57 per cent. Rio's David Peever warned that changing the rules mid-stream for multi-billion–dollar projects was 'the worst possible message Australia could send to investors'.[52] Rio chief executive Tom Albanese described Australia as the top sovereign risk in the world for his company. Some of these claims were industry exaggerations—yet they could not excuse the tax's defects.

Rudd's friend and adviser on infrastructure, Rod Eddington, a Rio director, would appeal to the government to start again. A month into the brawl he said a new process 'must begin now'. In private, Eddington was dismayed at the scale of Labor's blunder.[53] Yet Rudd's initial response had been to play the populist foreign company card.

'BHP is foreign owned, Rio Tinto is more than 70 per cent owned,' Rudd said. 'That means these massively increased profits built on Australian resources are mostly, in fact, going overseas.' It was a throwback to the politics of a past generation. Mining was a state-of-the-art industry where foreign financing of some of the world's biggest projects was an imperative. Interviewed for this book, Swan slammed Rudd, saying that 'Kevin went off the reservation; this was not part of our script.'[54]

Rudd was never able to explain the tax and many of his formulations were tortuous. At a private dinner in Perth in early May, Rudd dropped a bombshell: the RSPT aimed to slow the mining sector since the high dollar was hurting too many other industries—including financial services, tourism, educational services and wine exports. The idea that Labor was trying to slow resources development was lethal. This was not the official position; Swan was forced to clarify.[55]

Fortescue boss Andrew Forrest, a friend of Rudd, was enraged by the RSPT. 'It showed we would have a negative cash flow after paying interest,' he said. 'It would lead Fortescue to a default situation. Our company would not exist under the RSPT.'[56]

Kloppers assumed the leadership role in the anti-tax campaign. The 'war room' was established at Lonsdale Street in Melbourne with

Gerard Bond in charge. BHP Billiton believed it had been 'set up'. It felt the RSPT had global ramifications: if this was done in Australia, other nations would follow.

The Minerals Council–paid advertising campaign began on Friday 7 May, five days after the announcement. The campaign was run from its Canberra HQ through a taskforce chaired by Brendan Pearson. Spanning fifty-four days, the campaign cost $25 million, with its advertising director being Neil Lawrence, the director of Rudd's 2007 election campaign. It ranks with the ACTU's anti-WorkChoices paid campaign as the best special-interest campaign in recent decades.

An early priority for Kloppers was to persuade the Business Council of Australia to line up against the tax. The miners put a priority on the financial analysts—ensuring that the analysts for the big broking and banking houses attacked the tax. In effect, the financial sector was recruited. Kloppers' aim was to dismantle the RSPT by a punitive assault, an extraordinary step for his company. It revealed the complete break-down between the world's biggest mining company and the Rudd Government.

Rudd, however, was now in a terrible trap.

He had just staged his great climate change retreat. Attacked for lack of conviction, Rudd could not retreat again. Another sign of weakness might be fatal. It might risk his job. A Newspoll published just after the RSPT release showed, for the first time since Howard's 2007 loss, the Coalition in an election-winning position of 51 to 49 per cent, the result of Rudd's climate change retreat. It sent shivers down Labor's collective but weak spine. On 10 May the Neilson poll in Fairfax papers reported a 50–50 two-party–preferred split, enough for Labor to lose an election. Rudd felt he must use the RSPT battle to re-establish the 'strength' credentials he had lost. He had to play the tough guy—yet it was the wrong decision. Phillip Coorey was soon reporting 'almost universal concern within the ALP' about Rudd's communications problem.[57] He was losing this contest.

In late May, Peter Hartcher wrote a revealing column:

> One of the most mistaken ideas to take hold in politics in recent weeks is that Kevin Rudd has somehow been shocked that the big miners are reacting ferociously to his proposed new mining tax. To believe this, you'd have to think Rudd some sort of moron …
> Rudd wanted a fight. That's the whole point.

Hartcher said Rudd 'wants to be the little Aussie David fighting the greedy foreign Goliaths on behalf of his people'.[58]

In truth, Rudd had completely misjudged. He got neither the policy nor the politics right. Rudd bargained for a fight—not a war he would lose. 'They woke up a sleeping giant,' Hooke said.[59]

Meanwhile Abbott had wrong-footed Labor, yet again. Abbott saw the RSPT as a gift, not as the trap for him that Labor and most of the media had assumed. Indeed, Abbott could hardly believe his luck: Rudd had just delayed his ETS (what Abbott called his 'great big new tax') and within days had embraced a mining tax that Abbott branded as another 'great big new tax'. How good was this? And Abbott was supposed to be thrown onto the defensive!

At 10 a.m. on 5 May, just three days after the policy release, Kloppers met the Coalition's team: Abbott, Hockey, Bishop, Robb and MacFarlane. At 11.30 the same day, on a recommendation from Bishop, a Western Australian, shadow cabinet decided to oppose the RSPT. Abbott would enshrine the RSPT as an election-defining issue. 'The die is cast,' he said. 'The only way to stop this great big new tax on the people who saved us from recession is to change the government.'

Abbott had wedged Rudd: if Rudd kept his nerve Abbott would attack him for undermining the industry but if Rudd retreated then Abbott would accuse him of lacking conviction. It was the same story again: Rudd had handed Abbott another crusade. Penny Wong was puzzled. Her climate change strategy had been to ensure that Labor avoided any united attack from the coal sector and the steel sector together—but Labor now faced an attack from the entire resources sector. 'We ditched one cost-of-living argument for another,' she said. Abbott was on a roll.

'As campaign director I was told nothing beforehand,' said ALP National Secretary Karl Bitar of the mining tax.[60] Why tell Bitar? He was only running the re-election campaign. Labor was a party of phoney toughs: it pretended it wanted to fight the industry but it had no plans for the fight that occurred. AWU boss Paul Howes was briefed on the tax by Rudd at Kirribilli House before the announcement. 'I rather naively assumed this proposal had already been negotiated with the industry and had its general support,' Howes said. He was shocked upon realising this was not the case. 'Picking a fight of this scale just before an election was not brave; it was foolhardy,' Howes said. He began to think Rudd couldn't do the job.[61] Neither the ALP nor the unions expected a war with the miners.

Labor never properly addressed the role of the states. Rudd kept saying the people owned the mineral resources. Arising from the common law, however, ownership of mineral resources in Australia resides with state and territory governments. Labor was imposing a new tax on resources it did not own with the intent of eventually replacing royalties imposed by the states on assets they did own.

There was no formal consultation with all the states. This is because the problems would have required protracted dialogue with little prospect of agreement. Swan did meet with Barnett to try to sort out the issue. But Barnett told Swan he was 'fully opposed' to the tax. The package provided for the national government to compensate mining companies for state royalty obligations up to the time of the resources tax announcement. The aim was to tackle industry alarm that it might face a double tax. This meant the national government wanted state royalties frozen at current levels but, critically, it would have to negotiate with the states to achieve this result. From the announcement, however, this was unacceptable to Barnett. The unresolved 'hole' in the package was that if the states continued to raise royalties, a certainty, and the national government compensated the companies, then the quantum of the RSPT would be diminished.

With Western Australia raising more than 50 per cent of all state royalties, Barnett's opposition was lethal. He told Labor the Crown's ownership of minerals was vested in the states and then declared war on the RSPT. Treasury documents reveal Labor's tactic: the idea was 'to put the tax in place before negotiating a new intergovernmental agreement'.[62] In short, let's fight the miners first and the states second. Frankly, it was a no-brainer: the absence of state agreement up front undermined the political viability of the tax. Rudd and Swan had been contemptuous of the states and they paid a price.

Their greatest difficulty was rejection of the RSPT design by the mining and finance sectors. The conceptual key to the tax was government as a silent partner in a project sharing the risks and receipts. It would receive 40 per cent of super profits and refund losses when a project closed. The miners would lend the money to the government for its 40 per cent share and the government would pay interest on the loan. An economist who reviewed the tax, Sinclair Davidson, said: 'This loan took the form of a contingent liability that could be cashed in if the project failed. The government seemed to think this option was valuable while the miners thought it was worthless.'[63]

Chris Barrett said: 'Having the government take a 40 per cent share was an elegant position but the 40 per cent rebate was not bankable. It was not valued by the market, so it didn't work as intended.'[64] Interviewed in 2012, Swan said: 'We didn't necessarily get the design right. It became clear from the initial contacts with the industry that refundability was never going to fly.'[65] Rio chief Albanese said: 'I don't think you can take that promise to the bank.'[66] Ferguson was appalled by the Treasury design, calling it 'a textbook proposal you would apply to an immature mining industry such as Nigeria or Mozambique'.[67] Peever explained the situation: you cannot go to your board saying we have this new project but don't worry because if we lose money the taxpayer will look after it.

With the miners in revolt and financial analysts now permanent critics, the share market turned south. ANZ chief Mike Smith warned of the risk to investor confidence. David Murray, chair of the Future Fund, said the tax must be redesigned or abandoned. Ross Garnaut, a resource tax expert, advocated a major reversion towards Hawke's petroleum resources tax model.[68] High-profile market analyst Charlie Aitken wrote to his clients: 'Foreign investors believe we have lost our way. It is that simple.'[69]

In a lament, Hooke said of Labor and the industry: 'We appear destined to follow the same path as the debate over an emissions trading scheme—comparable objectives, failure to consult, failure in design, public conflict, real or perceived increasing sovereign risk of doing business in Australia and ultimately a lose–lose for all concerned.'[70]

By early June there was a mutual hardening of position. Rudd called the industry's claims 'a load of balderdash and absolute bunkum'. He boycotted the Minerals Council annual dinner but hosted pre-dinner drinks in his suite for leading executives. It was not a success. Rudd boasted to the miners about his knowledge of the industry. At the dinner Minerals Council vice-chair Ian Smith, from Newcrest Mining, told a highly charged audience: 'It is almost inconceivable that our industry should find itself so maligned and so misrepresented for its contribution to the social and economic welfare of Australians.' Kloppers said: 'I have never seen such anger in the room.' He called the RSPT the greatest threat he had seen to the industry in seventeen years. Forrest accused Rudd of 'trading the sovereign status of his country for a chance at improving an election process'.[71] Peever said: 'In thirty-three years working in the resources sector I had never seen such anger on the part of mining companies. There was a determination to deal with this issue because, first, we had been blindsighted and second, it was such devastatingly poor policy.'[72]

A sense of disbelief mounted across the Labor Party at the almost uncontrolled nature of the conflict and Rudd's inability to address it.

An early-June Newspoll broke 48 to 28 per cent against the tax, with 78 per cent wanting it modified or abandoned. Newspoll director Martin O'Shannessy said: 'The government is not winning its argument.'[73]

Ferguson, Swan and Rudd were involved at various times in negotiations with the industry. 'You're working for me now,' Rudd told Ferguson. 'I want you involved and sorting this out.'[74] Rudd grew angry with Swan: 'It became harder and harder to find the Treasurer as he progressively distanced himself from the debate. I said to my staff: "Why is he overseas? Where is he?"'[75] Ferguson had recurring resignation thoughts. 'I think the industry worked out I was tossing up pulling the pin,' he said. 'Don Argus and Marius Kloppers were wonderful to me. Don rang me and said, "You've got to hang in, we need you to settle it."'[76]

Interviewed for this book, Rudd made an explosive claim: 'There was an initial effort to land a position with Kloppers. He was then overruled, as he told me directly himself, by his chairman, [Jac] Nasser. From that point on, it became virtually impossible to engage the three majors.'[77] Ferguson said an understanding had been reached with Kloppers but he subsequently got a midnight phone call from Kloppers saying he had been 'countermanded' by Nasser.[78]

Convinced the BHP route was a dead end, Rudd tried to split the industry by cutting a deal with Fortescue and Andrew Forrest. The final week of Rudd's leadership saw hectic meetings with Rudd, his staff, Forrest and his CFO, Stephen Price, to strike a deal. The main Rudd–Forrest session was at the Lodge on the night of Sunday 20 June, Rudd's fourth-last night as prime minister. They met again on the Monday night. Forrest later said an agreement had been reached—yet this could not equate to an agreement with the industry or the 'big three'.[79] Swan was dismissive, saying the talks with Fortescue were 'not going anywhere' and only revealed 'how mad' things had become.[80]

The truth is that Rudd was far too slow at seeking a breakthrough with the industry. This should have been done weeks earlier, with BHP Billiton at the top of the list. Rudd exaggerated his strength and underestimated the damage being done to his government. For six weeks after the May 2010 pre-election budget, Labor's war with the miners was the consuming story. The government looked incompetent and chaotic. Rudd's tragedy is that his leadership had become dependent upon a mining tax that was untenable.

Interviewed for this book, Lachlan Harris said Rudd should not have tried to impose the tax before the 2010 election but instead should have sought an election mandate for the government's principles.[81] Harris is correct. It was a further blunder by Rudd and Swan. Given their insistence on the resources tax they should have put the broad principle of the tax, without rate, design or numbers, to the 2010 election seeking a mandate to be followed by a post-election negotiation. Fought out as an issue of principle, they could have won.

Swan grew enraged at the industry reaction. He saw something bigger and more menacing at work: an array of corporate power, mining and media, against Labor: 'You had all the briefings of the News Ltd papers, they [BHP] threatened people in the business community, did a thuggish number on their suppliers. They decided the government was weak enough they could go for our throat.' It had a lasting impact on Swan.[82]

There is a myth—a good government falling prey to an evil multinational industry. The miners were ruthless, self-interested and ugly. In the end, however, they had few options. Labor picked this fight at the wrong time in the wrong way with a flawed policy. Its ineptitude undermined a tax policy idea that should have attracted wide political support. There was always a template: the Hawke Government's negotiation of the offshore petroleum tax.

Watching Rudd and Swan struggle to explain and sell their RSPT, Ken Henry's mind went to another treasurer: 'Peter Costello knew the detail of the GST better than I did.'[83] It tells so much.

Karl Bitar pointed out that the real problem was not the tax but the perception of an incompetent government.[84] Consider this project: Labor had rushed the tax onto the stage, ambushed the industry, declined the consultation option, misjudged the design, fudged the problem with the states, fooled itself into thinking redistribution against a rich industry was a guaranteed winner and, when it lost the contest, refused a tactical retreat by summoning the parties to the table. It was a fusion of bad judgement and bad process.

Ferguson said: 'The industry would have accepted a profits-based tax. That was their submission to us. They were ready to work with us. My view is if you engage in an open and honest way then you always come out better. We lost the mining tax dispute not because of the mining industry's response but because we created the mess.'[85]

When Rudd was deposed by the caucus on Thursday 24 June, the RSPT still hung in his closet, unchanged and unresolved.

CHAPTER 21

THE DEMISE OF RUDD

Kevin Rudd was blind to the fatal manoeuvrings of his enemies. Like Caesar in the forum, he never sighted the assassins until the knives were unfurled. For Rudd, removal in an act of political violence was inconceivable and the aftershock never left him.

His grief at losing the leadership was compounded by his shock at misjudging Julia Gillard. She had been his deputy, his friend and his collaborator—now Gillard had betrayed him. Rudd never saw this prospect. His hatred for Gillard would now be driven by anger at his misjudgement of her.

A competent prime minister would not have been deposed. Rudd was removed by a groundswell of personal animosity and mass panic. Never in Australia's history has a prime minister been deposed with so little party debate, with such marginal influence from the cabinet and to the complete surprise of the public.

The execution of Rudd was a brilliant yet unconscious exposure of modern Labor—it would sacrifice any leader to stay in power. And it was weak: a two-month wobble in the opinion polls was enough to stampede a faint-hearted caucus. Rudd was removed by a right-wing push only because he had lost the confidence of his caucus.

Rudd faltered at his point of supposed strength: as a policy leader. His first failure was not to govern well. This is where he came undone. Governing well was the pivot that held his prime ministership together. Rudd's mishandling of frontline issues—climate change, the mining tax, asylum seeker boats, the home-insulation program and hospitals—reveals that by 2010 his system of prime ministerial government had malfunctioned. By June 2010 many caucus members knew something had gone seriously wrong, even if they were unable to identify the exact problem.

Poor governing led to Rudd's slide in the polls. This created the fear that Labor might lose the election and individual Members of Parliament lose their seats. It meant the caucus lost faith in the leader. Once Rudd was exposed in the polls, he suddenly became vulnerable. He had no internal system of factional protection or networking loyalists to guard his interests. Rudd was a loner in his office. Greg Combet described the uneasy mood:

> I could see his support was very weak. This is because of the way he was governing. A lot of tension, frustration and declining confidence in him as leader had been building for some time. There was soft talk in the corridors, a perplexed feel about the place, talk of how well Gillard was going.[1]

Gillard, seeing Rudd's drift, had become more assertive. After Copenhagen, Gillard felt Rudd had entered a psychological slump; her account of their Kirribilli House meeting in January 2010 makes this clear. She was frustrated over the hospitals saga and the climate change fiasco. 'I was having any number of conversations about the situation of the government,' Gillard said. Her main worry was Rudd's inability to get an election strategy in place. Gillard had developed plans but felt she was getting nowhere with Rudd or his office.[2]

Bruce Hawker, having recently joined Rudd's staff, felt that 'dealing with Julia was seen in terms of "placating" her rather than taking her concerns seriously.'[3] Gillard was pushing, yet Rudd and his office were resistant. 'I had done everything I could to mitigate the chaos,' Gillard said.[4]

Sean Kelly said: 'I think Rudd was angry at Gillard's interventions.' Yet Kelly felt that, after the mining tax issue, 'Kevin was finding it difficult to function and take decisions'.[5] The dislocation confirmed Gillard's bedrock view: 'By 2010 there was paralysis in the government and Kevin was not capable of leading the government out of its difficulties.'[6] Once Gillard believed this, self-justification for a challenge was near. Rudd loyalists began to say 'she wants to run everything' but Gillard's view was that virtually nothing was being run properly. The terrain for an explosion was laid.

Gillard's disillusionment was shared. The Right faction leaders in New South Wales and Victoria had become hostile to Rudd. Their influence was marginalised; they were rarely privy to decisions; their advice, when sought, was usually rejected. They were being provoked. Rudd's relations with Mark Arbib, the most influential Right powerbroker, were severed after a series of tensions. The Victorian Right in the form of Bill Shorten, Stephen Conroy and David Feeney was alarmed at Rudd's poor judgement. The culture of the Right, notably in New South Wales, is entrenched—it existed to exert power and influence with ALP leaders. Rudd was denying that culture.

The irony is that the Right could have been Rudd's Praetorian guard. Arbib had functioned as de facto protector before they fell out. So the people who could have saved Rudd would lead the insurrection. Rudd's lack of attention to ALP power realities was astounding, Gillard joking that once Arbib was 'in the freezer' there was no line of defence.

ALP National Secretary Karl Bitar believed Labor faced defeat. Over 4–9 June, Bitar did a benchmark study for the election. It showed Labor 35, Coalition 44 and Greens 14 per cent, translating into a Coalition victory of 52 to 48 per cent. Labor was losing votes to both left and right. The Green vote revealed the price Rudd was paying for his climate change retreat. Bitar tested the question: Does the Rudd Government deserve to be re-elected? Only 38 per cent said 'yes'. 'I was convinced we would lose the election under Rudd,' Bitar said, adding: 'I was not convinced that, if Gillard was leader, it would enable us to win.'[7]

On 7 June the Fairfax papers published an ACNielsen poll showing a 53 to 47 per cent two-party–preferred lead for the Coalition. A weak caucus began to buckle. The unthinkable prospect—that Labor, having suffered for eleven years in the wilderness under Howard, might succumb as a one-term government—now loomed. Arbib said later that this poll was an important catalyst.

Nielsen director John Stirton said: 'It looks like a protest against Kevin Rudd.' Feeney felt the public had decided he was a phoney. He saw no evidence of any viable re-election strategy. 'Caucus members don't expect much,' Feeney said. 'But they want to know the place is being run properly.' He likened the Rudd Government to an authoritarian regime. Arbib felt Rudd had lost the plot; his political antenna had gone missing. Shorten's view was that Rudd 'was taking the party over a cliff'.

Widely seen as a future leader, Shorten, a former AWU National Secretary, had a powerful base and influential backers. Rudd's ministerial decisions proved he preferred Combet over Shorten. Kevin and Therese had little time for Shorten while Shorten had judged Rudd and found him to be wanting. Shorten met Gillard on the morning of 15 June, eight days before the crisis erupted. He told Gillard that Labor was facing defeat, possibly a bad defeat. He asked her to consider, in the party's interest, the leadership issue. Gillard listened but held her counsel. The logic was inescapable: if Gillard refused to move then Rudd stayed in place. But Gillard could see the earth moving.[8]

When the push came, South Australian right-wing faction leader Don Farrell would be an enthusiastic backer. In early 2010 Farrell had travelled to Israel with former New South Wales right-wing powerbroker John Della Bosca. 'He was the first person to say to me the voters had woken up to Kevin,' Farrell said. 'In caucus there was no love for Kevin. He had done so many dreadful things to so many people.' Farrell judged that by mid-June 'the bulk of the caucus felt we could not win an election'.[9]

Cabinet minister Tony Burke was conducting his own private dialogue with Gillard, having decided Rudd 'couldn't have an honest conversation with you'. One evening he got a bottle of red and said to Gillard, 'Let's have a talk.'[10] It was the start of an influential dialogue. 'The whole conversation was about trying to fix things,' says Burke. At the end Burke said to Gillard: 'There is one issue we haven't raised. If you get to the point where you want to discuss it, then I am happy to do that.' Gillard said 'thank you'. Nothing more. Burke had put his line out on the leadership. He wanted a new prime minister.[11]

Gillard was smart, playing it tight, not exposing herself. As a political animal, she knew the leadership temperature was heating up. Gillard said, 'People did come to me—Arbib, Burke, you know, a few others, in a kind of desperation to try to open a conversation about the leadership. I would always say, "I am not having this conversation."'[12]

Before the crisis, Burke had held another two or three sessions with Gillard. Again, leadership was not canvassed; it was the elephant in the room. Burke later testified with feeling about Gillard's loyalty. 'We didn't have a candidate, that was the problem,' he says. But Burke had not given up.[13]

Rudd's office knew there were problems but missed their intensity. Lachlan Harris felt that 'from the moment of the CPRS decision the leadership became a risk'. Alister Jordan had invited Bruce Hawker into the office on a temporary basis to assist with political communications and improve ties with the New South Wales Right. 'Bruce, this is more serious than you think,' Arbib told Hawker after his arrival. 'Kevin isn't talking to people.'

The New South Wales and Victorian branches resorted to research. Over 16–17 June the New South Wales branch commissioned Labor's pollster, John Uttings from UMR, who went into four marginal seats—Eden–Monaro, Greenway, Hughes and Page. The result showed a Labor primary vote of 35 per cent, with the Coalition's 47 per cent. The swing against Labor was 7 per cent and the two-party result showed a Coalition lead of 55 to 45. Abbott was closing the gap on Rudd as preferred prime minister—to just 42 to 37 per cent Rudd's way. It showed a rout in

New South Wales, the biggest state. The marginal seats were in deeper trouble than the published polls suggested. Asked which way the nation was heading, 49 to 38 per cent answered on the 'wrong track'.[14]

The Victorian research by UMR was done from 4 June and yielded a better result than New South Wales. Maxine McKew, who sighted the results for her 2012 book, said the two-party–preferred vote was 52 to 48 for the Coalition but McKew believed this was based on sampling 'soft' voters. Gillard was shown to have an eight-point 'favourability' rating over Rudd, hardly surprising in Victoria. The poll, overall, was hardly an argument for a change of leader.[15] Such polls, however, made for a more nervous party.

The astonishing feature of the crisis and its prelude was the sheer lack of assessment of Gillard as alternative prime minister. It was all about Kevin, his problems, his defects, his behaviour. There was a universal assumption among the anti-Rudd camp that Gillard would be better. The big questions were never tested. How would Gillard do better? How would Gillard explain the assassination of Rudd? In politics, loose ends can be fatal and this operation would have surplus loose ends.

The move against Rudd had another element: to reclaim the party. The ABC's Barrie Cassidy captured this sentiment in his 2010 book *The Party Thieves*, where he argued there was a feeling that Rudd had 'hijacked' Labor and 'either ignored or abused key people within it for too long'.[16] This was a restoration of Labor norms, procedures and internal power arrangements. Gillard would govern *with* the party, not against it.

When it erupted, the revolt had the surge of a runaway bushfire. The Labor mob was virtually running amok in the building on the night of 23 June, delirious at the prospect of executing its demon leader. This was not an impressive event. It reeked of an institution lurching out of control. There is one certainty: due diligence was not done on this operation. Its energy came from below, fanned by anti-Rudd hostility. It had scarcely begun before it was over. Rudd's cabinet was useless as the fire break. Cabinet minister after cabinet minister was told on the evening of Wednesday 23 June that the leader was being terminated and the numbers had been assembled. Their impotence mocked their status. They were a cabinet of silos, knocked over with ease.

As the sole source of authority Rudd became the sole source of blame when things went bad. Wise leaders guard their behaviour but Rudd succumbed to the intoxication of power. In the end, he was isolated at his desk. Family and staff could not save him.

The danger zone for Rudd was the final sitting week before the winter break. Led by Burke and Arbib, the anti-Rudd forces talked up their prospects. On Saturday 19 June there was a state by-election in the safe Labor seat of Penrith, an epicentre of Western Sydney in the federal seat of Lindsay. The vote would expose the malaise of the dying New South Wales Labor Government. The morning of the vote Dennis Shanahan reported that key figures were preparing to challenge Rudd.[17] In Penrith the anti-Labor swing exceeded 25 per cent, worse than many had feared. Lifelong Labor voters were voting Liberal; the ALP brand was toxic.

Arbib was supposed to meet Rudd on the Sunday, courtesy of Hawker's effort to get them to reconcile, but the meeting was cancelled. Hawker made four efforts to organise a meeting and none eventuated. Arbib was national convenor of the ALP Right but Hawker couldn't get him in the door.[18] Put crudely, instead of meeting Rudd, Arbib decided to depose him.

Sensing the risk of a leadership meltdown, Swan tried to stabilise the party. He made several phone calls that weekend. Swan was backing Rudd—not out of love, merely out of pragmatism. His message was: calm down, it's no time for a leadership crisis. Interviewed for this book, Swan said:

> I thought it was a big thing to change leaders. There had been newspaper reports that weekend about a possible change. I spent some time that weekend on the phone, letting people know that in my view it was a bad idea. I spoke to Steve Smith about it. I'm pretty sure I spoke to Albo. I told people it was too late. Kevin had asked me earlier, when we had been on a plane together, about my view on a leadership change. I told him: 'I'm not for it, but I don't think it's got any serious momentum.' I didn't have an inkling things were that advanced. In my mind it wasn't going to happen.[19]

Smith had the same view. 'Wayne and I agreed a leadership change would be a mistake,' he said. 'This was the view of everybody in cabinet that I spoke with.'[20]

Ferguson, as usual, was suspicious of Gillard. She offered him a flight to Canberra in her VIP plane. 'All the way she kept nudging me about what's going on, she kept talking about the polls, she was up to something,' he said.[21] But that evening Gillard had a long discussion with a political journalist: no mention of leadership. Gillard was not destabilising via the press.

The following morning Gillard sent an email to Rudd and Jordan revealing her belief that Labor was heading towards defeat and her alarm about the asylum seeker issue. Gillard wrote:

> To state the obvious—our primary is in the mid-30s, we can't win an election with a primary like that and the issue of asylum seekers is an enormous reason why our primary is at that low level. It is an issue working on every level—loss of control of the borders feeding into a narrative of a government that is incompetent and out of control. As you know, I have been raising this with a great deal of anxiety and I remain desperately concerned about lack of progress.[22]

Gillard said Rudd had previously agreed with her that a policy revision document would be prepared for ministers. She had later found this had been derailed. Gillard listed other examples where neither herself nor senior ministers were involved in necessary policy reassessments.

The email reveals the depth of Gillard's frustration that Rudd and his office seemed unable to lead the government into adequate election preparations. Her frustration was near breaking point. Clearly, she felt Rudd was failing as a leader. This was the email of a deputy still trying to fix things yet suffering a profound loss of confidence in Rudd.

The Monday Newspoll had a poor ALP primary vote at 35 per cent, the lowest since March 2006, but Labor leading 52 to 48 on the two-party–preferred vote. This would later become a famous poll, the last before Rudd was deposed and showing Labor would still have won an election with him as leader.[23]

But Newspoll had surveyed five marginal seats across New South Wales and Queensland and found Labor's position worse than was revealed by the national result. In the Queensland seats the two-party–preferred result was a 54 to 46 per cent Coalition lead. In New South Wales there was a huge anti-ALP swing in Lindsay. Shanahan concluded that, on these figures, Labor would lose office on the anti-government swings in New South Wales and Queensland.[24]

The right-wing caucus met in Parliament House on Monday 21 June in a mood of anger mixed with frustration. The feeling was that Rudd was disengaged, he wasn't listening, he seemed divorced from the electoral crisis. The boat arrivals and the mining tax had become lightning rods for discontent. The danger signs were flashing.

The full caucus met at 9.30 a.m. the next day, Tuesday—the final meeting before the mid-year break. This was the danger moment for Rudd—but there was no move. Bradbury said of the Penrith vote: 'Yes, it was a by-election but we were being sent a message. It would be folly to think otherwise.' But former ALP Secretary Bob McMullan said the historical experience was that Labor would be re-elected with the current polls. The caucus broke unhappy and unresolved. The focus became the end-of-session parties.

That afternoon Arbib and Feeney had a dismal exchange. Both believed Labor was facing election defeat, yet they were fatalistic about how to stop the death march. Arbib lamented: 'People felt the chance to change leaders was gone.'[25] Gillard still kept control. Burke spoke to her but Gillard offered nothing on the leadership. Arbib said Gillard 'never signalled she was moving against Rudd' until the last moment.[26] Gillard's integrity is built upon her repeated claim that she was loyal to Rudd until the events of Wednesday 23 June. Many Labor figures testify to this.

But Kim Carr rejects this in a version of events that is highly contested. Carr claims that after the caucus meeting on Tuesday 22 June, at about 11.30 a.m., Gillard asked him to her office. He made a note of the event. Carr said:

> She told me she rejected some of the comments made in the caucus. She used the phrase 'we are sleepwalking to defeat'. She asked me, 'Do you think it would make a difference if I was leader?' She produced party research and showed me the material. She was asking me if I thought she would make a better leader.[27]

He said they discussed the state of the caucus. 'She asked me to find out how deep feelings were in the caucus,' Carr said when interviewed for this book. He had no doubt—Gillard was sounding him out on the leadership.[28] Carr said he subsequently went to Arbib's office and they had a discussion. He said Arbib was pessimistic but keen to move. Carr said Arbib told him he feared Rudd might 'go to the Governor-General and seek an election' to save himself. Carr said he then reported back to Gillard that the Right was still keen to change.[29]

Both Gillard and Arbib categorically denied these conversations when asked by the author. Gillard was adamant: 'Did I ever ask Kim Carr to check leadership numbers for me? Absolutely not, no. That did not happen.'[30] Arbib said: 'I'm not sure who Kim Carr spoke to at this time but it wasn't me.'[31]

That night Rudd, scheduled to address BCA chief executives over dinner, was met by BCA president Graham Bradley. With business alarmed over the mining tax war, Bradley offered a deal: if the government pulled its advertising campaign the BCA would persuade the mining industry to pull its own campaign. He got a blunt and cool response from Rudd. The PM followed with a highly aggressive speech—a frontal attack on the mining industry combined with praise for his government's performance in the GFC. Mark Arbib was one of the last to leave the dinner. 'I can't believe it's come to this,' he said to Bradley over the plight of Labor–business relations. That night Arbib feared that Labor faced another long stretch in the wilderness.

However, the situation was transformed the next morning, Wednesday 23 June. The trigger was a *Sydney Morning Herald* story written by Peter Hartcher and Phillip Coorey saying that Rudd's office chief, Alister Jordan, had sounded out almost half the caucus to bolster Rudd's leadership. The critical reference concerned Gillard. The report said Rudd 'does not fully trust the public assurances of his deputy' that 'she is not interested in the leadership'.[32]

It was a deeply damaging story for Rudd. He was being framed as the betrayer of Gillard's loyalty. Rudd's advisers later denied the story. They said neither Jordan nor other staffers had sounded out caucus members about their loyalty to Rudd.[33] 'The story was planted—no doubt about that,' Lachlan Harris said. 'It was a peg for a challenge.'[34] Albanese was scornful, saying the notion that the leadership changed because of an article that morning 'is in my view not credible'.[35]

Gillard told the author:

> The story was important. My first reaction to it was an emotional upset reaction. I actually asked Faulkner to come round because there are not that many people, as deputy prime minister, you can get upset with and it goes no further. I was very hurt, emotionally upset. What it said to me was I wasn't trusted. What it said to me was in all this chaos the one thing that had always worked, even if it had moments of tension, was my relationship with Rudd. And I thought if that's ruptured then there is nothing in this place that works.[36]

But Gillard got over the upset. The recollection of others is that upset, anger and punitive action followed in sequence. Gillard felt she had refused a series of approaches to challenge Rudd. Now her loyalty was being met with claims of disloyalty from Rudd's office. She was 'the angriest I have ever seen her', according to one confidant.

The article changed the atmospherics. Gillard was entitled to be upset. Rudd's camp, however, saw the article as a plant. Arbib and Feeney moved fast: they decided to push for a leadership change. Farrell recalled: 'David Feeney walked into my room and said, "I think we need to move against Rudd. I'm meeting with Arbib."' Farrell joined the push.

Arbib and Feeney visited Gillard about 9.30 a.m. and found her upset and angry. They went for the jugular: they said Rudd had lost their confidence, the party faced defeat and she should challenge. 'You have our support,' they told her. They set out the options: Gillard could act now or become Opposition leader post-election. Gillard said she wanted to talk with Rudd and had asked Faulkner to intervene. She made no commitment to challenge. She was still holding back: she would not commit until she knew the numbers were there. Arbib was frustrated but Feeney left 90 per cent sure Gillard would run.

The Gillard forces sought to ignite the powder keg. Arbib told one caucus member the story was a 'fuck you' message from the Rudd camp to Gillard. He reported that Gillard was 'devastated'. Gillard's refusal to be satisfied was highly convenient; she had found a justification for forcing the issue.

About midday Burke was asked to go to Gillard's office. 'Have you read the *Sydney Morning Herald*?' she asked him. Now Gillard opened up. 'We've skirted around this issue for a long time,' she said. Burke recalls her exact words: 'In my view that article effectively means Kevin's office had put out there publicly that they don't have faith in me as deputy. To my way of thinking that gives me only two choices: I either have to resign or I have to challenge.'[37]

Gillard asked Burke where he stood. He had been waiting for this question for months. 'I am an unequivocal supporter of Julia Gillard,' he said. He offered to go public if required. When he suggested doing a 'weather report' on the caucus, Gillard agreed—she was authorising a test of the numbers. Burke returned to his office and spoke to Arbib. 'Mate, I don't think she'll do it,' Arbib said. But Burke had good news: 'No Mark, I have just been down there with her. It's on. We need to start counting.' Burke related his conversation with Gillard.

Rudd came to Gillard's office before Question Time. The Prime Minister was worried; he wanted to secure peace. Gillard told Rudd she felt the story was an act of disloyalty. She believed she had been loyal and did not deserve this. With these words Rudd's position became endangered. It was a short meeting but not a good meeting. They would meet again later that day. Rudd's leadership was now at risk but everything depended upon Gillard. She had not decided to challenge, not yet.[38]

However, the direction was apparent: Gillard was heading into show-down territory. The momentum was irresistible. Burke knew Gillard had drawn a line on relations with Rudd. That afternoon Alister Jordan was told the Right was moving on the leadership. Rudd told Hawker it was 'disgraceful' that a challenge might be mounted so close to the upcoming G-20 meeting in Canada. He said Gillard was too inexperienced to become leader.[39] Their partnership was dying. Rudd was losing control of events. Few people in the building knew of the drama that was coming.

Who leaked the story? As always, the source is unknown but subject to endless speculation. Rudd's camp had no interest in such a leak but anti-Rudd forces, keen to provoke Gillard, had every motive. Faulkner believed the story was a 'stitch up' and called it 'bullshit'.[40] Interviewed two years later, Rudd said: 'I had no real concept of any possibility of a push against the leadership until that Wednesday morning. Prior to that it was just the usual sort of "noises around the shop" and increasing tetchiness on the part of Arbib and Bitar.'[41] Rudd had misread the caucus and Gillard, but he would deny any disloyalty towards Gillard:

> What a nonsense proposition. The accusation was that my chief of staff, Alister Jordan, had the previous day spoken to caucus members about their position on the leadership. The reality was that Alister, as you would expect from any political chief of staff, was always out there, sensing the mood, seeing how things were going. Someone deliberately exaggerated the extent of that to Peter Hartcher, who dramatised it ... This nonetheless was, in my judgement, just a pretext to advance the core proposition that had been discussed among the conspirators for a long period of time.[42]

It was Rudd's last Question Time as prime minister—until 2013. But the Rudd era was dying. The faction leaders were busy. A number of people spoke to Gillard that afternoon and a critical meeting was convened of the Gillard backers. Kim Carr pledged support from the Left, a decision he would forever regret, saying later he should have gone to speak to Rudd. 'I wasn't a principal party to the challenge,' Carr claimed.[43] It is not what others said. Burke said: 'The bizarre thing was that, as we called people, not one of them picked up the phone to Kevin's office to warn him.'[44] Arbib, Feeney, Farrell and Shorten were active. There were different assessments about Gillard's commitment. Farrell said: 'She didn't sign up but she didn't say "no".' But Gillard was sanctioning the lobbying in her cause; she let the momentum build. She never killed it. She was heading towards a challenge.

The faction organisers considered whether it was too late to change leaders and decided it wasn't. They were not sure Gillard could win an election but they agreed that Rudd would lose the election. The plan was to take Rudd out in one sharp, brutal strike.

A group of right-wingers went to Swan's office to brief him. The outcome was predictable: if Gillard became leader from a Right faction push then Swan would become the new deputy. Swan said: 'When it became apparent to me late in the afternoon that it was overwhelming, my view was "It ought to be clean and quick." I didn't have any sentimentality about this.'[45]

The story broke on the ABC news that evening. Burke had confirmed the story for ABC TV's political correspondent, Mark Simkin. He then rang three other senior gallery correspondents to brief them. That evening Rudd and Gillard met a second time, with Faulkner present. The story had an electric impact. 'What put the spear in was the leak to the ABC news,' Stephen Smith said. Most politicians and staff were rocked by the reports. Sky News began its sustained account of the crisis, lasting many hours.

Burke was stunned by the running tide: 'People now started ringing in to say, if it's true, then I'm in.' He called the support 'overwhelming and immediate'. What made the difference was having the candidate. When the caucus was given a choice, people deserted Rudd. 'The mood was unstoppable,' Burke says.[46]

Gillard, unsurprisingly, wanted to avoid any political bloodletting. Rudd later described what happened:

> When the Deputy Prime Minister came to see me within a reasonably short period of time the nub of her proposition was her request that I stand down as PM because, in her view, I could not win the next election. That's the proposition that was put—there was nothing else. John Faulkner was a witness to this.

Fighting for his political life, Rudd offered a compromise to purchase several months of grace. Interviewed by the author he said: 'I had worked long and hard for the election of a Labor government ... If I had actually concluded as we got close to election time that I was an impediment to the government's re-election then, of course, I would not jeopardise that.' He proposed Faulkner as arbiter: 'John Faulkner is a very professional individual. His ultimate interests are for the Labor Party. I said if he was of the view that I was an impediment to the government winning the election come when the election was due, six months hence, then of course I would vacate the position.'[47]

The way Rudd describes the idea, it was bizarre. How could one person, despite his integrity, be vested with this discretion? According to Rudd, Gillard agreed. Rudd said: 'The words I actually used at that point were "So we are agreed upon that?" And she said "yes".'[48]

Gillard will provide her own version of these events and that version is likely to have differences from Rudd's. But Rudd believed he had cut a deal. Towards the end Albanese entered the room. He said: 'I told them the Labor Party was melting down. They had to end it and they said to me, "We're almost there."' Albanese said when Rudd came out, his message was: 'It is resolved.'[49] There was no challenge. Rudd felt he had saved his leadership. Albanese began to spread the word: it's the status quo.

But Rudd was fooling himself. There was no goodwill left in the caucus. Gillard went to another section of the prime minister's office and rang her backers. She was told that the caucus had declared: the time for compromise was gone. The party wanted a leadership change. A majority wanted Gillard as leader. The rupture had become public; it was too late to restore the public façade.

Gillard had relied upon the legitimacy of caucus support when she asked Rudd to resign. But she did not control that support. It had a life of its own, bequeathed by two and half years of Rudd's poor behaviour.

After ten minutes Gillard returned to Rudd's office. Rudd said: 'She came back and said, "I am now advised that you no longer have the confidence of the caucus and I am therefore requesting a leadership ballot."' Rudd was shocked. His version is that he protested, saying: 'We just had an agreement ten minutes ago that we shook on in the presence of Faulkner that these matters would not be dealt with till the end of the year.' Rudd said he reminded Gillard that Faulkner was to be the arbiter and that she had accepted this.

Interviewed by the author, Rudd said: 'By the way, when she was out I had communicated to Albanese that everything was okay. So Albanese goes and tells Tanya Plibersek and everyone else that it's peace in our time. But she then comes back and reneges on the deal. There's not a word of exaggeration, it's exactly as it transpired.'[50] Albanese said: 'He was angry that it had been resolved and that she changed her mind.'[51]

Rudd saw his edifice crumbling. The glorious prime ministership that embodied all his ambitions and dreams had turned to ashes. The deputy he once praised for her loyalty had become the agent of destruction. His office was in shock. His daughter, Jessica, was in the office distraught. Staff had stopped taking media calls. The truth is that Rudd's compromise deal would not have worked. Hawker saw this: 'It would have been very difficult for Kevin to come back once the media knew a challenge was underway.'[52] Rudd's deal with Gillard assumed caucus tolerance of his position. But such tolerance was gone.

When Gillard returned to her office it was flooded with back-benchers and ministers. The office had become an organising centre for the challenge. Arbib, Feeney and Farrell agreed: 'The key was the spontaneous response of the caucus.' Gillard walked around to Swan's office, where he was talking with Stephen Smith. They confirmed Swan would run as deputy prime minister.

'We did the first count,' Burke said. 'It was a conservative, hard count. We just looked at one another: there was a majority from the start.'[53] Gillard was calm throughout. Later she went into her office, closed the door and got on the phone. By mid-evening it was all over. Rudd had barely lobbied a single person. Gillard, the Right and the caucus had seized back the leadership they had given Rudd in 2006.

At mid-evening Rudd held a press conference to announce a 9 a.m. caucus meeting the next day to resolve the leadership. From the moment he agreed to this meeting, Rudd was finished, sleepwalking to his execution. Rudd defended his record, declared faction leaders wanted him out and made a naked appeal for the left-wing vote. 'I will be very clear about one thing,' Rudd said. 'This party and this government will not be lurching to the right on the question of asylum seekers.' He identified the fatal flaw in Gillard's position: Rudd said he had been elected by the people, not ALP faction leaders. Before losing his job he had branded her challenge a violation of the people's will.[54]

Gillard's elevation was tarnished by her backers—factions and unions. On the night of the crisis, a youthful Paul Howes went on ABC TV's *Lateline* program backing Gillard in his role as AWU chief. AWU National President Bill Ludwig, previously devoted to Beazley's leadership, had an enduring hostility towards Rudd. Howes described his discussion with Ludwig:

Frankly, there was a high degree of hatred towards that man [Rudd] across the movement. I said to Bill, 'Well, you always back

the leader mate.' We have always done, except for Hawke–Hayden.
And he goes, 'But this is a different type of leader.' And then we
decided not to back him.[55]

Howes' intervention was a mistake. It gave Rudd a cause: he became a
victim of factional and union powerbrokers.

Rudd was angry about Swan. He had to ring Swan himself to find
that the Treasurer, too, had abandoned him. 'Can you believe it?' he
lamented to Hawker that night. The Right had closed behind a Gillard–
Swan ticket against Rudd.

At 9 a.m. Rudd addressed the party room. It was a sombre anticlimax.
In a calm and rational speech, he accepted responsibility for his failures,
including climate change, and declared the party should 'return to
our position on the emissions trading scheme and embrace it without
ambiguity'. He warned of the New South Wales disease: the declaration
of a challenge followed by the argument that stability could only be
achieved by removing a leader weakened by that challenge. He thanked
the party and said he would resign as leader and prime minister. He
would not contest the ballot. Rudd said this was in the best interests of
the party and government. He refused his enemies the satisfaction of his
humiliation. Gillard and Swan were elected unopposed.

Later that day in the prime minister's courtyard Rudd, surrounded
by family, made his long and choking farewell statement to the nation.
He started by saying: 'I was elected by the people of this country to bring
back a fair go for all Australians and I have given my absolute best to do
that.' Relying on the phrase 'I'm proud of the fact', he listed achievement after achievement. Bruce Hawker, in the main foyer of the building,
saw members of the public weeping. It was a national and personal tragedy that reinforced the sense of public confusion. That weekend Albanese
attended a function at the Cyprus Community Club in his electorate. He
said: 'People were coming up to me saying, "What happened to our prime
minister? What is this coup?" Even, "Who is this person?" They didn't
get it.'[56]

The feature of the event was the irrelevance of the cabinet and ministry. Stephen Smith said the coup was organised 'at the parliamentary secretary and backbench level'.[57] Kim Carr called it a 'sergeant major's coup'.

Swan had merely followed the mood. His firm initial instinct had
been that a change would be too disruptive. Lindsay Tanner was taken
by surprise and stayed loyal to Rudd; he felt the party had panicked.
Senate Leader Chris Evans was never in the loop. He said: 'I had two

or three ministers walk in and ask me, "What's going on, Chris?" I said, "No bloody idea."' Evans felt 'no change' was the safest option, though he eventually signed up to Gillard.[58] Stephen Smith was at a Government House dinner and was alerted by text. Referring to his talks with Swan, Smith said of the Gillard push: 'It wasn't our preference. But now there was no option—we had to make the change.'[59] Combet was taken by surprise. 'I hadn't before the event thought Rudd should be removed,' he said. 'But in any ballot I would have voted for Gillard.'[60] Ferguson found out at dinner. 'I was outraged,' he said. 'I went to Faulkner's room. We were both in disbelief about what our great party was doing to itself. John and I knew we had just killed ourselves.'[61] Faulkner opposed the change but, recruited by Gillard as honest broker, he was removed from the action. Chris Bowen discovered the challenge when rung by ABC journalists en route to a function. 'By the time I got back from dinner, it was all over,' he said.[62] Nicola Roxon had no role as an architect but quickly made up her mind and lobbied for Gillard. Simon Crean, a friend of Gillard, opposed the change and believed Rudd would win the election. Penny Wong did not push for change; only when the contest was joined did she feel there was no option but Gillard. Craig Emerson, another friend of Gillard, opposed any leadership change and was publicly backing Rudd the next morning. Albanese was Rudd's main, perhaps exclusive, cabinet adviser on the night; he was aghast, believing the challenge was a fatal mistake.

The conclusion from this sample is irrefutable: the cabinet would not have initiated a leadership change. It is an extraordinary situation. The cabinet's preference was to stay with Rudd. Indeed, this had been Swan's preference. The cabinet was hijacked, not all of them, but a majority. The faction leaders and caucus sentiment swamped the cabinet. Once Gillard's momentum was established, then a number of cabinet ministers accepted reality. They swam with the tide but they would not have smashed the dam wall.

Smith has captured its essence: 'The view was that Rudd's position had been trashed. It wasn't something we wanted.'[63] Chris Evans saw Gillard the next morning and recalls that he told her: 'I didn't think this was a good idea. Despite my concerns with Rudd, I felt this was an enormous step. I was deeply worried.'[64] Albanese offers a more extreme view: 'I think a majority of caucus did not want this to happen.' He feels an idea took hold: that because it was happening and because Rudd was damaged then the only viable solution was to make Gillard leader.[65] The start guaranteed the end. For Ferguson it was more elemental: Gillard's backers 'were consumed by hatred of Kevin'.[66]

The leadership change was a collective cabinet failure. It reflects on Rudd: how could he lose the leadership when the cabinet preference was for him to stay? But it also reflects on cabinet: how could it be taken by surprise on the night? Many cabinet ministers felt Rudd could still win the election. This split was fundamental. Karl Bitar said there was 'no doubt' Rudd would have lost. But many ministers, while aware of Rudd's problems, did not dismiss his strengths. The public is loath to vote out a first-time prime minister. And many ministers believed the transition to Gillard should happen in the second term.

Bob Carr saw the operation as proof of the catastrophic instinct of the New South Wales right-wing machine to solve problems by executing leaders. The New South Wales disease was imported to Canberra. 'There was no justification for what happened,' Carr said. 'Rudd should have been put on a warning.'[67] David Feeney later reassessed the politics of the change: he believed it was the correct decision but felt its tactical efficiency became a negative because the public was completely unprepared.

Lachlan Harris felt the party has misunderstood the volatility of new politics:

> What Labor missed in 2010 is that this is the new norm. We were running around saying, 'Oh my God, we're so unpopular, 2GB hates us, the *Australian* is trying to kill us.' But this is how politics now works. You don't respond by cutting off the prime minister's head. Labor couldn't handle the pressures of government. It is too easy to attribute all our problems to the personalities of Rudd and Gillard. Labor's problems as a party go far beyond that.[68]

Reflecting on the Rudd era, Chris Evans reminded that Rudd 'had never had the majority support of the caucus'.[69] Asked who was influential in her decision Gillard hesitated and said: 'Burke is significant.' Referring to her friend, she said that 'Brendan [O'Connor] is significant. I always take a lot of notice of Brendan's advice.'[70]

Did Gillard conspire against Rudd? She makes an unequivocal denial. Gillard says she only decided to cross the Rubicon on Wednesday 23 June: 'When people had sought to raise the matter with me earlier I had declined to have the conversation with them. I made my decision to ask Kevin Rudd for a leadership ballot on the day that I spoke to him and asked him for that leadership ballot.'[71]

Her version is backed by enough politicians to give it authenticity. Yet her office had been preparing a 'victory' speech over the previous ten days. It testified to an expectation that Gillard may become leader. She knew it might happen. While she was trying to get better decisions from Rudd's office she was aware it might culminate in a leadership showdown. But Gillard didn't background against Rudd and many political journalists know this. It is one reason why so many people felt nothing would happen. The spark for the crisis did not come from Gillard. She was correct in saying later that she merely acted on the will of the party. Yet the decision was Gillard's responsibility. It was her choice, and the consequences belong to her. Gillard, of course, never recanted.

Admitting that Gillard had got the leadership too early, Combet asked: 'What would have been better? A week later, a month, a year, fifteen years or never? Events come along. She grabbed an opportunity when it came and I'm not critical of her for that. We had a lot of problems. Something had to break.'[72]

Paul Howes offered a savage reappraisal:

> It was the right thing to do and the absolute wrong way to do it. We somehow thought you could, in the middle of the night, roll a person still a relatively popular prime minister, without any conversation with the Australian public about what's occurred over the past two years and gone wrong, and just wake up and expect that naively the Australian people are going to say, 'Oh, that's okay.' I don't know how we ever thought this was a strategy that would work.[73]

It could happen only in an institution obsessed by itself and distant from the nation.

Gillard stated her core justification: 'It is about more than winning an election. The government wasn't functioning. I had been surrounded by chaos for a long period of time. Kevin was not going to be able to come out of the spiral.'[74]

Rudd, family, staff and loyalists had their wake at the Lodge. There was grief yet pride. People got drunk; Kevin was thrown into the pool. Lachlan Harris said:

> At one point everyone, staff and family, gathered around the stairwell in the Lodge and Kevin spoke. One of his messages was 'this is not the end'. He said, 'We'll be back.' He wasn't saying this

will happen tomorrow. But I think he did mean he would be back as PM. It showed his determination—he wanted to return.[75]

That mission never left Rudd. Convinced he was cut down midstream in an act of treachery, he would never forgive Gillard and would often refer to her as 'that bitch'. Rudd had unfinished business.

GILLARD IN OFFICE: ALIVE BUT DOOMED

CHAPTER 22

THE FATAL INHERITANCE

From the moment she was elected leader, Julia Gillard was struggling—she had no persuasive explanation for her challenge, no developed idea of how to solve the problems besetting the government and no notion of how to manage Rudd. Gillard got the prime ministership too early, in circumstances that were too difficult.

Every arduous path that Gillard would transverse in the coming months had its origins in the misjudgement of her career—she failed to grasp the scale of the problems in deposing Rudd. This misjudgement was not limited to Gillard; it applied to the Labor Party. The caucus destroyed Rudd but imposed a fatal burden on Gillard. It ruined the past and crippled the future.

Asked later if she was ready for the job, Gillard shot back: 'I think I was as ready as you can be. You don't get a bloody manual for it.'[1] The answer is typical Julia. Yet Gillard was unable to escape the curse imposed by her role as political assassin. Her enemies would not allow it.

Wayne Swan said: 'I didn't operate under the illusion this wasn't going to lead to resentments. But I must admit that even me, with all of my knowledge of Kevin, underestimated his capacity for revenge. The way Rudd fuelled it over a long period of time was breathtaking.'[2]

Chris Evans said:

The problem was the circumstances of her coming to be job, the leaking during the campaign, and then having to form minority government. They really prevented her from being able to succeed in the role. It was like being in a Greek tragedy. You knew there was going to be a lot of blood, a lot of murders, a lot of grief, and you couldn't do anything about it.'[3]

Greg Combet said: 'The problems originated in how she got the leadership. Her authority and legitimacy were impaired from the outset.'[4]

Simon Crean said: 'Maybe she got it too early, maybe she took it too early.'[5] Anthony Albanese said: 'She got the job under the wrong circumstances. Was she up to the job? Absolutely.'[6] Asked if Gillard had been over-rated, Kim Carr said: 'Yes. In retrospect, we misjudged her. But she had been a very effective deputy.'[7] Stephen Smith said 'the PM's job came too early' but agreed with Swan: 'The nail in the coffin wasn't the leadership change. It was Kevin's enduring response. This was the real turning point in the six-year history of the government.'[8]

Sean Kelly, who served both leaders, said: 'I think both changes of prime minister were a mistake. The Labor Party underestimated the problems involved in changing a prime minister. The new leader was unable to campaign on the policy agenda of the leader just deposed. It made the campaign more difficult.'[9]

The party acted on Gillard's record as an effective deputy. Yet the gulf between deputy and leader is a chasm. Most competent ministers cannot succeed as prime minister. It demands a unique skill set. The party made no assessment of Gillard's plausibility as prime minister, her weaknesses and strengths, her inexperience in economic and foreign policy or how the public would react to Rudd's execution. Her factional backers, remote from cabinet power, were clueless about how to make the transition work. Not only did they lack the answers; they never put the questions.

Gillard was more a Labor traditionalist than Rudd. She pledged to restore teamwork and a proper cabinet system and to respect her colleagues. It was music to Labor's ears. Yet Gillard's problem would be rapport with the public. Unlike Labor, most people had not really thought of her as prime minister. She had never been an Opposition leader or treasurer, or even a minister for a full term. Suddenly, she was prime minister and Rudd was in exile.

Gillard conceded she didn't have a plan. The reason was obvious: she had not been plotting. Gillard said: 'If I had decided twelve months earlier I was going to bring down a prime minister then, of course, I would have had a plan. But that's not how it happened.'[10]

Devoid of any plan, she made a courageous start.

Gillard accepted responsibility for Labor's decision. 'I asked my colleagues to make a leadership change,' she said at her opening media conference on the morning of 24 June. This statement of responsibility was vital since the leadership change had been neither essential nor inevitable. What reason did she offer the Australian public? In words that became famous, Gillard said: 'I believed that a good government was losing its way.' As a result Gillard felt that 'I had a responsibility to step up, to take control and to make sure that this government got back on track.' Rudd had many achievements, she said, but at times the Rudd Government 'went off track' and 'did not do all it said it would do'.[11]

The problem was that saying Labor was merely 'losing its way' was feeble. It did not justify her act of political assassination. Gillard was trapped, unable to fully justify her decision or fully explain why she was prime minister. Indeed, the problem was insoluble. After losing office Gillard admitted the difficulty: 'I compounded the problem by deciding the best way of handling Kevin and mitigating his hurt was not to tell the story. What is abundantly clear is that the proxy language of a good government that had lost its way didn't cut it.'[12]

In future years it became the orthodoxy that Gillard should have come clean, exposed Rudd and told the truth about the reason for the change. Such retrospective rationalisations are nonsense. That would have inflamed the party and discredited the government even more. Such a tactic would have backfired on Gillard. As Rudd's deputy, Gillard could not denounce his performance. She had been involved in every vital decision of the Rudd Government. With Rudd's political body still warm, she could not engage in a 'chapter and verse' account of his travesties. She had to move cautiously. Swan saw the difficulty: it was impossible to give an explanation of Rudd's failings 'while he was still there and a Member of Parliament' but that left Gillard 'looking like a political assassin'.[13]

The upshot is that Gillard was unable to offer a convincing explanation for Rudd's removal and, as the years unfolded, events suggested she had made the wrong call.

'I'm very happy in my home in Altona, I'm very happy in my flat in Canberra,' Gillard told her inaugural media conference. She announced she would not move into the Lodge until she had earnt the trust of the people—that is, until she had won an election. It was a wise decision. But it revealed another problem: Gillard felt doubts about her legitimacy. When Keating rolled Hawke as prime minister in 1991 he moved into the Lodge; nobody doubted his legitimacy. Yet Gillard lacked the longevity in high office and the public acceptance of her prime ministerial destiny that Keating enjoyed.[14]

She introduced herself to the public via the bedrock of her life—her hardworking family. Her father, John, was the second-youngest of seven, she said. Most of his bothers and sisters were back in Wales. 'They breed them tough, the Gillards, they bred them tough,' she said with pride. Her parents 'taught me the value of hard work' and treating people decently.

These would be her values as prime minister. She might not have children of her own, but she knew the reality of family life. Gillard offered respect for ordinary people who 'set their alarms early, get their kids off to school, stand by their neighbours and love their country'.[15] It was evocative and showed Gillard trying to bond with the public.

Despite being deputy prime minister, Gillard had rarely advertised her private life and family background. But the public wanted to know about its new leader. And Gillard's personal life failed the test of conservative social values. Because she was unmarried, childless and involved in a long-term de facto partnership, her presentation to the public was difficult. But harping on the notion of 'hard work' wasn't enough. There was no touch of inspiration, no emotional engagement, no image akin to Latham's 'ladder of opportunity'. For most, it seemed Gillard did not reach out. She would be hardworking and perhaps she would be formidable.[16] It was never enough. Nobody had a plan for the marketing of Julia, an absence from which she never recovered.

Even more revealing in retrospect, Gillard did not project the concept of being Australia's first female prime minister. She was a politician first and a woman second. While Gillard was a feminist in her life and outlook, she rarely played the feminist card in politics. 'I didn't set out to crash my head on any glass ceilings,' Gillard said. Australia's first female PM was deeply reluctant to be limited by this definition. She got the job on merit, not quotas, which was entirely admirable. Yet the idea that Labor would not devise a strategy to sell Gillard as first female prime minister seems absurd in retrospect. In truth, there was no time.

From the start the contrast between the private and public Julia was marked. It would become one of the most baffling aspects of her leadership. Julia was a down-to-earth person who mixed easily with people from all walks. She was persuasive, friendly, witty and self-deprecating. People relaxed when talking with her. Paul Howes said: 'I am yet to meet anyone who engages with her on an individual basis who doesn't walk away impressed.'[17] When journalists were asked 'What's she really like?' members of the public were astonished to hear that, one on one, Julia was warm, authentic and engaging. Outsiders rarely saw the real Julia. Too often in her public speeches and interviews she was bloodless and grating.

Within days Gillard said she didn't believe in God. 'I was brought up in the Baptist church,' she said. 'But during my adult life I've, you know, found a different path. I am not going to pretend a faith I don't feel.'[18] A sign of the nation's maturity, there was almost no commentary about a female unmarried atheist PM. But it was noticed in much of a conservative electorate, along with the contrast with Rudd. And Gillard's greatest vulnerability was management of Rudd.

Unsurprisingly, Rudd was shocked, traumatised and angry. He felt a profound sense of betrayal. Therese shared these sentiments and, for a while, they became a wounded couple carrying an unfathomable griev- ance. Over the following weeks Rudd's face looked different, revealing the depth of his loss. His personal relations were strained, conversation with some people became impossible and for weeks he made his resent- ment plain to certain people in politics and the media.

At his farewell press conference the day he lost the job, Rudd announced he would re-contest Griffith. He wouldn't be leaving politics, unlike Hawke when rolled by Keating in 1991. In the teeth of humiliation, Rudd was staying. At an early stage Gillard's office had spoken to Alister Jordan about Rudd's ministerial intentions and Jordan informed them that Rudd was interested in a cabinet position. These were momentous steps: Rudd intended to pursue his political career and he wanted a cabi- net place. The job he preferred was obvious: Minister for Foreign Affairs.

Within hours of the caucus decision, Gillard confronted a serious Rudd management problem. Many ALP figures had assumed that Rudd, once deposed, would quit politics, even though they had no basis for this convenient assumption. He was still relatively young, was anxious to prove his opponents wrong and had been in office less than three years. Why wouldn't he stay? Yet there were expectations that Rudd 'would do the right thing'. Stephen Smith said: 'As a defeated leader he should have either left the Parliament or gone to the backbench for a considerable period of time.'[19] Gillard's prime ministership would have been trans- formed had Rudd quit the Parliament.

Announcing her ministry on 28 June, Gillard omitted Rudd. She revealed she had spoken to him and told him she would be 'absolutely delighted' to see him serve as a senior minister if Labor was re-elected. The message was clear: Gillard and her allies didn't want Rudd in the cabinet in the near future. Rudd said he would 'take a break' but he was unhappy. He knew there was a strong mood to drive him out. Gillard had rejected Rudd's desire to be in cabinet.[20] She did not offer Foreign Affairs and her supporters said later that Rudd would never get that prize. Rudd felt he was cast into an exile of unknown duration, a decision he believed Gillard took after talking with Swan and Smith. As a former ALP prime minister, one of only three people since the Great Depression to have brought Labor from Opposition into office, Rudd felt he was being treated with contempt; there was no respect for him.

Gillard's public explanations about denying Rudd a cabinet place were trite. 'I thought the appropriate thing was for him to have an opportunity for a bit of rest and recuperation,' Gillard said. She felt Kevin could spend 'more time with his family'. She sounded like the local therapist. More to the point, Gillard said she wanted a stable and steady ministry. ABC interviewer Jon Faine put it to Gillard: 'One minute he's chairing cabinet, the next minute you don't even want him in the cabinet at all.' When Faine said the reality is 'you wanted a break from him rather than him wanting a break from being a minister', Gillard said it was an 'unkind remark'.[21] But Faine had nailed it. Rudd, dumped as Labor leader, was going to be marginalised.

Through his grief Rudd found his steel: he would fight them.

It would have suited Gillard for caucus to have voted on the leadership. That would have documented the scale of Rudd's rejection by the party. Gillard's political adviser, John McTernan, said: 'There is a difficulty with defeated leaders staying on. It would have been best for Rudd to have left politics and to have been treated generously by being given an international posting. The government could not be stabilised with the two of them in caucus.'[22]

For the party, however, the untested numbers were conclusive: Rudd was finished. There was a nasty euphoria in the caucus. After Rudd's overthrow there was a breakout of celebratory back-slapping as people danced on his grave, swapped stories about what a low life he had been and competed to see who had the worst account of his bastardry. It was a celebration notable for its ugliness. However Rudd, alienated and rejected, believed Gillard was not equipped for the job and would falter. Perhaps in a strange, irrational way, he believed the monstrous injustice he felt would be redeemed. Incredibly, the Gillard backers felt they were doing Rudd a favour. Tony Burke said they extended a 'courtesy' to Rudd by not telling the truth about his administration. 'I knew he would be hurt by it,' Burke said of the coup. 'But it never occurred to me he would think he could turn it around.' These comments from a tough-minded New South Wales warrior betray the hole in the project.[23]

The coup leaders never devised a 'Rudd strategy', an unforgivable blunder. Gillard had no plan for managing Rudd, an essential step in any violent transfer of power. The brains trust who organised Rudd's demise seemed to assume it would sort itself out. How could people be so ignorant of Rudd's will-to-power? An incredulous Paul Howes asked: 'How did they not think he might actually try to extract revenge?'[24]

What should Gillard have done? She had to either eliminate Rudd or keep him close. But eliminating him from Parliament was not feasible. If Rudd was staying then Gillard had to bring him inside the tent. If Rudd was dangerous in the cabinet then he was more dangerous on the backbench. He should have been offered Foreign Affairs at the start. Instead Gillard was forced to make this offer under duress and from weakness after an election campaign calamity in a desperate bid to save her prime ministership. Enough said. In 1983 when Hawke rolled Hayden the peace deal was substantial: Hayden would be Foreign Minister with the option of becoming High Commissioner to London. This was a different situation but Gillard never tried. The victors felt it wasn't necessary, thereby misjudging Rudd.

In politics and in life it is rarely hard for the victor to behave in a generous manner. Would bringing Rudd inside the tent have stopped his retaliation? No, but it was still the best response. Gillard chose neither to eliminate Rudd nor to keep him close. She left Rudd isolated, angry and with every incentive to create havoc.

Labor polling commissioned by Bitar on the weekend after Gillard's elevation showed Labor with a two-party-preferred lead of 54 to 46 per cent. 'The initial polls showed the switch was working,' McTernan said.[25] Yet such a lift was only to be expected. The test was: would it be sustained? The political class was about to be shocked.

The caucus assumed it 'owned' the office of prime minister because it could make or break ALP leaders. This proved to be a simplification. While the public had no say in ALP processes, it disliked being treated with contempt. Caucus members got irresistible feedback: the public was unhappy about the overnight shock execution of Rudd. Sam Dastyari said the people 'want to feel part of the journey'.[26] It helps if the public is pre-conditioned for a party-room change of prime minister. Albanese said: 'The entire press gallery said the secrecy of the change was an act of brilliance. The exact flaw in the strategy was heralded as a success.'[27]

Gillard wanted to prove herself as prime minister. Her impulse was to show she could govern better than Rudd. 'I'll be seeking first and foremost to govern the country,' she said.[28] Reading her words more than three years later is a bizarre exercise in parallel politics. They coincide almost exactly with Rudd's declaration about governing after his June 2013 return and his determination to prove he could govern better than Gillard. Their partnership had surrendered to competition.

For Gillard, three Rudd policy failures had to be 'fixed': climate change, the mining tax and asylum seekers. Fixing these defects was the justification for her prime ministership. But on that first bright June morning when she spoke to the media, Gillard could never have imagined the tale of woe each would visit upon her doorstep. This goes to the next tragedy of her prime ministership.

'You see Julia Gillard in the first part of her prime ministership unable to define a Gillard agenda,' McTernan said. 'She had a policy legacy of problems which had to be dealt with first. She had a clear agenda but it only came out towards the end of her prime ministership.'[29] Gillard, in fact, was destroyed by the same issues that destroyed Rudd, though they took a different form—she was undermined by her carbon tax policy, her inability to halt boat arrivals and an embarrassing mining tax.

Gillard could never win clean air as prime minister. There was no blue sky, just rolling clouds of grey from Rudd's legacy. The timing of her ascent was horrible. The Rudd inheritance became a slow political strangulation. It dominated from Gillard's first day in office and, when she was removed three years later, it was still not fully resolved. The astonishing Labor tragedy is that in June 2013, when Rudd was recalled, he had to 'fix' the Gillard inheritance. Two of Rudd's opening moves were to modify Gillard's carbon scheme and radically toughen her boats policy. It was a bizarre cycle: the successor kept having to 'fix' the predecessor's mistakes.

On climate change there was a Gillard doctrine: before acting 'we will need to establish a community consensus'. She came to hasten slowly. Her goal was clear: 'If elected as prime minister, I will re-prosecute the case for a carbon price at home and abroad.'[30] Yet such a consensus would be hard to define and difficult to achieve. Her position was code for having flexibility on when and how to push for a scheme. Gillard shunned the rhetoric of moral challenges. When questioned by Laurie Oakes, she talked about the need for 'a deep and lasting community consensus'. It sounded a century away. 'We're not there yet,' Gillard said. 'I'm someone who believes that you've got to take the community with you.'[31] She wanted to neutralise Abbott's attack.

After calling the election she invited ridicule by proposing a citizens' assembly to assess the case; it was the flesh on the bones of her consensus policy. The notion was ludicrous; it was satirised as a grand ALP focus group and evidence of what Simon Crean would call Gillard's 'tin ear'.

A prime minister who felt the planet was under threat would have announced modifications to the CPRS and sought an election mandate but Gillard had no confidence in the saleability of the policy. While Rudd had retreated on carbon pricing, Gillard merely formalised that retreat. She was buying time. In July 2010, Gillard felt Labor could not win a fight over carbon pricing yet post-election she would be driven to the opposite conclusion.

On the mining tax, Gillard would purchase some success. She cancelled the government's mining tax advertisements and called upon the industry to cancel its own campaign. It was a stitch-up. BHP Billiton knew what was coming. The most lethal government–corporate war for decades was thus terminated within hours of Rudd's removal. Gillard would offer more than just peace; it became a fiscal surrender.

The optics were powerful: Julia had come to fix Kevin's mess. The negotiations were conducted with the big three miners, BHP Billiton, Rio Tinto and Xstrata Coal. The miners opened their books, and much of the work was done in Treasury. The government was in a weak position: Gillard needed a revised tax, she needed it fast, and she needed an agreement with the 'big three' that would constitute political peace. The reason the tax failed to raise much revenue lies in this political imperative.

The miners operated as co-authors of the tax. Labor had gone from excluding the industry to gifting it the tax model it preferred. On 30 June senior BHP Billiton executive Gerard Bond sent a draft tax agreement to Swan's office. The main company was involved in drafting the deal. The 'heads of agreement' dated 1 July was signed by the big three miners plus Gillard, Swan and Ferguson. The new Minerals Resource Rent Tax (MRRT) was no ordinary government decision; based on formal agreement with the 'big three' it was a shared decision.

Swan said:

> BHP opened up for us their bottom-line projections on volume and price. We found their market estimates were far above ours. This is why they had been so upset. They thought the RSPT was going to raise a lot more revenue than we had put in the budget. I told them we had never been in this for stupendous amounts of revenue. The irony is the tax arrived at the time the terms of trade turned down.[32]

According to Ferguson, 'Marius [Kloppers] was keen to settle the issue. He put some ideas down. Wayne and his staff went through them. They had to run the numbers in Treasury based on their modelling. The word came back: "It's okay, do the deal."'[33] Kloppers said later the MRRT was 'closer to our frequently stated principles'. Mitch Hooke from the Minerals Council said it was 'broadly consistent with the minerals industry's underlying principles'.[34]

The brilliance of Gillard's 2 July 2010 MRRT announcement is that she had negotiated peace with the industry at virtually no price. The MRRT was estimated to raise $10.5 billion, just short of the $12 billion over two years estimated for Rudd's detested RSPT that had precipitated the great crisis with the mining industry. How had Gillard and Swan pulled off such a trick? It seemed too good to be true—and it proved not to be true.

Within days Ken Henry explained what had happened: the Treasury had revised upwards its forecasts for future commodity prices based on latest trends. This underpinned the $10.5 billion revenue. The revenue was a function not of the tax but of commodity price forecasts. And commodity prices, always hard to forecast, would travel south, not north.

The biggest story was the tax design. The 'heads of agreement' specified that the miners would value their assets at market value on 1 May 2010 as the basis for depreciation over the mine life, a concession that proved greater than Labor realised. Giving evidence to a Senate committee, Henry called the tax design 'very generous'. The then shadow assistant treasurer, Mathias Cormann, said: 'The way this tax was negotiated was a disgrace. The government had a responsibility to act in the public interest but it didn't.'[35] Treasury documents released under FOI on 14 February 2011 showed that over the nine years to 2020–21 the MRRT was projected to raise $38.5 billion, a figure that soon looked completely improbable.

Gillard said the government was 'proceeding with the great bulk of the original proposal'. This was false—virtually every major industry concern had been met. The design and rate were different. Gillard seized credit for what she called a 'breakthrough' saying she had won 'consensus' with the miners where Rudd had got nowhere for weeks.[36] Swan said the large miners would be paying 'significantly more tax', a claim not validated. When the tax became operative the revenue was only $126 million in the first half year, but later forecasts were stronger over 2013–14. The $1.5 billion revenue shortfall was found via a range of decisions, including cutting the corporate tax rate to 29 per cent, not 28 per cent as originally envisaged in the Rudd package.

Interviewed for this book, Ferguson said: 'If there had been proper consultation with the industry at the start, when the RSPT was devised, then we would have done better. We could have kept the industry on side and got a better tax outcome.'[37] But that was history. He defended the new compromise: 'It's a profits-based tax. Nobody expected commodity prices to fall as quickly as they did. The numbers were right at the time but the world changed.'[38]

Gillard had negotiated in broken traffic and pulled off a win. She said the mining deal was delivering her pledge 'to get the government back on the track'. Projecting strength, she said: 'I'm not shy of a fight if a fight needs to be had.'[39] This had to be a joke; the MRRT was a political fix. In this mutual love-in Swan praised Gillard as a prime minister who 'gets things done'. Rudd must have watched in fury as the Treasurer became a beneficiary of the rewritten mining tax. Rudd had lost his job while Swan had been elevated to deputy prime minister.[40]

The announcement proved to be multiple political fraud. The overestimation of MRRT revenue at $10.5 billion was highly conve-nient for Gillard and Swan—it made the MRRT seem a credible tax at the 2010 election; it kept credible Labor's repeated claim that the tax would 'spread the benefits of the boom'; it concealed the sell-out to the miners to win political peace; and it assisted Labor's return-to-surplus by 2012–13 pledge, later revealed to be unobtainable.

Abbott retained his opposition to the tax but his position had weakened. The big miners, in effect, had changed sides. Having fought the RSPT with fury, they became Gillard's partners in the MRRT. They didn't like the tax but they were neutralised.

The third policy review—the arrival of asylum seeker boats—was the most intractable. Gillard unrolled her empathy. 'I can understand that Australians are disturbed when they see boats arrive on our shores unan-nounced,' she said. 'This country is a sanctuary, it's our home, so we've got a responsibility to manage our borders.' She denounced Abbott for fear-mongering but pledged to be a 'strong' border protectionist.[41] This was her abiding principle for three years as prime minister. Gillard's trag-edy is that she never found a policy to realise her goal. When she was deposed by Rudd in June 2013 the flow of boat arrivals was more than three thousand a month, meaning Australia had long since lost control of its borders.

Addressing the Lowy Institute just twelve days after becoming leader, Gillard delivered her initial asylum seeker response. It was sincere, naïve and a fiasco. The initiative was the establishment of a regional process-ing centre in East Timor. The tactic was to deny the people smugglers by sending boat arrivals to East Timor based upon cooperation with the United Nations High Commissioner for Refugees. People found to be refugees would be settled in Australia or other regional nations.[42]

Gillard launched this initiative without speaking to the Prime Minister of East Timor, Xanana Gusmao. She had spoken to President Ramos Horta, who was not part of the government. As a friend of Australia, Horta was encouraging. Yet the amateurism of Gillard's initiative and failure to conduct the proper dialogue with East Timor was patronising. It revealed her inexperience, poor judgement and inept staff. Rudd spent much of the next six months privately bagging Gillard's initiative, aware from the start that it was doomed.

Chris Evans said East Timor had been a 'policy option' for some time. He advised against it but the issue had been kept alive.[43] Gillard was searching for principles 'that can unite us'—a bid to foster yet more consensus. She wanted to stop the boats yet retain the moral high ground, a Labor fantasy. Gillard believed that higher numbers were driven by push factors rather than Australian policy. She recognised the boats had to be stopped on humanitarian grounds. Her principles were the acceptance of people in genuine need, denying boat arrivals an unfair advantage and ensuring that people smugglers were punished.

As the weeks unfolded and East Timor's politicians opposed the concept, Gillard had to row back. Abbott mocked her idea as a 'thought bubble'. She kept the notion of regional processing but downplayed East Timor's role. This was the position she took to the 2010 election. Experience would show that the people smuggling industry was far ahead of Gillard. Labor was not ready, politically or psychologically, for the harsh policies required to stop the boats.

From the start Gillard had acted with speed and ruthlessness to neutralise Rudd's problem legacy on climate change, boats and the mining tax. It led to inevitable blunders. Gillard was better organised than Rudd. But the task was too great. She could mitigate but not eliminate the damage done.

Time and circumstances were her enemies. Most new prime ministers come to power at a general election. They enjoy a three-year term to mould their agendas. Gillard had neither. And most new prime ministers don't have their predecessor sitting behind them with a knife. Yet Gillard's difficult circumstances raised an intriguing question: could Gillard have actually won an election as Opposition leader? It must be doubted.

Once installed, Gillard had to win public acceptance of her elevation. There were times when she almost scaled this mountain, only to fall back. She was unable to escape the 'political assassin' tag. If Rudd had left politics, that would have been possible. But Rudd's presence was a permanent reminder of Gillard's treachery. A majority of the party believed she had acted from high motives but the public was less charitable. As the campaign advanced, the public saw another reality: that the Rudd–Gillard war was ongoing.

Tony Abbott said Labor had dumped its leader but hadn't changed its product. Despite Gillard's tactical adaptations, Abbott got it right. Gillard was a transactional not a transformational leader. Labor had no wish to be transformed; it just wanted to win an election. It wanted a leader to honour the movement, uphold the faith and sell the product. Gillard's task was to return the party to itself. That gave Abbott hope since he believed Labor's problem was not the leader but the product.

'We never had a philosophical narrative,' John McTernan said.[44] That was Gillard as a transactional leader: solve each issue as it comes and move on. It is true that Gillard was a victim of events; it is equally true she never devised a successful view of how Labor should govern. Perhaps she could have accomplished that in a more favourable setting than that of mid-2010. But Gillard had chosen her political inheritance and it proved to be fatal.

CHAPTER 23

THE TRAGEDY OF MINORITY GOVERNMENT

Apart from her first twelve weeks, Julia Gillard's time in office was as a minority-government prime minister. Minority government branded and undermined her, denying her political oxygen while revealing her remarkable tenacity. It was a challenge no other prime minister had faced in the postwar period.

Her political capital was destroyed by two interconnected events: minority government and beating off Rudd's push. These torments darkened Gillard's door each day. The wonder is not that she succumbed in June 2013 but that she survived for so long.

ALP National Secretary George Wright said:

> We were a government whose efforts and energy were almost entirely focused on internal issues. All Julia Gillard's energies had to be directed at keeping a workable caucus and her minority government alive in the Parliament. And [in Abbott] we faced an opponent who was focused on the voters to win an election.[1]

Gillard was made leader to save the government at the 2010 election. She did not fail in this mission but neither did she win re-election in her own right. The paradox of the August 2010 election is that the manner of Gillard's victory doomed her. Her negotiating ability brought an ALP minority government into existence and kept it alive for a full term. She succeeded with the crossbenchers but was unable to master either Abbott or Rudd.

Minority government demanded endless fixes and deals, accentuated hostility towards Gillard via the roles of Craig Thomson and Peter Slipper, devastated the Labor brand through its alliance with the Greens, drove Gillard to disastrous decisions in the cause of survival, demanded a carbon pricing policy with a design that destroyed her integrity as prime minister, created an entire political/media industry focused on whether or not Labor could survive full-term and was linked in the public's mind with some of the worst sleaze in political life.

Gillard's political adviser, John McTernan, said: 'All of the flack of minority government was sucked into her prime ministership because she was so central to the deals and maintaining the deals. In my view, minority government became hugely damaging for her.'[2] Bob Carr said of Gillard: 'Many of her problems arose because of the exigencies of the hung Parliament. Any prime minister wheeling and dealing with the independents and the green party was going to be diminished.'[3]

The leader of the House, Anthony Albanese, when asked whether he thought minority government could last for the full term, said: 'I thought it was possible but I wouldn't say probable.'[4] Here was the dilemma: Gillard made the Parliament last three years but that finished her in the country. It didn't matter how many bills were passed; the public had a visceral dislike of this Parliament. In the end Gillard fell but the Parliament outlasted its architect, a cruel outcome that seems unfair.

Gillard outsmarted Abbott in the post-elections negotiations yet she gave too much away. David Feeney said: 'We could have played a tougher game of brinkmanship with the Greens. They had nowhere to go. They could either support a Gillard government or cast themselves into political oblivion. Instead we elected to wear them like a crown of thorns for the next three years.'[5] Her alliance with the Greens became political poison: it hurt Labor's image, confused its supporters and diminished its primary vote. The proof is Abbott: he loved it. He spent three years painting Labor as tied to Green demands and values.

While the management of the minority government was a success on the floor—Gillard was astute and Albanese held the operation together—as a communications project it was a catastrophe. This began with the infamous press conference seventeen days after the election when rural independents Tony Windsor and Rob Oakeshott declared for Gillard. It was a euphoric moment for Gillard and Labor; they had saved their government. Yet the optics created on this day lasted three years, with Windsor and Oakeshott going against the disposition of the conservative seats they represented. They decided to sustain a Labor government and became permanent reminders that Gillard's survival depended upon two independents overriding the wishes of their constituents. In the end, Windsor and Oakeshott walked away; but Labor could not walk away.

Minority government intensified the insiders-versus-outsiders fault line in Australia's political culture. Tabloid papers and talkback radio had a rich load of material and created the narrative of Gillard, living off Canberra, generating fixes and broken promises behind closed doors in defiance of the wishes of the public. It was perception that took hold, contaminating Gillard's profile to the extent that nothing she did could eliminate this impression or arrest the downward trajectory of her minority government.

On Saturday 17 July 2010, Gillard called the election early, for Saturday 21 August. 'The election was obviously too early,' Tony Burke said. 'It was the policy work and the announcements—they weren't ready to go.' Burke said the timing was 'entirely' driven by the need to strengthen Gillard by a public mandate.[6] 'The decision to call the election so promptly succeeded in ambushing the Labor Party,' David Feeney said.[7]

Interviewed in late 2013, Gillard said: 'I am happy about the timing in the sense I don't think I was ever going to be given a period to govern and show what I could do. The media was in one of its fevers. I was not going to be given any space.'[8] It is a remarkable insight. After just four weeks as prime minister, Gillard felt the media turning against her, a damaging omen for Labor.

The entire reputation of modern Labor was on the block: its record, its policies and its leadership change. Defeat after just one term would be too horrible to imagine. The central question of the campaign was: would the public accept Gillard? The answer was equivocal.

The Liberals, meanwhile, were enjoying their 'get out of jail' phase. The election was in August, not March. 'My strong view is that if an election had been held in early 2010 there would have been a further swing to Labor,' Liberal director Brian Loughnane told the author. Loughnane knew Labor had blown its big chance.[9]

Abbott had used the Labor chaos to build his foundations. He had two achievements—he had united the Liberal Party and he had framed a strong election agenda. 'Tony Abbott was able to define the terms of the debate,' Loughnane said. Abbott stuck to a narrow, focus-driven message, pledging to 'end the waste, repay the debt, stop new taxes and stop the boats'. He lived off Labor's blunders. As Opposition leader, Abbott substituted discipline for flair. The insiders (the political class) mocked his limitations but Abbott's message meant outsiders (the voters) knew what he stood for.

On voting day Labor suffered a 2.6 per cent swing towards the Coalition. In the end Gillard shaded Abbott on the two-party–preferred vote 50.1 per cent to 49.9 per cent. Labor lost 16 seats, with Rudd's 88 seats in 2007 reduced to Gillard's 72 seats in 2010. The Liberals had

73 seats, with four independents and one Green. This guaranteed a negotiation for a minority government.

For Labor, it was a death scare. This was the first time since the Great Depression in 1931 that a government had failed to win re-election in its own right at the end of its first term. Wayne Swan said: 'We came within a whisker of losing government despite the best-performing advanced economy in the world, despite substantially increasing the pension, despite fairer workplace laws, despite record investments in human capital and despite cutting income taxes three times.'

The truth is, Rudd's over-reach and ineptitude had weakened Labor's economic credentials. Loughnane called Rudd 'one of the most effective framers of a message we have ever seen in this country' but said this was the core of his problem: Rudd didn't deliver on the hopes he engendered. Gillard could neither fully capitalise on Rudd's successes nor fully neutralise his mistakes. The election timing proved that Gillard's standing as a new prime minister was in jeopardy. Karl Bitar's research showed high levels of dissatisfaction with Labor and weak recall of Labor's achievements.

The campaign revealed the downside of changing leaders late in the term. Media adviser to Rudd and Gillard, Sean Kelly, said: 'In its leadership changes of 2010 and 2013 Labor didn't factor in the costs. It forgot the new leader felt unable to campaign on the previous leader's policies. We got a new prime minister but we lost the momentum from the government's agenda.'[10]

As a campaigner Gillard was not in Rudd's class. Her election announcement was flat and uninspiring: she pledged a strong economy, better health and education and the values of 'hard work'. The magic of Labor's 2007 pitch had flown. The party's slogan, 'Moving Forward', was a shocker, easily satirised when endlessly repeated by Gillard. Labor entered the contest with Newspoll showing a misleadingly high 55 to 45 per cent lead. Gillard's task was to defend her lead, exploit doubts about Abbott and conceal the government's panicked improvisation. The Abbott-led Coalition was not ready to govern, yet Abbott's muscular populism and genius for destabilising Labor gave him a real chance in a volatile setting.

It was a fascinating but dispiriting campaign. Its real theme was the Australian retreat into introspection, caution and focus-group dominance. Gillard abandoned action on carbon pricing and Abbott abandoned any industrial relations reform. The power of the negative was too lethal. The scale of Abbott's IR retreat—refusing to even exempt small business from the unfair dismissal laws—took the Liberals back to a pre-Howard era. In an immortal declaration Abbott said WorkChoices was 'dead, buried and cremated'.

Gillard came with one new idea, a cynical ploy courtesy of the focus groups: she wanted 'a sustainable Australia, not a big Australia'. Gillard became the first prime minister to seek re-election for a slower growing Australia. Abbott played a similar politics by promising to cut net overseas migration. These constituted some of the most blatant genuflections before focus-group research in history. 'I don't believe in simply hurtling down a track to a 36 million or 40 million population,' Gillard said three days into the job.[11]

Rudd had been unwise enough to endorse the 'big Australia' phrase and Gillard exploited this for her own gain. In fact, the 36 million referred to the future population at 2050 on current trends. Gillard recycled an earlier Rudd request in asking Tony Burke to investigate a framework for a sustainable Australia. Indeed, a feature of Gillard's prime ministership was playing the immigration card in the prelude to both the 2010 and 2013 elections. The former focused on sustainability and the latter on trade union hostility to workers under the 457 visa program.

'Let's slow down, let's take a breath and let's get this right,' Gillard said. The imagery was powerful yet the meaning was vague. 'For my part I have said that I do not believe in the idea of a "big Australia",' she said. 'I will focus on preserving the quality of life of our Australian sanctuary.' Gillard said it was time to 'reconsider whether our growth model was right' because Australia faced water supply constraints, energy supply challenges, under-investment in major cities, and housing prices that put at risk 'the great Australian dream'. She asserted there was 'an Australian way of life' typified by 'clean beaches and precious open spaces' and she would protect it.[12] It was gesture politics to exploit public worries.

Abbott had pledged 'direct action to get our population growth under control' by cutting net immigration by 100 000 to 170 000 by the end of his first term. This was largely sleight of hand because the numbers were falling from a temporary high anyway. 'Tony has promised the Australian people what I'm already delivering,' Gillard said in their race towards smaller Australia rhetoric.[13]

The flaws in the Gillard/Abbott position were long known because this was an old debate. Given Australia's strong economic growth projections, a high future migrant intake was essential. The real problem was a failure of infrastructure management, but rather than address the infrastructure issue the leaders focused on the migrant intake. In the end, they fought each other to a futile stalemate on the issue but Labor paid a price: its vote fell in seats heavily populated with migrants.

The first and only leaders debate of the campaign, held on Sunday 26 July at the National Press Club in Canberra, was won by Gillard but became a threshold event for Abbott. Gillard was measured but had no new script and no new ideas. As challenger, Abbott exceeded expectations, proved he would not implode and projected as a possible prime minister.

The ghost of Rudd was ever present. A Nielson poll found more than two-thirds of voters disapproved of the way Rudd had been dumped. The Rudd issue dominated the opening weeks of the campaign.[14] Interviewed later, Rudd said: 'When Prime Minister Gillard said the government had lost its way under my leadership they, at that point, conceded, lost and trashed the opportunity to campaign effectively on having saved the national economy. This was a grave strategic error. It was a failure of politics.'[15]

The turning point of the campaign came over 27–28 July, with stories broken by Laurie Oakes and Peter Hartcher that were assumed to come from either Rudd or the Rudd camp. It was the sabotage moment; the shadow cast over Labor would last for three years.

The Oakes story was that Gillard in cabinet had opposed both an increase in the pension rate and a paid parental leave scheme. The Hartcher story said Gillard felt the big rise in the pension was excessive and had said 'old people never vote for us'. The report said she 'wanted to kill the idea of paid parental leave altogether'. Gillard was overruled in cabinet on both counts. Hartcher's story contrasted Gillard's views in cabinet with her campaign championing of both policies.[16]

Gillard's office did not deny the story. Gillard said that cabinet discussions were 'confidential' and added that 'if the Liberal Party have allegations to make, they should put their names to them'. This comment was unwise. It provoked Oakes to report: 'Prime Minister, you know this information didn't come from the Liberals. You'll need to look much closer to home.' Hartcher said his sources were 'government members'.[17]

The stories were explosive. Rudd and his camp were instantly blamed. This was a strike not just against Gillard; it was sabotage of the Labor campaign and, even in the annals of Labor's rich history of betrayal, an act of particular treachery.

Tony Burke captured the near-universal view: 'It was the worst behaviour I have ever seen from the Labor Party.' Burke delivered the ultimate assault on Rudd, saying, 'he appeared more comfortable with a Liberal government than a Labor government that wasn't his own'.[18]

Swan said: 'I had wanted to believe better of him. The leaks came from Kevin. There's no doubt they came from Kevin. I don't think anyone seriously contests that.'[19] Yet Rudd denied being the source of the leaks.

At the time of the February 2012 Rudd challenge, Gillard said: 'The 2010 election was sabotaged … we were in a winning position in that campaign until the sabotage that knocked that campaign very, very solidly.' For Gillard, Rudd was a saboteur, pure and simple.[20] Interviewed for this book, Gillard alleged that Rudd's behaviour transcended the tolerable norms of Labor in-fighting:

> This is actually the corrosion in Labor culture that Kevin Rudd has delivered. In all my Labor days—from manning booths, letter boxing, through to the 2007 campaign—it didn't matter what you thought, who you hated, you just got on with it and campaigned. I could not have foreseen, going into 2010, that anyone would do that to a Labor campaign.

Asked if she believed the leaks—that is, the Rudd camp—cost her re-election as a majority Labor government, Gillard said: 'Yes, I do. Our polling showed that. We didn't have an easy campaign. But the track polling had us basically in a winning position and then goes whoosh! It certainly looked like we might lose at that point.'[21] Gillard blamed Rudd for casting her into minority government, an unprecedented accusation for one Labor prime minister to make against the previous Labor prime minister.

Swan makes the same accusation. 'It was character assassination of her. You rewrite the whole history of the period at this point. It absolutely cost us majority government. We were lucky we fell over the line, given what he had done. It was a murderous thing.'[22] Stephen Smith had the same view: 'The leaking in the campaign was unforgivable treachery. It cost us the campaign and majority government.'[23] Mark Arbib said: 'The leaks destroyed Labor's campaign and sent us into free fall. It was an unforgiveable action.'[24] Greg Combet said: 'I can't forgive them. No matter what the manner of Rudd's removal you don't do that. Now he is widely suspected in the Labor Party as having leaked against the party and its leader in an election campaign.'[25] One of the faction chiefs in Rudd's removal, Don Farrell, said: 'I wasn't surprised by Rudd's tactic. I was at the Stag Hotel in January 2011 when he told anybody who would listen that it was Kevin 11, the comeback year. It was apparent to me he wasn't going to stop.'[26]

Labor members had to stay disciplined: to accuse Rudd openly would have ignited a public brawl guaranteeing Abbott the election.

Contemplating an ignominious end to her career, Gillard now revealed the quality that would define her prime ministership: tenacity in the face of the intolerable. Answering a barrage of media questions about the leak, Gillard went on the offensive. She was no 'soft touch' when it came to taxpayers' money. 'Of course I wanted to see a pension increase, of course I wanted to see paid parental leave,' she said. 'The question at the forefront of my mind was, are they affordable? If people want a prime minister that will have $50 billion of expenditure put before them and sign away without even a question asked, well I'm not it.'[27]

The crisis showed Gillard now depended on Rudd to win the election: she needed his loyalty. Yet it was just six weeks since her political assassination of Rudd. How could the political wheel spin so fast to deliver such humiliation? The party had already asked Rudd to assist by campaigning in Queensland seats. The media now sensed her vulnerability. Sections of the media focused on her hair and clothes, her de facto relationship and child-absent life. The sexism arose in part because she was vulnerable. When asked whether her partner, Tim Mathieson, would live with her at the Lodge, she said, 'Wherever I'll live, he'll live.'[28]

The Nielson poll published on 31 July showed, for the first time since the leadership change, that Labor would lose office with a 52 to 48 Coalition lead. Labor's primary vote had fallen six points in a week. Peter Hatcher wrote: 'The Julia Gillard experiment is failing … On this trajectory, Labor will have burnt through two prime ministers and ended up with a one-term government.' He said Rudd's ghost 'has stalked Gillard's every moment'.[29] Queensland, Rudd's home state, was a debacle, with a Coalition primary vote lead of 48 to 36 over Labor. With a deft touch, Rudd announced he had to enter hospital for an operation (poor Kevin) but on his return he would campaign in his own seat and 'elsewhere in Queensland and the rest of the country as appropriate' (loyal Kevin).

Travelling on the campaign with Gillard, Faulkner concluded that Labor was facing defeat. Unless there was a form of Gillard–Rudd rapprochement the public would abandon Labor. He spoke to both sides. The Gillard camp had to staunch the political bleeding. Rudd was willing to campaign but deeply suspicious of Gillard. Faulkner persisted. He believed rapprochement needed two elements: a genuine deal and some form of public event.

The television footage was priceless. Rudd and Gillard met in Brisbane, sitting robotic at a table covered with electoral maps. It had to be filmed as proof that it happened. There was no eye contact, no relationship whatsoever. They could barely disguise their mutual loathing.

But it was peace of sorts. The media made fun of the tension between them. Faulkner, by contrast, believed the meeting was a triumph because it stopped an Abbott victory. There were no more leaks.

Stephen Smith had already told Gillard he was prepared to surrender the Foreign Ministry if required in order to appease Rudd. When Gillard had been campaigning in Perth she and Smith had shared a car ride back to the city. 'I know this bloke's killing us,' Smith said of Rudd. 'If you need to offer him the Foreign Ministry then I am at your disposal.' Gillard said that Faulkner was trying to settle Rudd down. She told Smith: 'You and I would both rather win the election and have Rudd as Foreign Minister rather than see Abbott win.' From this time Smith assumed he would surrender the job.

Gillard's supporters say that pivotal to the stabilisation was an understanding that Rudd would be Foreign Minister in a new Gillard government. It was the olive branch Gillard should have offered the day she deposed Rudd. The Gillard camp insists the deal was done and confirmed by Gillard, yet the Rudd camp denies any agreement on the Foreign Ministry post; it says Rudd had no such assurance and was unsure post-election of his position.

Smith, however, was under no doubt the deal had been done. He recalls that after Gillard's campaign launch in Brisbane they had a brief discussion. 'Sorry, I've had to do this,' Gillard told him. 'You can have any portfolio you want apart, of course from Treasury and Foreign Affairs.' Smith said there were two natural vacancies, Finance or Defence. But Gillard was adamant: Smith could nominate what he wanted. In the end, Smith took Defence. But in this discussion Gillard also told him that if the Foreign Ministry became vacant in future then he was 'first cab off the rank'.

Five days before the Rudd–Gillard meeting, Gillard, aware she was facing defeat, decided to take 'personal charge' of the campaign. She told a stunned political class: 'I think it's time for me to make sure that the real Julia is well and truly on display.' Abbott said the 'real' Julia must be replacing the previous 'fake' Julia. The media had fun with the question: 'Who is the real Julia?' Gillard told the author: 'We had to press a reset button and maybe it was clumsily done. I take responsibility for it.'[30]

At his policy launch Abbott offered a restoration of order, his embrace of John Howard pointing to the restoration he envisaged. The romantic Abbott, whom Peter Costello once said loved to 'take on lost causes and fight for great principles', had surrendered to a disciplined, restrained Abbott. While Abbott was killing the idea that he was unelectable, his inexperience showed in a disastrous interview with Kerry O'Brien over the NBN, with Abbott declaring he wasn't a 'tech head'. Nobody watching this interview could think Abbott was ready for office. Apart from a generous paid parental leave scheme, Abbott was modest in his promises, relying on the Liberal orthodoxy: lower taxes and smaller government. His tactic was to win off the multitude of Labor mistakes.

Towards the end of the campaign, Gillard, her composure regained, was sharper and almost plausible. With spending constrained post-GFC, Gillard seized the idea of the NBN as Labor's latest signal of the future. Her real message was 'give Labor a second chance'. The great hopes vested in the leadership change had faded to quiet desperation. The truth was obvious—Julia was a warrior leader, a Labor traditionalist, but devoid of policy flair. Gillard might be able to save Labor, maybe, but asking her to rehabilitate the Labor Government was a bridge too far.

The 2010 campaign confirmed that the post-1983 reform age had terminated. Australia seemed a timid nation psychologically divorced from the crisis in the North Atlantic economies but reluctant to canvass the dilemmas inherent in its success as a high-immigration, high-growth, China-dependent, flexible economy, short on savings and needing more economic reform to sustain its prosperity. The campaign revealed the emerging crisis of Australian politics: the real needs of the nation were not addressed in political debate. This decoupling would be repeated at the 2013 election with far more serious consequences, bequeathing a deadly legacy for the Abbott Government in 2014.

The 2010 result exposed Australia as a divided, unsure nation. The south (Victoria, Tasmania, South Australia and the ACT) was a pro-Gillard paradise zone; the development states (Queensland and Western Australia) were a lost cause for Labor; while New South Wales was tipping to the Coalition (it got 51.2 per cent of the two-party–preferred vote) it didn't tip far enough for Abbott. A poor Liberal on-ground effort in New South Wales cost Abbott the Lodge.

Only Gillard loyalists could argue the leadership change had worked. The ALP primary vote had fallen 5.4 per cent to 38 per cent after one term of government—a lower primary vote than Keating had obtained at Labor's historic 1996 loss to Howard. Labor faced a structural crisis with its core vote.

At the Liberal election-night gathering in Sydney, Abbott was hailed as a hero. He told the audience that Labor 'had forfeited its moral claim to government'. But Gillard had begun to lobby. 'She rang me on election night,' Greens leader Bob Brown said. He was non-committal but impressed. When Brown met Abbott a couple days later he felt insulted. 'He had his feet on the table and I was sat down to look at the soles of his boots,' Brown said.[31]

Gillard was fixated as never before: 'I got back to Canberra and I thought I am going to stay here for as long as it takes.'[32] She felt she had a chance because Windsor and Oakeshott were not typical Nationals. And she felt the NBN was a big Labor plus. Her problem was that the seat count favoured Abbott 73 to 72 if the WA National Tony Crook was counted with the Coalition. Gillard's aim was to reverse this seat count: she told the Press Gallery to count Crook on the crossbench, given his comments to this effect. And she locked in the Greens, thereby securing their single member of Parliament, Adam Bandt. She argued that made the numbers 73 to 72 Labor's way.[33]

The Labor–Greens alliance was formalised in a five-page written agreement dated 1 September. It specified a full-term Parliament. The key step was recognition of the need to price carbon, with a multi-party committee created to this effect. 'It was a predetermined outcome that we were going to get a carbon price during this period of government,' Brown's successor Christine Milne said.[34] Gillard's aim was to show her mastery of minority government negotiations. It worked. Most media made the miscalculation of assuming the terms of the deal were unremarkable.

In fact, on the climate change issue, Gillard had changed policy: she moved from the flexibility of consensus to a process that meant legislating a scheme acceptable to the Greens. It was a major concession— understandable, yet eventually disastrous. Beyond that, Gillard had entered into an alliance relationship with the Greens with pledges on regular meetings with Brown and giving the Greens access to the major departments. The Labor Party was escorting the Greens into the corridors of executive power.

Since the world knew the Greens were never going to support Abbott, they gave Gillard nothing she would not have got anyway. Yet Gillard made two pivotal sacrifices: she lost flexibility on carbon pricing and she was saddled with the crippling burden of an alliance with the Greens. The idea that the Australian public would endorse at the ballot box a Labor–Greens legislated carbon policy was always improbable. And if they didn't, Labor would wear the consequences for years.

Judged by substance, it was a rotten deal for Labor. The author wrote on the day, 'the once great Labor Party passes into history with this deal'. The alternative for Gillard was to have extended an olive branch to the Greens but shunned a formal agreement and put nothing on paper.

Judged by circumstances, however, Gillard won momentum. She ended up with a piece of paper proving the numbers had changed and that strengthened her negotiating position.

'In the end, you buy the ticket, you take the ride,' McTernan said of the deal.[35] Gillard and Brown felt confident about working together. 'I found her surprisingly good,' Brown said. He was the axle that kept the brittle Labor–Greens wheels greased.

Labor views on the deal are divided.

'I don't think there was any alternative,' Swan said. 'Julia was putting it together block by block. If you didn't get the first block it wouldn't work.'[36] This is the view of many ministers. But the ALP Right, initially sceptical, became fierce opponents. Stephen Smith said: 'Julia did a great job in the negotiations. At the time I felt the formal arrangement with the Greens was unnecessary.'[37] Chris Bowen believed it was a mistake and said later Labor must govern 'alone or not at all'. Howes said the deal was 'nonsense' and should not have been made with Labor's enemies. Dastyari called it 'an unmitigated mistake'.[38]

The next day Gillard formalised her eight-page agreement with Tasmanian independent Andrew Wilkie. The next block was in place. Again, Abbott bombed out. But Wilkie was following the inclination of his seat. The Wilkie deal included commitments to Royal Hobart Hospital and, critically, a process for the Gillard Government to implement a pre-commitment scheme to limit damage from poker machine addiction. Gillard, a Victorian, did not fully comprehend its significance.

Looking back, Greg Combet said of minority government:

> The real problem for us was the pokies deal with Wilkie. That became a corrosive political problem in our own constituency. For my electorate, a working-class area in the Hunter, the pokies issue was a worse problem than asylum seekers. It mobilised all the RSLs. In a lot of Labor working-class areas the clubs are the only community infrastructure. You go to the club for food, exercise and entertainment. To align with what can be perceived as a do-gooder, middle-class, patronising social reform is pretty volatile politics for Labor.[39]

The New South Wales club culture is Labor. The Wilkie deal was an attack on that culture.

While Bob Katter backed Abbott, the joint Windsor–Oakeshott decision gave Gillard majority government 76 to 74, the tightest possible margin. Reflecting on the alienation of both MPs from the National Party, Abbott said: 'I realise asking them to work with us for the sake of the conservative side of politics was a bit like asking divorced parents to get together again for the sake of the kids.'[40] In fact, Gillard exploited the negotiation to damage the Coalition by forcing the release of Treasury costings of both Labor and Coalition programs, exposing a major 'black hole' in Coalition numbers. Abbott and Hockey were infuriated; Gillard had played them for mugs. Windsor later alleged Abbott said he would do anything short of 'selling my arse' to get a deal, forcing a denial from Abbott ('I just don't use that kind of language').[41] The longer the minority government ran, the more committed Windsor and Oakeshott became to Gillard.

The Gillard–Swan–Windsor–Oakeshott written agreement ran to thirty-three pages in addition to letters to both members of Parliament. Its main themes were a full-term Parliament, special deals for their seats and new funds for regional Australia. Windsor said it was 'about using the political system to advantage the people we represented'. It was a sterling effort to surpass the old Country Party at pork-barrelling. The total cost of bringing the minority government into existence with all its deals was a touch under $4 billion and would probably have been higher under Abbott.

Central to her success was Gillard's philosophy of locking up a three-year Parliament. This is what Windsor and Oakeshott wanted. They feared that if Abbott became prime minister he would seek an early election to become a majority prime minister and rip up the deals. Of course, they were right on this point. Gillard's vulnerability meant she had no interest in another election.

Neither Rudd nor Abbott could have managed minority government as effectively as Gillard. Labor got most of its agenda legislated, notably the NBN, carbon pricing and the National Disability Insurance Scheme. It was a legislative success but a political failure. Gillard hoped that making it work would mean a reward from the voters. But the reverse happened.

Feeney said: 'The burden of minority government—managing the Greens, eccentrics like Wilkie, tainted MPs like Thomson, adding to the effects of Abbott and Rudd—just overwhelmed the government.'[42] Combet said:

> The minority government collar had to be worn. The problem is the community felt we were running agendas that were not our own. They were seen as somebody else's. That was a real negative.

We passed a lot of legislation but we didn't get credit for the things we did. What did people see? They saw crossbenchers dictating various policy initiatives.[43]

For McTernan, it kept Labor on the brink: 'It meant every crisis had the potential to bring down the government,' he said.[44] 'I don't think we were doomed by minority government,' Swan said. 'Funnily enough, we actually handled minority government pretty well. The problem was the white-anting.'[45] For Swan, the real difficulty was Rudd.

Losing this negotiation was the best thing that happened to Abbott. In the end, he waited another three years and won in 2013 with a large majority. He hated the minority government, tried to bust it but failed.

The 2010 election revealed Gillard lacked the leadership skills her backers had expected. Her judgement was faulty and her relations with the public were fraught. Gillard failed to deliver on the hopes of the leadership change—to win re-election in Labor's own right. She kept Labor alive for a second term but in conditions so difficult that a third term was an unlikely option.

CHAPTER 24

SIGNING THE DEATH WARRANT

On 24 February 2011, six months after the election, a proud Julia Gillard announced agreement in principle between Labor and the Greens on a carbon pricing scheme for Australia. The Greens and the independents stood beside her in the prime minister's courtyard, Bob Brown given virtually equal status. Gillard was making minority government work. In the process she signed her death warrant as prime minister.

'The Greens pushed for this press conference,' Gillard said. Her retrospective view was that 'it cost us badly politically'.[1] John McTernan said 'it was a terrible look'.[2] Swan said that 'it was pretty bad'.[3] Chris Bowen fingered the problem: it wasn't Labor's policy; it was a Labor–Greens policy.

For Gillard, a deadly chain reaction was underway. The deal with the Greens had led to minority government, and that led directly to the carbon pricing announcement. This event shaped the next three years of politics: Gillard as reform zealot for carbon pricing against Abbott as crusading opponent of a carbon tax.

Abbott's media conference the same day saw one of the most brutal assaults by an Opposition leader in a generation. Labor never saw it coming. Abbott called Gillard's position 'an utter betrayal of the Australian people' and predicted a people's revolt. He enshrined the issue as trust: 'If the Australian people could not trust the Prime Minister on this, they can't trust her on anything.' He said 'the price of this betrayal will be paid every day by every Australian' in terms of higher power prices. Abbott launched a campaign that would make Gillard unelectable. Yet most of the ALP thought they had just negotiated a minority government triumph.

Only in retrospect can the scale and unfairness of Gillard's tragedy be comprehended. She was a victim of history and Rudd's failures. In politics a prime minister rarely gets three opportunities but Gillard was now chasing that third opportunity. Rudd had squandered the first two. A more astute Rudd would have legislated his carbon scheme with

Turnbull's support in 2009. Given that opportunity was missed, a more courageous Rudd would have won an early 2010 election on his scheme after Abbott voted it down in Parliament. Given that opportunity was also missed, Gillard in 2011 was left with the dregs, batting on a difficult wicket that was not her preferred choice.

Gillard's carbon crisis must be seen in that context. She had a superior policy design to Abbott's—her carbon pricing versus his direct action. The Productivity Commission found, in principle, that carbon pricing was superior. Abbott's policy did not reduce emissions at least cost and created its own uncertainties for industry. Economist Saul Eslake said Abbott 'can't find a single economist who supports his policy'. But Gillard's insuperable problem was that by 2011 the political window for carbon pricing had shut. Labor had missed its chance.

Consider the real world. Kyoto had failed to tackle the emissions issue. Prospects for any new global binding agreement were dead and were unlikely to return for many years. Climate change had become the perfect wedge splitting the ALP's industrial base from its urban progressives. That a Labor government would now promote a policy with this consequence was astonishing. Minority government, in effect, had created a phoney reality zone, remote from public opinion and international realpolitik.

The similarity with WorkChoices was striking. Gillard, like Howard, had announced the principles for a new policy only to find the political contest lost before the details were even formulated, let alone the legislation passed.

Insiders understood the reason for Gillard's latest guise as carbon pricing zealot, yet many outsiders saw it as betrayal. A weak Opposition leader would have allowed Gillard to escape. But Abbott was ruthless and he felt aggrieved. 'Once Gillard announced the carbon tax she destroyed the understanding on which she had been elected,' Abbott said. He believed she lacked legitimacy because she lacked integrity.[4] Abbott used carbon to accentuate the idea of dishonesty in the public's mind. Tony Burke said: 'From the moment of the Laurie Oakes leak, at the National Press Club there was a view Julia had been dishonest to Kevin. The dishonesty tag hit and it hit hard.'[5] Abbott felt Gillard and the independents had formed an unholy alliance to deny him office and that carbon policy was its main instrument. He saw Gillard's problem was saying one thing in the campaign but doing another after taking office.

The optics of Gillard's 24 February media conference revealed Gillard was no longer in command. This was not a Labor prime minister announcing one of the most important ALP policies since Federation.

It was a Labor prime minister sharing power. She shared power with the politicians who flanked her: Brown, his deputy Christine Milne, independents Windsor and Oakeshott. McTernan said later that if Gillard had won majority government there would have been no ETS at this time.[6]

In the campaign Gillard had been caution on steroids, saying an ETS would not be introduced short of a 'deep and lasting community consensus' on an ETS. But a Labor Government now became the willing vehicle for the Greens to realise their goals. Put more kindly, Gillard had changed her mind because the situation had changed.

Milne seized the moment. 'We certainly have ownership of this scheme because it's the one we put on the table ourselves,' Milne said. 'We argued for it during the election campaign. And it's because of Greens in the balance of power that we've got it. So it's our proposal, our idea … we own the idea. We own the process.' Abbott loved the imagery: it was a Labor–Green fix. Labor was handing Abbott the gun fully loaded. On day one Abbott said: 'It's pretty clear who is leading this government—it's Bob Brown.' What else would he say?

Combet said the 'real negative' was the release of the carbon framework without the detail:

> We weren't naïve about this. We discussed it with Julia and Wayne. We all felt we had to do it. We wanted to avoid a repeat of the mining tax by giving business the chance for genuine input. The downside was that Abbott drove a truck through it. The *Daily Telegraph* and Alan Jones just went crazy with the scare campaign. It hurt us a lot.[7]

Gillard called the media conference because she was a prime minister of honour; she was keeping her deals. So Julia Gillard, once the sceptical sentry warning Rudd against action, was now a convert due to self-interest.

'It's the right time to act,' Gillard told the media. 'History tells us that you need to be on the wave of change. You cannot afford to be stranded and left behind.'[8] The scheme would start on 1 July 2012, to enable its bedding down before the next election. There would be an initial fixed price, between three and five years, then transition to an ETS with a floating price. Bob Brown said work was 'on time and on target'.

Gillard was seizing the opportunities inherent in minority government. With Labor and the Greens in alliance the probability of passing bills actually increased. Milne said 'only minority government' could deliver a carbon scheme. Gillard saw that the Greens, having sunk Rudd's scheme, could not be wreckers a second time. In addition, she sensed Brown was in 'legacy mode'.

It was the final chapter in a remarkable career. Over thirty years Brown had moved from inspiring a bunch of angry anti-dam Tasmanian protesters to being an astute leader of the third force in politics holding the balance of power in the Senate. He wanted a carbon scheme for the nation. Gillard said: 'I felt we had this unbelievably unique political window where the Greens would be more sensible than [in] their general oppositionist role. I felt we could really manage the politics.' Gillard knew there is no substitute for statute. A law is a law is a law. Once you legislate, your opponents face an uphill task to repeal your law. 'I felt at the time the Greens were going to be in the balance of power position in the Senate for the foreseeable future,' Gillard said. In short, Abbott would find it hard to unravel the scheme once legislated.[9]

Explaining the scheme, Gillard wanted to be honest. The 'whole point' was to have a price impact to boost cleaner energy options. Gillard would be frank with the people.

That night, interviewed by Heather Ewart on ABC TV's *7.30 Report*, Gillard's effort to be honest led to political catastrophe. Ewart asked the killer question: 'You do concede it's a carbon tax, do you not?' Gillard said: 'Oh, look, I'm happy to use the word tax, Heather. I understand some silly little collateral debate has broken out today. I mean, how ridiculous. This is a market-based mechanism to price carbon.' To ensure nobody was in doubt Gillard then repeated that the scheme had 'a fixed-price period at the start' and said 'that is effectively a carbon tax'.[10]

Shock tremors went through Labor. Milne was aghast. Yet there was no need to call the policy a tax. 'If I had to pick the big error, the more telling error, it was not contesting the tax label,' Gillard said after leaving politics. 'We should never have conceded it was a tax. We did debate this internally. I made a deliberate choice. I made the wrong choice.'[11]

As Gillard conceded, it looks obvious in hindsight. Labor should have said: this is an ETS with an initial fixed price; it is not a carbon tax as an alternative to an ETS. That would have been accurate and defensible. So what was Gillard thinking? She reveals she was thinking of the May 2009 budget when Rudd and Swan, embarrassed by the size of the budget deficit, refused to use the words 'billions' and 'deficit' together and it became a discrediting farce. She feared being lampooned all around the country for refusing to say 'tax'. So Gillard decided 'Let's not play a game "tax or no tax", let's just argue about the substance.'

This overlooked Gillard's campaign comments ruling out a carbon tax. She repeated these remarks several times in her final week, notably telling Channel Ten: 'There will be no carbon tax under the government I lead.' Each time she was categorical. The danger, therefore, should have been obvious: by conceding the word *tax* Gillard exposed herself to the breach-of-trust campaign. Abbott stamped her as a Lady Macbeth. 'We will fight this tax every second of every minute of every day of every week of every month,' he said. Yet the first question to Abbott from a sceptical media at his press conference was whether he could keep his own party united behind this attack.[12]

Abbott said enactment of carbon pricing 'would be a conspiracy by the Parliament against the people'. It became a powerful idea. He would use carbon pricing to undermine the legitimacy of the minority-government Parliament.

His allies in this project would be the Macquarie radio network and the News Corporation tabloids spearheaded by Sydney's *Daily Telegraph*. The day after Gillard's media conference she conducted a confrontational interview with 2GB's Alan Jones, the highest-rating breakfast announcer in Sydney. Jones said: 'Do you understand, Julia, that you are the issue today, because there are people now saying your name is not "Julia" but "Ju-liar" and they are saying that we've got a liar running the country.'[13] It set a vicious tone.

Abbott, in fact, felt Gillard had stolen the election with her false promise and took this accusation into the Parliament. Given the small number of votes that decided the result, he asked Gillard at Question Time: 'Does she honestly believe that she would be in the Lodge today if, six days before the last election, she had been straight with the Australian people and said upfront to them, "Yes, there will be a carbon tax under the government I lead"?'[14]

Did Gillard tell a lie? No. It was not her intention in the campaign to introduce as fast as possible a de facto carbon tax. Did she break faith with the public? Yes. She changed her mind because of minority government.

The degeneration of public debate was displayed at the No Carbon Tax rally outside Parliament House a month later, on 23 March. Abbott, initially reluctant, addressed the rally of a couple of thousand people. But he was condemned by association when, after he began talking, placards were raised behind him saying 'Bob Brown's Bitch' and 'Ditch the Witch'. They framed the event. Having called for a people's revolt, Abbott could not dodge the rally. Labor demanded that he apologise. He refused, saying some people had gone 'a little over the top'. Gillard slammed Abbott for 'associating himself with One Nation, with the League of Rights, with anti-Semitic groups and with grossly sexist signs'. The fault line was drawn: Labor denigrated the sexism against Gillard while Abbott said people were justified in being angry over a deceitful prime minister. The poison had entered the minority Parliament.

They were tearing each other apart. 'You sit behind a climate change denier,' Gillard taunted the members of Parliament opposite her. 'Australians are disgusted by his negativity and revolted by his arrogance.' Abbott was a 'hollow, bitter man' who goes about 'spreading fear' and leading the Liberal Party 'down the wrong path'. And Abbott mocked her: 'We have seen real Julia; we have seen fake Julia. We have seen wooden Julia; we have seen teary Julia … The one thing we have never seen is truthful Julia.'[15]

Gillard's aim was to turn Abbott's strength against him—to convince people his destructiveness made him unfit for office. She had to ruin Abbott's credibility because he was bent upon destroying her. Abbott's purpose was to smash the minority government alliances and, by forcing somebody to lose their nerve—just one member of Parliament—bring down Gillard and procure the election he wanted. The chamber became a whirlpool of personal assault. They were both damaged by it but Gillard was more damaged. ALP National Secretary George Wright said 'the broken bond of trust' with the public was such that 'Julia never recovered'. The trust issue destroyed her in the first six months of the minority Parliament.[16]

The multi-party committee that Combet chaired was a cabinet sub-committee. It was the engine room to negotiate the decisions: the price, the coverage, industry assistance and tax-cut compensation. A tough negotiator, Combet was made for the task. He went to cabinet on more than forty issues to seek authorisation for Labor's negotiating position. 'The workload was absolutely crushing,' he said. 'To be honest, it nearly killed me.'[17]

He had little respect for the Greens. He found their analysis extreme and their grandstanding counterproductive. 'Even I found myself a little bit naïve about the extent of the ideology they operated on,' he said.[18]

The differences between Labor and the Greens were enormous. The Greens wanted to close the coal industry. They were opposed to gas as the answer. They sought a 100 per cent renewable-energy economy. This was an ideological stand untenable on costs and fatal to industry competitiveness. It was linked to the Greens' insistence that Australia's 5 per cent emission reduction target by 2020 from 1990 levels was far too modest and must increase to 40 per cent. Such positions were unacceptable to Labor. In this context the deal was a major achievement.

Combet did the negotiating back and forth, working with Milne, then Windsor and Oakeshott. The deadlocks were sorted between Brown and Gillard. 'We did the deal on price,' she said.[19]

'Price was always going to be the hardest issue,' Combet said. With time running out, Gillard and Brown had a short meeting and cut the deal at $23 a tonne, a straight horse-trade. 'There was an impasse and time was up,' Brown said. 'It was a considerable concession from the Greens. The Senate bells were ringing, so we shook hands and I had to rush off.'[20] It was marginally above the $20 a tonne price Combet had figured was about right. The European price was not much below $20 a tonne but it went south rapidly from 2011.

The fixed price was essential but fatal. 'It's the only way we could get it through the Parliament,' Combet said. Because the fixed price would run for three years, it deferred the debate over the carbon reduction targets, where Labor and the Greens had different positions.[21] The fixed price was the condition for parliamentary passage but also the flaw that destroyed the scheme politically.

The subsequent 11 July package was a huge achievement in rapid public policy–making. Gillard boasted she was outdoing Rudd. 'Pricing carbon is this government's biggest reform yet,' she said. Chasing a place in history, she compared the package with the Hawke–Keating float of the dollar and said it 'decoupled the growth of carbon pollution from the growth of our economy'.

Gillard presented herself as a carbon pricer, a tax reformer and a renewable energy champion. Yet she had to reverse the hostile political climate that had fermented since February. The package rested on two beliefs. First, the science was right, with Labor and Greens contemptuous of doubters. The message was alarmist: global temperatures 'could rise' up to 6.4 degrees Celsius by 2100. Global warming had become a Labor faith. Second, the policy was based upon the conviction that the rest of the world was taking assertive action. Labor was relying upon the more recent Cancun conference, when nations agreed to hold the average temperature increase to below 2 degrees above pre-industrial levels. These were strictly voluntary commitments. On this basis Treasury assumed a world carbon price of $29 a tonne in 2016 and this is the price it assumed for Australia at the 2016 transition to a flexible price.

Such assumptions were convenient and heroic. The arrogance was extraordinary: that there would be a 'smooth' transition from the fixed to floating price. Labor merrily claimed that, because other nations were acting, Australia's price was its 'fair share' in global terms. Such claims were essential for Gillard's political protection. Criticised at the time, in hindsight they seem absurdly misconceived. In 2014, ANU economist and carbon policy specialist Warwick McKibbin said: 'The assumptions in the policy design about the future of climate change action and the price of carbon globally were badly wrong.'[22]

The package was a hybrid: a carbon price with an ETS in parallel with a government-inspired industry policy to build a huge renewables sector. Pricing carbon was not enough; government intervention was deemed essential. 'I always said it is the carbon price plus plus plus,' Milne said. 'The carbon priced on its own will not do the job.'[23] But this was also Labor's view, though Combet said of the Greens that at times they seemed 'more concerned about renewable energy than emissions reductions'.

The package would create a new bureaucracy and several new agencies. Gillard envisaged a $100 billion investment in renewables by 2050. The plan to 2050 meant conventional coal falling from 70 to 10 per cent of the energy mix, with the big leap being renewables increasing to 40 per cent of electricity generation. For the Greens, it was still too low. A new Clean Energy Finance Corporation would fund renewables to $10 billion investment over five years, offering loans and loan guarantees—a de facto green bank. While the Greens claimed ownership, Combet said: 'We proposed it to them.' A new statutory body, the Australian Renewable Energy Agency, would administer $3.2 billion in government backing for R&D and provide renewable energy grants. These were to buttress the Renewable Energy Target, the bipartisan industry policy to deliver renewables to 20 per cent of the energy market by 2020.

The carbon price would affect about five hundred of the nation's biggest polluters, requiring them to buy a permit for each tonne of pollution they produced, thereby creating incentives to reduce pollution in the cheapest way. In the post-2016 flexible price period the number of permits issued by government would be limited by the cap on annual carbon pollution. The system was a market price but defined and ruled by government-determined caps. A new body, the Climate Change Authority, designed to be prestigious and headed by former Reserve Bank governor Bernie Fraser, would advise on progress towards targets and revised national targets.

Over half of Australia's emissions would be covered directly by the carbon price mechanism. Agriculture was excluded and Tony Windsor succeeded in having petrol excluded. But aviation was included, an important decision for Qantas. The economic justification was that the long-run cost of action was less than the costs of inaction. The scheme was a negative for economic growth and income growth but only a modest negative estimated to knock off annual income growth by 0.1 of a percentage point. The initial Consumer Price Index impact was far below the impact of the GST under Howard. It was estimated at a first-year increase in household weekly spending of $9.90, or about $510 yearly.

All the revenue went into three areas—assisting households, assisting business and funding clean energy programs. Emissions-intensive and trade-exposed entities would receive either a 94.5 per cent or 66 per cent shield from the carbon price. This was similar to Rudd's scheme. The biggest support went to households via pensions and family payment increases and income tax cuts in two stages. The tax-free threshold was trebled to $18 200. Support was directed to low- and middle-income earners.

Of Australia's 9 million households about 6 million would receive benefits to cover the average price impact. The bottom 4 million of these households would be overcompensated, with benefits exceeding carbon costs by 20 per cent. About a third of households would be worse off, a not-insignificant figure. Swan was happy with the package.

Across the forward estimates the cost to budget was $4.3 billion. It became a politically driven agenda to increase government spending. If the carbon price was below the estimates, the cost to the budget would skyrocket. In reality, once the tax cuts and transfer compensation were law, the politics of their abolition became too hard. In the end, Abbott would pledge to abolish the scheme but keep the benefits.

Journalist Marcus Priest described the result as a compromise struck between 'a party of ruthless pragmatists and a party of stubborn idealists'. In truth, it was compromise piled upon compromise. Such compromises delivered the numbers in Parliament. But they could never deliver the numbers in the country.

Speaking at the National Press Club, Gillard tried to explain herself to the people. 'It doesn't come easy to me to expose my feelings,' she said.

> I was the shy girl who studied and worked hard. I've brought a sense of personal reserve to this the most public of professions. If that means people's image of me is one of steely determination, I understand why ... In the moment I truly believed I was going to be prime minister I told myself: don't ever put off a hard call because it will only get harder every day.[24]

Then she made a bizarre detour that revealed her frustrations. Gillard said she would consider an inquiry into the Australian media, in particular newspapers, going to ethics and editorial standards. It was a direct strike at her media critics, notably the News Corporation papers, and followed the crisis that had engulfed Rupert Murdoch over the phone-hacking scandal in Britain. Gillard said she was 'shocked and disgusted' by the British revelations. She was responsive to Bob Brown's call for a wide-ranging investigation after he had branded the Murdoch press the 'hate media'. Gillard was serious; she knew there was anger in the caucus. 'If I could put it as clearly as I can … don't write crap,' she said. The line got traction. Labor would set up an inquiry.

A majority of business and industry would turn hostile as the EU carbon price collapsed. Gillard tried to pretend otherwise. She said, once legislated, business would want certainty and its message to Abbott would be 'don't do this, don't repeal it'.[25] Labor's tactic was to build a structure of carbon pricing, property rights, climate change governance and community compensation too entrenched to repeal. Any reasonable person would accept it. But Abbott was an unreasonable man.

The May 2011 Productivity Commission research report had good and bad news for Gillard. Its criticism of Abbott's 'direct action' principle implied that, sooner or later, his policy would demand revision. The bad news was that no nation had an economy-wide tax on greenhouse gas emissions or an economy-wide ETS. It found most existing ETS schemes were limited and it contradicted Labor's line that Australia was being left behind by the world on climate change action. The commission found that Australia was paying too much for too little abatement, while noting many other nations were far worse. Green politics had corrupted public policy. Budgets were being rorted for little environmental gain, the worst examples being solar photovoltaic subsidies, biofuel subsidies and renewable energy target (RET) schemes.

The Coalition made merry hell with the idea of Greens dictating to Labor. In reality, the package was largely a Labor package with necessary concessions to Greens and independents. 'Labor did the design,' Combet said. 'This has been Labor policy for a very long time. It is a Labor reform in strong Labor tradition.'[26] His message was: Labor is a serious government while Abbott is a stuntman.

For Gillard, the politics were too difficult. By late July the Nielson poll had Labor's primary vote at 26 per cent, the lowest in the poll's 39-year history. Newspoll conducted two polls in July—one before and one after the package, with Labor's vote at 27 and 29 per cent respectively, again record lows.

No major policy since World War II had been followed by such dismal ratings for its government. In the three months July to October, after release of the package, Newspoll showed the Labor vote across six successive polls to be in the 26 to 29 per cent range. This was beyond a landslide; it was obliteration. Bob Brown was smiling; benign Bob saw the Green vote lift into the 12 to 14 per cent range, just under half the ALP vote. Meanwhile the Coalition vote surged into the 45 to 50 per cent zone. Abbott was the biggest winner as Labor lost votes to both sides.

The backlash that Abbott cultivated had deep roots. People were alert to global warning—but they were suspicious of Labor's scheme. The recent Lowy Institute poll showed that, while 41 per cent of people felt global warming was a pressing problem, 59 per cent felt action should either be modest or delayed. Idealism was fading. The drought had broken. The climate change lobby's relentless and institutionalised campaign to scare the public had failed. It had become an epic political blunder. Depicting catastrophes fifty and a hundred years hence is a poor basis for public policy action now. When politicians like Rudd failed to honour his own warnings the public knew such warnings did not need to be taken at face value. Insisting that 'the science is settled' and that further debate was irrational (or immoral) was itself an irrational position and patronising of the public. When advocates were cavalier about the costs involved and promoted schemes that were rip-offs, they invited public cynicism.

Polls suggested people saw climate change as a problem. But they had to judge how much sacrifice to make now for uncertain gains in the future and how much to prioritise climate change action against a list of other challenges such as jobs, power bills and (for families) the kids' education—let alone population ageing. And this was a different Labor reform: it would have a negative impact on national income and economic growth.

The first question Gillard faced was how to reverse community rejection. Her answer was the 'lived experience'—once the people experienced the scheme from 1 July 2012, Abbott's scare would collapse. Combet said: 'The sting went out on 1 July 2012 when the world was just the same. The most potent issue came down to trust.'[27]

Nothing matched the euphoria of the Greens. For the first time they were changing the nation as governors. Milne said the Coalition was unable to cope with the 'psychological shift from the fossil-fuel past to a renewable-powered future'. Brown said it was an 'historic day' for

7 billion people on the planet. In case Labor missed what it had done, Brown told them: 'What we are doing here today is legislating—albeit with reserve—to hold back the great nemesis of climate change for the whole future of humanity and indeed of our millions of fellow species on this planet.'[28] He was putting Green values all over this law.

It was no surprise the climate change tide was running out. Great reforms are not endlessly available for incompetent governments that squander their opportunities. This is what happened with Labor.

Seen in this context the claims of some commentators that Abbott should have backed Gillard's policy in the national economic interest are absurd. That would have meant betraying his own position, accepting Gillard's betrayal of her position and abandoning a growing constituency that felt neither the scheme's design nor timing were right. Abbott could not have supported the scheme and remained leader.

In reality, the Coalition had won the politics yet assumed a large responsibility for the policy dead-end the country faced on climate change. The Coalition, having abandoned carbon pricing in 2009, had no viable alternative policy. Its direct action framework, as assessed by Treasury, was less efficient than a market-based mechanism. Under direct action the cost of emission reduction was higher; the option of cheaper internationally sourced abatement was not available; and the loss of national income to achieve a bipartisan target was greater. Abbott's destruction of Gillard's scheme had a long-run consequence—it locked a future Coalition government into a third-best policy answer unlikely to be durable.

The related problem was that carbon pricing stability could only be obtained from a Labor–Coalition agreement. Rudd was right in negotiating with the Coalition in 2009. Gillard was conscripted by history with the Greens as her partner. She could carry the Parliament but not the people. The AIG's Heather Ridout said the absence of consensus means 'this legislation may not do much to reduce the policy uncertainty that is strangling long-term investment in efficient electricity generation'.

The success of carbon pricing depends on global events beyond Australia's control. By 2012, when the policy started, the EU confronted recession, and US legislation for 'cap and trade' was more unlikely than ever. The international compact for carbon pricing was broken. It was beyond Labor's power to re-activate the global process. These trends guaranteed growing hostility from business. Ross Garnaut, the architect of two climate change reports, attacked business for promoting sectional interests and sacrificing the public interest. This would become a mantra from Labor and many commentators.

The truth is that business had genuine concerns. The AIG said the price was 'close to double those in major international markets'. Ridout said the scheme must be amended, its timing 'couldn't be worse' and the costs for manufacturing were far higher than in the EU. BCA chief Jennifer Westacott said the scheme was 'neither workable nor responsible'. The price was 'far ahead' of the world price. Industries that would have been competitive under a global price now faced decline. If Treasury's estimates at the floating price stage proved too optimistic then a major fiscal problem could result.[29] The Australian Chamber of Commerce and Industry called the package an 'economic mistake', while the resources sector was implacably hostile.

Interviewed for this book, Westacott went further. She dismissed any claims that the scheme was genuinely reformist.

> It is one of the worst pieces of public policy I can recall. Where have we ended up? We have very little impact in terms of emissions reductions. We have a deeply confused public in terms of the right response to climate change. We have a renewable energy target on top of the carbon price and it's the RET that really drives high prices. This is a policy mess. Companies are saying: how can we make long-term investments when we are uncertain about the future of these policies? Consider the tests: policy design, the process, communication with the public, budget consequences and industry certainty. There aren't many better examples of bad public policy than this.[30]

It had been the BCA under Michael Chaney in 2006 that encouraged the Howard Government to embrace an ETS. Now, six years later, the hostility of the BCA towards Gillard's scheme testified to the transformation in the international outlook and the utility of such a scheme for Australia.

Labor's decision to enshrine climate change action as the defining reform of its second term was a strategic and political blunder. Climate change was the priority for neither Australia nor the world at this point. The scheme was unlikely to prove enduring and revealed Labor's obsession with its own agenda and view of the world. It was the most important consequence of minority government but it arose only because of Gillard's alliance with the Greens. In 2013 the policy was pivotal to her removal as prime minister by the caucus and to Labor's election defeat.

CHAPTER 25

PHONEY VICTORY

'It was neither afraid to have a ballot nor conniving to have one,' Julia Gillard said, explaining her tactics in the February 2012 smashing of Kevin Rudd's leadership bid.[1] Gillard's victory revealed that Rudd's challenge was as dysfunctional as his government had been. In reality, Rudd was suckered into a contest and cut to pieces. If Rudd had not misjudged at this point there is a high probability he would have returned as prime minister earlier than June 2013.

This contest was startling for its brutality. Gillard secured a tactical victory over Rudd in a 71 to 31 vote as Labor released its pent-up hatreds. Given Gillard's aim was to complete the unfinished business of June 2010, her camp engaged in spectacular 'truth telling' about Rudd. After the bloodletting, Rudd languished on the backbench, his ambitions still beating but submerged. Gillard and Rudd would never serve in the same ministry again. It was the final severing of that once brilliant 2006 union from those happy days when Kevin and Julia, in blissful fidelity, danced Labor into office.

As Rudd went down, he laid his curse upon Gillard. He told the party room: 'We have been on track to suffer the worst electoral defeat in our history. And I refuse to stand idly by while the next generation of Labor leaders is wiped out.'[2] This cut into Labor's heart.

As Labor MPs voted for Gillard, their secret terror was that Rudd was right. The ballot, more anti-Rudd than pro-Gillard, came after six months of Labor's primary vote being locked in a 28 per cent to 33 per cent death zone. The dilemma was insoluble: Gillard was master of the party yet loathed in the nation while Rudd, the most popular politician in Australia, was loathed by his party.

Rudd told journalists before and after the ballot that he had 40 votes lined up. Rudd and his backers fed this number to the media and fell for their own propaganda. In the end Rudd looked a mug. He said later he lost a stack of votes in the final days. Martin Ferguson said: 'With the

February ballot a lot of people had given commitments to Kevin. But when the pressure came on they faded.'[3]

The Rudd campaign had been building for several months—it relied on the polls, intense briefings of journalists and editors, and spreading panic across the caucus. As usual in Labor leadership contests, the Gillard–Rudd war had nothing to do with policy or ideas; it was about Labor self-preservation. The ballot left a broken government.

Rudd resigned as Foreign Minister at a 1 a.m. media conference melodrama at the Willard Hotel in Washington, DC and then flew home. The location and timing were crazy. One of his most sympathetic backers, John Faulkner, was appalled. There was a mystery: why didn't Rudd wait until after the March 2012 Queensland state election, where Labor faced a debacle? He never gave a satisfactory explanation, for such an obvious blunder. In truth, Rudd misread Gillard.

It was in Gillard's interest to stage a showdown when she had overwhelming numbers. But she needed to avoid being the aggressor and making Rudd a public martyr. John McTernan said:

> You could hear the drum beats. You knew he was coming. But if Gillard moved against him first and that looked unprovoked, then Rudd would turn it into a victimisation process for his own electoral benefit. Rudd's tactics made us weaker and weaker. Yet we had to avoid being seen as the aggressor.[4]

Rudd solved Gillard's problem by moving first, resigning, and implying he would challenge. The Rudd challenge was forever hostage to the whims, moods and contradictions of its author. It was a concoction of revenge, hubris, self-belief, a quest for vindication and manipulation of a mostly willing media. It prospered only because of Gillard's inability to break the cycle of bad polls. After her victory, Gillard had to translate her caucus strength into a revival of her government's position. Within weeks her failure was apparent: she couldn't achieve this. Rarely has such a huge leadership win been lost in the sand so rapidly. The bedrock reason Gillard was vulnerable was summarised by a private remark from Bill Shorten: 'bad judgement'.

The December 2011 ALP National Conference had backfired for Gillard despite her wins—securing approval for offshore processing and selling uranium to India. The leadership issue had been pervasive. In her uninspiring leader's speech, with its infamous 'we are us' phrase, Gillard conspicuously omitted Rudd from her list of past iconic ALP leaders as

he sat expressionless in the front row before her. It was a stupid and pro-
vocative insult. Gillard's poor judgement became the talk off the conference floor. She avoided humiliation on her refusal to endorse same-sex
marriage only when her backers secured a narrow win on a conscience
vote. The National Conference ended in resentments and the deepening
of Rudd–Gillard tensions.

Gillard promptly went into a ministry reshuffle that promoted
Shorten and Combet and sought to consolidate her position. An angry
Kim Carr, a Rudd backer, was dumped to the outer ministry. Another
Rudd supporter, Robert McClelland, was dumped from attorney-general
to a lesser job but refused to be demoted outside cabinet. Now Rudd was
openly defiant. He said Carr had done an excellent job and was 'largely
responsible' for saving the car industry. Carr and McClelland went public
in defending their records.

Even Gillard's minority government victories were contaminated by
the Rudd factor. With Albanese's support, Gillard in late 2011 had consolidated her government by the recruitment of Liberal 'rat' Peter Slipper
to the office of Speaker. Labor's Speaker, Harry Jenkins, had told Gillard at
7.30 a.m. on 24 November, the last sitting day of the year, that he was quitting. Albanese, the leader of the House, rang Slipper at 8.30 a.m. to offer
him the post, having previously engineered Slipper into the deputy speak-
ership after the 2010 election. Slipper's career was about to be terminated
by the Liberal National Party in Queensland dumping his pre-selection.
Repudiated by his own side and courted by Labor, Slipper took the bait.

It was a play engineered by Albanese. During the 2010 negotiations
for minority government, he obtained the agreement of Liberal MP Alex
Somlyay to be Deputy Speaker. Indeed, Albanese says he had 'direct and
indirect' talks with four Coalition MPs at that time over the Speaker and
Deputy Speaker roles and they included both Slipper and Somlyay. On
the eve of the AFL Grand Final lunch, Somlyay, under pressure from his
own side, rang Albanese to apologise and say he had to pull out. 'By the
time lunch was over, we had Slipper in the field,' said Albanese. Slipper was
elected Deputy Speaker at the start of the minority government. 'He was
ours from that point,' Albanese said. 'There was no deal but Slipper was in
the back pocket.'[5] The subsequent elevation of Slipper to Speaker meant
that Gillard's position on the floor of Parliament was strengthened and
the minority government had a 76 to 73 majority when its declared
crossbenchers voted with it.[6]

Gillard's aspiration for a full-term parliament was now virtually
guaranteed. More immediately, Gillard had purchased critical protection

in case disgraced Labor MP Craig Thomson was charged and convicted or in case Andrew Wilkie repudiated his agreement with Gillard because of Labor's failure to honour its pledge on mandatory pre-commitment for poker machines.

This was critical because Wilkie did walk away. Less than eight weeks later, on 15 January 2012, Gillard told Wilkie that the 2014 deadline for his poker machine law was unachievable. She said it was impossible because she could not muster the numbers on the floor. This broke their agreement, on which Gillard had formed government eighteen months earlier. It gave relief to desperately worried New South Wales members of Parliament. 'The raw politics of poker machine gambling in New South Wales were shocking for us,' Greg Combet said. 'I come from Rooty Hill—the high school was next door to the RSL club.'[7]

Not surprisingly, Rudd was playing politics on pokies. New South Wales and Queensland members of Parliament were under pressure from the licensed clubs lobby trying to kill the Wilkie deal. Stephen Conroy alleged that 'Rudd's supporters were walking around caucus saying "Look, dump Wilkie."'[8] Gillard was under pressure from the backbench to weaken the policy. On 19 January, Wilkie saw Gillard at the Lodge and the next day he saw her in Melbourne: he tried to negotiate a fallback but Gillard now had the safety of numbers. There would be no mandatory pre-commitment law. She offered a damp squib: a trial run in the ACT. Gillard wanted Wilkie to bow before this reality. He refused.[9]

At the weekend Wilkie went public: 'A deal's a deal and it must be honoured. Our democracy is simply too precious to trash with broken promises and backroom compromises. So I will walk, take my chances, and so be it.' His agreement with Gillard was finished. Wilkie said he was 'disappointed and shocked that she [Gillard] was not true to her word'. He accused her of dishonour.

Asked the deadly question by the media—Had she broken a promise?—Gillard said it was 'very clear that there's not the parliamentary support' from the crossbench, an accurate view. Albanese reported that Gillard was 'white-hot angry' at Wilkie's repudiation and attack on her integrity.[10] On Sunday 19 February, Wilkie said on Sky News's *Australian Agenda* program that he had discussed the leadership with Rudd in November. Every fracas led back to leadership.

Asked about the importance of Slipper, Albanese said: 'It was critical. The government would not have continued had that change not happened. An election at that point in my view would have resulted in a significant defeat. It's as simple as that.'[11]

By late January/early February 2012 the Rudd camp media briefings reached a new intensity. A number of senior correspondents were predicting a challenge and reporting a shift in caucus support to Rudd. Newspoll had Labor's primary vote flat at 30 per cent. There was no summer lift. Union leaders began to publicly declare for Gillard. On Sunday 19 February, backbencher Darren Cheeseman said Gillard should quit.

Even more bizarre were the events of the previous night: a YouTube video was posted showing Rudd as prime minister losing his temper and swearing, the implication being, here is the ugly face of real Kevin. It was a turning point. Bruce Hawker contacted Sky's David Speers, who was at a dinner party, and the upshot was that Speers conducted an interview with Rudd at about 11 p.m. before his early departure for North America the next morning. Rudd turned the leak into a counterattack. He blamed Gillard's office, saying the footage would have been held by her office or department. This was promptly denied. But Rudd put much store by this leak: he felt the Gillard camp was moving against him.

In the best confessional tones, Foreign Minister Rudd, three days before his resignation from that post, told Speers he had changed his ways. He had reflected a lot. 'I don't want to walk away from some of my own failings in the past,' Rudd said. He had tried to learn, to delegate, to do less, to consult. 'You'd be a mug if you didn't learn anything from the past,' he said.[12] Leaving the message that he was a reformed man, Rudd flew to Washington. It was classic Kevin.

Some of Gillard's advisers urged her to strike to end the political haemorrhage. Her supporters started to go public. David Bradbury said that 'if it means getting a tattoo, I'd consider it'. Political correspondents reported that Rudd was ready to challenge. Few reported seething caucus resentment at his tactics. 'Kevin was always on high volume,' said Gillard. 'His supporters were on high volume. They always over-claimed their support with the media.'[13] Yet the gallery rightly judged that a showdown was coming. Labor was consumed by fear and treachery.

On Monday 20 February, Crean tried to forced the issue: he said Gillard must confront Rudd and secure his loyalty or his dismissal. 'He's been undermining Gillard for months,' Crean said. 'Simon went off on a mission of his own,' Gillard said. 'But it raised the temperature and, yes, that suited me.'[14]

The Gillard people now gave Rudd some of his own medicine: they took resort to the media. 'My view was this had to be brought to a head,' Tony Burke said.

We had a member of the cabinet working to bring down the
Prime Minister. I walked up to the press gallery and told a number
of journalists this couldn't go on. I did not say Kevin should be
sacked. But I made clear the undermining must stop. The stories
that went up online did go a step further than what I said.[15]

The reports based on Burke's briefing captured the aggression pulsating through Gillard's backers. They said Gillard was prepared to dismiss
Rudd.[16] But it was Gillard's supporters led by Burke, not Gillard herself,
who had briefed.

Would Gillard have sacked Rudd? Interviewed for this book, Gillard
left the impression she had taken no such decision. It must, however,
be doubted—sacking Rudd would have been counterproductive. Her
backers were astute in turning up the heat. The Rudd camp contacted the
journalists to check the situation. Rudd was unnerved; the temperature
had got too hot.

Meanwhile the discussion in Gillard's office was about the need to
secure a Gillard–Rudd meeting when the Foreign Minister returned to
the country.[17]

Gillard rejects the idea she orchestrated a 'Machiavellian plan' to trap
Rudd into resignation. But Rudd's supporters confirm that in phone
discussions with him from Washington he was worried Gillard would
dismiss him as Foreign Minister. Rudd pulled the plug; he became victim
of the political hysteria partly induced by his own campaign.

At his bizarre 1 a.m. press conference Rudd said: 'Minister Crean
and a number of other faceless men have publicly attacked my integrity
and therefore my fitness to serve as a minister in the government. When
challenged on these attacks, Prime Minister Gillard chose not to repudi-
ate them. I can only reluctantly conclude that she therefore shares these
views.' Rudd said he could not serve as Foreign Minister without the
Prime Minister's support. He resigned and was returning at once. Before
leaving the United States, Rudd said he was 'encouraged' by people
urging him to contest the leadership.

In words that enraged pro-Gillard ministers, in particular Swan,
Rudd said: 'I can promise you this, there is no way—no way—that I will
ever be party to a stealth attack on a sitting prime minister elected by the
people.'[18]

'I don't know what was going through his mind,' Gillard said.[19] She
told colleagues the media-generated mood at the time was 'crazy, absolutely
crazy'. Yet resigning from Washington made no sense. Questioned by the

author,[20] Rudd said he had no option but resignation and it was a matter of principle. It is an unpersuasive explanation. He announced a challenge only after his return, another blunder. The sequence was that Gillard said she would declare the leadership open and Rudd then said he would stand against her. From the time of Rudd's resignation the Gillard camp was most anxious that he challenge and operated on the assumption that he would—and Rudd foolishly obliged them. He realised he had no chance. 'He rang me and said, "Otherwise I'll be seen as a coward",' Martin Ferguson said.[21]

Rudd had chosen to fight—and Gillard and Swan would give him a fight beyond his worst nightmare. Their anger was now given licence. Most rivals need two strikes to win—witness Keating against Hawke. Gillard and Swan wanted to kill the two-challenge tactic. They decided to finish Rudd forever. Swan issued one of the most inflammatory statements in Labor history.

He said Rudd had put 'his own self-interest ahead of the interest of the broader labour movement and the country'. The ALP had given Rudd 'all the opportunities in the world and he wasted them with his dysfunctional decision making' and his 'deeply demeaning attitudes towards other people'. Swan moved to the central charges: 'He sought to tear down the 2010 campaign, deliberately risking an Abbott prime ministership and now he undermines the government at every turn. He was the party's biggest beneficiary then its biggest critic; but never a loyal or selfless example of its values and objectives.' While Rudd 'does not hold any Labor values', Gillard by contrast had 'a good Labor heart'. Colleagues were 'sick of Kevin Rudd driving the vote down by sabotaging policy announcements', Swan said. 'The Labor Party is not about a person, it's about a purpose. That's something Prime Minister Gillard has always known in her heart but something Kevin Rudd has never understood.'[22]

Gillard and Swan believed Rudd was unfit to be ALP leader or prime minister. These views were widely shared in the cabinet. Over the next two years many people would puzzle about Labor's resistance to recalling Rudd as leader given his popularity. This was the reason.

In an interview for this book, Gillard confirmed that the aim was to finish Rudd. At her media conference in Adelaide on 23 February, Gillard said there would be a leadership ballot the next Monday to settle the issue 'once and for all'. If defeated she would retire to the backbench and renounce future leadership ambition. She expected the same from Rudd. Gillard now revealed why she challenged Rudd in 2010.

She said government 'requires consistency, purpose, method, discipline, inclusion, consultation' and that Rudd, as prime minister, lacked those qualities. He had 'very difficult and very chaotic work patterns' and his government 'had entered a period of paralysis'. Rudd had been 'very, very focused on the next news cycle, on the next picture opportunity, rather than long-term reforms for the nation's interest'. She had not revealed the sordid details in June 2010 out of respect for Rudd. She now accused Rudd of sabotaging the 2010 campaign. 'We were in a winning position in that campaign until the sabotage,' she said. Gillard said it was her own effort after the sabotage that saved the government. She reached out to the media: 'I think people who know me, and many people standing in the press pack do, people who know me would know my stoicism and personal fortitude and a sense of calm under pressure.'

The most passionate part of this media conference, however, was her insistence that, as Rudd's deputy, she had been loyal to him, worked her guts out and tried to keep the ship afloat—in contrast to Rudd's campaign of destabilisation against her. Gillard announced she was absolving all journalists of their professional obligation to protect her: if any journalist knew of her private undermining of Rudd then they could reveal that. 'To a person they will say "no" because I never did,' Gillard said.[23]

The flood gates now opened. It became a Roman amphitheatre spectacle. Minister after minister denounced Rudd, with some refusing to serve under him again—Roxon, Burke, Conroy, Garrett and obviously Swan. The Labor Party was being ripped apart.

Yet Rudd had a minority of senior ministers with him: Albanese, Ferguson, Kim Carr, McClelland and Bowen. They believed Labor faced defeat at an election and Rudd was the best option. Implicit in their stand was a view that the June 2010 leadership change was a mistake. The party should have stuck with Rudd then; it should return to him now.

The contest was about the future and the past. But all roads led back to June 2010. At stake was the issue of responsibility: who carried responsibility for the divisions ripping apart the government? Rudd believed the June 2010 decision was a travesty; Gillard believed Rudd never accepted the party's decision and set about wrecking her government.

Rudd's public pitch was adroit: he called for an end to personality warfare. Rudd said the decision was not just about the ALP; it was about the Australian people. He spoke to the media before leaving Washington, on his arrival in Brisbane and later the same day to announce his candidature. 'I do not believe that Prime Minister Gillard can lead the Australian Labor Party to success in the next election,' Rudd said. 'That is a deep belief. I believe it's also a belief shared right across the Australian community.'

What was the core issue for caucus members? Rudd said it was trust and confidence: 'Rightly or wrongly, Julia has lost the confidence of the Australian people.' The vote was not about 'who you like and dislike'. The vote was about the public trust. Gillard had lost that trust and, once lost, it was gone forever.

Declaring he was 'shocked and disappointed' by the personal attacks, Rudd urged his supporters 'not to retaliate'. He wanted to set higher standards. Rudd was Mr Principle. Arriving in Brisbane, Rudd said, 'it's good to be back home with Therese and the family'. Rudd was Mr Family Man. He said the issue for Labor was: who is best equipped to defeat Mr Abbott at the coming election? Rudd was Mr Popularity.

He made his own disclosures about June 2010, in effect accusing Gillard of breaking her word. Rudd said they had 'explicitly agreed' in the presence of a witness (Faulkner) to delay the issue and 'revisit the question [the leadership] before the election was due in late 2010'. But ten minutes later Gillard 'came back in the room and said all bets are off, that agreement doesn't hold'. Rudd was puncturing the notion of Saint Julia; his charge was that Gillard got the leadership by breaking her promise.[24]

Rudd was sensible in setting out his policy priorities: restoration of business confidence, commitment to manufacturing and an earlier move to a floating carbon price. He pledged reform of the Labor Party and returning to caucus the power to elect the ministry. He bowed to Gillard's request: if he lost he would accept the decision. Nobody took this pledge seriously. Most journalists shared Peter Hartcher's view that Rudd, if he lost, 'will repair to the backbench and prepare for a second challenge'.

But Rudd's strongest argument was his repudiation of claims that 'all of the government's problems are the result of one person called K. Rudd'. He said: 'It wasn't K. Rudd who made a pre-election commitment on a carbon tax. It wasn't K. Rudd who made a particular commitment to Mr Wilkie on the question of poker machines. It wasn't K. Rudd who had anything to do with the East Timor solution or the Malaysia solution.' Blaming him for Gillard's leadership problem was 'simply unsustainable'. The government's accumulated problems, Rudd said, 'have been of its own making'. He was right. It was a fatal flaw in the assault upon him.

In this bizarre encounter, therefore, both Gillard and Rudd campaigned on a truth. Gillard was correct to argue that Rudd had undermined the government but Rudd was correct to argue that Gillard's problems, ultimately, went to her own defects. It was an exercise in mutual destruction. Both were totally open that the originating issue was June 2010. Rudd simply said: 'I want to finish the job the Australian people elected me to do.' In life, however, the past cannot be resurrected. Rudd's mission—part nostalgia, part vindication—sprang from his belief that the natural order had been violated in 2010, that Labor must re-create the past to claim the future.

Nicola Roxon did the most damage to Rudd. For the first time she revealed the chaos of hospitals policy in early 2010 and Rudd's quest for a referendum to help win an election. She said: 'If Kevin succeeds I won't serve in his ministry.'[25] She was destroying one of Rudd's treasures: his claims as a policy wonk. Conroy was lethal: 'Kevin Rudd had contempt for the cabinet, contempt for the caucus, contempt for the Parliament and ultimately what brought him down was the Australian public worked out that he had contempt for them as well.' Burke said it was an open secret that Rudd had been campaigning for the leadership. He believed 'some pretty significant lies' had been peddled to journalists. 'This has been a covert operation,' Crean said. 'Because he never sleeps, he's always manipulating something.' The day before the vote, Swan said: 'I noticed this morning on television Mr Rudd was talking about how he has changed. I don't believe he has changed.' Craig Emerson said journalists and editors had told him about Rudd's destabilisation. 'Kevin's saying it must stop,' Emerson said. 'Well, he can actually stop it.'

Kate Ellis, her voice quivering, went public with an account of events at Adelaide's Stag Hotel in February 2011 when Rudd was invited by his friend, Premier Mike Rann, to a social function. Addressing a group with Don Farrell, one of his prime opponents, Rudd is reported to have said: 'I've been wondering how you reconcile your conservative brand of Catholicism with a childless, atheist, ex-communist as Labor leader.' His spokesman denied these claims and called them 'lies'. When the story appeared Rudd denied it. Ellis said: 'I know for a fact he was talking down the Prime Minister. He was telling anyone who would listen that it was his mission, that he was going to get his revenge and come back. He should be honest about what he's been doing.' Ellis said guests had gone out of their way later to compare notes on Rudd's comments.[26]

Combet had turned against Rudd. In late 2011 they had a heart-to-heart conversation. Combet felt Rudd was in bad shape; before the sun set Rudd had poured them both a scotch and they ruminated on their futures. 'I didn't come into this place to be leader,' Combet told him. He said he would like, if events worked out, to be treasurer some day.

'It wasn't a talk about me supporting Kevin; I supported Gillard,' Combet said. 'There was no deal.' Yet Rudd and his camp peddled to journalists for two years that Combet was prepared to back Rudd for the Treasury job. 'We were just having a conversation,' Combet said. 'But he goes out and starts telling people, and journalists begin ringing me saying you've done a deal. Would I support somebody who behaves like that? That's just dishonest.'[27] Combet found against Rudd on character grounds; he never changed his mind.

Rudd's backers were restrained. Bowen said it was a contest between two 'very good candidates', both of whom deserved respect. The drama came when Albanese, close to breakdown, said he had opposed this contest just as he opposed the June 2010 contest. 'I believe the government's difficulties can be traced to that night,' Albanese said of Rudd's removal. 'It was wrong.' The coming ballot was the only opportunity Albanese had 'to express my dissent from the actions of that night and I intend to do so'.

Albanese had rung Gillard, said he would vote for Rudd and offered his resignation as leader of the House. Gillard declined to accept it. She needed Albanese to keep the minority government alive.[28]

Newspoll on the morning of the vote showed people preferred Rudd over Gillard 53 to 28 per cent. But Gillard won 70 per cent of the caucus. After the caucus vote Rudd said he bore no malice. He told Gillard: 'You will have my absolute support in your efforts to bring us victory. I will not under any circumstances mount a challenge against your leadership'—a pledge he would break. Flanked by his family at a media conference, Rudd said that 'on behalf of Therese and myself and the family' he wanted to thank the people for their 'extraordinary wave of public support'.

Rudd's ineptitude had been extraordinary. It was one thing to resign as Foreign Minister; it was another to challenge at that point. He should have gone to the backbench and waited, patiently and loyally. That would have denied Gillard victory in a ballot and deepened her frustration. The proof that this challenge had weakened Rudd was his subsequent fallback: he decided he could only become leader by overwhelming draft. And that would never happen.

For Gillard, the gains were limited: the party had gifted her more time. Nothing more. If Gillard was good enough, she could recover as prime minister. Within forty-eight hours the pessimistic omens came when Gillard mismanaged the transition to Canberra of former New South Wales premier Bob Carr, to become Foreign Minister. Gillard, acting on advice from New South Wales ALP Secretary Sam Dastyari, settled on Carr and spoke to him about filling a New South Wales Senate vacancy. She then backtracked, cognisant of her promise to Stephen Smith that he would be 'first cab off the rank' for the Foreign Affairs ministry if a vacancy arose. Carr was furious at having been encouraged and then denied. Finally, Gillard reverted to Plan A, Smith took a hit for the team, and Carr and Gillard conducted a media conference straight from the pages of Monty Python.

The realists knew the Gillard–Rudd conflict was elemental. While they both sat in the Parliament it was never ending. 'It didn't matter what you did to him,' Don Farrell said. 'It's like the *Terminator 2* movie—shoot him, run him over, crush him in a machine, he just keeps coming.'[29]

The *Financial Review* called for an election.[30] It was the last thought in Gillard's mind. She took solace from having exposed Rudd's true weakness in the caucus. Rudd's incompetence heartened the Gillard camp. As Stephen Smith said: if Rudd had ever conducted a 'no treachery' policy then he 'would have maximised his chances for a recall earlier'.[31] Burke identified the ongoing problem: 'Every time Julia started to get a head of steam Kevin would be reinserted into the media cycle.'[32] There was no escape.

Gillard promised to be a more 'forceful' advocate for the cause. But she had no new direction for the government. Abbott nailed the issue—nothing would actually change.[33]

CHAPTER 26

THE COLLAPSE OF BORDER PROTECTION

With boats arriving faster than ever, Chris Bowen was rung by Julia Gillard after the 2010 election and offered the job of Minister for Immigration, the 'poisoned chalice'. Bowen was surprised; he had hoped he would get Finance. 'She said it was the toughest job in the government,' Bowen said of Gillard's offer. Despite their differences over the leadership, Gillard and Bowen had a common cause: halting the boats by abandoning Rudd's caution.

They were brought undone by an unsurpassable troika—the High Court, the Abbott-led Coalition and the 'open door' boat policy of the Greens. This transcended a failure by Labor. It constituted one of the most comprehensive failures of Australia's system of governance in decades. The nation, in effect, lost control of its borders in a betrayal of the public interest.

Unburdened by the dead hand of the *Tampa*, Bowen operated on a clean slate. The Immigration Department found him fresh and intelligent. His first move was to convene a conference of the wise men—in Bowen's words, 'the council of elders'. This involved Andrew Medcalfe from Immigration and deputy Peter Hughes; DFAT chief and former ASIO boss Dennis Richardson; national security adviser Duncan Lewis; Ambassador for People Smuggling Issues James Larson, plus the heads of the intelligence agencies ASIO and ASIS, plus the head of Customs. They were the best brains on how to halt the surge of boats. 'My message to them was: I need you to tell me what will work and what won't work,' Bowen said. He had no ideological fixation. Gillard's play on East Timor had drawn a blank. The council of elders moved fast.

Bowen said:

They said Nauru didn't work and won't work. They said Temporary Protection Visas didn't work and won't work. Turning back

the boats did work; it worked under Howard, because of its simplicity—you end up where you started from. But they argued:
'Minister, you can't do that now because Indonesia won't accept it.
They turned a blind eye before, but life has moved on. The people
smugglers would sink the boats, there's a rescue at sea, you go to
the nearest land and that is Australia. So, it's not a workable policy.'[1]

It is a startling insight into the extent to which the Abbott–Morrison 'turn
back the boats' policies were rejected by the public service establishment.
Abbott's policy for much of the Parliament was to reopen Nauru, rein-
troduce Temporary Protection Visas and turn backs boats. Labor decided
Abbott talked loud but was a fraud.

The breakthrough idea was fly back, not tow back. The concept was
to remove people from Australia's processing and settlement system. The
elders wanted Bowen to think laterally. The options went to a National
Security Committee (NSC) meeting. As the idea took hold, the critical
question became: which nations might accept it? Bowen said: 'You got
the same result as turning back the boats without turning back the
boats. You could fly people back to Indonesia if you got agreement with
Indonesia. In return you'd take genuine refugees from Indonesia who
weren't getting on boats.'[2]

The government tested the concept with Indonesia but got nowhere.
Malaysia and Pakistan were the alternatives they contemplated. Bowen
got NSC authorisation to proceed. In October 2010, during a visit to
Malaysia, he met the Home Affairs Minister, Hishammuddin. They fired
off each other and felt they could do business, with Bowen later calling
Hishammuddin 'a real action man'. Australia mounted a major diplo-
matic effort with Malaysia involving Dennis Richardson, Medcalfe and
Australia's high commissioner in Malaysia, Miles Kupa.

The urgency was underlined on 15 December 2010 when a boat
carrying about ninety people foundered in huge seas off Christmas Island
amid terrible scenes, with fifty adults and children drowning. This was
one of the rare occurrences when a boat got through undetected. Bowen
had to rebut the appalling conspiracy theories surrounding such tragedies,
with pro-refugee elements blaming the Australian Government.

About five thousand people arrived by boat in 2010, an increase on
the previous year. Australia was a prized target, with people coming from
outside the region and transiting through several nations to arrive here.
The benign situation Rudd had inherited in 2008 was long gone. The
people smugglers now had plenty of demand and Australia had failed to

put disincentives in place. Given the unlimited demand, numbers would keep rising without policy action. Gradually but relentlessly, Australia was losing control of its borders. Gillard knew this was an untenable situation for any prime minister.

Bowen was putting in place a dual policy: easing punitive detention arrangements for families and striving to achieve a meaningful regional agreement. In early 2011 a number of violent and criminal events erupted in detention centres pressed to capacity. On 7 May Gillard and Bowen announced that they were close to signing an agreement with Malaysia under which 800 asylum seeker boat arrivals would be transferred to Malaysia upon their arrival in Australia and Australia, in turn, would accept 4000 people from Malaysia's refugee pool.

This is when Labor buried its *Tampa* legacy, courtesy of Gillard and Bowen. Labor now accepted the relevance of 'pull' factors in the boat trade. It embraced a new principle: the key to halting boats was to deny people processing in Australia by returning asylum seekers to the region as fast as possible. This was tied to the notion of 'people swap' based on regional cooperation.

'I expect protests, I expect legal challenges, I expect resistance,' Bowen said. The finalised policy was announced by Gillard on 25 July 2011, the day Bowen and Hishammuddin signed the agreement in Kuala Lumpur. She predicted it would 'smash the business model of the people smugglers'.

The policy meant that the next 800 boat arrivals would be sent to Malaysia, where Gillard said 'they will have to wait alongside more than 90 000 other asylum seekers for their claims to be assessed'.[3] They would get no preferential treatment. The disincentive and hardship would be real. The key to success was ensuring the policy did not require implementation in full.

Once boat people were flown immediately back to Malaysia en masse, and this was communicated across the region, the disincentive for people to board boats to Australia would be high. Medcalfe called it a 'virtual tow-back'. The boat journey to Australia ended in a long queue in Malaysia. The smugglers had to recruit 800 victims for futile voyages before they got clear passage again. For Bowen, a threshold beyond 800 would have been preferable but his policy would have an impact once the planes were returning boat people. The head of Australia's Customs and Border Protection Command, Mike Pezzullo, said it would kill the smugglers' business model 'stone dead'.[4]

There would be no 'blanket exemptions'—so men, women and children would be flown out. The government knew people might need to be forced onto the planes. Bowen's justification was to halt more children drowning on boats. No new legislation was needed; Howard's laws would suffice. The presentation effect was vital, so Bowen sold a tough message. 'Taking the decision to pay $20 000, for example, to a people smuggler to, in many cases, risk the lives of your family to get to Australia won't work.'[5]

The agreement specified that transferees would be lawful in Malaysia, be allowed to live in the community, have work rights and have access to health and education. Their refugee claims would be processed by the UNHCR. The agreement came under a broader regional framework finalised at Bali earlier in 2011. Gillard said Australia was increasing its offshore refugee intake, but for many the numbers were a problem: 800 being sent and 4000 being received from Malaysia equated to 1000 refugees each year for four years.

Shadow Minister Scott Morrison branded the deal an act of 'panic and desperation'. He said Australia would be meeting all the costs and that 'the human rights protections simply aren't there'. He campaigned against the agreement on human rights grounds, arguing that conditions in Malaysia were unacceptable. The Opposition complained that Malaysia was not a signatory to the Refugee Convention. As a solution Morrison said Nauru was better.[6]

The problem with Morrison's argument at the time was that being processed on Nauru did not rule out settlement in Australia while being sent back to Malaysia extinguished this option. When the Rudd Government dismantled the Pacific Solution it said that of 1637 people detained over 2001–08 in the Nauru and PNG facilities, 705 had been resettled in Australia.[7]

For political reasons Bowen had wanted Labor to embrace the Nauru option with Malaysia. He was right. He believed doing both would maximise the scope for Coalition support. 'The principle involved was saying to the Liberals, "You think this policy [Malaysia] won't work and we think that policy [Nauru] won't work, so why don't we do both?"' Bowen said. 'I was attracted very early to that idea.'[8] But he was overruled by Gillard.

The public debate focused almost exclusively on the plight of the 800 boat people being sent to Malaysia. There was scant attention paid to the humanitarian bonus of accepting another 4000 offshore refugees. The Greens declared political war on the agreement and formed a unity ticket with the Coalition to veto it on human rights grounds. The Australian Human Rights Commission, the Refugee Council of Australia and

Amnesty International also attacked the agreement. Much of the media coverage was sceptical. The right-wing shock jocks were hostile, raising the plight of children and the risks of returned asylum seekers being caned or whipped. Their overnight compassion for boat people was deeply moving. Abbott branded it a 'dodgy deal'. He said: 'I have nothing against Malaysia. But their standards aren't ours.'[9] He branded Labor's policy as 'far more brutal' than anything Howard had done.[10]

The Department of Immigration was preparing to send the first batch of people back on a plane when an asylum seeker asked to see a lawyer, a request that the department was legally obliged to honour. It led to refugee lawyer David Manne initiating a case before the High Court. The government's Malaysia policy had been based on supporting legal advice from the solicitor-general, Stephen Gageler. The High Court judgment was brought down on 31 August 2011 and found 6 to 1 against the government. It made permanent all injunctions that had been granted earlier. This prevented the removal of people to Malaysia and restricted the minister from removing unaccompanied minors. 'We had been 24 hours from getting the first group back to Malaysia,' Medcalfe said.

Gillard, Bowen and the Immigration Department were devastated. Labor had worked for a year to devise a viable policy, only to find it vetoed. In 2001 the High Court had upheld Howard's *Tampa* policy and in 2011 the High Court had gutted Gillard's Malaysia policy, a decision from which Labor's border-protection strategy never recovered.

'It was a huge blow and the rest is history,' Gillard said.[11] According to those who saw him in private, Bowen was shattered. The decision undermined Gillard's authority, left Bowen without a policy, encouraged the boats and solidified the political opposition. Bowen said all policy options were now on the table. The government refused to concede that the Malaysia agreement was finished.

This decision injected the High Court into the heart of public policy: the majority substituted its own policy for that of the Gillard Government. It was a decision heavy with hubris and short on wisdom. At the time Gillard said the judgement was 'deeply disappointing' and singled out the chief justice, Robert French, for criticism. She said the court had 'rewritten the Migration Act'. This may have been an unwise remark but it seemed accurate. The majority argued that the intent of the Migration Act as a whole is 'to facilitate Australia's compliance' with the Refugee Convention. That was a dubious claim with little historical evidence to sustain it from either parliamentary debate or administrative practice. The single dissenting judge, Dyson Heydon, attacked this interpretation, saying the Migration Act had not incorporated the Refugee Convention into Australian law 'so as to make it a direct source of rights and obligations under that law'. He argued that Bowen acted consistently with Parliament's original intention, a view that seemed persuasive on the history.

The effect of the court decision seemed to rule out offshore processing agreements with nations that had not signed the Refugee Convention—in other words, most of Australia's neighbours. It became a serious inhibition on Australia's ability to negotiate agreements to safeguard its borders. It implied even more severe tests—nations might have to prove their 'practical compliance' with convention requirements. The court found against Malaysia because it had not signed the Refugee Convention and its domestic laws did not have sufficient safeguards. A spooked solicitor-general said the decision meant PNG might not comply and there was a doubt about Nauru.

The decision confirmed migration policy as one of the defining struggles in Australian history between the judiciary on one hand and the Parliament and executive on the other. The institutions were locked in conflict—the courts and lawyers expanding the rights of non-citizen asylum seekers while governments and parliaments sought to limit such rights and curtail illegal arrivals in the national interest. Unable to win in the court of public opinion, the human rights lobby was more successful in asking the courts to deny governments the power to honour the declaration made by Howard that 'We will decide who comes to this country and the circumstances in which they come.' The High Court now told Bowen how to exercise his discretion in relation to third-country processing; its constructed legalisms were removed from the common sense of the public and interests of the nation.

The court also said an unaccompanied minor cannot be removed without the minister's written agreement reviewable in the courts. This applied even if a refugee claim had been rejected. Aware of the likely court judgement in such reviews, Bowen said this was 'not sustainable as public policy'.

It is obvious what should have happened next. The Parliament should have exercised its law-making powers to amend the Migration Act to restore appropriate authority to the executive government to negotiate offshore processing agreements. This is how democracies work. It would re-arm the current and future governments.

But Abbott's instinct was to offer Labor no concession. 'Whether it is pink batts, the NBN, live cattle or border protection, it is just one bungle after another,' he said. Shadow Attorney-General George Brandis advised Abbott that, with Nauru about to ratify the Refugee Convention, the Coalition's offshore processing plan at Nauru remained consistent with current law.

Labor was being taught again the main political lesson of the era: when the Coalition and Greens combined, Labor was the loser.

The Gillard Government now proposed amendments to allow off-shore processing with a wide discretion for the minister to determine the countries. Medcalfe, national security and DFAT officials were asked to brief the Coalition on Labor's amendments. At the end of the briefing Abbott thanked them politely but offered no solace. He disagreed with them. It was an extraordinary situation. This was the best advice on how to stop the boats, but Abbott would kill Gillard's amendments.

In Parliament Gillard stated the issue: 'Whether or not executive government, any executive government, should have the power and authority it needs to put in place and beyond legal doubt offshore pro-cessing measures'. She said Abbott's position would deny offshore pro-cessing options to a future Coalition government. Her argument was that Labor could do Malaysia and Abbott could do whatever countries he wanted.[12]

But Abbott had other priorities. 'Malaysia is a proven failure,' he said. 'Nauru is a proven success.' Why, he asked, was Gillard persisting with a proven failure? Gillard had formed minority government—if she was incapable of getting the numbers for her legislation then 'there are other options that are open to her and she should take them'.[13]

With Labor's latest Newspoll primary vote at 26 per cent, Dennis Shanahan analysed Abbott's tactics. 'His main aim is to spark an election,' Shanahan said, 'an election he would be certain to win.' Abbott's associated aim was to destroy Gillard and precipitate the transition to Rudd sooner rather than later. Abbott believed Gillard could not survive. He felt if Labor was going to change leaders, the sooner the better. 'If Abbott has to face Rudd, he wants time,' Shanahan said.[14]

In policy terms Abbott's stance would weaken border protection. It would largely permit the judiciary, not the government, to determine offshore policy—a violation of Coalition philosophy. It would guarantee more boat arrivals. It would align Abbott with the political Left in embracing the High Court judgement. It stranded Abbott in the uneasy position of pledging to stop the boats but taking a stronger stand on human rights than Labor. Abbott's position, in effect, meant tolerating more boats in his quest to undermine Gillard.

Gillard was dismayed by Abbott's stand. She asked: How could Abbott turn back boats to Indonesia but not fly people back to Malaysia? Why was one acceptable and the other a terrible immorality?

Yet Gillard had mismanaged the tactics. She was too aggressive with Abbott when she needed a concession from him. Gillard's only hope had been to announce, simultaneously with her bid to amend the Migration Act, a willingness to re-open Nauru, thereby giving Abbott a victory.

The Greens were never going to support Gillard's bill. As ideological dogmatists they were unprepared to accept political responsibility arising from the flow of boat arrivals. The onus for Labor's parliamentary defeat and the subsequent deadlock lay with Abbott. The *Australian's* foreign editor, Greg Sheridan, said this was Abbott's 'worst mistake' in the minority government parliament. But Abbott knew the political blame would be sheeted home to Gillard.

The cabinet was now forced to re-assess the situation.

Gillard's dilemma came to a head on 13 October 2011 with one of the most dramatic cabinet meetings of her prime ministership. Bowen pushed to secure a commitment to re-open Nauru in return for Abbott changing his position and accepting Labor's amendments. Gillard began the cabinet meeting by outlining the options and the debate quickly centred on Bowen's proposal. His push revealed the agitation of the ALP Right over the boats. Bowen was supported by Conroy, Burke and Shorten as well as Albanese from the Left. The New South Wales and Victorian Right, the factional base that made Gillard leader against Rudd, united behind Bowen. 'We've reached an impasse over whether it should be one or the other—let's do both,' Bowen said of Nauru and Malaysia. He wasn't naïve enough to think Abbott might succumb. But this would make Abbott's hypocrisy less tenable and more difficult politically since he would be voting against Nauru authorisation.[15] Bowen added an appeal to the Left—a substantial increase in the offshore humanitarian intake to 20 000 over four or five years.

Gillard wanted a full expression of cabinet views. As the debate continued, Burke noticed that Kim Carr was taking detailed notes. 'I was watching him,' Burke said. 'I realised he wasn't taking notes on the decision. Kim was writing down the initials of different cabinet ministers and writing down what they said.' It made Burke uneasy.[16]

Senior ministers from the Left—Combet, Macklin and Carr—opposed Bowen's proposal. So did Craig Emerson from the Right. Crucially, Rudd also opposed Bowen, arguing that Abbott would never accept the deal and Labor would make the concession for little gain. He believed Labor must stick with onshore processing. Combet said there was ten years of television footage of Gillard opposing Nauru and to switch now would deliver Abbott a political gift. Gillard said they would reconvene later.[17]

When cabinet met a second time Gillard said she could not endorse Nauru; it was a bridge too far. The government, therefore, would revert to the only option left: onshore processing. She knew it was a humiliating retreat from the stance she and Bowen had proposed initially. Yet they had been denied first by the High Court, then by the Parliament.

It was Gillard's call; Bowen was upset. Her argument was: Abbott will still say 'no' and there would be no breakthrough for Labor. That evening Gillard and Bowen announced their retreat at a joint media conference.

Their plight now transcended humiliation. Gillard wore her tragedy as a badge of stoicism. She said Labor remained committed to the Malaysian deal, to restoring the powers of executive government and to offshore processing. In the interim, however, it would recommit to a new onshore processing regime. The extent of the full political horror was almost incomprehensible. Gillard had two policies: the one in which she believed but could not implement and the one she could implement but in which she did not believe. Now she exposed this contradiction to the world.

'I do want to say this,' Gillard said. 'We are at a real risk of seeing more boats.' De-coded: I know my policy cannot work. Bowen was left with the difficult explanation. With detention centres heading to capacity, Bowen unveiled plans for a further shift to community-based detention. People would be processed quickly and given a bridging visa with limited work rights as they lived in the community. The upside was the hope of tackling the serious mental problems, depression and self-harm that were rife in many detention centres from months and years of incarceration, as documented in a range of official and informal reports.

Morrison now accused Gillard of capitulating to the Greens. He said releasing people into the community with a series of rights and benefits just guaranteed more boats. Morrison said Gillard should call an election. The iron now entered Labor's soul about Abbott: from this moment it was obvious he would get nothing, absolutely nothing, in office from Labor.[18]

Two days later Peter Hartcher had a detailed account of the cabinet meeting in the *Sydney Morning Herald*. Referring to the leak, Burke said: 'I knew. Because of where I sat in the cabinet room, I was the only one who knew. I let the Prime Minister know.' He told Gillard that Kim Carr was the leak.[19]

Gillard subsequently dumped Carr from cabinet. Asked if Carr had leaked, Gillard said: 'I don't know so, but I think so.' In truth, Gillard was finished with Carr: she felt he was disloyal in personal and policy terms.[20]
Burke said:

> At the next cabinet meeting the PM said the detailed notes of what everyone says are taken by the official note takers. There is no reason for cabinet ministers to be doing that. Later we were discussing something and the PM threw to me. Then I noticed Kim was doing it again, taking down detailed notes. I said there is an additional note taker in the room and I am not prepared to make a contribution. The room went silent. Kim Carr looked up, put down his pen and closed his notebook.[21]

Interviewed for this book, Carr said: 'I categorically deny the claim that I was responsible for the leak. The leak was against Chris Bowen, a person I am close to. I was infuriated by this allegation that she [Gillard] never put to me.'[22]

The Parliament was stalemated yet the stalemate was untenable. Labor and the Coalition both wanted offshore processing but could not agree on the terms. In November 2011 about nine hundred people arrived by boat, the highest monthly figure since Labor had taken office in 2007.

Those moral guardians of open borders remained unmoved in their morality, the most solemn being the *Age* newspaper: it now reassured its readers there was no boat people problem. That would have been news to the Prime Minister. Gillard, it editorialised, must have the 'honesty and decency' to concede 'what she must know'. Asylum seekers were not a 'political issue' at all but only a 'humanitarian issue'.[23] There are few limits to the irresponsibility of media moralists.

The December ALP National Conference proved that the Gillard–Bowen transformation of Labor policy would endure. The ALP Left and Labor for Refugees were routed by the ALP Right as the party embraced offshore processing, the policy it once assailed as immoral. Bowen and the Minister for Home Affairs, Brendan O'Connor, gave powerful speeches to the conference on this historic change. 'People smugglers are not modern-day Oscar Schindlers,' O'Connor said. 'Nothing could be further from the truth. The organisers and facilitators take their money, take their life savings, sometimes they take their lives.' The government judged that as many as 4 per cent of those who attempted the journey drowned in the Java Sea. Bowen now drew the once unthinkable nexus for the ALP: strong border protection equated to a humanitarian position.[24] Perhaps he had stopped reading the *Age*.

The ALP had now formally abandoned one of its most intense policy critiques of the Coalition in the past half-century: that Howard's 2001 *Tampa* venture was an immoral gimmick to win votes. Once Labor embraced offshore processing, this self-righteous pretence fell away. The reality was undeniable: governments had a responsibility for border protection conceived in security and humanitarian terms.

Under the Refugee Convention, Australia has obligations of non-refoulement: not to return refugees to places where they would be threatened again. These obligations apply when Australia is transferring people to third countries. It is also true, however, that refugees have no right under international law to self-select the country in which they make their claim.

The Scanlan Foundation's 2012 Social Cohesion report dissected at length public attitudes towards people movements. It found majority support for a strong immigration program, support for the long-established offshore refugee program and intense rejection of boat arrivals. The problem was not refugees as such but the mode of arrival. The public saw boat people as 'illegal immigrants' seeking a better life. Less than one in four respondents believed they were entitled to permanent residency.[25]

In December 2011, Bowen urged Gillard to write to Abbott seeking a circuit breaker, a private negotiation. There was an exchange of letters between Gillard and Abbott. Abbott's letter to Gillard was biting: 'You could, of course, declare this to be a matter of confidence and require your Green alliance partners to support your legislation. Alternatively, you could adopt our policy.'[26] Abbott's contempt was fuelled by Labor's post-2007 moral vanity when it had set about dismantling Howard's policies.

On 17 December 2011 another boat sank and 201 people drowned.[27] Cabinet, in retreat mode, now authorised Bowen to offer up Nauru in exchange for Malaysia in any negotiations.[28] Abbott refused to budge.

In January 2012 the author had dinner in Sydney with Abbott and Morrison. They came with a powerful message. Abbott systematically laid out a radically different policy to halt the boats: he would turn them on the water. He said this was a non-negotiable issue of Australian sovereignty. It was not dependent on Indonesia's cooperation. 'It is time for Australia to adopt turning the boats as its core policy,' he said. 'What counts is what the Australian Government *does*, not what it says.' Where Labor looked

to regional agreement, Abbott preferred unilateral action.[29] His approach
had one big advantage: it offered no opportunity for judicial veto.

The acting head of the Immigration Department, Martin Bowles,
told Senate estimates that smugglers watched every Australian move:
'Word of mouth is unbelievable … the network is phenomenal.' People
smuggling was a low-risk, high-profit business and a global industry with
annual profits in the range of US$3 billion to US$10 billion. Practices
were entrenched: up to 90 per cent of people reaching Australian territory
by boat destroyed documents and passports to maximise their chances
and deny their prompt return.[30] A cross-parliamentary group from all
parties began to agitate for a solution.

Reflecting her responsibility to find a breakthrough, Gillard declared
in Parliament that she would reopen Nauru in tandem with Abbott
accepting Malaysia. Yet the Coalition had convinced itself the Malaysia
option was a gulag. Morrison, repelled by what he had seen when visiting
Malaysia, said sending people to Malaysia was 'abominable'. The Greens
were high-minded in a way that could only provoke astonished admiration:
hundreds of deaths would not stain the purity of their principles.

How many deaths before the Australian Parliament would confront
its shame and end the deadlock? On 21 June 2012 another boat got into
trouble north of Christmas Island, with ninety-two people lost.[31] On
27 June news emerged of another sinking; this time the boat carried
about one hundred and fifty people; many were recovered, four drowned.
Gillard suspended Question Time to allow independent Rob Oakeshott,
seeking a compromise, to move a long-prepared bill that would allow
a government to send asylum seekers for processing to the forty-plus
nations that were signatories to the Bali process. Both Nauru and Malaysia
met this test. 'We have seen too much tragedy,' Gillard said in forcing the
debate. She was now willing to review the return of TPVs.

This triggered the most extraordinary and emotional debate in
the life of the minority Parliament. Feelings of complicity in death and
compassion for survivors drove a turbulent debate that saw members
of Parilament weeping and losing control. The emotionalism created an
unpredictable climate. The bill was carried 74 to 72 in the Lower House
with the support of crossbenchers. It was opposed by the Coalition and
the Greens.

It was a Gillard victory but, as Abbott said, a pyrrhic one. The
Coalition and the Greens had the numbers in the Senate to defeat the bill.
During the Senate debate, Chris Evans said: 'I was the one who closed
Nauru. I find this very difficult. But if we allow ourselves to be swayed by

the baggage we bring to the debate, we won't be doing our job.' Watching from his Adelaide sick bed, independent Senator Nick Xenophon said: 'The stink of compromise is better than the stench of death.'[32]

Bowen had asked the Parliament: 'Is there one single member of this House who could argue with any conviction, with any responsibility, that implementing the Malaysia arrangement and a detention centre at Nauru could not save lives?' But Abbott answered another question. 'Yesterday, today, forever—the Malaysia deal is a dud deal,' he said. 'We will never, ever support it.'[33] Abbott had a solution: change the government.

The Coalition stood on its new principle that offshore processing was only tolerable in nations that had endorsed the Refugee Convention. Consider the absurdity of the situation. Labor, having opposed offshore processing for years only to embrace the idea, now found its policy ruined by the Coalition who, under Howard, had devised offshore processing.

The defeat of Oakeshott's bill in the Senate was the nadir in this saga. The Australian Parliament was inviting the people smugglers to increase their trade to Australia. It was an unmitigated failure of Australian governance and betrayal of the public interest. The human rights concerns of Coalition MPs was not in question. But their sincerity was convenient because it defeated the Oakeshott bill, deepened Gillard's humiliation and kept the boats arriving in the knowledge that Gillard would be blamed.

The deadlock now provoked a flow of hostility towards the Greens, whose high moralism had been a feature of the debate. They paraded their compassion but closed their minds. The lion of the Labor Left, Senator Doug Cameron, savaged them. On display was a rarely analysed contemporary phenomenon—the debasement of human rights on the altar of human rights ideology. Many tears had been shed in the national Parliament. But for what result?

The result guaranteed more boats and more deaths. For the Greens, offshore processing was an immoral act, not to be tolerated under any circumstances. The vote was a triumph of ideology over common sense and of party politics over national interest. The ignominy of the minority Parliament knew few bounds.

From the trough of her ritualistic torment, Gillard kept her head. Has any prime minister borne such excoriation with such fortitude? Trying to keep the pressure on Abbott, Gillard announced an 'eminent persons' panel to assess the crisis and make fresh recommendations. It was a panel of rare quality: former chief of the Defence Force Angus Houston, former Howard adviser and DFAT chief Michael L'Estrange, and refugee advocate Paris Aristotle. Abbott said Gillard was wasting her time.

The report was unveiled six weeks later, on 13 August 2012. A sophisticated document, the Houston Report constituted the best that Australia's policy establishment could engineer. Its principles challenged both sides. The report said doing nothing was unacceptable; 'pull' factors were important; the national interest and humanitarian concerns dictated the need to dissuade boat arrivals; and regional cooperation was essential.

The report found that in the past three years more than six hundred people had drowned, a profound human tragedy. Boat arrivals had risen from twenty-five in 2007–08 to 8092 in 2011–12, four years later. They were increasing at a rapid rate. The report enshrined the idea of a long-run grand bargain—Australia must aim to have all boat arrivals processed offshore and, in return, accept refugees from the region. This report was the work of practitioners who came to terminate the deceptions that had enjoyed currency for too long. In the short term it unlocked the Nauru/ Malaysia impasse.[34]

It recommended legislation to allow offshore processing. Country designation would be achieved separately as an instrument needing parliamentary approval. Nauru and PNG should be established as venues as fast as possible. The Malaysian agreement should be re-negotiated to improve human rights protections, an unlikely prospect any time soon. The report, therefore, gave Abbott his victory and gave Gillard cover to concede his victory.

Gillard, emotional and fed up, knew what to do: her government endorsed the entire report in principle. 'Australians are sick at heart,' she said of the impasse. 'They're over it. I am over it. We're all over it.' Gillard said she would accept whatever compromises the report imposed on Labor. Legislation would be introduced immediately.[35]

Abbott would get Nauru and PNG without Malaysia, a smashing victory. Gillard was now ringing the President of Nauru and Prime Minister of PNG, as Abbott had long demanded. Australian military teams were soon in the air. Gillard said processing could begin within the month, shades of Howard in 2001. The Coalition spent the first day rubbing Labor's nose in the mud and the rest of the week crowing. Abbott was vindicated in spades. It was the final Labor repentance after the policy delusions and self-righteousness of the Rudd era.

Abbott said Labor's recant was 'four years too late'. The Coalition was supporting the bill because it was 'effectively the Opposition's bill'. Abbott threw at Gillard years of Labor's denunciation of Nauru, the Pacific Solution and offshore processing. He said Gillard had problems of character and judgement. There was a Westminister tradition, he said: given the magnitude of this reversal, 'as a matter of honour, this government should resign'.[36]

But the report's 'big picture' was unpalatable to the Coalition: it envisaged a regional model, where Indonesia and Malaysia were pivotal. Australia would increase its humanitarian intake from 13 750 to 20 000 people at once and then to 27 000 to persuade the region to embrace offshore processing for boat arrivals in Australia's territory. The panel took the 'people swap' from the Malaysia deal as the foundation for a regional strategy. Abbott and Morrison were unimpressed. This was not their vision. Abbott declined to endorse the document. He distrusted the views of the policy establishment. The report, in fact, constituted a far more serious questioning of Coalition thinking than of Labor thinking. It was specific on tow-backs: the conditions to make them viable did not yet exist. It struck at the heart of Abbott's policy.

The report enunciated a new moral concept: boat arrivals should not be accorded an advantage over people pursuing legal pathways to Australia. This became the 'no advantage' principle; it drove the human rights lobby wild. It went to the core issue: those advocates of international law who rejected government-imposed disincentives were giving preferential treatment to boat arrivals. The report said this was neither moral nor equitable. In effect, it said illegal asylum-seeker boat arrivals were chasing an advantage over more desperate people without funds to pay the smugglers. This had always been obvious. The report said asylum seekers coming by boat should wait the equivalent number of years that offshore refugees in the UN system had to wait. This was harsh, contentious and probably impractical. Yet enunciation of the principle was fundamental.

Gillard and Bowen embraced this principle. Bowen said: 'The whole panel's ethos, their outlook, their insight, is that you need to equalise treatment for asylum seekers so you don't get a better deal if you get on a boat.'[37] For Bowen, anybody who rejected this principle simply wanted to prioritise the people smugglers' option. The Greens denounced the report for espousing policies based on brutality, punishment and deterrence. Amnesty International said it was 'appalled' that the right of asylum seekers was being ignored. Panel member Paris Aristotle said his thinking had changed because he had been confronted by the reality of people missing or drowned at sea. Having dealt with families whose loved ones had left Indonesia and never arrived, he said, 'I can't really live with myself on that basis.'[38]

The Coalition backed Labor's new laws. Facilities at Nauru and PNG's Manus Island were re-opened by Labor. Gillard was authorising a new Pacific Solution based on offshore processing. Any asylum seeker arriving by boat after 13 August 2012 was liable to be sent offshore. Labor had accepted this ignominious policy retreat.

Given the delay in preparing facilities, the new policy was tested and overwhelmed by the smugglers. At the end of 2012 only 155 people had been transferred to PNG and only 414 had gone to Nauru. How the 'no advantage' principle would work was unknown.[39]

The deadlock in Australia's political system had given the people smugglers huge momentum. The policy change was too little, too late, given the asylum seeker fleets. Regional arrangements were grossly inadequate. The boats kept coming over the rest of 2012 and during 2013. The Houston Report was only partly implemented. Its grand bargain with the region never saw the light of day.

Labor's road to Damascus had been agonising: it had gone from seeing boat arrivals as a political issue to be managed (under Rudd) to realising that the boats had to be stopped as a national policy priority (under Gillard). This transformation involved a change in Labor attitudes towards boat arrivals and set the scene for an even tougher Labor commitment to offshore processing from June 2013 when Rudd returned to office.

The damage to the national interest from the stalemate was immense. Like so many of the failures of the Gillard era, the blame attaches in part to Gillard but in part to events beyond her control. The truth is that Gillard, from the time she became prime minister, knew policy must be geared to halting boat arrivals but she found this objective plagued with many obstacles.

The saga left Abbott with a special obligation. Boat arrivals triggered his most aggressive politics as Opposition leader, tougher even than his tactics on the carbon tax. There would be only one justification for Abbott's behaviour: proving in office that his own policies for stopping the boats would work. Nothing else would suffice to absolve his destruction of Gillard's policy. The early signs in 2014 were that Abbott and Morrison were more successful in halting boats that the 'experts' had predicted.

There is an enduring reality. Unless a framework for stopping the boats is effective, Australia's long-established offshore refugee intake will be wilted away and support for legal immigration will be relentlessly eroded. The public expects its government to control people movement to Australia. Rudd and Gillard were partly destroyed on this expectation.

CHAPTER 27

FEMINIST HEROINE

A s 2012 advanced, Julia Gillard took a personal and political decision: she would fight the hatred directed at her and promote her status as the first female prime minister. It was, literally, the 'coming out' of Julia, who had long declined to market her 'first woman' status. Gillard was sick to death of the sexism and misogyny.

This was a political strategy. Her adviser, John McTernan, said:

> Julia never made a fuss about being the first female prime minister of Australia. She took that decision a long time ago and she stuck to it. But while I was working for her, it got to the point where she concluded, she had none of the benefits but almost all of the dis-benefits. It wasn't working in her favour.[1]

It was time for a new approach. Sean Kelly said: 'The office had urged her for some time to make far more of her historic standing as the first female prime minister.'[2]

Gillard had previously told Emily's List, Labor's support program for progressive women candidates, that 'I never conceptualised my prime ministership around being the first woman to do this job.' She had a down-to-earth pragmatism: 'it was so obvious' she was the first woman PM 'that I didn't need to harp on about it'.[3] Yet the extent of vilification helped her to reassess.

The decision Gillard took was subtle but transforming: to publicise her private experience. She was aware of two related phenomena. Men and women would ask her to sign mementoes 'for my daughter'. Often, they would add the disclaimer 'I'm not a Labor voter, but ...' Invariably, they liked Julia. The connection as the first woman to be prime minister was real. It meant something to people. Yet this prized asset had never been properly mobilised. The compulsion to act was also driven by the hostility to Julia, notably from social media. The political logic became irrefutable: Gillard was being undermined as a woman and was not obtaining the benefit from being a woman.[4]

In politics vacuums will be filled. Neither Gillard's office nor Labor had marketed Gillard to the Australian public as a new prime minister by encompassing her story, character and passions. This was politics 101. The upshot is that her enemies did the job.

The famous misogyny speech was spontaneous. But it did not fall out of a clear blue sky. It sprang from the political context of the minority-government Parliament being the most venomous since 1974–75 under Whitlam. Many of Gillard's critics focused on her gender, a sad and contemptible feature of the time.

But gender fed into other dimensions. Gillard once told Barrack Obama: 'You think it's tough being African–American. Try being me. Try being an atheist, childless, single woman as prime minister.'[5] Gillard knew this profile was a negative for her. But she also appreciated Australian tolerance, aware that if born American it would have been 'inconceivable' that she would have become US president. American values on the matters of religion and family would never have allowed that. It was, therefore, 'very nice' that Australians did not disbar her just for being atheist, single and childless.[6] Yet these characteristics were relevant; many Australians did not like them.

It was stereotype piled upon stereotype. The manifestations and tone changed from social media to mainstream media to parliamentary combat. On Facebook and internet postings, Gillard was depicted naked with a strap-on dildo, her face was superimposed on a naked woman masturbating, she was presented as a slut having affairs with married men and was vilified and demeaned in numerous ways. 'You wouldn't be human if you had no reaction to it,' she said.[7] In August 2012, Gillard named former newspaper cartoonist Larry Pickering for his 'vile and sexist website' about her and for the material he sent to federal parliamentarians.

Feminist and Gillard champion Anne Summers tied the Liberal Party and Abbott to the sexist campaign but not to its worst features. She referred to Abbott's line that Gillard should 'make an honest woman of herself' by taking the carbon tax to an election. Liberal Senator Bill Heffernan had claimed she chose 'to deliberately remain barren'. CEO of the Australian Agricultural Company, David Farley, indirectly likened Gillard to a 'non-productive old cow'.[8] In July 2011 broadcaster Alan Jones said on his program: 'Quite frankly they should shove her and Bob Brown in a chaff bag and take them as far out to sea as they can and tell them to swim home.'

During her time in office, Gillard's hair, appearance, body shape and clothes excited much commentary. She was targeted not just by men but by women—witness Germaine Greer's comments on ABC TV's *Q&A* about her 'big arse', to much laughter from the ABC audience. This complicated the situation: evidently the reaction to abuse was a function of who delivered it. That could determine whether it was smart or deplorable. Gillard took great care with her appearance; it was part of her disciplined professionalism. Yet the double standard became more obvious, something that struck Gillard even after losing office.

She could hardly avoid noticing how Rudd was treated when he returned as prime minister. Did the media comment about his appearance? No. Did the media remark he had put on weight? No. Gillard's appearance was a constant story but Rudd's appearance was a non-story. Gillard was not criticising Rudd. But she felt most of the media had double standards according to gender.

Treatment of Gillard mirrored the coarsening of private space and public debates. Language and images that once carried heavy sanction were either tolerated or acceptable or presented as funny. On mainstream media, the ABC led the way. It ran a television series designed to belittle her, part of its wider cultural disposition to break established norms. The death of shame became the chorus on social media, where people advertised their hates, prejudices, secrets and sexual lives. This process was far from limited to Gillard; within politics Abbott, for years, was a constant target on two fronts—his religion and his alleged misogyny.

Academic Susan Mitchell, who wrote a book about Abbott, accused him of an 'innate and deeply embedded sexism and misogyny'; regular ABC literary critic Marieke Hardy said on her blog: 'I hope your cock drops off and falls down a plughole'; comedian and former Fairfax columnist Catherine Deveny mocked his ears, religion and views on virginity. Respected journalist David Marr referred to Abbott as a 'loudmouth bigot' and 'homophobe' at university. The abuse of Abbott, usually by women, was prominent in the mainstream media, reflecting prejudice towards his 'man's man' masculinity, Christianity and social values. It was becoming more acceptable to attack public figures for their appearance and values.

From August 2012, Labor's campaign against Abbott's attitude to women reached a new intensity, orchestrated by senior female cabinet ministers. It was buttressed by a media strategy devised by Gillard's office to exploit her status as a female prime minister. The ALP detected a rising current against Abbott as more prominent women attacked him.

Tanya Plibersek said Abbott had a problem with 'women in positions of authority'. Gillard branded him 'Jack the Ripper' in Parliament but had to withdraw. Nicola Roxon said Abbott was 'not very comfortable with capable women'. It was an assault on Abbott's character. On the defensive, Abbott replied that 'I take directions from women every day.' His defence became that he had a wife, three daughters, a woman as his chief of staff and a woman as his deputy leader.

The polls showed Abbott had a 'women problem'. It was the flip side of Gillard's even more serious 'men problem'. Gender had become an electoral fault line in the Gillard–Abbott minority-government contest. With Labor facing defeat, its weakness drove reliance on a tactic of discrediting Abbott. The technique was to mobilise all the vilification directed at Gillard and turn it back at Abbott. It was a problem for him because 'Have you stopped being a misogynist yet?' was the question that had no acceptable answer. Labor's risk, however, was that its ministerial 'handbag' hit squad might signal a poor government unable to campaign on its record.

At this point the Liberals replied with a calculated intervention by Margie Abbott, an intensely private person. In political terms she had no choice. 'I won't stand by and let others claim that the man I love and the father my children adore has some agenda against women,' she said in a double spread interview in the *Daily Telegraph* five days before Gillard's misogyny speech. 'I know these distortions are not true and [I] have decided to speak up in response to these personal and groundless attacks.' The script was perfect: she said Abbott, far from being a misogynist, actually 'gets women'. She talked about their home life: the mortgage, caring for family, enjoying work and community.[9]

These events precipitated the 'coming out' of Margie and, over time, the Abbott daughters, Louise, Frances and Bridget. To the extent that Labor forced Abbott's hand with the projection of his family, it was a blunder. The framing of the family in 2013 became a tangible factor in softening Abbott's image.

The trigger for Gillard's speech was the death of her father, whom she loved dearly. On Saturday 22 September, Alan Jones had spoken at a Sydney University Liberal Club private function. 'The old man recently died a few weeks ago of shame,' Jones told his audience of Gillard's father. 'To think that he had a daughter who told lies every time she stood for Parliament. Every person in the caucus of the Labor Party knows that Julia Gillard is a liar.'

It was inexcusable. When the comments were published, Jones had no option but to apologise. The backlash was ferocious. An effective social media campaign was organised against Jones and the main advertisers on his program. The Macquarie network was forced into pre-emptive action and suspended all advertising for a week to prevent death by a thousand cuts. Jones survived but the revenue was damaged. Gillard said she would never speak to him again; Swan said he should be removed from the airwaves.

Abbott mishandled the issue. His criticism of Jones, demanded by the media, was too weak and too delayed. It became an open invitation for cabinet ministers to hammer his 'women problem'. It revealed an Abbott characteristic—loyalty to friends. His lame criticism was that Jones was 'completely out of line'. It wasn't enough. Abbott was wrong on timing and content; wrong on his failure to condemn Jones.

Yet the campaign by senior cabinet ministers to nail Abbott as the real culprit became ludicrous. Roxon now blamed Abbott for Jones's remarks saying 'he has to be held responsible'. Albanese said that for Abbott there was 'nothing too low'. For Labor, the target was Abbott, not Jones.[10] The government was not dissuaded by Margie Abbott's intervention that same week. Indeed, Labor interpreted the response of the Abbott camp as evidence that he was being damaged. With Parliament about to resume on Tuesday 9 October, *Herald* correspondent Phillip Coorey reported that 'the climate of personal attacks is set to intensify'. Roxon insisted Abbott was 'fair game' because of his behaviour and comments about women.

Yet Labor was mugged from behind and left scrambling and embarrassed. As a result of a sexual harassment case against the Speaker, Peter Slipper, initiated by his former aide, James Ashby, a long series of text messages from Slipper were now released by the Federal Court. Slipper, a defector from the Coalition, had been recruited by Labor and installed as Speaker in a move that strengthened Gillard's numbers on the floor. Labor was now politically responsible for Slipper. He had stood aside from duties but remained as Speaker pending the outcome of the court case. Slipper was Gillard's man and detested as a 'rat' by the Coalition.

The text messages revealed a strange mind and became exhibits of sexism and misogyny. Slipper allegedly described female genitalia as 'shell-less mussells' [sic], made jokes about this notion and endorsed a description of Sophie Mirabella as 'an ignorant botch' [sic]. Shadow Attorney George Brandis accused Gillard of protecting 'the most vile, misogynist person it is possible to imagine'. Gillard was about to be caught by an ancient law of politics: only set moral standards you can uphold. At this point another woman emerged as enforcer.

Julie Bishop had grown close to Abbott and she was appalled by Labor's misogyny assault against him. She believed the motive was political gain, not concern about misogyny at all. Now the evidence stared her in the face. Bishop was furious. Her deepest anger was for female Labor ministers and what she saw as their manipulations. Bishop publicly called on Gillard to withdraw her support from Slipper because of his 'obscene, sexist and misogynist remarks'. Bishop was determined to nail Labor for its hypocrisy. She told shadow cabinet Slipper's position was 'untenable', that he had to be removed, that he had forfeited the respect of the office. The Coalition decided to strike.[11]

By Tuesday morning, 9 October, the media coverage of Slipper's remarks sealed the issue: he was finished. That the Labor brains trust missed this conclusion was extraordinary. Any political correspondent worthy of the name knew Slipper was terminal by 9.30 a.m. that day. The tidal wave of revulsion was irresistible—everywhere but inside the Gillard Government. It was so imprisoned by its propagandistic view of the world that it failed to perceive the world as it existed. Abbott planned to move against Slipper that afternoon but the Coalition feared that Labor would move first, aware that Slipper was now untenable.[12]

In fact, Abbott's 'no confidence' motion at 2.07 p.m., moving that Slipper be removed from office, took Labor by surprise. Abbott said Slipper was no longer 'a fit and proper person' to be Speaker. He quickly shifted the attack to Gillard: she had made Slipper the Speaker, an event engineered for self-preservation. Abbott declared that Gillard 'will lose her Speaker' and may soon lose her own job. Every day that Gillard defended Slipper would be a 'day of shame' for the Parliament and government. Abbott finished on this note.[13]

'How the women in this House can be expected to show respect to the Speaker when we are now aware of the views that he holds of women is beyond comprehension,' Bishop said following Abbott in debate. She said Gillard's selection of Slipper for Speaker was now exposed as a 'grave error of judgement'. Slipper was still drawing his salary. In a speech sharper than Abbott's, Bishop turned the knife against Gillard. She said it was a matter of pride for Gillard to refuse to admit mistakes. But this issue went beyond Gillard—the office of Speaker was at the heart of democracy.[14]

Gillard had no defence. She was backing Slipper but had no argument. Occasionally in a major debate the argument is so overwhelming that no tenable case can be mounted. This was such an occasion. Slipper

was exposed as a sexist, violating the same principles Gillard and her ministers had invoked to attack Abbott. But Gillard's political frustration came
second to another instinct: outrage at being lectured on sexism by Abbott.
She sat there fermenting: how dare he give her lectures about sexism.

Julia now let go. She released the pent-up rage accumulated over
two years of insults from Abbott, from Jones, from Pickering. She spoke
not just for herself; she was honouring her father. McTernan said: 'I think
Julia felt, "You can say what you like about me, but don't touch my dad.
Don't you come anywhere near my father." This was a reaction from the
grieving period.'[15]

From her opening sentence Gillard issued a cry from the heart, a
cry of anger and accusation. 'I will not be lectured about sexism and
misogyny by this man,' she thundered, pointing across the table. 'I will
not. The government will not be lectured about sexism and misogyny
by this man—not now, not ever.' She had no prepared speech, just a
few quotes from Abbott. It was an authentic outpouring. Gillard made it
deeply personal. 'I was very offended,' she said, by Abbott's past statements
on abortion, his remarks about housewives doing the ironing, when he
talked about making 'an honest woman of herself' and when he stood
near the rally sign saying 'Ditch the witch'.

'It is misogyny, sexism, every day from the Leader of the Opposition,'
she said. Ripping open her pulsating emotions, Gillard now plunged the
knife into Abbott. 'The government is not dying of shame,' she said. 'And
my father did not die of shame.' The Coalition benches were silent and
shocked. Yes, Gillard said, she was offended by Slipper's messages, but there
was a court case underway and the Parliament should let that conclude
first. It was a fig leaf.

This was a speech without precedent in the Parliament. It revealed
Gillard, above all, as the political professional. Holding a weak hand, she
threw the switch to high emotion and took the misogynist accusation to
a new intensity. Gillard was angry but it was controlled anger. She knew
what she was doing. After she sat down Gillard said she wanted to do
some correspondence. Swan told her: 'Listen, you have just given one of
the big speeches, the Australian version of *J'accuse*, so you might want to
sit there for a while.'[16]

Yet Slipper was finished. As the debate raged, Tony Windsor and Rob
Oakeshott went to see Slipper in his office. Windsor had previously read
the reports of Slipper's messages and was alarmed. Oakeshott believed
Slipper's position was untenable as soon as Abbott moved his motion.
They told an emotional Slipper that waiting for the court process to

finish (the Gillard fig leaf) was no longer feasible; he would have to resign. Windsor and Oakeshott were right: time had expired. They cut a deal—the independents would vote against Abbott's motion so Slipper would not be humiliated but he had to resign before the day was out. The independents had taken responsibility; they had done the job and procured the essential outcome.[17]

Abbott's motion was defeated 70 to 69 but unbeknown to most MPs, that victory was a face-saving formula to allow Slipper to resign. He resigned with a choking voice just after 7 p.m., offering an apology for his text messages. This is the result Labor should have negotiated that morning. The upshot is that Labor got the result it needed—it denied Abbott any victory but saw Slipper accept the inevitable. On the merit of the case, Gillard was caught out, having launched a ferocious speech in defence of Slipper only to see him quit a few hours later.

There were two opposing views of Gillard's speech. The political correspondents found against her on hypocrisy. Peter Hartcher said Gillard chose to defend her numbers, that she made an 'unprincipled' decision and by excusing Slipper's sexism she 'chose to defend the indefensible'. Dennis Shanahan said Slipper had shown better judgement than Gillard.

The alternative feminist/social media view was that Gillard had inspired women all around the world. 'Here was a woman saying "It happened to me and I don't like it",' said Anne Summers. She argued it was 'empowering for women everywhere'. Gillard had given women the strength to take a stand.[18] From Gillard's office Sean Kelly said: 'I think the speech did her good—she came over as human and passionate.'[19]

Gillard had redefined her leadership. Asked about her speech she said: 'I've had enough. Australian women have had enough. When I see sexism and misogyny I'm going to call them for what they are.'[20] Her female ministers closed ranks behind Gillard; that meant intensifying their attacks upon Abbott. Wong said Abbott should take responsibility for his sexist remarks by resigning, like Slipper. Plibersek said Abbott's language was the same as Slipper's. Jenny Macklin said Abbott's behaviour showed it was 'true' to say he had a hatred of women and girls.[21] The misogyny speech had seen reason fly out the window.

Julie Bishop retorted: 'Labor is trying to inoculate Julia Gillard against any criticism. She trashed her own public support and the sense of national pride in having the first female prime minister.'

Contrary to feminist claims, the speech did not help Gillard survive. It was seen as a triumph only within the progressive and social media classes. ALP National Secretary George Wright delivered the realism:

'We needed women with three kids working part-time to pay off the mortgage in the outer suburbs—"What does that mean to me? I'm still getting up at 6 a.m. to make the sandwiches."There was no point of connection with her.'

Wright nailed the paradox:

> The speech was seen through the lens of politics but I don't think its power came from either politics or Tony Abbott. Why did a million people look at it [online]? Because they saw an identification with their own life. It was more about gender relations than politics. There's nothing in the research to show it had a large impact on the political situation.[22]

The gender polarisation remained till Gillard was deposed nine months later. She substituted feminism for female stoicism. She held meetings with mummy bloggers, fired up the feminist lobby and ignited what had been lacking: passion about her identity. Gillard was proud of the stand she took. Something of her inner self had been released.

Gillard's tragedy is that she defined herself as a female prime minister by accusing Abbott of misogyny. This should not have become the benchmark. There should have been a better, more celebratory way. Launching a gender war made her feminist heroine to a minority but only deepened the suspicions of the majority. Yet the honour she showed her father's memory cannot be denied.

It was a political speech and needs to be assessed as a political speech. Judged by this standard it failed to change the dynamic in the country. It worried Abbott because its fallout was unpredictable. Yet Gillard played too many blame games—against business, media and misogynists. Labor got too hooked on the 'demonising Abbott' drug. In June 2013, when Gillard was deposed, the Labor vote had sunk to rock bottom. It had a lethal gender split. Stony and silent, men moved with grim determination to vote Gillard down. The collapse in the male vote was a factor in her demise.

CHAPTER 28

CHASING THE SURPLUS

O n 20 December 2012, in the shadow of Christmas, Treasurer Wayne Swan announced what every good economist knew: that Labor's three-year-old pledge to return the budget to surplus by 2012–13 was dashed. This was more than a fiscal miscalculation. It was the first and longest policy commitment made by Julia Gillard as prime minister. Labor failed its own test. It bet the house on the return to surplus and lost.

Treasury Secretary Martin Parkinson had warned Swan and his office since July that the surplus was most unlikely. Swan had suspected he would need an 'exit' strategy. The embarrassment was acute. 'Failure is not an option,' Gillard said in 2010 of the surplus goal. More recently, in a bizarre speech to the BCA annual dinner in mid-November, Gillard said Australia's budget was 'one of the seven economic wonders of the modern world.' But not wonderful enough.

Seven months earlier, in his fateful May 2012 budget speech, Swan had announced the surplus. He began with his famous declaration about the 'four years of surpluses I announce tonight'. Swan said he was delivering the 2012–13 surplus 'on time, as promised' and with 'surpluses each year after that'. The jeers from the Coalition benches were spontaneous and long. Shadow Treasurer Joe Hockey had long ago stuck his neck out, declaring that Labor would not achieve its surplus. He could have looked a mug. But Hockey was never persuaded by Swan, certainly not that May 2012 night when the budget forecasts showed the sunlit uplands of the surplus had arrived.

Five days before Christmas, Hockey would be vindicated. He had said the Rudd–Gillard era would never bring down a surplus budget and he was proved correct. Labor's failure on the surplus accentuated its core defect: over-promising and under-delivering.

The numbers Swan produced in the May 2012 budget had hardly been convincing—razor-thin surpluses of $1.5 billion and $2 billion for the first two years of the 'return to surplus' phase. Many analysts were highly sceptical. The slightest setback would sink the objective. The scale of the forecast turnaround was astonishing since a projected 2011–12 deficit of $44 billion (equivalent to 3 per cent of GDP) would become a $1.5 billion surplus in twelve months. This was fiscal acrobatics.

Announcing the failure in December, Swan said it was not Labor's fault. 'It's not because the government is spending too much,' he said. 'It's because we didn't collect the amount of taxes that we expected to collect.' There had been a 'sledgehammer' to revenues. Swan said the total revenue shortfall since the GFC had been $160 billion over five years. Again, in 2012–13 revenues had fallen away faster than forecast. Iron ore prices had fallen 38 per cent between June and September. He said Labor had kept making 'responsible savings' but it couldn't match the ongoing revenue downgrade. It was one of the biggest fiscal apologies in history.

Despite the excuses, it was the government's fault. It was Swan's fault as treasurer. In Australian politics governments are responsible for their budgets. The world is a volatile place and commodity prices are highly volatile. Treasurers must make provision for such volatility. Each budget since the post-GFC recovery, the revenue had fallen short; each budget Labor had miscalculated; each budget the 'bottom line' was worse than expected. Labor kept making the same mistake. Swan kept getting the forecasts wrong. The 'sledgehammer' was the flip side to excessively optimistic Labor forecasts.

From the position of December 2012, Swan said it would be irresponsible to impose more spending restraint to achieve a surplus. That would risk throttling the economy. At this point it was too late, the cause was lost. Cutting deeper and harder merely to realise the surplus goal didn't make sense. The business community and most economists agreed. More serious action should have been taken in the previous years.

There are two benchmark moments for Labor's economic policy. The first was its delivery of positive growth in the March quarter 2010, thereby averting a recession in the GFC. The second was this December 2012 abandonment of the budget surplus timetable. The narrative would be complete: in 2007 Rudd inherited a sizable surplus from Howard and in 2013 he passed on a sizable deficit to Abbott. The Liberal version of history—that its task is to clean up after Labor—would be vindicated. Labor will hate and dispute this statement but it is irrefutable. For Tony Abbott the abandoned surplus was money for jam: 'This is a government you simply can't trust. You can't trust it on the budget. You can't trust it with the truth.'[1]

A sympathetic Paul Keating said: 'I wouldn't have hung on to the surplus pledge for as long as Wayne did.'[2] Swan, in fact, had been trapped. He could have ditched the surplus pledge earlier, notably in 2011 using the European crisis as his rationale. That would have been superior timing to late 2012. But Swan, as treasurer, loathed the idea of bucking to failure. He held out until the end, hoping events would break his way. In fact, they broke against him, leaving Labor's fiscal credentials in tatters at the start of the 2013 election year. Swan was philosophical, telling the author: 'Maybe we would have been better to get out earlier, look that's probably right. I think it's a 50–50 judgement.'[3]

The media focus on the surplus retreat obscured the relatively sound condition of the economy. Unemployment was 5.2 per cent, growth was near trend and interest rates were low. Yet Labor would not recover from the consequences of its lost surplus.

Why was the surplus so important to Swan and Gillard? The short answer is that Labor had to prove its economic credentials. The surplus pledge was tied to Labor's fears and dreams. Rudd, Swan and Gillard came to office promising to be fiscal conservatives. Their 2008–09 stimulus to combat the GFC was justified on the basis that they would return to surplus; Gillard won office at the 2010 election on Rudd's surplus promise; the Gillard–Swan Government operated on this foundation; the pledge was invoked repeatedly by Gillard and Swan to vest their economic efforts with a golden glow. So frequent were Labor's surplus pledges that it seemed the government got confused into thinking promising the surplus equated to its delivery.

What was the origin of the pledge?

Once again, all roads lead back to the 2010 election and the pre-election May budget. Labor and Treasury had undergone a truly astonishing transformation. Having been far too pessimistic about the GFC downturn in 2008–09, warning about the deepest and darkest gloom since the Great Depression, Labor stumbled into a Pollyanna world of sunny horizons and glorious economic upturns. Once introduced to this world by the Treasury, Labor needed no encouraging. An impeccable source said: 'Having decided this would be a different and deeper recession because of its financial origins, Treasury now decided the recovery would be rather normal.' It was a serious mistake. The Treasury said the recovery would be V-shaped; it would be quick and steep.

The budget forecast a sharp growth resurgence—3.25 per cent in 2010–11 leaping to a remarkable 4 per cent in 2011–12. 'Our economy and fiscal position remain the strongest in the world,' Swan said. Having escaped recession, Labor was plunging into hubris territory. Swan announced the budget would return to surplus in three years' time. That was three years ahead of the schedule outlined during the GFC. Australia would return to surplus 'ahead of every advanced economy'. It would beat the world, yet again.

Swan's senior adviser, Jim Chalmers, captured the mood: 'There was lots of enthusiasm, including from me, for us to hit the more aspirational target and to go to the people in that year's election with a responsible plan to be back in surplus light-years ahead of comparable countries, within the term that was to follow.'[4] Chalmers said that, in putting the budget together, Treasury forecasts showed a return to surplus in three years or even two years, if more work was done. But this decision with its political consequences was Swan's responsibility. He decided to put the pledge up in lights. Labor invited judgement according to this test.

Treasury's optimism ran strong. In his post-budget speech Ken Henry predicted the accumulation of surpluses 'would likely be quite prolonged'.[5] Revealing a misplaced exuberance, Swan told the National Press Club: 'Growth is rebounding, revenues are returning and surplus is within sight.'[6] Unfortunately for Labor and the country, the surplus was not in sight. Indeed, it would eventually grow more distant. Swan called it a 'no frills' pre-election budget; he looked Mr Responsibility. Chalmers said the media sell in the budget lock-up was easy: 'back in black'.

The original mining tax was pivotal to Swan's surplus strategy. Anyone who doubts this should examine the 2010–11 budget. Across the forward estimates the mining tax provided $12 billion of $30 billion in so-called 'saves'. It was easily the main contributor. Labor's hopes for the mining tax were immense—yet it would suffer political detonation within weeks.

In 2010 nobody was demanding this faster surplus timetable. But for Labor, the political dividend was powerful. This could make a difference to the election result. It provided the perfect weapon to rebut the Abbott–Hockey attack over debt and deficits. It verified Swan's mantra that Labor 'would be Keynesians on the way down and Keynesians on the way up' (using public-sector stimulus when the economy was weak and winding spending back when the economy rebounded). This could empower Labor at the election: Rudd, having saved the nation during the GFC, was now reverting to fiscal conservative virtue. How clever was Labor? Gillard understood. As prime minister, she recruited the forecast surplus to bolster her reputation. It was guaranteed, she said—'no ifs, no buts: it will happen'. Her promise would be dishonoured two and a half years later.

Interviewed for this book former Finance Minister Penny Wong said what nobody else would admit: the May 2010 high-profile surplus pledge was a mistake. Wong was qualified but her meaning is unmistakable. She said: 'In hindsight, the strategic error Labor made was to turn an economic forecast into a political commitment. But this should not overshadow the substantive achievement of delivering growth during the world's biggest financial crisis since the Great Depression.'[7]

In hindsight, there seems no other way to see the promise. Nobody imposed it upon Labor and nobody but Labor was responsible for its non-delivery. Yet the pluses from Swan's decision were substantial. It imposed a discipline on the government and made its fiscal rules highly relevant: budget surpluses over the medium term, keeping tax as a share of GDP to the 2007–08 level (23.5 per cent of GDP) and holding real spending growth to 2 per cent a year until the budget returned to a distinct surplus. The cynics will scoff, but the surplus pledge meant the restraint in the Gillard years was firmer than it otherwise would have been.

An early warning of danger came from Deloitte Access Economics partner Chris Richardson: 'What many people don't realise is that our economy and—even more so—our budget have changed enormously since 2003. Where the budget balance settles from here is very much a function of where commodity prices settle from here. The budget comes with a "Made in China" stamp these days.' In late 2009, Ken Henry said the impact of the GFC on China and India 'hadn't been nearly as large as many feared' and that they seemed 'likely to support relatively high commodity prices, that is prices for Australian export commodities, for a considerable period of time, quite possibly for some decades'.

Richardson disagreed. 'We think the renewed commodity price crescendo won't last, even though it is currently back with a vengeance,' he said in September 2010. 'Australia's fiscal finances, both short-term and long-term, are hostage to the fate of commodity prices and hence to China's strength. If China (and other emerging economies) stumble badly, then the revenue landscape will resemble that of the Somme in 1916.'[8] In November 2011, Richardson issued another warning: the risk on commodity prices meant the budget might be 'a house of cards—an accident waiting to happen'.

Swan was aware of the risks. Who controlled the budget: the Treasurer or China? Swan, naturally, liked to think he controlled the budget enough to dictate the surplus timetable. Labor, in fact, was taking an optimistic bet on commodity prices. Swan understood.

Before the May 2011 budget, Swan gave a speech entitled 'A Tale of Two Booms' documenting how mining boom Mark Two following the GFC was different from mining boom Mark One during 2003–08. The exchange rate was now far higher, the competitive pressure on the rest of the economy was greater, the two-speed economy was more pronounced and, above all, the second boom would not deliver 'the surge in revenues' of the first boom. This was because the terms of trade, having escalated from 2003, would now fall back and because company and capital gains receipts were no longer so strong. It was a boom but Canberra's treasury chest was vulnerable.[9] This led to Swan's main message: tough budget decisions would be required to achieve the surplus. Never a truer word was spoken.

The problem, however, was that the decisions had to be tougher than Swan calculated.

As the financial headwinds got stronger after the August 2010 election, the government faced two viable options: it could have abandoned the surplus pledge earlier, as Keating suggested, or it could have made a more substantial policy effort to reach the surplus starting with the May 2011 post-election budget. But Labor did neither.

It hedged its bets; it offered a mix of spending restraint, tax increases and new programs. It tried to skate to surplus too easily and got caught. The pivotal budget issue in the Gillard–Swan era was whether Labor's spending could be sustained by the tax base. In the end, it couldn't. Labor's budgets—2011, 2012 and 2013—lacked the collective fiscal fortitude necessary to 'be Keynesians on the way up'.

Cabinet minister Craig Emerson told the author: 'I believe we should have done more in the early years of the final term. We should have gone earlier and harder on the surplus.' These are brave and defining comments, striking at the heart of the Gillard–Swan economic reputation. The evidence verifies Emerson's view.[10]

This conclusion does not deny Labor's achievements. It advanced a series of reforms with a keen eye for budget discipline, many driven by Jenny Macklin. It introduced means testing of Family Tax Benefit Part B at a $150 000 threshold. It pioneered a paid parental leave scheme, recognising this was an Australian social policy weakness. Labor's PPL model was limited, tied to the minimum wage, paid for eighteen weeks, did not involve any levy on companies and was geared to the less well-off. It tightened rules on the disability support pension and Macklin pushed the idea of income maintenance. Labor's means testing of the private health insurance rebate, one of the fastest growing areas of government spending—a move opposed by the Coalition—would deliver hefty structural savings.

From the 2011 budget, however, Labor failed to make the overall structural savings required. It was bringing down Labor-values budgets ('Labor to its bootstraps' was Swan's usual mantra) involving justified redistribution towards lower-income earners, often with a $150 000 threshold point dividing winners and losers. It was pouring funds into households (to counter 'it's not my mining boom' sentiment and to compensate for the carbon tax). There were extra family benefits, the schoolkids bonus, a new aged-care system, and income tax reforms to assist the low paid. Spending in the traditional Labor areas of health, education and welfare stayed strong. There was a redistribution from companies to households and from defence to social policy.

There were no horror budgets, no intense pain. While Labor was in political trouble, that did not originate from tough decisions in Swan's budgets. The cuts were cautious. It was sugar-coated austerity. The pre-budget bark was worse than the budget-night bite. There was a regular pattern: substantial savings would be partially offset by new spending. The biggest savings measure in the May 2011 budget was the flood levy. In the May 2012 budget the 'return to surplus' relied heavily on tax rises and defence cuts. Indeed, the defence budget was cut to below 1.6 per cent of GDP, the lowest since the Munich peace marches of the 1930s—a decision most unlikely to have come under Rudd.

At this point the economics editor of the *Financial Review*, Alan Mitchell, said the fiscal consolidation 'should have been started earlier' and have delivered a 'much larger surplus' than forecast.[11] The *Australian*'s David Uren warned 'many areas of spending are rising rapidly while revenue is weak'. He said the budget was designed 'to look good rather than be good'.[12] The mining tax and the carbon tax would quickly lose their revenue power while spending from current programs would grow strongly. The *Australian*'s Judith Sloan correctly warned that the strong forecast increase in tax revenues would not be delivered. Analysing spending from the early 2013 perspective, Chris Richardson said: 'Close to half of the total lift in spending recorded at the height of the GFC remains part of the most recent budget bottom line.'[13]

'We now started to see that none of the structural work had been done,' BCA chief executive Jennifer Westacott told the author of the May 2012 budget.[14] Business community scepticism reached new heights. Welcoming the surplus, the BCA said 'the test will be in the delivery'. The BCA had given up: it called for a commission of audit to do the job Labor had failed to do. Eventually Abbott would establish it.

Australia, in fact, had mismanaged the terms-of-trade boom on the way up and on the way down. On the way up the Howard Government had spent the proceeds of the boom when, despite its budget surpluses, it should have saved more. Because the revenue gains were temporary it was vital to save much of the windfall. That would have left the nation stronger to manage the fall in the terms of trade. Labor's fiscal laxity was probably not as great as Howard's post-2003.

Meanwhile Gillard set the scene for what is best called the end-of-empire collision. In 2012 Gillard broke free of Rudd's chains—she got the chance, beyond carbon pricing, to put her personal stamp on Labor policy and the nation. She embraced two reforms: a National Disability Insurance Scheme (NDIS) and a new model for school funding based on a report chaired by prominent businessman David Gonski. These reforms invoked Gough Whitlam in their scope and cost. Gillard wanted her own agenda for the 2013 election; she wanted these schemes negotiated and legislated, presenting any Abbott government with a fait accompli. She wanted to ensure that her time as prime minister would leave a legacy for the ages.

The NDIS was bipartisan, with Abbott committing at an early stage. The Gonski reforms were fought by the Coalition yet, at election eve, they beat a tactical retreat. These were Labor-values reforms, designed to rekindle Labor idealism and voting support. The origins of the NDIS lay in a Productivity Commission report initiated by Bill Shorten as parliamentary secretary; the Gonski report sprang from Gillard's early days as Education minister and her quest to find a better way to allocate public funds.

From 2012 Gillard pursued these goals with tenacity and aggression. At every point she sought to mobilise the reforms against the Coalition for electoral gain. With the ALP primary vote on 32 per cent, John McTernan explained Gillard's election tactics:

> We had to concede the public had turned away from us. We had to avoid a vote on our own record, which is what Abbott wanted every day. That meant finding a way to ask the public to think again, to take another look at Julia Gillard and at Abbott. Our plan was to have an election not about the past but about the future— Gillard's agenda versus Abbott's agenda. It is about the future. It is a binary choice.[15]

On these issues Gillard paraded as a transformational leader. The 2011 Productivity Commission report on disability was so powerful that both sides signed up. The report condemned the system for the disabled as 'inequitable, fragmented and inefficient'. Support was delivered by welfare, charity and family. Many carers were chained to this life till they died, often forced to re-prove their child's disability to every new agency. The report documented a policy shambles that diminished the lives of more than 400 000 disabled Australians and was a condemnation of the nation as a civilised place.

It made the status quo untenable. It recommended that disability shift from welfare to an insurance concept, that the national government take responsibility and that a new funding system was required. 'As I spoke to various groups it was obvious that they were poor and they lacked political power,' Shorten told the author. 'The case for reform had to be based in economics. It couldn't just rely upon emotion.'[16]

Responsibility fell to one of Labor's best ministers, Jenny Macklin, whose dedication to the cause and piloting of the process were impressive. 'This is the area of Australian social policy where the national effort has been the weakest until the last couple of years,' Macklin said. The commission recommended a national insurance scheme that gave all people coverage for long-term disability support (not for lost income). The insurance principle was designed to encourage best practice. The scheme would apply to people with current and future disability. The required extra funding would be huge. The commission recommended financing from consolidated revenue, with a tax levy an alternative but 'inferior' option.[17]

Gillard introduced the NDIS bill on the last sitting day of 2012, saying it was based on a 'simple moral insight: disability can affect any of us and therefore it affects all of us'. Launch sites would begin from mid-2013. Gillard called the scheme 'the greatest change to Australian social policy in a generation'. It would be a Labor achievement, like Medicare and universal superannuation. Gillard announced no funding mechanism. Abbott said: 'When it comes to the NDIS, I am Doctor Yes. There is no negativity in the Coalition towards the NDIS.' Abbott rejected the view that the NDIS 'uniquely represents the values of just one side of politics'. He had asked for a bipartisan parliamentary committee on the design but Labor refused.

Gillard brow-beat the Liberal states into agreement. The Liberal premiers, initially reluctant to put up funds for NDIS trials, were easy prey for Gillard as she accused them of not really caring about the disabled. They had no hope against her. Gillard dismissed the doubters as 'policy weaklings who lack the capacity or will for a change this fundamental'. She scorned those who doubted the nation could afford the reform.[18]

The Productivity Commission had estimated the full cost at about $13.5 billion each year, later revised upwards. It dwarfed virtually any other policy initiative of the Rudd–Gillard era. In mid-2012, Queensland Premier Campbell Newman suggested a tax levy to finance the scheme. Gillard declined. Labor had drunk from that well too often. Hockey saw the emerging train wreck: a May 2013 budget dominated by NDIS funding that would squeeze future Coalition government fiscal options for many years.

The May 2013 budget, Labor's last, provided an extra $14.3 billion over seven years to enable full implementation of the scheme, now called DisabilityCare, by 1 July 2019. State contributions would be extra, based on negotiated agreements. Gillard had reversed her earlier position and increased the Medicare levy from 1.5 to 2 per cent from July 2014 to buttress funding. Over the four years to 2018–19 the levy would raise more than $20 billion, about half the cost. This scheme would be funded by both higher taxes and higher spending. But the design flaw was obvious, the lack of financial controls threatening an untenable cost escalation. When introducing the Medicare levy bill Gillard shed tears. Her office said later her thoughts were with twelve-year-old Sophie, who had Down syndrome and was featured in a card sent to the Prime Minister. 'There will be no turning back,' Gillard declared of the policy. She was embraced by Macklin.

This was accompanied by another spending commitment, an extra $9.8 billion over six years from 2014–15 for the Gonski agenda. It was designed to deliver 'world-class education' as a key to economic success. Gillard was offering to meet 65 per cent of the total $14.5 billion and was asking all states to seal the deal. The 2011 Gonski report, commissioned by Gillard as minister, was high on ambition but weak on implementation and practical detail.

It sought to address Australia's declining school performance and the gap between high- and low-performing students. It attacked the current model and recommended an increase in total funds. The aim was to redistribute towards government schools and poorer students. A new schooling resource standard would apply across all schools, with loadings for special needs and disadvantaged students. Private schools would not face funding cuts. Gillard was genuine in seeking to transcend the old public–private funding brawl.

She embraced the report in principle. Abbott and his shadow minister, Christopher Pyne, opposed it as a dismantling of the Howard model. In the negotiating process much of the Gonski model was revised or amended. Gillard worked relentlessly to negotiate deals with the states—where responsibility for school education resided, a process that would continue when Rudd returned as prime minister. New South Wales Liberal Premier Barry O'Farrell rejected Abbott's pleas and signed up to Gillard's scheme. Invoking a 'national crusade' to transform lives and spread her own passion about education, Gillard called this a 'once-in-a-generation' reform. The evidence suggested its returns might be meagre.

This saga saw the repeat of an old story: a fight over funding models while standards were held hostage. Australia did not know how to conduct a debate about higher classroom standards. Grattan Institute expert Ben Jensen identified the problem: progress depended on the culture of student learning—that is, what happened in the classroom. Jensen said:

> If it is spent the way education money has been spent in the past, it will be a complete waste—and risk dooming further reform efforts for a generation. Across the past decade, education spending has increased by nearly three times as much as Gonski is proposing, yet our performance has stagnated or fallen. Australia is one of just four OECD countries in which 15 year olds went backwards on international assessments between 2000 and 2009.[19]

In short, if the classroom culture is wrong, money cannot fix the problem. Gillard's claim that it would 'ensure our schools are in the world's top five by 2025' was fantasy. The vehement support of teacher unions for the Gonski agenda was hardly encouraging as a pointer to classroom change.

Gillard wanted education as a frontline election issue; it was basic to rebuilding her political profile. Her method was to 'buy off' the private school sectors and then authorise big increases for government schools, a 'winners all round' technique. The more Abbott opposed her, the keener Gillard got about a Gonski education election (better than boats or carbon). 'Surely it's not too much to ask people to put kids first,' she said. Gillard was trouncing Abbott on the politics. For the Liberals, seeking a fight on school funding was little short of madness.

The final Gillard–Swan 2013 budget was a big-spending budget that looked responsible. It looked responsible because over the four years of forward estimates it was responsible, now projecting a surplus in 2015–16, ironically the original year nominated when the GFC fiscal stimulus was triggered. It was a big-spending budget because DisabilityCare and Gonski were rear-end loaded and the big dollars came beyond the forward estimates. Most of the extra Gonski funds came in years five and six, the last two years of the package, well into any Abbott second term. In a critical step, Abbott refused to honour the Gonski funding for these final years, thereby keeping open the option of major savings. The deferred funding for DisabilityCare was even more pronounced, with 85 per cent coming over the second and third term of an Abbott government, if there were to be such events.

This was a poison-pill budget, surely the greatest ever seen. The aim was to lock in Labor's agenda and deny Abbott's options in office for many years. Labor would get the credit for these icons but Abbott would have to finance them. The key to the fiscal sustainability of Labor's ambitious agenda was its assumption that real growth in spending could be limited to 2 per cent for a decade (think forever in political terms). It was beyond heroic. Abbott was locked into a fiscal straightjacket.

The budget looked too good to be true. Labor in late 2012 had been forced to make a choice: it abandoned its surplus timetable to keep DisabilityCare and Gonski. In truth, however, Labor was still fudging that choice. In its final budget it still wanted its prized surplus, now in 2015–16, plus DisabilityCare and Gonski.

Gillard and Swan were asking the budget to do too much, yet again. The settings were too optimistic. This time, senior Treasury officers dissociated themselves in private from Labor's budget and its forecasts. It was a Labor document, not a Treasury document.

There were lots of public warnings about the budget's flaws. Macroeconomics chief Stephen Anthony identified the core defect: 'The 2013–14 budget puts the cart before the horse.' DisabilityCare and the Gonski agenda were funded by high hopes off a precarious base—'on a promise of future spending discipline and by revenue growth which hinges on an optimistic view' of nominal GDP growth and the terms of trade. Anthony said the budget settings were 'a brave scenario' and, 'if wrong, the revenue estimates will tumble and there will be no surplus at the end of the forward estimates'.

Chris Richardson said:

> In the last few years the nation has simply been living on a promise that the budget would get better. Surpluses have been forecast rather than delivered. The shortfalls are so large and the siren call of election spending so compelling that it looks like deficits as far as the eye can see.[20]

The *Australian's* David Uren said the budget risk was that 'commodity prices and investment in the resources sector fall more sharply than expected'.[21]

But few expected the rapidity of the fall. In less than three months Treasury had stripped $33 billion from its revenue forecasts over the next four years. Tax receipts for 2013–14 were down an estimated $7.8 billion from the May budget. The budget was falling apart within weeks of being unveiled. The problem was Anthony's precise point: the terms of trade had fallen since the budget and the nominal GDP forecast had to be reduced.[22] The situation reminded of the remark by the economics writer for the *Financial Times*, Martin Wolf, when he had recently visited Australia: 'If I were running the Australian economy, I'd try to run it on the assumption that the commodity prices might halve.'

Labor didn't learn because it didn't want to learn and Treasury repeatedly overestimated the revenues. From the BCA, Westacott said: 'Our view was we'd had enough; this was now a disaster and the government had lost control of its fiscal strategy.'[23]

Consider the record. For 2010–11 Labor forecast a deficit of $41 billion that ended as a deficit of $48 billion. For 2011–12 it forecast a deficit of $23 billion that became an outcome of $44 billion. For 2012–13 it forecast a surplus of $1.5 billion that became a deficit of $19 billion. In 2013–14 it forecast a deficit of $18 billion yet less than three months later it was revised upwards to $30 billion. Too much spending was pledged on a vulnerable tax base.

In August, Rudd and Bowen, as the new prime minister and treasurer, had no option in the election prelude but to bring down a mini-budget. They had to account for the latest revenue slump and make new savings decisions to keep the 'bottom line' respectable. The return-to-surplus deadline was now delayed yet another year, until 2016–17, when the projected surplus was a razor-thin $4 billion. Obviously, the new timetable had no credibility.

Labor was like a beaten army, staging retreats as a prelude to more retreats. It had relied upon three different return–to–surplus deadlines: 2012–13, 2015–16 and 2016–17. The retreats were expected to continue.

A battle was being conducted over the budget. The battle, in effect, was between the economy and Labor. The economy, through slower growth and lower terms of trade, was weakening and depleting the budget's strength. Yet Labor was desperately pretending this was a powerful budget, strong enough both to finance its huge agendas and to get back into surplus. The strain was too great, the budget couldn't carry the burden, the forecasts kept buckling. Each time they buckled, Labor's political standing took another blow.

Reviewing this period, Stephen Anthony said:

> Over 2011 to 2013 Treasury's revenue estimates were too optimistic and the government failed to apply the spending discipline needed to repair the budget deficit. That demanded a tougher repair job to have any hope of getting near their 2012–13 surplus objective. The government, on the contrary, seemed to assume moderate savings and fiscal drag would get them there. That was a fantasy and it was never going to happen. There is no hindsight in this assessment; it is the judgement we and experts like Adrian Pagan made at the time. I think this is Labor's most important fiscal failure, more significant than its miscalculations during the GFC.[24]

Adrian Pagan, an economics professor and former RBA board member, had caused a stir at a May 2012 economics conference in Canberra when he accused Treasury of using 'unbelievable' forecasts post-GFC. He said the forecast kickback to 4 per cent growth had been 'ridiculous' and 'political'. That provoked a heated rebuttal from Treasury Deputy Secretary David Gruen, who said the claim was deeply offensive. Pagan insisted the forecasts were not plausible. 'I said it at the time and I still believe it.' He recounted how when his wife told him about the forecast he responded: 'Pigs can fly.'[25]

Chris Richardson was sympathetic to Treasury, saying weather forecasting was now much easier than budget forecasting. Swan stayed loyal:

> I'm not going to bag the Treasury. But it made life absolutely difficult. Our position just got undermined by revenue write downs above previous revenue write downs. There are economic effects here we don't fully understand—it's the combination of the dollar staying up and the terms of trade coming down. It put a squeeze on the profitability of our businesses.[26]

Australia's problem was that global central banks, led by the US Federal Reserve, boosted activity in their own countries by keeping interest rates low, thereby keeping the Australian dollar high and denying the depreciation that Swan wanted. 'Our problem was the exchange rate should have fallen but it didn't,' Craig Emerson said.[27]

Meanwhile the fiscal position kept deteriorating and warnings became more pronounced. In August 2013 the heads of Treasury and Finance released their pre-election outlook. It was a conspicuous attempt to flag the risks ahead. 'Treasury went out of its way to talk about the risks,' Richardson said.[28] The advisers were getting ready for a change of government.

Swan and Wong defend their record. Swan says:

> I held the line on spending pretty well. Even in the case of DisabilityCare and Gonski, we funded them for ten years in the budget. Some of the savings we did in the last budget were painful. We weren't on a spending spree. We didn't lose control of the budget. In fact, we kept fiscal policy in good shape. I stayed true to my values.[29]

Wong said: 'Criticism of Labor's economic management fails to acknowledge the central achievement of keeping Australia growing and maintaining its AAA credit rating when most advanced economies around the world experienced deep recessions and significant deterioration in their public finances.'[30]

This is a statement of the obvious. Nobody suggests Labor was on a post-GFC spending spree. The problem, however, is different: it is Labor's unsustainable fiscal legacy. On the reform front Labor failed to confront the structural defects in spending and tax essential to deliver a viable medium-term fiscal recovery. In 2014 that legacy casts a long and damaging shadow over the nation. Having promised a 2012–13 surplus, Labor has bequeathed a decade of deficits without policy correction.

In September 2013, Abbott came to power with his pledge to restore the budget position. In December, the Treasurer, Joe Hockey, released the mid-year review designed to document the dimensions of the task. The new government highlighted Labor's 'black hole', with discretionary spending by the Abbott Government also adding to upward revisions to the deficit. There had been a $68 billion deterioration in the budget across the forward estimates since August. Labor howled that it was being set up; some of this was a result of Abbott's decisions. There was, however, no gainsaying the structural budget problem that was Labor's legacy.

Labor had piled vast new spending programs (notably DisabilityCare and Gonski) on a tax base raising significantly less revenue as a portion of GDP than before. There was an imbalance between future revenue and future spending. Former Treasury chief Ken Henry warned in early 2014 of worries about 'the sustainability of budgets in Australia'. He said Labor's social commitments could not be funded by the existing tax system. They would require either offsetting spending cuts or more revenue sources.[31]

The most telling analysis came from Treasury chief Parkinson in April 2014. Parkinson said without policy change the budget was projected to be in deficit for the next ten years. The nation, in fact, was facing sixteen years of consecutive deficits since Rudd's response to the GFC. Labor's lost promise of a 2012–13 surplus now seemed one of the great fantasies of modern Australian politics.[32]

Parkinson said his projections were optimistic: they assumed no recession in the next decade and no tax cuts, an implausible result. He argued that restoration of a surplus would be harder than in the past because potential economic growth rates were lower, the terms of trade would ease and the ageing of the population would escalate spending demands.

His analysis documented problems on both the spending side and the revenue side. Parkinson said that, for the post-2002–03 decade, real spending had risen faster than real GDP. He offered a glimpse of huge new commitments: the disability scheme would cost the federal budget a net $64.5 billion out to 2023–24; health spending was projected to rise from $65 billion to $116 billion over the decade; the three main pension payments would cost an extra $52 billion annually by 2023–24. This obviously constituted a spending problem Labor had declined to address in its alleged long-run funding of its disability scheme and Gonski.

The mid-year review showed that, under Labor, spending had grown at 3.5 per cent annually in real terms, casting severe doubt on the assumption underpinning Labor's 2013 budget—that it could limit spending to 2 per cent in real terms for a decade. Stephen Anthony buttressed the Treasury argument. His work showed 'there is no possibility that existing policy settings will allow for sustainable spending growth rates at or below 3 per cent each year'.[33]

After the GFC, Australia faced a medium-term budget challenge arising from the gulf between locked-in spending and projected tax revenue. This threatens a fall in the growth rate of living standards of ordinary Australians. It was Labor's obligation to address this task. As Parkinson said, that demanded 'sustained discipline' on the spending front and tax reform to enhance growth. The judgement on Labor is that it failed to meet the challenge sufficiently on either side of the balance sheet.

Swan was Labor's third–longest serving Treasurer after Keating and Chifley. His record on balance is neither as good as his champions claim nor as bad as his critics claim. Swan avoided a recession during a period

of immense global volatility and wealth destruction. Australia moved up
to become the twelfth-largest economy, probably the highest place it will
reach. Unemployment was contained, nearly a million jobs were created
and the economy grew by 14 per cent. The contrast with the rest of the
industrialised world is impressive.

Chris Richardson said:

> Wayne Swan will rank well in the pantheon of treasurers. In his-
> torical terms I rate Keating as our best treasurer and Costello as
> our second best. But Swan ranks ahead of many others. The first
> point to make is that his crisis management was good. However,
> outside of the GFC his record is much more mixed. The economic
> recovery is not failing but it is not happy. Swan's reform achieve-
> ments are more modest.[34]

Swan said: 'Despite the carnage, we kept working on our big reforms:
NBN, education, carbon pricing and disability insurance.'[35]

The evidence, however, is more mixed. Swan, as treasurer, never
dominated by setting and imposing the economic reform agenda. He had
little influence on public attitudes or identifying the national challenges.
Labor's strategic difficulty was that the reforms it ventured—carbon
pricing and mining tax—were flawed while other pivotal reforms relating
to tax, spending and productivity were not attempted. The priorities
were misguided. The forecasting errors in Swan's budgets undermined
policy and political confidence in the government. In the end, depleted
of political capital, Labor had lost the confidence of the business and
investment communities. It is telling that Swan has left no identifiable
reform pathway as a guiding light for his Labor successors.

The paradox is that the 2008–09 global crisis made Labor's record
look much better because it triggered an event that demanded spending
and intervention as the solution. Without this success under its belt, Labor's
economic record would look much inferior. The ultimate irony is that
Labor survived the GFC only to fall victim to the resources boom. Each
year from 2010 it didn't have as much money to spend as it anticipated.
It applied spending restraints but they were insufficient to furnish Labor's
huge objectives: a return to surplus and financing end-of-empire social
edifices, potentially important for the nation yet bequeathing unresolved
fiscal issues.

Labor pledged to be 'Keynesians on the way down and Keynesians
on the way up'. It didn't keep this pledge—the 'word of honour' justifying

its GFC fiscal stimulus. The surplus Labor inherited in 2007 was never restored despite four budgets in the post-GFC recovery phase. This invites two conclusions. First, Labor misjudged the 2008–09 downturn, spent too much and sent the budget too far into deficit. More seriously, it misjudged the recovery from 2010. It got lost in contradictory economic and political priorities and left a structural fiscal problem that will challenge Abbott and stain Labor's economic credentials for years.

CHAPTER 29

FAR FROM ROOTY HILL

On 8 March 2012, Julia Gillard invited the editor-in-chief of Sydney's *Daily Telegraph*, Paul Whittaker, to Kirribilli House hoping to forge a better relationship with the tabloid and its boss. Gillard had peppermint tea and Whittaker had coffee. For Gillard, improved relations were critical to her government's standing in Western Sydney, the largest cluster of contested seats in the nation.

Gillard told Whittaker his paper had 'had its fun with Kevin and the leadership'. Her message was simple: forget Rudd, it's over. John McTernan had set up the meeting. 'I know Kevin was talking to you,' Gillard said. She left the impression she knew a lot more than that. Rudd had targeted the *Telegraph* in the prelude to the February 2012 challenge that he lost. Gillard told Whittaker she would lead Labor to the election. She wanted a new dialogue.

'It's time to move beyond the carbon tax,' she told Whittaker. The Prime Minister was steely eyed but friendly. Despite their differences Whittaker respected her; Julia was effective in these encounters. Outside it was a rainy day. Whittaker said the *Telegraph* wanted to see more transport infrastructure, more jobs and a new airport at Badgerys Creek. He wanted tax policies that gave people an incentive to earn higher incomes. The *Telegraph* championed the aspirational culture in the west.

In the end, Western Sydney would ruin Gillard. On 7 June 2013, a fortnight before Gillard lost her job, New South Wales right-wing organiser Sam Dastyari said the polling showed Labor losing every seat in Western Sydney. In Jason Clare's seat of Blaxland, Keating's old seat, the ALP two-party-preferred vote was at 44 per cent.[1] This was supposed to be ALP heartland. Down-to-earth Julia never connected with Western Sydney, a non-negotiable requirement for success as a Labor prime minister.

Gillard needed the media for her two battles—against Rudd and against Abbott. Swan never doubted the decisive role played by the newspapers: 'The media was 70 or 80 per cent of the problem in pro-moting Rudd and destabilising Gillard. In saying that I'm not suggesting we didn't make mistakes. Kerry-Anne Walsh has chronicled it pretty well. In my view her account is pretty accurate.'[2]

Nine months earlier, the week of Whittaker's appointment as chief, Gillard had texted him a message of congratulations from London. That led to an earlier meeting on 4 May 2011 on the patio at Kirribilli when Gillard asked what her government could expect from Whittaker. She hoped for better times, given the *Telegraph* had previously featured a mock-up of her as a pensioner on the front page at the time of the Laurie Oakes pension leak story. It was a friendly meeting. But Gillard's hopes faded within days with the *Telegraph*'s highly critical coverage of Swan's 2011 budget. She wasn't happy and rang Whittaker.

The following year McTernan arranged for Whittaker to meet Gillard in her office on budget morning, 8 May 2012. She had some good news. 'You're scrapping the carbon tax,' Whittaker joked. No, Gillard said; she wasn't scrapping the carbon tax—but the budget contained measures that would assist people with cost-of-living pressures. In truth, Gillard had no hope with the *Telegraph*. The problem was her policies and Labor culture.

The Gillard Government was lost in Sydney. In the nation's major city it was without powerful friends and without networks, influence or street savvy. None of Labor's four parliamentary leaders—Gillard, Swan, Conroy or Wong—came from New South Wales. Its ties with business were weak, often hostile. It was losing touch with the Rugby League net-works of the Western suburbs. Gillard tried but failed to deal effectively with the News Ltd headquarters at Surry Hills and, in the end, open war-fare broke out. Sydney was the city that Hawke, Keating and Bob Carr called home. Julia was a South Australian who became a popular Victorian.

John Alexander was a former editor-in-chief of the *Sydney Morning Herald* who had become a decisive figure in James Packer's empire. In February 2013 he told Carr over lunch that Gillard was not up to the job, she couldn't run a pie shop, the class war rhetoric was despicable and Rudd and Gillard had done enormous damage to the nation. 'This must be the conventional wisdom of the boardrooms,' Carr thought.[3] Alexander was a highly connected Sydney figure: his views represented an influential segment of Sydney opinion. Yet these were the same people who had backed former ALP giants Hawke, Neville Wran and, for quite a while, Keating.

Gillard was described as a great political fixer. It is an exaggeration; she was adept at internal fixes. But Gillard seemed clueless about how to cut deals with business, industry or media. The skills made famous and often infamous in Sydney politics were not her forte. In office as premier, Carr cultivated and won support from the Sydney *Daily Telegraph*, Gillard's nemesis, dining at Lucio's with its flamboyant editor, Col Allen; Keating as treasurer flattered and won the most powerful shock jock in the land, John Laws, to whom he gave the 'banana republic' interview; and Hawke installed John Singleton as advertising director for his campaigns, the same Singleton who owned the Macquarie radio network, employer of Alan Jones and Ray Hadley, the network that brought grief to Gillard. The Hawke Government had authorised Murdoch's takeover of the *Herald and Weekly Times*, a calculated move with the tangential hope of strengthening Labor's position.

Julia was not part of the Sydney networks. She could not do this job herself. By 2012 she had no Sydney lieutenant. Yet dealing with Sydney's power structure was not an option; it was not a luxury. It was a necessity, as former Labor leaders had demonstrated.

The extent to which Sydney was foreign territory was revealed early in the 2013 election year when Gillard relocated to Western Sydney for a week, sleeping overnight in a hotel annexed to the Rooty Hill RSL Club. The visit began with an unfortunate joke by one of her ministers, Mark Butler (a South Australian), who said he stayed at the Penrith Panthers when in Western Sydney because 'I'm not sure I could check into the Rooty Hill RSL with a straight face.' Butler said it conjured up Carry On films and Benny Hill episodes. The local mayor said the comment was 'disgraceful' and the people of the area 'couldn't be cheapened in any way'. Butler apologised. The *Daily Telegraph* had fun with the story at Gillard's expense.

The orchestration of the Rooty Hill visit left the impression of an outsider visiting the region. The optics were disastrous. Former New South Wales ALP secretary Graham Richardson said Gillard was toxic in the West. The Rooty Hill visit had its origins in a lunch meeting at Kirribilli House near Christmas, 2012, triggered by Sam Dastyari's warnings to Gillard. Dastyari had lethal research numbers for Western Sydney. 'Things are very bad in Sydney, we have to try something,' he told Gillard. The Prime Minister met six Western Sydney MPs—Chris Bowen, Tony Burke, Ed Husic, David Bradbury, Jason Clare and Michelle Rowland—along with Dastyari. It was not an easy meeting; some participants were pledged to Rudd. But Gillard would agree to a program and an agenda.

In the interim the corruption engulfing the New South Wales ALP off the back of a highly publicised ICAC inquiry involving two former state ministers, Eddie Obeid and Ian McDonald, only further contaminated the Labor brand, with virtually no hope for recovery. Smelling political blood, the media relocated to Rooty Hill to feast on Gillard's difficulties.

Launching her Western Sydney campaign on Sunday 3 March, Gillard pledged to stop foreign workers 'being put at the front of the queue with Australian workers at the back'. Presenting herself as a westie, she implied Abbott was a toff, saying: 'I didn't grow up on the North Shore or in the East either.' During the week her themes were jobs, traffic congestion, education and the cost of living. Her organisers were meticulous in keeping Gillard away from any spontaneous meetings with ordinary people. The media coverage was bad. Dastyari called the week an 'unmitigated disaster' but said he had to share responsibility. He told the author that this week was a 'turning point' for Gillard's leadership.[4]

Whittaker, along with other News Ltd editors, was caught up in the Gillard–Rudd political war. In February 2012, Rudd was in contact with Whittaker just before the leadership showdown; in August Rudd and Whittaker had dinner at Beppis in East Sydney, with Rudd keen to establish what were the *Telegraph*'s priorities for Sydney; Rudd stayed in regular phone contact with Whittaker; on Christmas Day 2012, Rudd texted Whittaker who was with his family in Queensland and they had a drink at Noosa the next day. Greg Combet mirrored ALP anger at Rudd's media tactics to undermine Gillard: 'Remember all the front pages on the *Telegraph*. It was like a hot line. I just can't cop that.'[5]

Foreign Minister Bob Carr called himself an elitist arriviste in the Gillard Government. He kept at arm's length and focused on foreign affairs. Sitting in the Gillard cabinet, he was struck by Labor's political ineptitude and singular failure in New South Wales. Carr, unsurprisingly, had proven ideas on how Labor should govern. He belonged to the most successful Labor Party tradition in Australia—the New South Wales Right, with its long list of luminaries. For decades New South Wales ALP success had been based on the McKell model, named after Sir William McKell, whom Carr called Australia's 'most effective state leader in the first half of the twentieth century'. McKell's two most famous successors were Neville Wran and Carr. Carr, deeply influenced by Wran, described the keys to his success: an acute grasp of public opinion, working with business and unions, staking out the middle ground and dominating the communications stream.

For Carr, there were four golden rules: fiscal responsibility, pro-business policies, cautious social reform ('keep the churches onside') and balanced environmental programs. 'You don't go to war with business,'

Carr said. 'Wran used to talk about "the big end of town" and I imbibed that. You don't go about creating enemies.' Or if you do create enemies, Carr said, ensure you have enough friends to prevail.[6]

Each leader is different but Hawke, Keating and Wran were shaped by the economic failures of the Whitlam Government. Carr loved to discuss McKell's style. A former boilermaker, McKell related to the wider community—the sportsmen, the archbishops, the farmers and the lawyers. Over time Carr pioneered what became, during the Howard era, a Labor model of government, with Carr in New South Wales, Bracks in Victoria, Rann in South Australia and Beattie in Queensland.

These leaders were not models of reform. Over time their governments disintegrated, some badly amid financial degeneration. But they had an electoral method, an art missing under Rudd and Gillard. Long-time adviser to ALP governments Bruce Hawker said:

> A new model of Labor government did emerge from the state capitals starting with Carr. He sold economic responsibility and personal security. Bob was often on the same page as John Howard. He wasn't interested in some of Labor's fashionable causes, was tough on law and order and focused on practical issues.[7]

Carr agreed with Howard on asylum seeker boats. As Foreign Minister, he said a responsible ALP government would halt illegal arrivals. Carr was struck by how proven methods and policies that delivered electoral success were repudiated or ignored by Gillard Labor.

There was a profound arrogance at work in the Rudd–Gillard years—a form of blind denial of how Labor succeeds in office. The final abandonment of sound electoral politics was the 12 March 2013 cabinet decision, without warning, to create a 'Public Interest Media Advocate', its task being to impose a new public interest test on media mergers and to retaliate against media companies that failed to meet appropriate editorial standards. The cabinet meeting had been a fiasco and the issue was rushed through. Most ministers did not understand what was being rubber-stamped. An incredulous Carr said: 'We are committed to a wholesale war with the newspapers'—six months from an election.[8]

In Carr's view the media policy was 'insane'. In the pre-election period Labor 'should be friends with all'. Carr told colleagues he had three rules with the media: persuade them, set their agenda and exploit the divisions between them. Going to war with the industry had slipped his mind as an option. It was recidivism to class-based tribalism.

Yet this decision had logic in the strange evolution of Gillard's government. Angry at coverage in News Corporation papers, notably the *Daily Telegraph*, Labor had commissioned a media inquiry by a former judge, Ray Finkelstein, assisted by a media academic. The 2012 report was a watershed: it rejected self-regulation of the industry via the Australian Press Council and proposed statutory regulation of media with a new body to adjudicate on editorial performance and fairness. The utopian philosophy in the 470-page report involved new laws to protect Australian democracy from biased journalists. This was justified by another assumption—you could not rely on the public's ability to make effective judgements in the marketplace. Finkelstein's mind was deeply in tune with Labor's disposition for more controls.

Gillard had nine months to sort out a response. Conroy and Swan led the charge but the government was divided. There was an obvious imperative: sort it out before the election year. And a sensible prime minister would do that. But it didn't happen. In the end, Gillard bowed to Conroy and gave him a diminished version of earlier proposals. The attack on the media industry became low-farce; the proposed bills were unworkable. There was no consultation with industry on the specifics, just as there hadn't been over the mining tax. The two Sydney-based media companies, News Corporation and Fairfax, were united in attacking the policy, a rare event and a distinct Labor achievement.

The chief executive of News Corporation, Kim Williams, called the proposal a 'modern-day Star Chamber'. He said the public interest test would become a political test and attacked the notion that the media advocate would be able to revoke the exemption afforded to journalists under privacy law. Fairfax chief executive Greg Hywood said Labor had resorted to the 'nuclear option'. It was a de facto system of newspaper licensing with the power to remove the licence. The key bill was called the *News Media (Self-Regulation) Bill 2013*, its title an Orwellian masterstroke, since it sought to impose a bizarre form of new regulation.

It was bad law and bad policy. Indeed, it failed every test. It was phoney reform; it lacked the numbers in Parliament and was abandoned; it created more hostility towards Labor; and, above all, it revealed Gillard's inability as prime minister to negotiate effectively with the power centres in Australian life. In essence, it was a conflict between Gillard and the Sydney-based newspaper groups. Rudd, of course, had told the senior editors at News that he would reject any such policy; they could rely on him!

There was a deep instinct in caucus for retaliation against News Corporation papers and this influenced Gillard. The situation, however, allows only one interpretation: Gillard felt this was necessary to bolster her leadership within caucus. Healthy governments do not operate this way. Labor was trying to damage its enemies, not save itself.

Interviewed in 2014, Carr said: 'The ineptitude of the media package destroyed any confidence I had in Julia Gillard's office and instincts.' He named the media decision as the point when he turned to Rudd. This is true but misleading. Carr was going to move with the New South Wales Right and the tide of Labor MPs in Western Sydney anyway. He called this a time of 'abnormally poor political management', a reference to Gillard's ineptitude.[9]

Gillard's dialogue with Whittaker had got nowhere. Her media policy merely intensified the conflict between Labor and News Corporation. The truth is, the policy and cultural gulf between Gillard Labor and News Corporation was too great. Other ALP leaders had forged highly effective working relationships with the Murdoch group—but not this Labor generation.

The final rupture between Gillard and Sydney politics came over the Palestinian issue. It is where Carr forced Gillard into a retreat, with her job otherwise at risk. With Palestine seeking to upgrade its position to observer status at the UN, Carr decided Australia should not oppose this bid. That meant a split from the United States and Israel. It signalled a change in Labor policy and in grass-roots ALP attitudes towards Israel and Palestine in Western Sydney. The New South Wales Right had long been a pro-Israel bastion but a new current was underway with the rise of Islam in many Labor seats.

Gillard was determined to oppose the Palestine bid yet failed to grasp the weight of her opponents. Bob Hawke, with an impeccable pro-Israel record, was backing Carr. Former Foreign Minister Gareth Evans told Carr that a 'no' vote 'would be the worst Australian foreign policy decision for a generation'. Tony Burke, whose seat included the Lakemba Mosque, told Carr Australia should vote 'yes'.

With the Right split between New South Wales and Victoria, political passions were engaged. Conroy told Carr his position was 'monstrous'. Gareth Evans said that if Carr was overruled it would warrant resignation. Carr and Rudd spoke on how to defeat Gillard's hard line. Aware that he would not prevail in cabinet, Carr encouraged Andrew Leigh MP to bring a motion to caucus; but, critically, Leigh's motion would favour an Australian abstention, a position easier to get up.[10]

It was a remarkable cabinet meeting. Gillard outlined her position and, at her request, Carr summarised both sides of the argument. Craig

Emerson spoke first, opposed Gillard and quoted Gareth Evans. Albanese, Bowen, Ferguson, Garrett, Burke, Butler and Crean all lined up against Gillard. Only Shorten and Conroy called for a 'no' vote. Carr could hardly believe what he was watching. With Stephen Smith having spoken at an earlier meeting, ten ministers were aligned against Gillard. Carr now declared his own hand: Australia should offer hope to the Palestinians and keep pressure on Israel to do the right thing. Gillard then announced it was her call; she would not change her position.

She was asserting her authority as prime minister against her cabinet. This came with the prerogative of being PM but it works only with the acquiescence of cabinet. Carr refused to acquiesce. He had to represent this position before the world. Carr pleaded for Gillard to rethink and to settle on an abstention.[11] Fighting for her position, Gillard asked Right convenor Joel Fitzgibbon to bind the caucus Right behind her policy. It was an extraordinary request; Gillard was trying to impose her will on half the party. But Fitzgibbon refused. 'I've been here seventeen years and I've never seen that happen,' he replied. The era of the New South Wales Right's near-uncritical support for Israel was ending.[12] The end of its support for Gillard would soon follow.

Carr lobbied against Gillard in the prelude to the next morning's caucus meeting. Carr had the numbers; Gillard faced defeat. Carr saw Gillard at 9.20 a.m., before the caucus meeting. He said she 'should— must—retreat to an abstention'. He pleaded with her to change her mind, saying it was the best means of protecting her leadership. The danger moment had arrived. Carr revealed that the caucus motion from Leigh would be to abstain. 'I saw fear dance in her eyes,' Carr said. He had conspired to defeat her. 'I can't vote against the Palestinians,' Carr told Gillard of the caucus meeting. This was high brinkmanship. Carr had no intention of resigning; he did not believe Gillard would sack him. He apologised for making her life difficult and left.[13]

Facing defeat, Gillard folded. Swan advised her to 'tap the mat'. She told the caucus she would favour abstention. Carr had forced her retreat off the back of the New South Wales Right. Gillard told the author: 'I think there is a real risk I would have lost.'[14] The campaign had been driven by policy and politics. Multicultural Sydney was changing. Dastyari said: 'You have to understand, Sydney's changed and the politics have changed. There are big and growing Islamic communities and they want their MPs to start expressing their views.'[15]

Burke said: 'If you take my electorate and the number of people of non–English speaking background, it is 72 to 74 per cent who don't speak English when at home. The multicultural character of Sydney is very different to the rest of Australia.'[16]

This political push had been driven by the needs of New South Wales Labor. It prioritised this issue but Gillard's priorities were elsewhere. The showdown symbolised the wedge between Gillard and the needs of Sydney Labor. This would assume a tangible meaning after Rudd's return as leader: in the 2013 election, Labor would save a number of critical seats across multicultural Sydney.

CHAPTER 30

LABOR TRADITIONALISTS

The breach of trust between Julia Gillard and Australian business was sealed on 6 December 2012 when, at the COAG Business Advisory Forum, Gillard pulled the plug on plans to rationalise the dual Commonwealth–state environmental project approval system. For business, this was a betrayal. The commitment to this reform originated at the April meeting of the forum. The national government, the states and business groups had been working towards a new model. The gains were going to be substantial—business sentiment was 'at last we're making progress somewhere'.

The forum, chaired by the PM, was a high-powered group that comprised the premiers, senior business figures and the peak business bodies. In the prelude to the meeting the Greens had waged a public campaign to kill the reform and at the penultimate moment Gillard reversed the government's position. Business leaders felt this was the final separation. Their remarks, based on separate interviews held in 2014, reveal a turning point.

Ai Group chief Innes Willox said:

This was the end of the relationship. The business community had pushed very hard. The signs were we would get meaningful changes. The PM had said it would be settled. Then at the final meeting it was reversed. We walked away with nothing. It was obvious the Greens had put a line through it.[1]

The head of the Australian Chamber of Commerce and Industry, Peter Andersen, said:

The Prime Minister just told the meeting the Commonwealth would no longer proceed with the 'in principle' agreement from last April. We concluded green politics were put before the economic

interests of the nation. I believe this was the highwater mark of the
Gillard Government acquiescence to the Green movement. There
was no pretence left.[2]

President of the Business Council of Australia (BCA), Tony
Shepherd said: 'We felt we had made a lot of progress.' Extensive work
had been done at public service level. The idea was to remove unneces-
sary Commonwealth–state duplication and have a single approval agency.
'We saw this as a tremendous breakthrough, saving time, energy and risk,'
Shepherd said.

> At the last minute we are told the PM does not believe this is a good
> idea and will not proceed. We were extremely upset. We felt we had
> been misled by the government. I saw this as a breach of trust. We
> were dealing with a government that was not trustworthy.[3]

Gillard said there had to be a national agreement with all states, not
separate arrangements with different states. Offers from the New South
Wales and Victorian governments to rationalise their approvals were not
taken up. The main business lobbies now reached a universal conclusion.
Willox said: 'The lesson we drew was that the government's main
priority was survival. It was about locking in the Greens, supporting
the trade unions, surviving minority government.'[4] On environmental
approvals, New South Wales Premier Barry O'Farrell said Gillard had
baulked after Green pressure. At the end of the meeting Gillard asked
Shepherd to attend the joint press conference. He refused.[5]
BCA chief executive Jennifer Westacott said:

> It was actually bigger than a breach of trust. This was a government
> saying 'these resource projects will pull us through'. They would
> talk a lot about their 'huge pipeline of investment' of $400 billion.
> Yet the policy decisions they made on fair work around greenfields,
> on refusing to tackle environmental approvals and on 457 Visas
> all worked against the resources projects. It was a massive policy
> contradiction.[6]

In 2012 the BCA launched its 'Pipeline or Pipedream?' report, arguing the resource projects pipeline was in jeopardy, with more projects
falling over on financial grounds. Commodity prices were easing and
Australia was a high-cost country. The former BCA president Graham

Bradley said the policy settings to deliver the pipeline were not in place; Australian projects were 40 per cent more expensive than those on the US Gulf Coast. Business wanted corrective action and felt Labor was not interested.

Gillard, unsurprisingly, looked inward not outward. Her focus was implementing her carbon deal, consolidating the unions, exciting the feminists, rolling out big-spending Labor reforms and beating off Rudd. 'There was a siege mentality,' Sam Dastyari said. 'When you're in the bunker there's a bunker mentality.'[7]

'The Prime Minister was always generally pretty courteous,' Westacott said. 'But you could tell she had a poor regard for the Business Council.' Gillard felt the BCA was too negative; she urged them to be positive. Yet this relationship sank in mutual distrust.

Reflecting on the attitude of the Gillard Government, Westacott said:

> There was no sense in which the business community was part of any compact with government. That idea never came through. On the contrary, the sense we got was that business had to be reined in, had to be controlled. It was not to be trusted. The government might say, from time to time, it wanted a partnership with business but it would not deliver policies to substantiate that. By contrast, I think Hawke and Keating knew business had to be part of the compact. We found virtually every piece of major reform was characterised in a derogatory way in relation to business. The carbon package was about the big polluters, as though there was an evil empire out there. The 457 Visa debate ran in terms of business exploiting and ripping off workers. It told us the government just had this antagonism towards the business community. It's easy to have a whipping boy in the big business sector.[8]

Willox, whose group represented 60 000 diverse companies in manufacturing, engineering and construction and transport, said:

> I think many business leaders in the final eighteen months gave up on the government. They were driven away. They just felt they couldn't get a serious engagement. To be fair, the Prime Minister never shut her door. But the weight of the government's position was always on the other side.[9]

Poor relations between business and a head of government can be offset by sound ties with the Treasurer, but this was not the case with Wayne Swan. From the mining tax fiasco, Swan's view of business grew jaundiced. He saw business as aggressive, self-interested and lacking reform commitment. The mining tax wounds were reopened by the carbon tax struggle. Swan said:

> The mining industry was able to utilise its supplier and media contacts to smash us over the mining tax. It was extraordinary. As a minority government we pioneered the carbon price reform. Did we get the support of the business community? No. Did we get the support of media organisations? No. We got absolutely smashed.

Swan dismissed any notion of business as a viable reform partner with Labor.[10] The alienation became forever. He attacked the resource majors: 'The companies went out and talked down the mining boom, it's what BHP and Rio and Xstrata did. It was brutal.' He said investors decided they didn't want to invest for the future; they wanted higher dividends now: 'So the decision was to "get" the Labor Government in Canberra by talking down the boom.'[11] This sentiment, deep and raw, was not unique to Swan. During the Labor years suspicion of the mining industry existed, to a greater or lesser extent, across much of government and in a public service divorced from the rest of the nation.

Swan and Gillard were convinced the big historical reforms had come from Labor. Indeed, this mentality had become an ALP fixation. But such hubris didn't help Labor in office. Interviewed for this book, Swan said:

> It has become much more difficult to get up a big long-term reform, particularly when you have such an irresponsible business community that cannot hold the line on basics like tax and climate change policy. There is too much romantic notion about business being on side for the reforms of the 1980s. Well, they weren't. They didn't back reform at the tax summit of the 1980s. They didn't back superannuation reform. By and large, they don't get on board.[12]

The alienation of Labor from corporate Australia ran deep.

The mutual distrust between Labor and business became irreparable and the consequences vast. Given this hostility, there was no prospect of

Labor running a political strategy from the centre. There was no hope of winning the middle ground, no duplication of the electoral methods of Hawke or Wran. Nobody expects Labor to love business but strategic cooperation is essential.

From early 2012 Swan broke out. In March he penned for *The Monthly* an article titled 'The 0.01 Per Cent' about the rise of powerful vested interests threatening the 'fair go'. His accusation was that 'a handful of vested interests' felt they had 'a right to shape Australia's future to satisfy their own self-interest'. In short, a small bunch of business rednecks were trying to derail the nation. Swan said such people would once have been laughed out of town but Australia had changed.

The threat came from Australia's own version of the Tea Party— deep industry pockets, biased newspapers, shock-jock ranting—with Abbott operating like a Tea Party Republican. Swan pointed the finger at Andrew Forrest, Gina Rinehart, John Singleton and Clive Palmer. These were his demons. Most businessmen, even miners, did the right thing; the problem was the tiny number blind to the national interest.[13]

Many people mocked Swan's article. But that was a mistake. He was creating a narrative that will carry much sway in Labor mythology—that Labor was sabotaged in office by greedy self-interested mining and media forces. It appealed to a rich lode in Labor history: the party of the 'fair go' assailed by ugly capitalists. The script is as old as Labor culture.

The argument gained fresh intensity in August 2012 when Swan delivered the John Button Lecture. It was a personal statement—Swan's version of the misogyny speech. The real Wayne was unveiled. He recruited that poet of working-class music Bruce Springsteen, his musical hero, to highlight the sea change in America—where ordinary people realised life wasn't getting any better and others were grabbing all the gains. Now Australia confronted a similar challenge to its values.

Did Swan regret his earlier criticism of our tycoons? 'Not for a second,' he said. 'In fact, my only regret is not going in hard enough.' The critics, he said, felt 'my day job was simply to shut up and to make the wealthiest Australians wealthier still'. Labor values were under attack: Palmer had threatened to run against him but had 'skulked away'; Forrest had used his money to buy full-page ads to promote himself; Rinehart wanted to buy the Fairfax media company. The Parliament, Constitution and independent journalism were being 'used as their playthings'.[14] Democracy and the 'fair go' were in jeopardy.

It was a class-based us-and-them polarisation. Swan later said Australia had reached 'a decisive point in our national story' because our ideals were 'under threat' from agents of mindless austerity. The coming election must be 'a referendum on the fair go'. Finally, he laid the ultimate charge: 'we are witnessing the Americanisation of the Right in this country';[15] those moderates Menzies and Howard had been replaced by extremists. This enabled Swan to cast Abbott and the self-interested tycoons into the same Tea Party pot—a fantastic concoction.

It was the authentic Swan, a party traditionalist with the beating heart of a Labor warrior. The words leapt from his personal life and political roots, roots validated by his time as Treasurer. Swan never forgave the assaults on his reforms: the mining tax, carbon pricing and his fiscal policy. He might talk about being a Hawke–Keating economic reformer but the veil was lifted. Swan's values, heart and passion lay elsewhere: deep in Labor traditionalism.

Only at this point did Swan begin to define the government. The brand was hostility towards miners, suspicion of business, polarisation by class. Ironically, the people identified had not wrecked the mining tax; that campaign was waged by the majors (BHP, Rio and Xstrata) and Swan had cut a deal with them anyway. Swan fanned class envy but his motive was not to attack the rich. This was a conflict about the national interest. Swan's real anger was that his opponents in the Coalition, business and media alleged that Labor had betrayed the national interest, that Labor in fact had become a party of sectional interests.

As this book argues, the difficulty facing Swan's reforms was not his opponents, though they were formidable. The real problem had been Labor. It was Labor's ineptitude that brought undone the mining tax and carbon pricing. The mythology about Australian Tea Party extremism was an alibi. It was resorting to an old technique: when failing, blame your opponent.

The public had conflicting perceptions of Julia Gillard. Yet the record is undisguised: Gillard was a passionate Labor traditionalist. Julia was a modern woman with rear-guard origins. Her political roots sprang from the soil of Labor families like her own and the eternal conviction that Labor carried the world's best hopes. 'Education and workplace relations were the two things that motivated me to enter politics in the first place,' she said in 2010.[16] Gillard had no interest in changing Labor's culture or structure. As prime minister, she needed the support of business but was unable to cross that bridge. Her policy conception was not sufficiently wide or creative to take her there.

In crude terms, Gillard ran a government that was too pro-union and too anti-business, and this branding became entrenched in public attitudes. Swan and Gillard, distant from each other till thrown together, shared the same Labor traditions. It is no surprise they got on. Labor would have done better had they complemented, not reinforced, each other.

The crisis Gillard faced was a governing crisis. From her first day to her last, the problem lay in how she governed. Much of the Labor Party denied this reality. Rudd's presence gained traction because of Gillard's difficulty in office. Indeed, she broke every rule in the Labor re-election book as perfected by Hawke and other successful ALP leaders. Gillard played to the Labor base at the expense of the middle—and lost her job for it.

She complained about Rudd's dysfunctional government but the truth is that Gillard had her own governing crisis as prime minister. Labor's tragedy is that both Rudd and Gillard failed to govern effectively.

Gillard was a willing prisoner of Labor's identity as a trade union party, as verified by her political adviser, John McTernan:

> Delivering for the labour movement was part of who she was. It wasn't really a transaction. It was simply a statement of how close she was to the unions. It is who she was. She was one of them. She was at one with them. She knew a Labor Government delivers for the labour movement.[17]

By contrast, Greg Combet said:

> The trade unions were deeply suspicious of Rudd. He didn't know the union movement or the people. He couldn't penetrate that. And that hurt him as Labor leader. Gillard knew how it worked from her time as a lawyer. She was involved in the movement in a way that Rudd wasn't. Julia could work the labour movement to gain and sustain its political support.[18]

Yet Gillard's strategy narrowed Labor's voting base. Teaming up with the Greens, appeasing the unions and dismissing the corporate sector did not make for a viable governing strategy. Yet there was no correction at work. Towards the end Gillard enacted more pro-union laws, sponsored class-based rhetoric, launched a crackdown on foreign workers with 457 Visas and sought to polarise the nation over Labor values. The result is that she polarised Labor into a minority position.

In February 2013, confronting a Nielson poll with a Labor primary vote of 30 per cent, Gillard attended the annual conference of the

Australian Workers' Union, the most powerful union inside the party. The Prime Minister offered a rallying cry. 'I'm not the leader of a party called the progressive party,' she said. 'I'm not the leader of a party called the moderate party. I'm not the leader of a party even called the social democratic party.' No, she led a different party. She came as 'Leader of a party called the Labor Party—deliberately because that is what we come from. That is what we believe in and that is who we are.' Her fidelity was to Labor as a trade union party. It is how she saw herself. It is how she governed. Yet it was fidelity to a sectional interest.

The corporate, entrepreneurial, small-business and self-employed communities concluded that Gillard was not their friend. Her loyalty lay elsewhere. With caucus unrest spilling through the media, outgoing AWU National President Bill Ludwig defiantly raised Gillard's arm. AWU chief Paul Howes praised her as a 'street tough' PM and said: 'I'm proud to lead a union that backs her 110 per cent.' Not for decades had the AWU assumed such a public role in defending an ALP national leader.

Such support helped Gillard in the party but weakened her in the nation. Yes, she was tough and tenacious. But on whose behalf? The irony for Labor is that, as trade union coverage of the workforce fell dramatically (to 14 per cent in the private sector), union influence within the party had grown. The talent pool for Labor politicians had shrunk to those with backgrounds as union officials, ministerial staffers or party advisers. Labor had narrowed as an institution while the society it aspired to govern grew more diverse.

There was, of course, another reason for Gillard's tactics. Combet said: 'Her capacity to work with the unions was the key to her survival as prime minister when the polls were bad and Rudd was destabilising her. The key union leadership didn't shift. From their point of view, she delivered for them.'[19] Yet it was a choice. Gillard was ready to challenge the teachers unions on school reforms; her appeasement of them on IR was her choice.

Chris Bowen, a Rudd champion, said: 'The AWU was her power base and it almost made her invincible.'[20] Caucus sources estimated that union power had the potential to influence up to 15 or 20 votes for Gillard. In his 2013 essay Mark Latham explained the system:

> Larger unions like United Voice, the Australian Manufacturing Workers' Union, the Australian Workers' Union and the Shop Distributive & Allied Employees Association ('the Shoppies') have purloined groups of MPs they can control, much like Britain's

eighteenth-century system of rotten boroughs. If any of these MPs defies a union directive, especially on major issues such as leadership ballots and industrial relations policy, they risk losing their pre-selection.[21]

March 2013 saw the explosion of a long-simmering sentiment: the attack on Gillard's governing ethos from within the party. It was a row over how Labor should govern and it came not from Rudd—though it was tied to leadership—but from the Hawke–Keating believers. There were three main critics—Crean, Ferguson and Bill Kelty—each a famous former union leader.

These men were a mixture of realists yet romantics. Realists because they had been architects of great events, including the ALP–ACTU Accord from the Hawke–Keating glory days; yet romantics because that age was dead and could not be resurrected. But they knew one thing: Gillard's was a bad way to govern.

For Crean, the disillusionment was deep and troubling. As a former leader he would talk to Rudd and Gillard, trying to awaken their minds to superior strategies. He hoped for a Labor relationship with unions to promote competitiveness, productivity and superannuation. 'The relationship with the trade unions was based around a legislative response, not a strategic response,' Crean said. 'It is the point I made time and time again. You cannot redistribute unless you have grown the cake.' Crean was dismayed that in the election year Labor was focused on 'right of entry' laws to help the unions. It was pathetic. Where, he asked, was the big picture?

Crean had no time for Swan. 'He doesn't have breadth of vision,' Crean said. 'He doesn't easily engage in conservation.' By late 2012, Crean felt Gillard had lost her way. Her model of government didn't work. For Crean, everything came back to Hawke. 'The success of modern Labor has been its ability to bring the show together,' Crean said. 'Bob's consensus model didn't shirk the hard decisions. Labor achieves its biggest reforms because it brings people with us.' But neither Rudd nor Gillard was Hawke. They were different; they had to find their own way.[22]

Gillard had ceased to take Crean seriously; she felt he suffered from 'former leader syndrome'—a problem with Bob Carr too. 'Simon's not in a good space,' she told colleagues. Many ministers got sick of Crean's harping about Hawke and Keating. Gillard felt she was kind to Crean; she tried to protect him in cabinet from the 'try and catch up' attitude others displayed towards him. Gillard decided Crean had never recovered from losing the leadership.[23]

When he called for a leadership ballot in March 2013, Crean invoked the Hawke–Keating model. He believed Gillard had to change. 'The class warfare thing was worrying me,' Crean said. 'Them-versus-us was the wrong sort of message.' He said the cabinet discussion about 457 Visas had been a good debate—but the public message of 'putting Australians ahead of foreigners' was dangerous and counterproductive.[24]

Ferguson's alienation was more intense. His resentment over the mining tax never died. Ferguson had been sidelined by Rudd and used by Swan. But his deepest hostility was reserved for Gillard, who he felt was over-promoted and over-rated. After Rudd's 'non challenge' of March 2013, Ferguson cut his ties, went to the backbench and spoke out.

'I am not reflecting on anyone,' Ferguson said. Of course, he was reflecting on Gillard. His message was that Gillard was not governing 'for all Australians'. Could there be a more lethal comment about a prime minister? 'The class war that started with the mining dispute of 2010 must stop,' Ferguson said, aiming at Swan. 'It is not doing the Labor Party good and it must reclaim the legacy of the Hawke–Keating [era] and, I might say, the then-ACTU leadership.' Ferguson knew the unions were at the heart of the problem. He complained that 'it's all ask and no give and take'. The unions were not seeking a strategic partnership. Ferguson, like Crean, sounded like a hopeless bygone-age romantic, except that he spoke the truth.[25]

Then Bill Kelty went public.

Kelty's thesis was that Labor must back responsible policies and 'reject the ideas and processes that have no home in the party'. He said it was 'too easy to blame the Opposition, the media or Kevin Rudd'. Labor must fix its own house. It had a good story on economic policy, low unemployment and strong living standards. 'The politics of the next few months is no longer about the result of the next election,' Kelty said. 'It is about the future of the ALP.' Gillard's task was to build on the foundations of past leaders, 'not put them at risk'.[26]

He complained about a litany of Gillard's attitudes—the trust-busting carbon tax, the reinvention of class warfare, the anti-foreigner rhetoric, pushing single mothers onto the dole—while he backed the Crean/Ferguson line on the need to create wealth before its redistribution. Kelty highlighted the previous ALP–ACTU Accord: increases in productivity were more important than fights over the share of the cake.

But Crean, Ferguson and Kelty were voices in the wilderness. The Gillard Government was in its twilight. Gillard was a different leader, Swan was a different treasurer; Labor's mindset had long departed the

Hawke–Keating era. Only the Crean/Ferguson/Kelty leftovers from that age actually grasped from their own experience how much Labor had changed and how much it had lost. The rest of the party recited empty slogans about following in the Hawke–Keating tradition without comprehending what that meant.

The trade unions had no wish to rekindle the 1980s-type arrangements. They remained tied to Labor but Labor seemed unable to reinvent this relationship. Hawke had recently let slip the truism about 'an almost suffocating union influence' on the Labor Party. What was Gillard's reaction? She pressed ahead with more pro-union IR laws.

ALP National Secretary George Wright said Labor must not 'maintain the union relationship to the exclusion of others'. Wright said that in the 2013 campaign, the single biggest ALP donation was through the internet. The party raised $70 000 via the internet in 2010 and $850 000 in 2013, which was 'a bigger contribution than any single union'. The future lay in a move away from the unions. But the Rudd–Gillard generation left this job to their successors.

The history of the ALP since the 1890s, as historian Graham Freudenberg identified, had been dominated by the question 'Who needs the other most—the unions or the party?' Under Gillard, the unions and Labor were devouring each other. The 2007 ACTU–ALP alliance that destroyed WorkChoices, so brilliant at the time, was now alienating Labor from the community. AWU chief Paul Howes said: 'For almost three years we did nothing but campaign against WorkChoices. Everyone was in it together. Opposing WorkChoices was our greatest strength but it also became our greatest weakness.'[27]

The 457 Visa issue became a study in Labor recidivism, creating agitation inside the party. It was sensible to eliminate abuses but cabinet's decision was presented with an 'Aussie jobs' xenophobic edge. In January 2013, under Labor, the scheme totalled 105 000 workers. The program was uncapped and driven by employer demand to meet skilled shortages, with visas lasting up to four years. It was a pathway to permanent migration. The program, initiated by Howard, had expanded under Labor. Gillard and Immigration Minister Brendan O'Connor decided to market the policy tightening as stamping out an odious foreign worker rort. This linked to the anti-457 campaign being run by Michael O'Connor, National Secretary of the CFMEU, who had called upon Labor to 'immediately suspend' the visas in all trades. O'Connor was the brother of the minister and a trusted long-time friend of Gillard. Labor could not meet his extreme demand but the government created a drumbeat of activity.

Minister O'Connor said there were 'too many rogue employers doing the wrong thing', that too many local workers were 'being discriminated against and missing out', that employers were preferring foreign workers because 'they'll be compliant' and that the government 'will not be influenced and lectured to by billionaires'. Australia's leading demographer, Professor Peter McDonald, a member of the minister's advisory council, said rorting was limited to 2 to 3 per cent of employers, rejected Gillard's claim that the program had been 'out of control' under Howard and said the scheme was essential to the entire immigration intake. Business could hardly believe what was happening.

Innes Willox from the Ai Group said the debate risked 'running completely off the rails and becoming an exercise in unfairly demonising companies'. Only three firms had been prosecuted since 2009 and 'xenophobes and zealots opposed to immigration in any form' were now being given a platform.[28] Business was stunned at the way it was targeted. 'The government just wouldn't let up,' Willox said. 'It was a politically driven union campaign by the CFMEU.'[29] Bob Carr said of the politics: 'Labor was staging a crackdown on workers coming legally to this country but failed to crack down on de facto economic migrants arriving illegally by boat.'

In Labor's final year, two issues intensified business alienation: the budget and more IR laws. On the eve of the May 2013 budget the four major business groups united, demanding a new approach to economic policy. The unity among different, often competing, business groups was conspicuous.

The BCA's Tony Shepherd said: 'Current policies, in our view, restrain and hamper business, making it harder to invest and harder to hire people and make us less competitive. They are risking our future. In industrial relations, we're going backwards. The tax system seems to be increasingly directed to discourage investment.' Jennifer Westacott said a return to policy transparency and 'proper processes' was essential to restore confidence. 'They have lost all credibility when it comes to economic projections,' said Innes Willox. There was agreement that economic reform was dead, and uncertainty about how to resurrect it. Mitch Hooke from the Minerals Council said: 'I've never seen anything quite so chaotic. The government has essentially shifted to a higher structural expenditure base off what is a cyclical revenue base.' Peter Anderson said the nation had a competitive problem and Labor's response was 'put a carbon tax on production and re-regulate the labour market'.[30]

This was the deepest and most sustained policy split between government and business since 1974–75, in the Whitlam era. The loss of trust and alarm about Labor policy became an unbridgeable chasm. Yet Labor refused to take such criticism at face value.

For business, tax reform was another flashpoint. In the May 2012 budget Labor scrapped a promised company tax cut from 30 to 29 per cent, blaming business for not persuading the Coalition to pass it (the measure was being financed by the mining tax). Labor set up a tax dialogue but said any business tax relief had to be offset by eliminating other corporate tax concessions. Westacott said: 'We saw this as a political set-up, we were being set up. There was no trust. Business figures would say to me, "If you offer them anything they will take it but not give you any company tax reduction."'[31]

With business, Gillard was often assertive, rarely persuasive. In her late 2012 speech to the BCA annual dinner she asked business to 'look at what the market is saying about us'. Labor had delivered economic growth, kept the AAA credit rating, finalised an Asian Century white paper, invested in education and skills, pioneered the NBN and advanced an infrastructure agenda. She ran a Labor government with 'an authentic Labor plan'. This was the problem: business felt it was being lectured outside any partnership.

In March 2013 a number of business groups combined to protest Gillard's plans for more pro-union amendments to the Fair Work Act covering union rights, workplace bullying, penalty rates and greenfields agreements. The message was blunt: this would damage small, medium-sized and large businesses and hurt jobs.

On 1 July 2013 Peter Anderson, dismayed and angered by Labor's policies, released a list of the impacts: an increase in the carbon tax, lifting of award wages, an increase in the superannuation levy, the fourth increase in four years in penalty rates, a lift in the unfair dismissal threshold and compensation, new parental leave obligations, new restrictions on recruiting overseas skilled workers, the requirement for employers to finance union travel and entry to remote workplaces, rights to sue employers for workplace bullying, and union rights to occupy lunchrooms.

Anderson said: 'While government politicians have spent months arguing about leadership, an unprecedented wave of anti-business decisions have been made, some rushed through and without due process.' Labor operated decision by decision. What mattered was the collective adverse impact. It was rarely, if ever, assessed.

For the Ai Group, the final year of the government's term was the worst. 'The situation got worse as the government went on,' said Willox.

The last year was very tough. We had Swan's rhetorical attack on billionaires. We had more changes to the Fair Work Act. We had a carbon price out of synch with the rest of the world. We ended up with an economy-wide tax that nobody else had. We were not allowed to have a floating price up-front because of politics. The tax was a serious extra regulatory import. Yet because of the Green alliance no argument, [of] no matter how much merit, could turn the debate.[32]

Acting on its mandate, Labor in 2012 abolished the Australian Building and Construction Commission, transferring its responsibility to a weaker regulator. The ABCC existed because of the Cole Royal Commission's finding that, in the building industry, 'the rule of law had little or no currency' in Western Australia and had 'long since ceased to have any significant application' in Victoria. A bitter series of militant building industry clashes reduced to farce earlier pledges by Rudd and Gillard to keep a 'tough cop on the beat'. Meanwhile the CFMEU's financial support for Labor election campaigns remained strong. Peter Anderson asked: 'How can it be that a parliament with independents promising to make the government accountable can just wave through a union plan to dismantle the legal framework recommended only a few years ago by the Cole Royal Commission?'[33]

ABCC abolition did not come with everything the union wanted. But it was a defining concession.

Interviewed after Labor lost office, Westacott said: 'I never saw from government a genuine effort to work with the business community, apart from efforts by ministers such as Simon Crean and Martin Ferguson. I think most people would say they just didn't get business at all.' Sometimes Penny Wong was mentioned favourably. When Swan's name was mentioned, Westacott said: 'There will be different views on this but I think the Treasurer did not have a good relationship with either the Business Council or many people in the business community. Whilst we got access and didn't get shouted at, you didn't feel that people were listening or there was respect for the view we were putting.'[34]

Gillard's senior ministers are unrepentant. Swan said: 'We were focused on the bread-and-butter issues but also putting in place the big reforms, like Hawke and Keating. The NBN is a big microeconomic reform. It deserves to be seen in the same breath as the floating of the dollar.'[35] Craig Emerson said: 'I felt under Julia there was a strong commitment to markets and an open economy and that she had no problem with this.'[36]

Drawing on his own experience, Combet complained about business: 'I think the business community lacked leadership on climate change. I mean every government in the world can't be wrong. If you assess it purely as an economic issue it is in our interest to reduce the emissions intensity of the economy.'[37]

The problem was not Gillard's toughness: 'I sit in this office and I say "no" to people because all the easy stuff, the nice stuff, is done somewhere down the chain. You can't be prime minister if you can't have those conversations.'[38] Asked about the motive for her 2013 trade unions laws, Gillard said: 'The motive is the legislation. It is good for working people and it is a natural extension of where we were going on IR. Was the trade union constituency happy about it? Yes.' This was No-nonsense Julia. She believed in the laws and believed they helped with the politics. She wasn't pretending to be a Princess Pure Heart. There was an ideological gulf: Gillard had a fundamentally different view from that of business.

Implicit in McTernan's explanation of Gillard's political strategy is the daunting nature of the task she faced:

> The research showed about 38 per cent of people said they were Labor supporters but only about 32 per cent said they were Labor voters. We had to win back what I called the U-turn voters. These were people who said 'Yeah, I'm Labor' but they were voting for the Coalition. Labor was a 'used to be' party. We had to win back these voters but at the same time appeal to the aspirational middle class.[39]

Gillard radiated conviction as an authentic ALP leader but was unable to persuade voters to 'think again'. She reinforced existing attitudes.

Gillard's conception of Labor was too limited. She failed, unlike Hawke, to reach across the divides. In politics you define yourself by your enemies. But in an election year Gillard had created too many enemies—notably across corporate Australia, large and small. Her brand of Labor traditionalism meant she did not govern from the centre. Gillard had polarised the nation, with Labor in a passionate minority.

CHAPTER 31

THE GILLARD DEMISE

O n 26 June 2013 the Labor Party, consumed by a desperation rare in its history, resurrected Kevin Rudd despite much loathing of its former leader—an admission that its survival as a viable political force was at risk.

Gillard called a ballot on the basis that the loser would quit politics, suffered a 57 to 45 defeat and bowed out, staying loyal and silent during Rudd's contest against Abbott. For Rudd, it was the sweetest vindication. The Labor Party, by its recall, made the implicit yet epic concession that his June 2010 removal had been a blunder.

Rudd supporter and future treasurer Chris Bowen captured the depth of Labor's plight:

> The view I reached was that the party faced an existential crisis. This went beyond losing a large number of seats. The issue was whether Labor could remain a competitive force after the 2013 election. I feared we might finish with closer to 20 than 30 seats and that would cast into doubt the historic mission of the party.[1]

Not since the Great Depression had Labor's mission been in such jeopardy. The ALP did not want Rudd. When faced with ballots, it had repelled him twice in the current Parliament. It was realistic about an election defeat but it could not tolerate its future being compromised. If Gillard had retained a shred of competitiveness the caucus would have kept her.

Rudd told the author: 'The first thing I said to my colleagues was, if you want me to return to the leadership, it is up to you to persuade the caucus. It is a matter for you.' Rudd said his message was that Labor had 'at best a one-in-four chance of winning this [election] because the odds are so stacked against us'. 'What I knew was we would produce at minimum a reasonable result that would enable the party to come back.

The alternative was Armageddon, the end of the Labor Party as a viable force in modern politics.'[2]

David Feeney, a Gillard backer who helped to make her leader, said:

> It had come down to a wretchedly difficult decision. We had to return Rudd in the interests of the party and government. That meant I had to vote against a woman I respect for a man I loathe who had engaged in political terrorism, and those tactics should not have been rewarded.[3]

Before the ballot, Penny Wong had come to see Gillard through the back door, distressed, in tears. She had never believed it would come to this. 'Pen, do what you think you have to do,' Gillard said. Wong was gone. Jason Clare told Gillard he had to vote for Rudd—he didn't want to see Labor hold no seats from inner Sydney to Perth. Gillard had a standard refrain: it is wrong to reward Rudd's bad behaviour. It was an ethical argument but, for many, the Labor crisis transcended any usual norms of ethics, love, loyalty or deals. Everything was stripped away.

A fortnight before, Swan had called Bob Carr to shore up support. 'Just let Rudd take over,' Carr said. 'There are only 100 days left.' He said Labor had to be left in some condition to fight back: 'It can't be rendered as weak as the New South Wales party.' Swan said they couldn't hand over the party to 'a madman'. Gillard's backers had run out of arguments.[4]

She lost, but the Gillard edifice didn't collapse. Julia got a solid vote. Not everyone accepted the 'existential crisis' proposition. On the final day, Tony Burke went to Gillard's office to say he wouldn't be shifting. 'I believe if there's a ballot now Rudd will win,' he told her. She asked Burke's view. 'I would rather you had control of a handover yourself than face defeat in the caucus,' he said.[5] But Gillard decided to force responsibility onto the caucus: she wouldn't do the job for them.

Combet was staying with Gillard. 'We were in a dilemma,' he said.

> It was assumed Rudd's return would deliver a better electoral outcome. And there is a moral logic to that—doing the best we can. On the other hand, the leaks in 2010 and destabilisation in 2012 and 2013 [were] so dreadful, damaging and devastating for the Labor Party that [such behaviour] couldn't be rewarded. I was more on that side of the argument.[6]

The young Paul Howes delivered a cry from the heart, angry at Gillard's fate, remorseful at the way Gillard's backers had made her leader:

> The view in the electorate is that this is a cold-hearted, mean-spirited bitch that stabbed her mate in the back. The irony, of course, is that I don't think there is anyone in that building who is nicer or more warm-hearted, on any side. I mean she is actually one of the genuine people in that building.[7]

There was no glory in the final Gillard–Rudd showdown, no 'Light on the Hill' idealism. It wasn't about the Australian people; it was about saving the Labor Party. This was a bunch of desperate politicians saving their necks. Past Labor leadership contests had a grander purpose: winning office or staying in office. There was no honour left. The Rudd–Gillard era had been reduced to a mad, self-interested scramble for survival.

It was the polls that ruined Gillard. Many caucus members felt Julia was a better person than Kevin. Labor knew the damage in 'revolving door' syndrome and the public's contempt for a party that kept assassinating its leaders. It had clung to Gillard, hoping the tide would turn, but the tide kept running out. Now Labor was stranded with a leader devoid of public credibility. Labor was at the nadir: it would change leaders to save some furniture.

For the waverers who defected from Gillard to make Rudd leader, there were no illusions. Did they believe Rudd was superior on policy? No. Did they like him more? No. Did they respect him more? No. They just knew one thing: it was over for Gillard.

Gillard's late 2012 polling recovery fell away. Newspoll ran two polls in November 2012, with Abbott's lead reduced significantly. But Gillard got no kick over summer. She began the political season with a bang: a confident Gillard told the National Press Club on 30 January 2013 that the election would be 227 days hence, on 14 September. The aim was to kill speculation over the date and vest her with more control of the agenda. This decision had logic but backfired. Gillard, inadvertently, was inviting the public to bring forward its judgement on her government.

She hoped for a period of 'cool and reasoned' governing before the campaign proper. It was a pipe dream. Abbott loved the announcement. He had longed for an election date; this was too far off but he was still grateful. That afternoon Abbott walked the press gallery in campaign mode.

Cabinet had not been told of the date. Gillard had consulted ALP National Secretary George Wright, who said it was her decision. On second thoughts, a few days later, Wright changed his mind and sent an email warning against it. He was prescient but too late. In that email, dated 29 January, Wright said:

> I am concerned the subtlety of the 'we are focusing on governing' message will not make it through the media and what we will be left with is 'we have just announced the longest election campaign in history' (a message that won't be welcomed by a public who feel they have been stuck in a 2 year election campaign already). Oppositions and Gov's move to a more equal standing once a campaign is called. Does announcing a date risk elevating Abbott rather than leave him looking irrelevant as we intend?

Wright said 'the Opposition want the campaign to start now', another reason for caution. Finally he said: 'We are not yet ready to start fighting the campaign. We have not worked long enough on framing the election the way we want it framed, we have nothing to launch.'[8] Events would vindicate Wright. But Gillard pressed ahead.

She was hit with setbacks—some just bad luck, some self-inflicted. The next day former Labor MP Craig Thomson was arrested and faced 149 fraud changes. He was bailed after appearing in a Central Coast court. That was bad luck. It followed the earlier charging of NSW union boss and former Labor Party National President Michael Williamson with multiple criminal offences.

Gillard now surprised by appearing at a weekend media conference flanked by two of her most senior ministers, Chris Evans and Nicola Roxon, to announce their resignations. What was going on? The timing was inept, putting it politely. The resignations and reshuffle should have been finalised pre-Christmas 2012. In both cases Gillard had been told twelve months earlier of their intentions. One reason she avoided any December announcement was because the caucus had to vote a replacement for Evans as Senate leader and Gillard wanted to pre-empt any leadership manoeuvring at that time. The leadership factor was ever present. Evans said he was not leaving 'sick, tired or bitter'. With Roxon there was a touch of emotion; she and Gillard were close.

But the media questions played badly. Journalists suggested it looked like a government in chaos. Leadership, pre-selection issues and confusion over the caretaker period dominated the questions. The media ran hard against Gillard. She was frustrated, sure that journalists were over-reacting. But the caucus was nervous.

For Gillard, it was the spectre of failed economic policy that was lethal. The Coalition was driving home the abandoned surplus promises, the collapsed revenue from the mining tax and reports that Labor wanted to tax superannuation payouts. The government was trapped; there were too many past blunders to defend and too many future budget difficulties to confront.

Julia kept her sense of humour. Paying tribute in Parliament to veteran political correspondent Michelle Grattan, who was moving from newspapers to an online position, Gillard spoofed her: 'What explains the timing of this announcement, who spoke to whom about this announcement, who was consulted about this announcement and how long can this chaos in the press gallery go on?'

Research conducted by George Wright in November had Labor close to the Coalition, around 49 to 51. It looked good but became a false dawn. The first two Newspoll surveys in February had Labor's primary vote at 32 per cent and 31 per cent respectively. The mid-February Nielsen poll, the first for 2013, had Labor's primary vote plummeting 5 percentage points since late the previous year to 30 per cent. These polls revealed a new 2013 trend that would be sustained. Labor's gains since the mid-2012 'lived experience' of carbon pricing were gone. Gillard's election-year plans were collapsing. Coalition MPs were agog at the rapidity of Labor's decline.

Rudd, aware of his over-reach the previous February, was controlled. Briefing journalists in February 2013, he had three messages on the leadership: this was an issue for Labor, not for him, since he meant his 'no challenge' declaration; he would only consider returning as leader 'if the party comes to me' or offers overwhelming support; and even then he would only return if he felt 'there was a serious prospect' of winning the election. Rudd was hanging tough.

The promotion of Rudd to the media by his caucus champions was misleading given that Rudd's tests for his return as leader were virtually unattainable. The uncertainty was whether Rudd was a candidate; 'Show me the numbers' was his mantra to his organisers. Rudd feared Labor's position was irrecoverable. He spoke privately of his predicament: becoming leader and taking the election loss that belonged to Gillard and was Gillard's fault.

Interviewed on Sky News's *Australian Agenda* program on 17 February, Rudd said there would be no challenge, he was not interested in any draft and it was time to put the leadership debate into 'cryogenic storage' because 'frankly it ain't happening'. Rudd wanted to force the party to come to him. But these comments reflected something deeper: Rudd was genuinely equivocal.

Greens leader Christine Milne went to the National Press Club on 19 February and terminated the Labor–Greens alliance while still supporting Labor in office. The Greens had decided they needed more product discrimination between themselves and Labor. They were just as cynical and unscrupulous as the major parties. With Gillard in her hour of weakness, Milne sunk in the knife. For its part, Labor was happy to be rid of the Greens for the rest of the term. That begged the inevitable question: if Labor was so happy about the divorce why was the marriage essential in the first place?

In early March, Gillard had her Rooty Hill campaigning week. For Sam Dastyari it confirmed her inability to recover. Dastyari said: 'Julia's narrative had been: give it time, give it time, give it time, it will get better. But it wasn't getting better. I think the realisation for a lot of MPs became: things are so bad we can't even do a re-start.'[9]

The Gillard camp was counting the numbers against Rudd. Craig Emerson was seeking to buttress her position. Julie Bishop had told the Coalition party room that Rudd 'has one more tilt left in him'. The Rudd camp claimed its vote had reached the low 40s, better but still short. Gillard's backers were adamant: they still had a caucus majority. But Dastyari knew the New South Wales Right was falling apart—it was heading to Rudd. Meanwhile Simon Crean, once a Gillard loyalist, was about to assume centre stage.

Crean met Rudd in late 2012 and continued the talks in 2013. Crean formed the idea of a Rudd–Crean leadership combination. His friend Martin Ferguson had been urging Rudd to link with Crean as his deputy. Ferguson's argument was that Rudd must unite the party and having Crean, a former leader, was the best option.

Rudd never accepted this argument. He told Crean that 'Albo' would be his deputy. 'I would like you to rethink that, Kevin,' Crean said. Rudd said: 'I can't, it's done.' Crean had no hope but he kept at Rudd. With the caucus worried about Rudd's style, Crean said: 'I am the insurance policy for the caucus.'[10] Crean saw himself as integral to remaking the government. He was prepared to go public. Yet Rudd was dismissive of Crean. 'If I am campaigning for the future, how can I link up with Crean?' he told confidants.

But the idea had lodged in Crean's head. It would be a final service to his party. And there was a personal element. Crean felt his leadership had been cut down prematurely in 2003. He still had a major contribution to make, even though Gillard refused to listen to him. Crean began dealing with the Rudd camp.[11]

There were multiple ironies. It was the New South Wales Right under former State Secretary Senator Mark Arbib that had led the June 2010 push to install Gillard as prime minister. Yet in 2013 it was the New South Wales Right under the fresh organisational management of young State Secretary Sam Dastyari that was pulling the rug from under Gillard's leadership. 'People will jump rather than face the firing squad,' Dastyari told Bob Carr. Arbib had ditched Rudd because of terrible polls in New South Wales; Dastyari now wanted Gillard ditched for the same reason.

Dastyari felt New South Wales Labor's future was at risk. It had been wiped out at the 2011 state election. With a 16 per cent swing against it, Labor was reduced to 20 seats in the worst defeat of a government in New South Wales history. The primary vote was a crushing 25.5 per cent. Dastyari said Labor had an obligation to minimise the damage at the 2013 election. The core Rudd group, nicknamed the Cardinals, comprised Chris Bowen, Alan Griffin, Joel Fitzgibbon, Kim Carr and Richard Marles. They began to target the fortnightly sitting that started on 12 March.

But at this point Gillard was misled by her faith in Conroy as Communications minister. She decided to back the Conroy media regulation package with its attempt to regulate editorial standards. 'There was a caucus appetite for doing something,' Gillard said.[12] Just before the 8.30 a.m. cabinet meeting to address the coal seam gas issue, ministers were told the agenda had changed to communications policy. Crean had his own complaint: he was angry that the policy gave major concessions on television licence fees without demanding appropriate standards for Australian drama content. As Arts minister he felt snubbed. 'The deal had been done behind my back,' Crean said. 'I was furious with Gillard.'[13]

Conroy said the package must pass Parliament in the next fortnight. The media reaction was predictable and incandescent, yet Labor misjudged it. Gillard said: 'I thought we would get a more benign reaction from Kerry Stokes than we got. I thought we would get a more benign reaction from Fairfax than we got.'[14] Labor had a collective tin ear. Conroy had misled Gillard. Bruce Hawker reported that 'angry backbenchers now have angry media outlets on their tails, including local papers'. The fiasco invited one conclusion: Gillard was destabilising herself.

On Monday 18 March the *Sydney Morning Herald* correctly reported that both Bob Carr from the New South Wales Right and Mark Butler, convenor of the South Australian Left, were leaving Gillard. Furious denials and qualifications were issued. Dastyari had been discussing with Carr how to bring the issue to a head but Carr, in Washington at the time, demurred. 'I am loyal to Julia Gillard,' he told the media. His denial was treated as a joke; his distaste for Gillard's leadership had become legendary. But Carr had no intention of becoming the Rudd camp's trigger. He would wait upon events. Carr was backing Rudd only because he was 'the least bad alternative'.

Rudd asked Bowen to negotiate with Crean. During their talks Crean was explicit: he wanted to remove Gillard and seek the deputy's job. This suited Bowen. His gameplan was an imminent strike to enable a Rudd government to bring down the budget and leave its policy imprint. He was also worried—he feared Therese was 'in two minds' about Kevin regaining the leadership.[15] A frustrated Bowen felt Rudd's numbers had hit a ceiling. He was keen to find a bloc of votes, and Crean seemed the best prospect.

Crean spoke to Rudd. 'There was a sense of urgency about bringing it to a head,' Crean said. Maybe. But the private briefings Rudd gave journalists remained the same. Rudd was unequivocal: he had not signed up to challenge. Rudd was not yet committed. In truth, Bowen was trying to get enough numbers to persuade him.

Crean saw Bowen and Fitzgibbon. 'They showed me their list,' Crean said. He offered to bring people across. Accounts differ on the numbers. Crean raised their hopes but Bowen and Fitzgibbon wanted evidence that Crean could deliver. Bowen said that if Crean ran as deputy they would try to deliver some votes for him. Bowen preferred Crean as deputy to Albanese. But the Gillard camp got Crean right: they saw him as a fading force.[16]

On the Wednesday evening, 20 March, Gillard initiated a meeting with Crean. 'You just can't blame it on destabilisation,' Crean said. 'You've got to look at your own contribution.' He made it clear he wanted a leadership vote. Gillard was standing firm. 'If he wants to challenge, let him do it,' Gillard told Crean. They finished without resolving anything. But Gillard was now alerted: a showdown was probable.[17]

Crean saw Gillard again next morning. 'What are you on about?' she asked. 'The word going around is you have done a deal with Rudd for deputy.' Crean replied: 'That's bullshit. If you want to know who he's supporting, it's Albo, so why don't you have a go at him.' Crean said the government wasn't functioning. He kept referencing the media issue. He asked Gillard to call a leadership spill. 'It is in the interests of the party that you bring this on,' he told her. Gillard was defiant. 'He hasn't got the numbers,' she said; it was up to Rudd to challenge. Crean indicated that he was prepared to force the issue and go public. Gillard warned Crean: he had a good reputation and this would tarnish it. She asked him to reconsider. He agreed to get back to her.

In the interim Crean had to negotiate a difficult 9.30 a.m. media conference. It was a bizarre event; he was polishing his rifle but unable to fire a shot. Bowen rang him afterwards. 'I saw you on TV but you weren't hard enough,' Bowen said. But Crean was now ready. He had reconsidered, as Gillard requested, and had rung Gillard. He told her: 'I want you to call the spill and if your answer to me is 'no' then I will go out and explain why I think you should.' Gillard didn't budge; the die was cast.[18]

Crean now pressed Bowen: 'If I pull the trigger, Chris, is this being supported by your people doing the count?'[19] Bowen wanted to press ahead. He knew it was a risk. If Crean delivered his numbers then Rudd should have a majority. Bowen knew it was a bizarre situation, with Rudd not yet committed. The two conditions Rudd specified to Bowen were: no challenge without a clear majority and a 30 per cent probability of him beating Abbott at the election.

But Rudd remained cautious. He distrusted Crean and his motives. At 9.20 a.m. he sent Crean a text message: 'Gidday Simon I'm told you saw the PM last night. If that's so and if it in any way touches on the leadership and if you are making any public comments please give me a call beforehand. My position is as before. All the best Kevin.'[20] While Bowen was ready to punt on Crean, Rudd was far more wary.

Crean didn't see Rudd's message and Rudd didn't think it important enough to phone him or ask to see him. At 1.20 p.m. Crean appeared before a throng of journalists in the Mural Hall at Parliament House. A shock to Rudd, Crean forced the showdown—and ruined his standing with both Gillard and Rudd.

In a rambling performance, Crean called on Gillard to have a ballot. He said Rudd must contest. 'I know the party will not draft him,' Crean said. He said Labor was looking for change—he would be backing Rudd. Crean had not spoken to Rudd in the past forty-eight hours. He offered himself as deputy but made clear he had no ticket with Rudd. As he spoke, a showdown became inevitable. With Crean now pledged to a leadership change, Gillard's position seemed at risk. She took two immediate decisions: she would call a ballot and she would eliminate Crean.

After the media event Gillard's office rang Crean's office seeking his resignation. 'You have got to be joking,' Crean told his staff. 'If they want my resignation, get her to ring.' Gillard rang Crean and requested his resignation. He refused. He said that if she won the ballot he would resign. But Gillard was finished with Crean. She had the letter ready on her desk—she said she was signing his dismissal letter for the Governor-General. Once her close personal friend, he was sacked.[21] Crean was stunned at her ruthlessness. Gillard went off to Question Time; Crean went to the backbench. Careers were being unmade by the minute.

Meanwhile, just before Question Time began at 2 p.m., Rudd told a senior figure from the media that he would not contest. The conditions he had outlined were clear; he would not change them. A few minutes later Gillard told the Parliament there would be a leadership ballot at 4.30 p.m. that day. Sudden death. Crean's colleagues now saw him on the backbench.

After Question Time, Rudd met his supporters—Bowen, Fitzgibbon, Griffin, Marles, Kim Carr—along with Albanese. He asked them three questions. The prospects for a significant majority? Answer: Zero. The prospects for a majority? Answer: Zero. He asked each what he should do. Answer: Don't run. It was a 'no brainer'. Rudd accepted the responsibility.

At 4.15 Rudd rang Crean to say he would not run. 'Kevin, you can't do that,' Crean implored. 'You've got to run.' Crean was dismayed.[22] Just before 4.30, as Rudd approached the caucus room, he stopped briefly before the TV cameras and announced he would not run. There was a collective roar of incredulity from the press gallery. A tiny number were 'in the know'. The jubilation was unrestrained in Abbott's office. The story was: Gillard stays, Labor in meltdown.

In public and private Rudd ridiculed Crean for his 'spontaneous combustion'. He claimed to have been caught 'off guard'. Rudd's attacks, mainly in private, were withering. Crean had misjudged badly, his intervention failing to tip Rudd's hand. Sadly, his declaration seemed to have carried no votes but his own.

Gillard was ebullient, ruthless and wary. She had stared down Rudd, yet again. Her message in lobbying caucus members went to Rudd's character: she said he lacked the strength to govern and, if elected, he would fold under pressure. Indeed, it seemed Rudd himself had done no lobbying. The Rudd 'no challenge' was mocked as a fiasco. Rudd was both derided as a coward and praised for keeping his word.

The psychological barrier to Rudd's return was too great. What is remarkable, given Labor's fatal poll numbers, is that the party refused to buckle before him.

The Labor Party now resembled the last days of Rome. Rudd supporters spoke to their families, then fell on their swords before being eliminated by Gillard. Gillard was on a purge, signalling she wanted Kim Carr and Bowen out of her ministry. In the next twenty-four hours, Bowen, Carr and Ferguson resigned, joining Rudd and Crean on the backbench. Marles resigned as parliamentary secretary; Fitzgibbon resigned as chief whip. Many attacked or slighted Gillard on the way out. 'Good riddance' was the Prime Minister's attitude. Most of the Rudd camp now gave up on the leadership. They believed in a pre-budget transition and they had blown it. They were smashed and despondent. Rudd looked a fool.

Retreating to Brisbane amid a backdrop of distant laughter, Rudd praised his supporters and called upon the party to unite behind Gillard. He said: 'There are no circumstances under which I will return to the leadership of the Australian Labor Party in future.' He had no option but to issue such an unqualified statement. But Rudd was disingenuous—the giveaway was that he would re-contest his seat. Laurie Oakes captured the contempt with which Rudd was viewed: 'He has no political future, even in Opposition,' Oakes said. He said Rudd should withdraw as a candidate at the September election and quit the Parliament.[23]

Labor was broken and discredited. It resembled two governments: one on the frontbench and an alternative on the backbench. It was unable to resolve the paradox of Rudd as the people's choice and Gillard as the party's choice. The Rudd challenge was over, yet the Rudd challenge was not over. The situation was that confusing. Its intensity meant the Gillard–Rudd war would not end while both sat as Labor MPs; it would end only when either Rudd or Gillard quit the Parliament. 'My view was that Kevin wouldn't give up, no matter what, no matter when,' Swan said.[24] 'I genuinely believed it was over,' Bowen said.[25] Kim Carr said: 'My initial response was deep despair. But within a relatively short period of time I felt there had to be another attempt.'[26]

On a jihad against treachery, Gillard restructured her ministry, promoted her supporters and tried to sell the 'it's over' message. Proof that it wasn't over came in the subterranean row over the numbers. McTernan said Rudd's decision not to run hurt Gillard by denying her public evidence of her superiority. The Gillard camp briefed every journalist that Rudd had only 37 to 38 votes, far short of the 52 majority needed. Gillard's people said that Shorten had been firmly in the Gillard bunker.

On the other hand, Bowen said Rudd had 43 to 45 votes. Kim Carr said 'well into the 40s'. Dastyari was higher: 'Kevin had 47 or 48 votes. I believe the New South Wales votes Kevin got in June were there in March.'[27] Dastyari had told Carr on 17 March that, of the 17 New South

Wales Right numbers, only 4 were still with Gillard. The Rudd backers said Shorten had flirted with a switch.

The weekend after the count, Labor royalty repaired to Byron Bay for a wedding. Swan's former office chief, Jim Chalmers, was marrying Laura Anderson from Gillard's office. At one point Swan went for Dastyari: 'You don't know Kevin, he is treacherous and evil.' Dastyari reflected: the government had become the Julia–Wayne–Conroy show.[28]

But Gillard felt it was 'diabolical' that there hadn't been a vote. The research showed Labor was now seen as an inept joke. 'The spill that never happened was a disaster,' McTernan said. 'Rather than seeing Julia dominant in the caucus, people now just saw a complete rabble.'[29] The Labor Party couldn't even organise a challenge. The public was contemptuous.

There was no polling recovery between March and June despite the budget. Fitzgibbon said the disability scheme and Gonski didn't bring voters over to Labor. The Rudd camp lay low, beaten but gradually aware they had another chance.

The focus now fell on Shorten. He had worked for Gillard in March. But Shorten was shocked by what he saw as her chronic bad judgement. His heart wasn't in the Gillard defence. Emerson said that as the year advanced, Shorten was: 'He was telling both camps what they wanted to hear. It didn't come as a surprise to anyone when he declared for Rudd at the end.'[30] Bowen felt the main difference between March and June was Shorten's shift to Gillard. But Shorten resented the public campaign conducted by the New South Wales Right to swing him and the Victorian Right to Rudd. The distrust between Rudd and Shorten was intense and enduring.

The Gillard camp was contemptuous of Shorten, considering him weak and duplicitous. In March, Swan had kept his eye on Shorten, suspicious about his loyalty to Gillard. Many Labor figures suspected that Shorten's real position in March was: I must support Gillard but I want Rudd to win. Neither side trusted him and neither side revised its view. 'I'll be staying with Julia,' was Shorten's frequent but unconvincing refrain. But Shorten didn't want the political blood of two leaders on his hands. He was thinking of his future.

In the end, polling in Victoria was too damaging. Bowen said: 'I think the big event between March and June was the Victorians deciding, based on their own research, that this wasn't mainly a New South Wales problem and they faced very heavy losses.'[31] Dastyari had the same view: 'The big difference after March is that bad numbers started coming out of Victoria.'[32]

Shorten, like Feeney, accepted the obligation to reinstate Rudd. The constant argument put to him was: since you are likely to be leader post-election, do you want to lead a rump or a competitive party? Shorten became a legitimising agent for some MPs to shift to Rudd.

On Sunday 9 June the host of the ABC's *Insiders*, Barrie Cassidy, announced that he believed Gillard 'will not lead the party into the next election'. The politicians knew that Cassidy would not have made this statement without impeccable guidance. It ignited a firestorm. The next day Dennis Shanahan wrote: 'It's now a question of how and when Julia Gillard's blighted leadership will end.'[33] Shorten had spoken to Cassidy before the *Insiders* program. He told Cassidy how serious the situation was and the extent of pessimism in the ranks. Swan made his own assessment: he felt sure Cassidy's remarks relaunched Rudd's bid and that Shorten was the key agent.

Rudd now abandoned his previous formula of ruling out any return to the leadership. After Cassidy's comments, Shorten told journalists he was still with Gillard. He would play a double game until the end.

But on 11 June Gillard revealed that her situation was irrecoverable. Addressing a 'Women for Gillard' meeting in Sydney, the Prime Minister said Labor was 'the party of women' and the election would decide whether 'we will banish women's voices from our political life'. Politicians from both sides were agog. Looking for a political circuit-breaker, Gillard was reviving the feminist cry from her misogyny speech. Labor was the party of equal pay, paid parental leave, childcare and dis-ability insurance. Moving into another assault on Abbott, she invited the audience to consider the situation where a prime minister, 'a man in a blue tie', goes on holidays only 'to be replaced by a man in a blue tie'. Gillard said 'very importantly' that 'we don't want to live in an Australia where abortion again becomes the political plaything of men who think they know better'.[34]

The speech took off. Gillard had introduced abortion into the campaign. She was tapping fears that Abbott as prime minister would threaten the status quo on abortion. There was no context, no hint to this effect by Abbott in four years as Opposition leader, though his past history revealed a concern to reduce the number of abortions.

The speech was too desperate—the final resort of a sinking leader—and it revealed Gillard's delusion. Her survival depended on better polling numbers, yet playing the abortion card would only deepen the trend against her. Kim Carr was incredulous: 'Our vote among men was down to one in four. We had got to the stage where the Labor Party's chance of surviving under Gillard's leadership was in trouble.'[35] Publisher and feminist Mia Freedman said Gillard's comments had 'felt manipulative [...] didn't feel genuine'. The former ALP pollster and chief of market researcher ANOP, Rod Cameron, said: 'Her credibility is absolutely zero in the electorate. Fairly or unfairly, the electorate is not listening to her. If they do listen to her—and not many do—but if they do, they get angry and it reinforces their decision not to vote Labor.'[36]

On Monday 17 June the departure bells were tolling for Gillard. The Nielsen poll in the Fairfax papers showed a Coalition lead of 57 per cent to 43 per cent on the two-party–preferred vote. But the story was gender. The primary vote for men recorded a 52 to 24 per cent Coalition lead. Men were voting for Abbott over Gillard in a 2:1 ratio. The *Financial Review* headline said: 'Men in Revolt against Gillard'. The resort to gender wars had become a catastrophe. The overall ALP primary vote was down to 29 per cent. Abbott led Gillard 50 to 41 as preferred prime minister.

The feminist/misogyny tactic was a tragic false step. How could Gillard have made these comments? With her leadership in jeopardy she had pulled the political suicide lever. In the teeth of these latest polls, how could the party now deny Rudd?

Bob Carr speculated that Gillard had been trying to duplicate Obama. Others assumed that progressive political fantasies had engulfed her office. The defect, as Dastyari identified, is that parts of the ALP believed 'there is a progressive majority in Australia'. In the United States, Obama had won on a progressive majority—Hispanics, Afro-Americans, youth, gays and other minorities.

Dastyari said:

> People argued that if we motivate our base and get progressives active in politics we will have a majority and win an election. There are two faults with this argument. First, the progressive group in Australia isn't big enough to win the election. We have no choice but to govern from the centre. And second, we have compulsory voting—everyone shows up regardless of how activated your base might be. The intensity of Gillard's support disguised the problem: she didn't have the middle.[37]

When cabinet met on the evening of Monday 17 June, Gillard said she would not be affected by the media and would stay as leader. Nobody commented. For Carr, this was surreal. 'Her selfishness struck me,' he said. 'If disastrous polling had been given to me—say, in my third year as premier—I would have handed over the leadership. What's going on in her head?' He concluded the motive could only be 'a deeply ingrained detestation of Rudd'.[38]

The next day at a meeting of the national Right, Dastyari told Carr: 'Shorten is resolved it must happen.' On 19 June, George Wright sent Gillard an update of a major research survey completed at mid-month. It read: 'Our identified losses stand at 34 seats, leaving us with 38 lower house members.' Yet it was even worse because 'the pollsters believe it is likely actual losses would exceed 40 seats'. That would leave Labor with around 30 members of parliament, a long-run structural problem. Wright felt this was a better guide. The defeat would be greater than Whitlam's in 1975 and 1977.

Interviewed for this book, Wright said: 'The core problems were the government's lack of stability, its perceived lack of competence and the public reaction to Julia personally.'[39] Two of the defining features were 'the huge damage done to the blue-collar vote' and the collapse of the ALP vote among men. 'There was a very definite gender difference,' Wright said. Changing leaders began to appear as an obligation.

Wednesday 19 June was the night of the mid-winter ball. At the urging of Richard Marles, Rudd and Shorten met face to face that night in Marles's office. Years of distrust lay between them. Shorten wanted to hear Rudd make his case; he wanted to know Rudd was commit-ted. Rudd, on the other hand, needed Shorten to sign up for change. Shorten had become a prize. But Shorten did not pledge to Rudd; he was too cautious, too distrustful. He would not show his hand until Rudd's challenge was declared. Both men knew their preferred positions had evaporated.

Rudd had to abandon his dream about a draft or an overwhelming surge. He had to knife Gillard; it would be an execution or nothing. 'He has to be prepared to fight for it,' Crean had said.[40] Gillard would never quit and Labor would never draft Rudd; the hatreds were too great. The truth was now revealed: Rudd's destabilisation of Gillard had been a disaster. Far from helping him to become prime minister again, it had hindered him, fanned hatreds and delayed his return. Stephen Smith got this right: he said a 'no treachery' tactic would have materially improved Rudd's prospect. Rudd had also been his own worst enemy.

Rudd's thirst for vindication was irresistible. He took resort to the sword. Rudd's hubris told him he would stand a chance against Abbott. Shorten's hopes that it could be resolved without blood on the floor were illusory. In the end, he would have to declare.

The next day Rudd's camp briefed that the challenge would occur the following week, the final parliamentary sitting before the election. Combet called for the issue to be settled. 'Essentially we had two leaders,' he said. 'I felt it needed to be resolved by a caucus ballot and I told Julia.'[41] At this meeting Gillard told Combet she would stand aside if he stood against Rudd. It is a remarkable offer but there was never any chance it would happen. Combet was ill and had already decided to leave the Parliament. Moreover, Combet knew that for the Labor Party, Rudd was the only alternative.[42] On Monday 24 June, Newspoll showed the ALP primary vote at 29 per cent, putting Labor's catastrophic situation beyond question. It was the third anniversary of the caucus vote that had made Gillard prime minister.

On 26 June, Carr went to see Gillard to discuss his Indonesia visit. At the end and speaking only for himself, Carr raised the leadership. Did Gillard really want to wake up the Sunday after the election facing the wipe-outs of Kristina Keneally or Anna Bligh? There were only ninety days to the election: 'It's not worth fighting about. But Gillard would not hand over.'[43]

Journalists reported that the Rudd camp was circulating a petition seeking a vote. Gillard met with her loyalists—Swan, Emerson, Brendan O'Connor, Conroy, Stephen Smith and Don Farrell. 'The show had been thrashed completely,' Gillard said. She knew Swan and Smith felt there had to be a ballot. She canvassed her prospects of winning if the leadership was spilt. There were two views: Gillard would probably lose but she would certainly lose if she waited beyond that day. Gillard decided to bring it on. Swan and Smith saw Albanese to ensure that the minority government ship stayed afloat.

Gillard's demeanour this fateful day was extraordinary. As she discussed the options she was disciplined, sharp, not without irony and devoid of self-pity. If the public could have seen the prime minister they loathed performing with such grace under pressure they would have been ashamed of their views. After Question Time, Gillard did an interview with David Speers on Sky News to announce the ballot. She radiated strength and confidence; she was an absolute professional. The loser, Gillard said, must quit politics. It was the final Gillard–Rudd contest.

Rudd promptly announced he would be a candidate. He said thousands of Australians wanted him to do this and to make the election competitive. Rudd conceded he had changed his position on the leadership. In short, he was breaking his earlier promise. Nobody seemed to care. Promises in the Labor Party had become worthless.

The final two hours must have been wretched for Gillard. People who had been unwaveringly loyal for three years now deserted. Wong was the only female cabinet minister to abandon Gillard, calling it her 'most difficult' decision. Shorten rang to say he could not support her. It was a brief discussion and she was unsurprised. Gillard never rated his defection as a significant event. Shorten made his public announcement in the corridor just before the party meeting. Neither side was impressed.

The 7 p.m. caucus meeting saw the final convulsion. 'The days since I stepped up in 2010 have not been easy ones,' Gillard told the caucus. She said the internal dissent had to end. Gillard lost the ballot 57 to 45, which meant she had lost 26 votes since her 2012 caucus victory. Her deputy, Swan, and Senate leader, Conroy, resigned. Emerson and Garrett stood down. They would not contest the election. Joe Ludwig quit the ministry. Combet brought forward a decision to quit for health reasons. Having agreed with Gillard that he would re-contest and then retire, Combet felt no such obligation to Rudd. Smith was in the same position. He had wanted to quit but decided that with Gillard he would re-contest. With Rudd now returned, Smith felt a free agent and decided to leave. Albanese defeated Crean 61 to 38 to become deputy prime minister. Wong became Senate leader and Bowen became Rudd's treasurer.

'The party should have stayed with Gillard,' Swan said. 'In my view she would have been a lot more stable in an election campaign. He was scathing of Dastyari's role and of the media. 'The media never properly held Rudd to account for his activities,' Swan said. 'He got away with political murder.' It is hard to dispute this assessment of the media.[44] Rudd's campaign to return was assisted by a permanent cheer squad in the media. Burke said there was a pattern: whenever Gillard began to make progress, Rudd destabilisation would erupt. Burke, Combet and Smith agreed that it was wrong to reward Rudd. 'This was the view of a wide range of cabinet ministers,' Smith said. 'We knew the damage Kevin had done and we should not have changed.'[45] 'My loyalty was to Julia,' Combet said. 'I think the public looked at us and said, this mob, the backstabbing, the undermining, it was terrible. So I thought "no revolving door".'[46]

Despite these comments Gillard's demise was of her own making. The caucus was prepared to extend extraordinary tolerance towards her, yet despite such tolerance her position became untenable. The caucus had no option. It was driven to the leadership change by Labor's self-interest, though Rudd's sabotage was unforgiving. Rudd's incompetence as a challenger was conspicuous. He returned as prime minister far too late, with too little time to display his credentials. Gillard's offer to stand down for Combet can be used to argue she was not clinging to the job at all costs. But it is unpersuasive. This offer was never a viable option since Rudd was the only alternative in the eyes of the party and the nation.

Gillard's tragedy was the absence of clean political air from the day she became prime minister. It became a protracted train wreck: the 2010 campaign leaks, minority government, the carbon tax, Rudd destabilisation, more boats, the disappearing surplus and entrenched public hostility. All roads lead back to Gillard's flawed decision on 23 June 2010 to depose Rudd. That was her responsibility, her fatal mistake. Gillard, however, is justified in drawing a contrast between herself and Rudd. She told the author:

> The difference is I formed my role in Kevin's government with loyalty. I asked him for a ballot. He didn't contest that ballot and I became prime minister. Kevin never accepted the outcome of the caucus decision. And he continuously destabilised the Labor Government. Obviously I didn't like it when caucus took another decision to put Rudd back. I accepted it and I have conducted myself in accordance with that decision.[47]

IX

THE DEMISE OF LABOR

CHAPTER 32

RUDD SUCCUMBS TO ABBOTT

Kevin Rudd came to bury much of the Gillard era and resurrect his own brand. Rudd's statement that he would 'resume' the office of prime minister was an act of assertion. He wanted to break free of Gillard–Abbott poisoned politics. His alienation from Gillard was now a gift. 'I was elected on a platform of new leadership,' Rudd said, investing a squalid ballot with the veneer of grandeur. Rudd wanted the public to 'think again' about Abbott.

The task was too great, the time too short. Impressions were too entrenched. And, critically, Rudd was too tarnished. The Rudd of 2007 would have had a chance; not the Rudd of 2013. Rudd won a honeymoon surge in the polls; that was to be expected. After that, the polls turned south against Rudd faster than many anticipated. By the campaign mid-point, Rudd was finished, short on ideas, reduced to negatives, running a dysfunctional operation. The flaws in Rudd's political nature were apparent—again.

The Rudd re-call had a meaning beyond saving the furniture. Rudd tried, with mixed results, to take Labor in new directions. Rudd told the author that Gillard betrayed the spirit on which he won the 2007 election. Rudd said:

> Regrettably after June 2010 a series of decisions were taken by the government which caused the community to conclude this was no longer new leadership and a new Labor government. It was a return to Old Labor, where the primary source of power was the unions and union-based factions. I believe the public looked at that and concluded that is not what they wanted for the future.[1]

He was scathing of Gillard's alliance with the Greens: 'It was not only politically unnecessary because the Greens had nowhere else to go. It was monumentally politically damaging for the re-election of the government because it involved a deep breach of her commitment to the Australian people.' By electing him in 2006, Rudd said, the caucus voted for a leader who believed in a 'new pro-business Labor approach' and who 'wouldn't simply tug the forelock and do what the unions wanted'.[2]

In critical areas Rudd wanted to purge Gillard's influence. Explaining his priorities, he said: 'Number one was the relationship with business, which had degenerated into class warfare. Number two, the government had gone flip-flop on asylum seekers and we weren't dealing with the core of the problem. The third thing that needed to be bedded down was the transition from a carbon tax to an emissions trading scheme.' Fourth, Rudd said he needed 'to change fundamentally the narrative on public finances' to invest the government with a more credible position. Finally, Rudd was more ambitious than before about party reform, determined to break through Gillard's legacy of resistance, sure this was now a mainstream issue for the public.[3]

The initial Rudd rebound was clean and strong. Labor polling showed a 51 to 49 per cent two-party-preferred lead after Rudd's first week. Newspoll showed 50–50 per cent after ten days. The Fairfax Nielson poll showed 50–50 per cent after a fortnight. Labor felt a thrill of excitement. For the Coalition, it was the moment when things could have unravelled. But Abbott kept his nerve; the Coalition stayed firm.

People tended to forget that Abbott had faced Rudd before. Abbott, Hockey and Bishop had assumed Rudd would return and for Abbott the sooner it happened, the better. In March 2012, when Crean broke out, Abbott thought that would be the day and he began to prepare.

'I remember sitting at my desk starting to write notes,' he said. 'I was very calm. I thought Rudd was at least as beatable as Gillard. I never saw the electoral alchemy with Rudd, whereas some of my distinguished advisers thought Rudd could transform Labor's fortunes. When Rudd did come back, I don't think I was particularly fazed by it.'[4]

For the Liberals, panic at this point could have been fatal. Brian Loughnane said: 'One of the advantages of the intensity of the previous three years was that, when Rudd returned, the party held its nerve when it could have become spooked.'[5] In senior ranks, Liberal confidence was anchored deep. Labor kept looking for cracks—namely, leadership tensions and Turnbull's resurgence in response to Rudd. They were more clueless than ever about Liberal politics. Abbott's consultative style meant he was entrenched.

'Think of Tony as the coach,' Julie Bishop said. 'The key is that even people who disagree with him on certain issues will follow Tony. It is part of his team ethos.'[6] Hockey and Abbott had long since agreed on the terms of their partnership.

The foundation of Liberal stability was the Abbott–Hockey relationship; it would be fundamental to the Abbott Government. The two first met about 1985 when Abbott was still at the Manly seminary. 'Tony was playing rugby for the seminary and I was playing for St John's College,' Hockey said. 'We played against each other with 400 priests as the sole crowd.' The 2009 leadership contest had left no personal rancour. Hockey, like virtually everyone, was surprised at Abbott's performance as leader.

Interviewed for this book after the 2013 election, Hockey said: 'I didn't think he [Abbott] had it in him. I don't know Tony thought he had it in him. He was unquestionably a better leader than I thought he would be. Tony is incredibly modest and easy to deal with.'[7] Their partnership was sealed in a discussion held before the 2010 election after Hockey's alarm at two Abbott initiatives—his paid parental leave scheme and his so-called green army.

'We had a "come to Jesus" discussion,' Hockey said. They reached a compact: Abbott, as leader, would respect Hockey's views and needs as shadow treasurer; and Hockey, in turn, would support Abbott's position as leader. 'Tony and I have worked very closely together,' Hockey said.

> We knew to be a successful Opposition there couldn't be a cigarette paper of difference between us. We reached an explicit understanding on that point. We knew there would be more scrutiny of our relationship than any other relationship in the Coalition. Tony is pragmatic and non-ideological. From my perspective, he has been the easiest person to work with.[8]

Rudd, operating in a situation of chaotic broken traffic, was initially impressive. He was camped down in Albanese's office trying to patch together a personal staff, running on instincts, talking endlessly to colleagues, projecting as a born-again leader, insisting that New Kevin, unlike Old Kevin, was no one-man band. Rudd talked up his conversion in favour of same-sex marriage, a sure vote winner with youth. Keen to nail Abbott, he raised the prospect of conflict with Indonesia over the 'turn back the boats' policy. Rudd was desperately keen to attend the upcoming G-20 meeting in St Petersburg but this notion horrified most of the ALP tacticians. How, they asked, did a trip to Russia fit into the election strategy?

Bruce Hawker became even more influential as the Prime Minister's political adviser. Hawker wanted an election framed around Rudd as the future and Abbott as the past. But Combet was alert to the danger: 'The public wanted the wrong that had been done to Rudd to be righted,' he said. 'But once it was righted, people's minds went back. "Oh, it's that guy again."'[9] There was a conflict between Rudd and the ALP tacticians. Rudd wanted to prove himself; he wanted to govern, at least for a while. He was sceptical of an immediate dash to the polls.

For Rudd, there was no higher priority than reframing the economic debate. 'My first action upon returning as prime minister is to reconstitute business in the middle ground,' he said. Yet too much damage had been done. 'The government had decided to define business as a class enemy,' he said. 'This had never been my view. It was certainly not the basis on which I was elected in 2007. My first instinct was to pick up the phone to [BCA President] Tony Shepherd and say we need to meet and work out what we can do together.'[10]

When Rudd met the BCA he ate humble pie. 'I think we've made missteps here,' he said. He pledged to 'fix the toxic relationship' with big business. He talked their language: competitiveness and productivity. 'It was very different to the conversations we were having with Gillard and Treasurer Swan,' Jennifer Westacott said.[11]

Rudd had the futile idea of creating a form of business–ACTU accord, literally out of the blue. Nothing better revealed his distaste of Gillard's governance. Yet a snap repair job for an election was not feasible. 'I said I would get the unions into the room and we would stop this ridiculous outdated language of class warfare,' Rudd said he told the BCA. 'And we are going to agree on common agendas for the reform of the economy based on productivity reform.' After conducting separate meetings with the ACTU and BCA, Rudd then convened a joint meeting. 'I'm simply telling you that if the government is returned at this election, this is how we will be approaching issues,' he told them. Both sides were wary; neither had any intention of being trapped in a formal deal.[12]

At the Press Club on 11 July, Rudd tried to reframe the economic debate, asserting that "the China resources boom was over". The boom had passed its commodity price peak and had gone through the intensity of the investment phase. Rudd wanted to trigger the urgent debate: what happens post-boom? His answer was that Australia needed a new competitiveness agenda to guarantee investment in the non–resources sector: manufacturing, construction, services and infrastructure. He identified a seven-point program: electricity price deregulation, removing workplace rigidities, more efficient business management, moving towards a single environmental approvals system, more investment in education and training, infrastructure initiatives and a better deal for small business. Rudd accepted the BCA policy of a 2 per cent productivity growth target. 'To us it was at least recognition the country did have a competitiveness and a productivity problem,' Westacott said. 'Prime Minister Rudd was willing to put things on the table. But he had no capacity to effect any changes.'[13]

This was a Rudd agenda, a modest wish list of reform. It was not an agenda to pass the minority government Parliament. In truth, it went nowhere, becoming instead a measure of the extent of Labor's past economic omissions.

The same judgement applied to Rudd's carbon tax reform package. 'We've taken the decision to terminate the carbon tax,' Rudd announced, flanked by Bowen and Butler, on 16 July. It seemed too good to be true. In fact, Rudd was bringing the floating price forward to 1 July 2014, fast-tracking the timetable by one year. There were no Greens in the vicinity. The float meant a lower price, helping households with cost-of-living pressures and costing the budget $3.8 billion over the forward estimates to be offset by new savings. Rudd said the savings for an average household would be about $380 in the coming year.

He did a brilliant sales job. But he did not terminate the carbon tax. It was still the law of the land. Rudd did not have the *power* to terminate the tax. There was no suggestion he would put his policy to the Parliament. It would be defeated since the Coalition and the Greens opposed it. Rudd was making a campaigning promise; he was not governing. He was campaigning against Gillard, who had legislated a scheme that the public disliked but that Rudd could not unscramble.

Rudd had produced a classic white elephant, big and enticing. Its deceptive beauty is that it would never exist: it would not pass the existing Parliament and, if Labor won the election, it would not pass the next Parliament since the eternal rule of climate change politics was that Labor needed either the Coalition or the Greens to pass its carbon policies and neither was volunteering on this occasion.

The BCA was not impressed. 'We had been saying for a long time the $23-a-tonne price had to be dropped immediately,' Westacott said.

> Every time we said it, the accusation became 'the Business Council is being hysterical, this [the price] is not having an impact'. Then we get the same government under a different leader announcing 'we cannot possibly keep this fixed price, it is hurting our

competitiveness'. We put out a press release that day saying this has got to stop, it's just a mess, go back to the Productivity Commission and sort out what to do.[14]

While Rudd's purpose was to undermine Abbott's anti–carbon tax crusade, he was conceding Abbott's argument—that Labor had been imposing an unjustified burden on the community. In policy terms Rudd was correct; his model was superior to Gillard's. The policy change invested Labor with a better legacy: it stood for an ETS, not a carbon tax. Finally, Rudd hoped to expose one of Abbott's great flaws: his 'direct action' scheme, likely to be high-cost and environmentally ineffective.

For Rudd, party reform was non-negotiable. Going into a Leadership Group meeting on the evening of Sunday 7 July, Rudd told Hawker that if his plans weren't endorsed 'they can find another leader'. The party, of course, had no option but to genuflect before Rudd. His changes were the most sweeping in the history of the caucus.

The legacy of June 2010 now assumed a new meaning—as an event never to be repeated. Rudd was not just taking revenge on the factional and caucus blocs that had killed his prime ministership three years earlier; he was torching the party system that brought him undone. Rudd wanted a fundamental change in power: weakening the caucus against both the rank-and-file and the public. It was a truckload of sweet satisfaction.

Under Rudd's rules the leader would be elected jointly with the rank-and-file and the caucus having a 50 per cent weighted share each in that vote. It was a step towards democratisation of the leadership vote. A Labor prime minister could be replaced only by 75 per cent of the caucus signing a petition requesting that the mechanism for a leadership vote be put in place. Under such an extreme threshold, Keating could not have replaced Hawke in 1991; it is doubtful whether Gillard could have replaced Rudd in 2010; and Rudd could not have replaced Gillard in 2013.

These were path-breaking reforms with the potential to change the nature of leadership and government. Under Rudd's system a Labor leader who wins an election would stay as prime minister for the full term. If Rudd won the 2013 election he would take the party to the 2016 election. In short, provided the people vote the ALP leader as prime minister then the caucus bows before that decision—it is a power transfer from the caucus to the public. Rudd said Labor had to fix the 2010 problem when the Australian public said 'we voted for this guy and then suddenly it all changed'. His rules would prevent someone strolling in and saying to a Labor PM, 'Okay, sunshine, it's over.'[15] Hawker saw this as 'possibly the most significant moment in the history of the modern Labor Party'.[16]

Rudd's tactic was to kill Abbott's line that Labor was run by faceless men. Abbott said that in 2007 people voted for Rudd but got Gillard; in 2010 they voted for Gillard and got Rudd. He asked: Who will you get if you vote Rudd in 2013? Rudd now answered: If you vote Rudd you get Rudd. It had a comic dimension—having spent three years bagging Rudd as a dysfunctional maniac, the caucus was voting to give Rudd more power than ever over his colleagues.

These were extraordinary days for Labor. Rudd had Albanese and Bowen with him as the ministry approved the proposals. The special caucus meeting was held at Balmain Town Hall, near the Unity Hall Hotel where the New South Wales ALP was born in 1891. It was agreed that the threshold to trigger a leadership vote when the party was in Opposition be only 60 per cent, still giving an Opposition leader a more stable platform than removal by 50-plus per cent of the caucus.

Final judgement on these reforms will take time. The 75 per cent threshold is too high, privileging stability before accountability. But a new threshold above 50 per cent was desirable because the 'revolving leadership door' had damaged Labor too much since 2001. The jury remains out on the larger change—the 50–50 arrangement for the leader's election to be split between the caucus and rank-and-file. Many senior ALP figures privately oppose this; it puts the leader under more pressure to appease the ALP rank-and-file whose views are somewhat distant from those of the public.

The most radical policy change Rudd made was on asylum seeker boats. It was revealed at a press conference in Brisbane on 19 July when Rudd and PNG's Prime Minister Peter O'Neill announced a regional resettlement arrangement between the two nations. It was the toughest boat policy embraced by a Labor government and constituted probably the most sweeping reversal by Rudd on any policy in his career. The deal followed Rudd's trip to PNG and his personal negotiations with O'Neill. Henceforth no asylum seeker arriving in Australia by boat would gain permanent residence in Australia. Neither Howard nor Abbott had gone this far. Boat arrivals would now be transferred to Manus Island in PNG or other Pacific Island states (Nauru signed a similar arrangement a few days later). PNG would conduct processing and any asylum seekers found to be refugees would be resettled permanently in that country or another Pacific nation. Those found not to be refugees would remain in detention in PNG or be returned home.

It was Rudd's *Tampa* moment; by this action he conceded all his past mistakes on asylum seeker policy. Rudd's policy was cruel and, for this reason, likely to dissuade. It was founded on the principle of regional cooperation—with PNG, then Nauru. It proved that Labor had delivered its soul to Rudd in a Faustian bargain. Virtually every humanitarian principle Labor had enunciated since 2001 in criticism of the Coalition was abandoned at this point. Rudd said he understood it was a 'very hard line' policy. His obligation, however, was to put in place 'a robust system of border security and orderly migration'. He sounded like Howard or Abbott. But Rudd said Australian policy remained within the Refugees Convention. PNG and Nauru were signatories to the convention; Australia would not return any refugee to persecution. 'I had spent some time thinking about a regional resettlement arrangement,' Rudd said. 'You needed time to negotiate it, announce it and bed it down. We did all that within a matter of weeks.'[17]

The problem, however, would become the appalling conditions on Manus Island as documented during 2014, an issue of ongoing Australian responsibility. Rudd said the initiative to do more had come from O'Neill—the upshot being a significant increase in Australia's financial support for PNG. Australia would continue to take 20000 offshore refugees annually.

At the cabinet meeting authorising the policy, Rudd said one adviser believed that, without effective action, boat arrivals could reach 50000 annually, a quarter of the migration intake being delivered by smugglers. Backing the decision, Bob Carr said:

> The irregular migration issue was not a tabloid beat-up or a nasty bit of xenophobia weaving its way through our political system. It is altogether legitimate for the Australian public to be concerned about whether people smugglers run our immigration policy. The notion that our immigration laws and practices are being subverted was disturbing and struck people as being unacceptable.[18]

Asked about Rudd's new policy, former Immigration minister Chris Evans said:

> I was deeply uncomfortable with it. If you are asking: Is it an effective deterrent message then the answer is yes. Do I think it is sustainable? No, I don't. I don't think either PNG or Nauru will long be able to maintain those people. The idea of resettling people

in conditions often better than enjoyed by their local populations will become intolerable for these governments.[19]

The policy would be run by new Immigration Minister Tony Burke, who had given Rudd a resignation letter after the leadership change; Rudd refused to accept it. Gillard had told Burke of his resignation: 'Don't you do something like that in my name; you go back, get that letter and tear it up.' Burke took the job.[20] Once a harsh Rudd critic, he was deeply impressed at the way Rudd negotiated and managed the PNG deal. 'Kevin was masterful at making it easier for the PNG Government to help us,' Burke said. Asked if Rudd was different the second time, Burke said: 'In his dealings with me, yes, fundamentally. None of the criticisms I made about him first time round [was] reflected the second time round.'[21]

On election eve Burke said the impact of transferring people to the Pacific had been dramatic. Boat arrivals had numbered 4236 in July and only 1585 in August. 'We have broken the back of their trade,' he said of the industry. 'The trade that we knew has now gone.'

That night at Kirribilli, Rudd had a drink with a few intimates. They believed the new policy would end the trade in human misery. Hawker now felt Rudd had closed off the big areas where Labor had been bleeding: the economy, party reform, the carbon tax and boats. The issue was whether they had done 'too much too quickly' for the public to absorb. Rudd campaigned against two images: Gillard's past and Abbott's future. Rudd's pace, travelling schedule and policy changes had energised the party. 'I'm not interested in saving the furniture, I'm in this to win the election,' Rudd told the author over breakfast at Kirribilli.

In the two major published polls, Newspoll and Nielson, Rudd never hit the front. On 21 July, Dastyari told Carr 'we can win this thing'. In fact, Rudd had peaked. The Newspoll taken over 19–21 July was crucial. With Rudd in the job just less than a month, the Coalition kicked back to a 52 to 48 per cent lead. On 24 July Hawker got disappointing results from Labor's pollster across 20 ALP marginal seats—on the primary vote the Coalition led, 50 to 37 per cent. Hawker was worried Rudd was doing too much, pushing himself too hard.

Rudd's instinct was to delay the election. He was keen to attend the G-20 St Petersburg meeting since Australia would host the event in 2014. But the final brick in Labor's poll preparation was the mini-budget to address the budget bottom-line deterioration since May—that meant ugly spending cuts.

It was the worst possible way to start an election campaign. The nation faced lower growth, rising unemployment and weaker terms of trade. In its May 2013 budget Labor had misread the economic trajectory, yet again. The mini-budget was a patch-up job, necessary because the pre-election statement from the heads of Treasury and Finance would document the deterioration, leaving Labor with no option but to address it first. The May deficit forecast of $18 billion for 2013–14 was now at $30 billion, a slide almost without precedent in such a short time. Chris Bowen said the mini-budget revealed 'not a crisis but a transition'.

The mini-budget savings included a tobacco excise, a bank levy and tightening of the fringe benefits tax on employer-provided cars, a move with adverse knock-on political consequences. The media reaction was universally tough. Disbelief about Labor's budget forecast was now undisguised. 'Let's be clear, the government's fiscal strategy is not on track,' said BCA chief Jennifer Westacott. Stephen Anthony from Macroeconomics said Labor should have 'fessed up' at budget time to the real situation. 'We think the situation is significantly worse than this document concedes,' Anthony said of the mini-budget. Rudd settled on a 7 September election; governing longer would not help.

Rudd's election slogan, 'A New Way', invited ridicule. Rudd talked endlessly of new challenges, asked the people to 'trust me' and went for the amnesia effect—hoping people would forget the past three years. Abbott's message was stronger: 'Don't vote for three more years like the past six years.' Rudd had to win seats to form majority government. From the start his dilemma was on display: he wanted to be positive, yet his only hope was to run a scare campaign.

The day after the election announcement, two papers, the *Daily Telegraph* and the *Financial Review*, published page-one editorials calling for a change of government. The Labor Party seemed shocked. Having worked endlessly to cultivate News Corporation support on his leadership contest with Gillard, Rudd now faced a sustained News Corporation attack on Labor's record.

Labor's blunders over three years had contributed to the 'making' of Abbott. He had become a proven Opposition leader, more formidable than in 2010. While not liking him, voters knew what Abbott stood for. By declaring the economy the main election issue, Rudd played to Abbott's strength.

Abbott, as leader, had two obstacles to combat in the two years before the election—that he was an extremist in his social conservatism and suspect in his economic competence. Fairfax's David Marr epitomised the progressive case against Abbott: 'The loudmouth bigot of his university days, the homophobe, the blinkered Vatican warrior, the rugger-bugger, the white Australian and the junkyard dog of parliament are all, he would have us believe, consigned to the past.'[22] This tapped into virtually every prejudice. Abbott became a hate figure among progressives, notably female progressives following Gillard's misogyny speech. Professional critics of Menzies and Howard now lamented that Abbott lacked the balance of these moderate and splendid Liberal leaders.

The response of Abbott's office to such branding was slow. In the end, the promotion of Abbott's family—his wife and three daughters—helped to create an image of stability and normalcy. At the 2013 launch his daughters virtually stole the show. Abbott began his speech with a personal homily to his family and values: 'I am so proud of my girls. I am so proud of my family that has given me so much. I am so proud of my team and so proud of my country.'

It was the face of conservative acceptability. Yet the memory of Abbott the wild man lingered below the surface; it helped with male votes but kept much of the female vote suspicious of him.

From 2009 the Liberal campaign for office had been the story of Abbott's personal journey. The question 'Who is Tony Abbott?' became the most asked and least satisfactorily answered question in politics. Abbott's pathway had been the opposite of figures such as Whitlam, Menzies, Hawke, Fraser, Keating and even Rudd. These politicians were quickly identified by their peers as future leaders. Abbott had enjoyed no such lobby. Indeed, many of his friends doubted he had the capacity to succeed as leader. The upshot is that his performance as leader exceeded the expectations of his peers.

Nick Minchin said, 'The hesitation about Tony has been based on the media characterisation of him as a limited individual and an arch conservative Catholic. What happens is people are then surprised to discover Tony is a much more balanced and rounded and educated and intelligent Australian.'[23] Abbott has flourished because he is a late developer; that meant more capacity for growth.

Ultimately, the progressive attack on Abbott's ideological and religious history did not prevent his 2013 election victory. Abbott's support for traditional values—Christianity, family, patriotism, the Anzac story and male valour—may have helped him more with mainstream voters than his critics could comprehend.

As the commentator Elena Douglas argues, Abbott possesses a social and cultural significance not as obsolete as his critics imagine. He presents an image of traditional masculinity in an age of the metrosexual man who gravitates to cooking, fashion and well-groomed eyebrows. Indeed, the sharpest image of his first day as prime minister is Abbott on his bike at 5 a.m. Provided he avoids Putinesque caricature, Douglas suggests Abbott's 'man appeal is the closest thing the Coalition has to a secret weapon'.[24]

Abbott's temperament was the key to his political success, and his exercise regime was pivotal to his temperament. 'Someone once said to me the challenge is to focus on the important, not the urgent,' he said.

> I assimilated that. Exercise is an important part of mental therapy for me. Howard was so much better as PM because he did those walks every day. For me, it's very hard to be consumed by the events of the day if you can see things in perspective. I think exercise is meditation for active people.[25]

The Abbott story rests on the conundrum of enduring values and flexible policies. It has provoked numerous failed efforts to define and discredit him. It is a long and contradictory list: that Abbott was a B A Santamaria–type protectionist; that Abbott was an Anglophile unable to deal with Asia; that Abbott's religion made him a reckless adventurer on social spending; that Abbott had no policy commitments at all and just cared about power; and finally, with the May 2014 first budget of the Coalition Government, that Abbott was a heartless pro-market economic ideologue. During Abbott's political journey it is entirely possible he was unsure exactly how the various aspects of his beliefs and character would fit into the whole. Tony was a work in progress—and that confused his critics, encouraged his supporters and left the public unconvinced.

During the 2013 campaign, Abbott's poll ratings as a leader were below those of Howard in 1996 and Rudd in 2007, the two previous Opposition leaders who became prime ministers. Abbott remained a polarising figure because of the political aggression he displayed in the pursuit and destruction of Gillard as a female prime minister. More than Howard, he is a trigger for 'culture-war' hostilities because of his muscular conservatism, religious values and cultural traditionalism. Abbott defies the recent orthodoxy that politics in Australia is becoming more feminised. The test in office is whether Abbott continues to evolve and becomes a prime minister who can reach across divisions, the usual requirement for political longevity.

The real tension within Abbott as Opposition leader was between his social vision and his economic policy. The proof of this tension was his paid parental leave (PPL) scheme imposed on the party as a leader's dictate before the 2010 election. It was a road-to-Damascus reversal. 'Not over my dead body,' was Abbott's retort when Sex Discrimination Commissioner Pru Goward pushed for the Howard cabinet to embrace a PPL scheme. Abbott was instrumental in killing the concept. He denounced the PPL policy as discrimination against women at home. But as leader, Abbott had other concerns: he needed an iconic symbol of his conversion on female issues.

The size of the scheme transcended policy logic because it had another function: to reposition Abbott with female voters. Denounced by many shadow ministers in private, the scheme at the 2013 election cost $9.8 billion across the forward estimates. 'I have grown, I have changed,' Abbott said as he mocked Labor's far more modest scheme.[26] Abbott offered twenty-six weeks at the wage rate up to $150 000 a year (later reduced to $100 000)—compared with Labor's scheme, which paid for eighteen weeks on the minimum wage. It was old-fashioned, big-spending, Whitlamist social policy in action. At the same time, Abbott had backed Gillard's NDIS, the biggest-spending social initiative of the Labor era. How was Abbott financing his PPL scheme? It was partly by a hefty 1.5 per cent levy on big companies (raising $4.4 billion across the forward estimates). The scheme was loathed by policy wonks inside the beltway but Abbott's eyes were outside the beltway.

With his PPL scheme Abbott was ready to pour money into households, transfer funds from companies to working women and give little regard to targeting in the cause of fairness. The scheme became a case study in Abbott's contradictory outlook—declaring a budget emergency but building his cherished social edifices. A leader this pragmatic was capable of very large policy swings and reversals. In fact, the cost of his PPL scheme was too great, and became a liability that exposed Abbott's problem in reconciling his social and fiscal priorities.

The central contradiction in Abbott is between his conservatism and his liberalism. As a conservative, Abbott made a promise to restore the established order. He would return Australia to a world where there was no carbon tax, no climate change–fixated government, no mining tax, no boat arrivals, no spending waste, no appeasement of trade unions, no red tape, no prolonged blocking of resource projects. His pledge was to purge the Labor excesses by 'changing the worst government in our history'.

Listening to Abbott in the 2013 campaign, the public felt clear about one thing: Abbott had no wish to impose harsh or abrupt change on the nation. Abbott was a conservative, not a radical. He loved the Australian way of life, its monarchy, its mateship, its social stability, its British heritage and its democratic institutions. His mantra was unmistakable: the real problem was Labor. By voting for change, the nightmare would end. 'The last six years will soon seem like an aberration,' Abbott said. His project was the great Australian restoration, the beating heart of his conservatism.

Yet the longer Abbott served as Opposition leader, the more he became an economic liberal. In a series of speeches made between 2011 and 2013, Abbott recast himself as an economic dry: he pledged to restore the budget, obtain a surplus, pay down debt and run a lower-tax, lower-spending, smaller-government model. He promised to 'end the bad blood' between government and business and to ensure that 'good policy should prevail over clever politics'.[27] Many people did not take him seriously but that was a mistake. In one sense Abbott was devising a policy for the times; in another sense it was the latest stage in his evolution. Such an economic liberal agenda was highly reformist. It meant Abbott, the liberal, was becoming a change agent. Only after he became prime minister did Abbott confront the extent of the changes that would be demanded. At that point he became an architect of liberal economic transformation—witness the first Abbott–Hockey budget.

As shadow treasurer, Hockey had forged a firm intellectual position on the post-GFC plight of Western democracies. He became the initial advocate of the compelling liberal alternative that shaped Coalition thinking. In his April 2012 speech in London, Hockey warned that the industrial West faced a fiscal crisis, and this led to an irresistible conclusion: 'the Age of Entitlement is over'. While talking about the West, Hockey made clear that his comments had relevance for Australia. He said Europe and the United States were living beyond their means, providing a lifestyle financed by debt since their tax base could not cover their spending. The economic future of many Western nations was now mortgaged by the huge array of entitlements. Hockey's messages were that fiscal discipline must be rebuilt, budgets must return to surplus, people must work longer before they accessed retirement benefits and more government services must come with a charge. He said: 'It is time for strong political and economic leadership to clean up this mess properly.'

Abbott, in his 2013 budget reply, said the coming election 'will not be an auction'. Outside his PPL scheme, he honoured this pledge. Abbott said the Coalition would pocket the savings from Labor's 2013–14 budget announcements. Hockey told the shadow cabinet that 'the easiest savings we get are those made by our opponents.' Hockey's campaign message was for the Coalition to get through the election keeping open as many policy options as possible. Abbott and Hockey devised what they saw as a measured timetable: achieving a budget surplus of one percentage of GDP within a decade (three election cycles).

In truth, the full extent of Abbott's campaign pledges was daunting. He was now both a conservative and a liberal. This synthesis became the new Abbott, perhaps the fully formed Abbott. In his election policy speech, Abbott the conservative let loose his icons: a PPL scheme costing $5.5 billion annually, full restoration of the private health insurance rebate within the decade (using public funds to subsidise choice) and, also within the decade, returning defence spending to 2 per cent of GDP, a hefty lift on Labor's current 1.6 per cent (for the Liberals, a repudiation of Labor's appeasement culture).

Abbott saw these as identity commitments; they went to the essence of the Liberal Party as a conservative party. Yet they stood with Abbott's liberal agenda: lower, simpler, fairer taxes (meaning a major tax reform), smaller government (meaning major spending restraint) and the return to surplus (meaning a growth economy off the back of microeconomic reform). Abbott famously said that 'no country has ever taxed its way to prosperity'. At face value, Abbott even looked more a classic economic liberal than Howard, since Howard in office made no such pledges about tax and spending. 'We had no quantitative commitments [on tax and spending],' Howard said of his government. But Abbott did make such commitments.[28] Abbott's election package was ambitious. It could only be achieved by substantial reductions in entitlements and a transformation in Australian life over a decade, far deeper than Abbott envisaged at the time.

In the end, Rudd ran the biggest scare campaign since Keating in 1993. Labor focused on the alleged $70 billion 'black hole' in terms of Coalition cuts to finance its programs and achieve a surplus. The figure was known to be false yet was used by Rudd to claim that Abbott's 'massive cuts risk throwing the entire economy into recession'. Recycling Keating from an earlier campaign, Rudd said: 'If you don't understand how Mr Abbott's $70 billion of cuts will affect your job, your school, your hospital—then don't vote for him.'[29] Having pledged to offer a positive vision, Rudd was reduced to fear and scares.

Final Coalition costings released two days before the election showed $42 billion in savings to finance tax cuts, pension rises and social spending while improving the budget bottom line by $6 billion across the forward estimates, little different from Labor's position. But Labor's negative campaign had an impact. In the final forty-eight hours before the vote, Abbott, on the brink of victory, made a series of sweeping statements ruling out cuts in office. Two days before the election, he told ABC Radio: 'I can assure your listeners that there will be no cuts to health, no cuts to education, no cuts to pensions, no change to the GST.' The day before the election, in an SBS interview, he promised 'no cuts to education, no cuts to health, no changes to pensions, no change to the GST and no cuts to the ABC or SBS.' These statements became pivotal when the first Abbott Government budget in May 2014 violated such pledges.

Yet Labor pushed too hard on the costings issue, with fatal consequences. In the second-last week of the campaign, the heads of Treasury and Finance, Martin Parkinson and David Tune, issued a statement repudiating Labor's claims on Abbott's costings. It was an unprecedented event, the biggest story of the campaign and a humiliation for Rudd as prime minister.

The background is that, before the election was called, Labor got the departments to cost proposals it felt approximated as best as possible the Coalition agenda. In the campaign Labor pounced. Rudd, Bowen and Wong released the departmental memos to claim that Treasury advice had 'exposed' Abbott's funding hole. Rudd accused Abbott of lack of truthfulness, the attack resting on departmental advice. Yet Parkinson and Tune had not costed the actual Coalition policies. The public service establishment felt Rudd was exploiting its advice in a misleading way. This became Labor's final ignominious failure in its manipulation of Treasury. Rudd had over-reached and been repudiated by his own advisers. The symbolism of a dying, dysfunctional and dishonest government was irresistible.

Labor's brand was stained beyond repair after six years of office. The Rudd revival had been designed, as far as possible, to substitute Rudd for Labor. The truth is that the task was far beyond Rudd's overrated 2013 campaigning ability. Towards the end, Rudd's campaign had become a shambles.

The defects of his first stint as prime minister now reoccurred: Rudd became erratic, failed to sort his priorities, delivered long and tedious press conferences and engaged in a series of disconnected, almost bizarre initiatives. He pledged to relocate navel assets away from Sydney to Queensland, sparking displeasure from New South Wales Premier Barry O'Farrell. In the Rooty Hill leaders' debate with Abbott, Rudd declared he was less free market than Abbott on foreign investment in land and, mocking the strategy required beyond the resources boom, warned about 'open slather', thereby raising the prospect that he wanted more foreign-investment restrictions. Rudd made a disastrous visit to the Northern Territory when, obviously unprepared, he pledged a special economic zone with reductions in the company tax rate but could not explain the details or costs. Unveiling Labor's commitment to the defence industry Rudd began to channel 'Black Jack' McEwen saying that 'I am at my heart of hearts an economic nationalist.' And he kept saying it. He seemed unable to comprehend how this trashed his economic credentials: Rudd had moved from being a fiscal conservative in 2007 to an economic Keynesian during the GFC to declaring himself an economic nationalist in the final 2013 apparition.

David Feeney complained that it was a campaign of 'no plans and no strategy'. By mid-campaign Bob Carr's disillusion was entrenched, telling his diary: 'Rudd appears as a tone-deaf campaigner who relies on notes, seems to expect to lose.' Swan said: 'You could feel the position falling away. He wouldn't run on any of the agenda we had set up.'[30]

Rudd's dysfunction revealed the hollowness at the centre of his campaign: it lacked an enduring theme. The downside of changing leaders on election eve was exposed. Rudd could not defend Gillard's record over three years. He campaigned like a recalled backbencher who disapproved of what she had done. He paid lip service to Gillard's schools and disability initiatives—where Labor had put its money. After the election Gillard was scathing—at least she had an established agenda over three years and would have fought for it. Rudd, she said, 'felt constrained in running on those policies where Labor had won the national conversation'—in short, schools and disability policy.[31]

It was only at the Labor launch six days before the vote that Rudd produced a coherent campaign theme: jobs versus cuts. Introduced by his wife, Therese, who called him a man 'who carries his country boy smile everywhere', Rudd, in fighting spirit, cast the choice in simple terms: Labor's jobs agenda versus Abbott's spending cuts. It was Labor's last desperate hope. And it was far too late. Rudd fought hard in the final week but he had no prospect.

Those journalists who felt Rudd had spent his time on the backbench working up new policies and visions were deluded. Rudd looked good when he returned as prime minister, but the longer he remained, the worse he got. Apart from his 'fix it' moves on carbon and his boat policy reversal, Rudd's cupboard was empty. He had little to offer in terms of new ideas.

Mid-campaign, Hawker reported, he and Rudd were frustrated 'by the shortage of strong breakthrough policies'.[32] It was a government running on empty. The Coalition was far ahead of Labor on economic policy and Rudd, in the campaign proper, was clueless about how to position on the economy. Having declared the poll was about the future, Rudd chopped and changed, sent different messages and, ultimately, proved Labor was better defined by its negatives—it existed to oppose Abbott.

The Coalition had a decisive victory with a two-party-preferred vote of 53.5 per cent to 46.5 per cent. Loughnane said that, over the two elections in 2010 and 2013, the Coalition had won 31 seats from Labor and achieved a 6.1 per cent two-party-preferred swing. The Coalition won 90 seats to Labor's 55 seats (the remaining 5 going to small parties and independents). There was a quasi euphoria in the Labor Party on election night at having averted obliteration; mere defeat was now blessed relief.

Rudd had the good sense to announce he would not contest the leadership again. That decision terminated the Rudd–Gillard era. Kevin celebrated with family and friends, sure he had justified his return. Gillard had a different election night.

In a shattering yet brave depiction of herself, Gillard wrote:

> I sat alone on election night as the results came in. I wanted it that way. I wanted to just let myself be swept up in it. Losing power is felt physically, emotionally, in waves of sensation, in moments of acute stress. I know now that there are the odd moments of relief as the stress ekes away and the hard weight that felt like it was sitting uncomfortably between your shoulder blades slips off. It actually takes you some time to work out what your neck and shoulders are supposed to feel like. I know, too, that you can feel fine but then suddenly someone's words of comfort, or finding a memento at the back of a cupboard as you pack up, or even cracking jokes about old times, can bring forth a pain that hits you like a fist, pain so strong you feel it in your guts, your nerve endings.[33]

Gillard slammed Rudd's campaign. After the change of leadership, 'no alternative purpose' had been injected into the campaign; there was 'not one truly original new idea to substitute as the lifeblood of the campaign'.[34]

The first question is: Was the return to Rudd the correct move?

National Secretary George Wright had no doubt. He said the return of Rudd saved as many as 25 seats, a view that Gillard supporters reject.

The next leadership generation—Shorten, Bowen, Burke and Clare—was saved. 'Our research in June showed we were looking at diabolical losses,' Wright said. 'We would have been reduced to a bit player in Parliament. It would have made the task of returning to government a long journey. I think Rudd made a very significant difference—we had a bad loss but we are still competitive as an Opposition. That was not the situation in June.'[35] Much weight should be placed on his assessment. If the 2016 election becomes highly competitive then Rudd's 'saving the furniture' strategy will be seen as vital in leaving Labor within striking distance in Abbott's first term.

Wright's view is buttressed by the Rudd backers. 'I have no doubt Kevin saved a very large number of seats,' said Chris Bowen. 'I do not believe I would have held my seat without the change of leadership.'[36] Bob Carr said: 'By every test the change to Rudd was vindicated.' He said the venom directed at Gillard would not have abated and the ALP primary vote could have fallen to 27 to 28 per cent.[37]

'The change saved the Labor Party from its worst election result since the very early days of the Commonwealth,' said Kim Carr.[38] Sam Dastyari said:

Kevin stopped it being a wipe-out in Sydney. I have no doubt the wipe-out we were facing meant not only a generation of conservative rule but that the people who are the crux of our rebuilding would no longer be there. I was looking at research that said there was a real possibility we would only be left with two or three seats in the whole of Sydney.[39]

But Swan dismissed the notion of Rudd as saviour: 'My view is that we wouldn't have been worse off and could have been better off with Julia. As someone who's been a marginal seat holder for a long period of time I reject fundamentally the claim that Rudd saved 25 seats.'[40] On balance, the evidence suggests the change was justified and that it made a difference, despite claims of the Gillard loyalists.

The second question is: How well did Abbott do?

He achieved a convincing victory, yet the Coalition would have liked more. And perhaps it needed more. Abbott fell just short of Howard's 1996 performance when he won 94 seats and 53.6 per cent of the two-party-preferred vote. By historical standards the result should deliver Abbott two terms, though no 'hard and fast' conclusions can be drawn. Abbott knocked Labor down; he did not knock Labor out.

The reason for the Coalition's success was Abbott's leadership—his discipline, judgement and calmness under pressure. 'Tony was exceptional in the 2013 campaign,' said Hockey. 'He was disciplined and focused with a steely resolve. He was indefatigable.' No other Liberal could have remotely matched Abbott's performance or got this result. After the experience of 2010 he felt confident against Rudd. 'For what it's worth I thought Rudd would fade in a campaign,' Abbott said.[41]

One of the few ALP politicians who seemed capable of rational analysis of Abbott was Greg Combet. 'As an Opposition leader, he was a dominant force,' Combet said.

> He exploited our weaknesses very effectively. He was a ruthless opportunist, populist politician prepared to do pretty much any-thing. I think he was under-estimated. Any person who can get to the leadership, dominate the way he did, dominate the political agenda the way he did, discipline his own side, get them moving in the same direction, perform so well in the 2010 election with only seven months as leader, a phenomenal achievement, and then to win in 2013, well that's not to be underestimated.[42]

In the Senate result Abbott scored a pivotal success by denying the Labor–Green combination an ongoing Senate majority. This would automatically have doomed his government's agenda and set the scene for guaranteed political crisis. But such relief was brief, with the Palmer United Party holding the balance of power in the new senate.

At its first outing the Palmer United Party polled 5.5 per cent of the primary vote, much of which would normally have gone to the Coalition. The Coalition primary vote was 45.6 per cent, about 12 points ahead of Labor, an increase of only 1.8 per cent on the 2010 poll. That was a disappointing result given Labor's woeful performance. It reflects doubts about Abbott in the community. But it also reflects the threat of Palmer, a populist breakaway with the potential to cause huge problems for Abbott in the nation and in the Parliament. Abbott's weakness was his Senate vote. The Coalition had 37 senators in Howard's first term while Abbott had only 33, a telling difference. At the Senate election Labor lost 6 seats and the Coalition 1 seat, evidence of disillusion with both major parties. By mid 2014 the prospect of a growing crisis loomed between the houses.

The third question is: What judgement does this result invite on the Rudd–Gillard–Rudd era?

George Wright said: 'Labor didn't so much lose the election as lose government.'[43] This is the essential point: Labor failed to sustain itself as a government. It is a damning judgement, yet it should not deny Labor's achievements.

In his gracious farewell speech to the Parliament, Rudd said he had set out to achieve many things as prime minister: 'In some of these I succeeded. In others I did not. Such is the nature of politics.' He mentioned the economic navigation through the GFC, assisting in the creation of the G-20 as the premier global forum, ratification of Kyoto, the apology to the Aboriginal people, delivering the first national curriculum, the first paid parental leave scheme and the biggest ever pension rise, as well as Australia's role in relations with China and the United States.

Asked about her main achievements, Gillard nominated the Gonski school reforms, the National Disability Insurance Scheme 'that wasn't inevitable until it was inevitable', the carbon pricing scheme (while admitting she was not sure if it would endure), the ongoing economic performance in delivering growth and jobs, and her international diplomacy—notably with China and the United States.[44]

Asked to evaluate the Rudd–Gillard–Rudd government, Stephen Smith said: 'It is a government that can hold its head up. The record shows it managed the economy and national security on a sound basis. It should have been a three-term (an eight- or nine-year) government. That failure is my generation's political responsibility.'[45]

The failure is really the responsibility of Rudd and Gillard. They were the best of their Labor generation; nobody disputes the dedication displayed by Kevin or Julia. Yet that generation underperformed, as Smith concedes. It should have governed better and for longer. The blame lies with the leaders. Their policy successes will endure, only to be overshadowed by their failures and missed opportunities. The defects and blunders of the 2007–13 Labor Government are sure to burn brighter and more permanently in public memory.

At the 2013 election the ALP primary vote, at 33.4 per cent, was the lowest for a hundred years. It was significantly below the 38.8 per cent vote when Labor lost the 1996 election. Between these two election defeats Labor had lost 5 percentage points of its vote. That is the responsibility of Rudd and Gillard. These numbers point to a structural, policy and strategic crisis—a sustained theme of this book.

The Rudd–Gillard leadership rupture ruined the government. But leadership is neither the start nor the end of the story. Pivotal political mistakes were fundamental in bringing Labor down. They were further compounded because Labor's policy framework was flawed and central to its destruction.

The evidence allows no other conclusion given the long series of disastrous policy problems in relation to climate change, economic reform, the mining tax, budget management and sustainability, boats policy and hospital policy. This Labor generation neither prepared sufficiently for office nor met the required standards of reforming government. At the heart of the government was an intellectual and strategic failure to devise and implement convincing policies for the times.

CHAPTER 33

THE AUSTRALIAN CRISIS

The deepest lesson of the Rudd–Gillard–Rudd era is that Australia's political system is failing to deliver the results needed for the nation, its growth in living standards and its self-esteem. The process of debate, competition and elections leading to national progress has broken down. The business of politics is too de-coupled from the interests of Australia and its citizens. This de-coupling constitutes the Australian crisis.

The erosion of Australia's political culture has deep and multiple origins. It will not be easily reversed. While discernible in Howard's final years, it exploded under Rudd and Gillard and now haunts Abbott in office. Unless the trend is reversed, Australia will undergo a steady economic and social deterioration until a circuit-breaker or nasty economic crunch arrives, offering the potential for a new course. The story of the Labor Government, as outlined in this book, is that major reforms are far harder to achieve and sustain. Such reform is the lifeblood of progress; it is the means to help realise Australia's immense potential.

The 2013 election offered a further illustration of the malaise. It was conducted in a fog of false optimism. The proof is that after its election the Abbott Government felt obliged to bring down a 'reality check' budget that shocked an unprepared nation largely unaware of the financial challenge facing the country and upset at the methods the Coalition used to address the problem. Seen in context, final judgement on the Abbott Government will invite one of two conclusions: it will either break the reform deadlock or succumb as another casualty to the contemporary Australian malaise.

Beneath the Rudd–Gillard war and Labor's political and policy tribulations lay a crisis of the system. At one level it is the modern dilemma in Western democracies: the inability of political decision-makers to address the problems of their nations.

Australia's worst delusion is that, because it has no immediate economic crisis, it has no political crisis. That would constitute the response
of a stupid country ignoring the evidence before it. The evidence is that
the political system has malfunctioned. The public senses this and the
examples are legion.

The Rudd–Gillard–Rudd era saw Labor buckle in government. The
Labor Government was broken by the pressures of the system. Neither
of its prime ministers nor Labor as an institution was able to hold the
line and assert sustained policy authority over a period of years. The
conclusion is not just the malaise afflicting the Labor Party; it is the crisis
afflicting the political process.

Australian politics is dominated by a poll-driven culture. It empowers negative campaigns, privileges sectional and special interests over
the national interest, struggles with a fragmented media less equipped
to facilitate sensible debate and confronts a conflict between long-run
policy and the short-term tyranny of the polling and media cycle. Every
serious blunder on the part of Kevin Rudd and Julia Gillard can only be
understood in this destructive context, where governing is more difficult,
reform far more difficult.

Political leadership is a more arduous task. A successful prime minister must master the art of politics and the art of governing, both skills
being essential. Reflecting upon his time as press secretary to Rudd and
Gillard, Sean Kelly said:

> The professionalism of politics conceals the magnitude of the
> transition to the job of prime minister. These days a competent
> minister learns to do two things—drive home the grab of the day
> and avoid making any mistakes. If you become PM these things
> aren't enough. People want something completely different from
> you. Their expectations are very high and I think our recent prime
> ministers have struggled with their transition to the top job.[1]

Leadership, as ever, is the pivotal factor. Rudd and Gillard were tested
as leaders and found to be wanting. Yet the pressures of the system are
making leadership more difficult.

Abbott was one of Australia's most successful Opposition leaders of
the past half century. As prime minister however, he will face the pressures that ruined Rudd and Gillard. This will test the strength, nerve and
belief of the Coalition parties.

The real challenge, however, is more daunting. It is whether the
political system can shift to address the genuine problems of the nation: a

fractured budget, an ageing population, a poor productivity performance, serious competitive pressures, declining relative school performance, the need for improved and better targeted infrastructure and the requirement for structural change as Australia's terms of trade fall away.

The recent results are discouraging. The political system is not delivering. Australia is living on borrowed time—courtesy of earlier reforms, the resources boom and the shift in global economic power to Asia. The most pathetic mantra from early 2014 is the bleat that 'Australia is not Greece'—the implication being that because Australia is not a smashed nation like Greece it has no need for painful repair to address its own problems. This is a backwards step to an immaturity that Australia was supposed to have left behind.

As this book argues, the post-1983 Reform Age of Hawke, Keating and much of Howard has long since terminated. It is romantic but unrealistic to think it will be revived. The danger, however, is that Australia is consigned to a state of weak public policy or even semi-paralysis. At a time when success in a competitive and globalised world demands flexible policy from government, the political system is hard-wired against change and reforms that disadvantage sections of the community as reforms invariably do. A nation that has lost the art of reform and self-improvement will finish on the path to decline—and Australia has stepped on to this escalator.

The tragedy is that reform seems to be a lost political art. Its essence lies in judgement: deciding what to discard and what to preserve. Australians are a practical people. In the past they have responded when arguments for change are grounded in common sense and pragmatic self-interest rather than ideology. History shows that in Australia the cause of economic reform and 'a fair go' can usually be reconciled. Yet over the past decade our leaders have lost this formula for success.

The last three prime ministers fell at the reform hurdle—Howard over WorkChoices and Rudd and Gillard on a mix of climate change policy, mining tax reform and flawed fiscal management. It would be wrong to deny the responsibility of these leaders for their own downfalls. It would be equally wrong to deny that their collective experience suggests a serious problem in Australia's political system.

Any remaining cross-party consensus for reform has been snapped by the combat of recent years. Will Abbott prevail or will he be overwhelmed, the fourth successive prime minister to succumb at the reform hurdle?

The message from the May 2014 budget is that Abbott, aligned with Joe Hockey, aspires to be a reforming prime minister. The challenges facing Abbott will not just test his own leadership but provide the latest

test of whether a reforming prime minister can succeed any more in Australian politics. The issue is whether the multiple forces at work—a negative Opposition, a collapse of reform consensus, a critical media, a coalition of community grievance, lack of control of the Parliament and the intensification of short-term poll pressures—will overwhelm Abbott just as a different matrix of these factors overwhelmed Rudd and Gillard.

There is no more important question for Australia's future: Has the political system become so internally destructive that the prospects for successful and reforming government have been seriously diminished? If the answer is 'yes' the only solution will come with a future economic crisis that arrests the erosion of the political culture. That means immense community pain and hardship in the process.

One issue is whether the shift against bold reform is because of defective leadership or whether the cause lies in the political system itself. The evidence suggests it is a dual problem. The Hawke–Keating era is rightly lauded. But it is by no means certain that Bob Hawke and Paul Keating would have succeeded in the contemporary system.

Volatility and fragmentation are the new driving forces. As the pace of personal and social life intensifies two terms may become the norm for a successful Australian government. People are more impatient. The leader they praised yesterday is the leader they condemn today. Politics has become far more competitive and brutal on a daily basis. This demands faster responses and those responses are invariably negative. The power of the negative only gains more clout—witness the ACTU campaign against WorkChoices, the corporate campaign against the mining tax, Abbott's campaign against the carbon tax and the Labor campaign against the first Abbott budget. It is true that campaigns often reflect a flawed policy but good policy earns no exemption from attack. Sectional interests have far more power than before—to raise funds, leverage media attention, lobby and pressure the system. Technology and campaign techniques mean that disaffected voters can be targeted and won. The result has been a strange polarisation—leaders either retreat in political fear (Rudd on climate change) or plunge ahead with a sense of crazy brave (Howard on WorkChoices).

Destructive internal pressures and the decline of tribal loyalty have taken a toll on the main parties as institutions. Good government hinges on competent parties. A strong prime minister can substitute for a weak party only for a limited period. The identity and policy crisis that hurt Labor in government is not just Labor's problem; it is the nation's problem.

Originating from the 1996 election defeat, if not earlier, Labor's tribulations as a party have only deepened for most of the past twenty years. It struggles with many dilemmas—its future as a trade union–based party, the schism on the Left with the rise of the Greens as an ideological rival, identifying new sources of true belief and deciding how Labor interprets economic reform to guarantee Australia's prosperity. The Rudd–Gillard era showed Labor in office was obsessed about its own problems rather than those of the nation. Rudd proved that a dysfunctional government will be exposed, while Gillard was simply unable to locate her government in the middle ground. Labor in office failed to manage the collective pressures of government and politics.

There will be no exemption for the Liberal Party from comparable pressures. The depth of the 2009 Coalition crisis over climate change and its almost miraculous resolution is one of the most astonishing events of 2007–13. A rare instance of snatching victory from the jaws of defeat, it exposed how the Liberal Party could fall into lethal dispute over belief, with the potential to immobilise it for years. Abbott as leader staged a recovery beyond the imagination of either side. In office, however, Abbott has been required not just to hold his own side together, but to emerge as a prime minister who can persuade the people to accept his own reform agenda. As Opposition leader, Abbott was brutally effective in destroying Gillard's authority—yet his tactics are now being duplicated by Labor in Opposition.

As prime minister, Abbott will be subjected to more demanding tests. Can the Liberal Party tolerate bad polls without losing its nerve? Will Abbott's leadership be called into question in a repeat of the Rudd saga? Will the Abbott Government have the strength to advance national interest policies in the teeth of a fierce backlash?

This task will be compounded by the eruption of the Palmer United Party at the 2013 election, where it eroded some of the Coalition primary vote. Clive Palmer defies categorisation or prediction. He may be a passing storm, but he may become a permanent presence on the populist Right, a Berlusconi-type figure with deep pockets and a loud voice, a quasi celebrity with the capacity to 'buy' votes and cause Abbott the heartburn the Greens have caused Labor over recent years.

Disillusionment with the main parties will create more difficulty for the government of the day—Coalition or Labor—to carry its agenda through the Parliament. Minor parties play to their sectional lobby. They lack any governing culture or responsibility for the national interest, yet their influence is becoming more important.

In Australia, there are only two pathways to national interest reform —bipartisanship or carrying the country. Bipartisanship is near dead, with Abbott, because of his aggression as Opposition leader, now a magnet for retaliation. In truth, bipartisanship has been close to death for many years. During its early years, the Howard Government's reforms in industrial relations, privatisation and the GST were carried on the votes of the Australian Democrats and independents, not Labor. In the same manner Gillard's reforms, spearheaded by carbon pricing, were carried by her voting alliances with the Greens and Independents.

In short, the much-extolled 1980s bipartisanship was an aberration. The Coalition and Labor are bitterly divided over the national direction and the meaning of reform. Yet it is extremely difficult for either major party to 'carry the country' and win a majority in both the House of Representatives and the Senate to legislate their respective policies. The system empowers the minor parties and independents, at present the Greens and Palmer United. Only a professional optimist could have confidence that these parties will be responsible agents in advancing national-interest reform through the Parliament.

The political system is plagued by a series of roadblocks. The breakdown in cross-party cooperation became far more traumatic in the Rudd–Gillard–Abbott period. The conflict over policy continues to deepen. It encompasses productivity, competitiveness, tax reform, industrial relations, climate change, spending entitlements, reform of Medicare, pension sustainability, higher education and industry policy. While such conflicts can be mitigated by electoral factors, their range and depth are conspicuous.

The political system, in fact, rewards division. It encourages one party to sink the other. These divisions are not just ideological; they are tactical. The politicians are given research showing that voters hate political squabbling yet the gains from negative politics are too great. In 2014 Labor's sweeping attack on the first Abbott Government budget—the most comprehensive assault on a budget for decades—was inspired by a mix of policy opposition and tactical calculation.

Superimposed upon this Liberal–Labor schism is the intensification of Australia's culture war, arising from conflicts over values, religion, history, symbols and single-issue campaigns (same-sex marriage, refugee rights and feminist agendas). For many progressives, Abbott is opposed as much for what he represents as for what he does.

Spanning the policy and culture conflicts is the intractable rift over climate change action. Abbott's leadership is tied to his rejection of carbon pricing and emphasis on energy efficiency rather than global warming.

He rode to power on this tide but he will be stranded if the world turns back to agreed climate change market-based pricing mechanisms.

Australia has had six years of disappointing though not disastrous government. It cannot afford another period of disappointing government, this time from the Liberal–National Coalition. But Abbott starts with a disadvantage: breaking promises from the 2013 election campaign. The extent of that broken trust is exaggerated but real. Abbott's mistake at the 2013 election was not what he promised but what he ruled out. Typically, if a politician rules out policies it probably means they are necessary. He ruled out pain and hardship: expansive spending cuts and tax rises. It was a variation of Gillard's mistake in the 2010 campaign: she ruled out a carbon tax.

These decisions testify to the power of the negative and the need to reassure. Yet the moral basis of this 'game' has become untenable. Leaders are questioned and probed until every policy option that might risk their election victory has been eliminated. The more options that are eliminated, the more worthless the commitments—the 'ruling out' pledges (no GST change, no tax rises, no social spending cuts) that are needed to win the election doom the victor to either weak government that honours promises or strong government that breaks promises. Neither is a satisfactory result.

It is true that leaders—Rudd, Gillard and Abbott—should be held to account; nobody disputes that. It is equally true that the system in practice operates as a zero-sum game trap that diminishes quality decision-making. The media loves 'playing this game' but usually refuses to discuss its lethal consequences.

Abbott's real solution to the dilemma was to devise a two-term strategy. He went to the 2013 election with agendas for a first term and a second term. At 2013 Abbott ran on a cautious, popular agenda, exploiting Labor's mistakes and seeking a substantial majority. Most of the big reforming challenges were deferred, consigned to inquiries during the first term—a white paper on tax, a review of the Federation, a Productivity Commission review of the industrial relations system and a competition policy review. There were many more. The idea was that Abbott would seek a more substantial mandate for change at the 2016 election. It was a variation of Howard's improvisations that saw him run on two different agendas: a cautious program at the 1996 election and a radical reform at the 1998 election.

The strategy adopted by Abbott is deeply revealing of the Australian political crisis. It showed that the Abbott-led Coalition believed reform could not be marketed from Opposition, that it was untenable (even for an Opposition in a strong position) to put before the public a full and honest appraisal of the nation's finances and the harsh medicine needed to repair them. To do this would be an act of political suicide. The power of negative politics was simply too lethal. In short, the political culture means it is difficult, even impossible, for leaders to talk honestly to the community. This breeds distrust and cynicism. Yet the price of honesty is too high.

The last prime minister to be successful in seeking a mandate for far-reaching reform was Howard, with his 1998 election GST-led tax package. It is, however, hard to imagine that this success could be replicated in the political culture fifteen years down the track. At the 2007 election Howard was destroyed on his ill-conceived WorkChoices reform. At the same election Rudd won a mandate on a carbon pricing policy but, when public opinion began to waver, he felt unable to market his policy in any 2010 re-election campaign. The consistent theme is the risk of reform. The system has moved decisively against change.

Abbott played the integrity card to great effect over the 2010–13 term. The more he punished Gillard for breaking promises, the more he tutored the nation on the value of trust. After the election he said: 'If there is one lesson to be learnt from the political quagmire that the previous government got itself into, it is: keep your commitments. So we will keep them.'

Yet Abbott was soon trapped by his pledges. When Abbott and Hockey examined the books, they concluded that their obligation was to bring down a tough first budget of structural change. Their dilemma was exquisite: they could keep their promises or address the broken budget. But they could not do both satisfactorily. They decided to address the nation's finances, the upshot being that Abbott will pay a high price for breaking his trust with the public.

The problems of the political system afflict the executive and legislative branches. Cabinet government is impaired. The quality of executive decision-making has declined. The rise of the ministerial office has run in parallel with the rise of political advisers and decline of policy advisers. Within the executive arm that old axiom—good policy is good politics—is deeply compromised. The concept of prime ministerial government, now the essence of the Australian executive model, went into malfunction under Rudd and Gillard. Whether it can be righted under Abbott remains to be seen.

The parliamentary system has entered precarious territory at the 2013 election, with a flawed Senate voting system delivering an unpredictable Senate crossbench. The test is whether the new Senate can deliver enough tolerable compromises in the cause of effective government or whether the Senate becomes integral to the Australian crisis. The situation is compounded because a prime minister's resort against an obstructionist Senate—the double-dissolution mechanism—has largely been destroyed since the mid-1980s with the expansion of the Parliament and reduction of the Senate quota at a double-dissolution election. The last double-dissolution election was in 1987. That is no accident. The problem at a double-dissolution election is the near certainty that it will lead to even more minor party candidates being elected because their quota for election is easily obtained.

Australia's contemporary problem lies in the intersection of a corrosive political culture with the need for hard and unpopular economic repair. It is the exact point the nation has reached since the 2013 election—the sunset poll for the age of prosperity that began with the terms-of-trade explosion in 2003. Prosperity is not being terminated but the fantastic national income lift from the terms-of-trade surge is dropping away significantly. Australia faces a certain hit in living standards—their rate of increase will fall, perhaps sharply over time. The Treasury has issued many warnings to this effect but the public has no real comprehension.

At the 2013 election Labor ran on an optimistic economic outlook while warning of a transition away from the resources sector. Abbott was far more alarmist, warning that the budget was in need of major repair down the track. It was no surprise that neither side sought an immediate mandate for the radical reformist policies demanded by these twin challenges: structural change to keep the Australian economy competitive along with a cut in entitlements and tax reform to support a more productive economy.

The 2013 election, in fact, was conducted in the afterglow of a resource boom fantasy land. The public was not told the terrible secret. After the election, economist Chris Richardson said:

> Mr and Mrs Average don't understand why the news on the economy is reasonable but the news on the budget is sackcloth and ashes. That lack of understanding by the electorate is a big problem. The resources boom of the last decade was good for the economy but stunningly good for the budget. The boost to the budget from the economy briefly peaked at over $80 billion a year just ahead of the GFC. And now we're back where we began. The bonanza delivered by the economy to the budget has now gone. Like every other boom in history it turned out to be temporary.[2]

Yet that temporary revenue surge had financed permanent benefits, tax cuts and entitlements, and they were huge. It had boosted household budgets and changed the political culture. Redistributing the boom's proceeds started in earnest in Howard's 2004 election year and ran unabated till Gillard's 2013 end-of-empire spending crusade in Labor's last budget that involved commitments running out for a further decade.

There is no denying the judgement: the political class spent too much of the boom and saved too little. That was compounded during the global financial crisis when the political class spent too much, yet again.

Despite their protests and the strong budget surpluses they ran, Howard and Costello must share the blame. In 2008 a Treasury analysis reviewing the Howard period said: 'Effectively, the additional revenue from the commodities boom has been spent or provided as tax cuts.'[3] Assessing the period under governments of both sides, Chris Richardson said: 'The rivers of gold are in full flood. The policy response of recent years can be summed up as 'spend the lot'. Australia has taken out no insurance for the future.'[4]

It is true that Treasury estimates over 2003–07 were too conservative on the revenue side, so the Howard Government found itself each year with more money than it expected. The funds went into family payments, health, education, defence, water and tax cuts. It is also true that Treasury under Ken Henry did not argue for higher surpluses beyond the 1.5 per cent of GDP surpluses being achieved, a very healthy outcome. This was confirmed by Henry in an interview for this book. He felt the surpluses were about right. In retrospect, however, Henry has changed his mind. 'I think we were wrong,' he said. 'I think there should have been significantly stronger surpluses.'[5] That is, more of the boom should have been saved, a critical point.

Labor's 2013 budget was the ultimate stage in this fiscal fantasy land. By this point the boom was running down—and revenue was falling short of forecasts on an annual basis. The surplus was more elusive than ever but Gillard engaged in a bout of Whitlamism with schools and disability spending agendas running beyond the forward estimates. The justification was the claim that for the next decade annual real spending would be kept to 2 per cent, a truly heroic notion given multiple demands on the budget. Richardson called it 'crude fiction'. Making a promise does not constitute delivery therof. Labor's spending record to that stage showed average annual increases of 3.7 per cent in real terms. In 2014, Ken Henry said the tax system could not pay for the big-spending budget agendas.

Richardson said of the 2013 budget: 'Just when the Treasury was accelerating the pace of its revenue write downs, the politicians were accelerating the pace of bipartisan promises. It was group denial at its most astounding. Australian electorate—we have a problem.'[6]

The 2013 campaign was based on a fracture between the artificial world of politics and the real world of national finances. This severance was not new; it had been a feature of post-2003 politics and had now reached its zenith. The budget was known to be in serious need of repair yet neither side was able to tell Australians that expectations must be reduced and harsher policies implemented. The Coalition said there was a serious problem. Labor remained in denial. The irony for Rudd is that many of the problems he faced in the 2013 campaign had their origins in his first stint as prime minister.

Post-election the reconciliation moment had arrived.

The corruption of the political culture had been substantial, with expectations far divorced from the ugly moment of accountability. After twenty-two years of economic growth plus a resources boom, bedrock complacency had taken hold. It had various manifestations: a decline in self-reliance, a culture of complaint, the rise of social envy, a growing dependency on government, a political system based on bidding up expectations about government's capacity to satisfy more needs and wants with the probability that people would only grow more dissatisfied. Finally, the public seemed to have lost any notion of the reason for Australia's prosperity and, as a result, of the steps necessary to sustain it. For the nation, this was an intellectual and a moral failure.

In early 2014 the 'accountability' documents were tabled. The Commission of Audit Report found spending was running at 25.9 per cent of GDP, virtually the same as spending during the fiscal stimulus at the peak of the GFC, while tax revenue was depressed, at 23.1 per cent of GDP. There was a hefty gap between spending and revenues. The country was living beyond its means. The solution meant action on both sides—spending and tax. Without policy change, the gap would endure, leading to more deficits and higher debt. The Audit Report found radical reforms would be needed in pension, health, welfare and education entitlements to achieve a healthy surplus by 2023–24. The backlash was fierce. The proposals were unacceptable to the community.

In April 2014 Treasury chief Martin Parkinson said the nation faced ten years of budget deficits on current policy settings. He said this was an optimistic outlook: it assumed no recession for a decade and no return of 'fiscal drag' via tax cuts. This would constitute sixteen years of successive deficits. He warned that major surgery would be required on both the spending and taxation sides. His speech seemed to have no impact on the media or the public.

Parkinson sounded the alarm on Australia's productivity performance, with the best measure—multifactor productivity growth—now negative, reflecting a trend across a range of industries. While conceding that productivity would lift in the mining sector, with more output coming from earlier investments, Parkinson said Australia's productivity performance was 'weak' by global standards. He repeated warnings long ignored: living standards had stayed strong only because the terms of trade had substituted for poor productivity growth. With the terms of trade peaking in September 2011, reconciliation time was now arriving. Future living standards were in jeopardy.

Australia faced a crunch from weak productivity, an ageing population and declining terms of trade. As a new treasurer, already convinced the 'entitlement culture' was poisoning the health of Western democracies, Hockey committed to an agenda of transformation. He issued three warnings. First, expectations embedded in the political culture were beyond the capacity of government and entitlements must be reduced. Second, there was no such thing as a free service and people had to pay more for government provisions. Third, it was time to end the 'borrow and spend' syndrome. Hockey offered a moral imperative: the more the current generation financed its lifestyle from borrowing, the more it robbed its children. The Treasurer was frank: it was time to prioritise the national interest over self-interest. This meant changing the social compact between the government and the people. His message was unmistakable—the political culture had to change.

In May 2014, Hockey brought down the sort of reform budget that had not been seen for nearly twenty years. It was a financial, political and culture shock, with structural reforms and punitive measures that struck pensioners, families, the sick, the young unemployed, university students, motorists and high-income earners. Hockey said Australians were 'a nation of lifters, not leaners'. Yet that judgement was in the balance. The nation had viewed the budget as a permanent war chest from which it took—not as a balance sheet for the future. Yet the actual fiscal consolidation proposed by Hockey was relatively modest: less than that of Costello in 1996 or the Hawke Government in the mid-1980s.

The budget was the latest evidence of the malaise of the system. There was a semi-permanent 'reality gap' between the public sentiment and economic need. The public was unprepared for such fiscal shocks. The cognoscenti had debated the task pre-budget but the Abbott Government had not prepared the public. Beyond this, its messages were too mixed (it preached fiscal restraint while backing an over-generous paid parental leave scheme); its measures breached the social compact (witness denying youths the dole for six months); and it made changes such as a Medicare co-payment without explaining how this fitted into its broader health policy vision thereby creating public alarm. The government's polling showed the public did recognise the need for fiscal repair yet the budget initiatives were flawed as a burden-sharing project.

Opposition leader Bill Shorten channelled Abbott from his days in Opposition and called it a 'budget of deceit' that attacked the pillars of Australian society. From the community there was genuine upset. Yet within the political system there was resentment, payback and cynicism. For Labor, the key to its revival was destroying Abbott's integrity. This was its political DNA—before, during and after the 2013 election.

Much of the political class now denied any budget problem whatsoever. The two minor parties—the Greens and Palmer United—said the fiscal dilemma was a fabrication by the Abbott Government for its ideological purposes. Such claims were a betrayal of the public and the national-interest obligations that politicians are supposed to assume. Labor denied any immediate problem that required such drastic fixing and insisted it had left the budget in splendid shape. Obviously, there could be no cooperation on any solution when the seriousness of the problem was denied. Every sign suggested that the polarisation in politics, the disintegration of shared ground and Liberal–Labor policy conflict would only intensify under the Abbott Government.

The trust between the political system and the public to sustain ambitious policy is close to being severed. If so, Australia faces an unhappy future. This is related to the decline in proper process and the apparent abandonment of the proven techniques of inquiry, debate, consultation and compromise, to carry policy reform. The changes in the media industry are part of the story. In the post-1983 reform age, the media was vital in backing national-interest policies. But that age is passing. With fragmentation of the traditional media and the rise of social media, the new values are fashionable narcissism and much less concern for national-interest policy.

Australia talks much about the opportunities in Asia and the coming so-called Asian century. But opportunity in Asia has to be won; it is not automatic. Australia cannot succeed in Asia with a political culture that is inflexible, resistant to change and tied to European-type regulations and entitlements.

In the post-1983 reform era, Australia won global renown because it devised a distinctive and unique approach to the challenge of globalisation. It settled about mid-point between the American and European models—a market-orientated, competitive economy with a sharing of benefits across the community. Both sides of politics have a bedrock instinct that this should be the enduring Australian strategy.

Australia's institutions and political system now face a test of their maturity. They have to do better. There is no guarantee that politics can emerge from its current trough to meet the challenges of the next decade. But failure would be a betrayal of the public interest. History suggests that Australia slumbers in prosperity but responds with resolution to crisis. Let us hope the crisis does not get too serious before the political system rises to the task.

NOTES

Introduction to the new edition
1   Julia Gillard, *My Story*, Random House, Sydney, 2014, p. 106.
2   Gillard, *My Story*, p. 98.
3   Gillard, *My Story*, p. 2.
4   Gillard, *My Story*, p. 2.
5   Gillard, *My Story*, p. 1.
6   Gillard, *My Story*, pp. 90–2.
7   Gillard, *My Story*, p. 92.
8   Gillard, *My Story*, p. 1.
9   Gillard, *My Story*, p. 95.
10 Gillard, *My Story*, p. 6.
11 Gillard, *My Story*, pp. 5–7.
12 Gillard, *My Story*, pp. 10–15.
13 Gillard, *My Story*, pp. 15–18.
14 Gillard, *My Story*, pp. 20–1.
15 Gillard, *My Story*, pp. 23, 37.
16 Gillard, *My Story*, p. 22.
17 Gillard, *My Story*, p. 22.
18 Gillard, *My Story*, p. 23.
19 Gillard, *My Story*, p. 43.
20 Gillard, *My Story*, p. 77.
21 Chris Bowen, interview with the author, February 2014.
22 Gillard, *My Story*, pp. 133–41.
23 Gillard, *My Story*, p. 461.

1   The Destruction of a Government
1   Kevin Rudd, interview with the author, June 2012.
2   Rudd, interview, June 2012.
3   Rudd, interview, June 2012.
4   Rudd, interview, June 2012.
5   Anthony Albanese, interview with the author, February 2014.
6   Tony Burke, interview with the author, June 2013.
7   Rudd, interview, June 2012.
8   David Feeney, interview with the author, February 2014.
9   Julia Gillard, interview with the author, October 2013.
10 UMR Research, June 2010.
11 Gillard, interview, October 2013.
12 Albanese, interview, February 2014.

13 Paul Kelly, *Australian*, 26 September 2012.
14 Simon Crean, interview with the author, May 2013.
15 Martin Ferguson, interview with the author, April 2013.
16 John Faulkner, interview with the author, January 2014.
17 Chris Evans, interview with the author, November 2013.
18 Chris Bowen, interview with the author, January 2014.
19 Paul Howes, interview with the author, April 2013.
20 Greg Combet, interview with the author, January 2014.
21 Craig Emerson, interview with the author, February 2014.
22 Stephen Smith, interview with the author, January 2014.
23 Wayne Swan, interview with the author, December 2013.
24 Bob Carr, interview with the author, June 2013.
25 Faulkner, interview, January 2014.
26 George Wright, interview with the author, February 2014.
27 Bill Shorten, interview with the author, February 2014.
28 Bruce Hawker, *The Rudd Rebellion*, MUP, Carlton, 2013, p. 11.
29 Sam Dastyari, interview with the author, January 2014.
30 Albanese, interview, February 2014.
31 Mark Arbib, interview with the author, February 2014.
32 Don Farrell, interview with the author, December 2013.
33 Kim Carr, interview with the author, February 2014.
34 Feeney, interview, February 2014.
35 Karl Bitar, interview with the author, February 2014.
36 Evans, interview, November 2013.
37 Howes, interview, April 2013.
38 Faulkner, interview, January 2014.
39 Mark Arbib, interview with the author, July 2010.
40 Kim Beazley, interview with the author, April 2009.
41 Julia Gillard, interview with the author, January 2010.
42 Gillard, interview, October 2013.
43 John Howard, personal discussion with the author, December 2007.
44 Faulkner, interview, January 2014.
45 Kevin Rudd, interview with the author, October 2008.
46 Gillard, interview, January 2010.
47 Peter Hartcher, *To the Bitter End*, Allen & Unwin, Sydney, 2009, p. 156.
48 Kim Carr, interview with the author, February 2013.
49 Paul Kelly, *Australian Magazine*, 27 October 2007.
50 Jacqueline Kent, *The Making of Julia Gillard*, Viking, Victoria, 2009, pp. 19–36.
51 Kent, *The Making of Julia Gillard*, p. 21.
52 Kelly, *Australian Magazine*, 27 October 2007.
53 Kent, *The Making of Julia Gillard*, p. 2.
54 This assessment draws upon Gillard's analysis in an interview in October 2013.

2 The Making of an Opposition

1 Tony Abbott, interview with the author, January 2014.
2 Nick Minchin, interview with the author, June 2011.

3 Brian Loughnane, interview with the author, March 2011.
4 Julie Bishop, interview with the author, January 2014.
5 Phillip Coorey, *Sydney Morning Herald*, 30 November 2001.
6 Abbott, interview, January 2014.
7 Abbott, interview, January 2014.
8 Malcolm Turnbull, interview with the author, February 2014.
9 Abbott, interview, January 2014.
10 Turnbull, interview, February 2014.
11 Minchin, interview, June 2011; and Tony Abbott, personal conversations with the author, November and December 2009.
12 Malcolm Turnbull, personal conversations with the author, November and December 2009.
13 John Howard, interview with the author, February 2009.
14 Tony Abbott, *Battlelines*, MUP, Carlton, 2009, pp. 183–4.
15 Malcolm Turnbull, ABC Radio National, 1 October 2009, and 2UE, 2 October 2009.
16 Abbott, interview, January 2014.
17 Abbott, interview, January 2014.
18 Laura Tingle, *Australian Financial Review*, 1 December 2009; Peter Hartcher, *Sydney Morning Herald*, 1 December 2009 and 30 January 2010; David Marr, *Sydney Morning Herald*, 2 December 2009; Phillip Coorey, *Sydney Morning Herald*, 5 December 2009.
19 Philip Coorey, *Sydney Morning Herald*, 9 December 2009 and 15 December 2009; Paul Kelly, *Australian*, 2 December 2009 and 5 December 2009.
20 Sean Kelly, interview with the author, October 2013.
21 Turnbull, interview, February 2014.
22 Turnbull, interview, February 2014.
23 George Wright, interview with the author, February 2014.
24 Lachlan Harris, interview with the author, February 2014.

3 Fighting on Two Fronts

1 George Wright, interview with the author, February 2014.
2 Bob Carr, interview with the author, January 2014.
3 Tony Abbott, House of Representatives, *Hansard*, 30 November 1995.
4 This calculation assumes Labor getting 80 per cent of Green preferences.
5 Malcolm Mackerras, interview with the author, June 2013.
6 Bob Brown, interview with the author, January 2014.
7 Lindsay Tanner, *Politics with Purpose*, Scribe, Melbourne, 2012, pp. 336–7.
8 Phillip Coorey, *Sydney Morning Herald*, 28 November 2011.
9 Cameron Stewart, *The Weekend Australian*, April 2012, pp. 14–15.
10 Brown, interview, January 2014.
11 Carr, interview, January 2014.
12 Tanner, *Politics with Purpose*, p. 336.
13 Mark Latham, *The Latham Diaries*, MUP, Carlton, 2005, p. 352.
14 Chris Bowen, *Hearts & Minds*, MUP, Carlton 2013, pp. 127–8
15 Paul Howes, interview with the author, April 2013.

16 Sam Dastyari, interview with the author, January 2014.
17 Greg Combet, interview with the author, January 2014.
18 Bob Brown, interview with the author, January 2014
19 John Faulkner, The Wran Lecture, 9 June 2011.
20 Gary Gray, interview with the author, mid-1996.
21 Andrew Robb, interview with the author, January 2004.
22 Paul Kelly, *The Weekend Australian*, 30 April 2011.
23 Paul Kelly, *The March of Patriots*, MUP, Carlton, 2009, chapter 21.
24 Tony Abbott, *Battlelines*, MUP, Carlton, 2009, p. 26.
25 Tony Abbott, interview with the author, January 2014.
26 Abbott, interview, January 2014.
27 Brian Loughnane, interview with the author, February 2014.

4 Shunning the Policy Challenge

1   Kevin Rudd, interview with the author, February 2014.
2   Troy Bramston, *Looking for the Light on the Hill*, Scribe, Melbourne, 2011, p. 81.
3   Sam Dastyari, interview with the author, January 2014.
4   Lachlan Harris, interview with the author, February 2014.
5   Paul Kelly, *Australian*, 22 October 2011.
6   Mark Latham, 'Not Dead Yet', *Quarterly Essay*, issue 49, 2013, p. 27.
7   Mark Latham, *The Latham Diaries*, MUP, Carlton, 2005, p. 187.
8   Latham, *The Latham Diaries*, p. 92.
9   Peter FitzSimons, *Beazley*, HarperCollins, Sydney, 1998, p. 414.
10 John Faulkner, interview with the author, January 2014.
11 Lindsay Tanner, *Politics with Purpose*, Scribe, Melbourne, 2012, p. 333.
12 Tanner, *Politics with Purpose*, p. 280.
13 Paul Keating, letter to John Robertson, 27 October 2008.
14 Martin Ferguson, interview with the author, May 2013.
15 Ferguson, interview, May 2013.
16 David Forman and Nicholas Way, *Business Review Weekly*, 3 March 1997.
17 Based on a personal discussion at the time with Kim Beazley.
18 Matt Price, *Australian*, 5 October 1998.
19 John Howard, interview with the author, February 2005
20 Julia Gillard, interview with the author, January 2010.
21 Latham, *The Latham Diaries*, pp. 140–1.
22 Tanner, *Politics with Purpose*, p. 291.
23 Paul Kelly, *Australian*, 4 July 2001.
24 Faulkner interview, January 2014.
25 Rodney Cavalier, *Power Crisis*, Cambridge University Press, Melbourne, 2010, p. 31.
26 Latham, *Quarterly Essay*, p. 12.
27 Mark Latham, *From the Suburbs*, Pluto Press, Sydney, 2003, p. 19.
28 Tanner, *Politics with Purpose*, p. 295.
29 Tanner, *Politics with Purpose*, p. 278.
30 Martin Ferguson, interview with the author, April 2013.

31 John Button, 'Beyond Belief', *Quarterly Essay*, Issue 6, 2002.
32 Cavalier, *Power Crisis*, p. 32.
33 Paul Howes, interview with the author, April 2013.
34 Chris Bowen, interview with the author, February 2014.
35 Dastyari, interview, January 2014.
36 Latham, *The Latham Diaries*, pp. 5–7.
37 Kevin Rudd, interview with the author, February 2014.
38 Harris, interview, February 2014.

5   The Death of Reform
1   Arthur Sinodinos, interview with the author, February 2009.
2   John Howard, *Lazarus Rising*, HarperCollins, Sydney 2010, p. 662.
3   Julia Gillard, interview with the author, January 2010.
4   Terry Moran, interview with the author, January 2014.
5   Innes Willox, interview with the author, February 2014.
6   Based on discussions with participants at the meeting.
7   Michael Chaney, interview with the author, February 2008.
8   Arthur Sinodinos, interview with the author, February 2009.
9   Kevin Rudd, *The Monthly*, February 2009.
10 Ross Garnaut, *The Great Crash of 2008*, MUP, Carlton, 2009, pp. 224–8.
11 Gary Banks, Stan Kelly Lecture, 15 August 2013.
12 Ken Henry, interview with the author, 2012 and CEDA Setting Public Policy, May 2013.
13 Moran, interview, January 2014.
14 Banks, lecture, 15 August 2013.
15 Wayne Swan, interview with the author, December 2013.
16 Lindsay Tanner, *Sideshow*, Scribe, Melbourne, 2011, pp. 2–7.
17 Greg Combet, interview with the author, January 2014.
18 Graham Richardson, *Australian*, 2 March 2012.
19 Combet, interview, January 2014.
20 Moises Naim, *The End of Power*, Basic Books, New York, 2013, pp. 1–2.

6   The Curse of Prosperity
1   Glenn Stevens, 'The Cautious Consumer', speech, 26 July 2011. compare note 14
2   Glenn Stevens, 'The Challenge of Prosperity', speech, 29 November 2010.
3   Ross Garnaut, *Dog Days*, Redback, Melbourne, 2013, p. 834.
4   Peter Costello, *The Costello Memoirs*, MUP, Carlton, 2008, p. 289.
5   Phillip Lowe, 'The Development of Asia: Risk and Returns for Australia', speech, 16 September 2010.
6   Martin Parkinson, speech to the Australia–Israel Chamber of Commerce, 7 March 2012.
7   Dean Parham, *Australian Financial Review*, 23 April 2013.
8   Gary Banks, 'Successful Reform: Past Lessons, Future Challenges', keynote address to the Annual Forecasting Conference of Australian Business Economists, Sydney, 8 December 2010.

9 Ross Garnaut, 2010 Hamer Oration, 5 August 2010, and 'Harder Choices Ahead', 2 November 2006.
10 Glenn Stevens, 'The Cautious Consumer', speech, 26 July 2011.
11 Ross Garnaut, 'Breaking Australian Great Complacency of the Early Twenty First Century', paper presented at the conference Sustaining Prosperity, New Reform Opportunities for Australia, 2005 Economic and Social Outlook Conference, Melbourne Institute and *Australian*, 31 March 2005.
12 Gary Banks, Stan Kelly Lecture, 15 August 2013.
13 Paul Kelly, *The End of Certainty*, Allen & Unwin, Sydney, 1992, pp. 210–13.
14 Stevens, speech, 26 July 2011.
15 Paul Kelly, *The March of Patriots*, MUP, Carlton, 2009, p. 536.
16 John Howard, *Lazarus Rising*, HarperCollins, 2010, p. 543.
17 Howard, *Lazarus Rising*, pp. 542–4.
18 Glenn Stevens, 'The Road to Recovery', speech, 21 April 2009.
19 Paul Kelly, *Australian*, 2 April 2005 and Paul Kelly, *Australian*, 4 November 2006.
20 Banks, keynote address, 8 December 2010.
21 Ken Henry, 'Treasury's Effectiveness in the Current Environment', speech, 14 March 2007.
22 Stevens, speech, 26 July 2011.

7 The Rudd–Gillard Pact
1 Mark Latham, *The Latham Diaries*, MUP, Carlton, 2005, p. 364.
2 Kelly, *Australian Magazine*, 27 October 2007.
3 Alexander Downer, *The Spectator Australia*, 19 June 2010.
4 Tim Gartrell, interview with the author, November 2009.
5 Mark Latham, *The Latham Diaries*, MUP, Carlton, 2005, pp. 218–21.
6 Julia Gillard, interview, January 2010.
7 Latham, *The Latham Diaries*, p. 391.
8 Kevin Rudd, personal discussion with the author, December 2008.
9 Kim Carr, interview with the author, January 2013.
10 Mark Arbib, interview with the author, July 2010; Kim Carr interview with the author, January 2013; Tim Gartrell, interview with the author, November 2009.
11 Arbib, interview, July 2010.
12 John Faulkner, interview with the author, January 2014.
13 Arbib, interview, July 2010.
14 Arbib, interview, July 2010.
15 Tony Burke, interview with the author, June 2013.
16 Gartrell, interview, November 2009.
17 Gartrell, interview, November 2009.
18 Arbib, interview, July 2010.
19 Julia Gillard, interview with the author, January 2010.
20 Gillard, interview, January 2010.
21 Carr, interview, January 2013.
22 Carr, interview, January 2013.

23 Carr, interview, January 2013.
24 Carr, interview, January 2013.
25 Gillard, interview, January 2010.
26 Gillard, interview, January 2010.
27 Kim Carr, interview with the author, February 2014.
28 Gillard, interview, January 2010.
29 Gillard, interview, January 2010.
30 Kevin Rudd, interview with the author, October 2008.
31 Kim Beazley, interview with the author, April 2009.
32 Arbib, interview, July 2010.
33 Gillard, interview, January 2010.
34 Gillard, interview, January 2010.
35 Chris Bowen, interview with the author, June 2012.
36 Stephen Smith, interview with the author, January 2013.
37 Wayne Swan, interview with the author, December 2013.
38 Chris Evans, interview with the author, November 2013.
39 Arbib, interview, July 2010.

8 Rudd and the Unions: An Alliance of Convenience

1 Julia Gillard, interview with the author, January 2010.
2 Greg Combet, interview with the author, February 2008.
3 Gillard, interview, January 2010.
4 Heather Ridout, interview with the author, July 2010.
5 Combet, interview, February 2008.
6 Tony Abbott, interview with the author, February 2008.
7 Kevin Andrews, interview with the author, February 2008.
8 Malcolm Mackerras, personal conversation with the author, 2008.
9 John Howard, interview with the author, February 2008.
10 Howard, interview, February 2008.
11 Nick Minchin, interview with the author, February 2009.
12 Jamie Briggs, interview with the author, April 2013.
13 John Howard, *Lazarus Rising*, HarperCollins, Sydney 2010, p. 584.
14 Howard, interview, February 2008.
15 Howard, interview, February 2008.
16 Bill Kelty, interview with the author, April 2008.
17 Minchin, interview, February 2009.
18 Briggs, interview, April 2013.
19 Howard, interview, February 2008.
20 Combet, interview, February 2008.
21 Kelty, interview, April 2008.
22 Peter Hartcher, *To the Bitter End*, Allen & Unwin, Sydney, 2009, pp. 91–5.
23 Combet, interview, February 2008.
24 Mark Skulley and Rachel Nickless, *Australian Financial Review*, 5 January 2007.
25 This is based on personal discussions with Brian Loughnane.
26 Hartcher, *To the Bitter End*, pp. 97–8.
27 George Wright, interview with the author, February 2014.

28 Howard, interview, February 2008.
29 Combet, interview, February 2008.
30 Ridout, interview, July 2010.
31 Combet, interview, February 2008.
32 Mark Davis, *Sydney Morning Herald*, 5 May 2007.
33 Andrew Robb, interview with the author, January 2008.
34 Joe Hockey, interview with the author, April 2008.
35 Ridout, interview, July 2010.
36 Gillard, interview, January 2010.
37 Mike Steketee, *The Weekend Australian*, 5–6 May 2007.
38 Kevin Rudd, conversation with the author, 15 May 2007.
39 Paul Kelly, *Australian*, 21 April 2007.
40 Rudd, conversation, 15 May 2007.
41 Gillard, interview, January 2010.
42 Combet, interview, February 2008.
43 Briggs, interview, April 2013.

9 Rudd's Triple Triumph
1   Kevin Rudd, interview with the author, February 2014.
2   Peter Costello, *The Costello Memoirs*, MUP, Carlton, 2008, p. 336.
3   John Howard, *Lazarus Rising*, HarperCollins, Sydney, 2010, p. 633.
4   Tim Gartrell, interview with the author, November 2009.
5   Lachlan Harris, interview with the author, February 2014.
6   Neil Lawrence, interview with the author, September 2013.
7   Paul Kelly, *Australian*, 27 October 2007.
8   Gartrell, interview, November 2009.
9   Julia Gillard, interview with the author, October 2013.
10 Paul Kelly, *Australian*, 23 November 2007.
11 Lawrence, interview, September 2013.
12 Mark Arbib, interview with the author, July 2010.
13 Howard, *Lazarus Rising*, p. 634.
14 Laura Tingle, *Australian Financial Review*, 13 November 2007.
15 John Howard, interview with the author, February 2008.
16 Kevin Rudd, interview with the author, October 2008.
17 Brian Loughnane, interview with the author, February 2009.
18 Peter Costello, interview with the author, February 2008.
19 Tony Abbott, personal conversation, September 2007.
20 John Howard, personal discussion, December 2007.
21 Nick Minchin, interview with the author, February 2009.
22 Howard, *Lazarus Rising*, p. 620.
23 John Howard, interview, January 2008.
24 Howard, *Lazarus Rising*, p. 618.
25 John Howard, interview, December 2007.
26 Alexander Downer, interview, December 2007.
27 Paul Kelly, *Australian*, 15 December 2008.
28 John Howard, interview December 2007; Alexander Downer, interview, December 2007.

29 Costello, *The Costello Memoirs*, p. 257.
30 Howard, *Lazarus Rising*, p. 625.
31 Gartrell, interview, November 2009.
32 Neil Lawrence, interview, September 2013.
33 Brian Loughnane, interview with the author, February 2009.
34 Kevin Rudd, policy speech, 14 November 2007.
35 Malcolm Turnbull, interview with the author, February 2008.
36 Gartrell, interview, November 2009.
37 Howard, interview, February 2008.
38 Kevin Rudd, House of Representatives, *Hansard*, 13 February 2008.
39 Rudd, interview, October 2008.

10 The Rudd Experiment: A Crisis in Governing
1   Graham Richardson, *Australian*, 22 November, 2013.
2   Julia Gillard, interview with the author, October 2013.
3   Terry Moran, interview with the author, February 2014.
4   Chris Barrett, memorandum, p. 2.
5   Gillard, interview, October 2013.
6   Gillard, interview, October 2013.
7   Gillard, interview, October 2013.
8   Chris Evans, interview with the author, November 2013.
9   Bruce Hawker, *The Rudd Rebellion*, MUP, Carlton, 2013, p. 4.
10 Greg Combet, interview with the author, January 2014.
11 Wayne Swan, interview with the author, December 2013.
12 Wayne Swan, interview with the author, July 2012.
13 Lindsay Tanner, *Politics with Purpose*, Scribe, Melbourne, 2012, p. 341.
14 Swan, interview, December 2013.
15 Gillard, interview, October 2013.
16 Moran, interview, February 2014.
17 John Faulkner, interview with the author, January 2013.
18 Chris Bowen, interview with the author, June 2012.
19 Anthony Albanese, interview with the author, February 2014.
20 Sean Kelly, interview with the author, March 2014.
21 Martin Ferguson, interview with the author, April 2013.
22 Gillard, interview, October 2013.
23 David Epstein, interview with the author, March 2014.
24 Evans, interview, November 2013.
25 Combet, interview, January 2014.
26 Gary Gray, interview with the author, June 2013.
27 Gillard, interview, October 2013.
28 Cameron Stewart, *Australian Magazine*, 7–8 November 2009.
29 Kelly, interview, March 2014.
30 James Button, *Speechless*, MUP, Carlton, 2012, p. 79.
31 Lachlan Harris, interview with the author, February 2014.
32 Gray, interview, June 2013.
33 Gray, interview, June 2013.
34 Gray, interview, June 2013.

35 Evans, interview, November 2013.
36 Simon Crean, interview with the author, May 2013.
37 Martin Ferguson, interview with the author, April 2013.
38 Evans, interview, November 2013.
39 Tony Burke, interview with the author, June 2013.
40 John Faulkner, interview with the author, February 2014.
41 Stephen Smith, interview with the author, January 2014.
42 Gray, interview, June 2013.
43 Moran, interview, February 2014.
44 Albanese, interview, February 2014.
45 Gillard, interview, October 2013.
46 Moran, interview, February 2014.
47 Smith, interview, January 2014.
48 Smith, interview, January 2014.
49 Barrett, memorandum, p. 3.
50 Interview with Barrie Cassidy, ABC TV *Insiders* program, 26 February 2012.
51 Burke, interview, April 2013.
52 Barrett, memorandum, p. 4.
53 Kim Carr, interview with the author, January 2013.
54 Faulkner, interview, January 2013.
55 Carr, interview, January 2013.
56 Crean, interview, May 2013.
57 Gray, interview, June 2013.
58 Evans, interview, November 2013.
59 Nicola Roxon, interview with the author, August 2012.
60 Paul Howes, interview with the author, April 2013.
61 Swan, interview, December 2013.
62 Carr, interview, January 2013.
63 Evans, interview, November 2013.
64 David Feeney, interview with the author, February 2014. This account also draws upon Barrie Cassidy, *The Party Thieves*, MUP, Carlton, 2010, pp. 123–4.
65 Combet, interview, January 2014.
66 Kelly, interview, March 2014.
67 Don Farrell, interview with the author, December 2013.

11 Rudd Finds His Mission

1 Kevin Rudd, interview with the author, June 2012.
2 Rudd, interview, June 2012.
3 Wayne Swan, interview with the author, February 2012.
4 Ken Henry, interview with the author, March 2012.
5 Henry, interview, March 2012.
6 Swan, interview, February 2012.
7 Rudd, interview, June 2012.
8 Henry, interview, March, 2012.
9 Henry, interview, March 2012; Lenore Taylor and David Uren, *Shitstorm*, MUP, Carlton, 2010, pp. 25–6.

10 Swan, interview, February 2012.
11 Swan, interview, February 2012.
12 Taylor and Uren, *Shitstorm*, pp. 74–5.
13 Swan, interview, February 2012.
14 Alistair Darling, *Back from the Brink*, Atlantic Books, London, 2011, p. 123.
15 Henry, interview, March 2012.
16 Swan, interview, February 2012.
17 Taylor and Uren, *Shitstorm*, p. 77.
18 Taylor and Uren, *Shitstorm*, pp. 78–81.
19 Chris Barrett, *Australia and the Great Recession*, pp. 35–6.
20 Wayne Swan, personal notes of the G-20 meeting.
21 Swan, interview, February 2012.
22 Swan, interview, February 2012.
23 Henry, interview, March 2012.
24 Kevin Rudd, joint press conference, 14 October 2008.
25 Swan, interview, February 2012.
26 Henry, interview, March 2012.
27 Henry, interview, March 2012.
28 Barrett, *Australia and the Great Recession*, p. 32.
29 Swan, interview, February 2012.
30 Swan, interview, February 2012.
31 Swan, interview, February 2012.
32 Taylor and Uren, *Shitstorm*, p. 136.
33 Swan, interview, February 2012.
34 Updated Economic and Fiscal Outlook, February 2009.
35 David Epstein, interview with the author, March 2014.
36 Swan, interview, February 2012.
37 Ken Henry, interview with the author, March 2014.
38 Rudd, interview, June 2012.
39 Wayne Swan, interview with the author, December 2013.
40 Rudd–Swan–Tanner, joint press conference, 3 February 2009.
41 Swan, interview, February 2012.
42 David Gruen, 'The Return of Fiscal Policy', address, 8 December 2009.
43 Barrett, *Australia and the Great Recession*, pp. 1–11.
44 Saul Eslake, interview with the author, March 2014.
45 Chris Richardson, interview with the author, March 2014.
46 Stephen Anthony, interview with the author, March 2014.
47 Henry, interview, March 2012.
48 Malcolm Turnbull, interview with the author, February 2014.
49 Wayne Swan, national press club speech, 13 May 2009.
50 Swan, interview, February 2012.
51 Gruen, address, 8 December 2009.
52 Swan, interview, February 2012.
53 Swan, interview, December 2013.
54 Rudd, interview, June 2012.
55 Swan, interview, February 2012.

12 Blunder at the Borders

1   Chris Evans, interview with the author, November 2013.
2   Julia Gillard, interview with the author, October 2013.
3   Wayne Swan, interview with the author, December 2013.
4   Paul Kelly and Dennis Shanahan in *Australian*, 23 November 2007.
5   Chris Evans, interview with the author, November 2013.
6   Kevin Rudd, *The Monthly*, October 2006.
7   Evans, interview, November 2009.
8   Chris Evans, speech, 29 July 2008.
9   Evans, interview, November 2013.
10 Chris Evans, speech, 17 November 2008.
11 Paul Kelly, *Australian*, 2 August 2008.
12 Evans, interview, November 2013.
13 Kevin Rudd, House of Representatives, *Hansard*, 26 November 2009, p. 13055.
14 Evans, interview, November 2013.
15 Gillard, interview, October 2013.
16 Evans, interview, November 2013.
17 Gillard, interview, October 2013.
18 Gillard, interview, October 2013.
19 Evans, interview, November 2013.
20 Stephen Fitzpatrick and Matthew Franklin, *Australian*, 29 October 2009.
21 Evans, interview, November 2013.
22 Gillard, interview, October 2013.
23 Evans, interview, November 2013.
24 Kevin Rudd, interview with Neil Mitchell, Radio 3AW.
25 Paul Kelly, *Australian*, 18 November 2009; Paul Maley, *Australian*, 29 December 2009.
26 Gillard, interview, October 2013.
27 Evans, interview, November 2013.
28 Australian Bureau of Statistics, *Migration, Australia, 2009–10*, no. 3412.0
29 Peter Shergold, interview with the author, May 2008.

13 Labor's New Cause

1   Howard Bamsey, interview with the author, March 2012.
2   Kevin Rudd, speech to the UN Bali Conference, 12 December 2007.
3   Bamsey, interview, March 2012.
4   Kevin Rudd, personal discussion, January 2008.
5   *Australian*, 14 December 2007.
6   Ross Garnaut, *The Garnaut Climate Change Review*, Cambridge University Press, Melbourne, 2008, p. xvii.
7   Garnaut, *The Garnaut Climate Change Review*, p. xxx and chapter 2.
8   ABC TV, *7.30 Report*, 3 July 2008.
9   All statements by Penny Wong in this chapter: interview with the author, December 2010.
10 White Paper, chapter 4.

11 White Paper, summary.
12 Bamsey, interview, March 2012.
13 Bamsey, interview, March 2012.
14 Bamsey, interview, March 2012.
15 Ross Garnaut, interview with the author, 2011.
16 Garnaut, interview, 2011.
17 Lenore Taylor and David Uren, *Shitstorm*, MUP, Carlton, 2010, p. 181.

14 The Quest for Control: From the Media to Yarralumla
1 Lachlan Harris, interview with the author, February 2014.
2 Sean Kelly, interview with the author, March 2014.
3 Lindsay Tanner, *Politics with Purpose*, Scribe, Melbourne, 2012, pp. 46–8.
4 David Epstein, interview with the author, March 2014.
5 Stephen Smith, interview with the author, January 2014.
6 Chris Barrett, memorandum, pp. 6–7.
7 Nicola Roxon, interview with Sky News, 24 February 2012.
8 Harris, interview, February 2014.
9 Harris, interview, February 2014.
10 Kelly, interview, March 2014.
11 Maxine McKew, interview with the author, March 2014.
12 Maxine McKew, *Tales from the Political Trenches*, MUP, Carlton, 2012, p. 109.
13 McKew, interview, March 2014.
14 Epstein, interview, March 2014.
15 Simon Crean, interview with the author, May 2013.
16 Tony Burke, interview with the author, June 2013.
17 Chris Barrett, memorandum, p 7.
18 James Button, *Speechless*, MUP, Carlton, 2012, p. 81.
19 Button, *Speechless*, pp. 48–9.
20 Harris, interview, February 2014.
21 Epstein, interview, March 2014.
22 Peter Blunden, interview with the author, March 2014.
23 Blunden, interview, March 2014.
24 John Lyons, *Australian*, 21 June 2008.
25 Chris Mitchell, interview with the author, February 2011.
26 Mitchell, interview, February 2011.
27 Mitchell, interview, February 2011.
28 Mitchell, interview, February 2001.
29 Kelly, interview, March 2014.
30 Greg Sheridan, *Australian*, 9 March 2009.
31 Gary Gray, interview with the author, June 2013.
32 Harris, interview, February 2014.

15 Australian Settlement Nostalgia
1 Ross Garnaut, *Dog Days*, Redback, Melbourne 2013.
2 Gary Banks, speech, 8 December 2010.

3 Ross Gittins, speech given to Australian Business Economists Annual Forecasting Conference, 8 December 2009.
4 Paul Kelly, *Australian*, 14 November 2009; Ross Garnaut, 2010 Hamer Oration, 5 August 2010.
5 Craig Emerson, interview with the author, March 2014.
6 Simon Crean, interview with the author, May 2013.
7 Bill Carmichael, *Australian*, 13 February 2012.
8 Martin Parkinson, speech, 5 October 2012.
9 Martin Parkinson, speech, 2 April 2014.
10 Jennifer Westacott, interview with the author, February 2014.
11 Paul Kelly, *Australian*, 24–25 November 2012.
12 Stephen Anthony, interview with the author, March 2014.
13 Ken Henry, ABC TV, *7.30 Report*, 12 March 2014.
14 *Australian Financial Review*, 7 June 2013.
15 Parkinson, speech, 2 April 2014.
16 Henry, ABC TV, *7.30 Report*, 12 March 2014.
17 Ross Gittins, *Sydney Morning Herald*, 27 July 2009.
18 Kevin Rudd, *The Monthly*, November 2006.
19 Productivity Commission position paper, January 2014, p. 39.
20 Kim Carr, interview with the author, February 2013.
21 Carr, interview, February 2013.
22 Gary Banks, Colin Clark Memorial Lecture, 6 August 2008.
23 Paul Kelly, *Australian*, 9 November 2013; Gary Banks, ACCI dinner, November 2011 and Stan Kelly Lecture, August 2013.
24 Productivity Commission, *Australia's Automotive Manufacturing Industry*, January 2014.
25 Banks, Stan Kelly Lecture, August 2013.
26 Banks, Stan Kelly Lecture, August 2013.
27 *Australian*, 18 March 2014.
28 Allan Hawke, Review of the Administration of the Home Insulation Program, 6 April 2010, p. x.
29 ANAO, Audit Report, no. 12, 2010–11.
30 Peter Garrett, interview with the author, 2013.
31 Greg Combet, interview with the author, January 2014.
32 Paul Kelly, *Australian*, 14 November 2009.
33 Parliamentary Library, NBN, budget review 2013–14.
34 Peter Hartcher, *Sydney Morning Herald*, 11 April 2009.
35 Malcolm Turnbull, interview with the author, February 2013.
36 Combet, interview, January 2014.
37 Peter Anderson, interview with the author, March 2014.
38 Innes Willox, interview with the author, February 2014.
39 Westacott, interview, February 2014.
40 Review of the Fair Work Act, June 2012.

16 Turnbull: The Fatal Assault

1 Nick Minchin, interview with the author, June 2011.
2 Malcolm Turnbull, interview with the author, February 2014.

3   Minchin, interview, June 2011.
4   *Australian*, 1 December 2007 and personal discussions with Malcolm Turnbull during 2007 and 2008.
5   Minchin, interview, June 2011.
6   Turnbull, interview, February 2014.
7   Minchin, interview, June 2011.
8   Brendan Nelson, *Australian*, 11 July 2008.
9   Joe Hockey, interview with the author, January 2014.
10 Minchin, interview, June 2011.
11 Minchin, interview, June 2011.
12 Lenore Taylor, *Australian*, 27 May 2009.
13 Penny Wong, interview, December 2010.
14 Chris Kenny, interview with the author, February 2013.
15 Sean Kelly, interview with the author, September 2013.
16 Turnbull, interview, February 2014.
17 Lenore Taylor, *Australian*, 26 May 2009.
18 Paul Kelly, *Australian*, 26 August 2009.
19 Kelly, *Australian*, 26 August 2009.
20 Kelly, *Australian*, 26 August 2009.
21 Tony Abbott, *Australian*, 24 July 2009.
22 Tony Abbott, speech, 27 July 2009.
23 Minchin, interview, June 2011.
24 Minchin, interview, June 2011.
25 Lenore Taylor, *Australian*, 26 November 2009.
26 Malcolm Turnbull, ABC Radio National, 1 October 2009 and 2UE, 2 October 2009.
27 Dennis Shanahan, *Australian*, 8 October 2009.
28 Stuart Rintoul, *Australian*, 12 December 2009. The author has drawn upon this article for his account of the meeting.
29 Rintoul, *Australian*, 12 December 2009.
30 Tony Abbott, *Battlelines*, MUP, Carlton, 2009, pp. 183–4.
31 Tony Abbott, interview with the author, January 2014.
32 Abbott, interview, January 2014.
33 These conversations are based on diary records.
34 Wong, interview, December 2010.
35 Wong, interview, December 2010; Ian Macfarlane, ABC TV, *4 Corners*, 9 November 2009.
36 Kevin Rudd, address to the Lowy Institute, 6 November 2009.
37 Julia Gillard, interview with the author, October 2013.
38 Chris Kenny, interview with the author, February 2013.
39 Kenny, interview, February 2013.
40 Mark Arbib, interview with the author, February 2014.
41 Sean Kelly, interview with the author, September 2013.
42 Malcolm Turnbull, interview with the author, February 2014.
43 Minchin, interview, June 2011.
44 Andrew Robb, personal discussion, 25 November 2009.
45 Malcolm Turnbull, personal discussion, 25 November 2009.

46 Minchin, interview, June 2011.
47 Turnbull, interview, February 2014.
48 Minchin, interview, June 2011.
49 Lenore Taylor and Matthew Franklin, *Australian*, 25 November 2009.
50 Paul Kelly, *Australian*, 28 November 2009.
51 Minchin, interview, June 2011.
52 Media statement, Cormann, Fifield, Mason, 25 November 2009.

17 Abbott: The Accidental Victory
1 Nick Minchin, interview, June 2011.
2 Dennis Shanahan, *Australian*, 26 November 2009.
3 Minchin, interview, June 2011.
4 Minchin, interview, June 2011.
5 Tony Abbott, interview with the author, January 2014.
6 Minchin, interview, June 2011.
7 Malcolm Turnbull, interview with the author, February 2014.
8 Abbott, interview, January 2014.
9 Turnbull, interview, February 2014.
10 Tony Abbott, personal conversations with the author, November and December 2009.
11 Malcolm Turnbull, personal conversations with the author, November and December 2009.
12 Paul Kelly, *Australian*, 28 November 2011.
13 Matthew Franklin and Dennis Shanahan, *Australian*, 27 November 2009.
14 Phillip Coorey, *Sydney Morning Herald*, 28 November 2009.
15 Coorey, *Sydney Morning Herald*, 28 November 2009.
16 Abbott, interview, January 2014.
17 Malcolm Turnbull, interview with Laurie Oakes, Nine Network, 29 November 2009.
18 Joe Hockey, personal conversations with the author, November and December 2009.
19 Minchin, interview, June 2011.
20 Minchin, interview, June 2011.
21 Minchin, interview, June 2011.
22 Minchin, interview, June 2011.
23 Minchin, interview, June 2011.
24 Joe Hockey, interview with the author, January 2014; Paul Kelly, *Australian*, 3 December 2009.
25 Minchin, interview, June 2011.
26 Paul Kelly, *Australian*, 3 December 2009.
27 Abbott, interview, January 2014.
28 Turnbull, interview, February 2014.
29 Minchin, interview, June 2011.
30 Minchin, interview, June 2011.
31 Turnbull, interview, February 2014.
32 Julia Gillard, interview with the author, October 2013.

33 Penny Wong, interview with the author, December 2010.
34 Minchin, interview, June 2011.
35 Turnbull, interview, February 2014.

18 How Rudd Gifted Abbott
1   Dennis Shanahan, *Australian*, 16 December 2009.
2   Tony Abbott, interview with the author, January 2010.
3   Abbott, interview, January 2010.
4   Sean Kelly, interview with the author, March 2014.
5   Malcolm Turnbull, interview with the author, February 2014.
6   Barnaby Joyce, Senate, *Hansard*, 30 November 2009, pp. 9576–80.
7   Christine Milne, Senate, *Hansard*, 30 November 2009, pp. 9590–4.
8   Bob Brown, interview with the author, January 2014.
9   Lachlan Harris, interview with the author, February 2014.
10 Phillip Coorey, *Sydney Morning Herald*, 3 December 2009.
11 Penny Wong, interview with the author, December 2010.
12 Wayne Swan, interview with the author, July 2012.
13 Julia Gillard, interview with the author, October 2013.
14 Howard Bamsey, interview with the author, November 2011.
15 Wong, interview, December 2010.
16 Wong, interview, December 2010.
17 Bamsey, interview, November 2011.
18 Bamsey, interview, November 2011.
19 Wong, interview, December 2010.
20 Bamsey, interview, November 2011.
21 Wong, interview, December 2010.
22 Julia Gillard, interview with the author, July 2013.
23 Swan, interview, July 2012.
24 Gary Banks, Garran Oration, 21 November 2013.
25 Karl Bitar, interview with the author, February 2014.
26 Swan, interview, July 2012.
27 Swan, interview, July 2012.
28 Mark Arbib, interview with the author, February 2014.
29 Kevin Rudd, interview with the author, June 2012.
30 Swan, interview, July 2012.
31 Rudd, interview, June 2012.
32 John Faulkner, interview with the author, January 2014.
33 Rudd, interview, June 2012.
34 Rudd, interview, June 2012.
35 Chris Evans, interview with the author, November 2013.
36 Wayne Swan, interview with the author, December 2013.
37 Kim Carr, interview with the author, February 2014.
38 Anthony Albanese, interview with the author, February 2014.
39 Harris, interview, February 2014.
40 Rudd, interview, June 2012.
41 Rudd, interview, June 2012.

42 Gillard, interview, October 2013.
43 Gillard, interview, October 2013.
44 Gillard, interview, October 2013.
45 Gillard, interview, October 2013.
46 Rudd, interview, June 2012.
47 Gillard, interview, October 2013.
48 Gillard, interview, October 2013.
49 Bitar–Jordan emails, 11 January 2010.

19 Climate Change Retreat
1   Karl Bitar, interview with the author, December 2012.
2   Karl Bitar, email to Alister Jordan, 12 February 2010.
3   Bitar, interview, December 2012.
4   Phillip Coorey, *Sydney Morning Herald*, 25–26 February 2012.
5   Kevin Rudd, interview with the author, June 2012.
6   Nicola Roxon, interview with the author, August 2012.
7   Nicola Roxon, ABC TV, *Insiders*, 26 February 2012.
8   Nicola Roxon, John Button Memorial Lecture, October 2013.
9   Roxon, interview, August 2012.
10 Nicola Roxon, interview with Sky News, 24 February 2012.
11 Julia Gillard, interview with the author, October 2013.
12 Roxon, Sky News, 24 February 2012.
13 Roxon, interview, August 2012.
14 Roxon, *Insiders*, 26 February 2012.
15 Roxon, Sky News, 24 February 2012.
16 Lenore Taylor, *Sydney Morning Herald*, 25 February 2012.
17 Kevin Rudd, interview with the author, July 2012.
18 Paul Kelly, *Australian*, 24 March 2010.
19 Kevin Rudd, National Press Club speech, 3 March 2010.
20 Terry Moran, interview with the author, February 2014.
21 David Epstein, interview with the author, March 2014.
22 Roxon, Sky News, 24 February 2012.
23 Paul Kelly, *Australian*, 14 April 2010.
24 Wayne Swan, interview with the author, July 2012.
25 ABC Radio, *AM*, 19 April 2010.
26 Rudd, interview, June 2012.
27 Swan, interview, July 2012.
28 Moran, interview, February 2014.
29 Rudd, interview, June 2012.
30 Kevin Rudd, Minutes of the Federal Parliamentary Labor Party, 24 June 2010.
31 Rudd, interview, June 2012.
32 Gillard, interview, October 2013.
33 This relies upon Geoff Kitney, *Australian Financial Review*, 25 July 2011.
34 Rudd, interview, June 2012.
35 Swan, interview, July 2012.
36 Kevin Rudd, press conference, 24 February 2012.

37 Rudd, interview, June 2012.
38 Personal conversation with Kevin Rudd, December 2010.
39 Rudd, interview, June 2012.
40 Gillard, interview, October 2013.
41 Gillard, interview, October 2013.
42 Mark Arbib, interview with the author, February 2014.
43 Gillard, interview, October 2013.
44 Lenore Taylor, *Sydney Morning Herald*, 27 April 2012.
45 Penny Wong, interview with the author, December 2010.
46 Martin Ferguson, interview with the author, April 2013.
47 Rudd, interview, June 2012.
48 Kim Carr, interview with the author, January 2013.
49 Sean Kelly, interview with the author, March 2014.
50 Lachlan Harris, interview with the author, February 2014.
51 Penny Wong, interview on 5AA Adelaide, 28 April 2012.
52 Rudd, interview, June 2012.
53 Rudd, interview, June 2012.
54 Swan, interview, July 2012.
55 Tony Burke, interview with the author, June 2013.
56 Ferguson, interview, April 2013.
57 Lindsay Tanner, interview with the author, September 2012.
58 Wong, interview, December 2010.
59 Wong, interview, December 2010.
60 Harris, interview, February 2014.
61 Wong, interview, December 2010.

20 The Mining Tax: The Fatal Blow
1   Terry Moran, interview with the author, February 2014.
2   Wayne Swan, interview with the author, July 2012.
3   Kevin Rudd, interview with the author, June 2012.
4   Swan, interview, July 2012.
5   Swan, interview, July 2012.
6   Wayne Swan, interview with the author, December 2013.
7   Swan, interview, December 2013.
8   Swan, interview, December 2013.
9   Martin Ferguson, interview with the author, April 2013.
10 Ferguson, interview, April 2013.
11 Dennis Shanahan and Matthew Franklin, *Australian*, 18 December 2010.
12 Swan, interview, December 2013.
13 Swan, interview, July 2012.
14 Ferguson, interview, April 2013.
15 Mitch Hooke, interview with the author, August 2012.
16 Hooke, interview, August 2012.
17 Hooke, interview, August 2012.
18 Hooke, interview, August 2012.
19 Minerals Council of Australia, private notes of meeting.

20 Rudd, interview, June 2012.
21 Chris Barrett to Ken Henry and David Parker, email, 30 March 2010, 9:06 a.m.
22 Paul Kelly, *Australian*, 18 April 2012.
23 Ken Henry, interview with the author, March 2012.
24 Rudd, interview, June 2012.
25 Swan, interview, July 2012.
26 Ferguson, interview, April 2013.
27 Hooke, interview, August 2012.
28 Marius Kloppers interview, ABC TV, *Inside Business*, 9 May 2010.
29 Dennis Shanahan and Matthew Franklin, *Australian*, 18 December 2010.
30 David Peever, interview with the author, May 2014.
31 Ferguson, interview, April 2013.
32 Ferguson, interview, April 2013.
33 Hooke, interview, August 2012.
34 Swan, interview, July 2012.
35 Ferguson, interview, April 2013.
36 Ferguson, interview, April 2013.
37 Swan, interview, July 2012.
38 Rudd, interview, June 2012.
39 Matthew Franklin and Sue Dunlevy, *Australian*, 25 February 2012.
40 Swan, interview, December 2013.
41 Swan, interview, December 2013.
42 Rudd, interview, June 2012.
43 Swan, interview, July 2012.
44 The Treasury, *The Resource Super Profits Tax*, May 2010; Paul Kelly, *Australian*, 5 May 2010.
45 Peter Anderson, interview with the author, March 2014.
46 Kevin Rudd and Wayne Swan, press conference, 2 May 2010.
47 The Treasury, *The Resource Super Profits Tax*, May 2010.
48 Rudd and Swan, press conference, 2 May 2010.
49 Hooke, interview, August 2012; David Crowe, *Australian*, 6 March 2012.
50 Hooke, interview, August 2012.
51 Ferguson, interview, April 2013.
52 Jennifer Hewett, *Australian*, 4 May 2012.
53 Dennis Shanahan and Jennifer Hewett, *Australian*, 3 June 2010.
54 Swan, interview, July 2012.
55 Jennifer Hewett, *Australian*, 15 May 2010.
56 Paul Kelly, *Australian*, 18 April 2012.
57 Phillip Coorey, *Sydney Morning Herald*, 15 May 2010.
58 Peter Hartcher, *Sydney Morning Herald*, 29 May 2010.
59 Hooke, interview, August 2012.
60 Karl Bitar, interview with the author, December 2012.
61 Paul Howes, *Confessions of a Faceless Man*, MUP, Carlton, 2010, pp. 8–10.
62 Treasury note to the Prime Minister's Office and the Treasurer's Office, 10 February 2010.
63 Sinclair Davidson, 'Evaluating the Resource Super Profit Tax in light of internal Treasury documentation', p. 13.

64 Chris Barrett, interview with the author, April 2012.
65 Swan, interview, July 2012.
66 Jennifer Hewett, *Australian*, 27 May 2010.
67 Ferguson, interview, April 2013.
68 Ross Garnaut, *The New Australian Resource Rent Tax*, 20 May 2010.
69 Charlie's morning thoughts, 16 June 2010, 8:31 a.m.
70 Mitch Hooke, speech, 9 June 2010.
71 Jennifer Hewett, *Australian*, 3 June 2010.
72 Peever, interview, May 2014.
73 Paul Kelly, *Australian*, 9 June 2012.
74 Martin Ferguson, interview with the author, July 2012.
75 Rudd, interview, June 2012.
76 Ferguson, interview, April 2013.
77 Rudd, interview, June 2012.
78 Ferguson, interview, April 2013.
79 Paul Kelly, *Australian*, 18 April 2012.
80 Swan, interview, July 2012.
81 Lachlan Harris, interview with the author, February 2014.
82 Swan, interview, July 2012.
83 Ken Henry, interview with the author, March 2012.
84 Bitar, interview, December 2012.
85 Ferguson, interview, April 2013.

21 The Demise of Rudd
1 Greg Combet, interview with the author, January 2014.
2 Julia Gillard, interview with the author, October 2013.
3 Bruce Hawker, *The Rudd Rebellion*, MUP, Carlton, 2013, p. 5.
4 Gillard, interview, October 2013.
5 Sean Kelly, interview with the author, March 2014.
6 Gillard, interview, October 2013.
7 Karl Bitar, interview with the author, December 2012.
8 Pamela Williams, *Australian Financial Review*, 16 July 2010; Barrie Cassidy, *The Party Thieves*, MUP, Carlton, 2010, p. 82.
9 Don Farrell, interview with the author, December 2013.
10 Tony Burke, interview with the author, June 2013.
11 Burke, interview, June 2013.
12 Gillard, interview, October 2013.
13 Burke, interview, June 2013.
14 UMB Research, June 2010.
15 Maxine McKew, *Tales from the Political Trenches*, MUP, Carlton, 2012, p. 188.
16 Cassidy, *The Party Thieves*, p. 115.
17 Dennis Shanahan, *The Weekend Australian*, 19 June 2010.
18 Hawker, *The Rudd Rebellion*, p. 8.
19 Wayne Swan, interview with the author, December 2013.
20 Stephen Smith, interview with the author, January 2012.
21 Martin Ferguson, interview with the author, April 2013.
22 Troy Bramston, *Looking for the Light on the Hill*, Scribe, Melbourne, 2011.

23 Dennis Shanahan, *Australian*, 21 June 2010.

24 Dennis Shanahan, *Australian*, 22 June 2010.

25 Mark Arbib, interview with the author, July 2010.

26 Arbib, interview, July 2010.

27 Kim Carr, interview with the author, February 2014.

28 Carr, interview, February 2014.

29 Carr, interview, February 2014.

30 Julia Gillard, interview with the author, October 2013 and February 2014.

31 Mark Arbib, interview with the author, February 2014.

32 Peter Hartcher and Phillip Coorey, *Sydney Morning Herald*, 23 June 2010.

33 Dennis Shanahan, *Australian*, 15 February 2012.

34 Lachlan Harris, interview with the author, February 2014.

35 Anthony Albanese, interview with the author, February 2014.

36 Gillard, interview, October 2013.

37 Burke, interview, June 2013.

38 Kevin Rudd, interview with the author, June 2012.

39 Hawker, *The Rudd Rebellion*, p. 10.

40 John Faulkner, interview with the author, February 2014.

41 Rudd, interview, June 2012.

42 Rudd, interview, June 2012.

43 Kim Carr, interview with the author, January 2013.

44 Burke, interview, June 2013.

45 Swan, interview, December 2013.

46 Burke, interview, June 2013.

47 Rudd, interview, June 2012.

48 Rudd, interview, June 2012.

49 Albanese, interview, February 2014.

50 Rudd, interview, June 2012.

51 Albanese, interview, February 2014.

52 Hawker, *The Rudd Rebellion*, p. 13.

53 Burke, interview, April 2013.

54 Kevin Rudd, press conference, 23 June 2010.

55 Paul Howes, interview with the author, April 2013.

56 Albanese, interview, February 2014.

57 Smith, interview, January 2014; Carr, interview, February 2014.

58 Chris Evans, interview with the author, November 2013.

59 Smith, interview, January 2014.

60 Combet, interview, January 2014.

61 Ferguson, interview, April 2013.

62 Chris Bowen, interview with the author, June 2012.

63 Smith, interview, January 2014.

64 Evans, interview, November 2013.

65 Albanese, interview, February 2014.

66 Ferguson, interview, April 2013.

67 Bob Carr, interview with the author, June 2013.

68 Harris, interview, February 2014.

69 Evans, interview, November 2013.
70 Gillard, interview, October 2013.
71 Dennis Shanahan, *Australian*, 15 February, 2012.
72 Combet, interview, January 2014.
73 Howes, interview, April 2013.
74 Gillard, interview, October 2013.
75 Harris, interview, February 2014.

22 The Fatal Inheritance
1 Julia Gillard, interview with the author, October 2013.
2 Wayne Swan, interview with the author, December 2013.
3 Chris Evans, interview with the author, November 2013.
4 Greg Combet, interview with the author, January 2014.
5 Simon Crean, interview with the author, May 2013.
6 Anthony Albanese, interview with the author, February 2014.
7 Kim Carr, interview with the author, February 2014.
8 Stephen Smith, interview with the author, January 2014.
9 Sean Kelly, interview with the author, March 2014.
10 Gillard, interview, October 2013.
11 Julia Gillard, press conference, 24 June 2010.
12 Gillard, interview, October 2013.
13 Swan, interview, December 2013.
14 Julia Gillard, press conference, 24 June 2010.
15 Gillard, press conference, 24 June 2010.
16 Julia Gillard, press conferences, 24 and 25 June 2010.
17 Paul Howes, interview with the author, April 2013.
18 Julia Gillard, interview with Jon Faine, ABC Radio, 774 Melbourne, 29 June 2010.
19 Smith, interview, January 2014.
20 Dennis Shanahan, *Australian*, 29 June 2010.
21 Julia Gillard, interview with Jon Faine, ABC Radio, 774 Melbourne, 29 June 2010.
22 John McTernan, interview with the author, July 2013.
23 Tony Burke, interview with the author, June 2013.
24 Howes, interview, April 2013.
25 McTernan, interview, August 2013.
26 Sam Dastyari, interview with the author, January 2014.
27 Albanese, interview, February 2014.
28 Gillard, press conference, 24 June 2010.
29 McTernan, interview, August 2013.
30 Gillard, press conference, 24 June 2010.
31 Julia Gillard, interview with Laurie Oakes, Nine Network, 27 June 2010.
32 Swan, interview, December 2013.
33 Ferguson, interview, April 2013.
34 Paul Kelly, *Australian*, 3 July 2010.
35 Paul Kelly, *Australian*, 13 February 2013.

36 Gillard–Swan–Ferguson, joint press conference, 2 July 2010.
37 Ferguson, interview, April 2013.
38 Ferguson, interview, April 2013.
39 Julia Gillard, interview with Neil Mitchell, 3AW, 2 July 2010.
40 Gillard–Swan–Ferguson, joint press conference, 2 July 2010.
41 Gillard, joint press conference, 2 July 2010.
42 Julia Gillard, Lowy Institute speech, 6 July 2010.
43 Evans, interview, November 2013.
44 McTernan, interview, August 2013.

23 The Tragedy of Minority Government
1 George Wright, interview with the author, February 2014.
2 John McTernan, interview with the author, August 2013.
3 Bob Carr, interview with the author, January 2014.
4 Anthony Albanese, interview with the author, February 2014.
5 David Feeney, interview with the author, February 2010.
6 Tony Burke, interview with the author, June 2013.
7 David Feeney, interview with the author, February 2014.
8 Julia Gillard, interview with the author, October 2013.
9 Brian Loughnane, interview with the author, February 2010.
10 Sean Kelly, interview with the author, September, 2013.
11 Julia Gillard, interview with Laurie Oakes, Nine Network, 27 June 2010.
12 Paul Kelly, *Australian*, 24 July, 2010.
13 Paul Kelly, *Australian*, 26 July 2010.
14 Phillip Coorey, *Sydney Morning Herald*, 24 July 2010.
15 Kevin Rudd, interview with the author, June 2012.
16 Peter Hartcher, *Sydney Morning Herald*, 28 July 2010.
17 Hartcher, *Sydney Morning Herald*, 28 July 2010 and Barrie Cassidy, *The Party Thieves*, MUP, Carlton, 2010, p. 163.
18 Tony Burke, interview with the author, June 2013.
19 Wayne Swan, interview with the author, December 2013.
20 Julia Gillard, media conference, 23 February 2012.
21 Gillard, interview, October 2013.
22 Swan, interview, December 2013.
23 Stephen Smith, interview with the author, January 2014.
24 Mark Arbib, interview with the author, February 2014.
25 Greg Combet, interview with the author, January 2014.
26 Don Farrell, interview with the author, December 2013.
27 Paul Kelly, *Australian*, 31 July 2010; Phillip Coorey, *Sydney Morning Herald*, 29 July 2010.
28 Phillip Coorey, *Sydney Morning Herald*, 28 July 2010.
29 Peter Hartcher, *Sydney Morning Herald*, 31 July 2010.
30 Gillard, interview, October 2013.
31 Bob Brown, interview with the author, January 2014.
32 Gillard, interview, October 2013.
33 Gillard, interview, October 2013.

34 Marcus Priest, 'Climate of Chaos', *Australian Financial Review*, 27 April 2013.
35 John McTernan, interview with the author, August 2013.
36 Swan, interview, December 2013.
37 Smith, interview, January 2014.
38 Sam Dastyari, interview with the author, January 2014.
39 Combet, interview, January 2014.
40 Tony Abbott, interview with the author, January 2014.
41 Abbott, interview, January 2014.
42 David Feeney, interview with the author, February 2014.
43 Combet, interview, January 2014.
44 McTernan, interview, August 2013.
45 Swan, interview, December 2013.

24 Signing the Death Warrant
1   Julia Gillard, interview with the author, October 2013.
2   John McTernan, interview with the author, August 2013.
3   Wayne Swan, interview with the author, December 2013.
4   Tony Abbott, interview with the author, January 2014.
5   Tony Burke, interview with the author, June 2013.
6   McTernan, interview, August 2013.
7   Greg Combet, interview with the author, January 2014.
8   Julia Gillard, joint press conference, 24 February 2011.
9   Gillard, interview, October 2013.
10 Julia Gillard, ABC TV, *7.30 Report*, 24 February 2011.
11 Gillard, interview, October 2013.
12 Tony Abbott, media conference, 24 February 2011.
13 Julia Gillard, interview with Alan Jones, 25 February 2011.
14 House of Representatives, *Hansard*, 23 March 2011.
15 House of Representatives, *Hansard*, 24 March 2011, pp. 58–62.
16 George Wright, interview with the author, February 2014.
17 Marcus Priest, 'Climate of Chaos', *Australian Financial Review*, 27 April 2013.
18 Priest, *Australian Financial Review*, 27 April 2013.
19 Gillard, interview, October, 2013.
20 Priest, *Australian Financial Review*, 27 April 2013.
21 Combet, interview, January 2014.
22 Warwick McKibbin, *Australian Financial Review*, 14 January 2014.
23 Priest, *Australian Financial Review*, 27 April 2013.
24 Julia Gillard, National Press Club speech, 14 July 2011.
25 Paul Kelly, *Australian*, 18 June 2011.
26 Combet, interview, January 2014.
27 Combet, interview, January 2014.
28 Senate, *Hansard*, 8 November 2011.
29 Paul Kelly, *Australian*, 15 October 2011.
30 Jennifer Westacott, interview with the author, February 2014.

25 Phoney Victory

1 Julia Gillard, interview with the author, October 2013.
2 Kevin Rudd, statement to the Parliamentary Labor Party, 27 February 2012.
3 Martin Ferguson, interview with the author, April 2013.
4 John McTernan, interview with the author, August 2013.
5 Anthony Albanese, interview with the author, February 2014.
6 Phillip Coorey, *Sydney Morning Herald*, 26 November 2011.
7 Greg Combet, interview with the author, January 2014.
8 ABC Radio, *AM*, 23 February 2012.
9 Pamela Williams, *Australian Financial Review*, 24 February 2012.
10 Williams, *Australian Financial Review*, 24 February 2012.
11 Albanese, interview, February 2014.
12 Kevin Rudd, interview with Sky News, 19 February 2012.
13 Gillard, interview, October 2013.
14 Gillard, interview, October 2013.
15 Tony Burke, interview with the author, April 2014.
16 Dennis Shanahan and Sid Maher, *Australian*, 23 February 2012.
17 McTernan, interview, August 2013.
18 Kevin Rudd, Statement of Resignation, 22 February 2012.
19 Gillard, interview, October 2013.
20 Kevin Rudd, interview with the author, February 2014.
21 Ferguson, interview, April 2013.
22 Wayne Swan, press release, 22 February 2012.
23 Julia Gillard, press conference, 23 February 2012.
24 Kevin Rudd, press conference, 24 February 2012.
25 Nicola Roxon, interview with Sky News, 24 February 2012.
26 Samantha Maiden, news.com.au, 26 February 2012.
27 Combet, interview, January 2014.
28 Albanese, interview, February 2012.
29 Don Farrell, interview with the author, December 2013.
30 *Australian Financial Review*, 27 February 2012.
31 Stephen Smith, interview with the author, January 2014.
32 Burke, interview, April 2014.
33 Paul Kelly, *Australian*, 3 March 2012.

26 The Collapse of Border Protection

1 Chris Bowen, interview with the author, June 2012.
2 Bowen, interview, June 2012.
3 Julia Gillard, press conference, 25 July 2011.
4 Paul Kelly, *Australian*, 3 September 2011.
5 Chris Bowen, interview with David Speers, Sky News, *PM Agenda*, 25 July 2011.
6 Scott Morrison and Julie Bishop, press conference, 25 July 2011.
7 The 'Pacific Solution', Parliamentary Library, 4 September 2002.
8 Bowen, interview, June 2012.
9 Tony Abbott, interview with Paul Murray, 2UE, 25 July 2011.

10 Tony Abbott, doorstop, 25 July 2011.
11 Julia Gillard, interview with the author, October 2013.
12 Julia Gillard, House of Representatives, *Hansard*, 12 September 2011, p. 9608.
13 Tony Abbott, House of Representatives, *Hansard*, 13 September 2011, p. 9899.
14 Dennis Shanahan, *Australian*, 22 September 2011.
15 Peter Hartcher, *Sydney Morning Herald*, 15 October 2011.
16 Tony Burke, interview with the author, June 2013.
17 This account of the cabinet meeting is based upon Peter Hartcher, *Sydney Morning Herald*, 15 October 2011.
18 Paul Kelly, *Australian*, 19 October 2011.
19 Burke, interview, June 2013.
20 Gillard, interview, October 2013.
21 Burke, interview, June 2013.
22 Kim Carr, interview with the author, February 2014.
23 *Age*, editorial, 15 October 2011.
24 Paul Kelly, *Australian*, 10 December 2011.
25 *Mapping Social Cohesion*, Scanlon Foundation survey, 2012.
26 Tony Abbott to Julia Gillard, 16 December 2011.
27 Report of the Expert Panel on Asylum Seekers, August 2012, p. 75.
28 Paul Maley, *Australian*, 24 December 2011.
29 Paul Kelly, *Australian*, 21 January 2012.
30 Paul Kelly, *Australian*, 9 June 2012.
31 Report of the Expert Panel on Asylum Seekers, August 2012, p. 75.
32 Peter Hartcher and Phillip Coorey, *Sydney Morning Herald*, 30 June 2012.
33 Paul Kelly, *Australian*, 30 June 2012.
34 Report of the Expert Panel on Asylum Seekers, August 2012.
35 Julia Gillard and Chris Bowen, press conference, 13 August 2012.
36 House of Representatives, *Hansard*, 14 August 2012, p. 17.
37 Gillard and Bowen, press conference, 13 August 2012.
38 'A Change of Heart', *The Age*, 15 August 2012.
39 Janet Phillips and Harriet Spinks, Boat Arrivals in Australia since 1976, Parliamentary Library, August 2008.

27 Feminist Heroine
1 John McTernan, interview with the author, August 2013.
2 Sean Kelly, interview with the author, March 2014.
3 Julia Gillard, interview with Anne Summers, 10 June 2013.
4 Julia Gillard, interview with the author, October 2013.
5 Phillip Coorey, *Sydney Morning Herald*, 2 April 2012.
6 Gillard, interview with Summers, 10 June 2013.
7 Anne Summers, Reports, Number 3, July 2013.
8 Anne Summers, *The Misogyny Factor*, Newsouth, Sydney, 2013, pp. 121–3.
9 *The Daily Telegraph*, 5 October 2012.
10 Paul Kelly, *Australian*, 3 October 2012.
11 Peter Hartcher, *Sydney Morning Herald*, 13 October 2012.
12 Phillip Coorey and Jacqueline Maley, *Sydney Morning Herald*, 13 October 2012.

13 House of Representatives, *Hansard*, 9 October 2012, pp. 28–30.
14 House of Representatives, *Hansard*, 9 October 2012, pp. 30–2.
15 McTernan, interview, August 2013.
16 Wayne Swan, interview with the author, December 2013.
17 Hartcher, *Sydney Morning Herald*, 13 October 2012.
18 Summers, *The Misogyny Factor*, pp. 148–51.
19 Kelly, interview, March 2014.
20 Julia Gillard, doorstop, 10 October 2012.
21 Dennis Shanahan, *Australian*, 12 October 2012.
22 George Wright, interview with the author, February 2014.

28 Chasing the Surplus
1 Tony Abbott, press conference, 20 December 2012.
2 Paul Keating, interview with the author, December 2013.
3 Wayne Swan, interview with the author, December 2013.
4 Jim Chalmers, *Glory Daze*, MUP, Carlton, 2013, p. 146.
5 David Uren and Chris Richardson, 'Temporary Boom, Permanent Waste', *Australian*, 10 August 2013.
6 Wayne Swan, National Press Club speech, 11 May 2010.
7 Penny Wong, interview with the author, March 2014.
8 Deloitte Access Economics, Budget Monitor, September 2010.
9 Wayne Swan, speech, 20 April 2011.
10 Craig Emerson, interview with the author, February 2013.
11 Alan Mitchell, *Australian Financial Review*, 8 May 2012.
12 David Uren, *Australian*, 16 May 2012.
13 Deloitte Access Economics, 15 January 2013.
14 Jennifer Westacott, interview with the author, January 2014.
15 John McTernan, interview with the author, August 2013.
16 Paul Kelly, *Australian*, 2 March 2011.
17 Disability Care and Support, Productivity Commission, July 2011.
18 Julia Gillard, speech, 3 December 2012.
19 Ben Jensen, *The Weekend Australian*, 23–24 February 2013.
20 Chris Richardson and Vik Khanna, *Australian Financial Review*, 8 May 2013.
21 David Uren, *Australian*, 15 May 2013.
22 Economic Statement, 2 August 2013, p. 32.
23 Jennifer Westacott, interview with the author, February 2014.
24 Stephen Anthony, interview with the author, March 2014.
25 David Uren, *Australian*, 12 May 2012.
26 Swan, interview, December 2013.
27 Emerson, interview, February 2014.
28 Chris Richardson, *Australian Financial Review*, 15 August 2013.
29 Swan, interview, December 2013.
30 Wong, interview, March 2014.
31 Ken Henry, ABC TV, *7.30 Report*, 12 March 2014.
32 Martin Parkinson, speech to Sydney Institute, 2 April 2014.
33 Report by Macroeconomics, December 2013.

34 Chris Richardson, interview with the author, November 2012.
35 Swan, interview, December 2013.

29 Far from Rooty Hill
1 Bob Carr, *Diary of a Foreign Minister*, Newsouth, Sydney, 2014, p. 381.
2 Wayne Swan, interview with the author, December 2013. The reference is to Canberra author Kerry-Anne Walsh's book, *The Stalking of Julia Gillard*, Allen & Unwin, Sydney, 2013.
3 Carr, *Diary of a Foreign Minister*, p. 293.
4 Sam Dastyari, interview with the author, January 2014.
5 Greg Combet, interview with the author, January 2014.
6 Bob Carr, interview with the author, June 2013.
7 Bruce Hawker, interview with the author, June 2010.
8 Carr, *Diary of a Foreign Minister*, p. 304.
9 Bob Carr, interview with the author, January 2014.
10 Carr, *Diary of a Foreign Minister*, pp. 225–35.
11 Carr, *Diary of a Foreign Minister*, pp. 235–6.
12 Peter Hartcher, *Sydney Morning Herald*, 28 November 2012; Troy Bramston, *Australian*, 29 November 2012.
13 Carr, *Diary of a Foreign Minister*, pp. 237–9.
14 Julia Gillard, interview with the author, October 2013.
15 Dastyari, interview, January 2014.
16 Tony Burke, interview with the author, April 2014.

30 Labor Traditionalists
1 Innes Willox, interview with the author, January 2014.
2 Peter Anderson, interview with the author, March 2014.
3 Tony Shepherd, interview with the author, January 2014.
4 Willox, interview, January 2014.
5 Shepherd, interview, January 2014; David Crowe, *Australian*, 7 December 2012.
6 Jennifer Westacott, interview with the author, January 2014.
7 Sam Dastyari, interview with the author, January 2014.
8 Westacott, interview, January 2014.
9 Willox, interview, January 2014.
10 Wayne Swan, interview with the author, December 2013.
11 Swan, interview, December 2013.
12 Swan, interview, December 2013.
13 Wayne Swan, *The Monthly*, March 2012.
14 Wayne Swan, John Button Lecture, 1 August 2012.
15 Wayne Swan, speech, 27 April 2013.
16 Gillard, interview, January 2010.
17 John McTernan, interview with the author, August 2013.
18 Greg Combet, interview with the author, January 2014.
19 Combet, interview, January 2014.
20 Peter Hartcher, *Sydney Morning Herald*, 19 November 2013.

21 Mark Latham, 'Not Dead Yet', *Quarterly Essay*, issue 49, 2013.
22 Simon Crean, interview with the author, May 2013.
23 Julia Gillard, interview with the author, October 2013.
24 Crean, interview, May 2013; Kate Legge, *Australian Magazine*, 27 April 2013.
25 Martin Ferguson, press conference, 22 March 2013.
26 Bill Kelty, *Sydney Morning Herald*, 28 March 2013.
27 Paul Howes, interview with the author, April 2013.
28 Paul Kelly, *Australian*, 9 March 2013.
29 Willox, interview, January 2014.
30 *Australian Financial Review*, 13 May 2013.
31 Westacott, interview, January 2014.
32 Willox, interview, January 2014.
33 Peter Anderson, interview with the author, February 2014.
34 Westacott, interview, January 2014.
35 Swan, interview, December 2013.
36 Craig Emerson, interview with the author, February 2014.
37 Combet, interview, January 2014.
38 Gillard, interview, October 2013.
39 McTernan, interview, August 2013.

31 The Gillard Demise

1 Chris Bowen, interview with the author, February 2014.
2 Kevin Rudd, interview with the author, February 2014.
3 David Feeney, interview with the author, February 2014.
4 Bob Carr, *Diary of a Foreign Minister*, Newsouth, Sydney, 2014, p. 382.
5 Tony Burke, interview with the author, April 2014.
6 Greg Combet, interview with the author, January 2014.
7 Paul Howes, interview with the author, April 2013.
8 George Wright, email to Ben Hubbard and Julia Gillard, 29 January 2013, 10.35 a.m.
9 Sam Dastyari, interview with the author, January 2014.
10 Simon Crean, interview with the author, May 2013; Kate Legge, *Australian Magazine*, 27 April 2013.
11 Crean, interview, May 2013.
12 Julia Gillard, interview with the author, October 2013.
13 Crean, interview, May 2013; Legge, *Australian Magazine*, 27 April 2013.
14 Gillard, interview, October 2013.
15 Carr, *Diary of a Foreign Minister*, p. 306.
16 Crean, interview, May 2013.
17 Crean, interview, May 2013.
18 Crean, interview, May 2013.
19 Crean, interview, May 2013.
20 Kate Legge, *Australian Magazine*, 27 April 2013.
21 Crean, interview, May 2013.
22 Kevin Rudd, press conference, 22 March 2013.
23 Laurie Oakes, *The Daily Telegraph*, 23 March 2013.

24 Wayne Swan, interview with the author, December 2013.
25 Bowen, interview, February 2014.
26 Kim Carr, interview with the author, February 2014.
27 Dastyari, interview, January 2014.
28 Peter Hartcher, *Sydney Morning Herald*, 16–17 November 2013.
29 John McTernan, interview with the author, August 2013.
30 Craig Emerson, interview with the author, February 2014.
31 Bowen, interview, February 2014.
32 Dastyari, interview, January 2014.
33 Dennis Shanahan, *Australian*, 10 June 2013.
34 Julia Gillard, speech, 11 June 2013.
35 Carr, interview, February 2014.
36 Peter Hartcher, *Sydney Morning Herald*, 15 June 2013.
37 Dastyari, interview, January 2014.
38 Carr, *Diary of a Foreign Minister*, p. 378.
39 George Wright, interview with the author, February 2014.
40 Crean, interview, May 2013.
41 Combet, interview, January 2014.
42 Greg Combet, *The Fights of My Life*, MUP, Carlton, 2014, pp. 282–4.
43 Carr, *Diary of a Foreign Minister*, pp. 399–400.
44 Swan, interview, December 2013; Burke, interview, April 2014.
45 Stephen Smith, interview with the author, January 2014
46 Combet, interview, January 2014.
47 Gillard, interview, October 2013.

32 Rudd Succumbs to Abbott
1 Kevin Rudd, interview with the author, February 2014.
2 Rudd, interview, February 2014.
3 Rudd, interview, February 2014.
4 Tony Abbott, interview with the author, January 2014.
5 Brian Loughnane, interview with the author, February 2014.
6 Julie Bishop, interview with the author, January 2014.
7 Joe Hockey, interview with the author, January 2013.
8 Hockey, interview, January 2013.
9 Greg Combet, interview with the author, January 2014.
10 Rudd, interview, February 2014.
11 Jennifer Westacott, interview with the author, February 2014.
12 Rudd, interview, February 2014.
13 Westacott, interview, February 2014.
14 Westacott, interview, February, 2014.
15 Kevin Rudd, joint press conference, 8 July 2013.
16 Bruce Hawker, *The Rudd Rebellion*, MUP, Carlton, 2013, p. 86.
17 Rudd, interview, February 2014.
18 Bob Carr, interview with the author, January 2014.
19 Chris Evans, interview with the author, November 2013.
20 Tony Burke, interview with the author, April 2014.

21 Burke, interview, April 2014.
22 David Marr, *Political Animal*, Black Inc. Melbourne, 2013, p. 7.
23 Nick Minchin, interview with the author, June 2011.
24 Elena Douglas, *Australian Financial Review*, 1 November 2013.
25 Abbott, interview, January 2014.
26 Paul Kelly, *Australian*, 21 August 2013.
27 Tony Abbott, speech to the Melbourne Institute/Australian Outlook conference, 2 November 2012.
28 Tony Abbott, 2013 campaign launch, 25 August 2013.
29 Paul Kelly, *Australian*, 2 September 2013.
30 Wayne Swan, interview with the author, December 2013.
31 Julia Gillard, the guardian.com, 14 September 2014.
32 Hawker, *The Rudd Rebellion*, p. 177.
33 Gillard, the guardian.com, 14 September 2014.
34 Gillard, the guardian.com, 14 September 2014.
35 George Wright, interview with the author, February 2014.
36 Chris Bowen, interview with the author, January 2014.
37 Carr, interview, January 2014.
38 Kim Carr, interview with the author, February 2014.
39 Sam Dastyari, interview with the author, January 2014.
40 Swan, interview, December 2013.
41 Abbott, interview, January 2014.
42 Combet, interview, January 2014.
43 George Wright, National Press Club speech, 29 October 2013.
44 Julia Gillard, interview with the author, October 2013.
45 Stephen Smith, interview with the author, January 2014.

33 The Australian Crisis

1 Sean Kelly, interview with the author, March 2014.
2 Deloitte Access Economics, Budget Monitor, 8 May 2014.
3 Treasury, Economic Roundup Summer 2008, *A perspective on trends in Australian Government spending*, Australian Government, Canberra, 2008.
4 Chris Richardson, interview with the author, December 2013; Deloitte Access Economics, Budget Monitor, May 2011.
5 Ken Henry, interview with the author, March 2012.
6 Chris Richardson, Budget Monitor, May 2014.

INDEX